THE NEW AMERICAN COMMENTARY

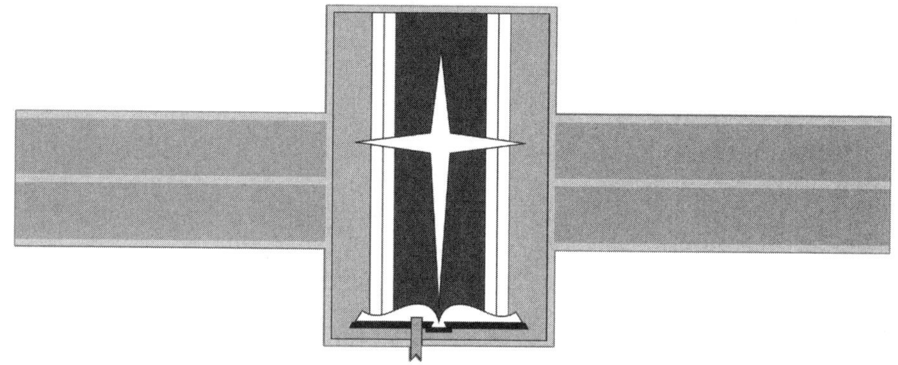

An Exegetical and Theological Exposition of Holy Scripture

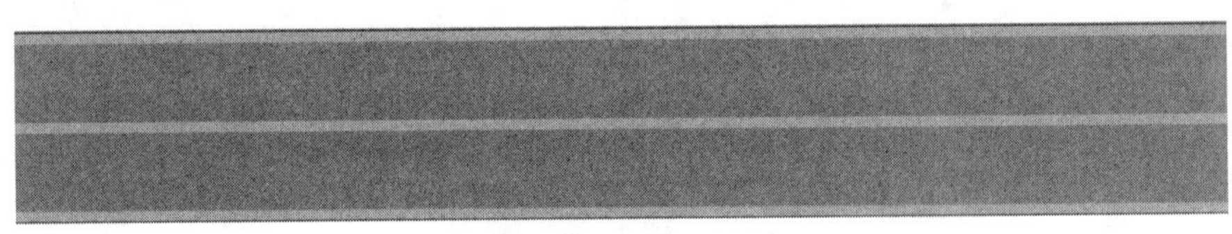

THE NEW AMERICAN COMMENTARY

Volume
37

1, 2 PETER, JUDE

Thomas R. Schreiner

PUBLISHING GROUP
Nashville, Tennessee

ISBN 978–0–8054–0137-0
Printed in the United States of America
14 15 16 17 18   22 21 20 19 18

To Diane

My Co-heir in the grace of life (1 Pet 3:7)

Editors' Preface

God's Word does not change. God's world, however, changes in every generation. These changes, in addition to new findings by scholars and a new variety of challenges to the gospel message, call for the church in each generation to interpret and apply God's Word for God's people. Thus, THE NEW AMERICAN COMMENTARY is introduced to bridge the twentieth and twenty-first centuries. This new series has been designed primarily to enable pastors, teachers, and students to read the Bible with clarity and proclaim it with power.

In one sense THE NEW AMERICAN COMMENTARY is not new, for it represents the continuation of a heritage rich in biblical and theological exposition. The title of this forty-volume set points to the continuity of this series with an important commentary project published at the end of the nineteenth century called AN AMERICAN COMMENTARY, edited by Alvah Hovey. The older series included, among other significant contributions, the outstanding volume on Matthew by John A. Broadus, from whom the publisher of the new series, Broadman Press, partly derives its name. The former series was authored and edited by scholars committed to the infallibility of Scripture, making it a solid foundation for the present project. In line with this heritage, all NAC authors affirm the divine inspiration, inerrancy, complete truthfulness, and full authority of the Bible. The perspective of the NAC is unapologetically confessional and rooted in the evangelical tradition.

Since a commentary is a fundamental tool for the expositor or teacher who seeks to interpret and apply Scripture in the church or classroom, the NAC focuses on communicating the theological structure and content of each biblical book. The writers seek to illuminate both the historical meaning and contemporary significance of Holy Scripture.

In its attempt to make a unique contribution to the Christian community, the NAC focuses on two concerns. First, the commentary emphasizes how each section of a book fits together so that the reader becomes aware of the theological unity of each book and of Scripture as a whole. The writers, however, remain aware of the Bible's inherently rich variety. Second, the NAC is produced with the conviction that the Bible primarily belongs to the church. We believe that scholarship and the academy provide an indispensable foundation for biblical understanding and the service of Christ, but the editors and authors of this series have attempted to communicate the findings of their research in a manner that will build up the whole body of Christ. Thus, the commentary concentrates on theological exegesis while providing practical, applicable exposition.

THE NEW AMERICAN COMMENTARY's theological focus enables

the reader to see the parts as well as the whole of Scripture. The biblical books vary in content, context, literary type, and style. In addition to this rich variety, the editors and authors recognize that the doctrinal emphasis and use of the biblical books differs in various places, contexts, and cultures among God's people. These factors, as well as other concerns, have led the editors to give freedom to the writers to wrestle with the issues raised by the scholarly community surrounding each book and to determine the appropriate shape and length of the introductory materials. Moreover, each writer has developed the structure of the commentary in a way best suited for expounding the basic structure and the meaning of the biblical books for our day. Generally, discussions relating to contemporary scholarship and technical points of grammar and syntax appear in the footnotes and not in the text of the commentary. This format allows pastors and interested laypersons, scholars and teachers, and serious college and seminary students to profit from the commentary at various levels. This approach has been employed because we believe that all Christians have the privilege and responsibility to read and seek to understand the Bible for themselves.

Consistent with the desire to produce a readable, up-to-date commentary, the editors selected the *New International Version* as the standard translation for the commentary series. The selection was made primarily because of the NIV's faithfulness to the original languages and its beautiful and readable style. The authors, however, have been given the liberty to differ at places from the NIV as they develop their own translations from the Greek and Hebrew texts.

The NAC reflects the vision and leadership of those who provide oversight for Broadman Press, who in 1987 called for a new commentary series that would evidence a commitment to the inerrancy of Scripture and a faithfulness to the classic Christian tradition. While the commentary adopts an "American" name, it should be noted some writers represent countries outside the United States, giving the commentary an international perspective. The diverse group of writers includes scholars, teachers, and administrators from almost twenty different colleges and seminaries, as well as pastors, missionaries, and a layperson.

The editors and writers hope that THE NEW AMERICAN COMMENTARY will be helpful and instructive for pastors and teachers, scholars and students, for men and women in the churches who study and teach God's Word in various settings. We trust that for editors, authors, and readers alike, the commentary will be used to build up the church, encourage obedience, and bring renewal to God's people. Above all, we pray that the NAC will bring glory and honor to our Lord who has graciously redeemed us and faithfully revealed himself to us in his Holy Word.

SOLI DEO GLORIA
The Editors

Author Preface

This commentary is written primarily for pastors and laypersons who are interested in serious study of the Scriptures. I hope that the commentary will be of interest to scholars, but I have tried to keep it short enough so that busy pastors will have time to read it. Commentaries are getting longer and longer, and I fear that only other scholars are reading such mammoth works. I have read representatively in commentaries, monographs, and journals on 1, 2 Peter and Jude, learning much from those that have preceded me. Another distinctive of the commentary is its theological slant. I understand the Scriptures to be a canonical unity. Hence, I attempt to explore at various junctures how the message of 1, 2 Peter and Jude coheres with the rest of the New Testament. No attempt is made in the commentary to defend the notion that the New Testament, despite its diversity, ultimately yields a coherent message. I believe such a defense can be made, but that would take another book.

I would like to thank Ray Clendenen for inviting me to contribute to the New American Commentary series and for his encouragement and friendship. I am also grateful for his keen editorial eye and his suggestions as to how the manuscript could be improved. It was a joy to teach 1, 2 Peter and Jude to a number of classes, and each class has made the commentary better than it would have been otherwise. Students in those classes spotted a number of errors in the manuscript that were corrected. Four students at The Southern Baptist Theological Seminary read the manuscript with special care and corrected errors: John Folmar, Michael Hardy, Randall Tan, and Brian Vickers. I thank each one for their labor of love. Philemon Yong and Jason Meyer helped me in countless ways by copying articles, chasing down references, and by their careful reading. Jason Meyer was an immense help in the proofing stage in checking references and giving the manuscript a final reading. Their friendship and help have been precious to me. John Glynn volunteered to read large sections of the commentary. He made innumerable suggestions that were remarkably helpful to me as I finished up the work. I cannot thank him enough for his labor of love on my behalf. Finally, I dedicate this book to the love of my life, Diane, who introduced me to the gospel of grace and is my co-heir in the grace of life (1 Pet 3:7).

—Thomas R. Schreiner
The Southern Baptist Theological Seminary
Louisville, Kentucky

Abbreviations

Bible Books

Gen	Isa	Luke
Exod	Jer	John
Lev	Lam	Acts
Num	Ezek	Rom
Deut	Dan	1, 2 Cor
Josh	Hos	Gal
Judg	Joel	Eph
Ruth	Amos	Phil
1, 2 Sam	Obad	Col
1, 2 Kgs	Jonah	1, 2 Thess
1, 2 Chr	Mic	1, 2 Tim
Ezra	Nah	Titus
Neh	Hab	Phlm
Esth	Zeph	Heb
Job	Hag	Jas
Ps (pl. Pss)	Zech	1, 2 Pet
Prov	Mal	1, 2, 3 John
Eccl	Matt	Jude
Song	Mark	Rev

Apocrypha

Add Esth	*The Additions to the Book of Esther*
Bar	*Baruch*
Bel	*Bel and the Dragon*
1,2 Esdr	*1, 2 Esdras*
4 Ezra	*4 Ezra*
Jdt	*Judith*
Ep Jer	*Epistle of Jeremiah*
1,2,3,4 Mac	*1, 2, 3, 4 Maccabees*
Pr Azar	*Prayer of Azariah and the Song of the Three Jews*
Pr Man	*Prayer of Manasseh*
Sir	*Sirach, Ecclesiasticus*
Sus	*Susanna*
Tob	*Tobit*
Wis	*The Wisdom of Solomon*

Commonly Used Sources for New Testament Volumes

AB	Anchor Bible
ABD	D. N. Freedman (ed.), *Anchor Bible Dictionary*
ACCS	Ancient Christian Commentary on Scripture
ACNT	Augsburg Commentary on the New Testament
AGJU	Arbeiten zur Geschichte des antiken Judentums und des Urchristentums
AJBI	Annual of the Japanese Biblical Institute
AJT	*American Journal of Theology*
AJTh	*Asia Journal of Theology*
ANF	Ante-Nicene Fathers
ANQ	*Andover Newton Quarterly*
ASNU	Acta seminarii neotestamentici upsaliensis
ATANT	Abhandlungen zur Theologie des Alten and Neuen Testaments
ATR	*Anglican Theological Review*
ATRSup	*Anglican Theological Review Supplemental Series*
AusBR	*Australian Biblical Review*
AUSS	*Andrews University Seminary Studies*
BAGD	W. Bauer, W. F. Arndt, F. W. Gingrich, and F. Danker, *Greek-English Lexicon of the New Testament and Other Early Christian Literature,* 2d ed.
BARev	*Biblical Archaeology Review*
BBR	*Bulletin for Biblical Research*
BDAG	W. Bauer, F. W. Danker, W. F. Arndt, and F. W. Gingrich *Greek-English Lexicon of the New Testament and Other Early Christian Literature,* 3d ed.
BDF	F. Blass, A. Debrunner, R. W. Funk, *A Greek Grammar of the New Testament*
BECNT	Baker Exegetical Commentary on the New Testament
BETL	Bibliotheca ephemeridum theologicarum lovaniensium
BETS	*Bulletin of the Evangelical Theological Society*
Bib	*Biblica*
BJRL	*Bulletin of the John Rylands Library*
BK	*Bibel und Kirche*
BLG	Biblical Languages: Greek
BLit	*Bibel und Liturgie*
BR	*Biblical Research*
BRT	*Biblical Review of Theology*
BSac	*Bibliotheca Sacra*

BT	*The Bible Translator*
BTB	*Biblical Theology Bulletin*
BVC	*Bible et vie chrétienne*
BZ	*Biblische Zeitschrift*
BZNW	Beihefte zur *ZAW*
CBC	Cambridge Bible Commentary
CBQ	*Catholic Biblical Quarterly*
CCWJCW	Cambridge Commentaries on Writings of the Jewish and Christian World
CNTC	Calvin's New Testament Commentaries
CO	W. Baur, E. Cuntiz, and E. Reuss, *Ioannis Calvini opera quae supereunt omnia,* ed.
ConBNT	Coniectanea biblica, New Testament
Conybeare	W. J. Conybeare and J. S. Howson, *The Life and Epistles of St. Paul*
CJT	*Canadian Journal of Theology*
CSR	*Christian Scholars' Review*
CTM	*Concordia Theologial Monthly*
CTQ	*Concordia Theological Quarterly*
CTR	*Criswell Theological Review*
Did.	*Didache*
DJD	Discoveries in the Judaean Desert
DNTT	*Dictionary of New Testament Theology*
DownRev	*Downside Review*
DSB	Daily Study Bible
EBC	Expositor's Bible Commentary
EDNT	*Exegetical Dictionary of the New Testament*
EGT	*The Expositor's Greek Testament*
EGNT	*Exegetical Greek New Testament*
EKKNT	Evangelisch-katholischer Kommentar zum Neuen Testament
ESV	English Standard Version
ETC	English Translation and Commentary
ETL	*Ephemerides theologicae lovanienses*
ETR	*Etudes théologiques et religieuses*
ETS	Evangelical Theological Society
EvT	*Evangelische Theologie*
EvQ	*Evangelical Quarterly*
Exp	*Expositor*
ExpTim	*Expository Times*
FNT	*Filologia Neotestamentaria*

FRLANT	Forschungen zur Religion und Literatur des Alten und Neuen Testaments
GAGNT	M. Zerwick and M. Grosvenor, *A Grammatical Analysis of the Greek New Testament*
GNBC	Good News Bible Commentary
GSC	Griechischen christlichen Schriftsteller
GTJ	*Grace Theological Journal*
HBD	*Holman Bible Dictionary*
HDB	J. Hastings, *Dictionary of the Bible*
Her	Hermeneia
HNT	Handbuch zum Neuen Testament
HNTC	Harper's New Testament Commentaries
HeyJ	*Heythrop Journal*
HTKNT	Herders theologischer Kommentar zum Neuen Testament
HTR	*Harvard Theological Review*
HUCA	*Hebrew Union College Annual*
IB	*The Interpreter's Bible*
IBS	*Irish Biblical Studies*
ICC	International Critical Commentary
IDB	*Interpreter's Dictionary of the Bible*
IDBSup	Supplementary Volume to *IDB*
Int	*Interpretation*
INT	Interpretation: A Bible Commentary for Preaching and Teaching
ISBE	*International Standard Bible Encyclopedia*
JAAR	*Journal of the American Academy of Religion*
JANES	*Journal of Ancient Near Eastern Studies*
JAOS	*Journal of the American Oriental Society*
JBL	*Journal of Biblical Literature*
JES	*Journal of Ecumenical Studies*
JETS	*Journal of the Evangelical Theological Society*
JJS	*Journal of Jewish Studies*
JOTT	*Journal of Translation and Textlinguistics*
JR	*Journal of Religion*
JRE	*Journal of Religious Ethics*
JRH	*Journal of Religious History*
JRS	*Journal of Roman Studies*
JSNT	*Journal for the Study of the New Testament*
JSOT	*Journal for the Study of the Old Testament*
JSS	*Journal of Semitic Studies*
JTS	*Journal of Theological Studies*

JTT	*Journal of Translation and Textlinguistics*
KEK	Kritisch-exegetischer Kommentar über das Neue Testament
LB	*Linguistica Biblica*
LEC	Library of Early Christianity
LouvSt	*Louvain Studies*
LS	Liddel and Scott, *Greek-English Lexicon*
LSJ	Lidell, Scott, Jones, *Greek-English Lexicon*
LTJ	*Lutheran Theological Journal*
LTP	*Laval théologique et philosophique*
LTQ	*Lexington Theological Quarterly*
LW	Luther's Works
LXX	Septuagint
MCNT	Meyer's Commentary on the New Testament
MDB	*Mercer Dictionary of the Bible*
MM	J. H. Moulton and G. Milligan, *The Vocabulary of the Greek Testament*
MNTC	Moffatt New Testament Commentary
MQR	*Mennonite Quarterly Review*
MT	Masoretic Text
Mus	*Muséon: Revue d'études orientales*
NAB	New American Bible
NAC	New American Commentary
NASB	New American Standard Bible
NBD	*New Bible Dictionary*
NCB	New Century Bible
NCBC	New Century Bible Commentary
NEB	New English Bible
Neot	*Neotestamentica*
NICNT	New International Commentary on the New Testament
NIDNTT	*New International Dictionary of New Testament Theology*
NIGTC	New International Greek Testament Commentary
NIV	New International Version
NorTT	*Norsk Teologisk Tidsskrift*
NovT	*Novum Testamentum*
NovTSup	Novum Testamentum, Supplements
NPNF	Nicene and Post-Nicene Fathers
NRSV	New Revised Standard Version
NRT	*La nouvelle revue théologique*
NTC	InterVarsity Press New Testament Commentary

NTD	Das Neue Testament Deutsch
NTI	D. Guthrie, *New Testament Introduction*
NTM	*The New Testament Message*
NTS	*New Testament Studies*
OTP	J. H. Charlesworth, ed., *The Old Testament Pseudepigrapha*
PC	Proclamation Commentaries
PEQ	*Palestine Exploration Quarterly*
PNTC	Pelican New Testament Commentaries
PRS	*Perspectives in Religious Studies*
PSB	*Princeton Seminary Bulletin*
RB	*Revue biblique*
RefTR	*Reformed Theological Review*
RelSRev	*Religious Studies Review*
ResQ	*Restoration Quarterly*
RevExp	*Review and Expositor*
RevQ	*Revue de Qumran*
RevThom	*Revue thomiste*
RHPR	*Revue d'histoire et de philosophie religieuses*
RSPT	*Revue des sciences philosophiques et théologiques*
RSR	*Recherches de science religieuse*
RSV	Revised Standard Version
RTP	*Revue de théologie et de philosophie*
RTR	*Reformed Theological Review*
SAB	*Sitzungsbericht der Preussischen Akademie der Wissenschaft zu Berlin*
SBJT	*Southern Baptist Journal of Theology*
SBLDS	SBL Dissertation Series
SBLMS	SBL Monograph Series
SBLSP	SBL Seminar Papers
Scr	*Scripture*
ScrB	*Scripture Bulletin*
SE	*Studia Evangelica*
SEAÛ	*Svensk exegetisk aΩrsbok*
SEAJT	*Southeast Asia Journal of Theology*
SecCent	*Second Century*
Sem	*Semitica*
SJT	*Scottish Journal of Theology*
SNTSMS	Society for New Testament Studies Monograph Series
SNTU	*Studien zum Neuen Testament und seiner Umwelt*
SPB	Studia postbiblica

SPCK	Society for the Promotion of Christian Knowledge
ST	*Studia theologica*
Str-B	H. Strack and P. Billerbeck, *Kommentar zum Neuen Testament*
StudBib	Studia Biblica
SWJT	*Southwestern Journal of Theology*
TB	*Tyndale Bulletin*
TBC	Torch Bible Commentaries
TBT	*The Bible Today*
TCGNT	B. M. Metzger, *A Textual Commentary on the Greek New Testament*
TDNT	G. Kittel and G. Friedrich, eds., *Theological Dictionary of the New Testament*
TEV	Today's English Version
Theol	*Theology*
ThT	*Theology Today*
TLZ	*Theologische Literaturzeitung*
TNTC	Tyndale New Testament Commentaries
TRE	*Theologische Realenzyklopädie*
TrinJ	*Trinity Journal*
TRu	*Theologische Rundschau*
TS	*Theological Studies*
TSK	*Theologische Studien und Kritiken*
TTZ	*Trierer theologische Zeitschrift*
TU	Texte und Untersuchungen
TynBul	*Tyndale Bulletin*
TZ	*Theologische Zeitschrift*
UBS	United Bible Societies
UBSGNT	*United Bible Societies' Greek New Testament*
USQR	*Union Seminary Quarterly Review*
VD	*Verbum domini*
VE	*Vox evangelica*
VR	*Vox reformata*
WBC	Word Biblical Commentary
WC	Westminster Commentaries
WEC	Wycliffe Exegetical Commentary
WP	*Word Pictures in the New Testament,* A. T. Robertson
WTJ	*Westminster Theological Journal*
WUNT	Wissenschaftliche Untersuchungen zum Neuen Testament
ZDPV	*Zeitschrift des deutschen Palästina-Vereins*
ZNW	*Zeitschrift für die neutestamentliche Wissenschaft*
ZRGG	*Zeitschrift für Religions- und Geistesgeschichte*
ZST	*Zeitschrift für systematische Theologie*
ZTK	*Zeitschrift für Theologie und Kirche*

Contents

1 Peter

INTRODUCTION OUTLINE

1. Author
   (1) Internal Evidence
   (2) External Evidence
   (3) Arguments against Petrine Authorship
   (4) Arguments Supporting Petrine Authorship
2. Date
3. Destination and Situation of the Readers
4. Character of the Letter
5. Purpose
6. Structure

INTRODUCTION

1. Author

(1) Internal Evidence

The letter claims to be from Peter as the first verse attests, "Peter, an apostle of Jesus Christ" (1 Pet 1:1).[1] No other direct reference to Peter exists in the letter. Some have seen a contrast between the readers and Peter in the statement that the readers have not seen Christ (1:8), with the implication that Peter has. Such an implication may be present, but it is hardly determinative for establishing authorship. A stronger piece of evidence is the author's claim to be "a witness of Christ's sufferings" (5:1). It is difficult to see how this could be said of someone outside the apostolic circle (but see the commentary on 5:1 for alternate interpretations of this expres-

[1] A resurgence of interest in Peter is traced in an article by J. H. Elliott, "The Rehabilitation of an Exegetical Step-Child: 1 Peter in Recent Research," *JBL* 95 (1976): 243–54. For a lucid and brief survey of scholarship on 1 Peter up until 1980, see D. Sylva, "1 Peter Studies: The State of the Discipline," *BTB* 10 (1980): 155–63. For an excellent summary of the history of research, see S. R. Bechtler, *Following in His Steps: Suffering, Community, and Christology in 1 Peter,* SBLDS 162 (Atlanta: Scholars Press, 1998), 1–22.

sion). The references to Silas, Mark, and Babylon (5:13) may reflect Petrine authorship, but by themselves they are unclear, for Silas and Mark in the New Testament are more closely connected to Paul than Peter (see the commentary on 5:12 and 5:13). Another important piece of evidence is suggested by 2 Pet 3:1, for there Peter says that he writes his second letter to the readers. Even if 2 Peter is pseudonymous (which I dispute), the reference is almost certainly to 1 Peter, suggesting that the first letter is genuinely Petrine. To sum up, the letter itself claims to be written by the apostle Peter, and the self-claim of the letter should be accepted unless there is clear evidence to the contrary.

(2) External Evidence

We turn from the internal evidence of the letter to the early tradition of the church regarding the letter. Some scholars have detected dependence upon 1 Peter in *1 Clement* (see *1 Clem.* opening; 7:6; 9:3–4; 21:7; 22:2–6; 49:5; 57:1), but none of the parallels clearly establishes dependence upon 1 Peter, and the evidence is insufficient to conclude that *1 Clement* knew or used 1 Peter. Neither do *Barnabas* or Justin's *Dialogue with Trypho* indicate dependence upon 1 Peter, despite the claims of some scholars. When we read Polycarp's letter to the Philippians, we have the first evidence of dependence on 1 Peter, and the date of Polycarp's letter is quite early (probably ca. A.D. 112–114). In four texts Polycarp's wording is remarkably close to what we have in 1 Peter, so there are good reasons for thinking that Polycarp used Peter as a source (cf. *Phil. 8:2* and 1 Pet 2:21; *Phil.* 1:3 and 1 Pet 1:8; *Phil.* 8:1 and 1 Pet 2:22,24; *Phil.* 2:1 and 1 Pet 1:13,22). Possibly the *Didache* also uses 1 Peter (see *Did.* 1:4 and 1 Pet 2:11), though certainty here is impossible. If the latter were to be established, the authenticity of 1 Peter would be strengthened.

By the end of the second century and beginning of the third century, the letter is explicitly identified as Peter's. Tertullian cites verses from Peter and explicitly identifies Peter as the author (*Scorp.* 12; cf. *Scorp.* 14; *Orat.* 20). Clement of Alexandria and Irenaeus also quote from 1 Peter and attribute the writing to Peter himself (e.g., *Paed.* 1.6.44; *Strom.* 3.11.75; 4.7.33–47; and *Adv. haer.* 4.9.2; 4.16.5 respectively). First Peter is not listed in the Muratorian Canon, but the omission may be due to the destruction of part of the document, so not much can be gleaned from this. We do learn that the external evidence for 1 Peter being authentic is quite early, and no doubts were raised about its authenticity.

(3) Arguments against Petrine Authorship

Despite the self-claim of the book and the early tradition attesting Petrine authorship, many scholars doubt that Peter is the genuine author of the letter. Various reasons are given for denying the authenticity of 1 Peter, though scholars who dispute authenticity differ on what arguments are persuasive and the weight that should be assigned to the different arguments.[2]

First, the cultivated Greek of the letter convinces many that the letter could not have been written by a Galilean fisherman.[3] In Acts 4:13 Peter is described as "unlearned" (*agrammatos;* NIV "unschooled"), and hence it seems quite improbable in the eyes of many scholars that the sophisticated knowledge of Greek grammar evident in the letter can be traced back to the apostle. Indeed, scholars generally agree that the Greek in Peter is among the best in the New Testament. Further, how do we explain the different quality of the Greek in 2 Peter if both letters were composed by Peter?

Second, and related to the first, the citations of the Old Testament in the letter come mainly from the Septuagint, and this does not seem to fit with Peter, whose native language would not be Greek.[4]

Third, scholars have often remarked that 1 Peter is noticeably Pauline in theology.[5] Peter focuses on the death of Christ, the need to suffer with Christ, obedience to governing authorities, the responsibility of wives to submit to their husbands, and other themes. The apparent dependence upon Paul seems especially strange, given that Peter and Paul disagreed in Antioch about how to relate to Gentiles (Gal 2:11–14).[6]

---

[2] For a concise summary of the arguments against Petrine authorship, see W. G. Kümmel, *Introduction to the New Testament*, rev. ed. (Nashville: Abingdon, 1975), 423–24; cf. also N. Brox, *Der erste Petrusbrief,* EKKNT, 2d ed. (Zürich: Benziger/Neukirchen-Vluyn: Neukirchener Verlag, 1986), 43–47. Kümmel says it is "undoubtedly a pseudonymous writing" (p. 424). For a recent rejection of Petrine authorship, see J. H. Elliott, *1 Peter: A New Translation with Introduction and Commentary,* AB (New York: Doubleday, 2000), 120–30.

[3] F. W. Beare, *The First Epistle of Peter: The Greek Text with Introduction and Notes* (Oxford: Blackwell, 1947), 27–28; L. Goppelt, *A Commentary on I Peter* (Grand Rapids: Eerdmans, 1993), 50; P. J. Achtemeier, *1 Peter: A Commentary on First Peter,* Her (Minneapolis: Fortress, 1996), 4–5. Beare argues from Acts 4:13 that the historical Peter was illiterate.

[4] E.g., Achtemeier, *1 Peter,* 6–7.

[5] So Beare, *First Peter,* 25–26.

[6] In a study comparing Ephesians and 1 Peter, C. L. Mitton concludes that the author of 1 Peter knew of Ephesians and depended upon it at some points ("The Relationship between 1 Peter and Ephesians," *JTS* 1 (1950): 67–73. K. Shimada carefully analyzes the evidence adduced by Mitton and rightly concludes that he has not proved his case ("Is I Peter Dependent on Ephesians? A Critique of C. L. Mitton," *AJBI* 17 [1991]: 77–106). Shimada conducts a similar study on whether 1 Peter is dependent upon Romans, showing again that dependence cannot be established ("Is I Peter Dependent on Romans," *AJBI* 19 [1993]: 87–137). Indeed, clear evidence that Peter drew on any Pauline writings is lacking. See also the careful discussion of Achtemeier, *1 Peter,* 15–19; Brox, *Der erste Petrusbrief,* 47–51; Elliott, *1 Peter,* 37–41. The commonalities between the two are better explained in terms of shared traditions. For a collection of Shimada's essays on 1 Peter see his *Studies on First Peter* (Tokyo: Kyo Bun Kwan, 1998). A recent work that argues for 1 Peter's independence from the Pauline letters is J. Herzer, *Petrus oder Paulus? Studien über das Verhältnis des ersten Petrusbriefes zur paulinischen Tradition*, WUNT 103 (Tübingen: Mohr, 1998).

Fourth, conservative scholars often appeal to Silvanus, arguing that he functioned as Peter's amanuensis (1 Pet 5:12). The quality of the Greek, therefore, derives from Silvanus rather than Peter. Scholars who reject Petrine authorship argue, however, that the formula in 1 Pet 5:12 does not indicate that Silvanus functioned as the secretary. The phrase "to write through someone" *(graphein dia tinos)* regularly refers to the *bearer,* not the secretary of the letter. We know from 1 Pet 5:12 that Silvanus carried the letter, but there is no evidence that he was its author. Further, even if he functioned as the secretary, on what basis can we say that his knowledge of Greek was advanced? Silvanus's facility in Greek is unknown, and hence any appeal to him is conjectural and does not advance the argument.

Fifth, some scholars question Petrine authorship because the letter says very little about the historical Jesus, and this is deemed incredible if the author is the historical Peter who walked and talked with Jesus.

Sixth, some scholars argue that the persecution described in the letter stems from Rome itself and is empirewide (1 Pet 5:9). Some conclude from this that such persecution can only be assigned to the reign of Domitian (A.D. 81–96). The late date of Domitian's reign, obviously, excludes any reference to Peter. Similarly, some scholars think that the mistreatment of believers in 1 Peter fits well with the correspondence between Pliny the younger and the emperor Trajan (A.D. 98–117).[7] Pliny was the legate to Bithynia in Asia Minor, and he wondered how he should respond to Christians in his province. On the one hand, he was quite sure he should execute believers who refused to sacrifice to the emperor and curse Christ. He suspected, however, that he should not impose punishments upon those who were labeled as Christians and agreed to curse Christ. Furthermore, he wondered if Christians should be actively sought out and anonymous charges accepted, or if he should only prosecute Christians who confessed their faith. Trajan responded by recommending a conservative course. He did not want a witch-hunt in which Christians were sought out since this would undermine stability. Christians who cursed Christ and sacrificed to the emperor were exempt from any punishment, whereas those who were stubborn and obstinate in their devotion to Christ and who refused to sacrifice to Caesar were to be put to death. If 1 Peter is dated during Trajan's reign, the apostle Peter cannot be the author at such a late date (A.D. 98–117).

Many scholars opt, then, for pseudonymity in the case of 1 Peter.[8] The

[7] See *Ep.* 10.96–97. Cf. J. Knox, "Pliny and 1 Peter: A Note on 1 Pet. iv.14–16 and iii.15," *JBL* 72 (1953): 187–89; F. G. Downing, "Pliny's Prosecutions of Christians: Revelation and 1 Peter," *JSNT* 34 (1988): 105–23.

[8] E.g., Beare says, "There can be no possible doubt that 'Peter' is a pseudonym" (*First Peter,* 25). Cf. E. J. Richard, *Reading 1 Peter, Jude, and 2 Peter: A Literary and Theological Commentary,* RNT (Macon: Smith & Helwys, 2000), 9–10.

letter claims to be written by Peter, but it was actually authored by someone else. P. Achtemeier's recent commentary functions as an example of those who espouse such a theory.[9] Achtemeier notes that pseudonymous writings were rejected in the early church, but he insists that the writings that were rejected were dismissed because of their *content,* not because they were pseudonymous. He thinks that a pseudonymous author felt justified in writing in Peter's name since there was a tradition that disciples wrote in the name of their teacher. This tradition is reflected in rabbinic literature, among the Pythagoreans, and is reflected in Tertullian. Further, Achtemeier appeals to evidence in both the Greco-Roman world and in the early church fathers supporting the notion of a "therapeutic lie."[10] Such a theory fits with the work of Donelson,[11] who argues that pseudepigraphers defended lying on the basis that some lies were "noble." Others would depart from Achtemeier and Donelson and argue that it was apparent to all that Peter did not write the letter and that there was no attempt to deceive. They would say that such an expedient was a "transparent fiction."[12] Others argue that the letter was composed by a Petrine group or a Petrine school.[13] This last theory is possible, but it suffers from lack of evidence.[14] No early tradition suggests that the letter derived from a group of writers, and it is difficult to believe that such a beautiful piece of literature could be composed by a group, as anyone who has served on a committee writing a report knows rather well. Ascribing the letter to a group evades the challenge of supporting Petrine authorship but often attempts to situate the letter within a Petrine circle.[15] The vagueness of the theory makes it difficult to refute, while at the same time suggesting that it can never be substantiated. Furthermore, Elliott's own theory ascribes the work to a fictive Peter (since he

---

[9] Achtemeier, *1 Peter,* 39–42.

[10] Plato, *Republic* 389b–c; Cicero, *Brutus* 11.42; Clement of Alexandria, *Strom.* 7.9.53.2; Chrysostom, *De paen.* 49.331; Origen, *In Jer.* 19.15. These references derive from Achtemeier.

[11] L. R. Donelson, *Pseudepigraphy and Ethical Argument in the Pastoral Epistles* (Tübingen: Mohr, 1986), 11.

[12] Cf. Beare, *First Peter,* 29. This represents R. Bauckham's view of 2 Peter (*Jude, 2 Peter* [Waco: Word, 1983]). See the introduction of 2 Peter for the discussion of Bauckham's view.

[13] E.g., E. Best, *1 Peter,* NCB (Grand Rapids: Eerdmans, 1971), 32–36, 64–65; Goppelt, *I Peter,* 48–53, 368–71; J. H. Elliott, "Peter, Silvanus and Mark in 1 Peter and Acts: Sociological-Exegetical Perspectives on a Petrine Group in Rome," in *Wort in der Zeit: Neutestamentlichen Studien: Festgabe für Karl Heinrich Rengstorf zum* 75. Geburtstag (Leiden: Brill, 1980), 250–67; R. P. Martin, "1 Peter," in *The Theology of the Letters of James, Peter, and Jude* (Cambridge: University Press, 1994), 92.

[14] See the criticisms of D. G. Horrell, "The Product of a Petrine Circle? A Reassessment of the Origin and Character of 1 Peter," *JSNT* 86 (2002): 29–60. Horrell's own claim is that the letter represents a consolidation in Rome of early Christian traditions.

[15] E.g., J. H. Elliott, *A Home for the Homeless: A Sociological Exegesis of 1 Peter, Its Situation and Strategy* (Philadelphia: Fortress, 1981), 270–80; Elliott, *1 Peter,* 127–30.

did not write it) but a genuine Mark and Silvanus. It is difficult to see how the latter can be accepted as historical while dismissing the former. A more consistent approach would accept the reference to all three as historical or understand each person named to be fictional.[16]

(4) Arguments Supporting Petrine Authorship

Despite the above objections to Petrine authorship, good and substantial reasons exist for accepting such authorship.[17] In answering the objections we will proceed backwards, beginning with the last argument and proceeding step by step to the first.[18] We should begin by noting again that the letter claims to be written by the apostle Peter. This point should be emphasized, for the earliest evidence we have on the matter supports Petrine authorship. Further, we have already seen that the tradition of the early church also supports Petrine authorship. There is no evidence that anyone in the early church believed that the letter was written by anyone other than Peter. Hence, any notion that the letter is a transparent fiction can be rejected confidently. We have no evidence from antiquity that the letter was recognized as pseudonymous or as being written by one of Peter's disciples. If the letter was a "transparent fiction," it was apparently a failure, for no one identified it as fictional. The historical evidence for a transparent fiction therefore is lacking.

More credible than the transparent fiction theory is the notion that the

[16] Elliott thinks the significance of the three named persists even if they are all fictional (*Home for the Homeless*, 279–80). It is difficult, however, to see how this could be the case since now the personal references are loosed from any historical anchor. Hence, we have no reason to think that the readers would think of the historical work of these three persons if the reference to them is sundered from history.

[17] Cf. C. L. Winbery, "Introduction to the First Letter of Peter," *SwJT* 25 (1982): 8–14; W. J. Dalton, "'So That Your Faith May also Be Your Hope in God' (I Peter 1:21)," in *Reconciliation and Hope: New Testament Essays on Atonement and Eschatology Presented to L. L. Morris on His Sixtieth Birthday* (Exeter: Paternoster, 1974), 262–66.

[18] R. H. Gundry supports Petrine authorship by arguing that the letter often evinces a dependence on the words of Christ in the gospel tradition, particularly appealing to texts where Peter is a major character in the story (see "'Verba Christi' in *I Peter: Their Implications concerning the Authorship of I Peter and the Authenticity of the Gospel Tradition, NTS* 13 [1967]: 336–50; and "Further *Verba* on *Verba Christi* in First Peter," *Bib* 55 [1974]: 211–32). Gundry's evidence is severely questioned by E. Best, who argues that in most instances dependence upon gospel traditions is not clearly established in 1 Peter (see "1 Peter and the Gospel Tradition," *NTS* 16 [1970]: 95–113). For a view that is quite similar to Gundry's, see G. Maier, "Jesustradition im 1. Petrusbrief," in *Gospel Perspectives: The Jesus Tradition Outside the Gospels*, vol. 5 (Sheffield: JSOT Press, 1984), 85–128. In my judgment the evidence warrants a view somewhere between Gundry and Best, for Peter uses gospel traditions more than Best grants but less than Gundry claims. I am not persuaded that the references to gospel traditions are sufficient to function as a further argument for Petrine authorship.

letter was written as a "therapeutic lie" or as a "noble lie." At least this theory recognizes that there is no evidence that the letter was ever understood to be a transparent fiction. On the other hand, there are serious problems with the notion that we have a therapeutic lie in terms of authorship. The letter itself criticizes deceit (2:1,22; 3:10), and this is quite inconsistent if the writer practices it himself. The high premium placed on truth in the early Christian movement does not square with such deceitful practices.[19] In the early church both the *Gospel of Peter* and the *Acts of Paul and Thecla* were rejected because they were pseudonymous.[20] To say they were rejected as authoritative only because of their content is reductionistic, since both Eusebius and Tertullian report that the books were rejected because of their content *and the false claim of authorship*. Cyril of Jerusalem rejects all the gospels except four, since the others are "falsely written and hurtful."[21] Indeed, Achtemeier's attempt to legitimize pseudonymity by appealing to ancient practice fails. Donelson rightly observes: "No one seems to have accepted a document as religiously and philosophically prescriptive which was known to be forged. I do not know a single example."[22]

Another problem surfaces with the noble lie theory in the case of 1 Peter. If Peter died in the 60s and the letter was written in the 70s or 80s (or even later), one wonders how the attempt to pass off the letter as a noble lie would have any chance of success.[23] Certainly the believers in Asia Minor could not have thought that Peter was still alive ten to thirty years after his death. It must have been a well-known fact that he was deceased. Hence, it seems quite unlikely the readers would have actually been deceived by a letter purporting to be by Peter. We are left, then, with a person writing in Peter's name with an intent to deceive, but the likelihood of success was minimal. There is no evidence, for instance, that the letter claims to be a missive from Peter composed many years before it arrived in Asia Minor, for the letter addresses current circumstances in the church.

Referring to the practice of the Pythagorean school does not solve the problem, for the issue is whether such a practice was accepted in the Jewish and Christian community.[24] Appeal to rabbinic practices does not advance the argument either, for the rabbinic sayings do not have the same personal

---

[19] For a helpful and up-to-date discussion of pseudonymity, see T. L. Wilder, "Pseudonymity and the New Testament," in *Interpreting the New Testament: Essays on Methods and Issues* (Nashville: Broadman & Holman, 2001), 296–335.

[20] See Eusebius, *Hist. eccl.* 6.12.3; Tertullian, *Bapt.* 17.

[21] Cyril, *Cat.* 4.36.

[22] Donelson, *Pseudepigraphy and Ethical Argument,* 11.

[23] This objection was suggested to me by one of my students, Matt Perman, in a discussion on the text.

[24] Cf. the comments of D. Guthrie, *New Testament Introduction*, 4th ed. (Downers Grove: InterVarsity, 1990), 777–79; Wilder, "Pseudonymity and the New Testament," 301.

allusions as the New Testament letters. Further, it is questionable whether the category of pseudepigraphy is appropriate for what we find in rabbinic literature. Surprisingly, Achtemeier points to examples where lying or deception were defended by the early church (e.g., the case of Rahab). These examples, however, are not really applicable to the subject before us. Even today Christians debate whether there are some instances in which the truth should be withheld from another person in order to preserve someone's life. Such exceptional circumstances and statements from the fathers do not suggest that the therapeutic lie was routinely accepted. Further, they provide no evidence that the same standard applies to literary documents and, in particular, to epistles. In conclusion, the theory of pseudepigraphy either involves outright deception or it was rejected by the early church. The ancient evidence indicates that the latter is more convincing. Since the same issue is even more pressing in 2 Peter, I refer the reader to the more detailed discussion in the introduction to that letter.[25]

We now turn to the matter of persecution in 1 Peter. Some scholars in the past have seen in the setting of 1 Peter an empirewide persecution, positing that it occurred either during the reign of Domitian (A.D. 81–96) or Trajan (A.D. 98–117). Today, however, a new consensus is emerging, and it is acknowledged that an official policy of persecuting the church was not enforced under Nero (A.D. 54–68), Domitian, or Trajan.[26] We can consider each emperor in turn. Nero, of course, blamed Christians for the fire in Rome to stave off the notion that he intentionally started the fire.[27] Certainly the persecution of believers was intense in Rome, but no evidence exists in Nero's reign that the persecution extended beyond Rome and became official policy toward Christians. Scholars have often argued in the past that Domitian launched an official policy of persecution against Christians. Domitian probably did persecute believers, for his reign was marked by terror, and he put opponents to death among the nobility and extradited

[25] See also the convincing article by D. A. Carson, "Pseudonymity and Pseudepigraphy," in *Dictionary of New Testament Background* (Downers Grove: InterVarsity, 2000), 857–64.

[26] See e.g., Achtemeier, *1 Peter,* 28–36; J. N. D. Kelly, *A Commentary on the Epistles of Peter and Jude*, Thornapple Commentaries (Grand Rapids: Baker, 1981), 5–10; Elliott, *Home for the Homeless*, 80–81; P. H. Davids, *The First Epistle of Peter,* NICNT (Grand Rapids: Eerdmans, 1990), 10; Elliott, *1 Peter,* 98–101 Brox, *Der erste Petrusbrief*, 24–33. W. L. Schutter, however, thinks that legal proceedings are still in view (*Hermeneutic and Composition in I Peter,* WUNT 2/30 [Tübingen: Mohr, 1989], 14–17). For a convincing response to Schutter, see Bechtler, *Following in His Steps*, 87–94. I am not saying that Christians were spared from petty lawsuits and other legal proceedings. The point is that the language is vague and refers to general mistreatment and discrimination of believers in everyday life. Lawsuits, then, may have been part of what believers experienced, but the text does not focus on legal proceedings.

[27] So Tacitus, *Ann.* 15.44. Cf. Suetonius, *Vit.* 6.16.

philosophers.[28] What the evidence does not indicate, however, is that official steps were taken against the church by Domitian. His discrimination against the church was of a piece with his mistreatment of all who opposed him, and certainly Christians would resist calling him "our god and lord" *(deus et dominus noster)*.[29] The sources do not support the claim that an organized and systematic repression of Christians occurred, nor is there evidence that such official action extended to Asia Minor.[30] What we see instead are local or spasmodic eruptions against believers, which could even lead to loss of life (e.g., Rev 2:12; 6:9; 16:6; 17:6; 18:24; 19:2; 20:4).[31] The situation was tense and life threatening in Rome, but one was not subject to official persecution for being a Christian, nor is there evidence of such a state of affairs in Asia Minor.

The last emperor we need to consider is Trajan. We have summarized briefly above the correspondence between Pliny the Younger and Trajan. It is apparent immediately that no official policy of persecuting Christians was in force, for Pliny does not know how he should respond to charges against Christians. He would scarcely have such a question if an official edict had been passed against believers. Nor does Trajan enact a policy that moves officially against Christians, in the sense that they are to be sought out and put to death. But when Christians were encountered who refused to curse Christ and express their devotion to the emperor, they were to be put to death. Such a situation is terrifying enough, surely, but it is not the same as a policy that seeks out believers, demanding their recantation or their death.

There is no reason, on the basis that the persecution in 1 Peter was empirewide during the reigns of Domitian (A.D. 81–96) or Trajan (A.D. 98–117), to locate the date of Peter during the rule of these emperors.[32] Nor does 1 Peter even indicate that an empirewide persecution was underway. Some have detected an official setting from the need to make a defense when asked about one's faith (3:15), the charges that were brought against Christians (4:14–16), and the reference to believers suffering all over the

---

[28] See Suetonius, *Vit.* 8.3.2; 10.2–3; 11–12; Tacitus, *Ann.* 6.29; *Agric.* 3.44. For hostility against Christians see Eusebius, *Hist. eccl.* 3.18.4–19.1; 4.26.9; *1 Clem.* 1:1.

[29] See Suetonius, *Vit.* 8.13.2.

[30] This is now the consensus among scholars. See D. Warden, "Imperial Persecution and the Dating of 1 Peter and Revelation," *JETS* 34 (1991): 203–12; W. C. van Unnik, "The Teaching of Good Works in I Peter," *NTS* 2 (1954): 102; E. G. Selwyn, *The First Epistle of St. Peter,* 2d ed. (Grand Rapids: Baker, 1981), 52–56; Goppelt, *I Peter,* 29; W. Grudem, *The First Epistle of Peter,* TNTC (Grand Rapids: Eerdmans, 1988), 31. See also n. 26.

[31] I am assuming here that Revelation was written during Domitian's reign, but it is possible that it was written under Nero.

[32] Indeed, F. V. Filson indicates that placing Peter within Trajan's reign is quite unlikely since there were some martyrs under Pliny, but there is no evidence of martyrdom in 1 Peter ("Partakers with Christ: Suffering in First Peter," *Int* 9 [1955]: 404).

world (5:9). None of these texts, however, point to an official state-sponsored policy of persecuting Christians. The questions and charges brought against believers in 3:15 and 4:14–16 were typical of the everyday questions believers would encounter because of their faith. In some instances, naturally, the resistance might lead to some kind of official action, but even in these cases it was a local and restricted response to Christians. We know from Acts that Paul was often punished by local authorities as he traveled from city to city and province to province. Such opposition should not be equated with an empirewide proscription of the Christian faith.[33] Nor does the reference to believers suffering throughout the world signal that the Roman Empire had promulgated a decree against the Christian faith. This verse simply reveals that the faith of believers was under threat in the entire Greco-Roman world. Threats, discrimination, and occasionally loss of life were the lot of Christians everywhere. Hence, Peter reminds the believers in Asia Minor that their situation is not unique.

When we examine 1 Peter carefully, an interesting fact emerges. Peter emphasizes throughout that the believers were suffering for their faith. Yet nothing is said about any believers actually dying because of their Christian commitment. It is possible, of course, that some believers were suffering death at the hands of local authorities. Still it seems that Peter would refer to death if this were actually occurring.[34] The only specific suffering noted is discrimination and mistreatment and verbal abuse from former colleagues and friends (1 Pet 4:3–4). The line between discrimination and mistreatment and physical punishment is often a thin one, and hence the former could easily lead to the latter. It must be observed that no specific statement in the letter reveals that believers were being executed in the provinces Peter addresses. We should also note that the Christian faith would be frowned upon because "it was an inferior upstart lacking an authentic, ancient heritage. . . . Furthermore, Christianity's claim to sole possession of the truth violated an important tenet of Roman society, what Goppelt calls 'conforming tolerance, i.e., reciprocal acceptance.'"[35] In other words, Christians were viewed as alarming because of their exclusivism. Apparently matters have not changed much since the first century. Indeed, Christians were under suspicion because they engaged in proselytism, which Goodman says was "a shocking novelty in the ancient world."[36]

The setting of 1 Peter therefore does not exclude a time period within

---

[33] Rightly Filson, "Partakers," 403.

[34] See also Achtemeier, *1 Peter,* 49. This point indicates that dating the letter when letters were exchanged between Pliny and Trajan (ca. A.D. 112–114) is unlikely.

[35] Bechtler, *Following in His Steps*, 84–85.

[36] M. Goodman, *Mission and Conversion: Proselytizing in the Religious History of the Roman Empire* (Oxford: Clarendon, 1994), 105.

Peter's lifetime. The letter easily could have been written during Nero's reign, when opposition to the Christian movement was localized. Those scholars who appeal to the nature of the persecution in 1 Peter and insist the letter must be dated during the time of Domitian and Trajan misinterpret the evidence in both 1 Peter and during the reign of these emperors. In neither case is there evidence of empirewide persecution. Hence, those who dismiss Petrine authorship on this basis fail to make their case.

Others find it incredible to think that Peter is the author since there are so few references to the historical Jesus or allusions to his words. Scholars debate, however, whether Peter alludes somewhat regularly to the words of Jesus. Gundry detects quite a few allusions, whereas Best contests Gundry's evidence.[37] We do not have space to negotiate this detailed discussion here. Suffice it to say that some verses appear to allude to sayings of the historical Jesus, but the number of such verses is not large. Peter seems to draw more on common Christian tradition instead of appealing clearly and indisputably to dominical tradition. In any case, the objection made against Petrine authorship does not seem compelling. The objection is a psychological argument, for it posits what someone who knew the historical Jesus would do if he indeed wrote 1 Peter. Arguments like these are not as compelling as they might appear to be on first glance, for we must beware of asserting what Peter would certainly do as an apostle of Jesus Christ.[38] We might *think* he would appeal quite often to events in the life of Jesus and his sayings, but such assertions have left the realm of evidence and belong to the realm of psychological conjecture. We need to remember that 1 Peter is a short letter in which Peter does not communicate all that he knows to his readers. He writes for a limited and specific purpose to address the concrete circumstances of his readers. Thus nothing can be concluded about Petrine authorship from what is left out of the letter.

The most significant objection against Petrine authorship is the quality of Greek in the letter. We noted earlier that many scholars avoid this problem by suggesting that Silvanus served as Peter's amanuensis on the basis of 1 Pet 5:12.[39] As noted earlier and in the commentary on 5:12, the formula used in 5:12, "through Silvanus . . . I have written this short letter" (NRSV) most naturally refers to the *carrier* rather than the secretary of the letter. There is no basis to posit that Silvanus served as Peter's secretary from this verse. Of course, it is possible that Silvanus was Peter's amanuen-

---

[37] See n. 18.

[38] On this point see also Guthrie, *New Testament Introduction,* 765.

[39] E.g., Selwyn, *First Peter,* 10–11, 27; C. E. B. Cranfield, *I & II Peter and Jude: Introduction and Commentary,* TBC (London: SCM, 1960), 13–16, 18; B. Reicke, *The Epistles of James, Peter, and Jude,* AB (Garden City: Doubleday, 1964), 69–71. Kelly comes close to embracing Petrine authorship but declares himself uncertain (*Peter and Jude,* 32–33).

sis anyway, and Peter says nothing about it. Moreover, it could be the case that someone else with Peter served as his secretary, and we are not told about this matter. Nevertheless, we have no internal evidence that Peter used a secretary. A secretary who knew Greek well could have assisted Peter in the writing of the letter, and this would explain the cultivated Greek in the epistle. Such a theory cannot be dismissed, but neither can it be proved. In any case, Peter may have used a secretary, which could explain the excellent Greek used in the letter.[40]

The preference for Greek instead of Hebrew also seems strange to many, for the citations and allusions to the Old Testament come from the Septuagint rather than the MT in 1 Peter. Some scholars are convinced that Peter, as a Galilean Jew, would not have cited the Greek Old Testament. The argument fails to convince. It is quite natural that Peter would appeal to the Septuagint since that is the Bible his readers would use in Asia Minor.[41] Peter wrote to communicate to his readers, and therefore it is hardly surprising that he relayed his message in their idiom.

We return to the objection that the cultivated Greek in the letter does not fit with Peter as a Galilean fisherman. This piece of data raises the most serious questions about Petrine authorship. As noted above, it is possible that Peter used an anonymous amanuensis, and the quality of the Greek could then be ascribed to the secretary. On this scenario Peter may have given orally the substance of his message, and the secretary composed it. Presumably Peter himself would have reviewed the first draft and suggested changes before sending out the letter. Such a review fits with the design and beauty of the letter. The disadvantage of this view is that it cannot be established on the basis of any firm evidence. On the other hand, it is possible that Peter used a secretary and did not inform the readers that he did so.

The argument can be pressed further. There are solid grounds for thinking that Peter himself, as a Galilean fisherman, could have written 1 Peter.[42]

---

[40] J. R. Michaels rightly says, "The assumption that Peter had professional help in the composition of this letter by no means requires that the name of his amanuensis be known" (*1 Peter,* WBC [Waco: Word, 1998], lxii). Similarly, Davids remarks that the "hypothesis does not depend upon the scribe's being Silvanus" (*First Peter,* 6, n. 4). Grudem makes this mistake, arguing that Silvanus is the bearer rather than the scribe of the letter (*1 Peter,* 23–24). He concludes that since Silvanus is not explicitly identified as the scribe, Peter must have written the letter himself. Such a conclusion cannot be proven given the present state of the evidence. The possibility remains that Silvanus or someone else functioned as the scribe. D. B. Wallace makes the same point, arguing that the difference in style between the two letters almost requires an amanuensis; he then suggests that either Silvanus or Luke may have served as such ("First Peter: Introduction, Argument, and Outline," at http://www.bible.org/studies/soapbox/2petotl.htm).

[41] Rightly Guthrie, *New Testament Introduction,* 767–68.

[42] In this regard see the remarks of F. Neugebauer, "Zur Deutung und Bedeutung des 1. Petrusbriefes," *NTS* 26 (1980): 72.

First of all, Greek was the language of commerce and had penetrated into Galilee.[43] Hellenism, as M. Hengel has demonstrated, was quite influential in Palestine by the time the New Testament documents were composed.[44] Furthermore, Galilee was near the Gentile Decapolis, and linguistic contact and overlap between the two areas was inevitable. Indeed, the city of Sepphoris in Galilee was a Hellenistic city in which both Aramaic and Greek were spoken. Peter, as a person of business, would almost certainly have known Greek, and it would have been necessary for him to know the language to advance his business interests. Porter rightly remarks, "Greek was the prestige language of Palestine, and anyone wishing to conduct business on any extended scale, including any successful fishermen from the Hellenized region of Galilee and probably any craftsmen or artisans who would have come into contact with Roman customers, would have needed to have known—indeed would have wanted to know—Greek."[45]

J. N. Sevenster argues that several lines of evidence suggest that ordinary people in Israel, particularly Galilee, would have known Greek.[46] In Jerusalem and Beth Shearim many ossuaries (stone coffins containing bones of the dead) have Greek inscriptions rather than Hebrew or Aramaic. One of the letters written by Simon bar Cochba (A.D. 132–135) or one of his assistants was written in Greek, which is surprising in a nationalistic movement, suggesting that Greek was quite well known. Some Greek has also been found in Qumran, even though Aramaic and Hebrew dominate. Josephus seems to indicate that other Jews could write Greek well if they were so motivated (*Ant.* 20.262–65). An imperial inscription warning against the robbing of tombs was published in Greek (found in Nazareth) in the first century A.D. This inscription was likely intended for Galilee, indicating again, presumably, that many Galileans could read what was inscribed. Inscriptions in Greek have also been found in a number of Jewish synagogues.

Greek certainly was known and commonly used in Palestine. The question, then, should be posed more sharply. The question is not, "Did Peter know and use Greek?" He almost certainly knew Greek and used it as well. The question is, "Is it plausible to say that Peter as a Galilean wrote such beautiful Greek?"

---

[43] Kelly, *Peter and Jude*, 31.

[44] M. Hengel, *Judaism and Hellenism: Studies in Their Encounter in Palestine during the Early Hellenistic Period* (London: SCM Press, 1974).

[45] S. E. Porter, "Greek of the New Testament," *DNTB*, 430–31.

[46] J. N. Sevenster, *Do You Know Greek? How Much Greek Could the First Jewish Christians Have Known?* NovTSup 19 (Leiden: Brill, 1968). For similar arguments see J. M. Fitzmyer, "The Languages of Palestine in the First Century A.D.," *CBQ* 32 (1970): 507–18. Much of the evidence is probably from the second to fourth century A.D., but it is quite likely that there was cultural continuity in the use of the language, and hence the later dates are not decisive against the thesis argued for here.

Some confidently say that he could not do so since he came from the business class. After all, he is labeled as "unschooled" *(agrammatos)* by the Sanhedrin in Acts 4:13. The epithet *unlearned* does not mean that Peter was uneducated or illiterate.[47] The Sanhedrin did not know Peter so intimately. What they did know was that Peter was not trained rabbinically. He did not have the equivalent of a seminary education, so how could he instruct them in theological matters? Grudem rightly observes that manual laborers who are untrained may have remarkable linguistic gifts. He points to John Bunyan, who wrote the masterpiece *Pilgrim's Progress*, even though he was merely a Bedford tinker.[48] Grudem also notes the example of Joseph Conrad (1857–1924), a Polish sailor whose first language was Polish, his second French, and who began learning English at twenty-one years of age. Nevertheless, he wrote the classic *Lord Jim* in English.[49] Some may respond by saying that the latter example is extraordinary and should not be introduced as evidence. But as Grudem observes, the point is not that Peter was as gifted as Joseph Conrad, since Peter was raised in a culture that probably was trilingual (Aramaic, Greek, and probably Hebrew). The purpose of the illustration is to say that if a person who did not learn English as an adult can write beautiful English, then Peter may have had the capability to write excellent Greek. Wand remarks, "I have known an ex-lumberjack in Australia . . . who could write better English than the average university don."[50] We must beware of an educational snobbery that refuses to recognize the intellectual and literary gifts of those in business.

Others insist that Peter could not have written the letter because the theology is too similar to Paul's.[51] The matter of Peter's relationship to Paul is quite complex, deserving further analysis than can be presented here. We can say that the Petrine letter does not show evidence that he used Paul's letters as a literary source.[52] Peter's wording is not exact enough to suggest that he wrote with any of the Pauline letters before him. Furthermore, important Pauline themes are lacking in 1 Peter: justification, the role of the law, Pauline Christology, and others. We can also point to some matters held in common: (1) salvation is an eschatological gift (1 Pet 1:3–9; Rom

[47] Rightly Dalton, "Your Hope in God," 263; Grudem, *1 Peter,* 26; Guthrie, *New Testament Introduction,* 764.

[48] Grudem, *1 Peter,* 30.

[49] Ibid., 31.

[50] J. W. C. Wand, "The Lessons of First Peter: A Survey of Interpretation," *Int* 9 (1955): 391.

[51] Others have objected that Peter would not have written to Pauline churches, but Guthrie rightly remarks that it is not evident that the churches addressed were established personally by Paul. Furthermore, even if they were planted by Paul (which is doubtful), Peter may have written these churches after Paul's death (see Guthrie, *New Testament Introduction,* 773–74).

[52] I am not denying that Peter knew some of the Pauline letters, for that is evident from 2 Pet 3:15–16. Nevertheless, the evidence is insufficient to conclude that any of the Pauline letters were used as a literary source for the contents of 1 Peter.

5:9–10); (2) believers will suffer for their faith (1 Pet 1:6–7; 3:13–17; 4:12–19; 2 Tim 3:12); (3) believers should live holy lives (1 Pet 1:13–2:3; Rom 6:1–23; Eph 4:1–6:9; Col 3:5–4:6); (4) Jesus is God's cornerstone (1 Pet 2:6; Rom 9:33); (5) believers should submit to governing authorities (1 Pet 2:13–17; Rom 13:1–7); (6) wives should submit to husbands (1 Pet 3:1–6; Eph 5:22–24); (7) husbands should treat their wives kindly (1 Pet 3:7; Eph 5:25–29); (8) Christ is exalted as Lord over angelic powers (1 Pet 3:18–19,22; Eph 1:20–23; Col 1:16; 2:10,15); (9) the end is near (1 Pet 4:7; Rom 13:11–14). Other doctrines held in common could be noted, but none of the items mentioned reflect dependence of Peter upon Paul. Indeed, the most probable conclusion is that they shared common Christian tradition on these matters.[53] Peter and Paul are not carbon copies of each other, and 1 Peter is distinct enough to make this clear.

We must also beware of a Tübingen overemphasis, in which the shared theology of Peter and Paul is erased (cf. 1 Cor 15:11).[54] The incident in Antioch (Gal 2:11–14) does not suggest fundamental and long-standing disagreements between Peter and Paul. If we take the written text seriously, Peter acted hypocritically and fearfully, not from conviction. Many scholars, of course, dismiss Paul's explanation and contend that Peter differed from Paul theologically. The text certainly indicates that Peter was more concerned and sensitive to Jewish objections than Paul. Still, no evidence exists that he differed with Paul's theology. I am not denying that Peter and Paul had different emphases in their theology, nor should we cancel out the diversity of the New Testament witness. The point being made here is that the "Pauline" character of 1 Peter does not rule out Petrine authorship.

I conclude by saying that there are no decisive grounds to reject Petrine authorship for the letter. Both internal and external evidence supports such a view, and there was no controversy over whether Peter wrote the letter in the early church, showing that there is no evidence from antiquity that the letter was a "transparent fiction." The objections raised against Petrine authorship are not compelling, and credible responses can be given to each one. The cultivated style of the Greek is the most important objection to authenticity, but a number of pieces of evidence indicate that it is quite possible Peter knew Greek well and could have written a letter like 1 Peter. It is unnecessary to say that Peter had visited the churches personally,[55] though we cannot rule out such a visit since we know little about Peter's travels. The reference to Babylon (see the com-

[53] Elliott remarks that "the theory of a Petrine dependence upon Paul must now be rejected in favor of a common Petrine and Pauline use of a broadly varied (liturgical, parenetic, and catechetical) tradition" ("Rehabilitation of 1 Peter," 247).

[54] So Guthrie, *New Testament Introduction*, 775–76.

[55] Rightly Davids, *First Peter,* 9.

mentary on 5:13) almost certainly refers to Rome, and therefore we can conclude that Peter wrote the letter while in Rome.[56]

2. Date

Discussion of the date of the letter can be quite brief since it depends upon the question of authorship.[57] Those who reject Petrine authorship typically date the letter in the time of Trajan (A.D. 98–117),[58] Domitian (A.D. 81–96), or even Vespasian or Titus (A.D. 69–81).[59] Most scholars now opt for the latter instead of the former. If Peter is the author of the letter and if he wrote from Rome, as the reference to Babylon in 5:13 suggests (see commentary on 5:13), the letter was likely written near the end of Peter's life when he was in Rome.[60] Assigning a specific date is conjectural, but it is likely that the letter was written in the 60s.[61] Arguments from silence are notoriously slippery, but there are good grounds for thinking that Peter would have mentioned the Neronian persecution if it had started, so that he could remind believers in Asia Minor of the intensity of suffering experi-

---

[56] See the excellent discussion in Guthrie, *New Testament Introduction*, 793–95. Cf. also Elliott, *1 Peter,* 131–34.

[57] Michaels follows Ramsey in suggesting a later date for Peter and its possible authenticity (after the Neronian persecution but before the reign of Domitian [*1 Peter,* lxii–lxv]). His arguments for a later date are not compelling (see comments of Davids, *First Peter,* 10, n. 12). He argues that the submissive attitude toward the state does not fit with either the Neronian persecution or the era when Domitian mistreated believers (lxiii). Such an argument is unpersuasive, for it ignores the fact that persecution and mistreatment were always hovering like storm clouds over the church. Such mistreatment did not alter the exhortation to be submissive to governing authorities. Achtemeier rightly says, "Long after severe persecutions had in fact broken out, Christians persisted in expressing their loyalty to the emperor and praying for the continued existence of the Roman state" (*1 Peter,* 46).

[58] A. T. Hanson, "Salvation Proclaimed: I. 1 Peter 3.18–22," *ExpTim* 93 (1982): 101; Beare, *First Peter,* 9–19 (A.D. 111–112).

[59] Kümmel, *Introduction to the New Testament*, A.D. 90–95; Elliott, A.D. 75–92 ("Peter, Silvanus and Mark," 254; *Home for the Homeless*, 87); he now says A.D. 73–92 (Elliott, *1 Peter,* 134–38); D. L. Balch (*Let Wives Be Submissive: The Domestic Code in I Peter,* SBLMS 26 [Chico: Scholars Press, 1981], 133–34) follows Goppelt (*I Peter,* 45–47) in narrowing the date to A.D. 65–80; Achtemeier, *1 Peter,* 50 (A.D. 80–100); R. Martin, "1 Peter," 94 (A.D. 75–85); Bechtler, *Following in His Steps*, 52 (A.D. 75–105); D. G. Horrell, A.D. 75–95 (*The Epistles of Peter and Jude*, EC [Peterborough: Epworth, 1998], 10).

[60] Elliott presents ten arguments for a Roman origin, acknowledging that not all of them are equally persuasive ("Peter, Silvanus and Mark," 253, n. 9).

[61] The reference to Babylon in 5:13 is not strong evidence for a post-A.D. 70 date as Michaels alleges (*1 Peter,* lxiii; rightly Davids, *First Peter,* 11, n. 13). The term was natural for one familiar with the OT. Nor, contra Michaels, does the reference to the congregation in Babylon suggest a different time frame in which there was a unified Christian community instead of house churches. The reference to the church in Babylon tells us nothing about how many congregations there were in Rome, nor does it preclude the existence of a multitude of house churches.

enced by Roman Christians. Therefore I would date the letter around A.D. 62–63 before the onset of the Neronian persecution.[62]

3. Destination and Situation of the Readers

The reference to Babylon in 5:13 is almost surely a reference to Rome, indicating that Peter wrote the letter from Rome to churches in Asia Minor.[63] We have corroborating evidence that Mark (5:13) was in Rome about the time Peter was written (Col 4:10; Phlm 24). The letter is addressed to believers dispersed in "Pontus, Galatia, Cappadocia, Asia and Bithynia" (1 Pet 1:1).[64] When Peter wrote the letter, Bithynia and Pontus were a single province (see commentary under 1:1), and hence Peter probably wrote generally, designating a geographic area north of the Taurus mountains (in what is now modern-day Turkey) as the recipients of the letter. It is likely that Peter designated the area by province instead of geographically; for if it were the latter, he probably would have included Paphlagonia, Phrygia, Pisidia, and Lycaonia.[65] The order in which the areas are listed probably designates the order in which the courier (Silvanus per 5:12) carried the letter.[66] The regions are roughly in a circle. We would expect a person coming from the sea to land at Bithynia first and then go on to Pontus. We cannot decipher the reason Bithynia was visited last. Perhaps Silvanus

---

[62] Selwyn, *First Peter,* 56–63 (A.D. 63 or early 64); N. Hillyer dates it in A.D. 63 before the outbreak of persecution (*1 and 2 Peter, Jude*, NIBC [Peabody: Hendrickson, 1992], 3). Kelly, *Peter and Jude*, 30; Cranfield, *I & II Peter and Jude*, 17 (A.D. 63 or 64); Guthrie, *New Testament Introduction*, 786–88 (A.D. 62–64); Wallace, "First Peter: Introduction, Argument, and Outline" (A.D. 64); Martin, *ISBE* (A.D. 64); Grudem, *1 Peter,* 37; Reicke, *The Epistles of James, Peter, and Jude*, 71–72 (A.D. 64 before Peter's death). Subsequent to persecution: J. A. T. Robinson (ca. A.D. 65), *Redating the New Testament* (Philadelphia: Westminster, 1976), 161.

[63] So Michaels, *1 Peter,* xlvii; Achtemeier, *1 Peter,* 63–64. Beare thinks the letter was written from Asia Minor itself and that the reference to Babylon is part of the pseudonymous dress of the letter (though he agrees that Babylon signifies Rome [*First Peter,* 31], but, according to Achtemeier, Beare later changed his view [*1 Peter,* 64. n. 657]). In support of Rome, see Kelly, *Peter and Jude*, 33–34. Goppelt sees the letter as hailing from Rome, even though he does not accept Petrine authorship (*I Peter,* 48).

[64] P. L. Tite suggests that the letter may not have been genuinely addressed to readers in five different provinces, so that the reference to the five locales may be metaphorical (*Compositional Transitions in 1 Peter: An Analysis of the Letter-Opening* [San Francisco: International Scholars Publications, 1997], 30). In my judgment there is no reason to doubt that Peter genuinely addresses readers in the locales named, for the metaphorical significance of listing five different locales is not evident.

[65] So Goppelt, *I Peter,* 3–4; Elliott, *Home for the Homeless*, 60; Kelly, *Peter and Jude*, 3.

[66] So F. J. A. Hort, *The First Epistle of St Peter: I.1–II.17* (New York: Macmillan, 1898), 167–84; C. Hemer, "The Address of 1 Peter," *ExpTim* 89 (1978): 239–43; Grudem, *1 Peter,* 37–38; Guthrie, *New Testament Introduction*, 784; R. Martin, "1 Peter," 87. Alternatively, Beare suggests that Pontus and Bithynia commence and conclude the list since the persecution was particularly fierce there, and the author was especially concerned about the church in these areas (*First Peter,* 22–24).

planned his visit to conclude in Bithynia so he could sail away to his next destination after completing the journey.

We know from the letter that the readers were facing suffering and persecution for their faith (1:6–7; 2:18–20; 3:1,13–17; 4:1–4,12–19; 5:10). It was explained earlier that the persecution was not state sponsored or an official policy of the empire. Instead, the suffering was local and sporadic.[67] Discrimination and mistreatment for Christian faith may arise at any time, but being a Christian was not formally illegal.[68]

Were the readers Jews or Gentiles? Peter assumed the readers knew the Old Testament since he quoted from it or alluded to it often (e.g., 1:16,24–25; 2:3,6–10,22; 3:10–12; 4:18; 5:5). A number of characters from the Old Testament are named: prophets (1:10–12), Sarah and Abraham (3:6), and Noah (3:20). Some in the history of scholarship, noting this emphasis on the Old Testament, conclude that the readers were Jewish.[69] Today, however, most scholars agree that the readers were mainly Gentiles.[70] The evidence in support of this conclusion is quite compelling.[71] To say that they lived in "ignorance" *(agnoia)* suggests an idolatrous and pagan past

---

[67] Michaels argues that Peter ignores the Jewish unbelievers in the letter (*1 Peter,* xlix). Elliott suggests that the Jews participated in the persecution of the church (*Home for the Homeless*, 80–81). Both of these views are speculative and lack evidence to substantiate the conclusion drawn (rightly Davids. *First Peter,* 8, n.7). More likely the power to discriminate and mistreat was not in the hands of the Jews who refused to believe in Christ but belonged to Gentile unbelievers.

[68] Reicke maintains that Peter wrote the letter to counsel readers against resisting the government, so that they would not engage in any activities that would overturn the government (*Epistles of James, Peter, and Jude,* 72–73). Such a reading of 1 Peter is quite improbable. See the critique by C. F. Sleeper, "'Political Responsibility according to I Peter,'" *NovT* 10 (1968): 270–86.

[69] E.g., Andreas in *James, 1–2 Peter, 1–3 John, Jude,* ACCS (Downers Grove: InterVarsity, 2000), 66; J. Calvin, *Commentaries on the Catholic Epistles* (Grand Rapids: Eerdmans, 1948), 25. For a current defense of the view see A. S. Sykes, "The Function of 'Peter' in I Peter," *ScrB* 27 (1997): 8–21; Elliott, *1 Peter,* 94–97, 721.

[70] So Kelly, *Peter and Jude*, 4; Best, *1 Peter,* 19; Davids, *First Peter,* 8–9; Achtemeier, *1 Peter,* 50–51; Winbery, "Introduction to First Peter," 6; Michaels, *1 Peter,* xlv–xlvi. Selwyn says the readers were mixed (*First Peter,* 42–44). Bechtler argues the letter addresses Gentiles only (*Following in His Steps,* 61–63). S. McKnight notes that the readers may have been God-fearers (*1 Peter,* NIVAC [Grand Rapids: Zondervan, 1996], 24).

[71] W. C. van Unnik argues that the readers were former God-fearers and proselytes who converted to the Christian faith ("Christianity according to I Peter," and "The Redemption in I Peter I.18–19 and the Problem of the First Epistle of Peter," in *Sparsa Collecta: The Collected Essays of W. C. van Unnik. Part Two: I Peter, Canon, Corpus Hellenisticum, Generalia,* NovTSup 30 [Leiden: Brill, 1980], 114–16 and 30–82). It is difficult to believe that all the readers in the various provinces addressed fit the paradigm. Further, clear evidence that Peter addressed God-fearers is lacking. Van Unnik relies on arcane and opaque terms to link 1 Peter to proselytes. Kümmel rightly says that identifying the readers as God-fearers "is an arbitrary assumption" (*Introduction to the New Testament*, 418). T. Seland argues that the readers were not actually former proselytes but that Peter used metaphors drawn from the social world of proselytes to communicate to his readers ("πάροικος καί παρεπίδημος: Proselyte Characterizations in 1 Peter?" *BBR* 11 (2001): 239–68.

(1:14).[72] Even more telling is the claim that they had been "redeemed from the empty way of life handed down to you from your forefathers" (1:18). Peter would scarcely say that Jewish forefathers lived vainly, since the Jews were God's elect people (cf. also 2:10,25). The Gentile origin of the readers seems clear from 4:3–4: "For you have spent enough time in the past doing what pagans choose to do—living in debauchery, lust, drunkenness, orgies, carousing and detestable idolatry. They think it strange that you do not plunge with them into the same flood of dissipation, and they heap abuse on you." It is difficult to believe that Peter would characterize Jews as indulging in such blatant sins, whereas the vices were typical of the Jewish conception of Gentiles.[73]

The citations and allusions to the Old Testament and the mention of certain characters from the Old Testament does not necessarily point to Jewish readers. We know from other letters (e.g., 1 Corinthians) that allusions and citations from the Old Testament are included in letters written to Gentiles. Apparently when Gentiles were evangelized, they received significant instruction in the Old Testament. This is not to say that the churches in northern Asia Minor were exclusively Gentile, for presumably some Jews were members of the churches. On the whole, however, the churches were Gentile, and texts like 1:18 and 4:3–4 indicate that they were mainly so.

What is particularly interesting is that the readers are identified as (NRSV) "exiles" (1:1, *parepidēmoi*), in "exile" (1:17, *paroikia*), "aliens and exiles" (2:11, *paroikous kai parepidēmous*).[74] In his sociological study of 1 Peter, Elliott argues that the terms refer to the political status of the readers before they became believers. The former refer to permanent strangers and the latter to

---

[72] Michaels suggests that the letter may reflect Gal 2:7–10, where Peter's ministry is to preach the gospel to the Jews. Even though the letter was addressed to Gentiles, "its genre is that of a diaspora letter to Israel" (*1 Peter,* xlvii; see also p. xlviii). The theory proposed by Michaels is quite implausible. We have no evidence that Peter reflects upon Gal 2:7–10. Furthermore, identifying the Gentile church as Israel seems like an artificial way to understand the agreement in Gal 2:7–10. It is much more likely that the agreement in Gal 2:7–10 was never intended to ban Peter from participating in the Gentile mission (cf. Wallace, "First Peter: Introduction, Argument, and Outline"). Finally, Davids rightly questions "whether the diaspora letter to Israel formed a distinct genre" (*First Peter,* 14).

[73] Sykes' claim that the readers were Jewish breaks down completely in his analysis of 1 Pet 4:3–4. He claims that Peter identifies the behavior of the persecutors, not the former lifestyle of the recipients ("The Function of 'Peter' in I Peter," 13). The text, however, clearly indicates that *both* the behavior of the persecutors *and* the former lifestyle of the recipients is in view. Sykes' view also fails in that he argues that describing the persecutors as Gentile is a rhetorical stratagem (p. 15). The other evidence in the letter, however, indicates that the recipients are Gentiles. Hence, no need exists to pit the rhetorical situation against the actual circumstances addressed.

[74] See also F. Schröger, *Gemeinde im 1. Petrusbrief: Untersuchungen zum Selbstverständnis einer christlichen Gemeinde an der Wende vom 1. zum 2. Jahrhundert* (Katholische Theologie 1: Passau: Passavia Universitätsverlag, 1981).

those who are living temporarily in the regions addressed in the letter.[75] Hence, for Elliott the readers were not aliens *by virtue of their faith.* They were literally resident aliens and visiting strangers in regions addressed by Peter.[76] This is an improbable reading of the evidence.[77] The pair of terms in 1 Pet 2:11 hearkens back to Gen 23:4 and Ps 38:13, showing that the church of Jesus Christ occupies the status of God's people throughout history.[78] In a thorough study of the evidence, Chin demonstrates that the terms cannot be distinguished so sharply from one another, based on his study of the LXX, Philo, the New Testament, and the early Fathers.[79] Hence, both words are used in a spiritual sense and should not be understood literally. Pryor rightly observes, "It is just not imaginable that a group of churches in Asia Minor at this time would be made up of one social class, 'resident aliens.'"[80] It must also be observed that 1 Pet 2:11 uses "as" *(hōs)* to introduce the words "aliens and exiles," indicating a comparison instead of a literal description of the status of the readers in society. The readers

---

[75] Elliott, *Home for the* Homeless, 37–49, 129–32; *1 Peter,* 100–102. So also B. L. Campbell, *Honor, Shame, and the Rhetoric of 1 Peter,* SBLDS 160 (Atlanta: Scholars Press, 1998), 21–22; McKnight, *1 Peter,* 25, 48–51.

[76] Bechtler argues that Elliott misreads the evidence, conflating the view that πάροικοι were both geographically displaced and noncitizens. In the LXX the πάροικοι were aliens geographically, but in Hellenistic literature, when used as a technical term, it designated those who were noncitizens. Hence, says Bechtler, many of the πάροικοι were natives of their region but were not part of the political process. Still, Bechtler concedes that the issue is difficult since the term is not always used technically (*Following in His Steps,* 70–74).

[77] Bechtler points out that Elliott is also faced with a problem in that παρεπίδημοι is taken literally by the latter in 2:11 when adjoined with πάροικοι, but the term seems to be understood metaphorically in 1:1 (*Following in His Steps,* 75). Now Elliott has taken the improbable step of arguing that the author begins by addressing some of the readers as literal aliens and then "enlarges" the concept so that it also applies metaphorically to all the readers (*1 Peter,* 102). Such a reading is impossibly complex, leading us to question why it is necessary to see a literal referent in the terms at all.

[78] So Bechtler, *Following in His Steps,* 78–81.

[79] M. Chin, "A Heavenly Home for the Homeless: Aliens and Strangers in 1 Peter," *TynBul* 42 (1991): 96–112. For a critique of Elliott, see R. Feldmeier, *Die Christen als Fremde: Die Metapher der Fremde in der antiken Welt, im Urchristentum und im 1. Petrusbrief,* WUNT 64 (Tübingen: Mohr, 1992), 203–10. Feldmeier remarks that the OT background sits awkwardly with Elliott's view (see esp. 208). Feldmeier examines the terms παρεπίδημοι and πάροικοι in Hellenistic and Jewish literature, including its usage in the Hebrew text, the LXX, the apocrypha, pseudepigrapha, Qumran, and Philo. He also discusses the term in other NT literature. Feldmeier devotes special attention to παρεπίδημοι, arguing that its placement in the prescript and in 2:11 herald its significance. He thinks Peter emphasized the nonentity of the readers in the world in which they lived. We can accept Feldmeier's conclusion here, though he goes too far in rejecting any notion of a heavenly homeland by contrast. The theme of a future inheritance is fundamental in 1:3–9 and, indeed, in the whole of 1 Peter.

[80] J. W. Pryor, "First Peter and the New Covenant (II)," *RTR* 45 (1986): 45; cf. also T. W. Martin, *Metaphor and Composition in 1 Peter,* SBLDS 131 (Atlanta: Scholars Press, 1992), 142.

are identified as aliens and exiles for theological reasons.[81] Further, as Bechtler notes, the term "scattered" *(diaspora)* in 1 Pet 1:1 derives from a Jewish rather than a Hellenistic background.[82] The word is used metaphorically in 1 Peter, for literally it designates the *Jewish* dispersion, but Peter applies it to Gentiles. The metaphorical use of the term calls into question Elliott's view that Peter used technical terminology from the Hellenistic domain when using the terms "strangers" and "aliens." The believers in 1 Peter are the new people of God, but as God's people they are disenfranchised, discriminated against, and mistreated. Their home is not earth but heaven.[83]

4. Character of the Letter

The structure of 1 Peter has been the subject of discussion from the earliest history of the church. Martin usefully surveys the different structures proposed from Pseudo-Euthalius up until the contemporary period.[84] The diversity of outlines illustrates that the task of exegesis is not merely a science but also an art. We will note here contributions that have been particularly important in the history of exegesis.

Some scholars see hymnic or creedal material in the letter (e.g., 1:3–12,18–21; 2:21–25; 3:18–22). Boismard maintains that there are four baptismal hymns in 1 Peter.[85] Possibly Peter draws upon such preformed material, but the criteria to establish such are anything but certain in the texts so identified.[86] Evidence that such hymns are "baptismal" is even more diffi-

---

[81] In his sociological study Bechtler argues that the fundamental issue in the letter is the issue of honor that faced the readers in their daily lives (*Following in His Steps,* 20; cf. also p. 103). "The essential problem, I shall argue, is that, in a society preoccupied with accumulation and loss of honor, the honor of the Petrine addressees is constantly at risk in their interactions with outsiders—interactions whose effects on the intended readers are characterized by the letter as 'suffering'" (p. 39).

[82] Bechtler, *Following in His Steps,* 75–77. The same point is made regarding Peter's use of the term ἐκλεκτοί. Originally it referred to Jews who were chosen by God, but Peter now appropriates the term and used it to refer to believing Gentiles (pp. 77–78).

[83] Achtemeier rightly argues that the evidence does not permit us to identify the readers with any particular social class, particularly the poor. Rather, the evidence we have indicates that the readers come from a broad and diverse social background (*1 Peter,* 55–57).

[84] Martin, *Metaphor and Composition in 1 Peter,* 3–39. See also the summary by Martin's student P. L. Tite, who argues that Martin's work is the best to date (*Compositional Transitions in 1 Peter,* 3–18. See Tite's adjustments on pp. 91–94. J. R. Slaughter laments that not enough work has been done on the structure of 1 Peter ("The Importance of Literary Argument for Understanding 1 Peter," *BSac* 152 [1995]: 72). Further work has been done since Slaughter wrote, though he himself does not set forth a detailed defense for his understanding of the letter (pp. 72–91).

[85] M.-E. Boismard, *Quatre hymnes baptismales dans la premiére Épître de Pierre,* LD 30 (Paris: Les Éditions du Cerf, 1961).

[86] Rightly Martin, *Metaphor and Composition in 1 Peter,* 83; Davids, *First Peter,* 12; Elliott, *1 Peter,* 32.

cult to defend. In any case, the texts are integrated into the fabric of the letter as a whole, and hence whether we have traditional material does not affect their interpretation unless we speculatively identify the setting of the hymns. The responsibility of the exegete is to explain how they fit into the context and argument of 1 Peter. If the texts are creedal, this would play a role in establishing the history of early Christianity but is not as important for interpreting 1 Peter.

Selwyn, in his outstanding commentary, defends the notion that Peter uses common catechetical traditions.[87] He demonstrates that Peter shares common themes and even common wording with both Old Testament texts and other epistles, especially the Pauline epistles. We can agree with Lohse, however, that the conclusions presented cannot be proven since "there will always be weighty objections that must be raised against such an attempt at reconstruction, because in doing this one too easily ventures into the realm of hypotheses that cannot be proven."[88] As Bechtler says, "No fixed schema of catechetical instruction can be discerned within or even behind the text."[89] Peter's letter demonstrates that early Christians shared common traditions, but it exceeds the evidence to postulate some kind of shared catechetical tradition.

A number of scholars have understood 1 Peter as a baptismal document.[90] Preisker even sees a baptismal service in progress when the letter was written, placing the baptism between 1:21–22. The theory is quite improbable, and we lack any convincing rationale why Peter would send the order of a baptismal service to churches in Asia Minor.[91] Cross identifies the letter as a baptismal liturgy for an Easter baptismal service, but this theory suffers from lack of evidence and is speculative.[92] The claim that baptism is fundamental in 1 Peter

---

[87] Selwyn, *First Peter,* 365–466.

[88] E. Lohse, "Parenesis and Kerygma in 1 Peter," in *Perspectives on 1 Peter* (Macon: Mercer University Press, 1986), 41.

[89] Bechtler, *Following in His Steps*, 4; so also Elliott, *1 Peter,* 29.

[90] W. Bornemann sees a baptismal sermon in the letter and sees Psalm 34 as the text for the homily ("Der erste Petrusbrief—eine Taufrede des Silvanus?" *ZNW* 19 [1919]: 143–65). O. S. Brooks identifies the letter as a baptismal sermon in which converts are given instructions on how to live the Christian life ("I Peter 3:21—The Clue to the Literary Structure of the Epistle," *NovT* 16 [1974]: 290–305).

[91] H. Windisch, *Die katholischen Briefe*, HNT (Tübingen: Mohr, 1951), 156–62.

[92] F. L. Cross, *I Peter: A Paschal Liturgy* (London: Mowbray, 1954). For a devastating and compelling critique of Cross, see T. C. G. Thornton, "I Peter, A Paschal Liturgy?" *JTS* 12 (1961): 14–26. Cf. also R. P. Martin, "The Composition of I Peter in Recent Study," *VE* 1 (1962): 36–40. T. W. Martin trenchantly remarks: "Indeed, constructing fanciful historical scenarios is a favorite method of these analytical traditions, but this method is unsatisfactory because of the subjective nature of the scenario. It is best to deal seriously with the text and avoid these fanciful reconstructions" (*Metaphor and Composition in 1 Peter,* 33). Indeed, Martin labels the views of Preisker and Cross as "sheer fantasy" (p. 36).

should be rejected, for the word only occurs in 1 Pet 3:21.[93] Scholars who read 1 Peter looking for baptism inevitably find it everywhere, but a more sober and critical reading shows the weakness of the hypothesis.[94] These theories were once quite popular in critical circles, but now most scholars reject them.[95] The disfavor with such theories, which were once embraced by many, reminds us that views that lack persuasion can seem quite compelling for a period of time.

Some scholars also have suggested that 1 Peter consists of two different letters, the first letter consisting of 1:3–4:11 and the second consisting of 4:12–5:14.[96] Those who defend a partition theory argue that the sufferings in 4:12 are present, while in 3:17 suffering is only hypothetical. Similarly, it is argued that joy is present in 1:6,8, whereas joy is confined to the future in 4:12–13. The "amen" in 4:11 signals the end of the first letter, as does the doxology in that verse. The claim to write a "short letter" (5:12) is only credible if 4:12–5:14 constitutes a separate letter.[97] This theory, though once quite popular, seems to be losing proponents, as scholars are becoming increasingly convinced of the unity of New Testament letters.[98] Convincing replies can be made to those who argue for partition.[99] First, it is

---

[93] So D. Hill, "On Suffering and Baptism in I Peter," *NovT* 18 (1976): 186. He also rightly remarks that "the baptismal theme [is] quite subsidiary, almost incidental, to the main purpose and meaning of I Peter" (p. 185). He goes on to say: "The baptismal tone of the letter is due, not to its being substantially a baptismal homily, or the liturgy of a just-completed rite, but to the fact that a Christian's baptism is the point of transition from an ancient, inherited system of religious practice (1:18) to a new faith and a consequent way of life that is marked by a totally new moral attitude and bearing." Cf. also his comments on p. 189. See also Lohse, "Parenesis and Kerygma in 1 Peter," 39–40.

[94] See C. F. D. Moule, "The Nature and Purpose of I Peter," *NTS* 3 (1956–57): 1–11. Even Moule, in my judgment, is too prone to see allusions to baptism in the letter.

[95] E.g., Kelly, *Peter and Jude*, 15–20; Goppelt, *I Peter*, 15–18; Michaels, *1 Peter*, xxxix; Davids, *First Peter*, 12; Achtemeier, *1 Peter*, 58–62. Michaels says that 4:12–5:11 elaborates and applies 4:7–11 to congregations ruled by elders. It is unclear from the text, however, that 4:12–5:11 has such a specific purpose.

[96] E.g. Windisch-Preisker, *Die katholischen Briefe*, 76–77; Cranfield, *I & II Peter and Jude*, 11–13; Beare, *First Peter*, 6–9.

[97] Moule argues that the letter was sent to different communities, one which was actually suffering and another that faced potential suffering, so that the letter was composed of two different parts originally, with 1:1–4:11 and 5:12–14 to the former group and 1:1–2:10 and 5:12–14 to the latter ("Purpose of I Peter," 7). He thinks the letter was later unified. J. W. C. Wand suggests that 4:12–5:11 may have been written when fresh news of impending persecution reached Peter (*The General Epistles of St. Peter and St. Jude*, WC [London: Methuen, 1934], 3). The structure of the letter, however, suggests a more unified composition and intention from the beginning.

[98] K. Shimada carefully compares the style of the alleged composite documents, concluding that there are no stylistic grounds for partition ("Is I Peter a Composite Writing? A Stylistic Approach to the Two-Document Hypothesis," *AJBI* 11 [1985]: 95–114).

[99] For arguments against partition and a careful analysis and outline of the letter's contents, see W. J. Dalton, *Christ's Proclamation to the Spirits: A Study of 1 Peter 3:18–4:6*, AnBib 23 (Rome: Pontifical Biblical Institute, 1965), 72–86.

clear from 1:6–7 that the sufferings of believers are not merely potential but actual in the first section of the letter (1:3–4:11). Hence, the reputed difference between 1:3–4:11 and 4:12–5:14 falls to the ground.[100] Second, it is a mistake to claim that joy is only present in 1:6–8 and exclusively future in 4:12–13. In 4:12–13 Peter called readers to "present" joy in light of their future joy. The imperative "rejoice" *(chairete)* is a present tense imperative. In fact, the theme of both 1:6–8 and 4:12–13 is remarkably similar. The reason believers are able to rejoice now is because of the eschatological joy laid up for them. Third, the presence of a doxology and "amen" in 4:11 does not necessarily signal the end of a letter. We see a similar formula in Rom 11:36, where a section of a letter concludes, but the letter itself does not end. Other examples also could be adduced (e.g., Gal 1:5; Eph 3:21). What the doxology and the "amen" do signal is that a section of the letter concludes at 4:11. Fourth, it is conventional at the end of letters to call them brief (cf. Heb 13:22), and hence such a statement says nothing about the length of the letter. In conclusion, there is no reason to doubt the unity of the letter, and it will be interpreted as such in this commentary.

Schutter argues that the body opening of the letter reflects "homiletic midrash" rooted in a Jewish hermeneutic.[101] He sees the closest parallels in Jewish apocalyptic sectarian groups, in which a pesher hermeneutic is employed. Schutter carefully observes the use of link words, inclusio, significant themes, and transitional devices. Martin detects much of value in Schutter's analysis. Martin argues that the letter fits the epistolary form and should be analyzed as a parenetic letter, arguing that the controlling metaphor in the letter is the diaspora.[102] The prescript is confined to 1:1–2. The blessing section follows next, consisting of 1:3–12. Martin locates the body opening at 1:13, arguing that the body middle includes 1:14–5:11. He subdivides the body middle into three discrete sections: (1) the elect household of God (1:14–2:10), (2) aliens in the world (2:11–3:12), and (3) sufferers of the dispersion (3:13–5:11). The body of the letter closes in 5:12 and concludes with a greeting (5:13–14a) and a farewell (5:14b).

Campbell argues that the letter should be understood as a species of Greek rhetoric.[103] He divides the letter into the *exordium* (1:3:12) and the concluding *peroratio* (4:12–5:14). The intervening sections (1:13–4:11) contain a number of rhetorical schemas, including *propositio, ratio, confir-*

---

[100] Rightly Brox, *Der erste Petrusbrief,* 35–38; Winbery, "Introduction to First Peter," 7.

[101] Schutter, *Hermeneutic and Composition in I Peter.*

[102] Martin, *Metaphor and Composition in 1 Peter,* 68–134, 144–60. Martin's thesis that 1 Peter is a parenetic letter is helpful, but the notion that the diaspora is the controlling metaphor for the letter is not as convincing. For an insightful review of Martin's work, see J. R. Michaels, *JBL* 112 (1993): 358–60.

[103] Campbell, *Honor, Shame, and the Rhetoric of 1 Peter,* 26.

matio, exornatio, and *conplexio.* It is doubtful that 1 Peter is patterned after the use of Greco-Roman rhetoric. The *peroratio* in Campbell's schema is inordinately long, and he does not convincingly demonstrate that the categories assigned actually fit 1 Peter. Moreover, there are serious questions about whether Greco-Roman rhetoric is practiced in any of the New Testament letters.[104]

5. Purpose

The purpose of the letter is to encourage believers to stand fast while they endure suffering and distress in the present evil age.[105] Achtemeier says that the letter is intended "to strengthen the readers in the 'now' of their suffering and persecution by assuring them that the future of glory will transform their present condition as surely as their present situation transformed them from their past."[106] They are encouraged to persevere, knowing that a great reward will be theirs on the day of salvation. Such perseverance is exhibited by living a godly life, living as good citizens, model slaves, gentle wives, and understanding husbands. When believers live in such a way, they indicate that they are placing their hope in God rather than in the joys and comforts of this world. Another way of describing 1 Peter is to say that those who hope and trust in God and in his future reward will have the strength to endure whatever comes their way in the present. When believers set their hope on the future, they reveal that their salvation comes from the cross of Christ, who bore their sins (2:24; 3:18). The Christ who suffered is also the Christ who is now exalted (1 Pet 3:19–22). Those who resist the church of Jesus Christ now will be judged on the last day (4:1–6). Since the end is coming soon, believers should imitate

[104] See, e.g., S. Porter, "Saul of Tarsus and His Letters," in *Handbook of Classical Rhetoric* (Leiden: Brill, 1997), 562–67; D. Stamps, "Rethinking the Rhetorical Situation," in *Rhetoric and the New Testament* (Sheffield: Academic Press, 1993), 193–210; J. A. D. Weima, "What Does Aristotle Have to Do with Paul? An Evaluation of Rhetorical Criticism," *CTJ* 32 (1997): 458–68.

[105] Wallace argues that Peter wrote the letter after Paul's death. The fact that Paul's sometime opponent, Peter, wrote the letter would encourage the readers, assuring them that Paul's gospel was truly legitimate ("First Peter: Introduction, Argument, and Outline"). The suggestion is stimulating, but evidence is lacking to support this specific reconstruction. Nothing is said about Paul's death, nor is there any indication that Peter wrote to reassure the readers of the legitimacy of the Pauline gospel.

[106] P. J. Achtemeier, "Newborn Babes and Living Stones: Literal and Figurative in 1 Peter," in *To Touch the Text: Biblical and Related Studies in Honor of Joseph A. Fitzmyer, S.J.* (New York: Crossroad, 1989), 235. Achtemeier argues that the controlling metaphor in the letter is the new people of God (pp. 222–31).

Jesus Christ and follow his example of suffering, for all those who suffer will also experience a great reward.

None of what Peter said should be construed as a call to works righteousness. Those who have had their sins forgiven by means of the cross and resurrection of Christ are now to set their hope on him and their future salvation. The message of Peter can be summarized as a call to stand in grace (5:12). Peter did not call on his readers to earn God's grace or strive to obtain a grace that is not theirs. No, they are to stand in a grace that is already theirs. Any grace received on the last day, on the day when hope becomes a reality, flows from the grace they received when God called them to himself (2:9; 5:10) as his people.

Peter wanted his readers to conceive of themselves as the people of God. They had become part of Israel by believing in Jesus Christ and were God's holy nation and special people (2:9–10). They were exiles and sojourners during their earthly journey. The encouragement to live as sojourners and set their hope only on God is also matched by the threat that they will be judged if they turn away from the gospel. The promise and threat are corollaries in the letter, for the threat of final judgment also spurs the readers to set their hope entirely on the promise. They realized that the future reward is also matched by future judgment and that hoping in God is not trivial but momentous.

6. Structure

The outline proposed below is not novel.[107] Peter has the conventional opening (1:1–2) and then begins the next major section (1:3–2:10) with a blessing (1:3).[108] The two succeeding sections are marked by "dear friends" (*agapētoi,* 2:11; 4:12), and as noted earlier the segment from 2:11–4:11 concludes with a doxology and "amen." The fourth section of the letter also ends with a doxology and "amen" (5:11) before the closing. In the commentary the flow of argument of the text will be explained before analyzing

[107] For a discourse analysis of the letter, see H. J. B. Combrink, "The Structure of I Peter," *Neot* 9 (1975): 34–63. Combrink's analysis is suggestive and insightful at many points. It seems unlikely, however, that the third and fourth sections of the letter comprise 3:13–4:19 and 5:1–11 respectively. Both the content and the marker ἀγαπητοί suggest a new section begins in 4:12. Nor is the presence of οὖν sufficient to indicate the beginning of a new section in 5:1.

[108] J. J. J. van Rensburg analyzes the letter as follows: 1:1–2 functions as the heading. The letter opening is comprised of 1:3–12. The letter body is composed of four inferences drawn from 1:3–12. The four subsections are 1:13–25; 2:1–10; 2:11–4:19; 5:1–11; and 5:12–14 is seen as the conclusion of the letter (see "The Use of Intersentence Relational Particles and Asyndeton in 1 Peter," *Neot* 24 [1990]: 298).

individual verses, and hence there is no need to extend the discussion of structure here.[109]

Kendall maintains that all the imperatives in the letter (1:13–5:11) flow from the introduction in 1:3–12.[110] He then divides the text into the following sections: (1) 1:13–2:10 explains generally what it means to be the people of God; and here we have three subdivisions, focusing on the need for holiness (1:14–21), love (1:22–2:3), and election in Christ (2:4–10). (2) He argues that the next major section (2:11–4:11) is more specific than the first section, in that the author now explains what holiness, love, and election look like in everyday life. (3) Finally, 4:12–5:11 functions as a "climactic summary" of the letter's contents, in which the author addresses the relationship with hostile unbelievers (4:12–19), community relationships (5:1–7), and God's purpose for believers in their conflict (5:8–11). He summarizes the message of 1 Peter as "a movement from present suffering to future glory and a fellowship of love."[111] Talbert, on the other hand, thinks the letter falls into two main sections: 1:13–2:10 and 2:11–5:11.[112] He sees

---

[109] For a similar understanding of the structure see L. Thurén, *The Rhetorical Strategy of 1 Peter with Special Regard to Ambiguous Expressions* (Åbo: Åbo Academy Press, 1990), 92. Thurén identifies the letter as epideictic (pp. 73, 96–98), but it is unclear that such an identification is demonstrable. The distinctive contribution of the work is to argue that Peter addresses two different types of implied audiences in his letter—both those who were tempted to assimilate with the secular society ("passive response") and those who were tempted to remove themselves from that society ("active response"). Thurén believes that the dual audience explains the ambiguous participles in the letter, concluding that the participles were intended as indicatives for some of the readers and imperatives for others. In a later work he expands his database to include all of 1 Peter, but he has not changed his view of the letter (see *Argument and Theology in 1 Peter: The Origins of Christian Paraenesis*, JSNTSup 114 [Sheffield: Academic Press, 1995]). Thurén's thesis is a creative attempt to bridge the debate between Elliott and Balch. Unfortunately, the theory hangs on a mirror reading that cannot be sustained from 1 Peter. We have no clear evidence that two different types of audiences are addressed. Tite rightly criticizes Thurén for basing his view on a speculative and unsubstantiated reading of the background (*Compositional Transitions in 1 Peter,* pp. 22–23, n. 41; cf. also Bechtler, *Following in His Steps*, 116). Tite also criticizes Thurén for relying on modern rhetorical theory instead of ancient rhetorical theory, arguing that the latter should base his study on a careful rhetorical analysis of the entire text that comports with the rhetorical schema of ancient texts. For similar criticisms of Thurén, see Campbell, *Honor, Shame, and the Rhetoric of 1 Peter,* 23–24. Campbell argues that the letter reflects deliberative rhetoric (p. 30). J. W. Thompson identifies it as a "persuasive sermon" ("The Rhetoric of 1 Peter," *ResQ* 36 [1994]: 237–50). Snyder argues that disagreement among scholars about whether participles are imperatives does not substantiate the view that they are ambiguous ("Participles and Imperatives in 1 Peter," 189, n. 10). In defense of Thurén's rhetorical analysis, his study of modern rhetoric and argumentation is of help in understanding the argument of 1 Peter, even though his work contains flaws that weaken his overall thesis. See his discussion on pp. 61–85.

[110] D. W. Kendall, "The Literary and Theological Function of 1 Peter 1:3–12," in *Perspectives on 1 Peter* (Macon: Mercer University Press, 1986), 103–120; so also van Rensburg, "The Use of Intersentence Relational Particles and Asyndeton in 1 Peter," 294–96.

[111] Kendall, "The Literary and Theological Function of 1 Peter 1:3–12," 115.

[112] C. H. Talbert, "Once Again: The Plan of 1 Peter," in *Perspectives on 1 Peter* (Macon: Mercer University Press, 1986), 141–51.

a pattern in the letter in which the first section explains the "ground of Christian existence (conversion spoken of in multiple metaphors like new birth, ransoming, tasting, election) and its ramifications, while 2:11–5:11 treats the norms of Christian behavior together with their warrants."[113] In the second major section of the letter Peter sometimes addresses all Christians, but he also addresses specific groups. Talbert sees a pattern:

A 2:11–17
B 2:18–3:7
A′ 3:8–4:6
B′ 5:1–5b
A′ 5:5b–11

Talbert argues that the pattern found here indicates that no break should be posited between 4:11 and 4:12. The words in 5:12 summarize the entire epistle, indicating that the entire letter is composed of declarations and exhortations. He argues that declaration refers to the ground and warrants of Christian existence, while exhortation refers to the behavior Christians should exhibit. Talbert distinguishes between grounds and warrants, seeing the former as the ultimate reason for godly living (such as new birth, conversion) and the latter as providing specific reasons for the paraenesis (e.g., the Christological warrant for submitting as slaves to unjust masters). Talbert believes that the author wanted to ensure both social cohesion and social adaptation and hence warned against adopting a false either/or on this matter. Without the first, Christians would lose their distinctiveness, but without the second they would have no avenue for evangelism.

OUTLINE OF 1 PETER

I. Opening (1:1–2)
II. Called to Salvation as Exiles (1:3–2:10)
   1. Praise for Salvation (1:3–12)
   2. The Future Inheritance as an Incentive to Holiness (1:13–21)
   3. Living as the New People of God (1:22–2:10)
III. Living as Aliens to Bring Glory to God in a Hostile World (2:11–4:11)
   1. The Christian Life as a Battle and Witness (2:11–12)
   2. Testifying to the Gospel in the Social Order (2:13–3:12)
   3. Responding in a Godly Way to Suffering (3:13–4:11)
IV. Persevering in Suffering (4:12–5:11)
   1. Suffer Joyfully in Accord with God's Will (4:12–19)
   2. Exhortations to Elders and the Community (5:1–11)
V. Concluding Words (5:12–14)

[113] Ibid., 142–43.

SECTION OUTLINE

I. OPENING (1:1–2)

I. OPENING (1:1–2)

[1]Peter, an apostle of Jesus Christ,

To God's elect, strangers in the world, scattered throughout Pontus, Galatia, Cappadocia, Asia and Bithynia, [2]who have been chosen according to the foreknowledge of God the Father, through the sanctifying work of the Spirit, for obedience to Jesus Christ and sprinkling by his blood:

Grace and peace be yours in abundance.

The opening greeting in 1 Peter is hardly a customary hello. It is theologically rich and densely packed with themes. The author, Peter, introduces himself as an apostle of Jesus Christ. He does not mean by this merely that he is a messenger of Christ. The word "apostle" is used in the technical sense. Jesus Christ designated Peter as an authoritative messenger and interpreter of the gospel. The letter does not represent good advice but a binding apostolic word for the church. It is written to God's pilgrim people, who are exiles in this world. Because they are God's elect and chosen people, therefore, they are pilgrims. Peter's letter is an encyclical, addressed to churches in areas in Asia Minor, all contained in modern-day Turkey. The order in which the provinces are listed suggests the order in which a courier would deliver the letter as he traveled roughly in a circle. The chosen pilgrims are foreknown by God the Father. Foreknowledge does not only mean that God foresaw that they would be his elect aliens. Foreknowledge should be understood in covenantal terms, and the foreknown are those upon whom God has bestowed his covenantal favor and affection. As elect sojourners, believers are also set apart or sanctified by the Spirit. Their entrance into the sphere of the holy, that is, their conversion, is the result of the Spirit's work. Finally, their conversion means that they have obeyed God and been cleansed by Christ's blood—forgiven of their sins. We note here the Trinitarian work of the Father, Spirit, Son. The opening closes with the prayer that grace and peace be multiplied in the lives of believers.

1:1 The letter begins with Peter identifying himself as the author. The name "Peter" was given to Simon by Jesus Christ early in his ministry (John 1:42; cf. Matt 10:2; 16:18; Mark 3:16; Luke 6:14). Peter designates himself as an apostle. The term "apostle" may simply mean "messenger," but here the idea is that Peter is one of the twelve apostles, specially chosen by Jesus himself for that office (Mark 3:13–19 par.). The special function and authority of the twelve is also communicated by the selection of Matthias in Acts 1:15–26. Grudem notes that "apostle" is the only office where the words "of Jesus Christ" are added, indicating, probably, the unique authority of the apostolate.[1] What Peter writes, then, is not merely his personal opinion. As an apostle he is commissioned by Christ and writes God's words to the churches (cf. 1 Cor 2:13; 14:37; Gal 1:8–9; 1 Thess 2:13; 4:8,15; 2 Thess 3:6,14; 2 Pet 3:2,16).

The letter is addressed to the "elect" *(eklektois),* and in the Greek text the term "elect" actually modifies the term "strangers" *(parepidēmois),* so we can translate "elect strangers" or "elect pilgrims." To speak of his readers as elect means that they have been chosen by God. Clearly (see introduction) the readers are primarily Gentiles. Often in the Old Testament, Israel is designated as God's chosen and elect people (Deut 4:37; 7:6–8; 10:15; 14:2; Ps 106:5; Isa 14:1; 41:8–8; 43:20; 45:4; 51:2; 65:9,15,23; cf. also *Wis* 4:15; *Sir* 46:1). Peter indicates at the outset, therefore, that the church of Jesus Christ is the Israel of God, his chosen people.[2] He forecasts here the theme of 1 Pet 2:9, where the church is called "a chosen people."[3]

The word "strangers" *(parepidēmois)* introduces a crucial idea in the letter, that is, that God's people are pilgrims, sojourners, and exiles on Earth. Again, a key theme of the letter is anticipated (cf. 2:11). The church is God's suffering people, having no place of rest in this world. The term *parepidēmos* is used in the New Testament only here and in 1 Pet 2:11 and Heb 11:13. In the Septuagint it is found only in Gen 23:4 and Ps 38:13. In the Old Testament, exile was Israel's punishment for their sin, when they were evicted from their land by Assyria (722 B.C.) and Babylon (586 B.C.). Any notion that Peter's readers are being *punished* as exiles is foreign to 1 Peter. Elliott, as we noted in the introduction, understands the exile in terms of the political status of the readers. By doing so he misses the theological point of Peter from the outset. Believers are exiles, not because they are displaced from their homeland. Many people in the Greco-Roman world no longer lived in their place of origin.[4] Believers are exiles because they suffer for their faith in a world that finds their faith off-putting and strange.

---

[1] W. Grudem, *The First Epistle of Peter,* TNTC (Grand Rapids: Eerdmans, 1988), 47.

[2] Rightly T. Lea, "I Peter—Outline and Exposition," *SwJT* 25 (1982): 20.

[3] J. W. Pryor suggests that Exodus theology informs all of 1 Peter in that they experienced deliverance through Christ as the Passover Lamb (1:18–19), are now experiencing trials as sojourners in the wilderness, and await their inheritance in the land of promise ("First Peter and the New Covenant (II)," *RTR* 45 [1986]: 46).

[4] See P. J. Achtemeier, *1 Peter: A Commentary on First Peter,* Her (Minneapolis: Fortress, 1996), 82.

Goppelt rightly observes that God's election is what accounts for their being exiles.[5] This interpretation is borne out in that the word "elect" modifies "strangers." They are not aliens literally; they are sojourners because they are elected by God, because their citizenship is in heaven rather than on earth.[6] Even though the sociological interpretation advanced by Elliott fails to persuade, he is correct in detecting a sociological implication from the elect status of the readers. Those who understand themselves as God's elect have the ammunition to resist the norms and culture of the society they inhabit.[7] Divine election reminds the readers that they have status, not because they are so worthy or noble but because God has bestowed his grace upon them.[8] Hence, they have the energy to counter accepted cultural norms and to live in accord with God's purpose.[9]

The location of the readers is communicated in the words "scattered throughout Pontus, Galatia, Cappadocia, Asia and Bithynia." The term "scattered" *(diasporas)* could be translated literally as "of the Dispersion" (NRSV). The term "dispersion" was often used of Jews who lived outside Palestine, who were scattered from their homeland because of their sin (Deut 28:25; 30:4; Neh 1:9; Ps 146:2; Isa 49:6; Jer 15:7; 41:17; cf. also *Jdt* 5:19; *2 Mac* 1:27; *Ps Sol* 8:28; 9:2). In the New Testament the word is used in only two other places, in both cases probably referring to Jews who were outside the land (John 7:35; Jas 1:1). In this instance, however, the word probably is used metaphorically. Peter was not writing to Jews but primarily to Gentiles, and hence he was hardly suggesting that they were the dispersed of Israel in the literal sense. And yet he signaled again that they were the people of God, who joined with believing Jews in the promises given to Abraham, Isaac, and Jacob. Dispersion belongs with the word "strangers" in that it communicates again that believers are distinct from the world.

---

[5] L. Goppelt, *A Commentary on I Peter* (Grand Rapids: Eerdmans, 1993), 64, 66. See his detailed discussion, including the self-perception of the Qumran community, on pp. 68–70. S. R. Bechtler confirms the idea that the readers are strangers because they are chosen by God (*Following in His Steps: Suffering, Community, and Christology in 1 Peter,* SBLDS 162 [Atlanta: Scholars Press, 1998], 137).

[6] J. R. Michaels, *1 Peter,* WBC (Waco: Word, 1998), 7–8.

[7] J. H. Elliott, *A Home for the Homeless: A Sociological Exegesis of 1 Peter, Its Situation and Strategy* (Philadelphia: Fortress, 1981), 122–23, 127.

[8] Elliott does not sufficiently emphasize the link between election and humility in that he overemphasizes the sense of status bestowed on the elect.

[9] T. Seland argues that the terms "aliens" and "strangers" are metaphorical and that the readers are described as if they were former proselytes. See "πάροικος καί παρεπίδημος: Proselyte Characterizations in 1 Peter?" *BBR* 11 (2001): 239–68. But Seland does not clearly establish that the terms "aliens" and "strangers" are intended to refer to proselytes. He shows that this may be the case, but this is quite different from establishing his thesis. Indeed, the connections are too loose and tenuous to buttress his interpretation since Peter does not clearly refer to proselytes anywhere in the letter.

Peter addressed believers from various areas in Asia Minor, in regions of modern-day Turkey. The area covered extends 300,000 miles, which is nearly all of Turkey.[10] We cannot be certain whether Peter intended to refer to Roman provinces or whether he simply referred generally to certain regions.[11] When the letter was written, Bithynia and Pontus were a single province.[12] So perhaps it is best to see a general reference to the areas included in the destination. Can we discern the reason for the order in which the areas are named? The most surprising element is the separation of Pontus from Bithynia since they were next to each other and constituted one province. Further, if the messenger came from Rome, we would expect him to travel to Bithynia first since it is closer to Rome than Pontus.[13] The most likely scenario is that the bearer of the letter traveled roughly in a circle, delivering it to churches in each region successively.[14] Perhaps Sylva is correct in suggesting that the letter was delivered to Pontus first because the persecution was especially intense there.[15] Certainty is not possible, but by ending up in Bithynia the courier could sail off to another destination.[16]

1:2 The NIV begins v. 2 with the words "who have been chosen," and interpretively this is fitting; but, in fact, those words do not appear in the Greek text of v. 2. The phrase "according to the foreknowledge of God the Father" actually modifies "elect aliens" in v. 1. The NIV repeats the concept since the phrases are separated by so many intervening words. Some scholars maintain, on the contrary, that God's foreknowledge here refers to all of v. 1.[17] It is unlikely, though, that every idea in v. 1 is modified by the prepositional phrases in v. 2. Even though "elect" is an adjective, it is

---

[10] So Michaels, *1 Peter,* 4; Achtemeier, *1 Peter,* 85.

[11] J. H. Elliott believes that the reference is to provinces (*1 Peter: A New Translation with Introduction and Commentary,* AB [New York: Doubleday, 2000], 84). His view that the letters are addressed particularly to rural communities cannot be demonstrated (p. 90).

[12] Achtemeier, *1 Peter,* 85.

[13] Ibid., 85.

[14] F. J. A. Hort, *The First Epistle of St Peter: I.1–II.17* (New York: Macmillan, 1898), 167–84; C. J. Hemer, "The Address of 1 Peter," *ExpTim* 89 (1978–79): 239–43; cf. also Michaels, *1 Peter,* 9; P. H. Davids, *The First Epistle of Peter,* NICNT (Grand Rapids: Eerdmans, 1990), 47; J. N. D. Kelly, *A Commentary on the Epistles of Peter and Jude,* Thornapple Commentaries (Grand Rapids: Baker, 1981), 42; Elliott, *1 Peter,* 91.

[15] D. Sylva, "1 Peter Studies: The State of the Discipline," *BTB* 10 (1980): 159.

[16] C. Hemer makes this remark about returning to Bithynia, "There on the Bosporus he could best intercept shipping returning direct to Rome before autumn closed the Black Sea" ("The Address of 1 Peter," *ExpTim* 89 [1978]: 241).

[17] Hort, *The First Epistle of St Peter,* 18–19; E. G. Selwyn, *The First Epistle of St. Peter,* 2d ed. (Grand Rapids: Baker, 1981), 119; F. W. Beare, *The First Epistle of Peter: The Greek Text with Introduction and Notes* (Oxford: Blackwell, 1947), 49–50; Grudem, *1 Peter,* 50.

likely that the three prepositional phrases in v. 2 modify it.[18] The term "elect," as we noted, is a common one for Israel as God's people. As an adjective it still carries significant weight in the sentence, and the prepositional phrases in v. 2 yield the most normal sense if they modify the word "elect."

The word "foreknowledge" *(prognōsis)* could simply mean that God foresaw whom would be his elect or chosen.[19] No one doubts, of course, that such an idea is included. The question is whether the term means more than this, whether it also includes the idea that God ordains whom would be elect. We should begin by observing the covenantal dimensions of the word.[20] The word "know" in Hebrew often refers to God's covenantal love bestowed upon his people (cf. Gen 18:19; Jer 1:5; Amos 3:2). The rich associations of that term continue in the New Testament. That foreordination also is involved is clear from Acts 2:23, where foreknowledge is paired with predestination.[21] Romans 11:2 drives us in the same direction. Paul queries whether God has "rejected his people whom he foreknew" (NRSV). The terms "rejected" *(apōsato)* and "foreknew" *(proegnō)* function as antonyms. We could rephrase the verse, "Has God rejected his people whom he chose?" Paul wondered if God had set aside Israel, upon whom he had set his covenantal favor. The same notion informs Rom 8:29, where we see that God has foreknown those whom he predestined. God foreknew "people," not objects or things. He has set his love upon them (cf. also 1 Cor 8:3; Gal 4:9). Probably the most important verse for Peter is 1 Pet 1:20, where it says that Christ "was chosen before the creation of the world." The term translated "chosen" by the NIV is actually "foreknown" *(proegnōsmenou)*. Peter was not merely saying that God foresaw when Christ would come, though that is part of his meaning. He was also saying

---

[18] So N. Brox, *Der erste Petrusbrief,* EKKNT, 2d ed. (Zürich: Benziger/Neukirchen-Vluyn: Neukirchener Verlag, 1986), 57; Goppelt, *I Peter,* 70; Michaels, *1 Peter,* 7; S. McKnight, *1 Peter,* NIVAC (Grand Rapids: Zondervan, 1996), 53. K. H. Schelke says it modifies ἐκλεκτοῖς παρεπιδήμοις (*Der Petrusbriefe—Der Judasbrief,* HTKNT [Freiburg: Herder, 1980], 20).

[19] This view has an ancient pedigree; see Origen in *James, 1–2 Peter, 1–3 John, Jude,* ACCS (Downers Grove: InterVarsity, 2000), 69.

[20] For an extended defense of the view propounded here see S. M. Baugh, "The Meaning of Foreknowledge," in *Still Sovereign: Contemporary Perspectives on Election, Foreknowledge, and Grace* (Grand Rapids: Baker, 2000), 183–200. So also Michaels, *1 Peter,* 10–11; cf. Hort, *The First Epistle of St Peter,* 19–20. For an exposition on the new covenant in 1 Peter, see J. W. Pryor, "First Peter and the New Covenant (I)," *RefTR* 45 (1986): 1–4; id., "First Peter and the New Covenant (II)," *RefTR* 45 (1986): 44–50.

[21] See especially the insightful discussion in Goppelt, *I Peter,* 73, n. 46; cf. also Lea, "I Peter—Outline and Exposition," 20. Goppelt draws our attention to the important parallels in CD 2:7 and 1QH 9:26–36. For OT background see Gen 18:19; Jer 1:5; Amos 3:2. In Acts 26:5 and 2 Pet 3:17 the term "foreknow" only means "know in advance." These two verses are distinct from the texts examined here since they refer to human foreknowledge instead of divine foreknowledge.

that God foreordained when Christ would come.[22] Indeed, God had to plan when he would come since Christ was sent by God. Christ's coming hardly depends on human choices. Therefore, when Peter said that believers are elect "according to the foreknowledge of God the Father," he emphasized God's sovereignty and initiative in salvation.[23] Believers are elect because God the Father has set his covenantal affection upon them.[24] The words "according to" *(kata)* may designate "result" or "cause."[25]

The second prepositional phrase, "through the sanctifying work of the Spirit" *(en hagiasmō pneumatos),* also modifies "elect." Not only does God the Father foreknow whom the elect will be, but the Spirit is the source of their sanctification.[26] The term "sanctification" often refers to the progressive growth of holiness in the lives of Christians (cf. 1 Thess 4:3). In this context, however, the focus is on conversion. Peter explained how believers came to be part of God's elect people. When believers are converted, they become God's holy and set-apart people (e.g., 1 Cor 1:2). Michaels probably is correct, then, in suggesting that this work of God accompanies the preaching of the gospel (1:12).[27] As the gospel is proclaimed, the Spirit sanctifies some by bringing them to faith, by bringing them into the realm of the holy.

The most difficult phrase to interpret is the last one. We begin with the preposition *eis,* translated "for" in the NIV. One could translate the phrase as causal. Believers are elect pilgrims because of the obedience of Jesus Christ and the sprinkling of his blood.[28] According to this view, "Jesus Christ" is a subjective genitive, that is, it refers to his obedience. This interpretation has two deficiencies that make it untenable. First, it is unlikely that the obedience described is that of Jesus Christ. Peter reflected on God's work in the lives of believers. They are foreknown, sanctified, and *obedient.* Indeed, Peter anticipated the theme of the believer's obedience, which was

---

[22] Rightly C. Spicq, *Les Épîtres de Saint Pierre,* SB (Paris: Gabalda, 1966), 69.

[23] Rightly Schelke, *Der Petrusbriefe—Der Judasbrief,* 20.

[24] Michaels wrongly restricts election to present status and future vindication, excluding past election (*1 Peter,* 7). The connection of "elect" with "foreknowledge" demonstrates that the past also is involved. Elliott completely misses Peter's theology by emphasizing voluntary choice, so that a synergism between foreknowledge and human choice is communicated (*1 Peter,* 318).

[25] See L. Thurén, *Argument and Theology in 1 Peter: The Origins of Christian Paraenesis,* JSNTSup 114 (Sheffield: Academic Press, 1995), 92.

[26] The word "Spirit" is a subjective genitive (Selwyn, *First Peter,* 119; Michaels, *1 Peter,* 11; Goppelt, *I Peter,* 73). Even though Peter thought of conversion here, Goppelt wrongly focuses on baptism (*I Peter,* 74). Baptism is part of the conversion process, of course, but there is no evidence that it was specially in Peter's mind.

[27] Michaels, *1 Peter,* 11.

[28] So F. H. Agnew, "1 Peter 1:2—An Alternative," *CBQ* 45 (1983): 68–73; E. J. Richard, *Reading 1 Peter, Jude, and 2 Peter: A Literary and Theological Commentary,* RNT (Macon: Smith & Helwys, 2000), 32; Elliott, *1 Peter,* 319.

central to his theology (1:14,22). Second, and even more decisive, the preposition *eis* occurs three times in the subsequent verses (vv. 3–5), and in every instance the preposition designates result. In this case, however, the result also includes the idea of purpose since Peter spoke of the outworking of God's saving plan. A causal reading of the preposition is unusual in any case, and it is more natural to understand it in terms of result/purpose. Another interpretation is suggested by the NRSV, "to be obedient to Jesus Christ and to be sprinkled with his blood" (cf. also RSV). In this case Jesus Christ functions as the object of the noun "obedient" and as the subject of "sprinkled with his blood." This interpretation should be rejected as awkward and "a grammatical monstrosity."[29] It is too confusing to imagine that Jesus Christ would be both an objective and subjective genitive in the same phrase.

The foreknowing work of God and the sanctifying action of the Spirit result in human obedience and the sprinkling of Christ's blood. This interpretation is the most satisfying. It separates the noun "obedience" and the phrase the "sprinkling of the blood of Jesus Christ." The first refers to human obedience; and the second, to Christ's work of cleansing and forgiveness. Grudem argues that obedience here refers to ongoing obedience in the Christian life, not the initial obedience of receiving the gospel.[30] He thinks Peter never used obedience to refer to conversion and that no clear example of obedience referring to conversion can be found in the New Testament. Grudem rightly maintains that the term "obedience" may refer to ongoing progress in the Christian life (e.g., Rom 6:16; Phlm 21; 1 Pet 1:14). He is mistaken, however, in saying that it never refers to conversion, and in fact, a reference to conversion is most likely in this verse.[31] First, the "obedience of faith" (NRSV) in Rom 1:5 and 16:26 most naturally refers to conversion. Second, the "obedience from the Gentiles" in Rom 15:18 (NRSV) refers to Paul's missionary work in bringing them to salvation. Third, in the context of Rom 10:14–17 the statement "not all have obeyed the good news" (Rom 10:16, NRSV; cf. Acts 6:7) clearly refers to conversion.[32] Fourth, the most natural way to interpret 1 Pet 1:22 ("Now that you have purified yourselves by obeying the truth") is to see a reference to conversion.[33] Fifth, that conversion is intended is confirmed by the parallel phrase on the sprinkling of Christ's blood. Two different sides of conversion are contemplated—the believers' obedience to the gospel and Christ's

---

[29] Achtemeier, *1 Peter,* 87.

[30] Grudem, *1 Peter,* 52.

[31] For this view see esp. Michaels, *1 Peter,* 11–12.

[32] The NIV, unfortunately, uses the verb "accepted" instead of "obeyed" and thereby diminishes the force of the text.

[33] See the commentary on that verse.

cleansing and forgiveness. What Peter said here is important. Conversion is not merely an intellectual acceptance of the gospel, nor is it faith with a blank slate. Conversion involves obedience and submission to the gospel, what Paul called the "obedience of faith" (Rom 1:5; 16:26).

To what does the sprinkling of blood refer? In the Old Testament the sprinkling of the blood is used for the cleansing of a leper (Lev 14:6–7), for the sprinkling of priests in ordination (Exod 29:21), and the sprinkling of the blood when the covenant with Moses was inaugurated (Exod 24:3–8). We can reject the sprinkling of blood in the ordination of priests immediately since the context suggests nothing about ordination. Grudem thinks the background is in the cleansing of lepers, arguing that it is an apt picture of the need of cleansing and forgiveness for the sins that disrupt fellowship with God after conversion.[34] In addition, he thinks a reference to sprinkling that occurs at conversion is unpersuasive since this sprinkling comes *after* sanctification and obedience.[35] Grudem's view is possible, but once again it is ultimately unpersuasive.[36] His objection about the order of sanctification and obedience only stands if both of these terms refer to life *after* conversion, but I have already argued that both of these terms refer to conversion as well. Sanctification, obedience, and the sprinkling of blood are three different ways of describing the conversion of believers in this context. Further, Exod 24:3–8 is the most probable background to the passage.[37] The covenant is inaugurated with sacrifices in which blood is shed and sprinkled on the altar (Exod 24:5–6). The people pledge obedience to the God of the covenant (Exod 24:3,7). The promise to obey matches the obedience Peter noted in the first part of the *eis* clause. Moses then sprinkled the people with the blood, stating, "This is the blood of the covenant that the LORD has made with you" (Exod 24:8). The blood of the covenant signifies the forgiveness and cleansing the people needed to stand in right relation with God. We see, then, that entrance into the covenant has two dimensions: the obedient response to the gospel and the sprinkling of blood. Similarly, God's work of foreknowing and the Spirit's work of sanctifying introduce the readers into God's new covenant.[38] Believers enter the covenant by obeying the gospel and through the sprinkled blood of Christ, that is, his cleansing sacrifice. Some scholars see a reference to

---

[34] Grudem, *1 Peter,* 52–54.

[35] Ibid.

[36] For views similar to my own see Michaels, *1 Peter,* 12–13; Achtemeier, *1 Peter,* 86–88.

[37] Michaels also draws attention to the sprinkling of the ashes of the red heifer in Numbers 19 (*1 Peter,* 12). It seems unlikely, though, that this is the most natural background since Exod 24:3–8 relates more directly to conversion, to the inauguration of God's covenant with his people.

[38] So Achtemeier, *1 Peter,* 89.

baptism in the sprinkling of blood, but the allusion is scarcely clear,[39] for nowhere else is baptism described as a bloody sprinkling.

The opening of the letter concludes with a prayer wish. The wording is similar to the prayer wish in 2 Pet 1:1, though in the latter instance the prayer wish is expanded. The use of the word "grace" *(charis)* is substituted for the typical Greek word "greetings" *(chairein)*. The message Peter proclaimed is one of grace, and he prayed that this grace would be the portion for his readers. Peter not only prayed for the dispensing of God's grace but also the bestowal of his peace. A prayer for peace was common in Jewish circles (*2 Mac* 1:1; *2 Bar* 78:3). God's peace is a result of his grace and signifies the holistic sense of well-being that belongs to those who are in a right relation with God. Peter prayed that both grace and peace would be multiplied in the lives of his readers, asking God to fill them with his grace and peace.

We should also note in the verse the reference to the Father, Spirit, and the Son. The Father foreknows, the Spirit sanctifies, and the Son cleanses. The idea is close to the traditional theological formulation of the Father as Creator, the Son as Redeemer, and the Spirit as Sanctifier. Similar triadic formulas are found elsewhere in the New Testament (Matt 3:16–17; 28:19; 1 Cor 12:4–6; 2 Cor 13:14; Eph 4:6; 2 Thess 2:13–14; Jude 20–21; Rev 1:4–5). Peter, of course, did not articulate in a full-fledged way the doctrine of the Trinity, but from verses such as this the doctrine was hammered out.

[39] So Goppelt, *I Peter,* 71–72, 74–75.

SECTION OUTLINE

II. CALLED TO SALVATION AS EXILES (1:3–2:10)
   1. Praise for Salvation (1:3–12)
      (1) A Promised Inheritance (1:3–5)
      (2) Result: Joy in Suffering (1:6–9)
      (3) The Privilege of Revelation (1:10–12)
   2. The Future Inheritance as an Incentive to Holiness (1:13–21)
      (1) Setting One's Hope on the Inheritance (1:13–16)
      (2) A Call to Fear (1:17–21)
   3. Living as the New People of God (1:22–2:10)
      (1) A Call to Love (1:22–25)
      (2) Longing for the Pure Milk (2:1–3)
      (3) The Living Stone and Living Stones (2:4–10)

II. CALLED TO SALVATION AS EXILES (1:3–2:10)

1. Praise for Salvation (1:3–12)

The opening highlights God's initiative and grace in the lives of believers, and vv. 3–12 continue that theme. In Greek one long and complex sentence comprises vv. 3–12. The main theme is introduced immediately in v. 3. God is to be blessed and praised for his saving work. It is an inestimable privilege and joy to be the object of God's mercy.

We can also divide the text into three main movements: vv. 3–5,6–9,10–12. Verses 3–5 focus on the end-time inheritance or salvation that belongs to believers. They should bless God because their future salvation is certain, and hence their lives should be marked by an undaunted hope. Second, the future inheritance gives them joy while they experience the difficulties and suffering of the present time (vv. 6–9). The trials they experience now are not meaningless but serve to refine and purify their faith; hence they will bring glory and praise to God when Jesus Christ reveals himself (vv. 6–7). Therefore their lives are now characterized by joy and by love for Jesus Christ, precisely because they know that eschatological salvation lies ahead of them (vv. 8–9). Finally, they should praise God because they live in the age of the fulfillment of the Old Testament promises regarding the coming of the Christ—his suffering and glory (vv. 10–12). The prophets anticipated and longed for his coming. The angels gaze from afar but have no first-hand experience of it. Peter's readers, however, live in the day of fulfillment. The words of the prophets were written *for them!* God is in control of history, and the Old Testament Scriptures point to the coming of Jesus Christ. Believers will praise God when they realize their privileged position in salvation history.[1]

(1) A Promised Inheritance (1:3–5)

[3]Praise be to the God and Father of our Lord Jesus Christ! In his great mercy he has given us new birth into a living hope through the resurrection of Jesus Christ from the dead, [4]and into an inheritance that can never perish, spoil or fade—kept in heaven for you, [5]who through faith are shielded by God's power until the coming of the salvation that is ready to be revealed in the last time.

1:3 Peter begins with the theme of the entire paragraph. God is to be blessed (*eulogētos*—the NIV translates the word "blessed" here as "praise") and praised for the salvation he has given to believers.[2] Many New Testament letters begin with a thanksgiving, but a blessing formula is also found in 2 Cor 1:3 and Eph 1:3. Blessing God, not surprisingly, is rooted in the Old Testament and is a pervasive feature of Old Testament piety.[3] The blessing is not a prosaic introduction but begins the section with joy, a gladness that fills the rest of the passage. The blessing is directed to God, "even" (*kai;* NIV "and) the "Father of our Lord Jesus Christ." The Father is the fount from which all goodness flows, and even the Lord Jesus Christ, as the Son, yields to the Father. We know from the Gospel of John that the Father commands and the Son obeys (John 5:19), the Father sends and the Son goes. And yet such a difference in role does not diminish the dignity of the Son, nor is there any notion that the Son is a creature (cf. John 1:1,18; 20:28).

The reason God is to be praised is now explained—"he has given us new birth." The term *anagennēsas* actually emphasizes "rebegetting or begetting anew rather than being born anew," though the latter idea is also implied.[4] This is borne out in 1 Pet 1:23, where believers are said to be begotten

---

[1] Also J. Calvin, *Commentaries on the Catholic Epistles* (Grand Rapids: Eerdmans, 1948), 38.

[2] Some scholars posit a hymn in vv. 3–12 (H. Windisch, *Die katholischen Briefe,* HNT [Tübingen: Mohr, 1951], 52 or D. Hill, "'To Offer Spiritual Sacrifices . . .' [1 Peter 2:5]: Liturgical Formulations and Christian Paraenesis in 1 Peter," *JSNT* 16 [1982]: 45–63), but the hymnic nature of the text has not been established (rightly L. Goppelt, *A Commentary on I Peter* [Grand Rapids: Eerdmans, 1993], 79).

[3] E.g., Gen 14:20; 24:27; Exod 18:10; Josh 22:33; 1 Sam 25:32; 2 Sam 18:28; 22:47; 1 Kgs 1:48; 5:7; 1 Chr 16:36; Ezra 7:27; Neh 9:5; Pss 28:6; 31:21; 41:13; 72:18–19; Dan 2:20.

[4] P. J. Achtemeier, *1 Peter: A Commentary on First Peter,* Her (Minneapolis: Fortress, 1996), 94.

(anagegennēmenoi) by the imperishable seed of God's word.[5] Begetting by "seed" directs our attention to the Father's role in producing children, with the means used being the word of God (1 Pet 1:23). The focus therefore is on God's initiative in producing new life. No one takes any credit for being born.[6] It is something that happens to us. The result of God's begetting is also included; believers are born anew (cf. John 3:3,7) and enjoy new life.[7] The begetting again of believers is "in his great mercy." The preposition "in" *(kata)* probably denotes the cause or reason for our new life.[8] Believers deserve judgment and wrath, but God is a God of mercy and grace, bestowing life upon those who are opposed to him (cf. Eph 2:4–5).

The goal or result of God's begetting is now explained with the first of three clauses beginning with the preposition *eis*. In v. 3 Peter mentions the living hope of believers, in v. 4 their inheritance, and in v. 5 their salvation.[9] He seems to have a fondness for triads, for we have already noticed the threefold work of the Father, Spirit, and Son in v. 2. A "living hope" is one that is genuine and vital, in contrast to a hope that is empty and vain.[10] The focus, of course, is on the word "hope" itself.[11] Those who are suffering

---

[5] The focus is not on baptism but conversion (against Goppelt, *I Peter,* 84; N. Brox, *Der erste Petrusbrief,* EKKNT, 2d ed. [Zürich: Benziger/Neukirchen-Vluyn: Neukirchener Verlag, 1986], 61; rightly W. J. Dalton, "'So That Your Faith May also Be Your Hope in God' (I Peter 1:21)," in *Reconciliation and Hope: New Testament Essays on Atonement and Eschatology Presented to L. L. Morris on His Sixtieth Birthday* (Exeter: Paternoster, 1974], 266).

[6] Goppelt rightly says, "Even in anthropological perspective, the basis for being a Christian is not a decision or the appropriation of a commandment, but the second birth established in God's mercy, the manifestation of a new being" (*I Peter,* 81). See also his discussion of parallels in the history of religion (pp. 81–83). Cf. also the comments of K. H. Schelke, *Der Petrusbriefe—Der Judasbrief,* HTKNT (Freiburg: Herder, 1980), 27.

[7] R. H. Gundry argues that Peter reflects dependence on John 3:3,7 here (and in 1 Pet 1:23; 2:2; see "'*Verba Christi*' in I Peter: Their Implications concerning the Authorship of I Peter and the Authenticity of the Gospel Tradition," *NTS* 13 [1967]: 338–39; "Further *Verba* on *Verba Christi* in First Peter," *Bib* 55 [1974]: 218–19). Contra Gundry, a clear parallel is not evident (rightly E. Best, "1 Peter and the Gospel Tradition," *NTS* 16 [1970]: 98).

[8] So BDAG, 512–13.

[9] Hence, hope is the consequence of God's begetting and not its cause (rightly J. Piper, "Hope as the Motivation of Love: I Peter 3:9–12," *NTS* 26 [1980]: 215).

[10] Cf. J. R. Michaels, *1 Peter,* WBC (Waco: Word, 1998), 23; Achtemeier, *1 Peter,* 95. So also M. Luther, *Commentary on Peter & Jude* (Grand Rapids: Kregel, 1990), 31.

[11] In his essay on eschatology in 1 Peter, E. G. Selwyn demonstrates that the tension between the already and not yet is maintained in the letter, even though he does not use this terminology. He also rightly emphasizes that the future hope is grounded in the inauguration of the end, an end that believers already participate in by virtue of the death and resurrection of Jesus the Messiah ("Eschatology in I Peter," in *The Background of the New Testament and Its Eschatology in Honour of Charles Harold Dodd* [Cambridge: University Press, 1956], 394–401). For agreement with Selwyn's view see P. L. Tite, *Compositional Transitions in 1 Peter: An Analysis of the Letter-Opening* (San Francisco: International Scholars Publications, 1997), 77. Contra D. C. Parker, who overemphasizes realized eschatology in the letter ("The Eschatology of 1 Peter," *BTB* 24 [1994]: 27–32).

persecution in Asia Minor are not dashed to the ground by their troubles. They look to the future with the sure confidence that inestimable blessing awaits them. Nor is their confidence baseless superstition. It is grounded in and secured by the resurrection of Jesus Christ. Their hope, in other words, is the hope of resurrection, triumph over death; hence, whatever happens to them in this world is trivial compared to the blessing of the future resurrection. Some scholars link the resurrection to being begotten by the Father instead of to the living hope.[12] This view is less likely for two reasons. First, the word order suggests that Christ's resurrection should be linked to the living hope since the former immediately follows the latter. Second, Peter emphasized that Jesus Christ was raised "from the dead." If Peter had wanted to emphasize our new life, he probably would not have added the words "from the dead." Their addition suggests he latched onto the hope believers have even after they die.[13] Third, the word "living" connects the hope to the resurrection.

1:4 The future hope of believers is now described more fully. Peter selects the language of "inheritance" *(klēronomia)* to describe what is in store for Christians. In the Old Testament the inheritance is the land God promised to his people (Num 32:19; Deut 2:12; 12:9; 25:19; 26:1; Josh 11:23; Ps 105:11; Acts 7:5). The word is especially common in Joshua for the apportionment of the land for each tribe or family.[14] Peter understood the inheritance, however, no longer in terms of a land promised to Israel but in terms of the end-time hope that lies before believers.[15] This hope is still physical, for we learn from 2 Peter that it will be realized in a new heaven and new earth (2 Pet 3:13; cf. Rev 21:1–22:5). But it transcends and leaves behind the land of Palestine. Paul's view of the inheritance was similar to Peter's, for the inheritance is the eschatological hope of believers (Gal 3:18; 4:30; Eph 1:11,14; 5:5; Col 1:12; 3:24). The author of Hebrews conveys a similar idea, saying that the patriarchs ultimately hoped for a heavenly country and city (Heb 11:13–16). We also see in the New Testament that the language of inheriting the kingdom is another way of saying that believers will receive eternal life (cf. Matt 19:29; 25:34; Mark 10:17; Luke 10:25; 18:18; 1 Cor 6:9–10; Gal 5:21). Grudem overreads the preposition "into" *(eis)* and suggests that believers may partially enter into the inheritance

---

[12] E.g., D. E. Hiebert, "Peter's Thanksgiving for Our Salvation," *Studia Missionalia* 29 (1980): 19; Michaels, *1 Peter,* 19.

[13] So also Achtemeier, *1 Peter,* 95, n. 27.

[14] Josh 11:23; 13:6,7,8,14,15,23,24,28,29,33; 14:2,3,9,13,14; 15:20; 16:4,5,8,9; 17:4,6,14; 18:2,7,20,28; 19:1,2,8,9,10,16,23,31,39,41,48,49; 21:3; 23:4; 24:30,32.

[15] See J. H. Elliott, *1 Peter: A New Translation with Introduction and Commentary,* AB (New York: Doubleday, 2000), 336.

now.[16] But that is not what Peter was saying. His point was that they are sojourners and aliens in this world, they face suffering now, and their hope is directed to the future inheritance. This inheritance "can never perish" *(aphtharton)* or be corrupted. Elsewhere we are told that God is imperishable (Rom 1:23; 1 Tim 1:17) and that our resurrection bodies are incorruptible (1 Cor 15:22). The inheritance cannot "spoil" *(amianton)* or perhaps better is "undefiled." The inheritance will not lose its luster and beauty. It will never become stained or filthy. The same word is used to denote Jesus' sinlessness (Heb 7:26), the purity of marriage (Heb 13:4), and genuine religion (Jas 1:27). Finally, the inheritance will never "fade" *(amaranton)*. It will last forever, just as the crown of reward that elders receive will never fade away (1 Pet 5:4). The verse concludes with the promise that the inheritance is "kept in heaven for you." The passive of the word "kept" *(tetērēmenēn)* is a divine passive, referring to God as the one who reserves the inheritance for believers. Peter emphasized in the strongest possible terms the security and certainty of the reward awaiting believers.

Marx complained that religion is the opiate of oppressed people. Was Peter making that mistake here by reminding those who are suffering of eternal life? Not at all. We should remind ourselves, first of all, that Peter was not exempt from suffering himself. He was not speaking as a rich and comfortable person to those who are experiencing difficulties. The promise of an eternal inheritance is abused if it becomes a means by which the poor are oppressed. And yet many of those who are suffering in this world find no relief and no justice. Marx offers nothing to them, since his only paradise is a worldly one—a paradise that most in this world never experience. The fundamental issue is that Marx did not believe in a heavenly inheritance. Peter did believe in it, and it provides a great incentive for those suffering, reminding them that the veil of tears will not last long, that a great reward is laid up for those who are faithful.

1:5 The living hope of believers, according to v. 4, is their inheritance, and v. 4 emphasizes that the inheritance is imperishable, beautiful, and reserved for believers. Now in v. 5 Peter considers whether his readers will certainly receive the inheritance.[17] Before we consider that theme, we should note that Peter now describes the inheritance in terms of "salvation" *(sōtēria)*. Salvation can be defined as being rescued from God's judgment or wrath on the last day (1 Pet 4:17; cf. Rom 5:9; 1 Thess 5:9). In popular circles salvation is usually conceived of as a past or present possession, and both of these notions are found in the New Testament (cf. Eph 2:8–9; 1 Cor

---

[16] W. Grudem, *The First Epistle of Peter,* TNTC (Grand Rapids: Eerdmans, 1988), 57.

[17] Contra M. C. Tenney, it simply cannot be established that Peter recalled here his own preservation after his denial of Christ ("Some Possible Parallels between 1 Peter and John," in *New Dimensions in New Testament Study* [Grand Rapids: Zondervan, 1974], 372–73).

1:18). In the majority of cases, however, salvation refers to the *future* glory believers will enjoy,[18] and it is clear that Peter conceived of salvation in future terms here.[19] Two pieces of evidence substantiate this judgment. First, it is clear in the context that "salvation" is another way of describing the believer's inheritance, and the latter is certainly future. Second, the salvation is "ready to be revealed in the last time." The passive of the verb "revealed" *(apokalyphthēnai)* is a divine passive, indicating that God will disclose this salvation on the final day. What is decisive, of course, is that Peter specifically informed his readers that the salvation will not be unveiled until the last day. In other words, it is a future event.

Peter assured his readers that they will certainly receive this inheritance, that future salvation will be theirs. The reason for this confidence is that they "are shielded by God's power." The word "shielded" *(phrouroumenous)* can be translated "guarded" or "protected." It is used of putting garrisons in a city to protect it from foes (cf. *Jdt* 3:6; *1 Esdr* 4:56; *Wis* 17:16; 2 Cor 11:22; see also Phil 4:7). How does God protect believers?[20] We know from the following verses that he does not exempt them from persecution or suffering. Believers may suffer agonizing pain, both physical and psychological, because of their faith. Peter must have meant that God preserves believers so that they will receive their final inheritance and experience the joy of eschatological salvation. The text does not merely say, however, that believers are protected by God to receive salvation. Peter added that believers are protected "through faith" *(dia pisteōs)*. Obtaining the final inheritance therefore does not bypass human beings, as if we are mere automatons in the process. Believers must exercise faith to receive final salvation. Faith here is "continuing trust or faithfulness."[21] Peter did not conceive of faith as a single isolated act; genuine faith persists until the day of redemption.[22] But if receiving the inheritance is dependent upon human faith, is it possible that some will fall short and be judged rather than saved?

There is no final salvation apart from continued faith, and thus faith *is a condition* for obtaining the eschatological inheritance.[23] It is imperative to understand that God's protection cannot be kept in a separate compartment

---

[18] Rightly C. Bigg, *The Epistles of St. Peter and St. Jude,* ICC (Edinburgh: T & T Clark, 1901), 102; Michaels, *1 Peter,* 23; Achtemeier, *1 Peter,* 97.

[19] Contra Parker, "Eschatology of 1 Peter," 28.

[20] Contra Brox the participle here is passive and not middle (*Der erste Petrusbrief*, 63).

[21] Michaels, *1 Peter,* 23.

[22] D. Horrell points out that it is possible that the reference here is to God's faithfulness, though he concludes (rightly in my view) that a reference to the faith of believers probably is more likely in context (cf. 1:7–9; see "Whose Faith[fulness] Is It in 1 Peter 1:5?" *JTS* 48 [1997]: 110–15).

[23] My discussion here comes from *The Race Set Before Us,* 246–47.

from our believing. We can get at the issue by asking, "How are we protected through God's power?" All of 1 Peter clarifies that we are not exempted from suffering or even death because of the power of God since the church experiences persecution. God's power does not shield believers from trials and sufferings, but it does protect us from that which would cause us to fall away. What would prevent us from maintaining our allegiance to Christ until the end? Surely the answer is sin, and we know that sin stems from unbelief—in failing to hope in God during our earthly sojourn. God's power, to be effective at all, must guard us from sin and unbelief. If his power plays no role in our faith, then it seems that his power accomplishes nothing in our making it to the end—since it is precisely unbelief and failure to hope in God that causes us to fall away from God. If God's power does not protect us from unbelief, it is hard to see what it does. How is God protecting us until the end if his guarding plays no role in our continuing faith? We are suggesting that 1 Pet 1:5 contains a glorious promise. God's power protects us because his power is the means by which our faith is sustained.[24] E. Best rightly discerns that the ultimate reason for our preservation must be God's gift rather than our faith since otherwise "the reference to God's power" is "unnecessary and provides no assurance to the believer since what he doubts is his own power to cling to God in trial."[25] We should not use this verse to deny that believers must maintain their faith until the end.[26] Its function is to encourage believers with the truth that God will preserve their faith through sufferings and the vicissitudes of life. Faith and hope are ultimately gifts of God, and he fortifies believers so that they persist in faith and hope until the day that they obtain the eschatological inheritance.

(2) Result: Joy in Suffering (1:6–9)

[6]In this you greatly rejoice, though now for a little while you may have had to suffer grief in all kinds of trials. [7]These have come so that your faith—of greater worth than gold, which perishes even though refined by fire—may be proved genuine and may result in praise, glory and honor when Jesus Christ is revealed.

---

[24] A further theological observation could be made, which I owe to a paper written by M. Perman in a class I taught on 1 Peter. Perman says the following in his exegesis of v. 5: "It must be admitted that God knows which external circumstances would lead any particular believer to apostatize. Consequently, even if the 'guarding' simply means that God protects us from attack, would not that necessarily imply that he will never allow to be actualized any circumstances or attacks in our lives that would lead to our apostasy?" Nevertheless, Perman agrees that the text says more than this, that Peter teaches that God is the one who sustains our faith.

[25] Best, *1 Peter,* 77.

[26] But we reject F. J. A. Hort's claim that "faith is the human condition which brings the Divine strengthening into operation" (*The First Epistle of St Peter: I.1–II.17* [New York: Macmillan, 1898], 38). Such a view sees human faith rather than God's preservation as ultimate.

[8]Though you have not seen him, you love him; and even though you do not see him now, you believe in him and are filled with an inexpressible and glorious joy, [9]for you are receiving the goal of your faith, the salvation of your souls.

1:6 The main theme in vv. 3–5 is that believers should praise God because of the certainty of their eschatological hope. The thought shifts slightly in vv. 6–9. Now Peter focuses on the joy (vv. 6,8) and love (v. 8) that fills the lives of believers, even though they are suffering. They are joyful because suffering is the pathway to a godliness that passes the test on the last day (v. 7), because suffering results in eschatological salvation (v. 9).

Verse 6 begins with the words "in this" *(en hō)*. Identifying a particular antecedent is difficult. The words "God" or "Christ" (v. 3) are too far removed to be likely candidates.[27] "The last time" *(kairō eschatō)* fits better, and it would require that the word "rejoice" *(agalliasthe)* be understood as a present tense with a future meaning.[28] It is preferable, though, to retain the normal sense of the verb tense, so that Peter referred to rejoicing now, not in the last day. This is the natural way to take the same verb in v. 8 as well. The strongest argument favoring this view is that the present tense verb "you love" *(agapate)* is clearly a present indicative and not a future.[29] Therefore the words "in this" should be understood as a general antecedent and can be translated "in which circumstances,"[30] or "for that reason."[31]

---

[27] Contra Hort, *The First Epistle of St Peter,* 40.

[28] So Goppelt, *I Peter,* 88–89; Michaels, *1 Peter,* 27–28; Horrell, *The Epistles of Peter and Jude,* 25; T. Martin, "The Present Indicative in the Eschatological Statements of 1 Peter 1:6, 8," *JBL* 111 (1992): 307–14. Martin defends this view by stating that the time of the aorist participle λυπηθέντες must precede the time of the main verb (*Metaphor and Composition in 1 Peter,* 62–63). It is incorrect, however, to argue that the aorist participle is necessarily antecedent temporally to the main verb. In this instance the participle and verb should be construed as contemporaneous.

[29] Contra A. B. du Toit, who takes the verb as an imperative ("The Significance of Discourse Analysis for New Testament Interpretation and Translation: Introductory Remarks with Special Reference to 1 Peter 1:3–13," *Neot* 8 [1974]: 70–71). Agreeing with du Toit is E. J. Richard, *Reading 1 Peter, Jude, and 2 Peter: A Literary and Theological Commentary,* RNT [Macon: Smith & Helwys, 2000], 45–46). The verb ἀγαπᾶτε is also most likely construed as indicative rather than imperative. Martin rightly observes that imperatives do not commence until 1:13 ("1 Peter 1:6," 307–8). First Peter 1:3–12 is the indicative segment of the letter, underlining the fact that the indicative is the foundation for the imperatives. Elliott observes that 4:13 also favors a reference to the present (*1 Peter,* 339).

[30] C. F. D. Moule, "The Nature and Purpose of I Peter," *NTS* 3 (1956–57): 131–32; Elliott, *1 Peter,* 338–39; du Toit suggests "herein" ("1 Peter 1:3–13," 68). So already Calvin, *Catholic Epistles,* 31.

[31] B. Reicke, *The Disobedient Spirits and Christian Baptism: A Study of 1 Pet. III.19 and Its Context,* ASNU 13 (Copenhagen: Munksgaard, 1946), 111; Achtemeier, *1 Peter,* 100; Grudem, *1 Peter,* 60; P. R. Fink, "The Use and Significance of *en hō* in I Peter," *GTJ* 8 (1967): 34; Brox, *Der erste Petrusbrief,* 63.

The phrase reaches back to the entire content of vv. 3–5, focusing on the eschatological hope of believers. They rejoice now because of the inheritance that most certainly awaits them.

The NIV rightly understands the participle *lypēthentes* as concessive ("*though* . . . you may have had to suffer grief").[32] Selwyn mistakenly identifies it as causal,[33] but this implies that suffering is intrinsically joyful, instead of seeing that suffering is valuable only for the benefits it brings. Suffering is still painful or it would not be described as suffering. Believers rejoice despite suffering because they know that it will not persist forever. It strikes "now" *(arti)* and "for a little while" *(oligon),* but it will be swallowed up by the eschaton.[34] Hence, when Peter said "a little while," he was not promising that suffering on this earth will be brief.[35] The difficulty is brief when compared to future glory, but it may endure for a lifetime. The diverse nature of the suffering is conveyed in the phrase "all kinds of trials."

Peter added the interesting phrase "if necessary" (NASB, *ei deon*), translated by the NIV "had to." The idea is that the sufferings believers experience are not the result of fate or impersonal forces of nature. They are the will of God for believers (cf. 1 Pet 4:19).[36] The New Testament regularly sees sufferings as the road believers must travel to enter into God's kingdom (cf. Acts 14:22; Rom 5:3–5; Jas 1:2–4).[37] We should not deduce from this that sufferings are somehow enjoyable or that a specific reason should be assigned to each suffering; nor should we minimize the evil actions of others in inflicting suffering (Acts 2:23). Peter assured his readers, however, that God is working out his plan even in their anguish.

1:7 Why is it God's plan for Christians to suffer? Verse 7 provides the reason. Sufferings function as the crucible for faith. They test the genuineness of faith, revealing whether or not faith is authentic. If faith proves to be

---

[32] In some manuscripts the text reads λυπηθέντας instead of λυπηθέντες, representing a grammatical change so that the text agrees with the implied ὑμᾶς.

[33] Selwyn, *First Peter,* 126.

[34] Calvin captures beautifully what Peter communicates, saying that "the faithful know by experience, how these things [joy and sorrow] can exist together, much better than can be expressed in words." He says believers "are not logs of wood" and hence are affected by sufferings, and yet this suffering is "mitigated by faith, that they cease not at the same time to rejoice" (*Catholic Epistles,* 32).

[35] For the apocalyptic and evangelistic character of the suffering in 1 Peter, see J. Holdsworth, "The Sufferings in 1 Peter and 'Missionary Apocalyptic,'" StudBib 1978: III. *Papers on Paul and Other New Testament Authors,* JSNTSup 3 (Sheffield: Academic Press, 1980), 225–32.

[36] So Goppelt, *I Peter,* 89–90, n. 29; Best, *1 Peter,* 78; J. N. D. Kelly, *A Commentary on the Epistles of Peter and Jude,* Thornapple Commentaries (Grand Rapids: Baker, 1981), 54; Achtemeier, *1 Peter,* 101; Schelke, *Der Petrusbriefe—Der Judasbrief,* 35.

[37] M. Dubis sees a reference to the Messianic woes that precede the end (*Messianic Woes in 1 Peter: Suffering and Eschatology in 1 Peter 4:12–19, SBL* 33 [New York: Peter Lang, 2002], 68–70).

real, the believer will receive "praise, glory and honor" when Jesus Christ returns. The idea is quite similar to *Wis* 3:5–6: "Having been disciplined a little, they will receive great good, because God tested them and found them worthy of himself; like gold in the furnace he tried them, and like a sacrificial burnt offering he accepted them" (NRSV). Also, "For gold is tested in the fire, and those found acceptable, in the furnace of humiliation" (*Sir* 2:5, RSV). Again we see the indissoluble connection between faith and faithfulness. Those who truly believe will persist in their faith, continuing to trust in God when difficulties occur. In a parenthesis authentic faith is contrasted and compared with gold. I understand, then, "of greater worth than gold, which perishes" as appositional to "the genuineness of your faith" (NRSV, *to dokimion hymōn tēs pisteōs*),[38] and not as the predicate of the verb "be found" (NRSV, *eurethē*).[39] Approved faith is more valuable than gold because the latter is temporary and perishes. But faith is also compared to gold, for like gold it is refined and proved through fire. Peter reminds believers again that the test may be intense and stringent. Life as aliens is anything but easy, and yet by God's grace the lives of believers are filled with joy, not gloomy moaning.

The focus here is on the value of genuine faith in God's sight on the day of judgment.[40] The words "may be found" (*heurethē*, NRSV) refer to the final judgment when God examines the life of each person (cf. 2 Cor 5:3; Phil 3:9; 2 Tim 1:18; 2 Pet 3:10,14; Rev 14:5). "Praise, glory and honor" are given on that day to the person whose faith has been tested and approved by fire (cf. Rom 2:7,10,29; 1 Cor 4:5). The eschatological reward will be given to them because of the genuineness of their faith, which is proved by the sufferings they endure. God brings sufferings into the lives of believers to purify their faith and to demonstrate its genuineness. The eschatological reward reveals that believers have been transformed by God's grace, inasmuch as they rejoice in God so much they are willing to undergo pain. Michaels correctly notes that the emphasis is on the reward believers receive; and yet praise, glory, and honor also, in a secondary sense, redound to God since he is the one who empowers believers to perse-

---

[38] A few manuscripts and 𝔓[72] insert the more common word δόκιμον, but it is clear that the unusual word δοκίμιον (with essentially the same meaning; cf. Jas 1:3) is original.

[39] Otherwise the verb εὑρεθῇ would have a second predicate clause (εἰς ἔπαινον καὶ δόξαν καὶ τιμὴν), which would be awkward. Moreover, it is unlikely that Peter's point is that God finds our faith to be more precious than gold as a result of our sufferings (rightly Michaels, *1 Peter,* 30; Achtemeier, *1 Peter,* 102, n. 40; contra Selwyn, *First Peter,* 129; Kelly, *Peter and Jude,* 54). The prepositional phrase with εἰς functions as the predicate with the verb εὑρεθῇ (rightly Michaels, *1 Peter,* 31; BDF 145.1).

[40] Michaels, *1 Peter,* 30.

vere (1:5).[41] The reward will be given at the second coming, "when Jesus Christ is revealed" (lit. "at the revelation of Jesus Christ," RSV).[42] Michaels rightly observes that the use of the term "revelation" demonstrates that Jesus is present with his people, but he is "invisible," and hence he must come and "be revealed" to them.[43]

1:8 Verse 7 concludes with the hope that animates believers—the revelation of Jesus Christ, his appearance at his second coming. Christ will be seen by all, and yet those to whom Peter wrote have never seen him. The first phrase ("though you have not seen him") relates to the past, indicating that Peter's readers located in Asia Minor never laid their eyes on the historical Jesus.[44] Nonetheless, they "love him." The verb "love" *(agapate)* should be construed as an indicative rather than an imperative. Peter was not exhorting the churches but commending them here. Their sufferings have not made them morose and miserable. They are filled with love for Jesus Christ. He is precious and lovely to them.

The believers have never seen the Lord Jesus, nor do they see him now. Nevertheless, they believe in him.[45] Believing is not based on seeing (cf. John 20:29).[46] Seeing will be their portion at the revelation of Jesus Christ. In the meantime the Christian life is marked by believing. We have an indication here that the "faith" in vv. 5,7, and 9 should not be restricted to "faithfulness." Those who truly believe are also faithful, but the latter is always rooted in the former. The main thought in this clause emerges with the verb "rejoice" (NRSV, *agalliasthe*) repeated from v. 6. Believers rejoice and exult in Jesus Christ, even

[41] Michaels: "In honoring he is honored, in glorifying he receives glory, and in praising he is praised. . . . Yet the priority is clear. Peter has in mind *explicitly* the praise, glory, and honor that God bestows on his servants, and only implicitly the praise, glory, and honor that is his in the act of giving" (*1 Peter,* 31). Cf. also Hort, *The First Epistle of St Peter,* 43; Goppelt, *I Peter,* 92; P. H. Davids, *The First Epistle of Peter,* NICNT (Grand Rapids: Eerdmans, 1990), 58; L. Thurén, *Argument and Theology in 1 Peter: The Origins of Christian Paraenesis,* JSNTSup 114 (Sheffield: Academic Press, 1995), 99.

[42] Contrary to Parker there is no suggestion here that Jesus Christ is revealed now by the behavior of believers ("The Eschatology of 1 Peter," 29). Peter thought exclusively of the second coming of Christ.

[43] Michaels, *1 Peter,* 32.

[44] A few manuscripts (A, K, P, Ψ, 33, 81, 614, *al*) support εἰδότες, but both the Alexandrian and Western texts support ἰδόντες. Further, the contrast is awkward if Peter said, "Though you have not known him, you love him" (cf. B. M. Metzger, *A Textual Commentary of the Greek New Testament,* 2d ed. (New York: United Bible Societies, 1994), 616; hereafter: *TCGNT.*

[45] Peter was not contrasting himself with his readers in this verse by reminding them that he as an apostle had seen the Lord (rightly Michaels, *1 Peter,* 32; contra Selwyn, *First Peter,* 131; Kelly, *Peter and Jude,* 56).

[46] But it is unclear that Peter drew here on the Jesus tradition reflected in John 20:29 (contra Gundry, "*Verba Christi,*" 338; "Further *Verba,*" 218; Tenney, "Parallels between 1 Peter and John," 373; G. Maier, "Jesustradition im 1. Petrusbrief," in *Gospel Perspectives: The Jesus Tradition outside the Gospels* [Sheffield: JSOT Press, 1984], 5:87; rightly Best, "Gospel Tradition," 98).

though they do not see him now.[47] The joy believers experience is a taste of heaven, an anticipation of the end, because it is "indescribable and glorious."[48] The word "glorious" *(dedoxamenē)* links back to "glory" *(doxan)* in v. 7, suggesting that eschatological glory is intended.

Peter's main point in the verse is clear. Believers who suffer are not dashed to the ground by their troubles. They love Jesus Christ and rejoice in him, even though they have never seen him and do not see him now. Their lives are characterized by a hope that fills the present with love and joy.

1:9 The participle "receiving" *(komizomenoi)* in v. 9 could be understood as attendant circumstances, and the phrase could be translated, "And you receive the outcome of your faith, the salvation of your souls."[49] Alternatively, it could be translated as temporal, "when you receive the outcome of your faith, your final salvation."[50] But the interpretation proposed by the NIV is most satisfying, understanding the participle as providing a reason, "For you are receiving the outcome of your faith, the salvation of your souls."[51] Peter was explaining why believers are filled with love and joy for Jesus Christ (the two main verbs from v. 8). They have love and joy because of the prospect of future salvation. The idea that the participle is temporal should be rejected because that requires that the verb "rejoice" in v. 8 be understood as a future. The present tense of the verb "rejoice" and the parallelism with the verb "love" in v. 8 indicates that "rejoice" describes the experience of believers now.[52] Salvation, as we have seen in v. 5, is eschatological, consummated only on the last day. The present participle *(komizomenoi)* does not necessarily indicate that the salvation in view here is present. Indeed, the word "outcome" *(telos)* suggests that a future gift is in view. It is possible that we have here the "now" and "not yet" tension that is so common in the New Testament. Believers now enjoy salvation and yet will experience it fully at the revelation of Jesus Christ.[53] In any case, believers are full of love and joy

---

[47] Contra du Toit ἀγαλλιᾶσθε should be understood as indicative, not imperative ("1 Peter 1:3–13," 70–71). The presence of ὃν ἄρτι and the participle πιστεύοντες in context indicate that the indicative is in view. I understand ἰδόντες to be attached to the verb ἀγαπᾶτε, and the particle δέ contrasts the two participles ὁρῶντες and πιστεύντες (so Achtemeier, *1 Peter,* 103).

[48] "Not even a thousand ironclad tongues can sound out the sweetness of the heavenly blessings," says Hilary of Arles in *James, 1–2 Peter, 1–3 John, Jude,* ACCS (Downers Grove: InterVarsity, 2000), 72.

[49] Grudem, *1 Peter,* 67.

[50] This is Michaels' translation and interpretation of the verse (*1 Peter,* 25, 35).

[51] So also Thurén, *Argument and Theology in 1 Peter,* 100. The pronoun ὑμῶν is missing altogether in B, a few manuscripts support ἡμῶν, but both the context and the majority of the manuscripts suggest that ὑμῶν is original.

[52] Michaels, again, wrongly restricts joy here to the future (*1 Peter,* 34). So also Luther, *Commentary on Peter & Jude,* 50.

[53] Grudem mistakenly emphasizes growth in salvation here instead of seeing the eschatological focus of the term (*1 Peter,* 67). Elliott notes that Peter shares the eschatological tension between inaugurated and consummated eschatology that is typical of NT writers (*1 Peter,* 337–38).

even now because of the hope of salvation.

Salvation of "souls" could easily be misunderstood by moderns, as if Peter referred to the salvation of our immaterial substance. The word "souls," however, refers to the whole person and does not suggest in any way that the body is left out. The reference is to "a person's whole life or self-identity."[54] We should also notice that such salvation is "the outcome of your faith." The word "outcome" *(telos)* has the idea of result here. Achtemeier wrongly says that faith means "faithfulness" rather than "belief."[55] We have already observed several times that such a judgment is mistaken, and the word "faith" here is closely linked to the participle "believing" (translated "believe" by the NIV) in v. 8. Faith and faithfulness were ultimately inseparable for Peter, but the latter is rooted in the former. We should sum up the main idea in the verse as we conclude. The love and joy of believers is rooted in the hope of eschatological salvation. They know, therefore, that despite present sufferings they will see Jesus Christ when he is revealed and enjoy him forever.

(3) The Privilege of Revelation (1:10–12)

10Concerning this salvation, the prophets, who spoke of the grace that was to come to you, searched intently and with the greatest care, 11trying to find out the time and circumstances to which the Spirit of Christ in them was pointing when he predicted the sufferings of Christ and the glories that would follow. 12It was revealed to them that they were not serving themselves but you, when they spoke of the things that have now been told you by those who have preached the gospel to you by the Holy Spirit sent from heaven. Even angels long to look into these things.

1:10 The link between vv. 9 and 10 is the term "salvation" *(sōteria)*. The salvation believers experience now, which will be consummated in the future, was also prophesied in the past. Believers in Christ represent the fulfillment of prophecy. They enjoy the great privilege of living in the days when the history of salvation is being fulfilled. The Old Testament prophets "prophesied of the grace that was to be yours" (NRSV).[56] The NIV translates the verse so that the repetition of "prophets" and "prophesied" is omitted, but in doing so one of the main emphases of the verse is blunted. What was predicted in the past was intended for Peter's readers. Their salvation is described as "grace" here, and the point is that such grace "was to come to you." God's favor and power were "meant for you"[57] and were not experi-

[54] P. G. Dautzenberg, "σωτηρία ψυχῶν," *BZ* 8 (1964): 273–75; Michaels, *1 Peter,* 35.

[55] Achtemeier, *1 Peter,* 104, n. 69.

[56] The word "grace" here is virtually equivalent to salvation (so S. R. Bechtler, *Following in His Steps: Suffering, Community, and Christology in 1 Peter,* SBLDS 162 [Atlanta: Scholars Press, 1998], 183–84).

[57] BDAG, 290.

enced in the same way by the Old Testament prophets. The prophets "searched intently and with the greatest care" (*exezētēsan* and *exēraunēsan*) into this salvation. The two verbs should be interpreted together, indicating how ardently the prophets investigated the salvation about which they prophesied.

Some scholars have argued that the prophets mentioned here are New Testament prophets.[58] They believe it makes more sense to conceive of New Testament prophets searching the Scriptures rather than the Old Testament prophets who actually wrote them. Most commentators agree, however, that the Old Testament prophets are the subject of discussion. The latter view is almost surely correct for a number of reasons.[59] First, searching need not be confined to the Scriptures. It can refer to seeking the Lord (Ps 119:2, LXX), and in this instance it likely refers to their attempt to discern the time when their predictions would be fulfilled.[60] Second, there is evidence that some of the prophets sought to comprehend their prophecies (Dan 8:15; 12:8). Third, possibly some Old Testament prophets reflected on earlier prophetic writings and attempted to grasp when they would be fulfilled. Fourth, the New Testament prophets knew the time of salvation as well as the Petrine community (v. 11). So it is difficult to perceive how they would be at any disadvantage in contrast to Petrine Christians. Selwyn thinks, however, that "the sufferings of Christ and the glories that would follow" (v. 11) refer to the sufferings of Christians.[61] This reading is just possible since the Greek could be read "the sufferings with reference to Christ" *(ta eis Christon pathēmata)* or the sufferings "designated or intended for the Christ."[62] We should reject this interpretation as well. In v. 10 a similar construction is used "grace . . . to you" *(eis hymas charis)*, and it refers to the grace that *belongs to Christians*. Similarly, the idea here is of the sufferings and glories that belong to Christ.[63] Further, the idea that Christ would suffer and then enter glory is a common feature of New Testament preaching (cf. Acts 2:14–36; 3:11–26; 13:16–41).[64] Note, for exam-

---

[58] Selwyn, *First Peter,* 134; D. Warden, "The Prophets of 1 Peter 1:10–12," *ResQ* 31 (1989): 1–12.

[59] So Michaels, *1 Peter,* 41; D. G. McCartney, "The Use of the Old Testament in the First Epistle of Peter" (Ph.D. diss., Westminster Theological Seminary, 1989), 27–31; Dubis, *1 Peter 4:12–19,* 108–10.

[60] So Michaels, *1 Peter,* 40.

[61] Selwyn, *First Peter,* 136–37, 263–65.

[62] McCartney, "The Use of the Old Testament in the First Epistle of Peter," 28; Elliott, *1 Peter,* 347–48.

[63] So Achtemeier, *1 Peter,* 110.

[64] Some scholars see a reference to the suffering and glory of both Christ and believers (Dubis, *1 Peter 4:12–19,* 113–17; W. L. Schutter, *Hermeneutic and Composition in I Peter*, WUNT 2/30 [Tübingen: Mohr, 1989], 107–8). But Peter restricted his vision here to Christ, even though he elsewhere taught that believers will experience glory because of their sufferings in Christ.

ple, "Did not the Christ have to suffer these things and then enter his glory?" (Luke 24:26); "This is what is written: The Christ will suffer and rise from the dead on the third day" (Luke 24:46); "I am saying nothing beyond what the prophets and Moses said would happen—that the Christ would suffer and, as the first to rise from the dead, would proclaim light to his own people and to the Gentiles" (Acts 26:22–23). Fifth, the phrase "have now been told you" in 1 Pet 1:12 indicates that the prophets belonged to a former era, one in which they did not grasp fully the things "now" revealed to believers.

1:11 Peter continued to emphasize that the Old Testament prophets had a predictive ministry and did not live in the days of fulfillment. Their prophecies were inspired by "the Spirit of Christ," showing that their words are authoritative and accurate. The prophecies were not the invention of the prophets or their best "guess." They were "revealed" (*edēlou,* my translation)[65] by the Spirit of Christ.[66] The "Spirit of Christ" does not refer to Jesus' human spirit but the Holy Spirit sent from Jesus (cf. Acts 16:7; Gal 4:6; Phil 1:19).[67] The same Spirit that inspired the prophets also speaks authoritatively (v. 12) through the gospel. I discussed in v. 10 the content of their prophecies, "the sufferings of Christ and the glories that would follow." We saw there that Christ's death and resurrection are a staple of New Testament preaching. Peter's point, of course, was that the prophets predicted these matters but did not know when they would be fulfilled, and they hoped upon hope that they would be fulfilled in their days.

We can infer Christ's preexistence from what is said here, since the subject is Old Testament prophecy. The preexistence of Christ is also implied in 1:20.[68] What the prophets desired to know and what they "searched out" (*eraunōntes,* note the link to the verb *exēraunēsan* in v. 10) fervently was "the person or time that the Spirit of Christ within them indicated" (NRSV). The words of the NRSV represent an interpretation of the Greek phrase *eis tina ē poion kairon,* and the meaning of this phrase is debated. The NIV provides another interpretation, "trying to find out the time and circumstances to which the Spirit of Christ in them was pointing." The NRSV favors the view that the prophecies were both about the person of the Messiah and the time of his appearing.[69] The NIV, on the other hand, sees only

---

[65] A number of manuscripts read ἐδήλουτο instead of the imperfect active ἐδήλου, but the former came about from wrongly combining the article τό with the verb.

[66] The words εἰς τίνα ἢ ποῖον καιρόν serve as the object of the verb ἐδήλου (so Achtemeier, *1 Peter,* 109).

[67] So McCartney, "The Use of the Old Testament in the First Epistle of Peter," 37; contra Richard, *Reading 1 Peter, Jude, and 2 Peter,* 54.

[68] Rightly Achtemeier, *1* Peter, 109–10. Against this view see W. D. Kirkpatrick, "The Theology of First Peter," *SwJT* 25 (1982): 75.

[69] Similarly, G. D. Kilpatrick, "1 Peter 1:11: TINA ' H ΠΟΙΟΝ ΚΑΙΡΟΝ," *NovT* 28 (1986): 91–92; N. Hillyer, *1 and 2 Peter, Jude,* NIBC (Peabody: Hendrickson, 1992), 41–42.

a reference to time, understanding the two pronouns as overlapping in meaning. A decision is quite difficult since both interpretations are sensible, and both can be defended lexically.[70] The pronoun *tis* is used both as an interrogative pronoun (e.g., 1 Pet 3:13; 4:17; 5:8; cf. Acts 8:34) and as an interrogative adjective (Matt 5:46; Luke 14:31; John 2:18; Acts 10:21; Rom 3:1).[71] Dogmatism should be avoided, but it seems to me that the interpretation proposed by the NIV is preferable.[72] First, Michaels probably is correct in noting that the prophets knew they were prophesying about the Messiah, and hence they would not be questioning that fact.[73] It seems unlikely that they were wondering precisely which person would fill that role. Second, the entire focus of the text is on the temporal difference between the Old Testament prophets and the Petrine Christians. The prophets prophesied about what was not fulfilled in their day. They "predicted" *(promartyromenōn)* Christ's suffering and glory (v. 11). His "glories" *(doxas)* refer here to his resurrection and triumph over evil powers (1:3; 3:19–22).[74] The prophets were serving Petrine Christians, not themselves, and the fulfillment is "now" announced to you (v. 12). Third, the great desire of the prophets was that the prophecies would be fulfilled in their days, that they would see what they promised coming to pass (cf. Dan 12:5–13; Hab 2:1–4). Therefore I suggest that the words (lit.) "which or what sort of time" are there for emphasis, to stress that the prophets did not know when the prophecies would be fulfilled, whereas Petrine believers live in the days of fulfillment.

1:12 Old Testament prophets longed to see and experience the fulfillment of what they prophesied. But God "revealed" (*apekalyphthē,* it is a divine passive) to them that their ministry of prophecy and foretelling would not be realized in their day. Their ministry was not ultimately directed to themselves or their own generation but to Petrine readers and all those who live on the other side of the death and resurrection of Christ. In other words, the Old Testament prophecies *do not only apply* to Peter's readers but were *intended* for them.[75] Further, Peter "claims not only that the Old Testament prophets were ministering ultimately to believers in the *eschaton,* but that the prophets *knew* it by revelation."[76] What the prophets

[70] Grudem objects that τίς is not an interrogative adjective with temporal words (*1 Peter,* 75). The question is whether such a usage is lexically defensible, and it surely is.

[71] The references are from Achtemeier, *1 Peter,* 109.

[72] Cf. Achtemeier, *1 Peter*, 109; Richard, *Reading 1 Peter, Jude, and 2 Peter,* 51; Schelke, *Der Petrusbriefe—Der Judasbrief,* 39.

[73] Michaels, *1 Peter,* 41.

[74] Christ's suffering and consequent glory blaze the pathway for believers, who will also experience glory after suffering (Bechtler, *Following in His Steps,* 179–80).

[75] I owe this point to J. Taylor, from an exegesis paper he wrote in a class I taught on 1 Peter.

[76] McCartney, "The Use of the Old Testament in the First Epistle of Peter," 41.

foretold has "now" *(nun)* been announced to believers through those who proclaimed the gospel. A distinction is drawn between the prophets who anticipated and predicted the coming of the gospel and those who have now actually proclaimed the fulfillment of the gospel to the believers in Asia Minor. Both are inspired by the Spirit. To say that the Spirit is "sent from heaven" is likely a reminder of Pentecost, when the Spirit was poured out on the church to bear witness to Jesus Christ.

We noted in v. 11 that the prophets prophesied by the Spirit of Christ, and here we are informed that those who proclaim the gospel do so by the power of the Holy Spirit.[77] We have an early indication here of the authority of the New Testament message, for the proclamation of the gospel is on the same level as the prophecies of the Old Testament. Indeed, the gospel fulfills what is found in the Old Testament, and in that sense the prophetic character of the Old Testament can only be grasped in light of the fulfillment now realized in Jesus Christ. It seems fair to conclude from what Peter said here that the fulfillment of the Old Testament in Jesus Christ is "*related to* but *more than* that which the human authors intended."[78] McCartney rightly argues that this text is paradigmatic for Peter's use of the Old Testament. The Old Testament Scriptures speak of Christ and those who belong to him. Since believers are united with Christ, the Old Testament prophecies are fulfilled with reference to Christ and those who believe in him.[79]

Peter's main point throughout is that believers in Jesus Christ are incredibly blessed to live in the time when the predictions of the prophets have come to pass.[80] A similar lesson was communicated to the apostles by Jesus himself: "Blessed are your eyes because they see, and your ears because they hear. For I tell you the truth, many prophets and righteous men longed to see what you see but did not see it, and to hear what you hear but did not hear it" (Matt 13:16–17).[81] Believers also stand in contrast to the angels, for they also long to glance at and reflect upon these truths. The point is that angels reflect with delight on God's saving actions. More specifically, angels do not experience the gospel in the same way as human beings since

---

[77] The preposition ἐν is missing in some important manuscripts (𝔓[72], A, B, Ψ, 33, *al*), but the majority of the witnesses support its inclusion. See the divided response of the committee in Metzger (*TCGNT,* 616–17). In any case, the meaning of the phrase remains unaltered. The dative may also be associative, signifying circumstances and manner rather than being instrumental (Michaels, *1 Peter,* 47).

[78] So D. J. Moo, "The Problem of *Sensus Plenior,*" in *Hermeneutics, Authority, and Canon* (Grand Rapids: Zondervan, 1986), 204.

[79] See the work of McCartney, "The Use of the Old Testament in the First Epistle of Peter."

[80] "A central purpose in the whole larger unit 1.1–12 is to make the addressees appreciate their status as Christians" (Thurén, *Argument and Theology in 1 Peter,* 102).

[81] Maier sees allusions to Luke 24:25–27; Matt 13:17; John 8:56 ("1. Petrusbrief," 88–89).

they are not the recipients of redemption.[82] Again, the privilege of enjoying and anticipating salvation comes to the forefront. Old Testament prophets saw it from afar, and angels also marvel when gazing upon what God has done in Christ, while the Petrine readers actually experience it.[83]

2. The Future Inheritance as an Incentive to Holiness (1:13–21)

Verses 1–12 celebrate what God has done for believers in Jesus Christ, featuring the saving work of the Father, Son, and Spirit (v. 2), emphasizing the certain inheritance of believers (vv. 3–5), focusing on their love for and joy in God (vv. 6–9), and highlighting how privileged they are to live in the days when God's promises are being fulfilled (vv. 10–12). In typical New Testament fashion Peter called believers to a holy life based on what God has done for them in Christ.[84] Hence, v. 13 begins with "therefore." Three imperatives mark this section (vv. 13,15,17). First, God has given them an unshakable hope in Jesus Christ, and so they are to fix their hope completely on what Christ has done (v. 13). Setting their hope on Christ means that they will reorient their thinking and live alertly and soberly. Second, Peter also summoned the readers to holiness (vv. 14–16), and this means that they will not capitulate to the desires that animated them formerly. Now they are to live different lives as God's pilgrim people, conforming their lives to God's very character. Third, believers are to live in fear (v. 17). The one they invoke as Father is also their judge, who will assess their lives and their eternal destiny according to their behavior. Fear is also fitting because they have been redeemed by Christ's precious blood (vv. 18–19), and his atoning work was destined by God for their benefit before history began (v. 20). In the meantime their lives are to be characterized by faith and hope, trusting his promises while they endure sufferings in the present age.

(1) Setting One's Hope on the Inheritance (1:13–16)

13Therefore, prepare your minds for action; be self-controlled; set your hope fully on the grace to be given you when Jesus Christ is revealed. 14As obedient children, do not conform to the evil desires you had when you lived in ignorance. 15But just as he who called you is holy, so be holy in all you do; 16for it is written: "Be holy, because I am holy."

---

82 Grudem rightly remarks that the point is not that the angels can only stoop and gaze for an instant.

83 Thurén rightly argues that both the prophets and angels highlight the privilege of Peter's readers (*The Rhetorical Strategy of 1 Peter,* 114).

84 As J. H. Elliott notes, the indicatives are the foundation for the imperatives (*A Home for the Homeless: A Sociological Exegesis of 1 Peter, Its Situation and Strategy* [Philadelphia: Fortress, 1981], 139).

1:13 The word "therefore" *(dio)* reaches back to all of vv. 1–12.[85] In the following verses the readers are exhorted to live a godly life. But all these exhortations are grounded in God's saving work as explained in vv. 1–12. Believers are to obey because they are God's chosen pilgrims, because they have been begotten by the Father, because they have an untouchable inheritance, and because of the greatness of their salvation. God's commands are always rooted in his grace. Another way of putting this is to say that the indicative (what God has done for us in Christ) is always the basis of the imperative (how we should live our lives).[86] To confuse the order here would be disastrous, and the result would be works righteousness instead of seeing holiness as the result of God's grace and power, as a response to the love of God in Christ.

Scholars have often argued that many participles in 1 Peter function as imperatives, and this is reflected in the NIV translation of v. 13.[87] Nevertheless, it is significant that only one verb is actually in the imperative mood in v. 13 and that the other verbal forms are participles. The one imperative in v. 13 is "set your hope *[elpisate]* fully on the grace to be given you when Jesus Christ is revealed."[88] It has often been observed that hope in 1 Peter is virtually equivalent to faith in Paul, and Piper remarks that the term "hope" reminds readers that one trusts God for the future.[89] The participles in the verse have an imperatival force, and hence the NIV translates them as "prepare *[anazōsamenoi]* your minds for action" and "be self-controlled" (*nēphontes,* RSV "be sober"). The participles should be understood, however, as subordinate to the main verb and thus should be construed as

---

[85] So J. J. J. van Rensburg, "The Use of Intersentence Relational Particles and Asyndeton in 1 Peter," *Neot* 24 (1990): 294.

[86] So Goppelt, *I Peter,* 102–5.

[87] See especially D. Daube, "Participle and Imperative in I Peter," in E. G. Selwyn, *The First Epistle of St. Peter,* 2d ed. (Grand Rapids: Baker, 1981), 467–88. Daube argues that NT writers follow the pattern of Tannaitic literature, where participles are used as imperatives. Other scholars argue that Daube's theory has not been sustained and that the development of the imperative from the participle in Greek, Hebrew, and Aramaic is to be explained by "independent development in each language." So S. Snyder, "Participles and Imperatives in 1 Peter: A Re-examination in the Light of Recent Scholarly Trends," *Filologia Neotestamentaria* 8 (1995): 188. Elliott commends Snyder's work but complains that he has not included the "influence of Christian hortatory tradition" (*1 Peter,* 358).

[88] The NIV correctly attaches the adverb τελείως to the verb ἐλπίσατε, so Selwyn, *First Peter,* 140; Achtemeier, *1 Peter,* 119; Tite, *Compositional Transitions in 1 Peter,* 67–68. Some commentators link it with νήφοντες (e.g., Hort, *The First Epistle of St Peter,* 65; Michaels, *1 Peter,* 55), and the adverb could modify either. It seems more likely it would modify the main verb.

[89] See Piper, "Hope as the Motivation of Love," 214; cf. also Goppelt, *I Peter,* 108.

instrumental participles.[90] Hence, the verse should read, "Set your hope fully on the grace . . . by preparing your minds for action and by being sober." This point is important because we can see more clearly the connection between the preceding paragraph and vv. 13–16. Peter emphasized in vv. 3–9 that the salvation of believers is eschatological, that it is an end-time hope. Now he urges them to set their hope completely on the grace that will be theirs "at the revelation of Jesus Christ" (RSV, *en apokalypsei Iēsou Christou*).[91] This latter phrase repeats in exact words the conclusion of v. 7. In each instance Peter reflects on the coming of Jesus Christ, the revelation of the one who is now invisible. The exhortation also reminds us that God's saving work in one sense is unfinished in believers. We await grace that will only be ours when Christ returns, and presumably that grace will finish the sanctifying work so that believers can no longer sin (cf. 1 John 3:1–3).[92] And yet no encouragement is given for sinning in the meantime. Believers are to live in hope even now, demonstrating that their greatest desire is for the consummation of the work that has begun in them.

The two participles, as noted, explain how believers are to set their hope completely upon Jesus Christ. First, they are to "prepare your minds for action." More literally, they are to "gird up the loins of your minds." The image of "girding up the loins" *(anazōsamenoi tas osphyas)* means that one tucks in one's long flowing garments to run or do serious work (cf. 1 Kgs 18:46; cf. also Exod 12:11; 2 Kgs 4:29; 9:1; Job 40:7; Jer 1:17; Nah 2:1; Luke 12:35).[93] Perhaps we have a reference to exodus traditions here, where Israel prepares itself to leave Egypt.[94] The NIV captures the sense well. Hope will not become a reality without disciplined thinking. Thinking in a new way does not happen automatically; it requires effort, concentration, and intentionality. Second, believers set their hope completely on the end by being sober. The NIV's "be self-controlled" is adequate, but the

---

[90] Cf. Snyder, "Participles and Imperatives in 1 Peter," 190. For a similar caution about identifying the participles as imperatives, see Achtemeier, *1 Peter*, 118. I think he wrongly identifies the participles as attendant circumstance or causal instead of seeing them as instrumental (p. 118, n. 11). Further, contrary to Achtemeier, it seems that some of the participles in 1 Peter should be understood as imperatival.

[91] Piper rightly observes that the imperative does not mean "demonstrate hope" but "have hope" ("Hope as the Motivation of Love," 216).

[92] The present participle φερομένην should be understand to denote the future (cf. Michaels, *1 Peter*, 56; Achtemeier, *1 Peter*, 119; contra Parker, "The Eschatology of 1 Peter," 29; Hillyer, *1 and 2 Peter, Jude*, 46).

[93] Peter probably alluded to Jesus tradition here (so Gundry, "*Verba Christi*," 339; "Further *Verba*," 224; Best, "Gospel Tradition," 104–5; Michaels, *1 Peter*, 54). More cautious is Maier, "1. Petrusbrief," 89–90.

[94] So McCartney, "The Use of the Old Testament in the First Epistle of Peter," 106; Hillyer, *1 and 2 Peter, Jude*, 44.

metaphor Peter used is lost. Peter was not merely saying that believers should refrain from drunkenness. There is a way of living that becomes dull to the reality of God, that is anesthetized by the attractions of this world. When people are lulled into such drowsiness, they lose sight of Christ's future revelation of himself and concentrate only on fulfilling their earthly desires.

1:14 The main verb is found in v. 15, where Peter calls on believers to be holy. Setting one's hope completely on Jesus Christ's coming (v. 13) means that one lives a holy life now (v. 15). The participle in v. 14 is literally translated "not being conformed" *(mē syschēmatizomenoi).* The NIV again translates the verb as an imperative, "do not conform." Once again some understand this to be an instrumental participle modifying the verbal clause "be holy."[95] Believers are to be holy by not being conformed to their former desires. The word "but" *(alla)* in v. 15 suggests, however, that the participle stands as an imperative in its own right, for the command not to conform to former desires is contrasted with the injunction to be holy.[96] These desires characterized the Petrine readers before their conversion (cf. 1 Pet 4:3–4). The reference to "ignorance" hearkens back to the pre-Christian past of the readers (cf. 1 Thess 4:5; cf. Acts 3:17; 17:30; Eph 4:18), suggesting also that they are Gentiles.[97] Peter recognized that the Christian life is not passive. Ungodly desires still beckon believers and tempt them to depart from God. They must refuse such desires and choose what is good. They are to do God's will just as "obedient children" obey their parents.[98] The phrase reminds us that believers are begotten by God (1:3,23; cf. 2:2). Hence, Peter did not summon believers to do God's will in their own strength. They are God's children, and as his children they are to obey him. We have already seen in 1:2 (cf. 1:22 as well) that obedience is necessary for conversion and cannot ultimately be separated from faith, though it flows from faith. Peter had no conception of the Christian life in which believers give mere mental assent to doctrines (cf. 2:13,18; 3:1,5,6; 5:5).

1:15 Instead of capitulating to evil desires, believers are to live holy lives. The pattern for holiness is God himself, who is unremittingly good.[99] The call to goodness is one of the distinctive emphases in 1 Peter (2:12–

---

[95] Cf. Achtemeier, *1 Peter,* 120; Martin, *Metaphor and Composition in 1 Peter,* 91–92; Snyder, "Participles and Imperatives in 1 Peter," 191, though Michaels rightly discerns an imperatival sense in context (*1 Peter,* 57).

[96] See the discussion of E. Lohse defending a participial imperative here ("Parenesis and Kerygma in 1 Peter," in *Perspectives on 1 Peter* [Macon: Mercer University Press, 1986], 45–46; cf. also Daube, "Participle," 482).

[97] So Michaels, *1 Peter,* 58.

[98] The genitive ὑπακοῆς in τέκνα ὑπακοης represents a Semitism, but at the same time it denotes a genitive of quality.

[99] Cf. Achtemeier, *1 Peter,* 120–21.

15,20,24; 3:6,11,13,17; 4:2,19). The holiness of their lives is to match that of God, who "called" *(kalesanta)* them to himself. "Calling" refers to God's effectual call in which he infallibly brings people to himself (1 Pet 2:9,21; 3:9; 5:10). This definition is borne out by 2:9, where God calls people "out of darkness into his wonderful light." Calling does not merely mean "invite" but conveys the idea of God's power in bringing people from darkness to light. Just as God's call creates light when there was darkness, so he creates life when there was death. The reference to "calling" is important, for again grace precedes demand. Otherwise the Petrine paraenesis could be confused with the idea that human beings attain their own righteousness or that they live morally noble lives in their own strength. All holiness stems from the God who called them into the sphere of the holy.[100] The command to be holy indicates that the pilgrim people of God (1:1; 2:11) are to live differently. They are to separate themselves from the evil desires of the world and live in a way that pleases God. Some scholars rightly point to Lev 18:2–4, where Israel is to distinguish itself from the evil practices of Egypt and Canaan.[101] To be holy is to separate oneself from what is evil. The injunction to holiness embraces all of life ("in all you do"). No sphere of life is outside God's dominion.

1:16 The summons to holiness is now grounded ("for," *dioti*) with a Scripture reference. McCartney perceptively notes that Peter typically closes sections with scriptural references instead of opening a new section with one.[102] Discerning where the citation comes from is difficult since a number of verses in Leviticus qualify (Lev 11:44–45; 19:2; 20:7,26).[103] Some commentators are convinced that the quotation comes from Lev 19:2 since Israel is called there to live differently from the people in whose midst they live.[104] But the same principle can be applied to 20:7 and 20:26. It is likely that Peter did not intend to refer to any one of these verses in particular but deliberately cited a theme that is suffused throughout all of Leviticus. God's people are to live holy and pleasing lives because God is holy and good. Verse 16 reiterates the notion that God's people are to model their lives after God himself. Pryor communicates well the theological impact of Peter's emphasis on holiness. "In the covenantal thinking of the O.T. blessing to the nations is important, but it is not the starting point.

---

[100] We probably should understand καλέσαντα as an attributive participle and ἅγιον as a substantive noun here (so Bigg, *Epistles of Peter and Jude,* 114; Best, *1 Peter,* 86; Michaels, *1 Peter,* 51). Achtemeier, on the contrary, sees καλέσαντα as a substantive (*1 Peter,* 121).

[101] So Kelly, *Peter and Jude,* 68; Achtemeier, *1 Peter,* 121.

[102] McCartney, "The Use of the Old Testament in the First Epistle of Peter," 99.

[103] It is difficult to discern whether ὅτι is original since it could represent assimilation from Lev 11:44–45.

[104] Achtemeier, *1 Peter,* 122; cf. Michaels, *1 Peter,* 59; Elliott, *1 Peter,* 365.

Israel must first be holy. And this appears to be Peter's emphasis as well. The minimal reference to evangelism (and dialogue) is not just because his primary concern is the church's survival in persecution (though this is a factor), but because he also sees the starting point as holiness in the covenant people (1.16)."[105]

(2) A Call to Fear (1:17–21)

[17]Since you call on a Father who judges each man's work impartially, live your lives as strangers here in reverent fear. [18]For you know that it was not with perishable things such as silver or gold that you were redeemed from the empty way of life handed down to you from your forefathers, [19]but with the precious blood of Christ, a lamb without blemish or defect. [20]He was chosen before the creation of the world, but was revealed in these last times for your sake. [21]Through him you believe in God, who raised him from the dead and glorified him, and so your faith and hope are in God.

1:17 The theme of the paragraph appears in the injunction to live their lives "in reverent fear."[106] Because of the inheritance and salvation believers anticipate (vv. 1–12), they should set their hope completely on Christ's coming (v. 13), devote themselves to holiness (v. 15), and live in fear (v. 17). The remaining verses (vv. 18–21) explain why believers should be fearful.[107] Did Peter mean that believers should live reverently or in terror? Most commentators opt for the former since the confidence believers have in Christ seems to be at odds with the idea of living in a terrified state.[108] Abject terror certainly does not fit with the joy and boldness of the Christian life. Reverence, however, can be watered down so that it becomes rather insipid. Peter contemplated the final judgment, where believers will be assessed by their works and heaven and hell will be at stake (see below). There is a kind of fear that does not contradict confidence. A confident driver also possesses a healthy fear of an accident that prevents him from doing anything foolish. A genuine fear of judgment hinders believers from giving in to libertinism. The background to such fear can be traced to Deuteronomy (e.g., Deut 4:10; 8:6) and the wisdom tradition (Prov 1:29; 3:7; 9:10; Job 28:28; Eccl 12:13), where the fear of the Lord informs all of life.[109]

Believers are to live in such fear while they are "strangers" *(paroikia)* on earth (cf. 1:1; 2:11). Some scholars insist that the term "strangers" refers only to the social dislocation of believers in this world.[110] Certainly believ-

---

[105] J. W. Pryor, "First Peter and the New Covenant (II)," *RTR* 45 (1986): 50.

[106] So also Thurén, *Argument and Theology in 1 Peter,* 114.

[107] Notice the link between the noun ἀναστροφῇ in v. 15 and the verb ἀναστράφητε in v. 17.

[108] E.g., Achtemeier, *1 Peter,* 125.

[109] So Pryor, "New Covenant," 46.

[110] Elliott, *Home for the Homeless,* 41–49; Richard, *Reading 1 Peter, Jude, and 2 Peter,* 63.

ers do not fit into the social order, for their values and behavior contradict the customs of unbelievers. The Petrine believers cut across the grain of the culture in a way that alienates them from the mainstream (Lev 25:23; 1 Chr 29:15; Ps 39:12). Their social dislocation is rooted, however, in their eschatological inheritance and their new birth (cf. 1:3–5). Their heavenly destiny raises a social barrier in the here and now between them and unbelievers. Hence, we need not choose between the options of seeing an emphasis on their present status or their future destiny.[111] Their experience of alienation in the culture can be traced to their shift in values. Their horizontal discomfort comes from their vertical commitment or, better, the end-time promise that awaits them. The parallel with Israel's sojourn in Egypt is apt (cf. Ps 105:12; *Wis* 19:10; Acts 13:17).[112]

The main admonition is to live in fear during one's earthly sojourn, but now we pick up the conditional clause that introduces the verse. The NIV translates the word "if" *(ei)* as "since," and this view is supported by others.[113] In one sense this interpretation is correct, for Peter did not wish to introduce any doubt into his readers' minds about whether God is their Father. Nevertheless, translating "if" as "since" is mistaken. Peter intentionally wrote the sentence as a hypothesis to provoke the readers to consider whether they call upon God as their Father, desiring, surely, that they would answer in the affirmative. The word "since" does not have the same effect, and therefore "if" should be retained. The word "Father" is used of God in the Old Testament (2 Sam 7:14; Ps 2:7; Jer 3:19; Mal 1:6; 2:10; cf. *Wis* 2:16; *3 Mac* 5:7). Indeed, the reference in *3 Mac* 5:7 uses both the term "Father" and the verb "call" *(epikaleomai),* as does 1 Pet 1:17.[114] It is likely, however, that Peter derived the term "Father" from the teaching of Jesus, where God's fatherhood is emphasized (cf. Matt 6:1,4,8–9; 7:11; 10:32; 11:25–27; 18:35; 23:9; John 5:19–20; 20:17). Whether it stems specifically from the Lord's Prayer (Matt 6:9) is harder to discern. What is remarkable here is that God's tenderness and love as Father is mingled with his judgment and the fear that should mark Christians in this world.[115] Apparently Peter did not think that the two themes negated each other but

---

[111] Rightly Michaels, *1 Peter,* 62.

[112] The term can also refer to exile to other lands (*3 Mac* 7:19; *Bar* 4:9,14,24).

[113] E.g., Best, *1 Peter,* 87; Kelly, *Peter and Jude,* 71; Achtemeier, *1 Peter,* 124.

[114] There is no basis for B. L. Campbell's view that the verb bears a legal significance, referring to an "an appeal for honor/vindication" (*Honor, Shame, and the Rhetoric of 1 Peter,* SBLDS 160 [Atlanta: Scholars Press, 1998], 67).

[115] McCartney rightly emphasizes that fathers also functioned as judges in ancient societies ("The Use of the Old Testament in the First Epistle of Peter," 130). Nevertheless, the three references he includes (Ps 89:26; Jer 3:19; Isa 63:16) focus on God's love and forgiveness as Father, not his judgment.

are complementary.[116] The relationship we have with God is both tender and awesome. Some have wrongly understood from the word *abba* that God is "daddy," applying it in astonishingly casual ways. J. Barr has demonstrated in two important articles that such an understanding is flawed.[117]

The motivation for living in fear is explained in the conditional clause. The one believers invoke as Father in prayer is also the one who will judge them impartially on the last day. Grudem concludes from the present participle "judges" *(krinonta)* that Peter referred to judgment and discipline in this life.[118] He adds that believers also have no reason to fear condemnation at the last judgment. His interpretation should be rejected for a number of reasons.[119] First, the tense of participles is not decisive and is not a clear indication of present time. The context in which the participle occurs is most important for determining its temporal referent. Second, judgment according to works is a pervasive theme in Jewish literature (cf. Pss 28:4; 62:12; Prov 24:12; Jer 17:10; 25:14; 32:19; 51:24; Ezek 33:20; 1QS 10:16–18; *Pss. Sol.* 2:15–17,33–35; 9:4–5; *2 Apoc. Bar.* 13:8; 44;4; 54:21). Such a theme is common in the New Testament as well and regularly refers to God's assessment of people, both believers and unbelievers, at the final judgment (Matt 16:27; Rom 2:6,11,28–29; 14:12; 1 Cor 3:13; 2 Cor 5:10; 2 Tim 4:14; Rev 2:23; 20:12–13; 22:14). It is doubtful that Peter said anything different here, especially since he referred in this paragraph to many other themes that are common in Christian tradition. Third, no dichotomy exists between judgment according to works and God's grace.[120] Good works are evidence that God has truly begotten (1 Pet 1:3) a person.[121] Perhaps Peter used the singular "work" to summarize the lives of believers as a whole. Peter reminded his readers that God is an "impartial" judge who does not reward people as one who plays favorites (cf. Acts 10:34; Rom 2:11; Eph 6:9; Col 3:25). Fourth, the fear of judgment still plays a role in the Christian life. Paul himself realized that he would be damned if he did not live the message proclaimed to others (1 Cor 9:24–27). Such a recognition inspires him to live faithfully; it does not paralyze him with fear. Paul himself taught that genuine faith always manifests itself in works (cf. Gal 5:21; 1 Cor 6:9–11).

---

[116] Richard notes that the command to fear one's parents (Lev 19:3) follows Lev 19:2, which is cited in 1 Pet 1:16 (*Reading 1 Peter, Jude, and 2 Peter,* 63).

[117] J. Barr, "'Abba, Father' and the Familiarity of Jesus' Speech," *Theology* 91 (1988): 173–79; id., "*'Abbā* Isn't 'Daddy,'" *JTS* 39 (1988): 28–47.

[118] Grudem, *1 Peter,* 81.

[119] That the judgment is the final judgment is rightly argued by Dalton, "Your Hope in God," 271.

[120] See here the helpful comments of Schelke, *Der Petrusbrief—Der Judasbrief,* 47.

[121] Luther says that "works are only the fruits of faith, by which one sees where faith is and where unbelief is" (*Commentary on Peter and Jude,* 69–70).

1:18 Verses 18–19 together form a negative/positive. Peter contrasted what did not redeem believers with the means by which they were redeemed. The participle "knowing" *(eidotes)* is rightly interpreted by the NIV as causal, giving the reason believers should "live . . . in reverent fear."[122] Verses 18–21 are written "to increase the addressees' appreciation of their new relationship to God and their new status as Christians."[123] Some scholars try to reconstruct confessional statements or hymnic fragments from these verses, but the evidence is insufficient to draw such a conclusion, and it is better to conclude that Peter himself used typical confessional language. Early Christians, presumably, often used their own words to express the fundamental elements of the faith, and no clear hymnic or poetic structure can be discerned here. Peter emphasized that believers were not "redeemed" with silver and gold. The term "redeem" *(lutroō)* and the word group recalls Israel's liberation from Egypt (Deut 7:8; 9:26; 15:15; 24:18). The term also is applied to the liberation of individuals (Pss 25:22; 26:11; 31:5; 32:7), and in Isaiah the return from exile is portrayed as a second exodus (Isa 41:14; 43:1,14; 44:22–24; 51:11; 52:3; 62:12; 63:9). In the Greco-Roman world those captured in war could be redeemed, and slaves were often manumitted, meaning that their freedom was purchased. In this context, in which many associations with the Old Testament are evident, we are safe in concluding that Peter derived his conception from the Old Testament.[124]

The word redemption signifies liberation, and here Peter spoke of redemption "from the empty way of life handed down to you from your forefathers." The "emptiness" *(mataias)* of life is a theme mentioned often in Ecclesiastes. In the Old Testament it is often associated with the idolatry of pagans.[125] Similarly, in the New Testament the word group depicts pre-Christian existence (Acts 14:15; Rom 1:21; Eph 4:17). The life of unbelievers before their conversion is futile, empty, and devoted to false gods. Such a way of life has been handed down from the forefathers, from generation to generation. The word "handed down from your forefathers" *(patroparadotou)* in Greek literature does not convey that which is wearing out or declining.[126] It signifies a vibrant tradition that is conveyed from generation

---

[122] So Michaels, *1 Peter,* 63; Achtemeier, *1 Peter,* 126.

[123] Thurén, *Argument and Theology in 1 Peter,* 115–16.

[124] Rightly Achtemeier, *1 Peter,* 127. Michaels thinks both ideas are included (*1 Peter,* 65).

[125] E.g., LXX Lev 17:7; 1 Kgs 16:2,13,26; 2 Kgs 17:15; 2 Chr 11:15; Ps 23:4; Hos 5:11; Amos 2:4; Jonah 2:9; Isa 2:20; 44:9; Jer 8:19; 10:15.

[126] The comments here depend on the study of W. C. van Unnik, "The Critique of Paganism in I Peter 1:18," in *Neotestamentica et Semitica: Studies in Honour of Matthew Black* (Edinburgh: T & T Clark, 1969), 129–42. A. R. C. Leaney mistakenly relates this verse to Jewish ancestors and to the fulfillment of the Passover in Christ ("I Peter and the Passover: An Interpretation," *NTS* 10 [1963–64]: 238–251). Contra Leaney it is not evident that the Passover motif played a significant role in Peter's theology. He never mentioned it explicitly. Rightly T. C. G. Thornton, "I Peter, A Paschal Liturgy?" *JTS* 12 (1961): 20.

to generation. Such tradition usually is described in a positive sense and is associated especially with religious traditions that are passed down from generation to generation. Here we have firm evidence that the readers were Gentiles (cf. 1 Pet 4:1–4), since the Jews were at least taught they should worship the one and only God. The verse also opens an interesting window on Peter's view of other religions. He did not see them as saving or even as noble, although I am not arguing that he was implying that every element in other religions is ignoble. In the final analysis, however, these religions are vanity and futility. They do not lead to faith and trust in the true God. The reference to silver and gold may be mentioned because of their association with idolatry (Deut 29:17; Dan 5:23; *Wis* 13:10; Rev 9:20).[127] They are "perishable" and do not persist through the ravages of time (cf. 1 Pet 1:4). They are greatly valued by human beings but end up being vain and useless, even to satisfy in this life (Eccl 2:1–11).

1:19 Verse 19 now communicates positively the means by which believers were redeemed. We learned from v. 18 that money was not the means. Instead, believers were purchased and ransomed by the blood of Christ. Peter contrasted here the perishability of money with the preciousness of Christ's blood.[128] The contrast is not an exact one, but neither is it difficult to comprehend.[129] Money is a thing that perishes, but Christians have been redeemed with the blood of a person. The shedding of blood signifies death, the giving up of one's life. Blood is precious because without it no one can live (Lev 17:11). L. Morris rightly argues that blood does not involve the release of life, as if life is somehow mystically transmitted by the spilling of blood.[130] Instead, the shedding of blood indicates that Christ poured out his life to death for sinners. What Peter teaches is that the blood of Christ is the means by which believers are redeemed. Some scholars have argued that in the Scriptures redemption always involves the notion of the payment of a price.[131] I. H. Marshall has demonstrated, however, that the idea of price is not invariably present, though there is always the idea of the cost or effort involved in redemption.[132] In some texts the emphasis is on deliverance, and

---

[127] Michaels, *1 Peter,* 65; Achtemeier, *1 Peter,* 128.

[128] The preciousness of Christ's blood may anticipate 2:4,6, where Christ is God's elect and precious cornerstone (so Michaels, *1 Peter,* 65).

[129] Bechtler overreads the word τίμιος when he tries to read the notion of honor into the word (*Following in His Steps,* 184–85).

[130] L. Morris, *The Apostolic Preaching of the Cross,* 3d ed. (1965; reprint, Grand Rapids: Eerdmans, 2000), 114–18.

[131] B. B. Warfield, *The Person and Work of Christ* (Grand Rapids: Baker, 1950), 429–75; Morris, *The Apostolic Preaching of the Cross,* 16–55.

[132] I. H. Marshall, "The Development of the Concept of Redemption in the New Testament," in *Reconciliation and Hope: New Testament Essays on Atonement and Eschatology Presented to L. L. Morris on His Sixtieth Birthday* (Grand Rapids: Eerdmans, 1974), 153–54.

nothing is said specifically about price (Luke 21:28; Rom 8:23; Eph 1:14; 4:30). On the other hand, some scholars are too eager to strike out any notion of price at all.[133] A number of texts indicate that believers were redeemed with Christ's blood (Rom 3:24; Eph 1:7; cf. Matt 20:28; Mark 10:45), and Peter plainly teaches that here. Achtemeier denies that believers were ransomed with Christ's blood by saying that the only point is that redemption came "by means of God's own act through Christ."[134] What Achtemeier affirms is true, but he passes over the specific wording of the text, which informs us that God ransomed believers with Christ's blood.

The term "blood" hearkens back to the sacrificial cultus in the Old Testament, where blood was necessary for atonement. The Old Testament imagery continues when Christ is compared to a lamb "without blemish or defect." The requirement that sacrifices are to be "without blemish" *(amōmos)* is often stated in the Old Testament (e.g., LXX Exod 29:1,38; Lev 1:3,10; 3:1,6,9; 4:3,14,23,28,32; 5:15,18; 12:6; Num 15:24; Ezek 43:22).[135] The word "without defect" *(aspilos)* is not found in the Old Testament, but it reinforces the thought that Christ was a perfect sacrifice. Indeed, as the fulfillment he surpasses the type. Animals were without defect physically, but Peter's point was that Jesus was sinless (cf. 2:22). He was a perfect sacrifice because of his perfect life. Some scholars try to restrict the background imagery here to exodus traditions, but the references above indicate that Peter referred to sacrificial language more generally.[136]

When Peter referred to Christ as the lamb, what Old Testament antecedent did he draw on? Some argue that he referred to the passover lamb (Exod 12:21–23), whose blood spared Israel from the wrath of the avenging angel.[137] In Exod 12:5 a "perfect sheep" *(probaton teleion)* is required.[138] Others see the reference to Isa 53:7, where the Servant of the Lord is led like a lamb to slaughter (cf. 2:21–25).[139] Still others think the reference is to the sacrificial cult in general, where the requirement that animals should be without blemish (see above) is often stated.[140] Some doubt that we have

---

[133] So F. Büchsel, *TDNT* 4:354–55.

[134] Achtemeier, *1 Peter,* 128.

[135] Van Unnik thinks the key to interpreting the two verses is seeing that the background does not depend on OT sacrifices but the offering of a proselyte ("The Redemption in I Peter I.18–19," 3–82). Against van Unnik, it is unclear that the proselyte's offering is alluded to in this text.

[136] So Achtemeier, *1 Peter,* 128–29.

[137] E.g., Calvin, *Catholic Epistles,* 51 (though he also includes the sacrificial cult); F. W. Beare, *The First Epistle of Peter: The Greek Text with Introduction and Notes* (Oxford: Blackwell, 1947), 80; Davids, *First Peter,* 73; Goppelt, *I Peter,* 116.

[138] Thornton notes that "a lamb was not the only possible Paschal victim" ("I Peter, A Paschal Liturgy?" 19).

[139] Kelly, *Peter and Jude,* 75.

[140] E.g., Achtemeier, *1 Peter,* 129.

a reference to the Passover since Israel was not redeemed by the blood of the lamb at Passover but by God's power. Further, the Passover blood was not redemptive but staved off God's wrath.[141] These objections are not decisive. A false dichotomy between blood and God's power is introduced since God's power in salvation is bestowed on those who applied blood to their homes. It is quite possible that the Israelites viewed the blood on the door as that which ransomed them. Against a reference to the lamb of Isa 53:7, it is objected that no other terms here indicate a reference to this text.[142] For instance, nothing is said about the blood of the victim in Isaiah 53. Though nothing is said about the blood, Isaiah 53 teaches that the Servant will die and that his death is a guilt offering (Isa 53:12), and we have already noted that blood signifies a life poured out to death. Hence, we could overemphasize the differences between the texts conceptually when it is clear that the same range of ideas is included. If one thinks of the sacrificial cult as described in Leviticus, it is evident that many of the sacrifices did not require a lamb, though in many cases a lamb "without blemish" is to be offered. To sum up, the text is too general to restrict ourselves to any one background, whether Passover, the Suffering Servant text, or the sacrificial cult. It probably is best to think of Peter as seeing the death of Christ as embracing all three ideas. Early Christians saw Passover, the Suffering Servant, and the sacrificial system as fulfilled in the sacrifice of Christ as God's sinless lamb.

1:20 With two participial phrases Peter contrasted Christ being foreknown before history began with his manifestation at the climax of salvation history for the sake of the readers.[143] In the Greek text of v. 19 the word "Christ" appears last, separated from the term "blood" by five words. The text was likely written in this way so that it would be clear that the Christ was the subject of the participle commencing v. 20. The Christ "was chosen before the creation of the world." The Greek word is not "chosen" but "foreknown" *(proegnōsmenou)*. This term has already been discussed in 1:2 (see commentary), and it was noted there that "chosen" is a reasonable way to translate it, though the covenantal overtones of the term may be overlooked with such a rendering. To say that something or someone is foreknown does not necessarily imply preexistence, for God foreknows and foreordains all that will occur in history. Nevertheless, to say that the

---

[141] Ibid., 128.

[142] Goppelt, *I Peter,* 116; Achtemeier, *1 Peter,* 129.

[143] R. Bultmann suggests that the participles signal a liturgical statement that is bound together with 1 Pet 3:18–19,22 ("Bekenntnis- und Liedfragmente im ersten Petrusbrief," ConBNT 11 [1947]: 10–12). The evidence for such a fragment here, however, is questionable since contrasting participles do not themselves signify the use of tradition. Even more speculative is the notion that the words used here should be attached to 1 Pet 3:18–19,22.

"Christ" is foreknown probably implies his preexistence.[144] Why did Peter state here that Christ was foreknown? How does it fit into the argument? The main theme of the paragraph is that believers should conduct their lives in fear. They should do so because they have been ransomed with the precious blood of Christ (vv. 18–19). Now the readers are informed that this is no afterthought. God determined before history ever began ("before the foundation of the world," NRSV; cf. Eph 1:4) that the Christ would appear at this particular juncture of history as redeemer.[145] This interpretation is confirmed by the last part of the verse. Christ "was revealed at the end of the ages for your sake." The "revelation" or "manifestation" of Christ refers to his incarnation. Peter emphasized that believers enjoy the blessing of living at the time when God is fulfilling his saving promises. The "end of the ages" *(ep eschatou tōn chronōn)* signals the last days of salvation history, which commenced with the ministry, death, and resurrection of Jesus Christ. Michaels rightly notes that the phrase here is to be distinguished from "in the last time" *(en kairō eschatō)* in v. 5.[146] The latter refers to the eschatological inheritance that awaits believers, but the phrase here indicates that the last times have commenced with the coming of Christ.[147] The stunning privilege of believers is communicated once again because all these things occurred "for your sake" (cf. vv. 10–12). What a tragedy it would be to throw all these privileges away by ceasing to live in the fear of God.

1:21 Verse 21 continues from v. 20, noting that believers who live in the days of the fulfillment of God's promises are "believers"

---

[144] Cf. also Michaels, *1 Peter,* 67; Davids, *First Peter,* 74; Schelke, *Der Petrusbriefe—Der Judasbrief,* 50. Hence, it is surprising that P. E. Davies says any notion of Christ's preexistence is "absent" in 1 Peter ("Primitive Christology in I Peter," in *Festschrift to Honor F. Wilbur Gingrich: Lexicographer, Scholar, Teacher, and Committed Christian Layman* [Leiden: Brill, 1972], 117; so also J. O. Tuñi, "Jesus of Nazareth in the Christology of 1 Peter," *HeyJ* 28 [1987]: 295; Elliott, *1 Peter,* 377). Some argue that the idea is merely that God's plan for the Christ and for salvation was preexistent, not the person of Christ himself. So J. D. G. Dunn, *Christology in the Making: A New Testament Inquiry into the Origins of the Doctrine of the Incarnation* (Philadelphia: Westminster, 1980), 238; E. Richard, "The Functional Christology of First Peter," in *Perspectives on 1 Peter* (Macon: Mercer University Press, 1986), 131. But the text does not refer to the plan being foreknown but the person, for the participle in v. 20 clearly modifies "Christ" in v. 19. Hence, it appears that the above-mentioned scholars follow a theological preference instead of the wording of the text in denying preexistence.

[145] Michaels rightly says, "What is decided from all eternity is not simply that Jesus Christ should come into the world but that he should fulfill a certain role, the role intimated already in v. 19" (*1 Peter,* 66–67). Cf. Grudem, *1 Peter,* 85–86.

[146] Michaels, *1 Peter,* 68.

[147] What we have here is inaugurated but not yet consummated eschatology (see Bechtler, *Following in His Steps,* 131–32).

(HCSB, *pistous*)[148] in God "through" (HCSB, *dia*) Christ.[149] They have put their faith in God because of the work of Jesus Christ, whose work is featured in vv. 18–19. Peter closed this section of the letter by reiterating themes already highlighted. The God in whom they believed raised Christ "from the dead and glorified him." We probably should understand the clause here to refer to an intended result, in that God purposed that people would put their faith and hope in him as a result of Christ's work.[150] Christ's resurrection of the dead is the foundation of the "living hope" of believers in 1:3, so too here the hope of believers is rooted in the resurrection of Christ.

The glorification of Christ after his sufferings is noted in 1:12.[151] The vindication and glorification of Christ after his sufferings is the paradigm for believers as well. As God's pilgrim people they suffer now, but their future hope is resurrection and glorification. They anticipate the day when sufferings will be no more, and they will experience eschatological salvation. It is likely that "faith and hope" are practically synonyms here. In the first part of the verse Peter emphasized that through Christ they are "believers" in God. "Hope" functions as an inclusio in this section, opening the discussion in v. 3 and closing it in v. 21. It also bounds vv. 13–21, for v. 13 begins with the call to set one's hope completely on future salvation. The close association between "faith and hope" also reaffirms that "faith" *(pistis)* in the earlier verses cannot be restricted to "faithfulness" (1:5,7,9).[152] Instead, Peter forged a unity between the two ideas, so that faithfulness flows out of faith.[153] What Peter said here is important for another reason. Three imperatives have dominated these verses: hope (v. 13), be holy (v. 15), and live in fear (v. 17). Verse 21 reminds the readers again that the holy life to which they are called is a life in which they are trusting in God's promises. Peter was not a moralist who trumpeted virtues for their own sake. A life of holiness is one in which God is prized above all things, in which believers trust and hope in his goodness.

---

[148] Most texts actually support the reading πιστεύοντας, probably because πιστοὺς (A, B, 398, Vg) is unusual. The latter should be retained as the harder reading (cf. *TCGNT,* 617).

[149] The NIV turns the substantival adjective into a verb—"you believe."

[150] Michaels, *1 Peter,* 70.

[151] Michaels rightly says, "The phrase 'gave him glory,' therefore, defines for the readers the significance of 'raised him from the dead' " (*1 Peter,* 69).

[152] See also Michaels, *1 Peter,* 68.

[153] Contra Dalton, it is unlikely that "hope" is a predicate adjective ("Your Hope in God," 272–74), and hence we should reject the translation "so that your faith may also be your hope in God." Rightly Achtemeier, *1 Peter,* 133.

3. Living as the New People of God (1:22–2:10)

We do not have a major break in the letter here, although the focus shifts from the individual to the community, from the call to live a holy life to proper relationships among church members. The three subsections are 1:22–25; 2:1–3; and 2:4–10. The first two paragraphs are marked by imperatives and the last one by an affirmation. First, Peter exhorted believers to love one another (1:22), grounding this call to love on their conversion (1:22a), on the fact that God has begotten them through his word (1:23). It is emphasized that the word is invincible, and this word is identified as the gospel proclaimed to the readers (1:24–25). The second section is also introduced with an imperative. Believers as newborn babes should long for the undiluted milk of God's word (2:2). The command to long for God's word is also grounded on v. 23, on God's begetting them to new life by means of his word. According to 2:1–3 the word is not only the means by which new life began (1:23) but also the means by which it continues, leading to salvation on the last day. Such spiritual growth also involves putting aside attitudes and actions that would poison the well of love within the community (2:1). Peter expected that they would long for the message of the gospel if they had tasted the Lord's kindness (2:3), for the initial taste would give them a desire to experience more of the Lord's beauty and goodness.

The transition to the next paragraph is not as clear (2:4–10), but it seems likely that in 2:4–10 Peter returned to what God has done for believers in Christ, as he did in 1:3–12. Hence, the structure of the text as a whole is a sandwich. The indicative of God's gracious work predominates in 1:3–12 and 2:4–10, but sandwiched in between are imperatives in 1:13–2:3. This structure emphasizes that all of the Petrine commands are rooted in and dependent upon God's grace. First Peter 2:4–10 emphasizes particularly that the churches in Asia Minor are God's chosen people, his new community in the world. Just as Jesus Christ was God's chosen one, so too those who trust in Christ are God's new temple and his chosen priests.

In the transition between vv. 3–4, faith is described as tasting the Lord's kindness in 2:3 and then as coming "to him" in 2:4. The Lord in view here is none other than Jesus Christ, who was rejected by his contemporaries but chosen and honored by God as is evident by his resurrection from the dead. What Peter emphasized, though, is an affirmation. As living stones, as a spiritual house, believers are being built by God so that they are now a spiritual priesthood (2:5). As God's priests animated by the Holy Spirit, they offer sacrifices that are acceptable to God through Jesus Christ. Most of vv. 6–10 is punctuated by citations and allusions to the Old Testament Scriptures. These verses elaborate and restate the themes articulated in vv. 6–10.

From Isa 28:16 we learn that God has divinely appointed Jesus Christ as the cornerstone of the new house (2:6). The house, therefore, takes its shape from him, and the one who believes in him (i.e., comes to him, v. 4) will not be put to shame on the last day. Hence, v. 7a does not merely mean that Christ as the living stone is precious. Instead, it means that God will honor and vindicate believers on the last day just as he honored and vindicated Jesus.[154] Conversely, unbelievers, fulfilling Ps 118:22, have rejected Jesus, even though he is the cornerstone of the building (2:7b). Hence, it is not surprising that they will trip over that stone and be judged on the last day (so Isa 8:14; 1 Pet 2:8a).

Here Peter reprises the theme that Jesus is rejected by human beings (2:4), but the theme of God's exaltation is also implied since unbelievers will stumble and be destroyed because of their rejection of Jesus. Their stumbling and disobedience have also been ordained by God (2:8b). Peter adds this theme to remind the readers that God controls all that will come to pass, that even their enemies are under his control. By way of contrast, the church of Jesus Christ now enjoys the blessings of Israel (2:9–10). The church is God's elect people, his royal priesthood, his holy nation, and his special possession. Ethnic Jews are not left out, but they must believe in Jesus as Messiah to be part of God's people. The purpose of this new people of God is to proclaim his praises and wonders, which probably restates the call to offer spiritual sacrifices in v. 5. The Petrine readers are truly blessed because they were formerly not God's people, nor were they the objects of his mercy as Gentiles (2:10), but now they belong to God's people and have experienced his bountiful mercy (Hos 2:23).

(1) A Call to Love (1:22–25)

22Now that you have purified yourselves by obeying the truth so that you have sincere love for your brothers, love one another deeply, from the heart. 23For you have been born again, not of perishable seed, but of imperishable, through the living and enduring word of God. 24For,

"All men are like grass,
and all their glory is like the flowers of the field;
the grass withers and the flowers fall,
25but the word of the Lord stands forever."
And this is the word that was preached to you.

1:22 The theme of the paragraph is found in the exhortation to love, and this command is bounded by two perfect participles, both of which give reasons or grounds for the command to love. The first participle uses the

[154] For the themes of honor and shame in 1 Peter, see J. H. Elliott, "Disgraced Yet Graced: The Gospel according to 1 Peter in the Key of Honor and Shame," *BTB* 25 (1995): 166–78.

language of the cult and purification (v. 22), while the second participle uses the image of begetting and fatherhood (v. 23).[155] The NIV translates the first clause, "Now that you have purified yourselves by obeying the truth." More literally the phrase could be translated, "Now that you have purified your souls by your obedience to the truth" (NRSV).[156] Both of these translations appear to understand "purified" *(hēgnikotes),* a perfect participle, as referring to conversion.[157] The perfect tense of the participle supports this view, signifying a past action that has ongoing consequences. Moreover, the phrase (lit.) "by obedience to the truth" *(en hypakoē tēs alētheias)* probably refers to "the truth of the gospel." Often in the New Testament the gospel is designated as "the truth."[158] We should not understand the phrase as "true obedience" (an adjectival genitive) but "obedience to the truth" (an objective genitive).[159] The word "obedience" (HCSB) describes conversion elsewhere in the New Testament, signifying submission to the gospel (Rom 1:5; 15:18; 16:19,26), and I have already argued that Peter had conversion in mind in 1:2 (cf. also 1:14) when he spoke of "obedience to Jesus Christ." Grudem argues vigorously, on the other hand, that the reference is to the ongoing process of sanctification.[160] First, he thinks obedience in every instance in the New Testament is postconversion. Second, he argues that obedience in 1:2 and 1:14 follows new life. Third, the verb "purify" describes the everyday life of discipleship in Jas 4:8 and 1 John 3:3. Fourth, the context is one of holiness. Fifth, Christians are never agents of their conversion but are agents in sanctification. Every one of these arguments fails to convince. The first two arguments are refuted by the evidence presented in v. 2.[161] Both in the New Testament and in Peter

---

[155] For an understanding of the participles similar to mine, see Richard, *Reading 1 Peter, Jude, and 2 Peter,* 69–70. M. Evang becomes more precise than the text allows in arguing that ἀναγεγεννημένοι functions as the ground only to the word ἐκτενῶς and that the participle ἡγνικότες modifies only ἐκ καρδίας ("Ἐκ καρδίας ἀλλήλους ἀγαπήσατε ἐκτενῶς: Zum Verständnis der Aufforderung und ihrer Begründungen in 1 Petr 1,22f," *ZNW* 80 [1989]: 117).

[156] The NIV rightly interprets the word "souls" to refer to the whole person and hence "yourselves." Contra Grudem, *1 Peter,* 88.

[157] So Piper, "Hope as a Motivation of Love," 214. The word is used often in cultic contexts especially in the OT (e.g., Exod 19:10; Num 6:3; 8:21; 19:12) but also in the NT (John 11:55; Acts 21:24,26; 24:18). It is not clear, however, that we have an allusion to baptism (against J. W. C. Wand, *The General Epistles of St. Peter and St. Jude,* WC [London: Methuen, 1934], 59).

[158] Cf. 2 Cor 6:7; Gal 2:5,14; 5:7; Eph 1:13; Col 1:5; 2 Thess 2:10,12,13; 1 Tim 2:4; 3:15; 4:3; 6:5; 2 Tim 2:15,18,25; 3:7,8; 4:4; Titus 1:1,14; Heb 10:26; Jas 1:18; 5:19; 2 Pet 1:12; 2:2.

[159] Rightly Selwyn, *First Peter,* 149; Achtemeier, *1 Peter,* 136–37; Beare, *First Peter,* 83–84; Kelly, *Peter and Jude,* 78.

[160] Grudem, *1 Peter,* 87–88.

[161] Achtemeier appears to think both are in view, "You are purified . . . by your acceptance of, and your living out, the Christian faith" (*1 Peter,* 137). The perfect participle, however, points to a past event.

obedience is used to refer to conversion. The third argument is not decisive since the issue is not whether other writers use the language of purification in other contexts to refer to one's ongoing life in holiness. In any case, two texts used elsewhere are insufficient to determine Peter's usage here, and so they can be set aside. The Petrine context suggests that conversion is in view since Peter clearly referred to the conversion of believers in v. 23, and in both this instance and in v. 23 the call to love would be rooted in their conversion. Probably the most important argument is the last one. Actually believers are called upon to repent, believe, be baptized, and confess Christ to be saved (e.g., Acts 2:38; 3:19; 13:39; 16:31; Rom 10:9). It is not surprising, therefore, that the notion of obedience is used as well. Of course, the New Testament clarifies elsewhere that faith, obedience, and repentance are the gift of God (Eph 2:8; 2 Tim 2:25; cf. esp. the commentary on 1 Pet 1:2), and so no idea of synergism is involved, nor was Peter suggesting that believers are the ultimate agent of their salvation.[162]

The goal or purpose of their conversion is a genuine love for fellow believers. The NIV translates the clause as if the goal has already been reached, "so that you have sincere love for your brothers." Peter's intention was not to comment on whether they were actually fulfilling the purpose.[163] Instead, he simply communicated the purpose for which they were converted, and so the RSV's translation is preferable, "Having purified your souls by your obedience to the truth for a sincere love of the brethren" (similarly ESV, HCSB, NASB). The term *philadelphia* indicates that fellow believers are in view (cf. 3:8; 5:9).[164]

Since love is the goal of conversion, the injunction to love from the heart follows naturally.[165] We should not draw distinctions between the verb "love" *(agapēsate)* and "love of the brethren" *(philadelphia)* here since they overlap semantically. In no way did Peter fall prey to works righteousness since the command to love is rooted in their conversion, in the purification of their hearts that enables love. The characteristic of a Christian commu-

---

[162] The NKJV translates, "Since you have purified your souls in obeying the truth through the Spirit in sincere love of the brethren." The remarkable difference is found in the words "through the Spirit," and διά πνεύματος is added by the majority text tradition. It is clearly secondary and may have been inserted to guard against any notion of works righteousness (cf. Achtemeier, *1 Peter,* 135).

[163] The εἰς indicates purpose here (cf. Best, *1 Peter,* 93; Achtemeier, *1 Peter,* 137), though Davids understands it as result (*First Peter,* 76).

[164] Contra Gundry it is not evident that Peter reflects the tradition found in John 13:34–35 and 15:12 in 1 Pet 1:22 and 4:8 ("*Verba Christi,*" 340; "Further *Verba,*" 215–16; cf. also Maier, "1. Petrusbrief," 90). Rightly Best, "Gospel Tradition," 96–97.

[165] It is difficult to know whether the word καθαρᾶς is original. The term is lacking in A, B, and Vg. Yet it occurs in 𝔓[72], ℵ, C, 86, 614. It could represent assimilation from 1 Tim 1:5 and 2 Tim 2:22. The meaning is not affected dramatically either way.

nity is fervent or constant love for one another. Probably the latter idea is intended here.[166] Peter emphasized the ideas of permanence, endurance, and incorruptibility in the near context. We should note that in vv. 21–22 Peter spoke of faith, hope, and now love. He did not summon a suffering church to anything other than the mainstream Christian life, to love for one another, and the flames of such love should not be extinguished by the winds of persecution.

1:23 The command to love, it is now explained, is rooted in God's prior saving work. Christians have been begotten *(anagegennēmenoi)* by the seed of God's word. Most versions translate the term as the NIV, "born anew." We saw previously in 1:3 that "begetting anew" rather than "born anew" is more precise.[167] The emphasis is on God as the one who granted them new life. This is particularly evident here since the means by which God begat them was the seed of his word. God begetting his children by the seed of the word is likened to a father begetting a child by the seed of his sperm. The idea of new life is present here as well since those who are begotten are born as a result of the divine begetting. Unfortunately, the RSV and the NRSV translate the verse in such a way that the relationship of v. 23 to v. 22 is completely obscured. The participle should be understood as causal. Peter's argument is that they should love one another *because* they have been begotten by God. The NIV captures the nuance by introducing v. 23 with the conjunction "for." In vv. 22–23, then, conversion is described from a twofold perspective—the act of human beings in purifying their lives and God's action in begetting them to a new life.[168]

The means by which God begat his people is "imperishable" rather than "perishable seed." The terms used here are among Peter's favorites. The heavenly inheritance of believers is "imperishable" (*aphthartos,* 1 Pet 1:4), and God is pleased when women have the "imperishable" *(aphthartos)* qualities of a "gentle and quiet spirit" (3:4). On the other hand, believers are redeemed with Christ's precious blood, not with "perishable" *(phthartos)* things like silver or gold (1:18). The human sperm of a father is perishable and earthly, and even if it produces children, they too will die eventually. The seed God uses to beget his people, on the other hand, is invincible and incorruptible. The term Peter used *(spora)* can be translated

---

[166] Scholars differ about whether ἐκτενῶς means "fervently" or "constantly." For the latter see C. E. B. Cranfield, *I & II Peter and Jude: Introduction and Commentary,* TBC (London: SCM, 1960), 57; Michaels, *1 Peter,* 75–76; Achtemeier, *1 Peter,* 137; Evang, "Zum Verständnis der Aufforderung und ihrer Begründungen in 1 Petr 1,22f," 116, 118; Elliott, *1 Peter,* 387. Richard says that the emphasis on fervency is already in the text in the expression "from the heart" and hence constancy is in view here (*Reading 1 Peter, Jude, and 2 Peter,* 71).

[167] Cf. Achtemeier, *1 Peter,* 139.

[168] So Goppelt, *I Peter,* 126; Piper, "Hope as a Motivation of Love," 214.

as "sowing" or "origin," and some scholars understand it to have this meaning here.[169] It makes better sense in the context, however, if the term refers to that which is sown, namely, seed, and so we should not distinguish the meaning from the usual term for "seed" (i.e., *sperma*).

But what is this seed? Some identify the seed as the Holy Spirit. Against this the Spirit is not mentioned elsewhere in the context. Most agree that the seed is the divine word *(logos),* which is immediately mentioned. According to this view we should not distinguish sharply between the prepositions "of" *(ek)* and "through" *(dia),* since both communicate the instrument by which God begat his children. A few scholars think the "word" *(logos)* refers to Christ as the divine Word, a meaning that clearly is found in John (John 1:1,14). We can be almost certain, however, that Peter used the term "word" *(logos)* to refer to the gospel. It often has this meaning in the New Testament (e.g., Eph 1:13; Phil 2:16; Col 1:5; 4:3; 1 Thess 1:8; 2:13; 2 Thess 3:1; 2 Tim 2:9; 4:2; Titus 1:3; 2:5; Heb 13:7; Jas 1:21) and bears this meaning elsewhere in 1 Peter (2:8; 3:1). Grammatically we could translate the last phrase as "the word of the living and enduring God."[170] But context indicates that the NIV is correct, "the living and enduring word of God" (cf. also Heb 4:12).[171] Verse 25 confirms our judgment here, for the word "endure" *(menō)* appears again (though this is not evident in the NIV translation), "the word of the Lord stands forever." In both v. 23 and v. 25, then, the abiding character of God's word is featured.[172] And to say that something "abides" is another way of saying it is "imperishable." That the spotlight is on God's word (and hence not the Spirit) is also conveyed by the last part of v. 25, where the word is identified with the gospel "that was preached to you." The means by which God begets his people is the seed of God's word, the preaching of the gospel. Peter's theology matches Paul's here, for the latter teaches that "faith comes from hearing the message" (Rom 10:17). Similarly, in Galatians 3 the reception of the Spirit is mediated through believing the preached message (Gal 3:2,5). Perhaps Peter used the word "living" because the word produces life, and he used the word "enduring" because the life once activated will never cease.[173]

1:24 The word "for" introduces the Old Testament citation (Isa 40:6–8), though Peter did not give any introductory formula, such as "it is writ-

---

[169] So Selwyn, *First Peter,* 150–51; Beare, *First Peter,* 86; Michaels, *1 Peter,* 76; E. A. LaVerdiere, "A Grammatical Ambiguity in 1 Pet 1:23," *CBQ* 36 (1974): 92.

[170] So LaVerdiere, "A Grammatical Ambiguity," 89–94; Michaels, *1 Peter,* 76–77; Richard, *Reading 1 Peter, Jude, and 2 Peter,* 72.

[171] For OT antecedents see Schelke, *Der Petrusbriefe—Der Judasbrief,* 53.

[172] Cf. Brox, *Der erste Petrusbrief,* 87–88.

[173] The addition of the words εις τόν αἰῶνα and εἰς τούς αἰῶνας in some manuscripts is clearly secondary.

ten," but plunged immediately into the Old Testament text. Typically the word "for" *(dioti)* signifies "cause," but it is difficult to see how the Old Testament quotation grounds what preceded. Contextually, it makes better sense as an explanation or restatement of v. 23, showing from the Old Testament that the word of God endures forever.[174] The Old Testament citation continues into the first part of v. 25. Peter probably cited the Septuagint here (LXX), for it omits part of Isa 40:7 from the Hebrew text (MT), and Peter did the same. Some minor differences exist between the Septuagint and Peter: Peter added "like" *(hōs)*, instead of "man" he used "their" (*autēs*, lit. "its"), in v. 25 the word "our" from Isa 40:8 is omitted by Peter, and contrary to both the Septuagint and the MT he replaced "God" with "Lord" *(kyriou)*.

The quotation comes from Isaiah 40, where comfort is proclaimed to Israel because God will work once again and restore them from their exile in Babylon. The "good news" for Israel (Isa 40:9) is that God fulfills his promises and that the nations of the world that seem strong cannot resist his promised word to deliver them from exile (Isa 40:6–8). Such nations are like grass and the flower of the grass, which perish when the Lord's wind blows upon them. Perhaps Peter thought of the persecutors of his day, who seemed invincible but whose glory was short-lived. Grass and flowers are beautiful in the springtime, but when fall arrives, one would never know that they thrived (cf. Jas 1:11).

1:25 The main point from the Old Testament quotation now emerges, "The word of the Lord endures forever" (NRSV). Isaiah therefore supports Peter's argument in v. 23 that the word of God is "living and enduring." It is an imperishable seed according to v. 23. Isaiah 40 emphasizes that no nation, regardless of its strength, can thwart his promises. Does Peter's use of the word "Lord" *(kyriou)* refer to Jesus Christ? In Isaiah the text shifts between "Lord" *(kyrios)* and "God" *(theos)*, and Yahweh is clearly the referent in each case (e.g., Lord: vv. 2,3,5[2x],10 and God: vv. 1,3,5,8,9). Probably Peter applied this text to Jesus Christ, as is the case with other New Testament writers when they cite Isaiah 40 (e.g., Matt 3:3; Mark 1:3; Luke 1:76; John 1:23; 1 Cor 2:16, but cf. Rom 11:34).[175] If this is the case, is the genitive subjective (the word spoken by the Lord)[176] or objective (the word spoken about the Lord)?[177] Both are sensible, but the next clause points us to the latter. The word of the Lord that stands forever was preached to them. The historical Jesus did not proclaim the gospel to believers in Asia Minor, and so the word of the Lord is the word about the

[174] Cf. Michaels, *1 Peter,* 77; Achtemeier, *1 Peter,* 141.

[175] Contra Richard, *Reading 1 Peter, Jude, and 2 Peter,* 74.

[176] Michaels, *1 Peter,* 79.

[177] Achtemeier, *1 Peter,* 141.

Lord Jesus, the gospel that was preached when these churches believed.

Verse 25 concludes with Peter's commentary on the Old Testament citation. The word of the Lord in Isaiah, which represents the promise that God will restore his people from exile and fulfill his promises to Abraham (Gen 12:1–3), is ultimately fulfilled in the gospel proclaimed *(euangelisthen)* to the churches in Asia Minor. The new exodus, the return from exile, and the fulfillment of all God's promises to Israel have become a reality through the gospel. Peter's use of the word *(euangelizō)* almost certainly comes from Isaiah as well since in Isa 40:9 (the very next verse from the section Peter cited) "the good news" for Zion and Jerusalem is that God will come and fulfill his promises to Israel. As previously observed, Peter argued that the promises preached by the prophets were not intended for the prophets but for Christian believers. Similarly, he argued here that the promises in Isaiah are fulfilled in the proclamation of the gospel. Such are the privileges of Peter's readers.

We should add one more comment to this verse. The word of God is identified as *logos* in v. 23 and *rhēma* in v. 25. The latter term is likely used in v. 25 because it occurs in the citation from Isa 40:8. Therefore we should not try to establish a different meaning for the two terms.[178] They are synonyms, both referring to the gospel. It is this gospel that God has used to beget them to new life, and on the basis of that life they are to love one another fervently and constantly.

(2) Longing for the Pure Milk (2:1–3)

[1]Therefore, rid yourselves of all malice and all deceit, hypocrisy, envy, and slander of every kind. [2]Like newborn babies, crave pure spiritual milk, so that by it you may grow up in your salvation, [3]now that you have tasted that the Lord is good.

2:1 The "therefore" *(oun)* is understood by some to reach all the way back to 1:13–25, and this is a possibility. But it seems more likely that it relates to what has just preceded, namely, the new life that believers enjoy by God's grace. They have been begotten by God (v. 23) by means of his word, and hence they are exhorted to lay aside all in their lives that quenches love for one another.[179] The participle translated "rid yourselves" *(apothemenoi)* is actually not an imperative, although most English translations render it in such a way. Understanding it imperatively is acceptable,

---

[178] Rightly Achtemeier, *1 Peter,* 142.

[179] E. Schweizer wrongly concludes from the aorist participle that once-for-all action is in view ("The Priesthood of All Believers: 1 Peter 2.1–10," in *Worship, Theology and Ministry in the Early Church: Essays in Honor of Ralph P. Martin,* JSNTSup 87 [Sheffield: JSOT, 1992], 286). Such an understanding of the participle has been overturned by recent research.

for it borrows, so to speak, its imperatival force from the main verb "crave" *(epipothēsate)* in v. 2.[180] We should observe, however, that the central command in this paragraph is the injunction to long for the "pure spiritual milk" (v. 2). The participle in this verse is loosely connected with the imperative and probably is best understood as attendant circumstances.[181]

Why did Peter begin with the call to put away evil attitudes and actions? Probably because such things destroy love, and responsibility to love was the main idea in vv. 22–25. What Peter referred to, as in vv. 22–25, is the need for love among fellow Christians.[182] We noticed the call to brotherly love in v. 22, and it was also specified that Christians should "love one another" *(allēous)*. In the next section of the letter (2:11–4:11) Peter explained how believers should relate to unbelievers, but here the focus is on community relationships. The word "rid yourselves" *(apotithēmi)* is often used in the New Testament for putting off sin or that which hinders Christian growth (Rom 13:12; Eph 4:22,25; Col 3:8; Heb 12:1; Jas 1:21). Some scholars see a reference to baptism, where believers removed their old clothes and then were clothed with new garments.[183] This practice, however, is not clearly attested in the New Testament, belonging to the later history of the church.[184] Even more important, the removal of these vices is not a one-time event in the lives of believers, and hence it cannot be restricted to baptism. The aorist may be ingressive, but it does not limit the action to one occasion. In fact, believers need to put aside these sins on a daily basis.

The sins listed tear at the social fabric of the church, ripping away the threads of love that keep them together. Peter signals thereby that no sin is to be tolerated in the community, that sin is to be rejected comprehensively. The first sin named could refer to wickedness in general, but the NIV rightly renders it "malice" *(kakian)* since the latter fits better with the social slant of these verses. Ill-will toward one another destroys the harmony befitting the community of believers. Guile and hypocrisy are closely related, for in both cases deceit and falseness have entered the community. "Sincere love" (v. 22) is to be the goal of believers, and deceit and hypocrisy introduce pretense and disingenuousness so that the trust necessary for love vanishes. Envy is also contrary to love, for instead of desiring the best for others, it hopes for their downfall or prefers the advancement of oneself to the joy of others. Slander is not limited to spreading false stories about oth-

---

[180] So Michaels, *1 Peter,* 84; contra Richard, who sees a reference to conversion (*Reading 1 Peter, Jude, and 2 Peter,* 77).

[181] So Achtemeier, *1 Peter,* 144; Snyder, "Participles and Imperatives in 1 Peter," 193.

[182] Achtemeier, *1 Peter,* 145.

[183] E.g., Kelly, *Peter and Jude,* 83–84.

[184] Rightly Grudem, *1 Peter,* 93, n. 1; Achtemeier, *1 Peter,* 144, n. 14.

ers but also involves disparaging others.[185] Well-timed words that carry insinuations about others are often all that is necessary. Love, of course, finds the good in others and avoids speaking what is negative.

2:2 The central admonition in the paragraph is communicated here. Believers are to long for the "pure spiritual milk" so that they will grow, resulting in their salvation. This longing for milk is compared to the craving for milk of "newborn babies" *(hōs artigennēta)*. The reference to "newborn babies" recalls the notion that Christians are "begotten" *(anagennaō)* by God (1:3,23), and here the result of that begetting (i.e., new life) is brought to the forefront. Some scholars conclude that the readers were new Christians since they are compared to newborns.[186] Such a judgment is mistaken, for the readers are not identified as infants in the faith.[187] They are compared to infants who have a longing for milk. They are not defined as new converts. Peter used an illustration, explaining one way in which all Christians should be like newborn babies. Achtemeier rightly comments, "The assumption that all the readers addressed in the vast area of northern Asia Minor would be recent converts all but defies the imagination."[188] The metaphor does convey that believers are dependent upon God for their lives.[189]

Peter's purpose was to say that all believers should be like infants in this sense—they should "crave" *(epipothēsate)* the "pure spiritual milk."[190] The word "crave" is a strong one, used of the ardent desire believers should have for God in the Old Testament (LXX Pss 41:2; 83:3). Babies long for milk that will sustain bodily growth, and similarly believers should desire milk for growth in salvation. The reference to "milk" *(gala)* in 1 Cor 3:1–3 and Heb 5:11–14 occurs in contexts where believers are indicted for spiritual immaturity, but we must beware of imposing those contexts on the Petrine usage. We must recall again that Peter gave an illustration of those who are newly born and used the image of milk to convey how believers grow.[191] Milk, then, becomes the very substance of life, comprising that which all Christians need to progress in their spiritual lives. The image of milk does not suggest, then, that believers in Asia Minor need elementary and basic teaching.[192] We conclude from this that this admonition applies

---

[185] Cf. Selwyn, *First Peter,* 153; Achtemeier, *1 Peter,* 144.

[186] E.g., Kelly, *Peter and Jude,* 84; Cranfield, *I & II Peter and Jude,* 61; Beare, *First Peter,* 88.

[187] Rightly Selwyn, *First Peter,* 154; Grudem, *1 Peter,* 94.

[188] Achtemeier, *1 Peter,* 145.

[189] Bechtler, *Following in His Steps,* 150.

[190] Again Schweizer overreads the aorist tense of verb here ("The Priesthood of All Believers," 287).

[191] Calvin rightly argues that "milk" here does not refer to simple teachings for the immature (*Catholic Epistles,* 63).

[192] Nor is there a clear allusion to the milk and honey of entering the promised land (contra Hillyer, *1 and 2 Peter, Jude,* 57).

to all believers throughout their lives. No believer in Asia Minor could exempt himself from the admonition by claiming spiritual adulthood.

What is the spiritual milk for which believers are to long? Two adjectives describe it, translated as "pure" *(adolon)* and "spiritual" *(logikon)* by the NIV. The word "pure" functions as a contrast to the deceit *(dolos)* believers are to put aside (v. 1), and the term refers to that which is unadulterated and uncontaminated. Contaminated milk produces sickness and even death, but this milk is health giving and pure. The word *logikos* is translated by the NIV and understood by many to mean "spiritual."[193] Usually, however, in Greek literature the term refers to that which is rational or reasonable.[194] It is not equated with the term "spiritual," even though it overlaps with it (cf. *T. Levi* 3:6; Philo, *Spec. Laws* 1.16; Epictetus, *Discourses* 1.16). Peter probably opted for the term to clarify that the milk he had in view was the word of God. The "word" *(logos)*, after all, was the means by which God begot believers. God's "word" *(rhēma)* abides forever, and that very word is identified as the gospel preached to the Petrine believers (1:25). Hence, Peter used *logikos* to define milk here, so that the readers will understand that the milk by which they grow is nothing other than the word of God.[195] The means by which God sanctifies believers is through the mind, through the continued proclamation of the word. Spiritual growth is not primarily mystical but rational, and rational in the sense that it is informed and sustained by God's word.

The purpose *(hina)* for desiring the milk of the word is now conveyed. By means of the word *(en autō)* they grow. The antecedent to *autō*, therefore, is the neuter noun "milk" *(gala)*. And we have just argued that the metaphor "milk" most naturally refers to the word, whether preached orally

---

[193] E.g., Best, *1 Peter,* 98; Goppelt, *I Peter,* 131; J. Francis, "'Like Newborn Babes'—The Image of the Child in 1 Peter 2:2–3," in *Papers on Paul and Other New Testament Authors,* StudBib 3, JSNTSup 3 (Sheffield: JSOT Press, 1980), 115; C. F. D. Moule, "Sanctuary and Sacrifice in the Church of the New Testament," *JTS* 1 (1950): 34.

[194] *TDNT* 4.142; rightly Wand, *Epistles of Peter and Jude,* 64–65. Against Elliott, *1 Peter,* 400.

[195] For similar views see Bigg, *Epistles of Peter and Jude,* 126; Kelly, *Peter and Jude,* 85; Grudem, *1 Peter,* 95; Achtemeier, *1 Peter,* 147; Davids, *First Peter,* 83; Brox, *Der erste Petrusbrief,* 92. Michaels identifies the milk as God's sustaining life which he gives to his children (*1 Peter,* 87–89). Others identify the milk as Christ (Wand, *Epistles of Peter and Jude,* 65; Beare, *First Peter,* 90). Richard sees it as God's love and kindness (*Reading 1 Peter, Jude, and 2 Peter,* 79–80). Luther argues that the milk is the gospel, and the gospel, of course, is certainly the content of the word (*Commentary on Peter & Jude,* 87). K. H. Jobes describes it as God's continuing grace through Jesus Christ (see "Got Milk? Septuagint Psalm 33 and the Interpretation of 1 Peter 2:1–3," *WTJ* 63 [2002]: 1–14). Jobes argues that milk cannot refer to God's word since in 1:23–25 it is metaphorically depicted as seed (p. 3). But the shifting of metaphors is not a problem since biblical writers mix metaphors with some regularity. She also says that Peter simply could have written "the milk of the word" if he desired to identify the milk as the word (p. 6). But her argument is not persuasive if there is a link between λογικος and λογος and if the former should be translated "rational," as I argue above.

or written, as the means of growth for believers. Such growth "results in" salvation. The NIV translates the preposition *eis* as "in," but it most likely denotes result here.[196] Spiritual growth is necessary for eschatological salvation. Understanding "salvation" as an end-time reality fits with 1:5 and 1:9, as we argued in the commentary on those verses.[197] Some commentators, however, make the mistake of saying that Peter referred to end-time salvation rather than spiritual maturity.[198] This is a false dichotomy. Peter's point is that spiritual growth is necessary for eschatological salvation. The evidence that one has been begotten by the Father through the word is that believers continue to long for that word and become increasingly mature. Such a view fits well, incidentally, with the argument of 2 Pet 1:5–11.

2:3 Believers are to long for the milk of God's word since it is essential to obtain salvation on the last day. This longing is fitting "if indeed you have tasted that the Lord is good" (NRSV). The NIV turns the conditional clause into a fulfilled condition, "now that you have tasted that the Lord is good."[199] Peter did not write "if" to sow doubts in the minds of the readers, but neither should "if" be confused with "since."[200] Peter wanted the readers to contemplate whether they have in fact experienced the kindness of the Lord, and he was confident that the answer would be affirmative. Translating the term "if" by "now" or "since," however, short-circuits the process, removing the contingency that the author wanted his readers to consider.

The words used here contain an allusion to Psalm 34. This psalm apparently was important to Peter, for he cited it again in 3:10–12, quoting vv. 13–16 of the psalm (Ps 33 in the LXX).[201] Here Peter alluded to v. 9 in the Septuagint. The selection of this psalm is intentional, and a number of echoes of this psalm reverberate throughout 1 Peter. We should note at the outset the theme of the psalm. When the righteous are afflicted and suffering, they can be confident that

---

[196] Cf. Achtemeier, *1 Peter,* 147. The Majority text omits the preposition either through oversight or because of rejecting the idea of growing into salvation (so *TCGNT,* 618).

[197] Cf. Davids, *First Peter,* 83.

[198] Rightly Michaels, *1 Peter,* 89; cf. Achtemeier, *1 Peter,* 147.

[199] For a similar view see Goppelt, *I Peter*, 132, n. 50; Michaels, *1 Peter,* 82, 90; Achtemeier, *1 Peter,* 143, 148; Richard, *Reading 1 Peter, Jude, and 2 Peter,* 80; Elliott, *1 Peter,* 402.

[200] Some later manuscripts insert εἴπερ instead of εἰ, but the Alexandrian manuscript tradition supports the latter.

[201] Kelly rightly says, "Our writer's citation of Ps. xxxiv.8 is not haphazard; the whole psalm was present in his mind as he wrote the letter, . . . Its theme is broadly the same as that of the letter" (*Peter and Jude,* 87). For a similar view of the influence of Psalm 34, see G. L. Green, "The Use of the Old Testament for Christian Ethics in 1 Peter," *TynBul* 41 (1990): 280–81; cf. also Jobes, "Got Milk?" 9–13. But we should reject the view of Bornemann that a baptismal sermon was constructed on the basis of the psalm ("Der Erste Petrusbrief," 143–65). Rightly, F. W. Danker, "I Peter 1:24–2:17—A Consolotary Pericope," *ZNW* 68 (1967): 94.

God will deliver them from all their troubles. Peter's suffering readers could take great encouragement from the message of this psalm. Further, the psalm calls on the readers to hope in God in the midst of their troubles (33:9,23, LXX), one of the central themes in 1 Peter.[202] The superscription of the psalm was also known to Peter's readers, and it informs us that David wrote the psalm when he fled from Abimelech after he feigned insanity. It is irrelevant for our purposes whether one thinks the superscription is accurate, for that is how the psalm was transmitted to the readers. Indeed, in the Septuagint version (33:5) David praised God for delivering him from all "his sojournings" *(paroikōn).*[203] This fits beautifully with the pilgrim people of God in 1 Peter, where the readers are "sojourners" (*paroikoi,* 1:17; 2:11; cf. 1:1). The blessing of God in 1 Pet 1:3 *(eulogētos)* is matched by the blessing of God in Ps 33:2 *(eulogēsō).*

Peter also emphasized the importance of fearing the Lord (1:17; 2:17–18; 3:2,14), and the psalmist often stressed its centrality of fearing the Lord (Ps 33:10,12). In the very next verse (1 Pet 2:4) Peter spoke of "coming" *(proserchomai),* which is the same verb used by the psalmist (Ps 33:6). Finally, both Peter and the psalmist said that those who trust and hope in the Lord, in contrast to unbelievers, will not be put to shame (1 Pet 2:6; 3:16; 4:16 cf. Ps 33:6). All of this indicates that Peter did not allude to Psalm 34 casually, but the themes of the psalm had made a powerful impact on him. Since Peter only alluded to the psalm here, we should not expect the exact wording of the psalm to be reproduced. Indeed, what is imperative in the psalm is a conditional statement in Peter, and the words "and see" *(kai idete)* from the psalm are deleted.[204]

We now come to the main idea of the verse. Believers should long for the Lord if indeed they have tasted or experienced his kindness. To see a reference to the eucharist reads the text too literally.[205] Longing to grow spiritually comes from a taste of the beauty of the Lord, an experience of his kindness and goodness. Those who pursue God ardently have tasted his sweetness. Christian growth for Peter is not a mere call to duty or an alien moralism. The desire to grow springs from an experience with the Lord's kindness, an experience that leaves believers desiring more.[206]

---

[202] See Piper, "Hope as the Motivation of Love," 212–31; F. Neugebauer, "Zur Deutung und Bedeutung des 1. Petrusbriefes," *NTS* 26 (1980): 73–74.

[203] K. R. Snodgrass rightly rejects the notion that 1 Peter is a baptismal sermon based on Psalm 34, but he goes on to say that the psalm played "a formative role in the composition of I Peter and especially of ii.1–10." Snodgrass identifies the themes from Psalm 34 echoed in 1 Peter ("I Peter II.1–10: Its Formation and Literary Affinities," *NTS* 24 [1977]: 102).

[204] A few manuscripts add καὶ εἴδετε, a clear example of assimilation (Ps 33:9).

[205] Contra Kelly, *Peter and Jude,* 87; Davids, *First Peter,* 83, n. 12.

[206] Some scribes accidentally inserted Χριστός for χρηστός, which is a natural mistake since the two words sound the same. We can be quite sure that the latter is original. Neither is it persuasive to suggest a play on words here. Peter selected the word because it was in the OT citation.

(3) The Living Stone and Living Stones (2:4–10)

**4As you come to him, the living Stone—rejected by men but chosen by God
and precious to him— 5you also, like living stones, are being built into a spiritual
house to be a holy priesthood, offering spiritual sacrifices acceptable to God
through Jesus Christ. 6For in Scripture it says:**

> **"See, I lay a stone in Zion,**
> **a chosen and precious cornerstone,**
> **and the one who trusts in him**
> **will never be put to shame."**

**7Now to you who believe, this stone is precious. But to those who do not
believe,**

> **"The stone the builders rejected**
> **has become the capstone,"**

8and,

> **"A stone that causes men to stumble**
> **and a rock that makes them fall."**

**They stumble because they disobey the message—which is also what they
were destined for.**

**9But you are a chosen people, a royal priesthood, a holy nation, a people
belonging to God, that you may declare the praises of him who called you out of
darkness into his wonderful light. 10Once you were not a people, but now you are
the people of God; once you had not received mercy, but now you have received
mercy.**

According to v. 4 the "Lord" of v. 3, who is clearly Yahweh in the Old Testament context of Psalm 34, is none other than Jesus Christ.[207] The use of the Old Testament is significant Christologically since it demonstrates that what is true of Yahweh is also true of Jesus the Christ. The present paragraph is challenging to interpreters since it is stocked with Old Testament allusions and citations. The first allusion emerges when Jesus is identified as "the living Stone." That Jesus is the stone is confirmed by the Old Testament references that follow in vv. 6–8 (see the commentary on these verses).[208] Jesus is doubtless called the "living" Stone because of his resur-

---

[207] So Michaels, *1 Peter,* 90, 98; McCartney, "The Use of the Old Testament in the First Epistle of Peter," 73; Elliott, *1 Peter,* 403; Brox, *Der erste Petrusbrief,* 93.

[208] As background Achtemeier points here to the texts where God is said to be our "rock" (e.g., Deut 32:4; 2 Sam 23:3; Isa 26:4; Ps 62:3,7; *1 Peter,* 154, n. 56). But in these texts Yahweh is never called λιθος, and interestingly, the LXX avoids using even the word "rock" in these texts. It is not clear, therefore, that the language of God being Israel's rock is appropriated here, though it is certainly possible.

rection.[209] Peter probably drew this theme from Ps 118:22, where the stone rejected by the builders becomes the cornerstone. In Acts 4:11 Peter appealed to this same verse to refer to Christ's death and resurrection/exaltation. The argument in Acts 4:10–11 demonstrates the connection. The religious leaders despised Jesus by crucifying him. But God made him the cornerstone by raising him. Such a reading of Ps 118:22 stems from Jesus himself in the parable of the tenants (Matt 21:33–46 par.).[210] The tenants slay the son to possess the inheritance—a clear reference to the crucifixion of Christ—fulfilling the prophecy that the builders would reject the cornerstone (Matt 21:42).[211] Matthew implied, however, that the slaying of Jesus is not the last word, for he becomes the cornerstone, which almost certainly points to his resurrection.

Peter continues to be informed by Psalm 118, for as the cornerstone of the building was rejected by the builders (see v. 7 below), so also Jesus was rejected by human beings. Some scholars maintain that Peter referred to the general rejection of Jesus by people rather than specifically to his crucifixion.[212] Perhaps it is better to say that the rejection of Jesus reached its climax in his execution. In Acts 4:10–11—where Peter also cited Psalm 118—it seems that the rejection of Jesus as the cornerstone was fulfilled in his death, whereas his vindication or being honored by God occurred at the resurrection. The same emphasis on Christ's crucifixion and resurrection of Christ is likely present here as well. The perfect tense of "rejected" *(apodedokimasmenon)* supports the notion of a past action with ongoing results.[213] In God's sight Jesus was not "rejected" but "chosen" *(eklekton)* and "honored" *(entimon)*. He is God's chosen and honored Stone, and since this is contrasted with his rejection by human beings, we probably have an allusion to the resurrection and exaltation of Christ. The life of Christ functions as a pattern for the Petrine Christians, for they too are despised by many, but they are chosen and honored in God's sight, destined for vindication after suffering.

2:5 Peter now draws the comparison between Christ as "the living

---

[209] Cf. J. H. Elliott, *The Elect and the Holy: An Exegetical Examination of I Peter 2:4–10 and the Phrase* βασίλειον Ἱεράτευμα," NovTSup 12 (Leiden: Brill, 1966), 34; id., *1 Peter,* 410. N. Hillyer provides a helpful summary of the Feast of Tabernacles in Jewish tradition, but his view that 1 Peter evinces a reference to the feast is quite speculative and lacking in evidentiary value ("First Peter and the Feast of Tabernacles," *TynBul* 21 [1970]: 39–70).

[210] Supporting dependence on gospel tradition here are Gundry, "*Verba Christi,*" 340; "Further *Verba,*" 221–22; Maier, "1. Petrusbrief," 90–91. Best's doubts are not compelling ("Gospel Tradition," 101).

[211] N. Hillyer argues that "stone" was a Messianic title among the Jews ("'Rock-Stone' Imagery in I Peter," *TynBul* 22 [1971]: 59, 69).

[212] So Michaels, *1 Peter,* 98; Achtemeier, *1 Peter,* 154.

[213] Contra Achtemeier, *1 Peter,* 154.

Stone" and believers as "living stones." Believers are "living stones" because of their faith in the resurrected Christ. Jesus' resurrection life becomes theirs, even while they live in the midst of a hostile world. They await their resurrection at the end of the age, but even now because they have come to Christ (v. 4) they have new life. Nowhere else in the New Testament are believers called living stones, though elsewhere they are described as God's temple or house (1 Cor 3:16; 6:19; Eph 2:19–22; Heb 3:6). The picture here is of a house in which believers constitute the building stones. The term "house" *(oikos)* alludes to the temple, which is commonly called a "house" in the Old Testament (e.g., 2 Sam 7:13; 1 Kgs 3:2; 6; 8, etc.) and is also designated as a house in the New Testament (Matt 21:13; 23:38; John 2:16–17; Acts 7:47,49). In particular, when the verb "build" *(oikodomeō)* is combined with "house" *(oikos)* in the Septuagint, the temple is often in view.[214] The house is "spiritual" *(pneumatikos)* because it is animated and indwelt by the Holy Spirit.[215] Despite the hesitation of some scholars, Peter clearly here identified the church as God's new temple.[216] The physical temple pointed toward and anticipated God's new temple, and now that the new temple has arrived, the old is superfluous.

The phrase "spiritual house" probably is appositional, and so the point of the text is not that believers "are being built into a spiritual house" but that they as living stones, as a spiritual house, are being built up.[217] The purpose of such building is that they function as a "holy priesthood" *(hierateuma hagion).*[218] We can summarize the verse as follows, You as a spiritual house are being built up "to be a holy priesthood" (NRSV).[219] Some might object that believers cannot be both the temple and the priests that minister in the temple, that the mix-

---

[214] E.g., 2 Sam 7:5,13; 1 Kgs 5:3,5,18; 6:1; 8:16,18–19; 9:1; 11:38; 2 Chr 36:23; Ps 69:9; Isa 56:7). Rightly Achtemeier, *1 Peter,* 156; E. Best, "I Peter II.4–10—A Reconsideration," *NovT* 11 (1969): 280; Bechtler, *Following in His Steps,* 140–41.

[215] So also Best, "I Peter II.4–10," 292–93; D. E. Johnson, "Fire in God's House: Imagery from Malachi 3 in Peter's Theology of Suffering (1 Peter 4:12–19)," *JETS* 29 (1986): 290; Elliott, *The Elect and the Holy,* 153–54.

[216] Contra Elliott, *The Elect and the Holy,* 149, 152–53, 157–59; id., *Home for the Homeless,* 165–266; id., *1 Peter*, 414–18. Elliott understands the motif to be domestic rather than cultic, but he wrongly underestimates the significance of the temple as God's house in the OT. Rightly Goppelt, *1 Peter,* 141; Michaels, *1 Peter,* 100; Achtemeier, *1 Peter,* 158–59; Best, "I Peter II.4–10," 280. See also T. Seland, "The 'Common Priesthood' of Philo and 1 Peter: A Philonic Reading of 1 Peter 2:5, 9," *JSNT* 57 (1995): 111.

[217] Contra Michaels, οἶκος πνευματικὸς is not a predicate nominative (*1 Peter,* 100) but appositional to the "you" of οἰκοδομεῖσθε (Achtemeier, *1 Peter,* 154).

[218] We have a divine passive here, and the word εἰς designates purpose (so Elliott, *The Elect and the Holy,* 160; id., *1 Peter,* 412–13). Achtemeier points out that εἰς denotes purpose when linked with οἰκοδομέω in 1 Chr 22:5; 28:10; *Tob* 14:5 (*1 Peter,* 156, n. 91). *Tobit* 14:5, however is temporal rather than purpose.

[219] The Majority Text omits εἰς, but it is surely original ($\mathfrak{P}^{72}$, ℵ, A, B, C, 5, 88, 307, 322, etc.).

ture of metaphors is intolerable. In reply it should be noted that the fulfillment in Christ transcends the types that anticipate it. Hence, we should not be surprised that believers are both priests and the temple. They are God's dwelling place by the Spirit and his new priesthood. No internal contradiction is involved since Peter did not refer to believers as priests serving in a literal temple. The spiritual nature of the house does not draw our attention to its immateriality but to a temple inhabited by the Holy Spirit.[220]

Before returning to the issue of the priesthood, we should note the NRSV ("like living stones, let yourselves be built into a spiritual house") understands the verb *oikodomeisthe* as an imperative so that believers are enjoined to build themselves up as God's people.[221] The passive of the verb, however, is never rendered as an imperative in its seven occurrences in the New Testament, and in the forty-eight uses in the Septuagint it is imperative only on two occasions (Ezra 6:3; Ps 50:20),[222] and hence we should take it as an indicative here. Furthermore, the parallel statements in v. 9 support the idea that affirmations or declarations rather than commands are found here. The passive of the verb signifies that God is the one building the church (cf. Matt 16:18) so that it will be a "holy priesthood." The notion of the church as a priesthood anticipates v. 9. Peter was not thinking mainly of each individual functioning as a priest before God.[223] The focus here is on the church corporately as God's set-apart priesthood in which the emphasis is likely on believers functioning as priests.[224] Western believers tend to individualize the notion of priesthood rather than seeing the community emphasis. In the Old Testament the priestly caste was limited to the tribe of Levi, and in that sense only a portion of Israel could carry out the priestly function (but see commentary on v. 9 below). All of God's people are now his priests. Despite the emphasis on the corporate priesthood, what Peter said applies by implication to individuals as well.[225] That is, all believers have direct access to God by virtue of the cross and resurrection of Jesus Christ. We must avoid, however, focusing on the individual, for

---

[220] Cf. Goppelt, *I Peter,* 140, n. 29.

[221] So also Goppelt, *I Peter,* 139–40; Martin, *Metaphor and Composition in 1 Peter*, 181; Richard, *Reading 1 Peter, Jude, and 2 Peter,* 85.

[222] So Selwyn, *First Peter,* 159; Elliott, *The Elect and the Holy,* 16; Michaels, *1 Peter,* 100; Achtemeier, *1 Peter,* 155; Davids, *First Peter,* 87.

[223] Rightly Elliott, *The Elect and the Holy,* 167; Achtemeier, *1 Peter,* 156.

[224] So Elliott, *The Elect and the Holy,* 68–69, 74, 167–68; id., *1 Peter,* 420, 451–54; A. T. M. Cheung, "The Priest as the Redeemed Man: A Biblical-Theological Study of the Priesthood," *JETS* 29 (1986): 274; Seland, "A Philonic Reading of 1 Peter 2:5, 9," 102–9; Brox, *Der erste Petrusbrief,* 104.

[225] Cf. also E. Best, "Spiritual Sacrifice: General Priesthood in the New Testament," *Int* 14 (1960): 279, 296–97. Luther rightly saw that all believers are designated as priests here, not simply those set aside for special ministry (*Commentary on Peter & Jude,* 93).

Protestants are prone to individualize the text in a way that blunts or even denies its corporate emphasis.

The purpose of the holy priesthood is "to offer spiritual sacrifices" (NRSV). The NIV does not as clearly indicate that we have a purpose clause here since it translates the infinitive as a participle ("offering"). The word "offer" *(anenenkai)* is regularly used to denote the offering of sacrifices in the Old Testament.[226] "Spiritual sacrifices" *(pneumtikas thysias)* are required, meaning that they are sacrifices offered by virtue of the work of the Holy Spirit.[227] Peter also implied that animal sacrifices are passé, though there is not an explicit polemic against such sacrifices.[228] Hence, the provisional nature of animal sacrifices probably was a settled issue in the Petrine churches. What sacrifices in particular were in Peter's mind?[229] The parallel with 2:9, where the royal priesthood proclaims God's wonders, suggests to some that this is the primary function of the priesthood (see commentary on 2:9 for further discussion). The priestly calling of the church is understood from 2:9 to be evangelistic, a praising of God's name so that people from all over the world will join in worshiping him.[230] Nevertheless, we should not limit the sacrifices here to any one item, for everything that is pleasing to God is probably included (cf. Rom 12:1; Heb 13:15–16).[231] Peter spoke generally and comprehensively of all that believers do by the power of the Holy Spirit.[232] Indeed, not any and every sacri-

---

[226] E.g., Gen 8:20; 22:2; Exod 24:5; 29:18,25; Lev 3:5,11,14,16; Num 5:26; Deut 12:13–14; cf. also Heb 7:27; 9:28; 13:15; 1 Pet 2:24.

[227] So Kelly, *Peter and Jude,* 91.

[228] Rightly Elliott, *The Elect and the Holy,* 220. Cf. Luther, *Commentary on Peter & Jude,* 94.

[229] To see a reference to the Eucharist as a sacrifice is unlikely and reflects the view of early church history rather than the NT era (contra Kelly, *Peter and Jude*, 92; Best, "Spiritual Sacrifice," 279; Hill, "Spiritual Sacrifices," 61). Rightly Elliott, *The Elect and the Holy,* 186–88.

[230] So Selwyn, *First Peter,* 292–93; Elliott, *The Elect and the Holy*, 185, 195; Achtemeier, *1 Peter,* 156. Best rejects this argument, contending that the argument moves in a new direction in v. 9. Hence, he sees the sacrifices in v. 5 as being general in nature. On this latter point Best is correct ("I Peter II.4–10," 287).

[231] Bechtler sees a reference to the ethic explicated in the rest of the letter (*Following in His Steps,* 168).

[232] Elliott defines such sacrifices as "the living of a holy life and the persistence in well-doing through the power of the Holy Spirit to the glorification of God" (*The Elect and the Holy,* 183). Bechtler argues that any reference to evangelism here is illegitimate (*Following in His Steps,* 159). Achtemeier rightly argues that evangelism cannot be excluded from the spiritual sacrifices Peter had in mind (*1 Peter,* 150, 156). S. McKnight suggests "something like the list of behaviors typical of early Christian churches (e.g., 4:7–11; *1 Peter,* NIVAC [Grand Rapids: Zondervan, 1996], 107). Michaels sees a reference to both worship and conduct (*1 Peter,* 101–2).

fice is pleasing to God, but only those offered "through Jesus Christ."[233]

2:6 Verse 6 begins with a word in Greek that usually is translated "because" *(dioti)* since it provides a reason or ground for what precedes. In this instance, however, the Old Testament citations appear to provide an explanation or restatement of what precedes, and hence the NIV's "for" is fitting.[234] Peter used an introductory formula, "in Scripture it says," for the scriptural citation.[235] The text cited is from Isa 28:16. In context Isaiah 28 is a message of judgment on Ephraim for their disobedience and unbelief. What Isaiah emphasized throughout the book comes to the forefront here. Those who trust in the Lord will escape judgment. Isaiah encouraged the people not to put their trust in foreign alliances or military strength (cf. Isaiah 30–31), but only the Lord. Those who do not trust in him will perish, but those who put their faith in him will triumph. It is possible in the original context that the stone refers to a Davidic king, to God's covenantal commitment to his people, and hence by extension it relates to Jesus as Messiah.[236] Interestingly, the citation does not match either the MT or the Septuagint.[237] Some maintain that the source of Peter's citation comes from Paul, who also cited the Isaiah text in Rom 9:33.[238] The Pauline quotation, however, differs rather significantly from Peter's, and so direct dependence is unlikely.[239] The text is alluded to in 1QS 8:7–8, where the council of the community is God's "precious cornerstone" and functions as the true temple of God. Nevertheless, the differences from Peter's citation are again remarkable enough to rule out any literary dependence. Interestingly, how-

[233] Achtemeier understands εἰς ἱεράτευμα ἅγιον to go with all that precedes, i.e., the offering of spiritual sacrifices to God that are acceptable (*1 Peter,* 156). Elliott restricts the phrase to the infinitive ἀνενέγκαι (*The Elect and the Holy,* 161). D. L. Balch restricts the word "acceptable" to "spiritual sacrifices" (*Let Wives Be Submissive: The Domestic Code in 1 Peter,* SBLMS 26 [Chico: Scholars Press, 1981], 134). The inclusive interpretation of Achtemeier seems most likely.

[234] Cf. Michaels, *1 Peter,* 102. There is no basis for Selwyn's view that Peter referred to a writing in general rather than the OT. He defends his interpretation by noting the omission of the article before γραφῇ (*First Peter,* 163), but this is insufficient grounds, especially when a particular text from Isaiah is cited immediately. Even more improbable is Martin's suggestion that it may signal reference to a hymn ("I Peter in Recent Study," 31); rightly Michaels, *1 Peter,* 102–3.

[235] Some manuscripts insert ἡ γραφή as the subject, but the external evidence favors ἐν γραφῇ ($\mathfrak{P}^{72}$, ℵ, A, B, Ψ, etc.).

[236] So McCartney, "Use of the Old Testament in the First Epistle of Peter," 80, 209; cf. Elliott, *1 Peter,* 424. D. A. Oss suggests that the stone in Isaiah may have referred to the remnant or Yahweh ("The Interpretation of the 'Stone' Passages by Peter and Paul: A Comparative Study," *JETS* 32 [1989]: 188). He notes, however, that a Messianic text is nearby in Isa 9:1–7, and hence, even though the text is not specifically Messianic, a Messianic reading is apropos (pp. 187–88).

[237] See the analysis of Oss, "The Interpretation of the 'Stone' Passages," 186–87.

[238] Hort, *The First Epistle of St. Peter,* 116; Beare, *First Peter,* 95.

[239] See especially K. N. Snodgrass, "I Peter II.1–10: Its Formation and Literary Affinities," *NTS* 24 (1977): 97–106; Hillyer, "Rock-Stone," 60–61.

ever, Peter argues that what is true of Christ is also true of the community. Just as Christ is the "living Stone," so also the church is comprised of "living stones." The text was understood Messianically by the Isaiah Targum, "Behold, I will appoint in Zion a king, a strong king, powerful and terrible."[240] All we can say with confidence is that Isa 28:16 was viewed by a number of sources as having an eschatological fulfillment and that Peter and Paul both see it as fulfilled in Christ, suggesting, perhaps, a common source. Some identify this source as a testimony book, in which a collection of Messianic prophecies was contained.[241]

The meaning of the citation is what is crucial for our purposes. God has "appointed" (*tithēmi,* see v. 8) Christ as a stone in Zion. The shift from the Septuagint "I lay" *(emballō)* to "I appoint" *(tithēmi)* places the focus on God's initiative. The Petrine use of "appoint" emphasizes God's election and points forward to v. 8.[242] He is God's elect and honored cornerstone.[243] That is, the entire building (i.e., the church) takes its shape from him. The Old Testament citation repeats the two terms "chosen" *(eklekton)* and "honored" *(entimon)* from v. 4, showing that Peter anticipated citing Isa 28:16 even in v. 4. I also argued in v. 4 that there is an allusion to Christ's resurrection. God made him the cornerstone of the building when he raised him from the dead. So the appointment in view here focuses on Christ's resurrection, which revealed that he was chosen and honored by God. The word "cornerstone" *(akrogōniaion)* is understood by some as referring to the top stone in a building or the keystone in an arch.[244] This interpretation should be rejected, for the reference to stumbling in v. 8 indicates that a stone on the ground is intended.[245] Furthermore, the Septuagint makes clear that the reference is to the foundation *(themelia).* We conclude by noting that the first part of the verse restates the idea from v. 4 that Christ was God's honored and chosen Stone.

The reference to "believing" *(pisteuōn)* in him restates the idea of "com-

---

[240] J. F. Stenning, *The Targum of Isaiah* (Oxford: Clarendon, 1949).

[241] E. E. Ellis, *Paul's Use of the Old Testament* (Grand Rapids: Eerdmans, 1957), 89–90. But this view is now doubted by most; see C. H. Dodd, *According to the Scriptures* (New York: Scribners, 1952), 41–43; Elliott, *The Elect and the Holy,* 130–33. Snodgrass rejects the idea of a testimony book but believes "there were texts that were grouped thematically to assist in worship, proclamation, teaching, and defense of the faith" ("I Peter II.1–10," 105; cf. also Best, "I Peter II.4–10," 270). Elliott sees the use of the OT here as reflecting a "common Christian tradition" (*The Elect and the Holy,* 32–33). Brox maintains it was formulated by the author of 1 Peter (*Der erste Petrusbrief,* 95).

[242] So Bauckham, "James, 1 Peter and 2 Peter, Jude," 311.

[243] Elliott sees election as the "unifying theme" of vv. 6–10 (*The Elect and the Holy,* 145).

[244] J. Jeremias, *TDNT* 1:791–93. Hillyer's view that both a capstone and cornerstone are intended is unlikely ("Rock-Stone," 70–72).

[245] See especially R. J. McKelvey, "Christ the Cornerstone," *NTS* 8 (1961–62): 352–59; so also Michaels, *1 Peter,* 103; Elliott, *1 Peter,* 425.

ing" *(proserchomenoi)* to him (see the commentary in v. 4). What Peter emphasized in citing this verse is that the one who believes in Christ "will never be put to shame." Just as Christ is the chosen and honored one of God and was so honored at his resurrection, so too believers will be vindicated on the last day. What is true of the Christ is also true of his people.[246] They will not experience the embarrassment of judgment but the glory of approval.[247] The phrase "will never be ashamed," therefore, is another way of saying they will be honored (*timē*, v. 7, rendered "precious" in the NIV).[248]

2:7 Peter now draws an inference (*oun,* translated "now" in NIV and "then" in NRSV) from v. 6 for believers. Unfortunately most English versions obscure the meaning of the verse by translating the word *timē* as "precious," although the word does not mean precious but "honor," and it actually stands as the subject of the sentence. We could translate it as follows, "The honor, therefore, is for you who believe" (cf. ESV, HCSB). By "honor," as we noted in the previous verse, Peter meant final vindication on the day of judgment.[249] This is confirmed by 1:7, where Peter referred to the eschatological honor that belongs to Jesus Christ on the last day and correspondingly to believers in him. Just as Christ was "honored" *(entimon)* by the Father (vv. 4,6) at the resurrection, so those who trust in him will be honored on the last day, even though presently they are suffering. We should also note that Peter has now used the verb for believing twice in the last two verses, reminding us again that the emphasis on "faith" in chap. 1 (vv. 5,9) should be interpreted in terms of trusting God and not just faithfulness. Of course, the latter idea is present as well, but faithfulness always flows from trust, and the two can never be reversed.

Conversely, those who disbelieve will face "shame" (v. 6) and dishonor (v. 7a) on the last day. The reason for this is that the stone that was disregarded by the builders has become the very cornerstone of the building. The establishment of the cornerstone likely refers to the resurrection of Jesus Christ (cf. Acts 4:11), as we noted earlier.[250] He has been vindicated by God and is the stone from which the building made of God's people takes shape. Peter cited Ps 118:22 at this juncture, and this psalm is cited often in

---

[246] So McCartney, "The Use of the Old Testament in the First Epistle of Peter," 81.

[247] Oss remarks that the insertion of "shame" rather than "will not hurry" in the MT puts the focus on judgment ("The Interpretation of the 'Stone" Passages," 186–87).

[248] Campbell rightly sees a reference to honor rather than preciousness here, though he emphasizes present honor without excluding the eschatological component (*Honor, Shame, and the Rhetoric of 1 Peter,* 86, 93, 95). Cf. also I. H. Marshall, *1 Peter,* NTC [Downers Grove: InterVarsity, 1991], 72. For the significance of honor and shame in 1 Peter, see also Elliott, "Disgraced Yet Graced, 166–78.

[249] Contrary to Beare, *First Peter,* 98. Rightly Goppelt, *I Peter,* 145; Michaels, *1 Peter,* 104; Hillyer, *1 and 2 Peter, Jude,* 64.

[250] So Michaels, *1 Peter,* 105.

the New Testament (cf. Matt 21:42; Mark 12:10–11; Luke 20:17; Acts 4:11). The psalm in its original context describes the return of the king to the temple to give thanks after his victory over his enemies. The stone rejected in the historical context of the psalm was the Davidic king, and the builders were the foreign nations that rejected the rule of the anointed king of Israel. The enemies of Israel thereby assured their own destruction, for the Davidic king was the stone by which Yahweh would carry out his plan in the world. Hence, the king cuts off God's enemies with confidence (Ps 118:10–14). Both Jesus and Peter (Matt 21:42; Acts 4:11) applied the psalm in a surprising way. The builders who reject the anointed king are not foreigners but the religious leaders of Israel. The religious leaders believe they are building God's building, but they have rejected the cornerstone for the entire edifice. By doing so they are behaving like the pagan nations of David's day and have assured their own judgment, for God has established Jesus as the cornerstone by virtue of his resurrection and hence vindicated him. The NIV understands the stone here to be the "capstone" rather than the "cornerstone." The Greek wording is literally "head of the corner" *(kephalēn gōnias)*. The word "head" here does not mean "top" but "end point, furthest extremity" (cf. 1 Kgs 8:8; 2 Chr 5:9).[251] Moreover, we note again that the next verse speaks of people stumbling over the stone, suggesting thereby a cornerstone that people trip over instead of a capstone (see comments on v. 6). In any case, the meaning is clear. God has vindicated and honored Jesus (vv. 4,6), even though people have rejected him (vv. 4,7). Those who disbelieve in him will face judgment.

2:8 Verse 8 continues the thought from v. 7. We can summarize the verses as follows: Those who disbelieve stumble over the stone, who is Christ. They stumble over Christ because they refuse to believe in him and obey him. People who stumble and disobey are responsible for their refusal to trust in Christ, and yet God has appointed, without himself being morally responsible for the sin of unbelievers, that they will both disobey and stumble.

The stone that sits at the head of the corner is one over which the disbelieving stumble and fall.[252] Peter alluded to (rather than cited) Isa 8:14 here. In the context of Isaiah 8, Israel and Judah are called upon to fear and trust the Lord rather than fear other nations. Apparently this section of Isaiah was important to Peter since he also alluded to Isa 8:12 in 1 Pet 3:14. He likely found it to be relevant to his readers since the churches in Asia Minor were tempted to fear those who mistreated and persecuted them. The allusion in this verse represents a literal translation of the MT and does not accord as closely with the Septuagint. Paul's

---

[251] Rightly Grudem, *1 Peter,* 105; cf. Selwyn, *First Peter,* 163.

[252] Elliott argues that the stone here refers to a stone or rock in open areas over which people may stumble, and the stone here refers to God (*1 Peter,* 430).

wording in Rom 9:33 is quite similar, but in Paul we have a mixed citation where Isa 28:16 and 8:14 are merged. The issue is raised again whether Peter used Paul as a source or whether they both drew from a common source, especially since both writers used Isa 8:14 and 28:16 together. It is doubtful that Peter used Paul as a literary source, but it is probably the case that these two texts were often used in early Christian preaching.

Peter then explained why some stumble and fall over the cornerstone. They fall "because they disobey the message." The "message" *(logō)* here is the gospel—the same word God uses as a seed to beget new life (cf. 1:23–25; cf. 3:1). The NIV rightly takes the participle "disobeying" *(apeithountes)* as causal, explaining why they stumble.[253] The participle "disobeying" is complementary to the participle "disbelieving" in v. 7. The two cannot be finally separated, though the latter is the root of the former since all disobedience flows from a failure to trust God. Their stumbling over the cornerstone is not accidental, as humans often trip unintentionally while walking. In this instance humans stumble because of rebellion, because they do not want to submit to God's lordship.

Peter added a provocative comment to conclude his comments about the disobedient, "which is also what they were destined for." The verb *tithēmi* often refers to what God has appointed to occur (Acts 1:7; 13:47; 20:28; 1 Cor 12:18,28; 1 Thess 5:9; 1 Tim 2:7). Some scholars argue that Peter merely meant that God has appointed that those who disobey the message of the gospel would stumble.[254] Such an interpretation fits with the theme that human beings decide their fate.[255] But the interpretation proposed is prosaic and obvious, and it is unlikely that this captures the meaning. Rather the pronoun "which" *(ho)* refers back to the entire thought that pre-

---

[253] The idea of the verse is that "they stumble because they disobey the word" rather than "they disobey because they stumble over the word." Hence the word οἳ should be construed as a relative pronoun and the subject of προσκόπτουσιν rather than modifying ἀπειθοῦντες (rightly Achtemeier, *1 Peter,* 162), and the dative τῷ λόγῳ is the object of the participle ἀπειθοῦντες rather than the verb προσκόπτουσιν. In support of this, ἀπειθέω takes τῷ λόγῳ as the object in 3:1 and τῷ τοῦ θεοῦ εὐαγγελίῳ in 4:17 (so Achtemeier, *1 Peter,* 162). Contrary to Michaels, τῷ λόγῳ is not the object of both verbs (*1 Peter,* 106).

[254] So Bigg, *Epistles of Peter and Jude,* 133; Michaels, *1 Peter,* 107; Campbell, *Honor, Shame, and the Rhetoric of 1 Peter,* 93; A. J. Panning, "Exegetical Brief: What Has Been Determined (ἐτέθησαν) in 1 Peter 2:8?" *Wisconsin Lutheran Quarterly* 98 (2001): 48–52; Elliott, *1 Peter,* 433–34; Marshall, *1 Peter,* 73. Hillyer suggests that perhaps the point is "not that individuals are predestined to stumble but that the stumbling of many against the rock is foretold in Scripture" ("Rock-Stone," 63). This is an unlikely interpretation since the text emphasizes the doom appointed for people, not the fulfillment of Scripture.

[255] So Didymus the Blind and Oecumenius in *James, 1–2 Peter, 1–3 John, Jude,* ACCS (Downers Grove: InterVarsity, 2000), 86–87.

cedes.[256] God has not only appointed that those who disobey the word would stumble and fall. He has also determined that they would disbelieve and stumble.[257] The idea that calamity also comes from God is often taught in the Old Testament. I will cite three representative examples since to modern people the idea is quite shocking: "Is it not from the mouth of the Most High that both calamities and good things come?" (Lam 3:38). "When a trumpet sounds in a city, do not the people tremble? When disaster comes to a city, has not the LORD caused it?" (Amos 3:6). "I form the light and create darkness, I bring prosperity and create disaster; I, the LORD, do all these things" (Isa 45:7). The worldview of the Scriptures is that God is sovereignly in control of all things, from the decisions made by kings (Prov 21:1) to the throw of the dice (Prov 16:33; cf. Isa 46:9–11). Even the cruelest and most vicious act in history—the execution of Jesus of Nazareth, was predestined by God (Acts 2:23; 4:27–28).[258]

It is imperative, however, that we add immediately another element of the biblical worldview. Biblical writers never exempt human beings from responsibility, even though they believe God ordains all things (cf. Rom 9:14–23). Peter indicted those who crucified Christ, even though the execution was predestined by God himself (Acts 2:23). It seems fair to conclude that Peter indicted them because in killing the Christ they carried out their own desires. They were not coerced into crucifying Jesus against their wills. No, in putting him to death they did just what they wanted to do. Similarly, Peter criticized those who stumble over Christ the cornerstone for their unbelief and disobedience. He did not argue that their unbelief is free from any guilt because it was predestined. He had already emphasized that they chose not to obey him and that they refused to believe in him. Peter articulated a common theme in the Scriptures that human beings are responsible for their sin and sin willingly, and yet God controls all events in history. The Scriptures do not resolve how these two themes fit together

---

[256] Rightly Hort, *The First Epistle of St Peter,* 123; Best, *1 Peter,* 106; Beare, *First Peter,* 100; Grudem, *1 Peter,* 107; Achtemeier, *1 Peter,* 162. Hort remarks, "All attempts to explain away the statement, as if e.g. it meant only that they were appointed to this by the just and natural consequences of their own acts, are futile." We should also note that Hort sees the antecedent particularly in the verb "stumble." Achtemeier observes that the plural ἐτέθησαν renders the former option unlikely.

[257] So Andreas in *James, 1–2 Peter, 1–3 John, Jude,* ACCS (Downers Grove: InterVarsity, 2000), 86. Davids rightly remarks that the emphasis here is corporate (*First Peter,* 90), but he wrongly sets the corporate in opposition to individuals. For a discussion of this matter see T. R. Schreiner, "Does Romans 9 Teach Individual Election unto Salvation?" in *Still Sovereign: Contemporary Perspectives on Election, Foreknowledge, and Grace* (Grand Rapids: Baker, 2000), 98–105.

[258] McCartney rightly says, "If God is absolutely sovereign in everything that happens, then God must be the one sending the suffering. Peter never refers to judgment or suffering as coming from anyone except God" ("The Use of the Old Testament in the First Epistle of Peter," 136).

philosophically, though today we would call it a "compatibilist" worldview. We must admit, however, that *how* this fits together logically eludes us, and hence theologians have often fallen prey to the temptation to deny one or the other truth. Why did Peter emphasize the theme of God's sovereignty here? He did so to comfort his readers, assuring them that the evil in the world is not sundered from God's control.[259] God still reigns, even over those who oppose him and the Petrine believers.[260]

2:9 The "but" *(de)* beginning v. 9 is most naturally understood as a contrast to what immediately precedes.[261] As Thurén says, "A negative example adds the appreciation of the positive."[262] God has appointed the disobedient to destruction, but on the contrary believers are a "chosen people" *(eklekton genos)*. They belong to God's people because they have been elected, chosen by him. We saw in the first verse of the letter that Peter introduced the theme of election to strengthen God's pilgrim people, and he returned to it here. The closest parallel to what Peter said here is in Isa 43:20, a context in which God promises to accomplish a second exodus for his people in bringing them out of Babylon.[263] Peter saw these promises as fulfilled in Jesus Christ, and God's elect nation is no longer coterminous with Israel but embraces the church of Jesus Christ, which is composed of both Jews and Gentiles.

The privilege of belonging to God's people is conveyed by Peter with a number of Old Testament allusions. Peter drew on Exod 19:6, using the exact words found there in identifying the church as a "royal priesthood" *(basileion hierteuma)*.[264] In Exodus the title applies to Israel, with whom God enacts his covenant at Sinai. Israel's priesthood was such that they were to mirror to the nations the glory of Yahweh, so that all nations would see that no god rivals the Lord (cf. also Isa 61:6). Unfortunately, Israel mainly failed in this endeavor as the Assyrian (722 B.C.) and Babylonian (586 B.C.) exiles demonstrate. The reason for the exile is that Israel failed to keep

---

[259] Rightly Schutter, *Hermeneutic and Composition in I Peter,* 134–35.

[260] Horrell reveals his presuppositions when he suggests that we can no longer accept what the Scriptures teach on this matter (*The Epistles of Peter and Jude,* 43).

[261] Contra Elliott, *The Elect and the Holy,* 143.

[262] Thurén, *Argument and Theology in 1 Peter,* 127.

[263] Elliott argues that "the Isaiah passage has been interpolated into the Exodus verse" (*The Elect and the Holy*, 142).

[264] The term βασίλειον is an adjective here modifying ἱεράτευμα (contra Selwyn, *First Peter,* 165–66; Elliott, *The Elect and the Holy,* 149–54; Kelly, *Peter and Jude,* 97; Best, "I Peter II.4–10," 288–89). Elliott understands Peter to be saying that the church is the house of God as King (*The Elect and the Holy*, 196; *1 Peter,* 436–37; cf. also Brox, *Der erste Petrusbrief,* 103). In *2 Mac* 2:17 both words are nouns, but this is clear because each word is preceded by the article τό, and the word καί also separates them. Supporting the idea that we have an adjective here is the fact the other two phrases in the verse have adjectives and the adjective in the phrase ἱεράτευμα ἅγιον in v. 5 (cf. Beare, *First Peter,* 104; Goppelt, *I Peter,* 149, n. 65; Michaels, *1 Peter,* 108–9; Achtemeier, *1 Peter,* 164; Davids, *First Peter,* 91–92, n. 30; Schweizer, "The Priesthood of All Believers," 291–92).

God's law. Now God's kingdom of priests consists of the church of Jesus Christ. It too is to mediate God's blessings to the nations, as it proclaims the gospel. We should note the comparison and contrast here. Both Israel as a whole and the church of Jesus Christ are identified as a "royal priesthood." There is no suggestion that only a portion of Israel served as priests in Exodus 19. The difference is not the extent of the priesthood but its identity, for now the royal priesthood is the church of Jesus Christ (cf. Rev 1:6).[265] As noted above, the priesthood here is corporate in nature, and yet this does not rule out the truth that individuals serve priestly functions. Best seems to strike the right balance here: "Christians exercise priestly functions but always as members of a group who all exercise the same function."[266]

Peter also replicated the exact words of Exod 19:6 in identifying the church as a "holy nation" (*ethnos hagion;* cf. Exod 23:22, LXX). The church of Jesus is a people now set apart for the Lord, enjoying his special presence and favor. The next phrase, "a people belonging to God" *(eis peripoiēsin),* does not allude as clearly to any Old Testament text. The term is used in Mal 3:17 of believers who respond to the Lord's rebuke and live righteously, and so in contrast to the wicked they constitute his possession, his special people. There is likely also an allusion to Isa 43:21. We noted above that the phrase "chosen people" may be drawn from Isa 43:20. The verb "I formed for myself" *(periepoiēsamēn)* in v. 21 is the verbal form of the noun "possession" (NASB, *peripoiēsis*).[267] Again the privileges belonging to Israel now belong to the church of Jesus Christ. The church does not replace Israel, but it does fulfill the promises made to Israel; and all those, Jews and Gentiles, who belong to the true Israel are now part of the new people of God.[268]

The purpose of the people of God is now explained. God has chosen them to be his people, established them as a royal priesthood, appointed them as a holy nation to be his special possession, so that they would "declare the praises of him who called you out of darkness into his wonderful light." Peter again probably alluded to Isa 43:21, for there we are told that God formed Israel for himself so that "they would recount my praises" *(tas aretas mou diēgeisthai).*[269] It should be noted especially that Peter, like the Septuagint, used the term "praises" *(aretas)* in the plural. As God

---

[265] Best is correct in arguing that levitical ideas of the priesthood merged with the nonlevitical nature of the priesthood in Exod 19:6 ("I Peter II.4–10," 283–86; contra Elliott, *The Elect and the Holy,* 173, 210, 219–20). For Luther's understanding that all believers are priests, see *Commentary on Peter & Jude,* 103–4.

[266] Best, "I Peter II.4–10," 287.

[267] It seems less likely, therefore, that the reference is to final salvation and preservation here (against Michaels, *1 Peter,* 109–10).

[268] Elliott remarks, "The sect, it is implied, is not the exclusive representative of the chosen people of God, the sole community where the prophetic hopes of Israel are fulfilled" (*Home for the Homeless,* 127).

[269] Rightly Achtemeier, *1 Peter,* 165–66.

formed Israel to praise him, now the church has been established to praise his wonders. God's ultimate purpose in everything he does is designed to bring him praise (Isa 43:7). The declaration of God's praises includes both worship and evangelism, spreading the good news of God's saving wonders to all peoples.[270] They proclaim God's praises for calling them "out of darkness into his wonderful light." This is a description of their conversion and employs the language of Genesis 1, where God utters the word and light becomes a reality (Gen 1:3–5), pushing back the darkness. Paul used the same picture of conversion in 2 Cor 4:6, where God shines in the heart of his people to give them knowledge of his glory through Jesus Christ. Conversion is often depicted in the New Testament as a transfer from darkness to light (Acts 26:18; 2 Cor 4:6; Eph 5:8; 1 Thess 5:4,5,8).[271] We also have noted previously (see the commentary on 1:15) that the calling described here is effectual. Just as God's word creates light, so God's call creates faith. Calling is not a mere invitation but is performative, so that the words God speaks become a reality. The beauty and glory of the new life is conveyed by the image of light in contrast to darkness. Hence, Peter identified the light as "wonderful" (cf. Ps 118:23).

2:10 Verse 10 returns to the status of the Petrine churches as God's people. Peter alludes to the words of Hos 2:23 here. Interestingly, Paul cited the same idea from Hosea in Rom 9:25–26, but Paul's wording differs from Peter's, and it is clear that no literary relationship can exist between the citations. In Hosea, Israel is repudiated as God's people because of their sin, but God pledges to have mercy upon them and form them again as his people. Such has been the experience of the church of Jesus Christ. The Petrine churches were composed mainly of Gentiles, living in darkness (2:9),[272] but now wondrously they are God's people. They did not deserve inclusion into God's people, but they have now received his mercy and rejoice at their inclusion. The message of mercy that opened the letter at 1:3 now closes a major section of the letter in 2:10.[273] Peter reminded the readers again that they are recipients of God's grace, that the foundation for obeying the imperatives is God's mercy in Christ.

---

[270] Cf. Elliott, *The Elect and the Holy,* 197; *1 Peter,* 439–40; R. Feldmeier, *Die Christen als Fremde: Die Metapher der Fremde in der antiken Welt, im Urchristentum und im 1. Petrusbrief,* WUNT 64 (Tübingen: Mohr, 1992), 167, 181, 186. It is mistaken, then, to limit what is said here to worship, though worship is certainly included. Those who restrict the text to worship only include Michaels, *1 Peter,* 110; Balch, *Let Wives Be Submissive,* 133; Seland, "A Philonic Reading of 1 Peter 2:5, 9"; Bechtler, *Following in His Steps,* 158–59. The notion that the eucharist is in view is farfetched (contra Kelly, *Peter and Jude,* 100–101). Cf. Cranfield, *I & II Peter and Jude,* 68; Davids, *First Peter,* 92–93.

[271] Since this language is typically used to denote the present state of believers, darkness and light here should not be understood as future (contra Michaels, *1 Peter,* 111).

[272] Cf. Michaels, *1 Peter,* 112.

[273] Cf. Schutter, *Hermeneutic and Composition in I Peter,* 29.

SECTION OUTLINE

III. LIVING AS ALIENS TO BRING GLORY TO GOD IN A HOSTILE WORLD (2:11–4:11)
   1. The Christian Life as a Battle and Witness (2:11–12)
   2. Testifying to the Gospel in the Social Order (2:13–3:12)
      (1) Submit to the Government (2:13–17)
      (2) Slaves, Submit to Masters (2:18–25)
         To Receive a Reward (2:18–20)
         To Imitate Christ (2:21–25)
      (3) Wives, Submit to Husbands (3:1–6)
      (4) Husbands, Live Knowledgeably with Your Wives (3:7)
      (5) Conclusion: Live a Godly Life (3:8–12)
   3. Responding in a Godly Way to Suffering (3:13–4:11)
      (1) The Blessing of Suffering for Christ (3:13–17)
      (2) Christ's Suffering as the Pathway to Exaltation (3:18–22)
      (3) Preparing to Suffer as Christ Did (4:1–6)
      (4) Living in Light of the End (4:7–11)

III. LIVING AS ALIENS TO BRING GLORY TO GOD IN A HOSTILE WORLD (2:11–4:11)

A new section of the letter begins here, marked by "dear friends" (1 Pet 2:11; *agapētoi)* and the "I urge" *(parakalō).*[1] The focus shifts from the relationship believers have with one another (1:13–2:10) to their relationship with the unbelieving world—an unbelieving world that is suspicious of and hostile to believers. In one sense the beginning of a new section is artificial because the foundation for the exhortations in 2:11–4:11 continues to be the gracious work of God by which he has bestowed upon believers new life and promised them an eschatological inheritance (1:3–12). The indicative of God's grace and salvation also undergirds the imperatives that dominate 2:11–4:11. Still, a new emphasis is evident in 2:11–4:11, for Peter did not emphasize how believers should love one another as he did in 1:13–2:10 but turned toward how they should relate to outsiders.

An inclusio (or envelope structure) functions as the boundary for 2:11–

[1] So also J. H. Elliott, *The Elect and the Holy: An Exegetical Examination of I Peter 2:4–10 and the Phrase* βασίλειον Ἱεράτευμα, NovTSup 12 (Leiden: Brill, 1966), 16.

4:11 since the text begins (2:12) and concludes with the theme of God's glory (4:11). The repetition of these words suggests that the next major section of the letter commences in 4:12. That the section ends with 4:11 is also suggested by the repetition of the words "dear friends" *(agapētoi)* in 4:12. The theme for 2:11–4:11 is explicated in 2:11–12. Believers should live as aliens in this world so that unbelievers will observe their godly lives and glorify God by coming to faith in Christ. According to the first major subsection believers please God by living in a way that adorns the gospel in the social order (2:13–3:12). Christians exemplify a godly lifestyle by submitting to those in authority (2:13,17; 3:1). Believers should submit to governing authorities (2:13–17), slaves should submit to masters (2:18–25), and wives should submit to husbands (3:1–6). The goal in every instance is to live in such a way that unbelievers will glorify God and repent and believe, and hence these sections flesh out the thematic statement in 2:11–12. Christ's suffering is the supreme example to imitate (2:21–25), for his own suffering was the means by which human beings returned to God. Another theme sounded in this section is that a godly life is necessary to receive an eternal reward. In the summary (3:8–12) Peter called on his readers to live in a way that pleases God so that they will obtain life on the last day.

The next major subsection is found in 3:13–4:11. Dividing these verses into a coherent outline is more difficult. The subject of suffering comes to the forefront, and the focus turns to the eternal reward of believers. Those who endure suffering will receive an eschatological blessing from God. First Peter 3:8–12 functions as a transition from the previous subsection since the theme of reward is also prominent in that paragraph. In this new section Peter emphasized that believers are blessed by God if they suffer for doing what is right (3:13–17). The suffering of believers leads Peter, as in 2:18–25, to the topic of Christ's suffering. The suffering of Christ was the pathway to glory and the means by which he triumphed over evil powers (3:18–22). Peter implied that the same pattern is true in the life of believers—their suffering is the prelude to eschatological glory. But in the interval between suffering and glory believers must prepare themselves to suffer and to make a clean break with sin (4:1–6). They will be rewarded in the last day if they do so. Finally, they are to live daily in light of the *eschaton* (4:7–11), which means that they must pursue a life devoted to prayer, vigilance, and ministering to others.

1. The Christian Life as a Battle and Witness (2:11–12)

11Dear friends, I urge you, as aliens and strangers in the world, to abstain from sinful desires, which war against your soul. 12Live such good lives among the pagans that, though they accuse you of doing wrong, they may see your good deeds and glorify God on the day he visits us.

Peter now addresses believers as aliens in this world and directs his attention to their behavior in a hostile culture. He summons them to conquer evil desires with which they struggle. Christians must live exemplary lives with the kinds of good deeds that will make unbelievers take notice. Hence, they will fend off any suggestion that they are practicing evil. Even more important, the goal is to provoke unbelievers to glorify God in the day of visitation. Peter's hope was that unbelievers will be compelled to admit that the lifestyle of believers is morally beautiful, and this admission will bring them to saving faith so that God will be glorified on the day of judgment. The introductory verses of this section show, then, that the good works of believers are intended for mission, so that those who are unbelievers will have the same experience Peter described in 1 Pet 2:9–10. They will be "called out of darkness" and "into his wonderful light" (1 Pet 2:9). They will praise God's saving mercy and proclaim his praises for rescuing them from the dominion of sin. Peter realized that not all will be saved when they observe the lives of believers (cf. 3:16). Nevertheless, he summoned believers to holiness with the confidence that some unbelievers will be brought to faith as they see the transformed lives of believers. Since 2:11–12 functions as the introduction to the following verses, the call to mission informs the entire section.

2:11 As noted earlier a new section begins with "dear friends" (*agapētoi;* cf. 4:12) and "I urge" *(parakalō).* The translation "dear friends" is unfortunate since what Peter emphasized in the term *agapētoi* is that they are "beloved by God" and chosen to be his people.[2] The emphasis now shifts to the relationship believers have with the world. Hence, they are identified as "aliens and strangers" *(paroikous kai parepidēmous).* These terms recall Abraham's status as a sojourner, for he describes himself as an "alien and stranger" *(paroikos kai parepidēmos)* in Gen 23:4 (LXX). Abraham uttered these words in a context in which he had no property on which to bury his wife. Similarly, the Petrine readers had no permanent home in this world. The two words also appear in Ps 38:13 (LXX). There the psalmist emphasized the shortness of life, a theme that fits well with Peter's themes.

There is no need to try to distinguish between the terms "aliens and strangers" (cf. 1:1,17; cf. Eph 2:19; Heb 11:13). Peter intended us to read them together to say that believers are aliens and strangers in this world. We should not read the words literally as if they depict the actual political sta-

[2] J. R. Michaels, *1 Peter,* WBC (Waco: Word, 1998), 115.

tus of the readers.[3] The language of strangers and exiles is appropriated theologically, signifying that the readers are *like* foreigners because of their allegiance to Jesus Christ. Achtemeier rightly observes, "It was precisely the precarious legal status of foreigners that provided the closest analogy to the kind of treatment Christians could expect from the hostile culture in which they lived."[4] But Achtemeier wrongly rejects the notion that Christians as exiles longed for their heavenly home, saying that they awaited the return of Christ instead.[5] He introduces a false dichotomy, for the inheritance of believers would only be theirs when Christ appeared. Nor should the inheritance be conceived of as ethereal and immaterial. The future inheritance, as 2 Pet 3:13 informs us, is a new heaven and new earth (cf. Rev 21:1–22:5), a new universe that is transformed by God's power. The author of Hebrews informs us that the patriarchs as exiles looked forward to the new world as well (Heb 11:13–16), to a heavenly city, a new country.

Peter now exhorts believers *(parakalō)* to live a certain way as aliens and strangers. Exhortations to godly living are often communicated in the New Testament with the verb "I urge" (cf. Rom 12:1; Eph 4:1; Phil 4:2; Phlm 10). Such exhortations are always grounded in the redemptive work of Christ already accomplished for believers. The infinitive "to abstain" *(apechesthai)* following "I urge" takes on an imperatival flavor (cf. Acts 15:20,29; 1 Thess 4:3; 1 Tim 4:3).[6] They are exhorted "to abstain from sinful desires," or more literally "desires of the flesh" *(sarkikōn epithymiōn)*. The meaning here appears to be close to the Pauline understanding of the term "flesh." These are the natural desires that human beings have apart from the work of the Spirit.[7]

---

[3] Contra J. H. Elliott, *1 Peter: A New Translation with Introduction and Commentary*, AB (New York: Doubleday, 2000), 458–62, 476–83; id., "Peter, Silvanus and Mark in 1 Peter and Acts: Sociological-Exegetical Perspectives on a Petrine Group in Rome," in *Wort in der Zeit: Neutestamentlichen Studien: Festgabe für Karl Heinrich Rengstorf zum 75. Geburtstag* (Leiden: Brill, 1980), 254. Elliott now says that the terms were used of both actual strangers and resident aliens and metaphorically were applied to the whole community. Such a conclusion calls into question the legitimacy of reading the terms at a literal level at all. E. J. Richard distinguishes the two terms and thus sees both ideas in the verse (*Reading 1 Peter, Jude, and 2 Peter: A Literary and Theological Commentary*, RNT [Macon: Smith & Helwys, 2000], 103), but this is unlikely, for it is unclear that Peter intended one of the descriptions to be read socially and the other spiritually.

[4] P. J. Achtemeier, *1 Peter: A Commentary on First Peter*, Her (Minneapolis: Fortress, 1996), 174; cf. Michaels, *1 Peter*, 116.

[5] Achtemeier, *1 Peter*, 175.

[6] The textual evidence is rather evenly divided between the imperative ἀπέχεσθε (𝔓[72], A, C, L, P, 33, 81, etc.) and the infinitive ἀπέχεσθαι (א, B, Ψ, 049, 1739, MT). But the meaning remains the same. The external evidence slightly favors the infinitive, but see Michaels, *1 Peter*, 114.

[7] Richard argues that "natural impulses" are in view, and so the injunction should be interpreted to say that believers should "abstain from natural impulses in as much as they [in their excesses] wage war against the soul" (*Reading 1 Peter, Jude, and 2 Peter*, 105). Against Richard nothing is said in the text about resisting fleshly desires in terms of excess. Richard introduces the idea of "excess" into the text, whereas the text simply says that believers must abstain from fleshly desires that wage war against us.

In 1 Peter the "flesh" *(sarx)* represents the weakness of human beings in this age (cf. 1:24; 3:18; 4:1–2). The verse is instructive because it informs us that those who have the Spirit are not exempt from fleshly desires. Such desires cannot be confined to sexual sins or sins of the body like drunkenness. We have already seen in 2:1 that believers are warned against "social" sins like slander and envy. The depth of the struggle in which believers are engaged is explained by the words "which war against your soul." Obviously the desires of the flesh that emerge in believers are quite strong if they are described in terms of warfare, as an enemy that attempts to conquer believers. Such desires must be resisted and conquered, and the image used implies that this is no easy matter.[8] The Christian life is certainly not depicted as passive in which believers simply "let go and let God." The "soul" here does not refer to the immaterial part of human beings.[9] The whole person is in view, showing that sinful desires, if they are allowed to triumph, ultimately destroy human beings.[10]

2:12 Verse 12 is connected to v. 11 by a participle that is translated as an imperative by the NIV as well as the NRSV, "conduct yourselves."[11] The participle may be better rendered as instrumental ("by keeping your conduct good among the Gentiles," *tēn anastrophēn hymōn en tois ethnesin echontes kalēn*).[12] If the latter is the case, it still has an imperatival sense by virtue of its relationship to the main verb. One of Peter's favorite words for expressing the new life of believers is "conduct" *(anastrophē)*.[13] In 1:15 it refers to the holiness of life required of Christians and in 1:18 to the evil way of life from which they have been delivered by Christ's death. It depicts the godly behavior of wives in 3:1–2 and the godly life of those suffering as believers in 3:16. The term is used broadly in Peter to designate

---

[8] M. Luther's comments are insightful: "As soon as the Spirit and faith enter our hearts, we become so weak that we think we cannot beat down the least imaginations and sparks of temptation, and we see nothing but sin in ourselves from the crown of the head even to the foot. For before we believed, we walked according to our own lusts, but now the Spirit has come and would purify us, and a conflict arises when the devil, the flesh, and the world oppose faith. . . . If thou then hast wicked thoughts, thou shouldst not on this account despair; only be on thy guard, that thou be not taken prisoner by them" (*Commentary on Peter & Jude* [Grand Rapids: Kregel, 1990], 112–13).

[9] Cf. W. Grudem, *The First Epistle of Peter,* TNTC (Grand Rapids: Eerdmans, 1988), 115.

[10] Rightly J. N. D. Kelly, *A Commentary on the Epistles of Peter and Jude,* Thornapple Commentaries (Grand Rapids: Baker, 1981), 105–6; C. E. B. Cranfield, *I & II Peter and Jude: Introduction and Commentary,* TBC (London: SCM, 1960), 72; Michaels, *1 Peter,* 115–16.

[11] W. Munro argued that 1 Pet 2:12–3:12 is a later interpolation (*Authority in Paul and Peter: The Identification of a Pastoral Stratum in the Pauline Corpus and I Peter,* SNTSMS 45 [Cambridge: University Press, 1983]). Her view is unpersuasive. See J. H. L. Dijkman, "1 Peter: A Later Pastoral Stratum?" *NTS* 33 (1987): 265–71.

[12] So Achtemeier, *1 Peter,* 177.

[13] For a discussion of the terms ἀναστροφή and ἀγαθοποιός, see Elliott, *The Elect and the Holy,* 179–82.

the new way of life demanded of Christians. Such "good conduct" (RSV) will appear beautiful to "pagans" (lit. "Gentiles," *ethnesin*). Using the term "Gentiles" for pagans indicates that the terminology of Israel is now applied to the church of Jesus Christ.[14] Hence, even though unbelievers are inclined to revile Christians as those who do evil, they will be constrained by the godly lifestyle of believers to reconsider.[15]

Some scholars think that formal legal charges are in view when unbelievers allege that Christians practice evil.[16] Hence, they include this verse in seeing an empirewide and formal persecution against Christians. It is more likely, however, that the language used here is more general. Peter reflected on the widespread cultural opposition to the Christian way of life, so that the charges here are not restricted to legal cases.[17] Unbelievers viewed Christians with suspicion and hostility because the latter did not conform to their way of life (4:3–4). Since believers did not honor the typical gods of the community, they were naturally viewed as subversive and evil in that social context.

Peter did not summon believers to a verbal campaign of self-defense or to the writing of tracts in which they defend their morality. He enjoined believers to pursue virtue and goodness, so that their goodness would be apparent to all in society. The evident transformation of their behavior will contradict false allegations circulating in society. Peter's hope is that unbelievers will glorify God because they see "your good deeds."[18] The verb "see" is a participle here *(epopteuontes)* and should be understood as causal ("because they see your good deeds).[19] The verb was used in mystery religions, but to see any such influence here falls prey to "parallelomania," where scholars impose the meaning of a term from one realm onto another.[20] Some scholars think the good works here refer to the honors and public recognition granted by public officials for behavior that was exem-

---

[14] See Elliott, *1 Peter,* 466.

[15] The phrase *en hō* here probably is temporal (so B. Reicke, *The Disobedient Spirits and Christian Baptism: A Study of 1 Pet. III.19 and Its Context,* ASNU 13 [Copenhagen: Munksgaard, 1946], 110–11; P. R. Fink, "The Use and Significance of *en hō* in I Peter," *GTJ* 8 [1967]: 34). Elliott thinks it is temporal or circumstantial (*1 Peter,* 467).

[16] E.g., J. Moffatt, *The General Epistles: James, Peter, and Jude* (New York: Harper & Brothers, 1928), 120–21.

[17] Rightly Michaels, *1 Peter,* 117; Achtemeier, *1 Peter,* 177.

[18] Achtemeier argues that ἐκ τῶν καλῶν ἔργων is partitive as in John 16:17 and Luke 21:16, so that the phrase can be rendered "some of your good works" (*1 Peter,* 178, also n. 78). It seems unlikely, though, that Peter restricted his idea to only "some" of their works.

[19] So Michaels, *1 Peter,* 118; Achtemeier, *1 Peter,* 178.

[20] E.g., F. W. Beare, *The First Epistle of Peter: The Greek Text with Introduction and Notes* (Oxford: Blackwell, 1947), 112. Rightly Kelly, *Peter and Jude,* 106. See S. Sandmel's famous article, "Parallelomania," *JBL* 81 (1962): 2–13.

plary, but Peter likely thought more generally of the good works of believers that permeate every dimension of life.[21]

Peter almost certainly alluded to the words of Jesus recorded in Matt 5:16, "Let your light shine before men, that they may see your good deeds and praise your Father in heaven."[22] Both Peter and Matthew drew a connection between "seeing" good deeds and the corresponding praise that is given to God as a result. But what did Peter mean by "glorify God on the day he visits us"? The RSV translates the verse literally, "Glorify God on the day of visitation." The "day of visitation" *(en hēmera episkopēs)* could refer to God's judgment or his salvation.[23] Peter may have been saying that they will glorify God in the day when they are judged, acknowledging at that time the good works of believers and vindicating God's justice. The NRSV clearly adopts this interpretation, "They may see your honorable deeds and glorify God when he comes to judge." It is argued that the word group for "visitation" when combined with a temporal idea refers to judgment. The idea of judgment is certainly present in a number of verses (Isa 10:3; 24:22; 29:26; Jer 6:15; 10:15; cf. also *Wis* 14:11; 19:15; *Sir* 16:18; 23:24).[24]

Van Unnik is also persuaded that condemnation is in view.[25] The day of visitation, he argues, refers to the eschatological day of judgment and cannot be understood as a reference to salvation that is experienced in this life, before the final day. He points out that "glorifying" God is not restricted to salvation. Condemned Gentiles will glorify God on the last day (Ps 86:9). He also argues that the wicked will glorify the Lord according to *The Testament of Judah* 25:5, though this verse is debatable and could refer to the salvation of the wicked. *First Enoch 62* also reveals that the wicked will honor and glorify God on the day of judgment but will not be spared from wrath.

Some strong arguments support a reference to eschatological judgment in

---

[21] E.g., W. C. van Unnik, "The Teaching of Good Works in I Peter," *NTS* 2 (1954): 99.

[22] So R. H. Gundry, "'*Verba Christi*' in *I Peter: Their Implications concerning the Authorship of I Peter and the Authenticity of the Gospel Tradition, NTS* 13 (1967): 340; "Further *Verba* on *Verba Christi* in First Peter," *Bib* 55 (1974): 224; E. Best, "1 Peter and the Gospel Tradition," *NTS* 16 (1970): 109–10; L. Goppelt, *A Commentary on I Peter* (Grand Rapids: Eerdmans, 1993), 160–61.

[23] In both cases it refers to the last day, contra D. C. Parker, "The Eschatology of 1 Peter," *BTB* 24 (1994): 30.

[24] Achtemeier, *1 Peter,* 178; cf. D. G. McCartney, "The Use of the Old Testament in the First Epistle of Peter" (Ph.D. diss., Westminster Theological Seminary, 1989), 140–41.

[25] Van Unnik, "Good Works in I Peter," 104–5; cf. also D. L. Balch, *Let Wives Be Submissive: The Domestic Code in I Peter,* SBLMS 26 (Chico: Scholars Press, 1981), 87–88. S. R. Bechtler argues that the verse does not speak of the evangelism and conversion of unbelievers, but he thinks it is possible that δοξάσωσιν refers to eschatological salvation (*Following in His Steps: Suffering, Community, and Christology in 1 Peter,* SBLDS 162 [Atlanta: Scholars Press, 1998], 159–60).

this verse, but there are good reasons to think Peter referred to salvation in this verse, and this is the view defended here. Achtemeier wrongly excludes the notion that "visitation" can involve salvation when a temporal notion is included (cf. Exod 13:19; Isa 23:17). That God's visitation is salvific in a temporal expression is clear from *Sir* 18:20, "Before judgment, examine yourself, and in the hour of visitation *[en hōra episkopēs]* you will find forgiveness." *Wisdom of Solomon* 3:7 speaks of the salvation of the righteous similarly, "In the time of their visitation *[en kairō episkopēs]* they will shine forth, and will run like sparks through the stubble," as does *Wis* 3:13, "For blessed is the barren woman who is undefiled, who has not entered into a sinful union; she will have fruit when God examines souls" (lit. "in the visitation of souls," *en episkopē psychōn*).[26] This evidence does not, of course, prove that the visitation in 1 Peter is salvific. It merely demonstrates that such a view cannot be ruled out by appealing to the phrase "day of visitation."

The reference to glorifying God suggests that the salvation of Gentiles is in view.[27] Typically in the New Testament people glorify God or give him glory by believing (cf. Acts 13:48; Rom 4:20; 15:7,9; 1 Cor 2:7; Eph 1:6,12,14; 2 Thess 3:1; Rev 5:12–13). Van Unnik finds a few examples where glorifying God refers to the end-time judgment of unbelievers, but usually God is glorified when people believe. Conversely, those who refuse to believe do not glorify God (Acts 12:23; Rom 1:21). We see the same contrast in Revelation between those who believe and glorify God (Rev 11:13) and those who refuse to repent and do not honor him (Rev 16:9). Peter exhorted believers to live noble lives because in doing so unbelievers will see their good works. Because they observe such works, some unbelievers will repent and believe and therefore give glory to God on the last day.[28] The use of the participle "see" (from the verb *epopteuō*) also suggests that salvation is in view, for the same term is used in 1 Pet 3:2, where the submission of wives is intended to lead to the salvation of unbelieving husbands. Peter was confident that some unbelievers will be saved when they notice the godliness of believers. The unbelievers may revile Christians, but as they notice the goodness in their lives, some will repent and be saved, and as a result of their salvation God will be glorified.

---

[26] For salvific character of God's visitation cf. Gen 50:24,25; Exod 3:16; *Ps. Sol.* 10:4; 11:1,6.

[27] So C. Spicq, *Les Épîtres de Saint Pierre,* SB (Paris: Gabalda, 1966), 99; Kelly, *Peter and Jude,* 106; Michaels, *1 Peter,* 118–20; S. McKnight, *1 Peter,* NIVAC (Grand Rapids: Zondervan, 1996), 128; I. H. Marshall, *1 Peter,* NTC (Downers Grove: InterVarsity, 1991), 82. Cf. Grudem, *1 Peter,* 117; Richard, *Reading 1 Peter, Jude, and 2 Peter,* 108; Elliott, *1 Peter,* 471; Bede in *James, 1–2 Peter, 1–3 John, Jude,* ACCS (Downers Grove: InterVarsity, 2000), 91). J. Calvin argues that unbelievers will be converted before Christ's return by the behavior of believers (*Commentaries on the Catholic Epistles* [Grand Rapids: Eerdmans, 1948], 79).

[28] Goppelt, *I Peter,* 160; J. R. Michaels, "Eschatology in I Peter iii.17," *NTS* 13 (1967): 397.

2. Testifying to the Gospel in the Social Order (2:13–3:12)[29]

The household code is interpreted variously by scholars. The background to such codes in the past was attributed to Stoic sources. Many scholars now seem to be convinced by Balch that the codes can be traced back to Aristotle, in which mutual responsibilities required in relationships were explicated.[30] The nearest parallels are in Hellenistic Judaism (Philo, *Decalogue* 165–67; *Hypothetica* 7.14; *Spec. Laws* 2.226–27; Josephus, *Ag. Ap.* 2.190–219; *Ps.-Phoc.* 175–227).[31] But as Michaels observes, the Petrine form is not clearly dependent on any particular source.[32]

Scholars also debate how the household codes should be interpreted in 1 Peter.[33] Balch sees the code as apologetic, contending that Peter counseled believers to conform to the social roles expected in society, so that unbelievers would not criticize their behavior.[34] Elliott, on the other hand, suggests that the household code was not intended to answer the objections of unbelievers but was given to promote social cohesion within the Christian church.[35] Believers are to live as exiles and hence should not conduct

---

[29] Goppelt identifies the instruction in 2:13–3:7 as "station codes" instead of household codes and provides a helpful survey of research (*I Peter,* 162–79). Recent scholarship, in particular, has located the origin of such codes in Aristotelian teaching, something Goppelt does not emphasize.

[30] Balch, *Let Wives Be Submissive.* Cf. Elliott, *1 Peter,* 504–7.

[31] These references are from Michaels, *1 Peter,* 122.

[32] Ibid.

[33] H. von Lips sees the household code in 1 Peter as similar in many respects to Titus and maintains that the code in 1 Peter and Titus represents a tradition that is parallel to what is found in Colossians and Ephesians ("Die Haustafel als 'Topos' im Rahmen der urchristlichen Paränese: Beobachtungen anhand des 1. Petrusbriefes und des Titusbriefes," *NTS* 40 [1994]: 261–80).

[34] Ibid., 109.

[35] J. H. Elliott, *A Home for the Homeless: A Sociological Exegesis of 1 Peter, Its Situation and Strategy* (Philadelphia: Fortress, 1981), 110–12, 213–18; see Elliott, *1 Peter,* 104–7. For Elliott's discussion of household codes see *Home for the Homeless*, 208–20. Balch and Elliott engage in a dialogue with each other in a volume titled *Perspectives on 1 Peter;* see J. H. Elliott, "1 Peter, Its Situation and Strategy: A Discussion with David Balch," *Perspectives on 1 Peter* (Macon: Mercer University Press, 1986), 61–78; D. L. Balch, "Hellenization/Acculturation in 1 Peter," ibid., 79–101. C. H. Talbert tries to split the difference, seeing some truth in the view of both Elliott and Balch ("Once Again: The Plan of 1 Peter," ibid., 146–48). Elliott continues to maintain that there is no indication in the letter of assimilation to secular values, whereas Balch persists in seeing such a theme. P. Achtemeier sides with Elliott, though he rejects Elliott's view that the readers are political exiles ("Newborn Babes and Living Stones: Literal and Figurative in 1 Peter," in *To Touch the Text: Biblical and Related Studies: J. A. Fitzmyer Festschrift* [New York: Crossroad, 1988], 218–22). B. L. Campbell suggests that the term "cultural adaptation" is preferable to "cultural assimilation" or "acculturation" (*Honor, Shame, and the Rhetoric of 1 Peter,* SBLDS 160 [Atlanta: Scholars Press, 1998], 126, n. 91). Bechtler raises four objections to Balch's view: (1) the language expressing the difficulty between believers and their opponents is too general to indicate a focus on the role of slaves and women; (2) the words to slaves function paradigmatically for all believers; (3) the "stereotyped" words to wives suggest they are not framed to counter specific criticisms; and (4) such a theory gives too much prominence to the household code in 1 Peter, which is confined to only a few verses (*Following in His Steps*, 104, n. 196). Bechtler asserts that the author of 1 Peter argues that believers are "neither fully within society nor completely removed from it" (p. 118).

their lives to please other human beings but to please God. Pryor advances still a third interpretation, arguing that the exhortations are given because they represent God's will.[36] Believers fulfill what God expects when they submit to those in authority. When we examine the evidence in 1 Peter, we find some evidence to support all three, for they are not necessarily mutually exclusive. Peter exhorted believers to behave in a certain way because it is God's will, but at the same time he anticipated that it would quell some of the objections and misrepresentations of unbelievers and lead some to repentance and salvation. Yet we can also see that such godly living would bind the community together as one that uniquely lives to please the Lord.

(1) Submit to the Government (2:13–17)

[13]Submit yourselves for the Lord's sake to every authority instituted among men: whether to the king, as the supreme authority, [14]or to governors, who are sent by him to punish those who do wrong and to commend those who do right. [15]For it is God's will that by doing good you should silence the ignorant talk of foolish men. [16]Live as free men, but do not use your freedom as a cover-up for evil; live as servants of God. [17]Show proper respect to everyone: Love the brotherhood of believers, fear God, honor the king.

How should believers respond to the social structures of the day? Since God is their Lord, should they ignore human and governmental institutions? Peter argues here that believers should submit to the emperor and those governing authorities appointed by him. They are to submit to governing authorities because of their relationship to God, for in obeying the government they carry out God's will. Further, by doing good in the public square they will contradict those who claim that believers practice evil. Peter did not see human authorities as ultimate. Christians obey governing authorities because such obedience is God's will. Hence, the supreme authority for Peter was not the emperor but God himself. Further, in v. 16 believers are to submit as those who are free in Christ and as slaves of God, and not from a subservient spirit. Peter only cautioned that their freedom should not become a pretext for evil. The section concludes with four imperatives in v. 17. Believers are to show respect and honor to all people, while a special affection for fellow believers is to be displayed. Only God is to be feared, but this does not rule out honor for the emperor.

2:13 The central theme of this section is found in the first word, "submit" *(hypotagēte)*. The idea that believers should be subject to governing authorities is a standard part of New Testament ethical exhortations (cf. Rom 13:1,5; Titus 3:1). The parallels to Rom 13:1–7 have led some scholars to see literary dependence, but the differences are as great as the simi-

[36] J. W. Pryor, "First Peter and the New Covenant (II)," *RTR* 45 (1986): 47.

larities. For instance, Peter did not explicitly say authorities are ordained by God, and nothing is said about paying taxes, both of which are prominent themes in Romans 13. The similarities probably are better explained in terms of common Christian tradition.

Some scholars define "submit" to refer to "deference" or "respect" rather than obedience.[37] It is lexically difficult, however, to wash the concept of obedience out of "submit."[38] Indeed, in 1 Pet 3:5–6 Peter glided from the verb "submit" in v. 5 to "obey" in v. 6 without any hint of discomfort. The idea of willing obedience (or failure to submit) is evident in a number of texts: Jesus' submission to his parents (Luke 2:51), refusal to submit to God's law (Rom 8:7), refusal to submit to God's righteousness, the church's submission to Christ (Eph 5:24), the need to be subject to God (Jas 4:7), and the submission of younger ones to elders (1 Pet 5:5). Other examples could be adduced, but the main point is clear. Michaels and Achtemeier criticize the translation "submit" by implying that it involves "total submission"[39] and "unquestioning obedience to whatever anyone, including governing authorities, may command."[40] Their interpretations confuse context with lexicography. Whether or not submission involves "unquestioning obedience" cannot be determined by the term but by context. Translations like "defer" or "be considerate of" are simply too weak to convey the meaning of the word. The injunction to submit does not rule out exceptions, for God is the ultimate authority.[41] They illegitimately use this point, however, to diminish the force of the command. Peter gave a command that represents a general truth, that is, he specified what Christians should do in most situations when confronting governing authorities. Believers should be inclined to obey and submit to rulers. We will see, however, that the authority of rulers is not absolute. They do not infringe upon God's lordship, and hence they should be disobeyed if they command Christians to contravene God's will.

The injunction to submit is not to "every authority instituted among

---

[37] Cf. Michaels, *1 Peter,* 124; Achtemeier, *1 Peter,* 182; Campbell, *Honor, Shame, and the Rhetoric of 1 Peter,* 110.

[38] Rightly Grudem, *1 Peter,* 135–37. See also E. Kamlah, "'ΥΠΟΤΑΣΣΕΣΘΑΙ in den neutestamentlichen 'Haustafeln,'" in *Verborum Veritas: Festschrift für Gustav Stählin zum 70. Geburtstag* (Wuppertal: Brockhaus, 1970), 240–41. Cf. also the helpful discussion in Elliott, *1 Peter,* 487. Richard's translation "recognize one's association with, relationship to, or duty toward" does not capture the call for submission that is contained in the term (*Reading 1 Peter, Jude, and 2 Peter,* 111). A. B. Spencer wrongly implies mutuality when she describes submission as "respectful cooperation with others" ("Peter's Pedagogical Method in 1 Peter 3:6," *BBR* 10 [2000]: 110).

[39] Michaels, *1 Peter,* 124.

[40] Achtemeier, *1 Peter,* 182.

[41] It was recognized early that there were exceptions. See Andreas in *James, 1–2 Peter, 1–3 John, Jude,* ACCS (Downers Grove: InterVarsity, 2000), 92.

men" (NIV) or "every human institution" (RSV, NRSV, NASB) but "to every human creature" *(pasē anthrōpinē ktisei).* The word "creature" refers to human beings or creation (Mark 16:15; Rom 1:25; Col 1:23; cf. also *Jdt* 16:14; *Tob* 8:5,15). No basis exists for defining it as "human institution." Some commentators therefore conclude that Peter exhorted believers to submit to every human being,[42] using this argument as well to modify the meaning of the verb "submit."[43] The interpretation offered fails to account for the context in which the command is given. Peter immediately defined "every authority" with the phrases "whether to the king, as the supreme authority, or to governors" (vv. 13–14). When Peter gave the exhortation, he reflected only upon governing authorities, not every single person.[44] Yet we must also explain the reason why these authorities are called human creatures. The reason is not hard to seek. The emperor cult was popular in Asia Minor, and Christians doubtless felt social pressure to participate. Peter reminded his readers at the outset that rulers are merely creatures, created by God and existing under his lordship. A fine balance is maintained, however, in that believers still have a responsibility to submit to these authorities. Their submission, however, is not obsequious or mindless. Believers are to submit "for the Lord's sake" *(dia ton kyrion),* which is likely a reference to Jesus Christ.[45] They obey the injunctions of governing authorities ultimately because of their reverence for and submission to the Lord. We have an implication here that the ruling powers should be resisted if commands were issued that violated the Lord's will. It is impossible to imagine that one would obey commands that contravened God's dictates "for the Lord's sake."

Seeing an allusion to the emperor cult is justified since the "king" *(basileus)* who has authority *(hyperechonti)* is almost surely a reference to the emperor (cf. John 19:15; Acts 17:7).[46] This interpretation is reflected in the NRSV, "For the Lord's sake accept the authority of every human institution, whether of the emperor as supreme." If another king is intended, whether David, Herod, or someone else, they are typically named or context specifies that the king of the Jews or Messiah is in mind.[47]

2:14 When Peter said "every authority" (v. 13), he meant both the

---

[42] So Kamlah, "ΥΠΟΤΑΣΣΕΣΘΑΙ," 237; Richard, *Reading 1 Peter, Jude, and 2 Peter,* 111.

[43] So Cranfield, *I & II Peter and Jude,* 74; Michaels, *1 Peter,* 124; Achtemeier, *1 Peter,* 182.

[44] Cf. N. Brox, *Der erste Petrusbrief,* EKKNT, 2d ed. (Zürich: Benziger/Neukirchen-Vluyn: Neukirchener Verlag, 1986), 119.

[45] So Michaels, *1 Peter,* 124. Contra Kelly, *Peter and Jude,* 109; Richard, *Reading 1 Peter, Jude, and 2 Peter,* 111–12.

[46] So Michaels, *1 Peter,* 125.

[47] Cf. Matt 1:6; 2:1,2–3; 14:9; 27:11,29,37,42; Luke 1:5; John 1:49; 12:13; 18:33,37,39; 19:14, 19,21; Acts 7:10,18; 12:1; 13:22; 25:13; 2 Cor 11:32.

emperor and governing authorities under the emperor. The word "governors" *(hēgomosin)* is not intended to be specific since it can include procurators, proconsuls, and officials who collect revenues.[48] Believers should submit not only to the highest authority (the emperor) but to all those who are in authority. When Peter spoke of governors as "sent by him," it is tempting to read this in light of Rom 13:1–7, where it is clear that God ordains ruling authorities.[49] Such an interpretation is unlikely here since the nearest and hence natural antecedent is the word "king," representing the emperor.[50] Governors, in other words, are commissioned by and under the authority of the emperor and are to be obeyed as his representatives.

The purpose of ruling authorities is then explained: the punishment of evildoers and the praise of those who do what is right.[51] Doing right here means that Christians behave as good citizens, that they do what is honorable in the world's eyes.[52] Peter hardly intended to say that rulers always fulfill such a purpose. He was quite aware from the Old Testament that rulers may resist God and his will (e.g., Pharaoh and Nebuchadnezzar). The persecution of believers indicates that rulers may be involved unjustly in oppressing believers (cf. 3:14,16; 4:14,16). Furthermore, Peter and early Christians could hardly forget that Christ was unjustly condemned under Pontius Pilate or that James was put to death by Herod Agrippa (Acts 12:2). Even the most oppressive governments, however, hold evil in check to some extent, preventing society from collapsing into complete anarchy. The ideas here are quite similar to Rom 13:3–4, though Peter did not identify the ruling authority as "God's servant."

Modern people are not familiar with governments praising those who do what is right. The Romans, however, would erect statues, grant privileges, or commend in other ways those who helped the community.[53] Still, evidence is lacking that Peter encouraged wealthy readers to engage in public benefaction. He addressed all believers and did not particularly focus on the well-to-do.[54] All believers should do what is right and strengthen the social

---

[48] Goppelt, *I Peter,* 185, n. 31; Achtemeier, *1 Peter,* 183, n. 53.

[49] So E. Best, *1 Peter,* NCB (1971; reprint, Grand Rapids: Eerdmans, 1982), 114; F. V. Filson, "Partakers with Christ: Suffering in First Peter," *Int* 9 (1955): 407.

[50] Rightly Kelly, *Peter and Jude,* 109; Michaels, *1 Peter,* 125–26; Achtemeier, *1 Peter,* 183.

[51] Luther remarks that Christians are to avoid taking vengeance, but the civil authorities have the responsibility of punishing evil actions (*Commentary on Peter & Jude,* 118).

[52] S. Légasse, "La Soumission aux Autorités d'après 1 Pierre 2.13–17: Version Spécifique d'une Parénèse Traditionelle," *NTS* 34 (1988): 388.

[53] Cf. B. W. Winter, "The Public Honouring of Christian Benefactors: Romans 13.3–4 and 1 Peter 2.14–15," *JSNT* 34 (1988): 87–103; Goppelt, *I Peter,* 185–86; Achtemeier, *1 Peter,* 184; Campbell, *Honor, Shame, and the Rhetoric of 1 Peter,* 112.

[54] Rightly Bechtler, *Following in His Steps*, 89, n. 153. Cf. also McKnight, who observes that nothing else is said in 1 Peter about doing things "for the civic good" (*1 Peter,* 147, n. 15).

fabric. Rulers help maintain order in society by commending good citizens.[55]

2:15 Peter now explains why believers should submit, arguing that they should do so "because" (*hoti*, "for," NIV) "it is God's will." The word "thus" *(houtōs)* is omitted by the NIV, but it is crucial for unpacking the meaning of the verse. Literally the Greek reads, "Thus is the will of God." The question that must be answered is whether "thus" is retrospective or prospective. Most English versions take it as prospective, and in this case we could translate the verse, "Because the will of God is that you should silence the ignorance of foolish people by doing good." If "thus" is retrospective, the verse should be translated, including the main verb of v. 13, "Submit because thus [the command to submit] is the will of God, with the result that you will silence the ignorance of foolish people by doing good." Achtemeier rightly argues that the latter option is correct.[56] It fits with the word *hoti,* meaning "because." The word "thus" *(houtōs)* is typically retrospective (cf. 1 Pet 3:5). By submitting to government, Christians demonstrate that they are good citizens, not anarchists. Hence, they extinguish the criticisms of those who are ignorant and revile them. Such ignorance is not innocent but culpable, rooted in the foolishness of unbelievers. To refer to unbelievers as foolish is no denigration of their intellectual capacities. Peter hearkened back to Proverbs, where the foolish are morally debased. They are foolish because they do not fear the Lord and walk in his ways (Prov 1:7), and hence their ignorance is culpable.[57] Such people will be silenced by the good deeds of Christians. The participle "doing good" *(agathopoiountes)* is instrumental, emphasizing how unbelievers are silenced.

We should note again that there is no conception of believers doing whatever a government enjoins. Indeed, Peter used the same verb *(agathopoieō)* in acknowledging that believers may suffer while practicing what is right (1 Pet 3:17). He did not envision society and governmental structures as always siding with believers or inevitably commending them for their good behavior. His point was that the good behavior of Christians will minimize slanderous attacks on believers, revealing that charges of moral debilitation have no basis. Opponents will be discovered to be animated by hatred, lacking any objective ground for their criticism of believers. Perhaps there is also the hint here that some would see the good conduct of believers and glorify God by believing in the gospel (cf. 1 Pet 2:12),

---

[55] Calvin observes that even tyrannical governments provide some measure of order in society (*Catholic Epistles*, 83).

[56] Achtemeier, *1 Peter,* 185; so also Elliott, *1 Peter,* 494. For the alternate view see Michaels, *1 Peter,* 127.

[57] Cf. E. G. Selwyn, *The First Epistle of St. Peter,* 2d ed. (Grand Rapids: Baker, 1981), 173; Beare, *First Peter,* 117; Kelly, *Peter and Jude,* 111.

though this point is not made explicitly here.

2:16 Peter was not merely concerned about the outward actions of believers but also the motivations that inform their submission. Three phrases explain the standpoint from which Christians should operate in subordinating themselves to governing authorities. In each case the implied verb is "submit" from v. 13 rather than "live" as the NIV renders it.[58] The Greek text lacks a verb, and hence as interpreters it must be supplied. First, they are to submit "as free people" (NRSV, *eleutheroi*).[59] Believers have been ransomed by Christ's blood (1:18–19) and are no longer subject to the futile lifestyle characteristic of this world.[60] Hence, the submission of believers is never servile or rendered out of weakness. Second, as free people they are not to use their freedom as an excuse to indulge in evil. Genuine freedom liberates believers to do what is good. Those who use freedom as license for evil reveal that they are not truly free since a life of wickedness is the very definition of slavery. Christians should never respond to the dictates of government slavishly, but they should obey out of strength and because of their freedom (cf. Matt 17:24–27). Third, believers should submit "as servants *[douloi]* of God." The word "servants" also could be rendered "slaves." Believers do not enjoy unrestricted freedom. Their freedom is exercised under God's authority. In fact, genuine freedom is experienced only by those who are God's slaves. One is either a slave of sin or a slave of God (cf. Rom 6:15–23). True liberty, according to the New Testament, means that there is freedom to do what is right. Hence, only those who are slaves of God are genuinely free. Believers are called upon to live under God's lordship, obeying the government as God's servants.

When we consider the freedom of believers and their subservience, ultimately, to God alone, it is evident that the government does not enjoy carte-blanche authority. Peter did not envision Christians submitting to government regardless of the circumstances, even if ruling authorities prescribe what is evil.[61] The ultimate loyalty of Christians is to God, not Caesar. They are liberated from fearing Caesar, and hence they do not feel compelled to do whatever he says. Believers are God's servants first, and thereby they have a criterion by which to assess the dictates of government.

---

[58] Michaels wrongly connects the clauses in v. 16 with v. 17 (*1 Peter,* 128). It is more natural to take the ὡς clauses with what precedes rather than what follows.

[59] Gundry wrongly posits a dependence on the Jesus tradition found in Matt 17:26–27 ("*Verba Christi,*" 340–41; "Further *Verba,*" 230; so also G. Maier, "Jesustradition im 1. Petrusbrief," in *Gospel Perspectives: The Jesus Tradition outside the Gospels,* vol. 5 [Sheffield: JSOT Press, 1984], 91–92). Best is more convincing in this instance ("Gospel Tradition," 110–11). Maier also sees an allusion to Matt 22:15–22 (p. 92).

[60] Against Elliott ἐλεύθεροι does not refer to the social and legal status of those addressed (*1 Peter,* 496).

[61] Luther recognized this long ago (*Commentary on Peter & Jude,* 123).

Ordinarily believers will submit to the commands of ruling authorities, for in the normal course of life governments punish evil behavior and reward good conduct. The inclination and instinct of believers, then, will be submission to government. Peter wanted to avoid anarchy and a kind of enthusiasm that rejects any human structures. Nevertheless, if governments prescribe what is evil or demand that believers refuse to worship God, then believers as slaves of God must refuse to obey.

2:17 The section concludes with four commands. Two of the commands remind us of Prov 24:21, "Fear the Lord and the king," though Peter reserved fear for God alone.[62] The command to "honor" *(timaō)* begins and concludes the list, but this is obscured by the NIV since in the first instance they translate the verb "show proper respect" and in the last case "honor." The NRSV more closely reflects the Greek here, "Honor everyone. . . . Honor the emperor." Interestingly, the first imperative is in the aorist tense, and the remaining three are all present tense imperatives. Some have tried to explain this by seeing the first command as summarizing the remaining three,[63] but it is unsatisfying to say that the command to fear God fits under the "all" *(pantas)* of "honor everyone" (NRSV).[64] Peter did not place God on the same plane as the others mentioned in this verse, for fearing God is fundamental and primary and hence cannot be equated with the honor due to all. Peter specifically distinguished one's attitude toward God ("fear") from one's attitude toward the emperor ("honor"). The verbs "honor," "fear," and "love" simply do not mean the same thing. It is preferable, then, to take each command separately, so that we have four distinct injunctions in the verse.[65]

What is the significance of the first command being in the aorist tense *(timēsate)* rather than the present tense? At first glance it is tempting to conclude that the following verbs "love" *(agapate)* and "fear" *(phobeisthe)* may have different tenses because of the nature of the verbs.[66] That is, "love" and "fear" are in the nature of the case ongoing attitudes. One could respond, of course, that the same is true of "honor." Most important,

---

[62] E. Best wrongly suggests that Peter introduced a different "verb to preserve the rhythm of his sentence" ("I Peter II.4–10—A Reconsideration," *NovT* 11 [1969]: 274), but he fails to see that fear is directed only to God in 1 Peter.

[63] So Campbell, *Honor, Shame, and the Rhetoric of 1 Peter,* 121–23; T. W. Martin, *Metaphor and Composition in 1 Peter,* SBLDS 131 (Atlanta: Scholars Press, 1992), 204–5; S. E. Porter, *Idioms of the Greek New Testament*, BLG 2 (Sheffield: JSOT Press, 1992), 54, 227; S. Snyder, "1 Peter 2:17: A Reconsideration," *FNT* 4 (1991): 211–15.

[64] Rightly E. Bammel, "The Commands in I Peter II.17," *NTS* 11 (1964–65): 280; Elliott, *1 Peter,* 498; Légasse, "1 Pierre 2.13–17," 384.

[65] Bammel proposes a chiasm ("I Peter II.17," 280). We can accept a chiasm if we see the injunctions at the beginning and the end as framing the entire verse (Elliott, *1 Peter,* 499).

[66] So N. Hillyer, *1 and 2 Peter, Jude,* NIBC (Peabody: Hendrickson, 1992), 80.

though, the verse concludes with the imperative "honor" *(timate)* in the present tense. Hence, any attempt to explain the variations in the tense by the meaning of the verbs fails since Peter used the same verb twice.[67] Indeed, it is difficult to come up with any satisfying explanation for the variation, for it is not evident why Peter would emphasize that the emperor should be honored in an ongoing way in contrast to all people. I conclude, therefore, that the difference in tense is not interpretively significant and that all four imperatives are generalizations that apply to one's entire life.[68]

The first imperative is the call to "honor everyone" (NRSV). Believers are to treat every person with dignity and respect since all human beings are created in God's image (Gen 1:26–27). Even sinners are to be accorded respect and honor as human beings. Interestingly, the same respect and honor that should be given to the emperor should be given to all human beings. Those with more power and dignity are not exalted over "ordinary" human beings. Michaels wrongly equates the verb "honor" with "submit," but the meanings of the verbs are quite different.[69] One should honor all people, but nowhere is it clearly taught that we should submit to all people. The word "submit" is used of hierarchical relationships. All human beings should be respected, but there is a special bond between fellow believers. Indeed, the union between fellow Christians is such that it is best described in terms of family, and hence we have the command to "love the brotherhood of believers" *(agapate adelphotēta).* The word "brotherhood" is only found in Peter in the New Testament, both here and in 1 Pet 5:9. It appears nowhere in the Greek Old Testament, though it is used seven times in the Maccabean writings (*1 Mac* 12:10,17; *4 Mac* 9:23; 10:3,15; 13:19,27). In the stresses and difficulties of life and the battle against fleshly desires (1 Pet 2:12), believers need to be reminded of the priority of love, of the need to love fellow members of the family.

The injunction to "fear God" is placed in contrast to honoring the king ("emperor," NRSV). Believers are to honor the king and show him respect because of his office, but they are not to fear him. Only God is to be feared (cf. 1:17). Peter may have been taking a swipe at the emperor cult here. Indeed, Peter was quite clear that his readers were not to fear other human beings (1 Pet 3:6,14) and that only God should be feared as the sovereign Lord. Goppelt notes that fear belongs only to God "because God alone determines existence and non-existence."[70] We are reminded again that ultimate loyalty belongs to God, not to the emperor, nor to husbands (1 Pet

[67] Contra Achtemeier, *1 Peter,* 187–88.

[68] So also P. H. Davids, *The First Epistle of Peter,* NICNT (Grand Rapids: Eerdmans, 1990), 103, n. 14.

[69] Michaels, *1 Peter,* 130.

[70] Goppelt, *I Peter,* 190.

3:6). The imperatives conclude with a call to honor the emperor. The literal word here is "king" *(basilea)* instead of "emperor" (NRSV). But as we noted in 2:13, the word "king" would certainly bring to mind the emperor to Peter's readers. Believers should continue to respect and honor the emperor, even though they are free citizens of God. Their freedom should not become a pretext for sin, as if they were free from giving the emperor the respect the office deserved.

(2) Slaves, Submit to Masters (2:18–25)

18Slaves, submit yourselves to your masters with all respect, not only to those who are good and considerate, but also to those who are harsh. 19For it is commendable if a man bears up under the pain of unjust suffering because he is conscious of God. 20But how is it to your credit if you receive a beating for doing wrong and endure it? But if you suffer for doing good and you endure it, this is commendable before God. 21To this you were called, because Christ suffered for you, leaving you an example, that you should follow in his steps.

22"He committed no sin,
and no deceit was found in his mouth."

23When they hurled their insults at him, he did not retaliate; when he suffered, he made no threats. Instead, he entrusted himself to him who judges justly.
24He himself bore our sins in his body on the tree, so that we might die to sins and live for righteousness; by his wounds you have been healed. 25For you were like sheep going astray, but now you have returned to the Shepherd and Overseer of your souls.

Peter continued the household code by enjoining slaves to submit to their masters, even if the masters are wicked people. The exhortation is addressed to slaves, but slaves function as examples for all Petrine Christians, and so the principle enunciated applies to all believers.[71] The motivation for the exhortation is given in v. 19. Those who endure suffering from masters while doing what is good will be rewarded by God. Given the emphasis on the eschatological reward in 1 Peter, the reward in view here is probably the end-time gift of salvation. Verse 20 explains v. 19 in more detail. Those slaves who endure punishment because they have sinned will not receive any approval from God. Only those who do what is good and experience suffering will be rewarded by God. Peter began v. 21 by reminding believers that they have been called to suffer, and he immediately turned to Christ as an example to be imitated. Therefore the suffering of believers may be like Christ's in that it will lead some unbelievers to repentance and conversion. The subsequent verses are richly informed by the Servant Song of Isaiah 53. Verse 21 also calls attention

---

[71] So L. Thurén, *Argument and Theology in 1 Peter: The Origins of Christian Paraenesis,* JSNTSup 114 (Sheffield: Academic Press, 1995), 140; Brox, *Der erste Petrusbrief,* 128.

to the distinctive nature of Christ's suffering, for he suffered "for you," implying his substitutionary work on the cross. It seems the exemplary quality of Christ's suffering is emphasized in vv. 22–23, while his atonement for sinners is featured in vv. 24–25. According to vv. 22–23, Christ did not suffer for wrongdoing since he was sinless. When he was criticized and threatened, he did not retaliate but entrusted himself and the whole situation into God's hands. Verses 24–25 advance the argument in that they focus on the unique character of Christ's suffering. His death was on behalf of his people so that he bore their sins on the cross. The purpose was to free people from sin so that they would live righteously. In v. 25 Peter reminds the readers that previously they were wandering from God like errant sheep, but now, by virtue of Christ's death as the Suffering Servant, they have returned to him as their Shepherd and Overseer.

TO RECEIVE A REWARD (2:18–20). **2:18** Peter began by exhorting believers to submit to the government (2:13–17). Now he turns to the responsibility of slaves.[72] People became slaves by being captured in wars, kidnapped, or born into a slave household. Those facing economic hardships might choose to sell themselves into slavery in order to survive. Many slaves lived miserably, particularly those who served in the mines. Other slaves, however, served as doctors, teachers, managers, musicians, artisans, and could even own other slaves. It would not be unusual for a slave to be better educated than the master. Those who are familiar with slavery from the history of the United States must beware of imposing our historical experience on New Testament times since slavery in the Greco-Roman world was not based on race and American slave owners discouraged education of slaves. Still, slaves in the Greco-Roman world were under the control of their masters, and hence they had no independent existence.[73] They could suffer brutal mistreatment at the hands of their owners, and children born in slavery belonged to masters rather than the parents who gave them birth. Slaves had no legal rights, and masters could beat them, brand them, and abuse them physically and sexually. J. A. Harrill remarks: "Despite claims of some NT scholars, ancient slavery was not more humane than modern slavery."[74] Slaves could purchase their freedom in the Greco-Roman world with the help of their masters, a procedure called manumission. Manumission, however, was available mainly for urban slaves, and most slaves had no hope of being manumitted.[75]

---

[72] On the nonretaliation theme in 1 Peter see M. H. Schertz, "Nonretaliation and the Haustafeln in 1 Peter," in *The Love of Enemy and Nonretaliation in the New Testament* (Louisville: Westminster/John Knox, 1992), 258–86.

[73] See S. S. Bartchy, "Slavery: NT," *ABD* 6.66.

[74] J. A. Harrill, "Slavery," *DNTB,* 1125.

[75] Ibid., 1126.

Just as citizens are to submit to the government, so slaves are commanded to submit to their masters.[76] A word should be said here about the common New Testament admonitions that slaves should submit to masters (cf. Eph 6:5–9; Col 3:22–25; 1 Tim 6:1–2; Titus 2:9–10; Philemon). Modern people often ask why New Testament writers did not criticize the institution of slavery or advocate its overthrow. The latter was completely unrealistic for the fledgling New Testament church in the Roman Empire. The young churches would be fighting the consensus of the Greco-Roman world, and hence any such attempt would be doomed to futility. Why was there not criticism of the practice? Again we must remember that New Testament documents address readers in the situation in which they live. Railing against slavery would not be of any help to ordinary Christians, for, as noted, the dissolution of slavery was out of the question. Furthermore, New Testament writers were not social revolutionaries (cf. 1 Cor 7:17–24). They did not believe that overhauling social structures would transform culture. Their concern was the relationship of individuals to God, and they focused on the sin and rebellion of individuals against their Creator. New Testament writers therefore concentrated instead on the godly response of believers to mistreatment. Peter fits this paradigm nicely, for he admonished his readers to respond in a godly way to persecution and oppression.

If enough individuals are transformed, of course, society as a whole benefits and the Christian faith begins to function as a leavening influence. We are keenly aware from history that Christians have too often failed to live righteously, and yet we may fail to see that the Christian faith also has been a force for good in Western civilization. History demonstrates the impact of Christian faith on social structures. One of the consequences, under Christian influence, was the eradication of slavery. Christians, of course, have inflicted evil on others throughout the centuries as well. As sinners we have left a legacy that is disappointing. A realistic appraisal of history, however, includes both the evil and the good that Christians have accomplished.

It is crucial to note that the New Testament nowhere commends slavery as a social structure. It nowhere roots it in the created order, as if slavery is an institution ordained by God. The contrast with marriage is remarkable at this very point. God ordained the institution of marriage, but slavery was invented by human beings. The New Testament regulates the institution of slavery as it exists in society, but it does not commend it per se. Hence, Peter's words on slavery should not be interpreted as an endorsement for the system, even if he does not denounce the institution.

---

[76] The word δεσπότης is used elsewhere of slave owners (cf. 1 Tim 6:1–2; Titus 2:9). Bechtler thinks non-Christian masters are in view (*Following in His Steps,* 165). They probably were the majority, but we cannot rule out the possibility that a few of the masters were believers.

Most scholars think the participle "submitting" *(hypotassomenoi)* is imperatival here.[77] Others suggest that the participle depends on the imperatives in v. 17 and should be construed as instrumental.[78] The problem with this latter view, however, is that it is difficult to see *how* the participle could relate to all four imperatives in v. 17. It hardly makes sense to say, "Love the brotherhood by submitting to pagan masters." In this case, therefore, we should simply construe the participle as an independent imperative, in which slaves are enjoined to submit themselves to their masters. The submission is to be carried out "with all respect." The Greek literally says "with all fear" *(en panti phobō)*. The NIV's "with all respect" and the NRSV's "with all deference" suggest that a proper attitude toward the master is in view.[79] But this interpretation is unlikely, and the NIV should have retained the meaning of fear. In every instance in 1 Peter fear is directed toward God, not human beings (1 Pet 1:17; 3:2,6,14,16).[80] In fact, Peter spoke against fearing human beings in 3:6 and 3:14. The phrase "conscious of God" in 2:19 also constitutes evidence for this view. The reason slaves are to submit to masters is because of their relationship with God. Hence, we have evidence that masters are not to wield absolute authority over slaves. If they commanded slaves to violate God's will, then slaves are obligated to disobey, even if they suffer because of their disobedience.[81]

Ordinarily, however, believing slaves will do what their masters dictate. Peter applied the injunction to submit to both good and kind masters and masters who are "harsh" *(skoliois)*. The word "harsh" is not the best translation, for the emphasis is on the moral bankruptcy of some masters (cf. Acts 2:40; Phil 2:15).[82] The evil of slavery is reflected in Seneca's criticism of

---

[77] E.g., Kelly, *Peter and Jude,* 116; Michaels, *1 Peter,* 138; D. Daube, "Participle and Imperative in I Peter," in E. G. Selwyn, *The First Epistle of St. Peter,* 2d ed. (Grand Rapids: Baker, 1981), 482–83; S. Snyder, "Participles and Imperatives in 1 Peter: A Re-examination in the Light of Recent Scholarly Trends," *FNT* 8 (1995): 197.

[78] Cf. C. Bigg, *The Epistles of St. Peter and St. Jude,* ICC (Edinburgh: T & T Clark, 1901), 142; Achtemeier, *1 Peter,* 194. Campbell maintains that the subsequent participles depend on all of 2:11–17 rhetorically and on ἀπέχεσθαι in 2:11 grammatically (*Honor, Shame, and the Rhetoric of 1 Peter,* 124).

[79] So also J. W. C. Wand, *The General Epistles of St. Peter and St. Jude,* WC (London: Methuen, 1934), 79–80; Grudem, *1 Peter,* 125.

[80] Rightly K. H. Schelke, *Der Petrusbriefe—Der Judasbrief,* HTKNT (Freiburg: Herder, 1980), 80; Bigg, *Epistles of Peter and Jude,* 142; Beare, *First Peter,* 121; Kelly, *Peter and Jude,* 116; Michaels, *1 Peter,* 138; Achtemeier, *1 Peter,* 195; Davids, *First Peter,* 106. Contra Brox, *Der erste Petrusbrief,* 131.

[81] Calvin rightly saw that there were exceptions to the injunction that slaves should submit to their masters (*Catholic Epistles*, 86).

[82] The term σκολιός in the OT denotes those who are wicked and considered to be morally bankrupt (Deut 32:5; Ps 77:8; Prov 2:15; 4:24; 8:8; 16:26,28; 21:8; 22:5,14; 23:3; 28:18; Job 9:20; cf. *Wis* 1:3).

harsh masters: "You may take (a slave) in chains and at your pleasure expose him to every test of endurance; but too great violence in the striker has often dislocated a joint, or left a sinew fastened in the very teeth it has broken. Anger has left many a man crippled, many disabled, even when it found its victim submissive" (*Ira* 3.27.3).[83] Harrill argues, however, that "such calls to kindness toward slaves were not criticisms of the institution but of its abuse by arrogant masters not abiding by Stoic ideals. These statements calling for humane treatment of slaves analogous to modern calls against cruelty toward animals were articulated to strengthen the institution, not abolish it."[84] Believers cannot opt out of obeying masters who are wicked and disreputable. Peter was scarcely saying that Christian slaves should participate in evil or follow a corrupt master in an evil course of action. His point was that slaves cannot exempt themselves from doing what a master says, even if the master is wicked. A word about how this would relate today will illustrate Peter's meaning. A secretary cannot refuse to type a letter for a manager simply because the manager is an evil person. Refusal to type the letter would be defensible only if the contents of the letter are evil.

2:19 In v. 18 slaves are called on to submit, and now Peter explains why ("for," *gar*) such submission should be practiced. The reason believers should submit is that such obedience is "commendable." What did Peter mean when he said it is "commendable"? We should note that the literal Greek word used is "grace" *(charis)*. Before answering the question on the meaning of the term "commendable" *(charis),* we need to examine the meaning of the verse in context. It seems that v. 19 states the general principle, and v. 20 explains or unpacks the principle in more detail. The principle articulated in v. 19 is that those who suffer unjustly are rewarded by God. In v. 20 Peter explained more fully what he meant. He remarked that those who are punished while doing wrong have no reason to congratulate themselves since they are simply receiving what they deserve. On the other hand, those who suffer while doing good and who endure such mistreatment will receive a reward from God. Verses 19–20 are marked by an inclusio, for v. 19 begins with the statement "this is grace" (literal translation), and v. 20 concludes with "this is grace in God's sight" (literal translation).[85] We are instructed by the inclusio to interpret the two verses together. It should also be noted that the injunction given to slaves becomes a model by which believers should respond to injustice, and hence what is

---

[83] I owe this reference to Elliott, *1 Peter,* 521.

[84] Harrill, "Slavery," 1125.

[85] So Michaels, *1 Peter,* 142; Achtemeier, *1 Peter,* 196.

said here is not applicable only to slaves.[86] The use of the word "one" (RSV, *tis*) also indicates that the instructions relate to believers in their various situations.[87]

Now we return to the question posed above. What is commendable in the lives of believers? It is "grace" *(charis)* if they endure pain while suffering unfairly. That such suffering comes because of their Christian faith is clear from the phrase "conscious of God." The word for "conscious" *(syneidēsis)* usually refers to the "conscience" in the New Testament (e.g., Acts 23:1; 24:6; Rom 13:5; 1 Cor 8:7,10,12; 10:25,27–29; 1 Tim 1:5,19; 3:9), and it even has this meaning in 1 Pet 3:16,21.[88] In these latter two instances the adjective "good" is used to show that the conscience is in view. But in the verse we are examining the word "God" *(theou)* is an objective genitive, signifying a different contextual meaning that is suitably rendered "consciousness of God."[89] Slaves are commended, then, if they suffer pain because of their relationship with God, a relationship that causes them occasionally to deviate from what masters desire.[90] So what is the main point Peter was trying to communicate? He was saying that slaves who endure unjust suffering because of their relationship with God will be rewarded by God. What reward did he have in mind? He probably was speaking of the reception of the future inheritance described in such detail in 1:3–5.

Some might think Peter simply said that such suffering is "evidence of

[86] So Michaels, *1 Peter,* 135; Achtemeier, *1 Peter,* 196–97; D. W. Kendall, "The Literary and Theological Function of 1 Peter 1:3–12," in *Perspectives on 1 Peter* (Macon: Mercer University Press, 1986), 119; E. J. Richard, "The Functional Christology of First Peter," in *Perspectives on 1 Peter* (Macon: Mercer University Press, 1986), 137; Campbell, *Honor, Shame, and the Rhetoric of 1 Peter,* 143; Elliott, "Reception of 1 Peter 2:18–25," 188.

[87] In saying that Peter's advice functions as a model for all believers, I am not denying that Christians should seek justice in society by working within the legal system of the country in which they reside. Indeed, Paul demanded an apology from the authorities in Philippi when they wrongly beat Silas and him (Acts 16:35–40). We should not conclude, then, that Christians must absorb injustice even if there is legal recourse to redress grievances. The admonition to slaves, however, becomes a model for believers when they face unjust suffering and the civil authorities stand on the side of injustice. Christians who have recourse to a justice system in which they can appeal legal decisions must beware that they do not fall prey to bitterness and rage when courts rule against them. Injustice may be perpetrated by the very systems of justice. Such, after all, was the experience of Jesus himself as 1 Pet 2:18–25 discloses.

[88] Some commentators see such a meaning in this verse as well (e.g., Goppelt, *I Peter,* 197–98; Davids, *First Peter,* 107).

[89] The unusual meaning for συνείδησις provoked some scribes to make changes, but the genitive θεοῦ is strongly attested (cf. *TCGNT* 619).

[90] This interpretation of συνείδησις is the majority view. Cf. J. Moffatt, *The General Epistles: James, Peter, and Jude,* MNTC (New York: Harper & Brothers, 1928), 126; Best, *1 Peter,* 119; Wand, *Epistles of Peter and Jude,* 80; Kelly, *Peter and Jude,* 116–17; Cranfield, *I & II Peter and Jude,* 83; Michaels, *1 Peter,* 140; Achtemeier, *1 Peter,* 196. Contra Selwyn, *First Peter,* 177.

God's grace" in one's life. Two pieces of evidence, however, indicate that Peter thought of rewards rather than evidence of grace.[91] First, the word "credit" *(kleos)* is parallel to the word "grace" *(charis),* and it can be defined as "credit," "fame," or "glory" (cf. Josephus, *Ant.* 4.105,115; 19.223; *1 Clem.* 5:6; 54:3). It refers to the reward believers will inherit (cf. *1 Clem.* 5:6), demonstrating that "grace" here is not "evidence of grace" but the divine favor, blessing, and reward given to believers on the last day. Second, the argument in v. 19 is quite similar to Luke 6:32–35, and Peter adapted that tradition here.[92] Jesus in Luke argued that if people bestow love only on their friends, they are no different from unbelievers. What distinguishes believers from others is their love for enemies and sinners. Similarly, Peter insisted that suffering for doing wrong deserves no credit, but if one suffers for doing what is right, a reward is fitting. Interestingly, three times in Luke the reward believers would receive for showing love is conveyed through the word "grace" *(charis),* translated "credit" by the NIV (Luke 6:32–34). We see from this that the word "grace" can be a synonym for the word "reward." Indeed, in the conclusion of the paragraph (Luke 6:35) Luke shifted from "grace" to "reward" *(misthos),* showing that the two terms are roughly synonymous here. Indeed, in the Matthean parallel (Matt 5:46) to Luke 6:32 the word "reward" *(misthos)* is used instead of "grace" *(charis),* constituting another piece of evidence that "grace" means reward in Luke 6:32. To sum up, when Peter said it is "grace" for someone to endure suffering because of their relationship with God, his point was that those who suffer in such a way will receive a reward from God and that the reward in context is their eschatological inheritance—future salvation.

2:20 Verse 20 elaborates on v. 19, explaining ("for," *gar*) in what circumstances believers will be rewarded and in which circumstances they will not. Peter began with the instance in which believers endure pain,[93] but they do so because they have "done wrong" *(hamartanontes)* and as a conse-

---

[91] Cf. Elliott, "Reception of 1 Peter 2:18–25," 189–90; *1 Peter,* 518, 520; Selwyn, *First Peter,* 176; Kelly, *Peter and Jude,* 116; Michaels, *1 Peter,* 139–41; Campbell, *Honor, Shame, and the Rhetoric of 1 Peter,* 61; Bechtler, *Following in His Steps,* 191–92. Contra Goppelt, *I Peter,* 195–96, 199; Martin, *Metaphor and Composition in 1 Peter,* 59. Although Bechtler rightly sees that divine approval is in view, he wrongly sees a reference to present approval, but the focus is on future reward.

[92] For support of the idea that Peter used Jesus tradition here, see Gundry, "*Verba Christi,*" 341; "Further *Verba,*" 226; Best (in cautious agreement), "Gospel Tradition," 106; Michaels, *1 Peter,* 135–36, 139.

[93] The verb ὑπομενεῖτε in both instances is in the future tense. Some manuscripts have the present tense (e.g., 𝔓[72], ℵ[2], Ψ, 69, 323, 614, 945, 1241, 1739), but the future is preferable both on the grounds of external evidence (ℵ, A, B, C, P, 049, etc.) and as the harder reading (cf. Michaels, *1 Peter,* 134). The meaning remains unchanged in either case.

quence received beatings.[94] In such cases they will receive no reward from God since they are simply receiving what they deserve. On the other hand, if they endure suffering as a consequence of "doing good" (*agathopoiountes*)—a favorite word of 1 Peter (2:15; 3:6,17; cf. 2:14; 3:11,16; 4:19) and translated "do right" by the NIV here—then one will receive a reward ("grace," *charis*) from God.

TO IMITATE CHRIST (2:21–25). **2:21** What is the logical relationship between vv. 18–20 and v. 21, which begins with the words "for to this you have been called" (NRSV; the NIV omits the "for," *gar*)? The words "to this" *(eis touto)* point back to the believers' experience of suffering,[95] even though they do what is right. The word "called" *(eklēthēte),* as we have seen elsewhere (see commentary on 1:15; 2:9), refers to God's effectual call that results in the faith of believers.[96] So what Peter said here was that believers were called to experience their final reward (vv. 19–20) through enduring suffering.[97] Suffering, in other words, is not a detour by which believers receive the inheritance to which they were called. It is God's appointed means for receiving the inheritance.[98]

Why are believers called to suffer in order to receive their final reward? The answer given is that this was also the way appointed for Jesus, the Messiah ("because Christ also suffered for you," NRSV).[99] It is likely that

---

[94] The word for "beaten" (κολαφιζόμενοι) is replaced by the more general "punish" (κολαζόμενοι), but the former is clearly original. Van Unnik argues from Greek parallels that the word "sinning" (ἁμαρτάνοντες) means "doing wrong" in a secular sense, not sinning against God ("1 Classical Parallel to I Peter II. 14 and 20," in *Sparsa Collecta: The Collected Essays of W. C. van Unnik. Part Two: I Peter, Canon, Corpus Hellenisticum, Generalia,* NovTSup 30 (Leiden: Brill, 1980), 106–10.

[95] Supporting the idea that εἰς τοῦτο points backward are Wand, *Epistles of Peter and Jude,* 81; Michaels, *1 Peter,* 142; Achtemeier, *1 Peter,* 198; Elliott, *1 Peter,* 523. Grudem, on the other hand, thinks τοῦτο refers to trusting God (*1 Peter,* 128).

[96] E.g., D. E. Hiebert, "Following Christ's Example: An Exposition of 1 Peter 2:21–25," *BSac* 139 (1982): 33. There is, however, no allusion to baptism (contra Kelly, *Peter and Jude,* 118).

[97] T. P. Osborne rightly observes that Peter did not merely summon believers to suffer, "but to perseverance in good actions even when unjust suffering accompanies these actions" ("Guide Lines for Christian Suffering: A Source-Critical and Theological Study of 1 Peter 2,21–25," *Bib* 64 [1983]: 390).

[98] Many scholars have detected an early Christian hymn or creedal formula in vv. 21–25 (K. Wengst, *Christologische Formeln und Lieder des Urchristentums* [Gütersloh, Germany: Gerd Mohn, 1972]; Goppelt, *I Peter,* 204–7; R. Bultmann, "Bekenntnis- und Liedfragmente im ersten Petrusbrief," *ConBNT* 11 [1947]: 12–13; D. Hill, "'To Offer Spiritual Sacrifices . . .' [1 Peter 2:5]: Liturgical Formulations and Christian Paraenesis in 1 Peter," *JSNT* 16 [1982]: 53–56), but the support for this is not compelling (see Michaels, *1 Peter,* 136–37). Osborne rightly argues that the features of the text are better explained by the view that Peter applied the message of Isaiah 53 to his readers ("Guide Lines for Christian Suffering," 381–408). For cogent arguments against seeing a hymn here, see Elliott, *1 Peter,* 548–50.

[99] The word ὅτι is clearly causal here.

the phrase Christ "suffered for you" *(epathen hyper hymōn)* refers to the vicarious sacrifice of Christ, especially since such an idea is explicitly taught in v. 24 and is clearly taught in 3:18.[100] By implication Peter may have been suggesting the unique benefits of Christ's death. Achtemeier, however, doubts that this idea is intended, for the word "also" *(kai),* wrongly omitted by the NIV, demonstrates that the logic of the verse is as follows: Christ *also* suffered for you, as you now suffer for him.[101]

Supporting this interpretation are the words immediately following. Christ's suffering functions as an example to believers. They are to follow his pattern and endure suffering in this present age. The word "example" *(hypogrammon)* is used of children who trace over the letters of the alphabet in order to learn to write the letters correctly. Christ's suffering functions as an example for this purpose *(hina),* so that believers would "follow in his steps." As Christ's disciples, believers are to suffer as he did, enduring every pain and insult received because of their allegiance to the Master.

Achtemeier rightly detects the emphasis on following Christ in his suffering, which is emphasized particularly in vv. 22–23. Still, the significance of the "also" is preserved without embracing his interpretation. We saw in 1 Pet 2:12 that the good conduct of believers while being reviled is intended to lead others to salvation. It is likely that such a theme is suggested here as well. Just as Christ's suffering led to the salvation of others, so too the unjust suffering of believers will draw some to faith in Christ. Believers are to suffer just as Christ also suffered, but Peter recognized and specifically taught that the suffering of Christ and believers is not comparable in every respect, in that Christ's substitutionary death is the sole basis of the relationship of believers with God (1:18–19; 2:24; 3:18). Further, he emphasized that Christ was sinless (1:20; 2:22–23), something that is not matched by any believer. Indeed, Christ's sinlessness is the basis upon which his death can function as a vicarious sacrifice for believers. The godly life of believers may win unbelievers to the faith, but Jesus' suffering and death are unique since he alone through his death atones for sin.

2:22 Peter now begins to elaborate on Jesus' exemplary suffering, depending significantly on Isaiah 53 in doing so.[102] His selection of Isaiah 53 is no accident since the focus in Isa 52:13–53:12 is the suffering of the

---

[100] A variant reading inserts ἀπέθανεν ($\mathfrak{P}^{81}$, ℵ, Ψ, 623, 2464, and some others), but both internal (the theme of suffering in 1 Peter) and external evidence ($\mathfrak{P}^{72}$, A, B, C, 33, 81, 614, 1739, and others) support the term ἔπαθεν. It is also difficult to discern whether ὑμῶν, ὑμῖν are original or ἡμῶν, ἡμῖν. The second person is preferable, given the second person plural verb that follows, and the external evidence also inclines one to the reading in NA27.

[101] Achtemeier, *1 Peter,* 198–99.

[102] O. Cullmann thinks the servant of the Lord is fundamental in Petrine theology (*Christology of the New Testament* [Philadelphia: Westminster, 1963], 75).

Servant of the Lord. By the time Peter wrote, Isaiah 53 was firmly established in Christian tradition as a text that pointed to the suffering and exaltation of Jesus the Messiah (cf. Matt 20:28; Luke 22:37; Acts 3:13; Rom 4:25; 1 Cor 15:3; Phil 2:7). Peter alluded in this verse to Isa 53:9, and the only variation is the substitution of the word "sin" *(hamartian)* for "lawlessness" *(anomian)*. Perhaps the word "sin" is used to harmonize the allusion with v. 24, where Isaiah 53 is again cited. In any case, the meaning is not affected. The distinctiveness of Jesus stands out here, for Peter was not merely saying that Jesus resisted sinning in suffering but that he never sinned. Jesus' sinlessness is widely attested in the New Testament (Matt 27:4; John 7:48; 8:29,46; 18:38; 2 Cor 5:21; Heb 4:15; 1 John 3:5). Peter's main purpose was to commend Jesus as an example. If Jesus as the servant of the Lord did not sin or use guile, despite suffering intensely as the righteous one, then believers should follow his example and refrain from sinning or using deceit when they are mistreated as Christ's disciples.

2:23 Verse 23 emphasizes that the sinlessness of Jesus was not easily attained. He did not live apart from the hostility and hatred of the world in an isolated bubble where he brooked no opposition. Rather he faced "insults" and severe suffering. Probably Peter thought of Jesus' whole ministry here but particularly his passion. Though we have no specific allusion to Isaiah 53, it is likely that we have a reference to Isa 53:7, which describes the servant as one who suffers in silence like a lamb. Jesus' silence in suffering is the most remarkable evidence of his nonretaliatory spirit since the urge for revenge can be almost unbearable when mistreatment takes place.[103] Further, in the ancient world people demonstrated their innocence by arguing passionately against accusers, and hence Jesus' silence reveals his confidence in God's vindication.[104] Jesus' lifestyle matched his own teaching, where love for enemies and a spirit of nonretaliation was central (cf. Matt 5:38–48).[105]

The NRSV captures the play on words of the first statement, "When he was abused, he did not return abuse." The same verbal root is used (*loidoroumenos* and *anteloidorei*, obscured in the NIV), showing that Jesus did not indulge in retaliation. Second, Jesus did not engage in threats while suffering. Even if physical harm cannot be inflicted on tormentors, it is tempting to intimidate them with words of future judgment, but Jesus refrained from doing so. Both of the main verbs are imperfect, expressing ongoing action in past time, demonstrating that the spirit of nonretaliation informed Jesus' entire life. What gave Jesus the strength to refrain from threatening and

---

[103] Achtemeier tries to distinguish the two by saying that the point of Isa 53:7 is silence rather than retaliation (*1 Peter,* 200), but the two themes belong together and should not be segregated.

[104] So Hill, "Spiritual Sacrifices," 55.

[105] See esp. J. Piper, *Love Your Enemies* (Grand Rapids: Baker, 1991).

abusing those who mistreated him? He "entrusted himself to him who judges justly." The verb "entrusted" *(paredidou)* is again imperfect, expressing ongoing activity that characterized Jesus' life and ministry and especially his passion. The NIV says that Jesus entrusted "himself," but the Greek text has no object, so scholars debate whether Jesus entrusted himself, his cause, his passion, or his enemies.[106] Since the object is unspecified, it would be a mistake to limit the object's sphere. Jesus kept "handing over" *(paredidou)* to God every dimension of his life, including the fate of his enemies.[107] In particular, he knew that God would judge rightly on the last day, both vindicating him and punishing his enemies if they refused to repent. The Scriptures nowhere teach that believers can refrain from retaliation because they become stoics in suffering and put on a brave face. Rather, believers triumph over evil because they trust that God will vindicate them and judge their enemies, putting everything right in the end (cf. Rom 12:19–20).[108] Jesus functions as an example for his disciples, for they too are to trust God, believing that he will ultimately reward them (see 2:19–20) and punish their enemies.

Peter also probably alludes here to Jeremiah's plea for justice and for God's judgment on his enemies in Jer 11:18–23. Jeremiah did not contradict the spirit of nonretaliation taught here, for it is precisely because Jeremiah could leave justice in God's hands that he was enabled to turn from personal retaliation. Hence, Jesus, like Jeremiah, was God's "gentle lamb" (Jer 11:18). The text in Jeremiah matches 1 Pet 2:23 in emphasizing that God judges righteously (*krinōn dikaia,* Jer 11:20), showing that God's justice includes both the vindication of his servant and the punishment of his enemies (cf. Jer 11:21–23).

2:24 Now the distinctiveness of Jesus' suffering and death comes to the forefront. Believers are to follow Christ in his suffering, but it must always be remembered that his suffering is unique and the basis of salvation for his followers. In the first clause Peter alluded to Isaiah 53. He actually alluded to three different verses in Isaiah 53, which can be translated from

---

[106] Defending "himself" are Bigg, *Epistles of Peter and Jude,* 146; Wand, *Epistles of Peter and Jude,* 82; Selwyn, *First Peter,* 179–80; his cause (Kelly, *Peter and Jude,* 121), his enemies (Michaels, *1 Peter,* 147).

[107] M. Dubis draws a connection between 2:23 and 4:19 because a number of similar terms and concepts are used in the two verses (*Messianic Woes in 1 Peter: Suffering and Eschatology in 1 Peter 4:12–19, SBL* 33 [New York: Peter Lang, 2002], 178–82). He concludes from this that 2:23 not only refers to Jesus entrusting himself to God but also to God's judgment of Jesus on the cross (cf. 2:24–25). Contra Dubis, v. 23 lacks any notion of God judging Jesus. Dubis overloads the verse in seeing such an idea. The substitutionary character of Jesus' death is communicated in vv. 24–25.

[108] For my understanding of these verses see T. R. Schreiner, *Romans,* BECNT (Grand Rapids: Baker, 1998), 673–76. This is contrary to Goppelt, who denies any reference to future judgment (*I Peter,* 212).

the Septuagint as follows: "He bears our sins" (*houtos tas hamartias hēmōn pherei,* Isa 53:4); "he will bear their sins" (*tas hamartias autōn autos avoisei,* Isa 53:11); "he bore the sins of many" *(autos hamartias pollōn anēnegken).* Compare this with a literal translation of 1 Pet 2:24: "He himself bore our sins" *(hos tas hamartias hēmōn autos anēnegken).* The word "our" in 1 Peter matches Isa 53:4; the word "himself" *(autos),* Isa 53:11;[109] and the past tense "bore," Isa 53:12. It is clear from these allusions that Jesus' death is the means by which sins are forgiven. Often the word "bore" *(anapherō)* is used of "offering" sacrifices (Heb 7:27; 13:15; Jas 2:21; 1 Pet 2:5; cf. Gen 8:20; 22:2; Exod 24:5; 29:18). We ought not to derive from the expression here that the cross is an altar to which Jesus carried up our sins.[110] Nor is it clear that the image of the scapegoat who was released in the wilderness is in mind (Lev 16).[111] In this instance the verb must mean "bore" rather than "offered" since the word "sins" is the object of the verb. The text does not say that "God offered Jesus" but that "Jesus bore our sins." Peter added that our sins were borne in Christ's body "on the tree." Peter's use of the word "tree" (*xylon;* cf. also Acts 5:30; 10:39; Gal 3:13) instead of "cross" contains an allusion to Deut 21:23. The idea that Jesus was cursed for the salvation of his people is probably implicit. Since Christ died for the sins of the people, it is fair to deduce that his death was substitutionary (cf. 3:18).

The purpose of Christ's death *(hina)* was not merely to provide forgiveness but to empower his people to "live for righteousness." This is the main point of v. 24, not Christ's atoning death, for Peter emphasized here the purpose of his death. Righteousness *(dikaiosynē)* is not forensic here, as is evident from its connection with the verb "live" *(zēsōmen).*[112] Living to righteousness becomes a reality by dying "to sins." The participle "departing from" (*apogenomenoi*—translated "die" by NIV) indicates how believers can live righteously. Peter envisioned freedom from the power of sin (cf. 4:1), a freedom that is purchased at Christ's death (cf. 1:17–19 for a similar argument).[113] The verse begins, then, with the basis upon which believers are forgiven: Christ's atoning death. Peter then emphasized the purpose of

[109] Peter's dependence on Isaiah probably explains the shift from the second person to the first person here. A few manuscripts, not surprisingly, insert the second plural, but the textual evidence overwhelmingly supports the first person plural, and it also represents the harder reading.

[110] Contra Schelke, *Der Petrusbriefe—Der Judasbrief,* 85.

[111] See Kelly's helpful comments on these matters (*Peter and Jude,* 122–23). Cf. also Elliott, *1 Peter,* 532.

[112] Rightly Michaels, *1 Peter,* 149; Achtemeier, *1 Peter,* 202–3.

[113] Michaels rightly argues that in using the word ἀπογενόμενοι Peter did not use the metaphor of death as Paul did in Romans 6. The participle here means "departing from" (*1 Peter,* 148–49). Cf. also Selwyn, *First Peter,* 181; Kelly, *Peter and Jude,* 123; Elliott, *1 Peter,* 535. Osborne thinks it means "die" in this context ("Guide Lines for Christian Suffering," 400–401).

his death: so that believers will live a new kind of life.

The verse concludes with another allusion to Isaiah 53, here to v. 5. The wording is quite close to the Septuagint. The first person plural verb has been changed to a second person plural, and the relative pronoun "whose" *(hou)* has been substituted for "his" *(autou)*.[114] Peter spoke of being healed by Christ's wounds, and the wounds probably refer by metonymy to his death, though it is just possible that every dimension of the suffering leading to death is involved, including scourging. The reference to wounds would speak to the situations of slaves who were threatened by physical abuse.[115] In any case, it would be a mistake to limit what Peter said to Christ's scourging. Was Peter referring to forgiveness of sins here or physical healing? Even though Isa 53:5 is used in Matt 8:17 in reference to Jesus' healing ministry, we can be quite sure that forgiveness of sins is the subject here. Nothing else in the context points to physical healing. The first part of v. 24, which refers to Jesus' bearing our sins, clearly points to forgiveness, and the content of v. 25 (see below) also implies forgiveness when it speaks of those who have returned to their shepherd and overseer.[116]

2:25 The "for" *(gar)* connecting vv. 24–25 indicates that the healing in v. 24 is from the punishment deserved for wandering in v. 25, demonstrating that the healing involves forgiveness of sins.[117] The reference to wandering as sheep hearkens back to Isa 53:6. The major difference is again the shift from the first plural to the second plural. The conversion of the readers is indicated by the word "you have returned" *(epestraphēte)*. Another allusion to Isaiah probably exists here, for in 6:10 Isaiah speaks of those who "return and I will heal them" (translated from the LXX, *epistrepsōsin kai iasomai autous*).[118]

The combination of "return" and "heal" is another piece of evidence that the healing in view involves the forgiveness received at conversion. Believers are no longer lost sheep but "have returned to the Shepherd and Overseer of your souls." We are reminded again of the uniqueness of Jesus' life and suffering. The moral goodness of the lives of believers should shine as an example to unbelievers (cf. 2:18–21) and draw them to a saving knowledge of God. And yet all those who are now believers were once condemned before God. Only Christ lived a sinless life, and he atoned for sins

---

[114] Support for the latter by a number of manuscripts is an example of assimilation to Isa 53:5.

[115] So McCartney, "The Use of the Old Testament in the First Epistle of Peter," 93.

[116] Cf. Michaels, *1 Peter,* 149–50; Goppelt, *I Peter,* 214–15; Kelly, *Peter and Jude,* 124.

[117] The MT and some other significant manuscripts (𝔓[72], C, P, Ψ, 33, 1739) support the reading πλανώμενα. The masculine plural πλανώμενοι is to be preferred (א, B, 1505, and some others) since the neuter plural was likely a correction to fit with πρόβατα.

[118] This allusion is noted by Michaels, *1 Peter,* 150; cf. Achtemeier, *1 Peter,* 204. Dubis detects an allusion to the shepherd, wandering, and return motifs in Ezekiel 34 (*1 Peter 4:12–19,* 57–58).

by his substitutionary death. With the words "Shepherd and Overseer," Peter reminded his readers that their ruler is not the emperor or slave owners but Christ himself. Christ is likely the shepherd here rather than the Father since only Christ is called a shepherd in the New Testament.[119]

The word "Shepherd" designates the leader and ruler over the souls (i.e., whole persons) of those in the church. The emphasis is not on Christ's tenderness, which often comes to our minds with the word "shepherd" but his authority. This is confirmed by the word "Overseer" *(episkopos)*. Elsewhere in the New Testament the term "overseer" refers to those who had authority in churches (Acts 20:28; Phil 1:1; 1 Tim 3:2; Titus 1:7). Here it refers to Christ as the ultimate "Overseer," who rules over the church. Conversion involves returning to Jesus Christ as ruler and lord.

(3) Wives, Submit to Husbands (3:1–6)

[1]Wives, in the same way be submissive to your husbands so that, if any of them do not believe the word, they may be won over without words by the behavior of their wives, [2]when they see the purity and reverence of your lives. [3]Your beauty should not come from outward adornment, such as braided hair and the wearing of gold jewelry and fine clothes. [4]Instead, it should be that of your inner self, the unfading beauty of a gentle and quiet spirit, which is of great worth in God's sight. [5]For this is the way the holy women of the past who put their hope in God used to make themselves beautiful. They were submissive to their own husbands, [6]like Sarah, who obeyed Abraham and called him her master. You are her daughters if you do what is right and do not give way to fear.

Peter concentrated in the household code on those in the relationship who have less power. For instance, masters are not addressed at all, and wives receive an exhortation of six verses, whereas husbands are addressed in one verse. It is probably also the case that the "weaker" member of the pair is addressed because their vulnerable stance is representative of the church as a whole. Just as slaves and wives lived under the rule of masters and husbands, so too the Petrine believers were subject to persecution from other members of their cultural circle. Achtemeier may be correct in suggesting that the exemplary role of slaves and wives, which fits the suffering in the Petrine churches, explains why masters are not addressed at all and husbands are instructed in one verse.[120]

Wives are enjoined to submit, and it is evident from v. 1 that the wives of unbelievers are particularly in view, although it is likely that all wives are in

[119] Matt 26:31; Mark 14:27; John 10:2,11–12,14,16; Heb 13:20; cf. John 21:15–17; Rev 7:17. But see Osborne, who thinks the reference is possibly to the Father ("Guide Lines for Christian Suffering," 403–5).

[120] Achtemeier, *1 Peter,* 54–55; so also Elliott, *1 Peter,* 559. It does not follow, then, that slaves and women are addressed because of their large numbers. Contra Michaels, *1 Peter,* 122.

view as well.[121] Peter hoped that submission and godly behavior would become the means by which unbelieving husbands would be converted to the Christian faith. In vv. 3–4 Peter gave advice that was quite typical for moralists in the Greco-Roman world. Wives should repudiate expensive attire and ostentatious and expensive hairstyles and jewelry. God desires inner beauty consisting of a gentle and quiet spirit. The exhortation to wives is supported in vv. 5–6 by an appeal to godly women of the Old Testament era. Such women obeyed and respected their husbands and focused on inner adornment. Peter concluded by saying that the women of the Petrine community were truly daughters of Sarah if they pursued a life of goodness and conquered any fear of others.

3:1 Peter continued to address various segments of the church, concentrating on those with less power, and so now he turns to wives, introducing the discussion with the words "in the same way" *(homoiōs).*[122] The term does not suggest that the relationship between wives and husbands is like that of slaves and masters. Instead, it should be understood as "a connective" meaning no more than the conjunction "and."[123] The address is not to women in general but to wives as the words "your own husbands" (NASB, *tois idiois andrasin*) demonstrate. Wives are exhorted to submit *(hypotassomenai)* to their husbands, just as citizens should submit to ruling authorities (2:13) and slaves to their masters (2:18).[124] Voluntary submission is in view here.[125] Husbands do not have the responsibility to ensure that wives submit to them. The participle "submitting" (translating literally) functions as an imperative here.[126] It is difficult to see, against Achtemeier, how the participle could modify the imperatives in 2:17, for the latter verse is quite distant from the present verse.[127] Peter did, however, continue in the vein of the instructions in 2:13–25.[128]

Peter's words are addressed in particular to wives with unbelieving husbands—"even if some of them do not obey the word" (NRSV). Still, all wives are addressed, not only those with disobedient husbands, for the

---

[121] So Richard, *Reading 1 Peter, Jude, and 2 Peter,* 126.

[122] The word is lacking in a few manuscripts, but it is original and supported by most of the manuscript tradition.

[123] So Michaels, *1 Peter,* 156. J. R. Slaughter thinks the term has a broader frame of reference, indicating that wives, like slaves, should submit for the sake of the Lord ("Submission of Wives [1 Pet. 3:1a] in the Context of 1 Peter," *BSac* 153 [1996]: 68); so also Elliott, *1 Peter,* 553.

[124] The comparison to the previous two texts is not established by ὁμοιώς but the repetition of the verb "submit."

[125] Slaughter, "1 Pet. 3:1a," 70; Spencer, "Peter's Pedagogical Method in 1 Peter 3:6," 109.

[126] So many commentators, e.g., Brox, *Der erste Petrusbrief,* 142

[127] Achtemeier, *1 Peter,* 209. Spencer holds a view similar to Achtemeier's ("Peter's Pedagogical Method in 1 Peter 3:6," 111).

[128] For the status of women in the Greco-Roman world, see Achtemeier, *1 Peter,* 206–7.

words "even if" (NASB) may indicate that the majority of the husbands were believers.[129] The NIV wrongly translates with the words "do not believe" instead of "do not obey," but the verb in question *(apeitheō)* focuses on disobedience rather than unbelief.[130] In fact, it is a favorite term of Peter's. First Peter 2:8 also refers to disobedience to the word; 4:17, to those who disobey the gospel; and 3:20, to those who disobeyed during the days of Noah. The "word" *(logos)* here, as in 2:8, refers to the gospel. All disobedience, of course, stems from unbelief, but the emphasis here is on the rebellion of husbands who refuse to adhere to the gospel. Again the parallel to what is said about slaves is noteworthy, for just as slaves are to submit to morally bankrupt masters (2:18), so Christian wives are called on to submit to unbelieving husbands.

Many commentators argue that Peter's advice to wives should be understood within the same framework as his counsel to slaves.[131] In both cases he commends submission, but in neither instance does he endorse the patriarchal institution that enforces submission.[132] Wives are to submit to unbelieving husbands because this is the means by which husbands can be "won" *(kerdēthēsontai)* for the faith.[133] Peter knew, according to this view, that it would be futile to try to overturn the social structure of his day, and his primary concern was the conversion of unbelieving husbands, not the pursuit of female rights. Hence, submission is commended for the sake of the mission of the church, but Peter, these scholars insist, did not actually sanction the idea that wives should submit to their husbands. He addressed a particular situation in which he explained how wives should relate to *unbelieving* husbands.

---

[129] J. R. Slaughter, "Winning Unbelieving Husbands to Christ (1 Pet 3:1b–4)," *BSac* 153 (1996): 199; cf. Richard, *Reading 1 Peter, Jude, and 2 Peter,* 127. Bechtler argues that the admonitions are directed particularly to wives with unbelieving husbands (*Following in His Steps*, 166).

[130] It is not clear that the term implies active and overt opposition to the gospel (contra Balch, *Let Wives Be Submissive,* 99).

[131] E.g., Cranfield, *I & II Peter and Jude,* 88–89; Achtemeier, *1 Peter,* 208–11. Goppelt argues that submission is not part of the order of creation and contradicts the fundamental equality of women (*I Peter,* 218–19). It is required, he contends, because of custom. Kelly, on the other hand, thinks the command derives from the creation order (*Peter and Jude,* 127).

[132] For a helpful discussion of the view of wives and women in the culture of Peter's day, see Elliott, *1 Peter,* 553–58, 585–99. Contra Elliott, I believe Peter's words are normative for today's world.

[133] For the Jewish antecedents to the term, see D. Daube, "Κερδαίνω as a Missionary Term," *HTR* 40 (1947): 109–20. After the particle ἵνα we expect a subjunctive instead of the future κερδηθήσονται. Boyer shows, however, that the future and subjunctive overlap. Further, he rightly argues that the future does not suggest that the conversion of unbelieving husbands is guaranteed. We have a purpose here, not a promise (cf. Mark 14:2; Luke 20:10; Gal 2:4–5; 4:17, where indicatives after ἵνα are equivalent to subjunctives). See J. L. Boyer, "The Classification of Subjunctives: A Statistical Study," *GTJ* 7 (1986): 3–19.

It is certainly the case that the wives of unbelieving husbands are addressed in these verses, and their primary objective is to win their husbands to the Christian faith. Peter engaged in a play on words, saying that those who are disobeying "the word" *(logos)* may be converted "without words" (lit., "without a word," *aneu logou*) by their wives' behavior. By "without a word" meant wives should refrain from badgering their husbands about their need for conversion. The spoken words of wives had not had an effect, and so they were called upon to live out the gospel before their husbands. The primary influence on husbands will not be the speech of wives but their godly behavior. The word "behavior" *(anastrophē)* was a favorite of Peter's, summarizing the godly conduct required of believers (cf. 1:15; 2:12; 3:2,16 and by contrast 1:18).

We can agree, then, with those scholars who emphasize that Peter addressed specific circumstances. The question is whether we should infer from this text that wives should submit to husbands in today's world. Is Peter's advice limited to a missionary situation and a culture that is quite different from ours? Indeed, some would argue that in our culture such advice would hinder the mission of the church rather than enhance it. Achtemeier summarizes well the view of women among the educated in the Greco-Roman world: "Dominant among the elite was the notion that the woman was by nature inferior to the man. Because she lacked the capacity for reason that the male had, she was ruled rather by her emotions, and was as a result given to poor judgment, immorality, intemperance, wickedness, avarice; she was untrustworthy, contentious, and as a result, it was her place to obey."[134] What is remarkable about this list is that nowhere did Peter or the rest of the New Testament teach that women are inferior to men, that they are intellectually substandard, or that they are more prone to wickedness. Indeed, Peter emphasized that wives are coheirs with husbands of eternal life (1 Pet 3:7), implying the fundamental equality of men and women. The equality of men and women is also proclaimed in Paul's affirmation in Gal 3:28. The New Testament was countercultural, therefore, in promoting the equality of women. Indeed, Jesus' treatment of women was revolutionary in that he treated them with dignity and respect, and hence his stance toward women was paradigmatic for the early church.

The question, therefore, is not whether women are equal with men, for the New Testament is clear on this matter. The issue is whether such equality is compatible with the call for wives to submit to husbands. One answer, as we have seen, is to argue that such submission represents an accommodation to ancient culture for the purpose of evangelism. Such a reading of the text is certainly possible, and it might even be preferable if the only text

---

[134] Achtemeier, *1 Peter,* 206.

we had on this matter were in 1 Peter. When we read the Scriptures canonically, however, it is doubtful whether the accommodation view can be sustained. It is clear from Eph 5:22–33 that submission of wives to husbands is grounded in theology—in Christ's relationship with the church. It is not an accommodation to culture. The submission of wives to husbands mirrors the church's submission to Christ, and hence it should be accepted as a norm that transcends the culture of the first century.[135]

We should also note a crucial difference between slavery and the admonition given to husbands and wives. Slavery, as argued above, is an evil institution developed by human beings, while marriage, on the other hand, was instituted by God at creation. It does not follow, therefore, that those who believe in the submission of wives would also endorse slavery. We must be careful to observe the distinctions between the two institutions, so that we do not confuse the human practice of slavery with the institution of marriage that was ordained by God. It must also be said that Peter gave no indication that the submission of wives is a temporary accommodation to the culture of his day. He firmly rejects, as we have seen, the notion that women are unequal to men. Nor is there any indication that he equates submission with inequality.[136] The same Paul who trumpeted the equality of women in Gal 3:28 also commanded them to submit to their husbands in Eph 5:22–33 (cf. Col 3:18; Titus 2:4–5). Peter's words to women are remarkably similar, in that he teaches the equality of women (v. 7) and counsels submission (v. 1). It seems fair to conclude that differences in role or function do not cancel out equality. Men and women are equally made in God's image (Gen 1:26–27), have equal access to salvation (Gal 3:28), and share the same destiny (1 Pet 3:7). Similarly, the Son of God, Jesus Christ, is equal to the Father in essence, but he submits to the Father (1 Cor 15:28), revealing that he has a different role. The submission of wives, therefore, does not imply their inferiority. A different function does not suggest that they are lesser beings. Those who argue that a different function implies inequality betray a secular worldview that identifies worth with stature and the exercise of authority.

3:2 Verse 2 elaborates on what is involved in bringing unbelieving hus-

---

[135] Schelke rightly sees marriage as a creation ordinance (*Der Petrusbriefe—Der Judasbrief,* 88). It is interesting to note, given current debates, that Calvin believed husbands were the head of their wives and yet argued at the same time for mutual submission (*Catholic Epistles,* 147). He apparently believed that husbands were the authority in a relationship, but such authority did not mean that husbands did not concede to the wishes of their wives when such was fitting. That Calvin was not thinking of mutual submission in the same terms as modern egalitarians is clear by his immediately succeeding words, where he argued that sometimes parents should occasionally submit to children. Clearly, Calvin did not think that such occasional bending to the desires of children subverted the authority of parents.

[136] Rightly Slaughter, "1 Pet. 3:1a," 70.

bands to faith. Wives should not focus on speaking words to their husbands in attempting to persuade them to believe. Husbands are apt to be impressed with the Christian faith "as they observe your pure conduct" (my translation). Peter commended "seeing" *(epopteusantes)* rather than "talking" as the means by which wives should influence their husbands.[137] The same term for "seeing" also appears in 2:12, and in both verses Peter also used the word "conduct" or "behavior" (*anastrophē,* "lives," NIV in 3:2). Unbelieving husbands may be alienated by wives who constantly beg them to become Christians. A better course is to live a faithful Christian life, and as they see the transformation of their wives, they are more likely to be inclined to adopt the faith of their wives.

When Peter spoke of the "reverence of [the wives'] lives," it should be noted that the word translated "reverence" is not actually an adjective, but in the Greek we have a prepositional phrase "in fear" *(en phobō),* so that a literal translation would be "as they observe your pure conduct in fear." What should be emphasized here is that the fear is not directed to the husband, but as we saw in 2:18 (see commentary) "fear" in 1 Peter is always directed toward God.[138] Peter was not suggesting, therefore, that wives should fear their husbands (cf. 3:6), nor was he even suggesting that wives should respect their husbands (though Paul commended such in Eph 5:33). Instead, Peter's point was that the good conduct of wives should stem from their relationship with God. Slaughter rightly says that wives do not submit in order to satisfy a husband's vanity or to promote his reputation. Neither do they submit to show how godly they are, nor to avoid conflict, nor to impress the neighbors, nor to manipulate their husbands, and not even because she thinks he is wise. She submits because of her relationship with and trust in God.[139]

We can also infer from this that the submission of wives is not absolute. If husbands require wives to disobey moral norms or follow another religion, then wives should disobey.[140] The exception implied here would be extraordinarily important to Peter's readers, for wives were expected to adopt the religion of their husbands in the Greco-Roman world. Plutarch said: "A wife should not acquire her own friends, but should make her hus-

---

[137] The textual evidence is rather evenly divided between the present and aorist forms of the participle, but the meaning is not affected significantly in either instance. Perhaps the present participle stems from 2:12. I think it is doubtful that we should stress that the aorist participle emphasizes "after seeing." Moreover, the participle could be construed as causal, temporal, or as means.

[138] So also Beare, *First Peter,* 128; Best, *1 Peter,* 125; Michaels, *1 Peter,* 158; Achtemeier, *1 Peter,* 210; Schelke, *Der Petrusbriefe—Der Judasbrief,* 88; contra Slaughter, "1 Pet 3:1b–4," 207; Brox, *Der erste Petrusbrief,* 143.

[139] Slaughter, "1 Pet 3:1a," 72–73.

[140] Rightly Slaughter, "1 Pet 3:1b–4," 203.

band's friends her own. The gods are the first and most significant friends. For this reason, it is proper for a wife to recognize only those gods whom her husband worships and to shut the door to superstitious cults and strange superstitions."[141] The wives Peter addressed, then, would be considered socially radical in Peter's day since they had adopted a different religion from their husbands. They are encouraged to submit to their husbands wherever possible, but there are limits to their submission. Even if it causes their husbands displeasure, they should continue to be part of the church of Jesus Christ.

3:3 The NASB represents a literal translation of the verse, "Let not your adornment be merely [added for clarity] external—braiding the hair, and wearing gold jewelry, or putting on dresses." The admonition here is quite similar to what we find in 1 Tim 2:9–10. We should also note that it was common in the Greco-Roman world to admonish women to dress modestly instead of ostentatiously or seductively.[142] Writers such as Seneca, Dio Chrysostom, Juvenal, Plutarch, Epictetus, Pliny, and Tacitus wrote about this matter (cf. also *1 En.* 8:1–2; *T. Reu.* 5:1–5).[143] For instance, Juvenal writes, "There is nothing that a woman will not permit herself to do, nothing that she deems shameful, when she encircles her neck with green emeralds and fastens pearls to her elongated ears; there is nothing more intolerable than a wealthy woman" (*Satires,* 6.457–60). Juvenal goes on to say about the hairstyles of women, "So important is the business of beautification; so numerous are the tiers and storeys piled one upon another on her head" (*Satires,* 4.501–3). In Plutarch we find a negative assessment of outward adornment and then the statement, "It is not gold or precious stones or scarlet that makes her such [i.e., decorous], but whatever invests her with that something which betokens dignity, good behavior, and modesty" (*Mor., Con. pr.* 141E). What Peter wrote here, therefore, would not come as a shock to his readers. His admonition was in accord with the standpoint of many within the Greco-Roman world. Peter did not prohibit women from wearing their hair nicely or from wearing any jewelry at

[141] *Conj. praec.* 19, *Mor.* 140D (the translation is taken from Elliott, *1 Peter,* 557–58). So also Michaels, *1 Peter,* 157; Achtemeier, *1 Peter,* 211; Balch, *Let Wives Be Submissive*, 84–85; B. Winter, "'Seek the Welfare of the City': Social Ethics according to 1 Peter," *Them* 13 (1988): 93.

[142] See D. Scholer, "Women's Adornment: Some Historical and Hermeneutical Observations on the New Testament Passages," *Daughters of Sarah* 6 (1980): 4–5; Balch, *Let Wives Be Submissive*, 101–2. Campbell argues that the women in Peter's community were inclined to dress ostentatiously or seductively, and hence Peter responded to such a situation (*Honor, Shame, and the Rhetoric of 1 Peter,* 154).

[143] Seneca, *Ep., Ad Helv.* 16.3–4; *Benef.* 1.10.2; 7.9.4–5; Dio Chrysostom, *Or.* 7.117; Juvenal, *Satire* 6.457–63; 490–511; Plutarch, *Mor., Con. pr.* 141E; Epictetus, *Enchir.* 40; Tacitus, *Ann.* 3.53; Ovid, *Amor.* 3.130–49.

all.[144] He prohibited them from spending an excessive amount of money on their outward adornment or from wearing clothing that is seductive.[145] Indeed, the Greek literally forbids the wearing of clothing at all ("the putting on of garments," *hē endysis himatiōn*). Obviously, Peter was not recommending that women wear nothing at all. His point was that they should not wear clothing that is exorbitantly expensive or immodest. Neither is there any contextual warrant for the notion that such adornment is forbidden because it was associated with idolatry, even though braiding of hair was featured in the cults of Isis and Artemis of Ephesus.[146]

3:4 The adornment God desires is not external but internal. Wives should not focus on hairstyle, jewelry, and clothing but on who they are in relationship to God, on their "inner self" (lit., "the hidden person of the heart," *ho kryptos tēs kardias anthrōpos*). What matters to God is not what people look like on the outside but their godly character. An echo of 1 Sam 16:7 may be found here: "The LORD does not look at the things man looks at. Man looks at the outward appearance, but the LORD looks at the heart." Goppelt remarks, "'The hidden person' is not the inner side of the person, but the whole human being as it is determined from within."[147] In other words, what a person is on the inside does not remain hidden (as if Peter thought about some private and interior Christian life hidden from the world) but manifests itself in the way wives behave in everyday life. In particular, women should strive for "a gentle and quiet spirit" inasmuch as these qualities are "incorruptible" (*aphthartos,* cf. 1:4,23), whereas clothing, jewelry, and braided hair are transitory and will fade away. A "gentle" *(praus)* spirit is not only incumbent upon women but all believers (cf. Matt 5:5; 11:29; see esp. 1 Pet 3:16). "Quietness" *(hēsychios)* is also required of women in 1 Tim 2:11 and is linked with submission. Gentleness and a quiet spirit evidence the kind of godly behavior that will attract husbands to the faith, and they contrast with a verbal witness, which unbelieving husbands tend to view as irritating. The word "which" may refer back only to the word "spirit,"[148] but it likely includes the whole thought of v. 4.[149] Peter

---

[144] Hilary of Arles says, "There is nothing wrong with these ornaments in themselves, but they are unnecessary extras for the believer and should be avoided" (*James, 1–2 Peter, 1–3 John, Jude,* ACCS [Downers Grove: InterVarsity, 2000], 98).

[145] Note already the wise comments on this matter by Calvin, *Catholic Epistles*, 96. It does not follow necessarily from the exhortation that many wealthy women were in the churches (rightly Goppelt, *I Peter,* 221; contra Kelly, *Peter and Jude,* 129; Beare, *First Peter,* 129). Still, the exhortation implies that at least some of the women were upper class (so Davids, *First Peter,* 117–18).

[146] Rightly Balch, *Let Wives Be Submissive*, 101–2; Michaels, *1 Peter,* 160; Achtemeier, *1 Peter,* 212.

[147] Goppelt, *I Peter,* 221.

[148] Kelly, *Peter and Jude,* 130.

[149] So Beare, *First Peter,* 129–30; Best, *1 Peter,* 126; Achtemeier, *1 Peter,* 214.

emphasized that a focus on internal adornment is not only attractive to husbands but is also "of great worth in God's sight." The words "great worth" translate a term *(polyteles)* that comes from the financial realm, indicating that such godly qualities are "costly" (cf. Mark 14:3; 1 Tim 2:9; Josephus, *Ag. Ap.* 2.191; *J.W.* 1.605). Peter likely used this word to distinguish these qualities from the expensive clothing and ornamentation desired by women in the Greco-Roman world. His use of the term is another indication that he opposed ostentatious clothing, hairstyles, and jewelry instead of forbidding such things altogether.

3:5 Verses 5–6 provide an example from holy women of the past to encourage the women of the Petrine churches to submit to their husbands with a gentle and quiet spirit. These women are called "holy" *(hagiai)* because they lived in a way that was pleasing to God; they were set apart for his purposes (cf. Matt 27:52; Mark 8:38; Eph 3:5; 2 Pet 3:2).[150] The reference to Sarah suggests that the women in view were Sarah, Rebecca, Rachel, and Leah, just as the patriarchs were Abraham, Isaac, and Jacob.[151] The most important comment in the verse is that these women "put their hope in God" *(hai elpizousai eis theon).* This comment is instructive, for it informs us that these women did not submit to their husbands because they believed their husbands were superior to them intellectually or spiritually. They submitted to their husbands because they were confident that God would reward all those who put their trust in him. A major theme of 1 Peter is sounded here, for the eschatological hope brings consolation in persecution (1:3–9), and believers are to set their hope completely on the future revelation of Jesus Christ (1:13; cf. also 1:21; 3:15). Such hope characterized the lives of the women of old, for they continued to hope in God during the vicissitudes of human existence.[152] These holy women "used to adorn themselves" (NRSV, *ekosmoun heautas*) with the virtues of a gentle and quiet spirit (v. 4), and hence they showed that their focus was not on external "adornment" (v. 3, NASB, *kosmos*) but on that which is internal. We should note here the contrast between the two different kinds of adornment, and the imperfect tense of the verb, reflected in the words "used to," demonstrates that their adornment represented ongoing and habitual action in the past.

The next phrase is wrongly translated by the NIV as an independent clause, "They were submissive to their own husbands." The NRSV rightly sees that the participle is instrumental, explaining *how* the women adorned

---

[150] Achtemeier wrongly understands their holiness only in terms of their membership in the people of God, and not their behavior (*1 Peter,* 214). Such a reading misses the emphasis of the verse, for Peter focused on their character here, not their righteousness by faith.

[151] So Best, *1 Peter,* 126; Michaels, *1 Peter,* 164; Achtemeier, *1 Peter,* 214.

[152] Rightly Beare, *First Peter,* 130; Achtemeier, *1 Peter,* 215.

themselves, "by accepting the authority of their husbands."[153] A better translation would be "by submitting *[hypotassomenai]* to their own husbands." Peter meant, of course, that they submitted to their husbands with the gentle and quiet spirit extolled in v. 4.

3:6 Verse 6 becomes even more specific, for now Sarah, the wife of Abraham, is introduced as an example for the women of Peter's day. We should notice the logical connection between v. 5 and v. 6. The holy women of old "submitted" to their husbands "as" *(hōs)* Sarah "obeyed" *(hypēkousen)* Abraham. The comparison demonstrates that the word "submit" includes the idea of obedience (cf. Luke 2:51; Rom 8:7; 10:3; 13:1; 1 Cor 14:34, etc.).[154] Some object that obedience is an example but not a definition of submission.[155] Surely submission includes more than obedience, for the right spirit and attitude are also commended in v. 4. What must be noticed, however, is that nothing less than obedience is required. In other words, submission does not merely involve being considerate or adapting to one's husband.[156] It is crucial to note that obedience and submission are different in various spheres. Peter was hardly suggesting that wives submit and obey in the same way as children, for the relationship is between two adults. We also learn from Paul that mutuality also characterizes the marriage relationship (1 Cor 7:3–5). Reading the whole marriage relationship through the lens of submission is liable to distort significantly the Scriptures. Nevertheless, what cannot be washed away is the responsibility of wives to follow their husbands' leadership.

The example of Sarah's obedience cited is when she called Abraham "master" *(kyrios)*. What is interesting is that the text alluded to is Gen 18:12, and it reflects an off-hand comment by Sarah to the idea that she will become pregnant by Abraham. What Peter found remarkable was that she still referred to him with respect and dignity instead of merely calling him an old man (though she did note his age!). We see from this that even in casual situations Sarah respected Abraham's leadership, revealing thereby that her honor of him was part of the warp and woof of her life.[157] Hence,

---

[153] Supporting an instrumental participle is Achtemeier, *1 Peter,* 215.

[154] Dijkman fails to note this point in his discussion ("1 Peter," 267–68).

[155] So Achtemeier, *1 Peter,* 215, n. 138. Richard simply departs from the meaning of the term and offers the meaning "show respect" (*Reading 1 Peter, Jude, and 2 Peter,* 133). He provides no lexical evidence for his interpretation, and hence his interpretation is not credible.

[156] Goppelt recognizes the connection here (*I Peter,* 224, n. 44).

[157] McCartney makes the same point: "Although Gen 18:12 does not give in itself a direct example of Sarah's obedience, the fact that even in this negative instance in Sarah's life she referred to Abraham as 'my lord' would have indicated to Peter, and it did to his contemporaries, that submission was her *customary attitude* toward Abraham" ("The Use of the Old Testament in the First Epistle of Peter," 146–47; cf. also J. R. Slaughter, "Sarah as a Model for Christian Wives [1 Pet. 3:5–6]," *BSac* 153 [1996]: 360).

we do not find here an arbitrary exegesis foisted upon the text but a reflection of Sarah's true character.[158] Kiley and Spencer argue that Peter's words here should be interpreted in light of Genesis 12 and 20, where Sarah followed Abraham's advice even when it placed her in an unfavorable situation.[159] We can agree that Sarah's behavior in those chapters matched what Peter praised here, but the text clearly alludes to Gen 18:12.

The wives in the Petrine community have become Sarah's daughters if they imitate her godly behavior. The past tense verb "you have become" (NRSV, *egenēthēte*) is obscured by the NIV's "you are." The time of conversion was likely in Peter's mind, though some think Peter simply referred to the kind of character required of wives.[160] But how should we understand the two participles that follow? The NIV takes them as conditional, "if you do what is right and do not give way to fear."[161] The NRSV introduces a temporal idea, though it is also implicitly conditional, "as long as you do what is good and never let fears alarm you." Some scholars reject a conditional idea, arguing that such a notion does not fit with the idea of conversion in the past and violates the teaching that conversion is God's

---

[158] Contra Davids, who says that the exegesis here would satisfy Peter's readers, even though it violates contemporary standards of interpretation (*First Peter,* 121). Campbell goes even further, saying that Peter "seems to misapply her story" (*Honor, Shame, and the Rhetoric of 1 Peter,* 159). Sarah may have been amused at the prospect of having children at such an advanced age, but even in the midst of her laughter she referred to Abraham respectfully.

[159] M. Kiley, "Like Sara: The Tale of Terror Behind 1 Peter 3:6," *JBL* 106 (1987): 689–92. D. I. Sly's attempt to read the Petrine account in light of the exegesis of Philo and Josephus is less persuasive ("1 Peter 3:6b in the Light of Philo and Josephus," *JBL* 110 [1991]: 126–29). T. W. Martin rightly says about Sly's view that "she offers no proof that the author of 1 Pet relied upon such traditions" ("The TestAbr and the Background of 1 Pet 3,6," *JBL* 90 [1999]: 141). Spencer's interpretation bears similarities to Kiley's, for she also thinks Gen 12:11–20 is the likely background ("Peter's Pedagogical Method in 1 Peter 3:6," 113–18). She notes a number of parallels between 1 Peter and Genesis 12, such as Abraham and Sarah were aliens in Egypt, Sarah's beauty is noted, Abraham was disobedient to God's word in traveling to Egypt, and Sarah obeyed Abraham's instructions. Spencer's exegesis is suggestive; however, it is difficult to know if Peter intended a reference to exile or her external beauty when he typified Sarah's obedience to Abraham. Abraham, however, was not disobedient in the same sense intended in 1 Peter, for in Peter the husbands are clearly unbelievers, and so the parallel seems forced in this instance. Possibly there is an allusion to Sarah being an heir, but one wonders if Sarah's suffering is viewed as vicarious and if Abraham's prayer for Pharaoh is alluded to in 1 Pet 3:7. Contrary to Spencer we should note that the only clear allusion is to Gen 18:12. In discussing Kiley's view, Martin points out the problem with the view shared by him and Spencer. In appealing to Genesis 12 (and 20) they wander from the evidence of the text, supplying a background that is not clearly in view since Sarah never calls Abraham "lord" in these texts ("The TestAbr and the Background of 1 Pet 3,6," 140). Martin's own solution, that Peter draws on *T. Ab.,* cannot be clearly established (see his defense of the view on pp. 141–46).

[160] So Slaughter, "1 Pet. 3:5–6," 361; Elliott, *1 Peter,* 573. Again Kelly wrongly sees a "specific reference" to baptism (*Peter and Jude,* 131).

[161] Beare suggests a conditional clause but appears inclined to understand the participles as instrumental or manner (*First Peter,* 130–31).

work.[162] The participles could be construed as instrumental, "You have become her children by doing good and not fearing."[163] Or they could be understood as temporal, "You became her children when you did good and did not fear."[164] The conditional notion is most likely in context. A conditional element does not sit awkwardly with conversion in the past. In fact, there are many statements in the New Testament where a past conversion is noted and then a conditional statement follows (e.g., Rom 11:21–22; 1 Cor 6:9–11; Col 1:21–23; Heb 3:14). What Peter said here is not unusual at all. Peter followed the standard New Testament view that perseverance is needed to obtain eternal life (cf. 2 Pet 1:5–11). Those who are Sarah's children "do what is right" *(agathopoieō).*[165] The term "doing good" (literally) is a favorite of Peter's (2:15,20; 3:17; cf. 2:14; 3:11,16; 4:19), expressing the Christian character of believers. Not only should believers do good but they should "not give way to fear." An echo of Prov 3:25 may exist here.[166] In particular, wives of unbelieving husbands would be prone to fear their husbands, who could treat them rather harshly and perhaps even violently because of their faith.[167] Believers are exhorted to fear God (cf. 1:17; 2:17–18; 3:2), but any fear of human beings, even in persecution (3:16), is to be avoided. The implication is that believing wives will not always behave in a way that pleases their husbands because at times their loyalty to God will transcend their duty to submit to husbands. In such cases they are not to fear but hope in God, trusting that he will vindicate them on the last day. The response of women to oppression by unbelieving husbands is exemplary and paradigmatic for all believers, just as the behavior of slaves points to the way all believers should react to persecution.

(4) Husbands, Live Knowledgeably with Your Wives (3:7)

[7]Husbands, in the same way be considerate as you live with your wives, and treat them with respect as the weaker partner and as heirs with you of the gracious gift of life, so that nothing will hinder your prayers.

---

[162] Michaels, *1 Peter,* 166–67; Achtemeier, *1 Peter,* 216; van Unnik, "Good Works in I Peter," 100.

[163] So Bigg, *Epistles of Peter and Jude,* 153–54.

[164] Achtemeier, *1 Peter,* 216. Michaels sees them as imperative (*1 Peter,* 166–67). Goppelt says that they demonstrate they are God's children by doing good and not fearing (*1 Peter,* 224). T. Martin thinks the participles designate purpose ("The TestAbr and the Background of 1 Pet 3,6," 144).

[165] Michaels departs from the context of 1 Peter 3 in saying that all believers are children of Sarah (*1 Peter,* 166). Theologically the statement is unobjectionable, but it strays from Peter's purpose here.

[166] See Michaels, *1 Peter,* 167.

[167] Hence, unbelieving husbands seem to be the focus here (so Bechtler, *Following in His Steps,* 165).

Husbands are exhorted to treat their wives with knowledge, according to the will of God. Women are physically weaker, and the wise husband considers the biological difference between his wife and him in the relationship. Husbands should honor their wives because they are coheirs of the eschatological gift of life. Both husbands and wives can expect the same heavenly destiny. The seriousness of bestowing honor upon one's wife is evident, in that husbands who refuse to do so will find that their prayers are hindered.

3:7 Only one verse is addressed to husbands, presumably because Peter focused on those who were liable to experience oppression from authorities (whether rulers, masters, or husbands) rather than those who actually exercised authority.[168] As noted above, the conduct of the oppressed functions as an example for all the Petrine churches as they face persecution. Nevertheless, husbands are also addressed briefly in this verse. The words "in the same way" *(homoiōs)* do not suggest that husbands are to submit to wives, as people submit to rulers (2:13), slaves to masters (2:18), and wives to husbands (3:1). The connective is loose, indicating that a new group is addressed.[169] The New Testament nowhere counsels husbands to submit to wives, and such an idea is not implied here. Instead husbands are to (literally) "live together with them according to knowledge" *(synoikountes kata gnōsin).*[170]

The participle *synoikountes* should be understood as an imperative.[171] Most English versions translate the verse so that husbands are exhorted to be considerate and kind in their relationship with their wives.[172] Such a reading is not incorrect, but it shifts the focus slightly away from the meaning of the text. I understand the phrase "according to knowledge" *(kata gnōsin),* like "in fear" (literal translation) in 3:2 and "conscious of

---

[168] Bechtler observes that the admonition to husbands undermines Balch's view that the household code served an apologetic purpose (*Following in His Steps,* 167–68). Peter was scarcely calling on husbands to assimilate to cultural norms. Nor is it evident that we have a polemic here against wives who adopted an egalitarian agenda (rightly Elliott, *1 Peter,* 584).

[169] Even though Lea does not argue that husbands should submit to wives, he overreads the connective here ("I Peter—Outline and Exposition," 34). Elliott rightly observes that the connective is loose and that Peter would not be thinking of wives submitting to husbands (*1 Peter,* 574).

[170] Kelly sees a reference to sexual intercourse (so also McKnight, *1 Peter,* 186) in the term συνοικοῦντες (*Peter and Jude,* 132), but this is unlikely in context (cf. B. Reicke, "Die Gnosis der Männer nach I. Ptr 3:7," in *Neutestamentliche Studien für Rudolf Bultmann zu seinem siebzigsten Geburtstag,* 2d ed., BZNW 21 [Berlin: Töplemann, 1957], 299). The word can refer to sexual relations (Deut 22:13; 24:1; 25:5), or living with someone in marriage, without the emphasis being on sexual union (e.g., Gen 20:3; Judg 14:20; *2 Mac* 1:14; *Sir* 25:8,16; 42:9–10; Isa 62:5).

[171] Contra Achtemeier, *1 Peter,* 217, who, in effect turns it into imperative. Rightly Selwyn, *1 Peter,* 483; Goppelt, *I Peter,* 226; Michaels, *1 Peter,* 167.

[172] Bechtler thinks that husbands should know their wives are weaker vessels (*Following in His Steps*, 174–75).

God" in 2:19, to refer to the relationship of husbands to God.[173] Husbands, then, should live together with wives informed by the knowledge of God's will, of what he demands them to do.[174] The wife is described here as the "weaker vessel" (NASB; *asthenesterō skeuei*).[175] The word "vessel" can also refer to men (Acts 9:15; cf. Rom 9:21–23),[176] and the comparative form suggests that women are weaker than men.[177] In what sense are women "weaker"? Nothing else in the New Testament suggests that women are intellectually inferior,[178] nor is it clear that women are weaker emotionally, for in many ways the vulnerability of women in sharing their emotions and feelings demonstrates that they are more courageous and stronger than men emotionally. Nor did Peter suggest that women are weaker morally or spiritually than men.[179] Such a view would suggest that men are actually better Christians than women, which is not taught elsewhere in the Scriptures, nor is it evident in history. The most obvious meaning, therefore, is that women are weaker than men in terms of sheer strength.[180] Peter used the word for "female" or "woman" *(gynaikeios)* rather than "wife."[181] He directed attention to what is uniquely feminine about women, pointing husbands to the knowledge that God would require them to have of the female sex.

A husband who lives according to God's requirement shows "respect"

---

[173] So also Spicq, *Les Épîtres de Saint Pierre*, 123; D. Senior, "The Conduct of Christians in the World (2:11–3:12)," *RevExp* 79 (1982): 435–36; Achtemeier, *1 Peter,* 218. Contra Richard, who thinks the knowledge is the husband's superior intellectual ability relative to wives (*Reading 1 Peter, Jude, and 2 Peter,* 136–37). Nowhere do the canonical Scriptures teach that men are intellectually superior to women. Therefore Richard's interpretation should be rejected.

[174] Kelly correctly observes that husbands are not called upon to submit to their wives but to exercise their authority properly (*Peter and Jude,* 132).

[175] The first use of ὡς here is not concessive (contra Reicke, "Gnosis," 302).

[176] The meaning of the term in 1 Thess 4:4 is debatable, though I incline to the view that wives are mentioned there as well.

[177] Bigg, *Epistles of Peter and Jude,* 155; Wand, *Epistles of Peter and Jude,* 93; Grudem, *1 Peter,* 144; Achtemeier, *1 Peter,* 217.

[178] Contra Campbell, *Honor, Shame, and the Rhetoric of 1 Peter,* 164.

[179] Neither, contra Grudem, does he refer to being weaker in terms of delegated authority (*1 Peter,* 144).

[180] This view has an ancient pedigree. See Hilary of Arles in *James, 1–2 Peter, 1–3 John, Jude,* ACCS (Downers Grove: InterVarsity, 2000), 100. So also Kelly, *Peter and Jude,* 133; Cranfield, *I & II Peter and Jude,* 91; Michaels, *1 Peter,* 169; Achtemeier, *1 Peter,* 217; Davids, *First Peter,* 122–23; Hillyer, *1 and 2 Peter, Jude,* 98. Elliott agrees but then observes that modern science has since disproved Peter's contention (*1 Peter,* 577–78). Against Elliott, Peter referred here to brute strength and did not intend to say that men are stronger than women in every conceivable way. Luther suggests that women are weaker physically and emotionally (*Commentary on Peter & Jude,* 140).

[181] In this context, however, he thinks only of wives, not other female members of the household (contra Reicke, "Gnosis," 302; Achtemeier, *1 Peter,* 216).

(timēn) for his wife (and by extension to all women).[182] The reason he does so is that women are "heirs with you of the gracious gift of life," showing that women are fundamentally equal with men.[183] Bechtler says that the admonition to husbands to honor their wives is unique in Greco-Roman literature.[184] The language of heirs points toward the eschatological gift (cf. 1:4; 3:9) that both men and women who believe will receive on the last day.[185] Men should honor women because they share the same destiny—an eternal inheritance in God's kingdom.[186] Any suggestion that women will receive a lesser reward is repudiated. The "life" in the phrase "gift of life" should be understood eschatologically (cf. 3:10), referring to the life that will be ours in the coming age.[187] Husbands who ignore such a command will find that their prayers are hindered, which means that God will refuse to answer their prayers. God does not bless with his favor those who are in positions of authority and abuse those who are under them by mistreating them.[188] Perhaps this verse anticipates v. 12, where the Lord attends to the prayers of the righteous but turns away from those who practice evil.

---

[182] Cranfield mistakenly concludes that showing honor is equivalent to subordination (*I & II Peter and Jude,* 91). Surely husbands are to honor their wives as equals, but this is not the same as saying that husbands are to submit to wives, for the latter is never commanded in the NT.

[183] In some manuscripts we find the nominative συγκληρονόμοι (A, C, P, Ψ, MT) instead of the dative συγκληρονόμοις ($\mathfrak{P}^{72}$, $\mathfrak{P}^{81}$, $\aleph^{2}$, B, 33, 69, 232, 141, 1739). The external evidence supports the latter, and contextually it makes better sense to say that wives are coheirs instead of stressing that husbands are coheirs.

[184] Bechtler, *Following in His Steps*, 175.

[185] Reicke, "Gnosis," 303. Reicke (pp. 297–98) also defends the nominative συγκληρονόμοι instead of the dative συγκληρονόμοις.

[186] C. D. Gross argues, however, that the wives in view here probably are unbelievers, arguing that both grammar and the rest of the household code in 1 Peter (2:18–3:6) point to such a conclusion ("Are the Wives of 1 Peter 3.7 Christians?" *JSNT* 35 [1989]: 89–96). This interpretation is unlikely, for wives were almost surely in view when Peter spoke of those who are "coheirs." Gross thinks the shift from the singular to the plural makes this view "extremely awkward." But shifts from the singular to the plural are found elsewhere in exhortations to men and women (e.g., Eph 5:22–24,28; 1 Tim 2:8–15).

[187] The genitive should be construed appositionally, "grace that consists in life" (Michaels, *1 Peter,* 169; Achtemeier, *1 Peter,* 21; Beare, *First Peter,* 132; Kelly, *Peter and Jude*, 134; Elliott, *1 Peter,* 580). Elliott rightly remarks that Peter did not conclude from this that men and women are equal in every sense, and hence an egalitarian agenda cannot be read out of Peter's words.

[188] It is quite improbable that Peter was saying the prayers of both men and women would be hindered. Some commentators argue that Peter referred to men and women (see Calvin, *Catholic Epistles,* 100; Beare, *First Peter,* 132; Goppelt, *I Peter,* 228; Michaels, *1 Peter,* 171; Elliott, *1 Peter,* 581; Davids, *First Peter,* 123, n. 20 [possibly]; Schelke, *Der Petrusbriefe—Der Judasbrief,* 92).

(5) Conclusion: Live a Godly Life (3:8–12)[189]

[8]Finally, all of you, live in harmony with one another; be sympathetic, love as brothers, be compassionate and humble. [9]Do not repay evil with evil or insult with insult, but with blessing, because to this you were called so that you may inherit a blessing. [10]For,

"Whoever would love life
and see good days
must keep his tongue from evil
and his lips from deceitful speech.
[11]He must turn from evil and do good;
he must seek peace and pursue it.
[12]For the eyes of the Lord are on the righteous
and his ears are attentive to their prayer,
but the face of the Lord is against those who do evil."

The conclusion to all of 2:11–3:7 is now drawn in these verses.[190] Verse 8 in a chiasm (see p. 164) summarizes appropriate relationships in the community, emphasizing particularly the need for brotherly love.[191] Verse 9 addresses how believers respond to those who inflict evil upon them. They are not to respond by inflicting evil in return but by praying that God will bless their tormentors. The reason believers are called to bless others is so that they themselves will inherit the eschatological blessing of eternal life on the last day. The Old Testament citation commencing in v. 10 confirms that blessing others is necessary to receive eternal life, being linked to v. 9 by "for." The life and good days of v. 10 are nothing other than eternal life and the future inheritance. Those who wish to enjoy such must refrain from speaking evil, make a clean break with evil in their lives, and live in the realm of goodness. They must be people who seek out peace and live peaceably. Verse 12 confirms the interpretation proposed. The Lord's favor rests on those who are righteous, but he turns his face forever against those who practice evil.

3:8 The conclusion to all of 2:11–3:7 is introduced with the word "finally" *(telos).*[192] Now the whole community is addressed as "all of you"

---

[189] What we have here is not a summary of what precedes but a conclusion of 2:11–17 (Michaels, *1 Peter,* 174, though he identifies it as the conclusion of 2:18–3:7).

[190] J. J. J. van Rensburg argues that δὲ with τὸ τέλος signals the conclusion to 2:11–3:7 ("The Use of Intersentence Relational Particles and Asyndeton in 1 Peter," *Neot* 24 [1990]: 288).

[191] Bechtler argues that in these verses Peter modified and softened the hierarchical ethic of his day (*Following in His Steps*, 171–76). He is correct in seeing that the relationship between husbands and wives is to be leavened with love. In that sense we have a modification. But he puts on modern glasses when he says that there is an implicit critique of hierarchical social structures.

[192] Some scholars think the similarities between Pauline and Petrine paraenesis suggest the literary dependence of the latter upon the former when we compare a text such as Rom 12:9–17 with 1 Pet 3:8–12. Evidence for such dependence, however, is not compelling (cf. Selwyn, *First Peter,* 407–13; Piper, "Hope as the Motivation of Love," 218–19).

(pantes). It seems that Peter addressed relationships within the church in v. 8 and relationships with unbelievers in v. 9, though certainty on this matter is impossible.

In the Greek of v. 8 there are five adjectives without any verb. The NIV supplies the verb "live," which captures well the implied imperative.[193] Probably the implied imperative comes from the "to be" *(eimi)* verb, and the text would read, "You must be harmonious," etc. When we look at all five words together, we see that obeying these exhortations would lead to smooth relationships within the church (and with outsiders in most cases). The call to "harmony" *(homophrones)* is common in the New Testament, even though this term only appears here (cf. Rom 15:5; 1 Cor 1:10; 2 Cor 13:11; Phil 2:1–2; 4:2). Presumably this admonition and others would be unnecessary if churches were not prone to suffer from division and dissension. Believers are also to be "sympathetic" *(sympatheis),* caring deeply about the needs, joys, and sorrows of others (cf. Rom 12:15; 1 Cor 12:26). The admonition to brotherly love *(philadelphoi)*—"love as brothers" in the NIV—is an indication that Peter addressed relationships among believers. The family love of believers for one another was important for Peter (cf. 1:22; 2:17; 5:9 and 2:11; 4:12). Their common relationship with Christ inducts them into the same family, and one evidence of genuine Christian faith is a warm love for others as brothers and sisters (cf. also Rom 12:10; 1 Thess 4:9; Heb 13:1; 2 Pet 1:7). Believers are also to be full of compassion *(eusplanchnoi)* to those who are experiencing pain. In Eph 4:32 such compassion is rooted in the mercy experienced in the forgiveness of sins. Again, one of the marks of the Christian life is compassion (cf. 2 Cor 6:12; 7:15; Phil 1:8; 2:1; Col 3:12; Phlm 7,12,20; 1 John 3:17). Finally, believers are also summoned to be "humble" *(tapeinophrones)*.[194] Humility means, of course, that others are considered more important than oneself (Phil 2:3–4) and that pride does not fill one's life (cf. Acts 20:19; Rom 12:16; 2 Cor 10:1; Eph 4:2; Col 3:12; Jas 1:9; 4:6; 1 Pet 5:5). Humility was scorned in the Greco-Roman world, and hence the distinctiveness of Christian vision for the moral life emerges.[195] It seems that there is an ABCB′A′ pattern in this verse, so that the verse functions as a chiasm.[196]

---

[193] Against Achtemeier it is difficult to believe that the adjectives relate back to the imperatives in 2:17 (*1 Peter,* 222). Hence, the adjectives are imperatival (Davids, *First Peter,* 124), or there is an implied imperative ἐστέ.

[194] The Majority text reads φιλόφρονες ("courteous"), but the variant is clearly secondary.

[195] See Elliott, *1 Peter,* 605.

[196] Bauckham sees a chiasm in which v. 8 matches 11b, 9 = 11b, 9a = 11a, 9b = 10b, and 9c = 10a ("James, 1 Peter and 2 Peter, *Jude,*" 312).

A Harmony
B Sympathy
C Brotherly Love
B′ Compassion
A′ Humility

Harmony and humility belong together, for the primary means by which harmony is disrupted is pride and self-assertion. Sympathy and compassion are closely related and even hard to distinguish from each other. Brotherly love is the middle term, showing that it is the most important of all the virtues and that the other virtues are embraced in the call to love one another as a family.

3:9 If v. 8 focuses on relationships among fellow believers, it seems that v. 9 directs attention to how believers should respond to unbelievers who mistreat them, one of the central themes of 1 Peter.[197] On the other hand, it is possible that both believers and unbelievers are in view, and in any case the admonition remains the same. Those who inflict evil or hurl insults at believers should not be repaid in kind, as tempting as it might be to strike back. The use of the word "insult" *(loidoria)* hearkens back to 1 Pet 2:23, where the verbal root of the same word is used. When Jesus was "insulted," he did not respond in kind. The first part of the verse is similar to Paul's injunction in Rom 12:17, "Do not repay anyone evil for evil." Similar wording is found in 1 Thess 5:15, "Make sure that nobody pays back wrong for wrong." The Pauline formulation in 1 Cor 4:12 is quite similar to Peter's: "When we are cursed, we bless" *(loidoroumenoi eulogoumen)*. These admonitions, of course, are rooted in the teaching of Jesus himself.[198] For example, in Luke 6:28–29 we find this exhortation: "Bless those who curse you, pray for those who mistreat you. If someone strikes you on one cheek, turn to him the other also. If someone takes your cloak, do not stop him from taking your tunic" (cf. Matt 5:38–42). Peter's wording does not match the Pauline or Jesus tradition exactly, but it is closer to the Pauline than the Matthean or Lukan tradition. Perhaps Paul and Peter drew upon the same Jesus tradition here.[199]

Instead of insulting others or responding in kind, believers are called on to bless others.[200] By "blessing" Peter means that believers are to ask God

---

[197] So McKnight, *1 Peter,* 201.

[198] So Piper, "Hope as the Motivation of Love," 220–22; Achtemeier, *1 Peter,* 224.

[199] Cf. Gundry, "*Verba Christi,*" 342; "Further *Verba,*" 226; Goppelt, "Jesus," 100; Piper, "Hope as the Motivation of Love," 220–22; Achtemeier, *1 Peter,* 224; against Best, "Gospel Tradition," 105.

[200] The participles ἀποδιδόντες and εὐλογοῦντες are both to be explained as imperatival (so Daube, "Participle," 483; Kelly, *Peter and Jude,* 136; Michaels, *1 Peter,* 223; Snyder, "Participles and Imperatives in 1 Peter," 195). Their distance from other main verbs precludes their dependence upon them. Therefore Achtemeier's view that they depend on the imperatives in 2:17 cannot be sustained (*1 Peter,* 223).

to show his favor and grace upon those who have conferred injury upon them.[201] The reason believers should bless is now explained ("because, *hoti*). They have been "called" to bless others. The words "to this" *(eis touto)* could point forward or backward.[202] If they point forward, then the idea is that God has called believers to inherit the blessing of eternal life. More likely, though, as in 2:21, the pronoun "this" when attached to the verb "called" is retrospective.[203] Believers have been called by God to bless others, so that they would inherit the blessing of eternal life (cf. also Gal 5:13; Eph 4:1,4; Col 3:15).

Peter's logic may seem strange at first glance. Christians are called to bless so that *(hina)* they will inherit the blessing of eternal life.[204] Is there the danger of works righteousness here, of suggesting that the blessing will be obtained by the merit of believers?[205] Peter had already explicitly taught that God has begotten believers to new life (1:3,23) and that he will preserve them to the end (1:5). Now he stressed the behavior that is necessary for those who identify themselves as Christians. He continued in the same vein in the subsequent verses (3:10–12), where good behavior is deemed to be necessary to obtain eternal life. Nor is such teaching foreign to the rest of the New Testament since good works are often introduced as evidence that one is truly redeemed (Rom 2:6–10,27–29; 1 Cor 6:9–11; 2 Cor 5:10; Gal 5:19–21; 2 Pet 1:5–11; 1 John 2:3–6; Rev 20:11–15).

3:10 In vv. 10–12 Peter cited Ps 34:12–16 (LXX 33:13–17). He did not use an introductory formula, but the wording is clearly dependent upon the Septuagint. The main difference is that Peter altered the text from the second person singular to the third person singular. It is difficult to know whether the change is intentional or whether the text is cited from memory.[206] It is also imperative to note that Psalm 34 focuses on suffering and the Lord's deliverance of those who are afflicted. Peter already had alluded to it in 2:3 and now returned to it again. The psalm was not selected arbi-

---

[201] Rightly Achtemeier, *1 Peter,* 224.

[202] For a forward reference see Kelly, *Peter and Jude,* 137; Davids, *First Peter,* 126–27.

[203] So Piper, "Hope as the Motivation of Love," 224–28; Michaels, *1 Peter,* 178; Achtemeier, *1 Peter,* 224; Elliott, *1 Peter,* 609–10.

[204] Rightly Michaels, *1 Peter,* 179; Spicq, *Les Épîtres de Saint Pierre,* 127.

[205] Cf. Goppelt, *I Peter,* 237–38; Best, *1 Peter,* 130.

[206] Selwyn thinks some changes of the OT in Peter can be explained by citations from memory (*First Peter,* 25), while Piper thinks the changes here are intentional ("Hope," 226).

trarily since it addresses the issue faced by Peter's readers.[207] The psalmist reminded his readers that the Lord rescues his own when they suffer and that he will judge the wicked. Meanwhile the righteous display their trust and hope in the Lord by renouncing evil and pursuing what is good. It is not difficult to see that themes that are central in 1 Peter are evident in the psalm: the suffering of God's people, their ultimate deliverance, the judgment of the wicked, and the notion that a godly life is evidence of hoping in God.

The most important feature for understanding the structure of the text is the "for" *(gar)* linking vv. 10–12 to v. 9. I summarize the logic of the text as follows:

> You were called to bless so that you will inherit the blessing of eternal life (v. 9).
> For anyone who wishes to experience the life of the age to come must shun evil speech and do good to all in order to receive that blessing (vv. 10–11). For the Lord's favor is on the righteous, but he will judge the wicked (v. 12).

In the historical context of the psalm, "life" *(zōēn)* and "good days" *(hēmeras agathas)* refer to life and blessing in this world. But for Peter this language almost certainly referred to the *eschaton,* to end-time salvation.[208] We have already seen in 1:4 that the "inheritance" refers to eschatological salvation. The language of the psalm, therefore, is understood typologically in that the promise of life and good days in the land points toward and anticipates life in the world to come. Similarly, the language of 3:7 also demonstrates that Peter thought of the coming reward since "joint heirs of the grace of life" (RSV) signifies life in the future age. It is doubtful, contrary to some, that a reference to *both* this life and the age to come is intended.[209] Peter was

---

[207] Bauckham says, "1 Peter was by no means content to relay isolated scriptural texts which came to him in the tradition, but studies whole passages of Scripture . . . in a way which combined christological-prophetic interpretation and paraenetic application" ("James, 1 Peter and 2 Peter, Jude," 313). So also McCartney, "The Use of the Old Testament in the First Epistle of Peter," 102–3. See the programmatic work of C. H. Dodd, *According to the Scriptures* (New York: Scribners, 1952), 78–82. Even though W. Bornemann overemphasizes the role of Psalm 34, he rightly discerns that it played a critical role in the writing of the letter ("Der erste Petrusbrief—eine Taufrede des Silvanus?" *ZNW* 19 [1919]: esp. 147–51; cf. W. L. Schutter, *Hermeneutic and Composition in I Peter,* WUNT 2/30 [Tübingen: Mohr, 1989], 44–49). But in my judgment Schutter underplays the significance of Psalm 34, so that the truth is somewhere between Bornemann and Schutter.

[208] So most commentators. E.g., Cranfield, *I & II Peter and Jude,* 96; Kelly, *Peter and Jude,* 138; Reicke, *The Epistles of James, Peter, and Jude,* 105; Piper, "Hope as the Motivation of Love," 226–27; Michaels, *1 Peter,* 180; Achtemeier, *1 Peter,* 226; Lea, "I Peter—Outline and Exposition," 35; Brox, *Der erste Petrusbrief,* 155; Schelke, *Der Petrusbriefe—Der Judasbrief,* 95. Grudem wrongly places the blessing in this life (*1 Peter,* 148–49; so also Richard, *Reading 1 Peter, Jude, and 2 Peter,* 141; Calvin, *Catholic Epistles,* 104).

[209] Against Goppelt, *I Peter,* 236–37; Achtemeier, *1 Peter,* 226.

not promising good days in this world since persecution and troubles are to be expected (1:6–7; 3:13–17; 4:12–19). He was providing a motivation for believers to bless those who persecute them and to live in a way that pursues peace. They are to refrain from speaking evil and from guile so that they will obtain the eschatological reward, eternal life itself. We must insist again that such a theology is not works righteousness, nor does it compromise the theme that salvation is by grace. Peter believed that those who have received new life from God will live transformed lives and that such lives provide evidence (necessary evidence!) that they have been converted. Michaels rightly says that the blessing "is not earned by the performance of good works, it nevertheless belongs to those who demonstrate good works."[210] To sum up, the good behavior enjoined in 2:11–3:7 is crucial for experiencing the eschatological inheritance of 1:3–9. That the tongue would refrain from speaking evil hearkens back to 3:9, "Do not repay evil with evil." And the exhortation to avoid deceit *(dolon)* reminds us of 2:1, where believers are enjoined to put aside "all deceit" *(panta dolon).*

3:11 The Christian life is not one of passivity for Peter. We have seen that he gives all the credit to God for the new life of Christians (1:3,23). They have been begotten by the Father, and no one can take any credit for being born. Yet the priority of God's grace can never be used to deny the need to take action. A life of goodness does not simply happen as believers meditate quietly in their rooms. Believers must make a conscious effort to "turn" *(ekklinatō)* from evil.[211] They must devote themselves to what is "good," and we have seen often in 1 Peter that goodness was especially prized by Peter (see commentary on 2:18). Peace can easily be disrupted, especially when others mistreat and even abuse us. Hence, believers must "seek" *(zētēsatō)* and "pursue" *(diōxatō)* peace. Such peace will only be preserved if believers do not insult and revile others, if they extend forgiveness to those who injure them.

3:12 Verse 12 differs from the Old Testament citation only in the addition of "for" *(hoti)* to the text.[212] Peter explained why good behavior is imperative. The reason is the same that we have already seen in v. 9 and in the relationship between v. 9 and vv. 10–11.[213] Achtemeier wrongly and surprisingly, given his recognition of the logic of the text, says that believ-

---

[210] Michaels, *1 Peter,* 182.

[211] The manuscript evidence is rather evenly divided over whether δέ should be included. It is probably original, being omitted because it is lacking in the LXX text.

[212] Some manuscripts add the remaining words from Ps 34:16, "to destroy their memory from the earth." Others add "to destroy them from the earth." The addition is secondary, but it reminds us that the punishment in view, from Peter's perspective, is eternal and definitive.

[213] Achtemeier, *1 Peter,* 226.

ers may be included in those who practice what is evil.[214] But the point of the text is that the Lord's favor is on those who live in such a righteous way.[215] In other words, he will bless them with the inheritance promised in vv. 7,9 and with the future life of the age to come noted in v. 10. The hearing of their prayers (cf. v. 7) reveals that they are truly members of God's people. Conversely, the Lord will turn away his face from those who practice evil, which means they will not obtain an eternal inheritance but God's punishment. Indeed, in the very next line of Psalm 34, which Peter did not cite here, it is said that those who are wicked will be destroyed by God. Peter's omission of this line dos not indicate that he diverged from the meaning of the psalm. What he included has already made that point clear. We have now seen on numerous occasions that living a godly life does not earn salvation but is an evidence of it. Peter was hardly suggesting that believers will live perfectly and that such perfection is necessary to obtain an inheritance. But he was insisting that a transformed life is necessary to obtain the inheritance.

3. Responding in a Godly Way to Suffering (3:13–4:11)

A new subsection of the text begins here, even though v. 12 is closely related to v. 13 (see below). In 2:13–3:12 the godly behavior necessary in various stations and realms of life is explicated. Peter then turned more directly to the call to suffer, arguing first that there is no need to fear suffering since it is actually the pathway to blessing (3:13–17), just as suffering was the pathway to blessing and triumph for Christ (3:18–22). Hence, he called on the readers to prepare themselves for suffering (4:1–6) since those who consent to suffer have made a clean break with sin. Believers may be criticized by unbelievers in this life, but the latter will be judged by God whereas believers will be vindicated on the last day. Indeed, the last day is coming soon (4:7–11). Therefore believers should devote themselves to prayer, to love, and to mutual service by using their gifts. Thereby they will glorify God.

(1) The Blessing of Suffering for Christ (3:13–17)

13Who is going to harm you if you are eager to do good? 14But even if you should suffer for what is right, you are blessed. "Do not fear what they fear; do not be frightened." 15But in your hearts set apart Christ as Lord. Always be pre-

---

214 Ibid., 227.

215 Some think the "Lord" here, as in the OT context, probably refers to God rather than Christ (Achtemeier, *1 Peter,* 227). Bauckham argues that "Lord" refers to Christ since Peter, when he cited Psalm 34 in 2:3, clearly identified the Lord as Christ ("James, 1 Peter and 2 Peter, Jude," 313). Bauckham's argument is persuasive since he takes into account the Petrine usage of the psalm.

pared to give an answer to everyone who asks you to give the reason for the hope that you have. But do this with gentleness and respect, [16]keeping a clear conscience, so that those who speak maliciously against your good behavior in Christ may be ashamed of their slander. [17]It is better, if it is God's will, to suffer for doing good than for doing evil.

Peter concluded v. 12 by promising that the Lord's favor is on the righteous, but he will punish evildoers. He drew an inference from v. 12 in v. 13. It follows, therefore, that no one can ultimately harm those who are zealous in doing good. The promise of the heavenly inheritance guarantees that the distresses of this life do not constitute the last word. Verse 14 restates the thesis of v. 13. Believers may be distressed by persecution now, but in actuality they are blessed by God himself and will enjoy the eschatological reward. Since no one can ultimately harm believers and since they live under God's blessing, they are exhorted in v. 15 not to fear. Those who have God's promise of blessing realize that any pain in this life is short-lived. Instead of fearing what unbelievers might do, believers are to set apart Christ as Lord in their hearts and to respond to those who ask them about their endtime hope with humility and the fear of the Lord. Their good conduct will be the basis for the eschatological shame of their opponents since the latter did not respond to goodness when observing it. Peter only wanted to be sure (v. 17) that believers suffer for doing what is good instead of deserving censure because of evil behavior.

3:13 Even though I begin a new section here, this verse is closely linked to the preceding verses. The word *kai,* which is left untranslated by the NIV, is usually translated "and" or "but." In this instance, however, it is almost equivalent to "therefore."[216] Peter had just affirmed in v. 12 that the Lord will look with favor on the righteous, but he sets his face against those who practice evil. He speaks here of the final judgment, where those who live righteously will be rewarded and the wicked will be judged.[217] A rhetorical question is employed to stimulate the thinking of Peter's readers. Who will inflict harm upon believers if they pursue what is good? The NRSV is a bit more helpful than the NIV in that it clarifies even more explicitly that the future is in view, "Now who will harm you if you are eager to do what is good?" Some commentators understand Peter to speak of this life, so the meaning is that people will ordinarily treat believers well

[216] Kelly, *Peter and Jude,* 139–40; Achtemeier, *1 Peter,* 229; van Rensburg, "Intersentence Relational Particles and Asyndeton in 1 Peter," 289. Michaels translates it "then" or "and so" (*1 Peter,* 185; cf. also Tite, *Compositional Transitions in 1 Peter,* 95–97).

[217] The link between the two verses is even clearer in Greek. Note the close proximity of the words κακά and κακώσων.

if they practice righteousness.[218] The logical connection between vv. 12 and 13 suggests that this interpretation is incorrect. Furthermore, the future tense of the participle *(ho kakōsōn)* probably refers to judgment day. The point of the rhetorical question, then, is that no one will harm believers ultimately on the day of judgment, for God (as 3:10–12 teaches) will reward them for their faithfulness.[219] The link with the previous verses is also indicated in the last clause of the verse, "if you are eager to do good." Godly behavior is also described as doing "good" in 3:11, which summarizes all that is required in 3:8–12. The word translated "eager" literally means "zealous" *(zēlōtai),* demonstrating an ardent pursuit of virtue, even in the face of persecution.[220] Peter was not promising, then, that believers would escape rejection and harm in this world. Some understand Peter to say that usually the righteous will escape harm but occasionally they will encounter suffering.[221] This view should be rejected, for Peter did not suggest that sufferings are rare. Suffering stalks the believer until this present evil age comes to an end. Instead, Peter assured believers that nothing can ultimately harm them if they continue to walk in God's paths, that the pain inflicted on them now is only temporary, and that they will be vindicated by God on the last day.[222] The thought is quite similar to Rom 8:31:[223] "What, then, shall we say in response to this? If God is for us, who can be against us?" Paul was scarcely saying that believers face no opposition. His point was that no one can ultimately and finally triumph over believers since God will vindicate them on the last day.

3:14 The conjunction "but" *(alla)* introducing v. 14 does not provide a contrast but a clarification of v. 13. Hence, it could be translated as "indeed."[224] The suffering of Christians might suggest that the assertion in v. 13 is false. Believers can be harmed, even killed, by opponents. Peter, however, did not conceive of the suffering of believers as contradicting the claim of v. 13. Those who suffer for the sake of righteousness, those who

---

[218] E.g., Davids, *First Peter,* 129–30; McKnight, *1 Peter,* 212–13; Marshall, *1 Peter,* 114.

[219] Rightly Cranfield, *I & II Peter and Jude,* 97–98; Kelly, *Peter and Jude,* 139–40; Michaels, *1 Peter,* 183–84; Achtemeier, *1 Peter,* 229; Martin, *Metaphor and Composition in 1 Peter,* 214; Bechtler, *Following in His Steps,* 164; Elliott, *1 Peter,* 620; Schelke, *Der Petrusbrief—Der Judasbrief,* 100.

[220] The word ἀγαθοῦ here is an objective genitive.

[221] E.g., Lea, "I Peter—Outline and Exposition," 35.

[222] F. Neugebauer remarks that there is also an emphasis on present reward here ("Zur Deutung und Bedeutung des 1. Petrusbriefes," *NTS* 26 [1980]: 78–79).

[223] Augustine says, "If you love the good, you will suffer no loss, because whatever you may be deprived of in this world, you will never lose God, who is the true Good" (in *James, 1–2 Peter, 1–3 John, Jude,* ACCS [Downers Grove: InterVarsity, 2000], 103).

[224] Michaels paraphrases the beginning of v. 14 as follows, "What is more (even if you should suffer . . .) you are blessed" (*1 Peter,* 185).

endure opposition because of their zeal for what is good, are "blessed" (*makarioi;* see also 4:14).[225] The blessing comes from God himself, showing that believers are beneficiaries when they are afflicted. In what sense are they blessed? Peter hardly could have meant that sufferings are themselves pleasant, for then, obviously, they would not be sufferings. He was almost certainly drawing on the Jesus tradition here, for Jesus himself taught in Matt 5:10–12 (cf. Luke 6:22–23) that those who suffer are blessed because of the eschatological reward they will receive.[226] We can see now why the word "but" should be translated "indeed." The train of thought is as follows: "No one will be able to harm believers on the future day if they are zealous for good" (v. 13). Indeed, even present suffering is not a sign of punishment but of God's blessing both now and especially in the future, in the day when he rewards his people with eternal life.

Peter used the optative form of the verb "suffer" *(paschoite),* which leads some scholars to the conclusion that suffering is unusual and a remote possibility for Christians.[227] Such an understanding of the verbal form flies in the face of the context of the rest of 1 Peter, where it is quite evident that Christians in Asia Minor were facing suffering (cf. 1:6–7; 2:12,19–21; 4:12–19; 5:9–10). Furthermore, such a view is difficult to square with the rest of Christian tradition, where suffering is part and parcel of the believer's life.[228] The purpose of the optative, then, is not to suggest that suffering is unlikely. Rather, the optative is used because suffering, though not a constant experience in the Christian life, is always a threat and could erupt at any time.[229] Peter was not teaching that suffering is rare, only that it is not perpetual. The suffering envisioned is "for what is right" *(dia dikaiosynēn)* and hence excludes trouble that comes because of ignorance or sin (cf. 2:20; 4:15). Righteousness is another way of describing "the good" for which believers are zealous in 3:13.

Peter now draws two implications (in this verse and the next) from the fact that suffering is an indication of God's blessing.[230] These two implications are the main point of the text and are expressed as imperatives. Since

---

[225] See also Kelly, *Peter and Jude,* 140; Achtemeier, *1 Peter,* 231.

[226] So Goppelt, *I Peter,* 241.

[227] Cf. Cranfield, *I & II Peter and Jude,* 98; Beare, *First Peter,* 137; Richard, *Reading 1 Peter, Jude, and 2 Peter,* 147.

[228] Cf. Acts 4:1–22; 5:17–42; 7:54–8:3; 9:29–30; 12:1–24; 13:45; 14:1–6,19,22; 16:19–40; 17:5–9,13–15; 18:12–17; 19:23–41; 1 Thess 3:1–5; 2 Thess 1:4; 2 Tim 3:11–12).

[229] So Kelly, *Peter and Jude,* 141; Selwyn, *First Peter,* 191; R. Omanson, "Suffering for Righteousness' Sake (1 Pet 3:13–4:11)," *RevExp* (1982): 439; Achtemeier, *1 Peter,* 231; F. W. Danker, "I Peter 1:24-2:17—A Consolatory Pericope," *ZNW* 68 (1967): 100, n. 38. Michaels suggests that the optative provides emphasis, so that the point is that even when believers suffer their future is better than unbelievers (*1 Peter,* 186).

[230] The connecting word is δὲ, but contextually we should discern an inference here.

believers are blessed by God when they suffer, they should not fear what unbelievers can do to them. The NIV understands the first phrase differently, translating it, "Do not fear what they fear."[231] The NIV rendering fits with the allusion to Isaiah, which will receive attention below. In the Petrine context, however, we probably have a reference to the fear that unbelievers could strike into the hearts of Christians.[232] This interpretation is reflected in the NASB, "Do not fear their intimidation." The second imperative, "do not be frightened," bears the same idea and simply restates the first imperative.[233] The admonition fits with Peter's emphasis on only fearing God. Fear of human beings, even of those who persecute, is forbidden. The reason fear is prohibited relates back to vv. 13–14a. Since no one can ultimately harm believers and since even their suffering is a sign of God's blessing, then it follows that they should not fear what others can do to them.

Peter alluded in this verse and the next to Isa 8:12–13. The text is reshaped slightly to fit Petrine themes, though we again do not know if the text was carefully altered or if it is cited from memory. Apparently the Isaiah text was important for Peter, for we saw in 1 Pet 2:8 that he appealed to Isa 8:14, in the texts collected on the stone. The context of Isaiah 7–8 is important. The Southern Kingdom of Judah was threatened by the Northern Kingdoms of Israel and Aram (approximately modern day Syria). These two countries were threatening to remove Ahaz as king of Judah and to install a certain Tabeel as king in his stead. The threat filled Ahaz and Judah with terror (Isa 7:2), but Isaiah promised that the Lord would preserve Judah, that Israel and Aram would be vanquished by Syria, and that the Lord would provide a sign to demonstrate the faithfulness of his word. Judah and Ahaz were to respond by trusting in the Lord's promise. In Isa 8:11–15 the Lord commands his people not to fear the plot hatched by Israel and Aram. They should only fear Yahweh, the God of Israel, and put their trust in him alone. Those who trust in him will find him to be a sanctuary, but those who fail to trust will stumble, fall, and be broken. We can see from this short synopsis of Isaiah that Peter appropriately applied the prophecy to his situation. Just as Judah had enemies in the days of Ahaz, so

---

[231] For this interpretation see Hillyer, *1 and 2 Peter, Jude,* 110.

[232] The pronoun αὐτῶν would then be a genitive of source (so also Achtemeier, *1 Peter,* 232, n. 45). Or similarly it could be an objective genitive (Kelly, *Peter and Jude,* 142; Michaels, *1 Peter,* 186–87). Calvin maintains that Peter shifted the meaning slightly from the original intention in Isaiah, but he argues that the difference in meaning is not significant in any case (*Catholic Epistles,* 106–7).

[233] The words μηδὲ ταραχθῆτε are omitted in a few manuscripts (𝔓[72], B, L) but are surely original. Perhaps Michaels is correct that they were omitted because of the similar ending on φοβηθῆτε (*1 Peter,* 183).

the Petrine readers faced opponents in their day. Just as Judah was tempted to fear their foes, so the Petrine readers were liable to fear what their persecutors might do to them. Hence, the words of Isaiah still spoke to Peter's day. Believers are not to fear the suffering unbelievers might administer to them. They are to trust in the Lord, believing that he will vindicate his own.[234]

3:15 Peter here stated the second implication from vv. 13–14a, continuing to allude to Isaiah 8. Negatively, believers are to refrain from fear. Positively, they are "to set apart Christ as Lord" in their "hearts." The differences from the Septuagint are more substantial than in v. 14. In Isa 8:13 the "LORD" *(kyrios)* is clearly Yahweh, but here Peter added the word "Christ" *(Christon).*[235] The words "in your hearts" are also lacking in Isaiah. The move from Yahweh to Christ is common in the New Testament, reflecting the conviction that Jesus the Messiah deserves the same honor as Yahweh. In addition, Peter's change reflects the situation his readers faced, for they were persecuted because of their allegiance to Jesus Christ as Lord. Peter exhorted his readers to continue to treat Christ as the holy one, fearing him instead of those who are harming them. Christ is already Lord in any case, but believers demonstrate and acknowledge his lordship in their lives by honoring his name (cf. Matt 6:9).

Some scholars argue that the construction should be translated as "set apart the Lord, namely, Christ."[236] The meaning does not change dramatically if this interpretation is correct, though more emphasis is placed on Christ's identification as Lord, so that Peter would have been stressing that what was said about Yahweh in the Old Testament was now true of Jesus Christ. But two arguments suggest that we should interpret the construction as it is interpreted in the NIV, "set apart Christ as Lord." First, "Lord" lacks the article, but "Christ" has one, and it would be more natural in an appositional relationship if both nouns lacked or retained the article.[237] Second, it seems more likely in context that Peter did not want to stress that Christ is Lord but that believers should set him apart and treat him *as Lord.* The place where Christ is to be set apart as Lord is "in your hearts." We should not understand the heart as our inner and private lives, which are inaccessi-

---

[234] McCartney observes that despite the minor differences between the OT and Peter, "the resultant force is actually quite similar. In both contexts the exhortation is on being afraid not of other people, but only of the Lord" ("The Use of the Old Testament in the First Epistle of Peter," 95–96).

[235] The MT inserts θεόν instead of Χριστόν. The external evidence supports the latter (𝔓[72], ℵ, A, B, C, Ψ, 33, 614, 1739), and perhaps scribes inserted θεόν because Christ was not in the LXX of Isa 8:13. See also *TCGNT* 622–23.

[236] Kelly, *Peter and Jude,* 142; Michaels, *1 Peter,* 187.

[237] So Achtemeier, *1 Peter,* 232.

ble to others. The heart is the origin of human behavior (cf. 1:22; 3:4), and from it flows everything people do. Hence, setting apart Christ as Lord in the heart is not merely a private reality but will be evident to all when believers suffer for their faith. The inner and outer life are inseparable, for what happens within will inevitably be displayed to all, especially when one suffers.

How the next sentence relates to the previous one is difficult to discern. The NIV understandably turns the adjective "prepared" *(hetoimoi)* into an imperative, "be prepared," for something needs to be supplied to make the construction sensible. Technically speaking, perhaps, a participle *(ontes)* links this phrase to the main verb above ("set apart," *hagiasate*).[238] In any case, the adjective ends up *functioning* like an imperative, and so the NIV is not far off. Believers are to be ready constantly to respond to those who ask about their faith. What Peter emphasized is that they were to be prepared to provide a "defense" (NRSV, *apologia*—rendered "answer" by NIV) to those who ask about the Christian faith. The word "defense" suggests to some scholars a reference to formal court cases in which believers responded to legal accusations (cf. Luke 12:11; 21:14; Acts 19:33; 22:1; 24:10; 25:8,16; 26:1–2,24; Phil 1:7,16; 2 Tim 4:16).[239] We have already seen in the introduction that the persecution in 1 Peter was sporadic and informal and does not represent the kind of state-sponsored persecution under Pliny and Trajan (see introduction). Hence, the text does not address primarily formal legal situations.[240] It envisions instead informal circumstances when believers are asked spontaneously about their faith.[241] This interpretation is supported by the words "everyone who asks you" *(panti tō aitounti hymas),* suggesting that believers respond to a wide variety of people, not exclusively in court situations.[242] The admonition here, of course, also applies to legal settings, nor does it preclude the possibility that believers occasionally faced legal charges.[243] What I am saying is that the admonition cannot be restricted to courtroom appearances.

The exhortation here is instructive, for Peter assumed that believers have

---

[238] So Achtemeier, *1 Peter,* 233, n. 54. Beare describes the adjective as imperatival (*First Peter,* 138).

[239] E.g., Beare, *First Peter,* 138–39.

[240] So most scholars. E.g., Omanson, "Suffering," 439; Selwyn, *First Peter,* 193; Kelly, *Peter and Jude,* 142–43; Michaels, *1 Peter,* 188; Achtemeier, *1 Peter,* 233; Goppelt, *I Peter,* 244.

[241] The words απολογία and ἀπολογέομαι are also used of private controversies (cf. 1 Cor 9:3; 2 Cor 7:11; 12:19).

[242] Some manuscripts (א², A, Ψ) insert ἀπαιτοῦντι instead of αἰτοῦντι. The latter is original, and it is just possible that the former emphasizes the forcefulness with which believers are challenged (cf. Achtemeier, *1 Peter,* 228).

[243] So Kelly, *Peter and Jude,* 143; Achtemeier, *1 Peter,* 233; Bechtler, *Following in His Steps,* 90–91.

solid intellectual grounds for believing the gospel. The truth of the gospel is a public truth that can be defended in the public arena. This does not mean, of course, that every Christian is to be a highly skilled apologist for the faith.[244] It does mean that every believer should grasp the essentials of the faith and should have the ability to explain to others why they think the Christian faith is true. Achtemeier remarks that in this respect we have an interesting difference between the Christian faith and mystery religions, for the latter required secrecy of their adherents.[245]

Interestingly enough Peter used the word "hope" *(elpis)* rather than "faith" here. We have already seen in 1:21 (see commentary) that the two words are closely linked. "Hope" was a central word for Peter, focusing on the eschatological inheritance that awaits believers (1:3; cf. 1:13).[246] The implication is that unbelievers will recognize by the way believers respond to difficulties that their hope is in God rather than in pleasant earthly circumstances. The "hope that you have" is literally "the hope that is in you" (NRSV) or "the hope among you" *(tēs en hymin elpidos)*. Some scholars favor the latter, arguing that the focus is not on the individual but the hope that is shared by the whole community.[247] Social scientific studies of the New Testament era have rightly emphasized the community in the ancient world. Modern Western culture is highly individualistic, and the emphasis on personal freedom sets us apart from our ancestors. Nevertheless, we must beware of an overreaction, for early Christians did teach that individuals needed to repent and believe and were responsible for their decisions (cf. Acts 2:37–38; 3:19; Rom 10:9, etc.). In this case the translation of the NRSV, "the hope that is in you," is to be preferred.[248] The phrase is parallel to "in your hearts," focusing attention on the inner life from which outward actions flow. The New Testament does not separate the inner from the outer, the private from the public, for whatever is on the inside is manifested on the outside. Here the hope that animates believers will become so evident that unbelievers will ask for an explanation.

When believers encounter a hostile world and are challenged concerning their faith, the temptation to respond harshly increases. Defending a position could easily be transmuted into attacking one's opponents. Hence, Peter added that the defense must be made "with gentleness and reverence" (NRSV, *meta prautētos kai phobou*).[249]

---

[244] Luther argues from this text that every believer needs to know God's word individually (*Commentary on Peter & Jude,* 158–59).

[245] Achtemeier, *1 Peter,* 234.

[246] So Brox, *Der erste Petrusbrief,* 17.

[247] Selwyn, *First Peter,* 194; Michaels, *1 Peter,* 189; Achtemeier, *1 Peter,* 233–34.

[248] Rightly Goppelt, *I Peter,* 244; Kelly, *Peter and Jude,* 143.

[249] In the Greek text this phrase is part of v. 16.

The NRSV translation is to be preferred over the NIV's "with gentleness and respect." The latter's use of the word "respect" suggests that Christians should treat unbelievers in a fitting way when questioned, and obviously Peter would not disagree. We have seen throughout the commentary, however, that "fear" in 1 Peter is always directed toward God (see the commentary on 2:18). Furthermore, "gentleness" or "humility" also becomes a reality when creatures consider themselves in relation to God.[250] Still, Peter probably had in view gentleness toward other people and reverence before God.[251] Such fear and humility are required for wives as well (3:2,4), suggesting again that the instruction for the wives functions as a pattern for all oppressed believers. Those who fear God and live in humility will treat their opponents with dignity and refrain from lashing out against them. What Peter emphasized, however, is the relation with God that enables believers to respond appropriately to unbelievers.

3:16 Verse 15 blends right into v. 16, being joined by a participle. We also have another piece of evidence that suggests that "gentleness and reverence" in v. 15 focus on the relationship of believers to God. The phrase "keeping a clear conscience" functions as an imperatival participle, even if it is technically instrumental. Again, Peter specified what is involved when believers defend their faith. When Peter spoke of a "clear conscience" (*suneidēsin agathēn,* lit., "a good conscience"), he referred to the relationship of believers to God. As Goppelt says, "They have the certainty of living by faith, without being perfect therein."[252] They live in God's presence in all they do, and hence they must not resort to revenge, anger, or sin when they are called upon to defend their hope.

Why should believers live in fear and humility before God and maintain a good conscience? In a purpose clause ("so that," *hina*) the intention is explicated, "so that" those who abuse the good conduct of believers will be humiliated on the last day. We receive further evidence that the primary form of persecution in 1 Peter was not physical but social. The situation addressed is "when you are maligned" (NRSV, *en hō katalaleisthe*).[253] Unbelievers are "those who speak maliciously" *(ho epēreazontes)* about Christians. Formal court cases are not envisioned here but negative verbal attacks in the public square. The latter, of course, can lead to the former, and when verbal opposition ratchets up, physical violence may not be far

[250] Rightly Michaels, *1 Peter,* 189.

[251] Elliott, *1 Peter,* 627. Cf. also Bechtler, *Following in His Steps,* 164.

[252] Goppelt, *I Peter,* 245.

[253] The RSV and others rightly translate this clause as temporal (so Reicke, *The Disobedient Spirits and Christian Baptism,* 110–11; Fink, "Use of *en hō* in I Peter," 34; Brox, *Der erste Petrusbrief,* 161). A number of witnesses substitute καταλαλοῦσιν ὑμῶν ὡς κακοποιῶν for καταλαλεῖσθε, but the former is almost certainly due to assimilation to 1 Pet 2:12.

behind. What unbelievers criticize, shockingly, is the "good behavior" of believers. The word for "behavior" *(anastrophēn)* was a favorite of Peter's, often designating the kind of conduct that is pleasing to God (1:15; 3:1–2; by way of contrast 1:18, and see the verbal form in 1:17). That the behavior in view is distinctively Christian is clear by the prepositional phrase "in Christ" *(en Christō)*. The "in Christ" language pervades the Pauline letters, with the phrase appearing seventy-three times, and it is used outside Paul only in 1 Peter (cf. also 5:10,14); but Peter did not develop the phrase in the same way as Paul, and here it is virtually equivalent to "Christian."[254]

Peter continued to emphasize that the conduct of believers is related to the Lord, where all conduct is in the sphere of Christ. Further, Christians should only be abused for their "good" conduct. Believers are to live righteously so that those who abuse their good conduct will "be ashamed" *(kataischynthōsin)*. Commentators are divided about whether unbelievers will feel ashamed during this life by recognizing the conduct of unbelievers or whether the shame is eschatological, referring to the humiliation experienced on the day of judgment.[255] In support of the former it seems that Peter expected unbelievers to recognize the good conduct of believers now.[256] When Christians persist in doing good and refrain from revenge even when censured, unbelievers cannot help but notice the goodness of those who claim to be Christ's. The first option is certainly a possibility; neither was Peter denying that some will take notice of the good conduct of believers. Still, his focus here was on the end time, the day of judgment.[257] Three pieces of evidence support this interpretation. First, the verb "put to shame" in 1 Pet 2:6 refers to the last day, and though the term does not always refer to the future, it often bears this meaning (Rom 5:5; 9:33; 10:11; 1 Cor 1:27). Second, and most important, believers are already abused and criticized for their good behavior in Christ. It is difficult to see how "more good behavior" would suddenly lead unbelievers to feel ashamed. Some non-Christians are persuaded, despite the godly conduct of Christians, that they are troublemakers. Peter called on believers to continue to live righteously when threatened. Peter probably had in view unbelievers who are hardened toward believers, who have made up their minds (come what may) that Christians are socially dangerous. Hence, he exhorted his readers to continue to please God and live in a godly fashion, so that on the day of judgment unbelievers will recognize that they were mistaken all along. Third, the language of 1 Pet 2:12 is parallel to 3:16 in a

---

[254] So Michaels, *1 Peter,* 190.

[255] Bechtler says that the shame of unbelievers is now recognized by the believing community (*Following in His Steps,* 195), but this would afford little encouragement to a beleaguered church.

[256] Cf. Achtemeier, *1 Peter,* 236; Richard, *Reading 1 Peter, Jude, and 2 Peter,* 151–52.

[257] So Michaels, *1 Peter,* 190–91; Elliott, *1 Peter,* 623–33.

number of respects: the call to good conduct, the maligning by unbelievers, and the need to continue to live righteously when oppressed.

We have seen that there are good reasons to think in 1 Pet 2:12 that the righteous conduct of believers will lead some unbelievers to salvation to the glory of God, and that some would respond with repentance is not denied here. But Peter emphasized another truth in this verse. Some unbelievers refuse to acknowledge the goodness of the lives of believers. On the last day, however, they will be put to shame by God himself and will be compelled to acknowledge that believers lived righteously. First Peter 2:12 and 3:16 do not contradict each other. They contemplate different responses to the godly lives of believers: some unbelievers will see their good conduct and glorify God by believing the gospel (1 Pet 2:12), but others refuse to believe and will only admit the goodness of believers on the day that God judges them.

3:17 The word "for" (NRSV, *gar*) links v. 17 to the preceding, though the connecting word is unfortunately omitted by the NIV. Scholars debate the meaning of the verse, and so we must pursue this issue before explaining how it relates to the preceding. Is the verse saying that it is better for Christians to suffer when they do good than it is for them to suffer for doing evil? Such a view is supported by many commentators.[258] Others object that such an interpretation is prosaic and so obvious that it hardly needs to be said. Therefore they understand the verse eschatologically. It is better to suffer now for doing good than it is to suffer on the day of judgment for practicing evil.[259]

Supporting this latter view is the eschatological focus of the argument in 3:10–12 and in 3:16. Further, the wording is parallel in some respects to Mark 9:43,45,47. Despite some provocative arguments favoring the latter view, I think Peter was not referring to the final judgment in this verse, even though I agree that eschatology informs 3:10–12 and 3:16.[260] Such an eschatological focus is not evident here. The parallels in Mark are hardly decisive since those verses explicitly refer to end-time judgment and salvation. The Petrine formulation lacks such eschatological language. Further, the idea expressed in this verse is also communicated in 4:15–16 (cf. 2:20). Such a sentiment may seem prosaic, but it may be said in response that Peter knew human nature, realizing that even Christians may be apt to explain all suffering as an indication of their righteousness, when some of it

---

[258] E.g., Brox, *Der erste Petrusbrief,* 163; Omanson, "Suffering," 440; Beare, *First Peter,* 140; Achtemeier, *1 Peter,* 237–38.

[259] So Michaels, *1 Peter,* 191; cf. id., "Eschatology in I Peter iii.17," 394–401; Martin, *Metaphor and Composition in 1 Peter,* 223.

[260] Rightly Brox, *Der erste Petrusbrief,* 162–63; Horrell, *The Epistles of Peter and Jude,* 68–69. Horrell notes that the author would not speak of judgment as the cause of suffering.

may be deserved and come to them because of their sins. Neither is the verse merely a secular sentiment since the suffering Peter envisioned was for the good done because of one's relationship with God. Further, nowhere else did Peter use the word "suffer" *(paschō)* to refer to eschatological judgment, but only to the difficulties faced during the present evil age. We have noted in the above verses that the good conduct of believers is rooted in their relationship with God. Verse 17, then, explains that the opposition Christians receive must be for good behavior, not their shortcomings.

Another feature of v. 17 must be noted. The suffering of believers is attributed to the will of God (cf. 1:6).[261] The optative of the verb "suffer" *(paschoi)* is used because Peter did not know the extent to which God wills the suffering of each believer. He realized that some will experience more vilification and even bodily harm than others. Such opposition, however, is not outside God's control.[262] The suffering each believer endures represents God's will for them. Peter did not deny the reality of Satan and his evil ragings in the persecution of the church (5:8), nor did he exempt from responsibility human beings who persecute the church (2:12; 3:16). Nevertheless, ultimately no one can touch God's children apart from his permission. This is also the message of the Book of Job. Satan could only inflict damage on Job with God's acquiescence. Naturally God's intentions and motives in allowing suffering are remarkably different from Satan's, and hence God remains unalterably good in the process, while Satan is irremediably evil.

(2) Christ's Suffering as the Pathway to Exaltation (3:18–22)

**18For Christ died for sins once for all, the righteous for the unrighteous, to
bring you to God. He was put to death in the body but made alive by the Spirit,
19through whom also he went and preached to the spirits in prison 20who disobeyed long ago when God waited patiently in the days of Noah while the ark was
being built. In it only a few people, eight in all, were saved through water, 21and
this water symbolizes baptism that now saves you also—not the removal of dirt
from the body but the pledge of a good conscience toward God. It saves you by
the resurrection of Jesus Christ, 22who has gone into heaven and is at God's right
hand—with angels, authorities and powers in submission to him.**

In vv. 13–17 believers are to be full of confidence and refrain from fear because of the promise of their eschatological inheritance. Now in vv. 18–22 Peter argued that Christ also traveled the pathway from suffering to glory. Suffering, then, is not a sign of divine displeasure. Precisely the

[261] Cf. Goppelt, *I Peter,* 246.

[262] Calvin rightly says our suffering is not due to chance but God's will (*Catholic Epistles,* 111).

opposite. Those who suffer for the Christ will be glorified as he was.[263] The paragraph is a difficult one, but it has three main points. First, Christ suffered for the unrighteous to bring believers to God (v. 18). Second, by the power of the Spirit he was raised from the dead and proclaimed victory over demonic spirits (vv. 18–19). Finally, he is now exalted on high as the resurrected and ascended Lord and has subjected all demonic powers to himself (v. 22). The main point, then, is that believers have no need to fear that suffering is the last word, for they share the same destiny as their Lord, whose suffering has secured victory over all hostile powers. Believers, then, are akin to Noah. They are a small embattled minority in a hostile world, but they can be sure that, like Noah, their future is secure when the judgment comes. The basis of their assurance is their baptism, for in baptism they have appealed to God to give them a good conscience on the basis of the crucified (v. 18) and risen (v. 21) work of the Lord Jesus Christ.

3:18 The main idea of the previous paragraph is that believers should not fear, even though unbelievers may inflict pain on them (3:14). Instead they should set apart Christ as Lord in their hearts and be prepared to respond to questions posed by unbelievers (3:15). The reason believers should not fear is that they will be rewarded and blessed by God for suffering (3:13–14). Hence, suffering is the pathway to glory. The word "for" *(hoti)* introducing v. 18 relates back to the constellation of ideas we have just traced from the previous paragraph. Believers should not become intimidated in suffering but continue to sanctify Christ as Lord because the suffering of Christ was also the means by which he was exalted. Just as suffering was the pathway to exaltation for Christ, so also suffering is the prelude to glory for believers. This paragraph, then, with all its interpretive difficulties does not veer away from the situation of the readers. Rather, the emphasis on Christ's victory reminds believers that the troubles of the present time are temporary, that victory is sure because Christ has triumphed over evil powers.[264] The theme of the text therefore is not the imitation of Christ, contrary to some scholars,[265] but his victory over evil.

---

[263] Campbell comments, "Peter's point is this: just as Christ who suffered innocently . . . was exalted to honor, so those who faithfully follow him can anticipate the divinely bestowed honor" (*Honor, Shame, and the Rhetoric of 1 Peter,* 179).

[264] Cf. also R. T. France, "Exegesis in Practice: Two Examples," in *New Testament Interpretation: Essays on Principles and Methods* (Grand Rapids: Eerdmans, 1977), 266; Achtemeier, *1 Peter,* 243; W. J. Dalton, *Christ's Proclamation to the Spirits: A Study of 1 Peter 3:18–4:6,* AnBib 23 (Rome: Pontifical Biblical Institute, 1965), 111–12.

[265] So Reicke, *The Disobedient Spirits and Christian Baptism*, 130–31 (who argues that believers should like Jesus proclaim the gospel); Selwyn, *First Peter,* 195; Thurén, *Argument and Theology in 1 Peter,* 164. Rightly Best, *1 Peter,* 139; W. J. Dalton, "1 Peter 3:19 Reconsidered," in *The New Testament Age: Essays in Honor of Bo Reicke,* 2 vols. (Macon: Mercer University Press, 1984), 1:97.

Peter did not summon his readers to follow Christ in these particular verses. He encouraged them by reminding them of Christ's victory over evil powers. Some scholars have postulated that Peter used traditional material in these verses.[266] There is little doubt that traditional themes are cited, but the text has too many unique features to be counted as traditional. And the syntax is too complicated to read a hymn or confessional formula behind the wording.

The subject in v. 18 turns toward the suffering of Christ. Many manuscripts read that Christ "died" *(apethanen)* rather than "suffered" *(epathen).*[267] The word "suffered" is likely original because the statement that Christ "died" for sinners was part of the common Christian confession (cf. Rom 5:8; 1 Cor 15:3; 2 Cor 5:14; 1 Thess 5:10), and the term "suffer" is unusual by comparison.[268] Further, Peter never used the verb "died" but used the verb "suffer" eleven times. Indeed, the connection with the previous verse is strengthened where the term "suffer" is also found. Peter was thinking of the death of Christ here, but the term "suffer" establishes a connection with the experience of his readers. The NIV omits the word "also" *(kai),* just as it did in 2:21. The idea, once again (see the commentary on 2:21), is that just as believers in Asia Minor were suffering, so also Christ suffered. Nevertheless, the uniqueness of Christ's suffering is also communicated, just as it was in 2:21. Christ's death was "for sins" *(peri hamartiōn).* This phrase probably is rooted in the Septuagint, where the singular noun "sin" with the preposition "concerning" *(peri)* refers often to the sin offering. Wright has demonstrated that it has this meaning in forty-four of its fifty-four occurrences in the Septuagint (cf. also Heb 10:6,8; 13:11).[269]

This interpretation is strengthened by the phrase "once for all" *(hapax).* The suffering of Christ was unique and definitive in that he offered himself as a sin offering once for all. The distinctiveness of Christ's sacrifice is featured here, for even though believers suffer, they do not suffer for

---

[266] See, e.g., Wand, *Epistles of Peter and Jude,* 99–100; Selwyn, *First Peter,* 325–26; K. Shimada, "Formula," 158–59; R. Bultmann, "Bekenntnis- und Liedfragmente im ersten Petrusbrief," ConBNT 11 (1947): 1–14; K. Wengst, *Christologische Formeln und Lieder des Urchristentums,* SNT 7, 2d ed. (Gütersloh: Gütersloher/Mohn, 1974); Dalton, *Proclamation to Spirits,* 96–100. Kelly restricts the liturgical elements to vv. 18 and 22 (*Peter and Jude,* 147). See the more detailed discussion of Achtemeier, *1 Peter,* 241–43; Elliott, *1 Peter,* 694–97.

[267] Support for ἀπέθανεν includes 𝔓[72], ℵ, A, C, Ψ, 33, 1739, etc. (so Kelly, *Peter and Jude,* 147–48). The word ἔπαθεν is supported by B, K, P, and the Majority text.

[268] So Achtemeier, *1 Peter,* 239; Dalton, *Proclamation to Spirits,* 119–21.

[269] N. T. Wright demonstrated in his magisterial work that "resurrection" in Judaism and the Greco-Roman world refers to resurrection of the physical body and cannot be equated with living in some kind of immaterial state (*The Resurrection of the Son of God,* in *Christian Origins and the Question of God* [Minneapolis: Fortress, 2003], 3:220–25); also France, "Exegesis in Practice," 267.

the sins of others, nor does their suffering constitute a sacrifice for the sins of others. Nor was Peter suggesting here that the suffering of believers is the means by which unbelievers are brought near to God.

The uniqueness of Christ's death continues to be emphasized, for he suffered on the cross as "the righteous for the unrighteous." The righteousness of Christ is an allusion to his sinlessness (cf. 2:22). His suffering therefore was undeserved. We saw earlier in 2:21–23 that the response of Jesus to unjust suffering functioned as an example for believers. Christ's role as an example is also implied in this text since in the previous paragraph believers are also exhorted to do what is right even if they suffer. Nevertheless, the uniqueness of Christ's suffering comes to the forefront here. That Christ was "righteous" *(dikaios)* is stressed elsewhere in the New Testament (Matt 27:19; Luke 23:47; Acts 3:14; 7:52; 1 John 2:1,29; 3:7; cf. Isa 53:11). Since Christ suffered as the sinless one (1 John 2:1; 2 Cor 5:21), his suffering is unique. Indeed, only Christ suffered "for the unrighteous" *(hyper adikōn)*. His death was vicarious and substitutionary and the basis upon which people become right with God.[270]

The reason Christ's death is sufficient is precisely because he was sinless. He could not have died on behalf of his people if he himself were stained by sin. His perfect obedience, therefore, is the basis for the sufficiency of his death. Peter shared common Christian tradition when he spoke of Christ dying for the unrighteous. Paul described it as Christ dying for sinners (Rom 5:8), adding elsewhere that he died for our sins (1 Cor 15:3). John said God's Son was the satisfaction for sins (1 John 4:10). And we have seen already in 2:24 that Peter drew upon Isaiah 53 in teaching that Christ "bore our sins."[271] The uniqueness of his death is also communicated in the purpose of his sacrifice. He died "to bring you to God."[272]

The word "bring" *(prosagagē)* communicates the notion that one has access to God (cf. the noun in Rom 5:2; Eph 2:18; 3:12 and the background in the LXX; e.g., Exod 19:4; 29:4; 40:12; Lev 8:24; 16:1; Num 8:9). Only Christ through his suffering died *for* the unrighteous, and the suffering of believers could not bring others to God. Indeed, Christ's suffering is the means by which the Petrine Christians were themselves brought to God, showing that they were formerly unrighteous and sinners.

---

[270] Rightly Davids, *First Peter,* 135–36; contra Dalton, *Proclamation to Spirits,* 122.

[271] The manuscript tradition has a plethora of readings. Most variants read that Christ suffered or died for "our sins" or "your sins." Such elaborations are hardly surprising, and the concise "for sins" is to be preferred.

[272] Manuscript tradition is divided in that a number read "us" rather than "you." Scribes were apt to confuse the two since they sounded the same. And cribes would be apt to use the first person plural to include all believers. Hence, the second person plural should be accepted as original.

Intense controversy over the text begins with the next phrase and continues through v. 21. We will take the text a phrase at a time and try to sort out what Peter was saying. We have a contrast between two phrases, "He was put to death in the body, but made alive by the Spirit." The contrast between the flesh and S/spirit in the New Testament is a common one.[273] The RSV renders the contrast differently, understanding the two dative nouns to be datives of sphere, "being put to death in the flesh but made alive in the spirit" (cf. also NRSV, NASB).[274]

This translation could support the interpretation that Jesus was put to death in his body but lived in terms of his human spirit. Other scholars argue that the point is that Jesus was put to death in the realm of flesh but was brought to life in the spiritual realm (cf. HCSB).[275] Still another possibility is that the two dative nouns "flesh" and "spirit" *(sarki* and *pneumati)* are both datives of agency. According to this view Jesus was put to death *by* human beings (the flesh) and was brought to life *by* the Spirit. Before attempting to resolve this issue, we can make some progress by establishing what is clear in the text. A contrast exists here between death and resurrection of Christ. The participle "being put to death" (RSV, *thanatōtheis*) obviously refers to the death of Christ, showing specifically *how* he suffered (cf. *epathen* earlier in the verse). The participle "being made alive" (literal translation, *zōopoiētheis*), on the other hand, refers to the resurrection of Christ. The verb refers to the resurrection in a number of texts in the New Testament (John 5:21; Rom 4:17; 8:11; 1 Cor 15:22,36,45; cf. also Eph 2:5; Col 2:13).[276] Elsewhere in the New Testament the death and resurrection of Christ are also communicated in the same text (cf. Rom 4:25; 8:34; 14:9; 1 Thess 4:14). We can be confident, therefore, that Peter did not envision Jesus merely living in the interval between his death and resurrection in terms of his human spirit. He thought here of Christ's resurrection from the dead.[277]

---

[273] Matt 26:41; Mark 14:38; Luke 24:39; John 3:6; 6:63; Rom 1:3–4; 2:28–29; 7:5–6; 8:4–9,12–13; 1 Cor 5:5; 2 Cor 7:1; Gal 3:3; 4:29; 5:16–19; 6:8; Phil 3:3; Col 2:5; 1 Tim 3:16; Heb 9:13–14; 12:9.

[274] The view that they are datives of reference (so Selwyn, *First Peter,* 196; Kelly, *Peter and Jude,* 151) does not differ remarkably from the idea that they are datives of sphere.

[275] E.g., France, "Exegesis in Practice," 267; cf. Dalton, *Proclamation to Spirits,* 134; Elliott, *1 Peter,* 645–46.

[276] The verb is used eleven times in the NT and in eight out of the eleven instances refers to resurrection, but only here to Christ's resurrection. A. T. Hanson wrongly concludes that if the text refers to the resurrection, then the resurrection is not a bodily one ("Salvation Proclaimed: I. 1 Peter 3.18–22," *ExpTim* 93 [1982]: 101).

[277] Rightly France, "Exegesis in Practice," 267–68; Davids, *First Peter,* 136–37.

Most scholars try to explain the verse by understanding the dative nouns "flesh" and "spirit" in the same way. Either both nouns are understood to refer to the person of Christ, both his body and spirit, or both nouns are understood to refer to a realm, so that the realm of the flesh and the realm of the spirit are in view. Or both nouns are construed as datives of agency, so that Christ was killed in the body by the "flesh" (i.e., human beings), and he was raised by the Holy Spirit. We can eliminate the first option because the text speaks of the resurrection of Christ, not of his human spirit. The second interpretation is ruled out by v. 19, for it hardly makes sense to say that Jesus "went" *(poreutheis)* and preached to the imprisoned spirits in the spiritual realm. But neither is the last option credible. It is doubtful that the singular "flesh" (NIV "body," *sarki*) refers to human beings. The NIV's interpretation that it refers to Christ's body is much more probable. The deadlock can be broken if we recognize that the two dative nouns are not used in precisely the same way; the first is a dative of reference, and the second is a dative of agency. Christ was put to death with reference to or in the sphere of his body, but on the other hand he was made alive by the Spirit. Interestingly, the parallel in 1 Tim 3:16 should be interpreted similarly. Jesus "appeared in a body" (*en sarki,* lit., "in the flesh") and "was vindicated by the Spirit" *(en pneumati).* I think the NIV's interpretation is correct here, and it is likely that the two nouns though preceded by the same preposition are to be rendered differently (cf. also Rom 1:3–4). The message for the readers is clear. Even though Jesus suffered death in terms of his body, the Spirit raised (cf. Rom 8:11) him from the dead. Similarly, those who belong to Christ, even though they will face suffering, will ultimately share in Christ's resurrection.

3:19 Before examining the details of this verse, the main interpretations that have been proposed will be summarized.[278] Luther wrote, "A wonderful text is this, and a more obscure passage perhaps than any other in the New Testament, so that I do not know for a certainty just what Peter means."[279] It should be noted that the main features of the various views are sketched in for the sake of clarity, and the differences of opinion among those who share the same view are not explained. First, Augustine, and since him many others, understood the text to refer to Christ's preaching through Noah to those who lived while Noah was building the ark.[280]

[278] For a more detailed history of interpretation, see Reicke, *The Disobedient Spirits and Christian Baptism,* 7–51; Dalton, *Proclamation to Spirits,* 15–41.

[279] Luther, *Commentary on Peter & Jude,* 166.

[280] Augustine, *Letter,* 164; J. S. Feinberg, "1 Peter 3:18–20, Ancient Mythology, and the Intermediate State," *WTJ* 48 (1986): 303–36; J. H. Skilton, "A Glance at Some Old Problems in First Peter," *WTJ* 58 (1996): 1–9.

According to this view, Christ was not personally present but spoke by means of the Holy Spirit through Noah. The spirits are not literally in prison but refer to those who were snared in sin during Noah's day.[281] If this view is correct, any notion of Christ descending into hell is excluded. Second, some have understood Peter as referring to Old Testament saints who died and were liberated by Christ between his death and resurrection.[282] Third, others understand the imprisoned spirits to refer, as in 4:6, to the sinful human beings who perished during Noah's flood. Christ in the interval between his death and resurrection descended to hell and preached to them, offering them the opportunity to repent and be saved.[283] Most of those who adopt such an interpretation infer from this that God will offer a second chance to all those in hell, especially to those who never heard the gospel. If salvation was offered to the wicked generation of Noah, surely it will also be extended to all sinners separated from God. Fourth, the majority view among scholars today is that the text describes Christ's proclamation of victory and judgment over the evil angels. These evil angels, according to Gen 6:1–4, had sexual relations with women and were imprisoned because of their sin. The point of the passage, then, is not that Christ descended into hell but, as in 3:22, his victory over evil angelic powers.[284]

I believe the last option is correct and will attempt to explain why in

---

[281] Some understand the spirits to refer to those who perished during the flood (Cranfield, *I & II Peter and Jude,* 102; id., "I Peter iii.19 and iv.6," 370) or those who perished before the coming of Christ (cf. Kelly, *Peter and Jude,* 153; E. Schweizer, "1. Petrus 4,6," *TZ* 8 [1952]: 78). Clement of Alexandria thought the reference was to righteous men and women who preceded Christ (*Strom.* 6.6.46–47), while other church fathers may have identified the spirits as the righteous of the OT (Ignatius, *Magn.* 9:2; Justin, *Dial.* 72:4).

[282] So Calvin, *Catholic Epistles,* 114. Cyril of Alexandria teaches that Jesus grants a second chance to those who did not sin grievously while on earth. See *James, 1–2 Peter, 1–3 John, Jude,* ACCS (Downers Grove: InterVarsity, 2000), 107–8. The view of Severus of Antioch is ambiguous. It could be interpreted to refer to release from hell only to those who had already believed in Christ, or alternatively he may be teaching a second chance for those in hell (see *James, 1–2 Peter, 1–3 John, Jude,* ACCS [Downers Grove: InterVarsity, 2000], 108).

[283] Cranfield, *I & II Peter and Jude,* 104; "The Interpretation of I Peter iii.19 and iv.6," *ExpTim* 69 (1957–58): 369–72; Goppelt, *I Peter,* 258–60. Cf. Wand, who suggests that such mercy is likely extended to all who have lived (*Epistles of Peter and Jude,* 111–12). Fink suggests the unusual view that Jesus' spirit preached victory over the spirits in prison during the three hours that he hung on the cross ("Use of *en hō* in I Peter," 37–38). Hanson adds that mercy was offered during this interval to both human beings and evil angels ("1 Peter 3.18–22," 102–3). For a survey of the early church tradition of Jesus' descent into hell, see Elliott, *1 Peter,* 706–10.

[284] McCartney essentially accepts this view but argues that Peter appealed to a legend to point to Christ ("The Use of the Old Testament in the First Epistle of Peter," 175–76).

what follows.[285] In the discussion that follows, the second and third view will be combined since both teach that Christ liberated people from confinement between his death and resurrection. First, the idea that Christ spoke by means of the Spirit through Noah suffers from a number of problems. First, it does not explain adequately the participle *(poreutheis)* translated "went" in v. 18 and "has gone" in v. 22. In v. 22 it is clear that it refers to Jesus' ascension to God's right hand, showing that it is a postresurrection event.[286] The word "went" seems out of place and strange for those who defend the Augustinian view, for Christ does not really go anywhere if he preaches "through" Noah. There are instances in the New Testament where the word "went" *(poreuomai)* refers to the ascension of Christ (Acts 1:10–11; John 14:2,3,28; 16:7,28), while it nowhere refers to his descent into the underworld. We also noticed in v. 18 a clear reference to the resurrection of Christ. The "going" in v. 19, therefore, also most naturally refers to what is true of Christ's resurrection body. It is obviously the case that Christ did not need his resurrection body to preach through Noah by means of the Spirit. Indeed, the reference to Christ "going" in v. 19 demonstrates the implausibility of the first view since it is difficult to understand how Christ needs to "go anywhere" if he speaks only through the Holy Spirit. This piece of evidence alone shows the first view is implausible. Second, the word "spirits" *(pneumasin)* fits much

[285] This is still the view of the majority of commentators. See Selwyn, *First Peter,* 198–200; Achtemeier, *1 Peter,* 245–46; Kelly, *Peter and Jude,* 152–56; Elliott, *1 Peter,* 648–50; Davids, *First Peter,* 138–41; D. E. Hiebert, "The Suffering and Triumphant Christ: An Exposition of 1 Peter 3:18–22," *BSac* 139 (1982): 146–58; A. J. Bandstra, "'Making Proclamation to the Spirits in Prison': Another Look at 1 Peter 3:19, *CTJ* 38 (2003): 120–21. Michaels argues that the "spirits" are the offspring of evil angels (i.e., the evil spirits often mentioned in the Gospels). He understands the "prison" to be their refuge, which Jesus declares now, as a result of his death and resurrection, to be under his sovereignty. The point is that the powers are now domesticated (*1 Peter,* 206–10). It is unclear, however, that Peter distinguished between the evil spirits of the Gospels and the imprisoned spirits, especially if the prison denotes their confinement to the earth and inability to cohabit with women after their sin. Further, that φυλακή refers to a place of refuge is unattested in the literature (so Davids, *First Peter,* 141, n. 39). Even if the term bears that meaning in some instances, the similarity to 2 Pet 2:4 and Jude 6 suggests that the meaning is not "refuge" here (so McCartney, "The Use of the Old Testament in the First Epistle of Peter," 170). If the imprisoned spirits refer to all demons and the imprisonment is metaphorical, this would also handle Feinberg's objection that it seems strange that Christ would proclaim victory over only *some* angels ("1 Peter 3:18–20," 329, 333). If the reference is metaphorical, we also need not trouble ourselves over the place in which the spirits were imprisoned since the tradition includes under the earth, to the ends of heaven and earth, and in the second of the seven heavens (see "1 Peter 3:18–20," 270–71). France rightly remarks, "Christ went to the prison of the fallen angels, not to the abode of the dead, and the two are never equated" ("Exegesis in Practice," 271).

[286] Cf. also Kelly, *Peter and Jude,* 155–56; Dalton, *Proclamation to Spirits,* 159–61; France, "Exegesis in Practice," 271; Achtemeier, *1 Peter,* 257–58; Richard, *Reading 1 Peter, Jude, and 2 Peter,* 158–59.

more plausibly with a reference to angels than to human beings,[287] for "spirits" *(pneumata)* in the plural almost without exception in the New Testament refers to angels.[288] The only place in which the term clearly refers to human beings is Heb 12:23, and in that instance the addition of the word "righteous" *(dikaiōn)* removes any doubt that human beings are in view. The normal use of the plural "spirits" points toward angels, not human beings.[289] Further, though, the word "prison" *(phylakē)* is often used to denote the place where human beings are held on earth (e.g., Acts 5:19; 8:3; 2 Cor 6:5; 11:23), but the word is never used to denote the place of punishment for human beings after death.[290] The term is used in Rev 20:7, however, for Satan's confinement for one thousand years (cf. Rev 18:2). That the evil angels are imprisoned is clearly taught in Jewish tradition (*1 Enoch* 10:4; 15:8,10; 18:12–14; 21:1–10; 67:7; *2 Enoch* 7:1–3; 18:3; *Jub.* 5:6).[291] Finally, it is difficult to see what relation preaching through Noah has to the present context. Nothing else in these verses emphasizes that the Petrine readers were also to preach to their contemporaries.

The view that Christ offered salvation to those who died in the flood suffers from some of the same weaknesses as the first. Such a view also reads the term "spirits" to refer to human beings, but we have seen that this is unlikely. If Christ descended into hell before his resurrection, the word "went" seems superfluous when used of Christ's "spirit."[292] If the journey below is placed after the resurrection, at least Christ has a body with which

---

[287] So most commentators (e.g., Dalton, *Proclamation to Spirits*, 145–50; Selwyn, *First Peter,* 198; Best, *1 Peter,* 142; Kelly, *Peter and Jude,* 154; Michaels, *1 Peter,* 207; Achtemeier, *1 Peter,* 255; "1 Peter 3:18–20," 269–70; Elliott, *1 Peter,* 657). Reicke thinks the primary reference is to angels, though human beings are also included (*The Disobedient Spirits and Christian Baptism,* 52–70).

[288] Cf. Matt 8:16; 10:1; 12:15; Mark 1:27; 3:11; 5:13; 6:7; Luke 4:36; 6:18; 7:21; 8:2; 10:20; 11:26; Acts 5:16; 8:7; 19:12–13; 1 Tim 4:1; Heb 1:14; 12:9; 1 John 4:1; Rev 16:13–14; cf. Heb 1:7. On four occasions πνεύματα appears to refer to spiritual gifts (1 Cor 12:10; 14:12,32; Rev 22:6) and four times in Revelation to what I believe is the Holy Spirit (1:4; 3:1; 4:5; 5:6).

[289] Michaels rightly objects that Feinberg's view requires that the spirits were embodied when they heard Christ preach through Noah, though they are *now* disembodied (Feinberg, "1 Peter 3:18–20," 320–21, 330). But this requires that the text move back in time, and no indication of such is supplied in the text (Michaels, *1 Peter,* 210–11). The same point is rightly made by Reicke, *Disobedient Spirits and Christian Baptism*, 96–97.

[290] Rightly Reicke, *Disobedient Spirits and Christian Baptism*, 53, 66–67; Dalton, *Proclamation to Spirits*, 157–59; Achtemeier, *1 Peter,* 256; Elliott, *1 Peter,* 657–58.

[291] For a survey of this tradition see Elliott, *1 Peter,* 697–705.

[292] The view that Christ descended into hell has a long history. Those supporting such a view, however, vary in terms of their understanding of the text as a whole. See Justin, *Dial.* 72:4; Clement of Alexandria, *Strom.* 6.6.45–46; Athanasius, *Ep. Epic.* 5:26–27. So also Beare, *First Peter,* 145–47; S. E. Johnson, "The Preaching to the Dead," *JBL* (1960): 48–51.

to make the trip. This interpretation has another fatal problem. It makes no sense contextually for Peter to be teaching that the wicked have a second chance in a letter in which he exhorted the righteous to persevere and to endure suffering.[293] Indeed, we have seen in many places throughout the commentary that eternal life is conditioned upon such perseverance. All motivation to endure would vanish if Peter now offered a second opportunity after death. The benefit of braving suffering is difficult to grasp if another opportunity to respond will be offered at death.

The best solution, therefore, is that the verse proclaims Christ's victory over demonic spirits after his death and resurrection.[294] The evidence supporting this view is impressive. First, as we have seen, the word "spirits" almost certainly refers to angels (evil angels in this context). Second, the notion that the spirits are imprisoned fits with Satan's imprisonment in Rev 20:7. Third, Gen 6:1–4 may possibly provide the reason for the spirits' punishment: their sexual relations with women. Such an interpretation of Gen 6:1–4 is debated of course. But fourth, this interpretation was standard in Jewish literature in Peter's day (see *1 Enoch* 6–19,21,86–88; 106:13–17; *Jub.* 4:15,22; 5:1; CD 2:17–19; 1QapGen 2:1; *T. Reu.* 5:6–7; *T. Naph.* 3:5; *2 Bar.* 56:10–14; cf. Josephus, *Ant.* 1.73).[295] The impact of this tradition is explained further in my commentary on Jude 6 and 2 Pet 2:4.[296] Some scholars doubt that Peter was influenced by such a tradition. Because of space constraints I can make only a few comments. Whatever one's understanding of the literary relationship between Jude and 2 Peter 2, it is clear that the texts are very similar. We know that Jude was influenced by *1 Enoch* (cf. Jude 14–15). Hence, it is to be expected that in v. 6 Jude relays an interpretation that is quite similar to the basic understanding of *1 Enoch*, though he does not ratify every detail of Enoch's view. It is quite implausible that 2 Pet 2:4 should be interpreted differently from Jude 6 since the texts share the same tradition. Further, those who believe in the Petrine authorship of both 1 and 2 Peter, as I do, have all the more reason to think that 1 Pet 3:19 draws on the same tradition. Indeed, as I note in the com-

[293] Elliott rightly says that such a view "would be completely inconsistent with the outlook of 1 Peter, which envisions divine judgment according to one's deeds (1:17; 4:17–18) and condemnation of the disobedient (2:7–8; 4:17–18). . . . And any notion of a possibility of conversion or salvation after death would seriously undermine the letter's consistent stress on the necessity of righteous behavior here and now" (*1 Peter,* 661–62).

[294] Cf. Dalton, *Proclamation to Spirits,* 184–86.

[295] For a brief synopsis of this tradition see Brox, *Der erste Petrusbrief,* 171–75.

[296] Dalton argues that evidence from 2 Peter indicates the author understood 1 Pet 3:19; 4:6 to refer to the proclamation of victory over angels and the preaching of the gospel to human beings who have since died respectively ("Light from 2 Peter," 551–55). This constitutes early evidence in support of the interpretation offered here. See also Dalton's commentary on the impact of Jewish tradition (*Proclamation to Spirits*, 163–71).

mentary on Jude, the understanding of the text in the New Testament and Jewish tradition probably is in accord with the meaning of the text in Gen 6:1–4.

Finally, such a view of the text, as I already have argued, makes best sense of 1 Pet 3:19 in its own context. The two uses of the participle *(poreutheis)* "went" in v. 19 and "has gone" in v. 22 most naturally refer to Jesus' exaltation. That it involves his exaltation is specifically taught in v. 22, where he is at God's right hand. Moreover, this interpretation understands the "spirits" of v. 19 to be another term for the "angels, powers, and authorities" in v. 22. In both cases evil angels are in view. Indeed, in both instances Christ's victory over them is featured. In v. 19 he proclaims his victory over them as the crucified and risen Lord, and in v. 22 he subjects them to himself as God's vice-regent. If this view is correct, we can eliminate the interpretation that Christ preached in the interval between his death and resurrection.[297] Again we note that the words "spirits" and "prison" fit most naturally with this interpretation. The greatest difficulty for such a view is the word "preached" *(ēkryxen)*. Usually this term refers to the preaching of the gospel, and such a definition fits better with the first two interpretations than with this one.[298] The word can be used, however, in a neutral sense (cf. Rom 2:21; Gal 5:11; Rev 5:2).[299] Context is decisive in defining the meaning of terms. Usually in the New Testament what one "heralds" is the gospel, but in this instance victory over demonic powers is heralded.[300] Such an understanding does not impose an alien meaning on the word, and it harmonizes with the emphasis on victory in this text (cf. Col 2:15). Further, this fits with Enoch's role in *1 Enoch* 12:4, where he goes and tells *(poreuou kai eipe)* the Watchers that they will be judged.[301] Another objection that can be raised is, Why would Christ proclaim his victory over only some angels, so that his victory is heralded only over the angels who sinned by having sexual relations with women? The question is an

---

[297] The notion that Christ preached between his death and resurrection has been widely held. See Beare, *First Peter,* 145; Reicke, *The Disobedient Spirits and Christian Baptism,* 116–18; Best, *1 Peter,* 140; Cranfield, *I & II Peter and Jude,* 103–4.

[298] Many scholars believe the gospel was proclaimed by Christ either personally or by means of the Holy Spirit through Noah. E.g., Best, *1 Peter,* 144; Grudem, *1 Peter,* 160. Some argue that Christ only announced salvation to Noah's generation, OT saints, or all the righteous (cf. Spicq, *Les Épîtres de Saint Pierre,* 138). Reicke gives cogent arguments, defending the view that Christ rather than Enoch did the preaching (*The Disobedient Spirits and Christian Baptism,* 98–100).

[299] So Dalton, *Proclamation to Spirits,* 150–57; Selwyn, *First Peter,* 200; Achtemeier, *1 Peter,* 260, 262; France, "Exegesis in Practice," 271; Elliott, *1 Peter,* 659–62.

[300] Dalton, *Proclamation to Spirits,* 186–91.

[301] Cf. Reicke, *The Disobedient Spirits and Christian Baptism*, 64; Dalton, *Proclamation to Spirits,* 166; France, "Exegesis in Practice," 270. But Reicke does not draw the same conclusion as Dalton and France regarding πορευθείς (see p. 65 in Reicke). Where Christ proclaimed this victory is debated. See the discussion in Dalton, *Proclamation to Spirits,* 177–84.

excellent one, though we must recognize that we cannot answer every question raised in difficult texts. It is possible, however, that the angels who sinned as recorded in Gen 6:1–4 represent all the evil angels.[302] Still, the text does not answer this issue definitively, and so unanswered questions remain.

Virtually every element of the verse has been discussed except for the phrase "through whom" *(en hō)*.[303] The phrase could be construed as temporal[304] (cf. 2:12; 3:16; see also 1:6 and 4:4, where the phrase probably is causal).[305] Or it could be construed as a general antecedent and be translated "wherein," thereby," or "thus."[306] Others take the antecedent to be the neuter noun "spirit" *(pneumati)*.[307] This last view is the most likely. If one understands the latter to refer to sphere, then Christ goes in the spiritual sphere, and this could even occur before his resurrection;[308] but as Achtemeier observes it is difficult to see how this understanding coheres with Christ going in his resurrection body. It is preferable to see the antecedent as "spirit" and to understand the dative clause as instrumental.[309] According to this view, Christ by means of the Holy Spirit went and proclaimed victory over the imprisoned spirits.[310] This interpretation explains the "also," for the Spirit not only raised Christ but also empowered him to herald victory.[311]

3:20 The interpretation of v. 20 depends, of course, on how v. 19 is understood. I have already argued that the imprisoned spirits in v. 19 refer to the angels who sinned by cohabiting with women in accordance with Gen 6:1–4. Such angels "disobeyed long ago." The participle "disobeyed"

---

[302] See the discussion in n. 284.

[303] Some scholars believe the original reading was ʼΕνώχ and that scribes accidentally introduced an error through haplography. See, e.g., E. J. Goodspeed, "Some Greek Notes: IV; Enoch in I Peter 3:19," *JBL* 73 (1954): 91–92. The reading has no manuscript support, and a reference to Enoch does not cohere with the rest of the context (see Reicke, *The Disobedient Spirits and Christian Baptism,* 94; Dalton, *Proclamation to Spirits,* 134–36; Achtemeier, *1 Peter,* 253–54).

[304] So Reicke, *The Disobedient Spirits and Christian Baptism*, 103–15; Fink, "Use of *en hō* in I Peter," 36–37; Elliott, *1 Peter,* 652; Brox, *Der erste Petrusbrief,* 170.

[305] Defending a causal reading is Skilton, "Some Old Problems in First Peter," 4.

[306] Goppelt, *I Peter,* 255–56.

[307] Dalton, *Proclamation to Spirits,* 137–39. France sensibly argues that this refers to the activity of the risen Christ ("Exegesis in Practice," 268–69). Feinberg thinks that Christ as a spirit, without his body, preached either through Noah ("1 Peter 3:18–20," 318) or after his death and before his resurrection (cf. Beare, *First Peter,* 144–45). Kelly identifies the antecedent similarly, but he adopts the view that Christ proclaimed victory over demonic spirits after his resurrection (*Peter and Jude,* 152–56).

[308] So O. S. Brooks, "I Peter 3:21—The Clue to the Literary Structure of the Epistle," *NovT* 16 (1974): 303.

[309] Rightly Achtemeier, *1 Peter,* 252. Michaels observes that a temporal interval between vv. 18 and 19 is preserved in almost all the interpretations proposed for ἐν ᾧ (*1 Peter,* 205–6).

[310] We should not see a reference here to Christ's human spirit.

[311] Again Achtemeier, *1 Peter,* 253.

(apeithēsasin) should be understood as causal, explaining why the spirits were imprisoned.[312] The disobedience, as Jude 6 and 2 Pet 2:4 also explain, is their transgression of boundaries God established, with the result that they engaged in sexual relations with women. Another confirmation of the proposed interpretation is the reference to Noah, since the incident between the "sons of God" and the "daughters of men" (Gen 6:1–4) immediately precedes the flood narrative. Indeed, it is quite plausible to understand the sin in Gen 6:1–4 as the climax of sin, the enormity of sin now being great enough to justify the extermination of all humanity.

The reference to God's patience fits with the reference to Noah and his preparation of the ark. The Lord could have wiped out the human race instantly and recommenced his plan with Noah. Instead God demonstrated his patience while Noah built the ark, presumably giving human beings an opportunity to repent during this interval (cf. Rom 2:4; 3:25; Acts 14:16; 17:30). Some might object that God's patience toward humans eliminates any reference to angels, but we need to recall that the angels sinned with human beings, so that the fate of human beings and angels becomes entangled in the one event. It is also likely that Peter reflected on God's patience toward the angels as well (Gen 6:3), for there is no evidence that God immediately judged the angels for their sin. He allowed them to commit sin with women, and it seems that some time elapsed before he responded in judgment.[313]

The judgment of the flood that destroyed all is prominent in the text, but so also is the salvation of the few. Peter emphasized that only a "few" *(oligoi)* were saved (cf. Matt 7:14) from the flood. Indeed, the number of those who were rescued was only "eight." The text literally reads "eight souls," but we should understand the word "souls" *(psychai),* as elsewhere in Peter (1:9,22; 2:11,25; 4:19), to refer to human beings as whole persons, not to the immaterial substance.[314] Indeed, the latter view would be incredibly strange here since the point of the story is that they did not perish in the flood, which would hardly call to mind the idea that only their "souls" were preserved. Some in the history of interpretation have been tempted to understand the word "eight" symbolically.[315] Any symbolic reading is mistaken in this instance, for Peter thought of the eight persons who literally survived the flood: Noah, his wife, their three sons, and their wives (see

---

[312] Ibid., 262. Skilton takes it as temporal ("Some Old Problems in First Peter," 2).

[313] Cf. the discussion in Dalton, *Proclamation to Spirits,* 204–5.

[314] Rightly Michaels, *1 Peter,* 213.

[315] Kelly, e.g., sees a reference to the eighth day as Christ's resurrection and the baptism of believers on Easter (*Peter and Jude,* 159). He falls prey to reading later church history into 1 Peter at this point. For a similar attempt to read the text symbolically, see Reicke, *The Disobedient Spirits and Christian Baptism,* 140–41.

Gen 7:13; cf. also 6:18; 7:7). An application is intended, of course, for Petrine readers. They were also sojourners and exiles on earth, a small community beset by opponents who mistreated them.[316] They should not be discouraged by the smallness of their numbers but must remember that God now extends his patience to all, but the day of judgment is coming in which their opponents will be ashamed and they will be vindicated. Hence, the appeal to Noah and God's patience reminds them to persevere. If God preserved Noah when he stood in opposition to the whole world, he will also save his people, even though they are now being persecuted.

A pattern or type between Noah's day and the experience of the Petrine readers is also established with reference to salvation. The eight saved in the ark were saved physically, of course. Their physical preservation points toward the eschatological salvation that has now dawned in Jesus Christ (cf. 1 Pet 1:10–12). Indeed, even in Genesis the physical is bound up to some extent with the spiritual, for those who perished in the flood were destroyed because of their sin, and Noah was preserved because he found favor with God (cf. Gen 6:8,12–13,18). The preposition used in Greek with the verb "were saved" *(diesōthēsan)* usually means "into" *(eis)*. It is difficult to see, however, how it can retain that meaning here, for it does not make much sense to say that they were saved "into the ark." We should understand the preposition as the NIV does to refer to salvation "in" the ark.[317]

Another preposition poses a problem interpretively. What did Peter mean when he said Noah and the eight "were saved through water" *(di' hydatos)?* If one takes the preposition as instrumental, then the water is the means by which Noah and his family were saved.[318] The objection to this interpretation is that the water was the instrument used to destroy the world, not the means by which Noah and his family were saved. Others understand the preposition in a general locative sense.[319] According to this view, Noah and his family were brought safely through the waters that threatened to submerge and destroy them. In the Old Testament water is often represented as a scourge that

---

[316] Rightly France, "Exegesis in Practice," 272; Michaels, *1 Peter,* 213; Dalton, *Proclamation to Spirits,* 190; Achtemeier, *1 Peter,* 265.

[317] So Dalton, *Proclamation to Spirits,* 207; Michaels, *1 Peter,* 212; Achtemeier, *1 Peter,* 264; Elliott, *1 Peter,* 665. Elliott rightly observes that εἰς was being used for ἐν in the NT period. Against D. Cook, "I Peter iii.20: An Unnecessary Problem," *JTS* 31 (1980): 73, 75. Cook thinks Peter was reflecting on Gen 7:6–7 and conceives of Noah and his family entering into the ark from the waters of the flood that had already begun to inundate the land. Grudem also opts for the translation "into" (*1 Peter,* 161).

[318] So Best, *1 Peter,* 147; Kelly, *Peter and Jude,* 159; Michaels, *1 Peter,* 213; France, "Exegesis in Practice," 273.

[319] So Goppelt, *I Peter,* 265; Cook, "I Peter iii.20," 75–76; Selwyn, *First Peter,* 202–3; Achtemeier, *1 Peter,* 265–66; Elliott, *1 Peter,* 667. Davids is confusing in presenting his own view, saying first that water is not "the means of salvation" and then later that "Peter's thought seems to view the water as a means of salvation" (*First Peter,* 142, n. 44).

destroys (Pss 18:4; 42:7; 69:1–2,14–15; 88:7; 144:7).[320] The flood waters represented God's judgment and fury at sin, and hence Noah and his contemporaries were also rescued from the judgment of sin. We can say, then, that Noah was actually saved through water if we understand Peter to be saying the following: "Noah's 'salvation' was brought about by the same act of judgment that destroyed the wicked. . . . The way God rescues the righteous is by destroying their enemies."[321] The water, then, also separated Noah and his family from their wicked contemporaries, who perished in the flood, and hence they were spared from the corruption of the society in which they lived.[322] When the waters subsided, they entered a new world, so to speak, one that was cleansed from sin and prepared afresh for life. The parallel to baptism is drawn in the next verse and will be discussed below.

3:21 The typological thrust of the text is now specifically stated, expressed in the NIV by the verb "symbolizes," though in the Greek the word is a noun that could be translated as "type" or "pattern" (*antitypon;* cf. Heb 9:24).[323] The water that deluged the world in Noah's day and through which Noah was saved functions as a model or pattern for Christian believers.[324] But to what is the water related in the new covenant? The answer is baptism. In fact, we have the surprising statement that "baptism . . . now saves you." Before examining that statement, we must consider in what way the flood waters prefigure or correspond to baptism.[325] The waters of the

---

[320] So McCartney, "The Use of the Old Testament in the First Epistle of Peter," 177.

[321] Ibid., 178.

[322] So L. Thurén, *The Rhetorical Strategy of 1 Peter with Special Regard to Ambiguous Expressions* (Åbo: Academy Press, 1990), 114. Reicke says that Noah and his family were saved "from his dangerous environment, the disobedient beings of his time" (*The Disobedient Spirits and Christian Baptism,* 143).

[323] Elliott opts for the dative ᾧ here instead of ὃ, arguing for a substitution on the basis of the similar sight and sound of the two terms (*1 Peter,* 668–70). But the external evidence overwhelmingly favors ὃ, and hence Elliott's suggestion should be rejected.

[324] The Greek pronoun ὃ in v. 21 most naturally goes back to the word "water" (ὕδατος), which is the word that immediately precedes the pronoun (so Brox, *Der erste Petrusbrief,* 176; Michaels, *1 Peter,* 213–14; Achtemeier, *1 Peter,* 266–67). Others understand the pronoun to be more general, referring to the phrase that precedes (see Cook, "I Peter iii.20," 77; Goppelt, *I Peter,* 266; Beare, *First Peter,* 148 (though Beare prefers the reading ᾧ to ὃ). Even more improbable is the view of F. C. Synge, who understands v. 20 as parenthetical and thus connects ὃ to the death and resurrection of Christ ("1 Peter 3:18–21," *ExpTim* 88 [1971]: 311).

[325] The word ἀντίτυπον is understood as an adjective by some ("this analogous baptism now saves you," Reicke, *James, Peter, and Jude,* 106; Elliott, *1 Peter,* 671; Dalton, *Proclamation to Spirits,* 212 [though Dalton does not concur with Reicke's overall interpretation [pp. 213–14]. Selwyn thinks the reference is to people ["and water now saves you too, who are the antitype of Noah and his company" [*First Peter,* 203]). Brooks moves the period, so that it is placed after ἀντίτυπον. He translates the verse: ". . . a few, that is, eight people were saved through water which even in reference to you (is) a pattern. Baptism now saves, not as . . ." ("1 Peter 3:21," 291). For the most natural reading see Davids, *First Peter,* 143–44. Davids shows that the distance between ἀντίτυπον and βάπτισμα makes it unlikely that the former is an adjective. Brooks's view should be rejected, for he is forced to take the pronoun ὑμᾶς in two different ways.

flood deluged the ancient world and were the agent of death.[326] Similarly, baptism, which was by immersion during the time of the New Testament, occurs when one is plunged under the water. Anyone who is submerged under water dies. Submersion under the water represents death, as Paul suggested in Rom 6:3–5. Jesus described his upcoming death in terms of baptism (Mark 10:38–39; Luke 12:50), indicating that submersion under the water aptly portrays death.[327] Just as the chaotic waters of the flood were the agent of destruction, so too the waters of baptism are waters of destruction. In New Testament theology, however (cf. Matt 3:16; Mark 10:38–39; Rom 6:3–5), believers survive the death-dealing baptismal waters because they are baptized with Christ. They are rescued from death through his resurrection (Rom 6:3–5; Col 2:12). Hence, we are not surprised to read in this verse that baptism saves "by the resurrection of Jesus Christ." The waters of baptism, like the waters of the flood, demonstrate that destruction is at hand, but believers are rescued from these waters in that they are baptized with Christ, who has also emerged from the waters of death through his resurrection. Just as Noah was delivered through the stormy waters of the flood, believers have been saved through the stormy waters of baptism by virtue of Christ's triumph over death. The word "now" refers to the present eschatological age of fulfillment. With the coming of Jesus Christ the age of salvation has arrived.[328]

It is clear from what has already been said, therefore, that Peter did not succumb to a mechanical view of baptism, as if the rite itself contains an inherent saving power. Such a sacramental view was far from his mind. The saving power of baptism is rooted in the resurrection of Jesus Christ.[329] Peter also added another comment, however, to ward off any misunderstanding.[330] He described what occurs in baptism. Baptism is not "the removal of dirt from the body." The NASB follows the Greek more closely here, "not the removal of dirt from the flesh," so that we see that the term actually used is "flesh" *(sarx)* rather than "body" *(sōma)*. The distinction is important, for some commentators conclude from the use of the word

[326] Still, R. E. Nixon is unpersuasive when he argues that baptism refers primarily to suffering rather than to water baptism ("The Meaning of 'Baptism' in 1 Peter 3,21," in *Texte und Untersuchungen zur Geschichte der altchristlichen Literatur,* vol. 102, *SE,* Vol. IV [Berlin: Akademie–Verlag, 1968], 437–41).

[327] Contra Dalton, who fails to see that the image of death applies to believers (*Proclamation to Spirits,* 203).

[328] So also Elliott, *1 Peter,* 674; Brox, *Der erste Petrusbrief,* 177.

[329] So Goppelt, *I Peter,* 267 (nonetheless Goppelt succumbs to a sacramental view; see p. 266); Achtemeier, *1 Peter,* 267–68.

[330] The two contrasting noun clauses (οὐ σαρκὸς ἀπόθεσις ῥύπου ἀλλὰ συνειδήσεως ἀγαθῆς ἐπερώτημα εἰς θεόν) are appositional to the clause where ὅ functions as the subject. So France, "Exegesis in Practice," 273; Achtemeier, *1 Peter,* 266.

"flesh" that Peter spoke in a moral rather than a physical sense.[331] According to this view, baptism does not involve the removal of moral filth or impurity (cf. Jas 1:21).[332] This interpretation should be rejected. Elsewhere baptism is connected with the cleansing and removal of sin (cf. Mark 1:4; Luke 3:3; Acts 2:38; Eph 5:26; Titus 3:5). It would be strange indeed if baptism did not represent cleansing from moral impurity. Others understand the verse even more symbolically, thinking that the removal of the filth of the flesh refers to circumcision since uncircumcision can signify uncleanness (cf. Lev 19:23; Jer 4:4; 1 Sam 17:26,36; Jer 9:26).[333] Baptism, on these terms, is not equivalent to physical circumcision and should not be understood merely as a physical and external act. This view at least has the merit of being a more sensible understanding of Peter's theology, for any sense that the physical act of baptism saves is removed. But the attempt to connect the expression with circumcision should be assessed as a failure. The language used is too remote to detect an allusion to circumcision. It is difficult to believe that Gentiles in Asia Minor would have seen any reference to circumcision, nor did Peter evince any interest elsewhere in Jewish rituals.[334] The simplest interpretation is to be preferred. Any notion that baptism is inherently saving is ruled out, for the point is not that the water itself magically cleanses.[335] Water removes dirt from the skin, but baptism does not save simply because someone has been submerged under the water.[336] The statement about the removal of dirt is made so that believers will not understand baptism mechanically or superficially. They must attend to what is really happening in baptism.

The meaning of baptism, then, is explained in the contrasting clause. It is not removing dirt from the flesh but "the pledge of a good conscience." The NIV translation represents one interpretation of a very contested phrase. The word translated "pledge" *(eperōtēma)* occurs only here in the New Testament and only once in the Septuagint (Dan 4:17). In the latter case it means something like "decree," which does not make sense in our passage. The meaning of the noun, however, can be derived from the verb

---

[331] E.g., Michaels, *1 Peter,* 215–16.

[332] So Richard, *Reading 1 Peter, Jude, and 2 Peter,* 162.

[333] Dalton, *Proclamation to Spirits,* 215–24; Kelly, *Peter and Jude,* 161–62; Achtemeier, *1 Peter,* 269; cf. also the more general view of Reicke, *The Disobedient Spirits and Christian Baptism,* 188.

[334] Cf. Goppelt, *I Peter,* 268; Michaels, *1 Peter,* 215; Davids, *First Peter,* 144, n. 49; D. Hill, "On Suffering and Baptism in *I Peter,*" *NovT* 18 (1976): 186–87; France, "Exegesis in Practice," 281, n. 59; Elliott, *1 Peter,* 678–79.

[335] So Selwyn, *First Peter,* 204; Grudem, *1 Peter,* 163; Davids, *First Peter,* 144; France, "Exegesis in Practice," 274; Elliott, *1 Peter,* 679.

[336] Calvin emphatically rejects any notion that baptism alone saves (*Catholic Epistles,* 118–19).

(eperōtaō), which often has the meaning of "ask" or "request" in the New Testament, occurring fifty-six times in the New Testament (e.g., Matt 12:10; 16:1; 17:10; 22:23,35,41,46; 27:11; Mark 7:5; 9:21; Luke 2:46; 3:10; John 18:7; 1 Cor 14:35).[337] If the meaning is derived from the verb, the translation "ask," "request," or "appeal" would fit. We see this interpretation in the NRSV, "an appeal to God for a good conscience" (cf. also RSV). The interpretation reflected in the NIV can be supported by the usage of the word in the papyri. In these instances the term can be used of stipulations found in contracts. One pledges or promises to abide by the terms of the contract and the stipulations found therein. Similarly, one can understand the text to refer to the promise or pledge made at baptism.[338] If one adopts this view, the genitive word "conscience" could be understood as subjective or objective. If subjective, the phrase says that the promise or pledge to abide by baptismal vows flows from a good conscience. Most scholars who adopt this view, however, understand the word "conscience" to be an objective genitive. If this is the case, the person being baptized promises to maintain a good conscience at baptism.[339] The one baptized pledges to live for the glory of God. This interpretation is certainly possible and does not necessarily contradict Petrine theology. I think it is more likely, however, that the meaning of the noun is derived from the verb. I reach this decision on contextual grounds. In other words, both interpretations of the word *eperōtēma* are possible lexically. In context, however, it seems more likely that baptism is associated with an appeal or request to God for a good conscience.[340] Once again the word "conscience" could be understood as a subjective genitive—an appeal to God arising from a good conscience. We can rule out the subjective genitive immediately, though, for then we cannot specify what the believer is praying for since he already has a good conscience.[341] But if the genitive is objective, as I think it is, believers at bap-

[337] So Senior, "The Conduct of Christians in the World," 72; Grudem, *1 Peter,* 163–64; Beare, *First Peter,* 149; Michaels, *1 Peter,* 217; Schweizer, "1. Petrus 4,6," 82; H. Greeven, *TDNT* 2:688–89; Schelke, *Der Petrusbriefe—Der Judasbrief,* 109

[338] So Fitzmyer, "First Peter," 367; Dalton, *Proclamation to Spirits,* 224–29; G. C. Richards, "I Pet. iii.21," *JTS* 32 (1930): 77; Kelly, *Peter and Jude,* 162–63; Achtemeier, *1 Peter,* 270–72; G. T. D. Angel, *NIDNTT* 2:880–81; Best, *1 Peter,* 148; Selwyn, *First Peter,* 205–6; Davids, *First Peter,* 145; D. H. Tripp, "*Eperōtēma* (I Peter 3:21): A Liturgist's Note," *ExpTim* 92 (1981): 267–70; Hill, "Spiritual Sacrifices," 59; France, "Exegesis in Practice," 275; Elliott, *1 Peter,* 679–80; Brox, *Der erste Petrusbrief,* 178.

[339] Alternatively, Brooks understands the phrase as a "declaration of the individual's appropriate conscious awareness in reference to God" ("I Peter 3:21," 294).

[340] Michaels suggests that the word εἰς following ἐπερώτημα might support "appeal" (*1 Peter,* 217).

[341] Scholars who support the subjective genitive even though they may not agree on the meaning of the word ἐπερώτημα include Cranfield, *I & II Peter and Jude,* 106–7; Best, *1 Peter,* 148; Selwyn, *First Peter,* 205; Michaels, *1 Peter,* 216; Richards, "I Pet iii.21," 77.

tism ask God—on the basis of the death and resurrection of Christ—to cleanse their consciences and forgive their sins.[342] The idea, then, is quite similar to Heb 10:22, where believers can draw near to God confidently because their "hearts" have been "sprinkled to cleanse us from a guilty conscience" (cf. Heb 10:2).[343] In Hebrews there is no doubt that a cleansed conscience is due to the cross of Christ. The interpretation adopted here fits with the context of 1 Pet 3:18–22, where Peter emphasized Christ's death as the means by which believers are brought into God's presence. Christ died for believers, the righteous for the unrighteous, and hence believers enter into God's presence on the basis of God's grace alone. So too Peter did not focus on promises believers make when baptized but the saving work of Christ and his resurrection. Believers at baptism can be confident on the basis of the work of the crucified and risen Lord that their appeal to have a good conscience will be answered.

3:22 The resurrection of Jesus Christ brings us back to the center of this passage, the victory of Christ over his enemies. Peter picked up again the word "has gone" *(poreutheis),* emphasizing Jesus' ascension after his resurrection. The same term in v. 19, I argued, also refers to Jesus' triumph over demonic powers after his death and resurrection. The emphasis here is on Jesus' entrance into heaven and rule at God's right hand. The reference to the right hand recalls Ps 110:1, where David's Lord sits at Yahweh's right hand and rules. Jesus applied the psalm to himself in his teaching (cf. Matt 22:44; 26:64; Mark 12:36; 14:62; Luke 20:42–43; 22:69), and the influence of the psalm is pervasive in the rest of the New Testament (Acts 2:34–35; Rom 8:34; 1 Cor 15:25; Eph 1:20; Col 3:1; Heb 1:3,13; 8:1; 10:12). The text circles back to v. 19 emphasizing that angels, authorities, and powers are subjected to Jesus. All three words refer to angels (for "authorities" *[exousia]* see 1 Cor 15:24; Eph 1:21; 3:10; 6:12; Col 1:16; 2:15; and for "powers" *[dynamis]* see Rom 8:38; 1 Cor 15:24; Eph 1:21). Trying to discern the hierarchy of angels from the different words lands us in unprovable speculation. The point is that Jesus reigns over all the hostile angelic pow-

---

[342] Supporting the objective genitive with this interpretation are Dalton, *Proclamation to Spirits*, 230–33;Grudem, *1 Peter,* 163; Beare, *First Peter,* 149; Moffatt, *James, Peter, and Jude*, 143; Schweizer, "1. Petrus 4,6," 82; Achtemeier, *1 Peter,* 271–72; Goppelt, *I Peter,* 268–69; Schelke, *Der Petrusbriefe—Der Judasbrief,* 109. Of course, one may favor the interpretation "pledge" and still argue for an objective genitive (see Kelly, *Peter and Jude,* 163). Contra to Campbell, believers are not asking to be honored or vindicated (*Honor, Shame, and the Rhetoric of 1 Peter,* 183), for the text links the plea to having a good conscience.

[343] Some might object that believers do not ask God to cleanse their consciences and forgive their sins at baptism since they are already forgiven and cleansed before baptism. But Peter did not attempt here to distinguish between the exact moment when sins were forgiven and baptism. Baptism, like going forward in many Baptist churches today, is portrayed as the time when sins are forgiven and one becomes a believer.

ers. Contextually it would make little sense to emphasize that Jesus ruled over good angels.[344] The message for Peter's readers is clear. In their suffering Jesus still reigns and rules. He has not surrendered believers into the power of the evil forces even if they suffer until death. Jesus by his death and resurrection has triumphed over all demonic forces, and hence by implication believers will reign together with him.

(3) Preparing to Suffer as Christ Did (4:1–6)

1Therefore, since Christ suffered in his body, arm yourselves also with the same attitude, because he who has suffered in his body is done with sin. 2As a result, he does not live the rest of his earthly life for evil human desires, but rather for the will of God. 3For you have spent enough time in the past doing what pagans choose to do—living in debauchery, lust, drunkenness, orgies, carousing and detestable idolatry. 4They think it strange that you do not plunge with them into the same flood of dissipation, and they heap abuse on you. 5But they will have to give account to him who is ready to judge the living and the dead. 6For this is the reason the gospel was preached even to those who are now dead, so that they might be judged according to men in regard to the body, but live according to God in regard to the spirit.

Peter drew a conclusion from the previous paragraph with the word "therefore." He argued in 3:18–22 that the suffering of the Christ was the pathway to his victory and exaltation. Hence, just as Christ suffered in the flesh (by dying, as 3:18 indicates), so too believers should resolve to suffer, for the decision to suffer indicates that they have ceased to let sin have dominion over them. Verse 2 supplies the purpose for the exhortation given in v. 1. Believers should resolve to suffer in order to live for the will of God during the rest of their lives. Peter remarked in v. 3 that they had already had more than ample time to live like the Gentiles, in a life of unrestrained licentiousness. Because the Petrine believers had broken with their pagan past (v. 4) and no longer pursued a dissolute life, their former friends were astonished and reviled both believers and their God. In v. 5 the readers are reminded that the reviling of unbelievers is not the last word. God, at the conclusion of history, will judge the living and dead. Ultimately, the wicked will be recompensed for their evil lives and their mistreatment of believers. Peter implied from this that it would be folly for believers to relapse into a pagan lifestyle, even though they currently faced hostility and criticism. At the end of the day they will be vindicated, and the wicked will be judged, and so they should resist any temptation to relapse and thereby join the company of those who will be judged. In v. 6 Peter took up another objection to the gospel he preached. Pagans probably dismissed the Christian

[344] Rightly Achtemeier, *1 Peter,* 274; Selwyn, *1 Peter,* 208; Kelly, *Peter and Jude,* 164.

faith by pointing out that believers died in the same way as unbelievers. Peter explained that the gospel was proclaimed to believers while they were still alive so that they would live in the spirit in God's presence, even though they experienced the temporal judgment of physical death. In other words, physical death is not the last word for believers. The gospel promises that they will ultimately be raised from the dead.

4:1 The word "therefore" draws a conclusion from the previous verses (3:18–22), where Christ's victory over hostile powers by virtue of his death and resurrection is featured.[345] The connection between the two sections is this: since Christ's suffering is the pathway to glory, believers should also prepare themselves to suffer, knowing that suffering is the prelude to an eschatological reward.[346] The main point of the verse is that believers are to arm themselves *(hoplisasthe)* with the intention to suffer. The term "arm yourselves" has military connotations, and in other texts the Christian life is compared to the life of a warrior (Rom 6:13; 13:12; 2 Cor 6:7; 10:4; Eph 6:11–17; 1 Thess 5:8). The martial language indicates that discipline and grit are needed to live the Christian life, particularly in view of the suffering believers encounter. Indeed, believers must arm themselves with the "attitude" that suffering is inevitable. The word translated "attitude" *(ennoia)* can be translated "intention" (NRSV) or "thought" (RSV). In most cases a translation like "insight," "thought," or "knowledge" suffices.[347] The connection with "arm yourselves," however, indicates that the insight becomes an "intention" and so the latter probably is the best translation. Like soldiers preparing for battle, believers should prepare themselves for suffering.

The first clause in the verse explains the reason the Petrine readers should expect to suffer. Christ also "suffered in the flesh" (NRSV). The wording hearkens back to 3:18, where both the verb "suffer[ed]" *(paschō)* and the noun "flesh" *(sarx)* occur (in NRSV).[348] We have further evidence confirming the interpretation of v. 18, for the "flesh" of Christ refers to his bodily suffering (cf. NIV). We noted in v. 18 that the verb "suffer" was a favorite of Peter's, and in both texts he links the suffering of Christ to the suffering of his readers, acknowledging, of course, the distinctiveness of Christ's suffering as well. Christ's suffering here focuses on his death as in 3:18 and 2:21–24. Further, as in 2:21–23 Christ's suffering is exemplary for believers, providing the pattern they should imitate.

---

[345] Van Rensburg, "The Use of Intersentence Relational Particles and Asyndeton in 1 Peter," 297.

[346] Michaels wrongly thinks that vv. 19–22 are skipped over when the argument resumes in v. 1 (*1 Peter,* 225).

[347] See BDAG, 337; I. T. Blazen, "Suffering and Cessation from Sin according to 1 Peter 4:1," *AUSS* 21 (1983): 30–32.

[348] The point made here is not damaged by the fact that the noun σάρξ is connected to θανατωθείς.

The most difficult part of the verse is the last phrase, "because he who has suffered in his body is done with sin." Once again the NIV translates *sarx* ("flesh") as "body," so that the connection between Christ's suffering and that of believers is preserved. Still the NIV captures the meaning by rendering both as "body." Some scholars also understand the word "because" *(hoti)* as an explanation of the word "intention" (NRSV) rather than causal.[349] But a causal meaning seems more likely syntactically.[350] Fortunately, the meaning is not affected significantly either way since a reason is given for why believers should prepare themselves to suffer. Scholars debate, however, on what reason is supplied. Three different interpretations are quite possible.[351] First, the one who suffered could be identified as Jesus Christ.[352] The objection to this view is that Jesus never sinned (cf. 2:22; 3:18), so how could it be said that he had ceased from sin?[353] This interpretation could still be defended if sin is understood in terms similar to Rom 6:8–10. By virtue of his death and resurrection, the power of sin was broken, and Christ ceased to have any relationship with sin. At the cross the sinless one took sin upon himself, but now that he has suffered, he no longer deals with sin. His triumph over it is complete. This interpretation is attractive in that it removes any implication that believers could somehow be sinlessly perfect. It is difficult to see how believers are done with sin in this life, but it makes good sense to say that Christ was done with sin once for all at the cross. Nevertheless, this interpretation should be rejected. It is scarcely clear that the phrase "he who has suffered" refers to Christ. The subject is almost surely believers, for the syntax of the text indicates that those who arm themselves are to be equated with those who suffer. The singular form here is generic and should not be pressed as if the reference were to a solitary individual. The need to posit Christ as the subject can be eliminated if we show that there are plausible ways of speaking of Christians as ceasing from sin without importing any idea that believers are sinless. Both of the following interpretations fit this requirement.

Second, the one who suffers in the flesh refers to Christians, but it should be understood in terms similar to Rom 6:7, "Anyone who has died has been freed from sin." In Romans 6 believers died with Christ, via bap-

---

[349] E.g., Calvin, *Catholic Epistles,* 121; Kelly, *Peter and Jude,* 166; Achtemeier, *1 Peter,* 278; Davids, *First Peter,* 148, n. 2; Dalton, *Proclamation to Spirits,* 241.

[350] So Michaels, *1 Peter,* 225–26; Goppelt, *I Peter,* 280; Elliott, *1 Peter,* 714. Elliott argues that the focus on action—ceasing from sinning—stands in favor of this option.

[351] Achtemeier mentions the notion that one's suffering could atone for sin but rightly rejects this as incompatible with Petrine theology (*1 Peter,* 279).

[352] So Michaels, *1 Peter,* 226–29; Hillyer, *1 and 2 Peter, Jude,* 120; cf. Richard, *Reading 1 Peter, Jude, and 2 Peter,* 167–68.

[353] Bechtler says the verse is ambiguous and both Christ and believers are in view (*Following in His Steps*, 196–98).

tism, to the power of sin. Similarly, the verse here says that the dominion of sin has been broken in the lives of those who have died with Christ.[354] The advantage of this interpretation is that it coheres with Paul and sensibly explains how believers cease with sin. Still, the interpretation should be rejected.[355] We must beware of imposing the Pauline writings on 1 Peter, and the two contexts are quite different. It is apparent in Romans 6 that the believer dies with Christ, but no such language is used in 1 Peter. Indeed, the word "suffered" in the last phrase of v. 1 cannot be equated with dying. As Elliott argues, Paul spoke metaphorically of dying with Christ whereas Peter had in mind actual suffering.[356] We should note that the verb used is "suffer" *(paschō),* not "die" *(apothēnskō).* The notion here is not that believers have died with Christ but that they should follow Christ in their daily lives by consenting to suffering. Further, Peter did not use the word "sin" *(hamartia)* to designate a power, something that is quite common in Paul. The word "sin" in Peter is used of acts of sin (cf. 2:22,24; 4:1,8).[357]

The third interpretation is most persuasive.[358] "He who has suffered" refers to believers and relates back to the imperative to prepare themselves for suffering. Peter explained why they should prepare themselves to suffer, seeing the commitment to suffer as evidence that they have broken with a life of sin.[359] The point is not that believers who suffer have attained sinless perfection, as if they do not sin at all after suffering. What Peter emphasized was that those who commit themselves to suffer, those who willingly endure scorn and mockery for their faith, show that they have triumphed over sin. They have broken with sin because they have ceased to participate in the lawless activities of unbelievers and endured the criticisms that have come from such a decision. The commitment to suffer reveals a passion for a new way of life, a life that is not yet perfect but remarkably different from the lives of unbelievers in the Greco-Roman world.[360]

4:2 The NIV understands the clause in this verse to designate result—

---

[354] So Calvin, *Catholic Epistles,* 121; Beare, *First Peter,* 153; Dalton, *Proclamation to Spirits,* 244–48; Kelly, *Peter and Jude,* 168–69; Cranfield, *I & II Peter and Jude,* 108.

[355] See Achtemeier, *1 Peter,* 279–80.

[356] Elliott, *1 Peter,* 716.

[357] Rightly Blazen, "1 Peter 4:1," 39–41.

[358] So Grudem, *1 Peter,* 167; Schweizer, "1. Petrus 4,6," 84; Omanson, "Suffering," 445–46; Achtemeier, *1 Peter,* 280; Bigg, *Epistles of Peter and Jude,* 167.

[359] Nor is it likely that the term "suffer" here refers to death, so that believers cease from sinning upon death (so Blazen, "1 Peter 4:1," 27–50). Blazen mistakenly imports the meaning of "suffer" in terms of Christ's specific suffering and reads the same meaning into the lives of believers.

[360] The view supported here should be distinguished from the idea that suffering itself breaks the inclination to sin in a person's life since people may respond to suffering negatively, multiplying rather than diminishing sin. Neither is there any reference to Jewish martyr traditions here, where suffering atones for sin (rightly Elliott, *1 Peter,* 715).

"As a result," but more likely it is a purpose clause.[361] Christians should arm themselves with the intention to suffer, so that they live the remainder of their lives in carrying out God's will instead of fulfilling the human lusts that dominated their lives before conversion. The purpose clause provides confirmation for the interpretation proposed for the last clause in v. 1. Believers are summoned to suffer in the sense that they are called to do God's will and to turn away from a life of sin. Some scholars think the remaining time on earth is understood as the short time before the second coming of Christ rather than the rest of one's life before death.[362] But we need not choose between these two options, for the text is not specific enough to warrant one or the other.[363] Peter realized that some Christians would likely die before Christ returned while still anticipating the imminent return of Christ. Whatever the span of life God grants, believers are to live zealously for God as long as life endures.

4:3 The "for" *(gar)* introducing v. 3 explains why believers should live the rest of their lives for God's will. They have already spent sufficient time *(arketos)* in the past carrying out "the will of the Gentiles" (translated "pagans" by NIV).[364] The use of the word "will" *(boulēma)* establishes a contrast between vv. 2 and 3. Believers should live for the "will" *(thelēma)* of God, but before their conversion they devoted themselves to the "will" *(boulēma)* of the Gentiles. The use of the word "Gentiles" *(ethnē)* for unbelievers, without comment, indicates that Peter understood believers in Jesus Christ as part of Israel, members of the new people of God (cf. 2:9–10). In saying that the time past is "enough" to have lived as unbelievers, Peter's point was that it is more than enough, that there is no room now for any dalliance with the lifestyle of unbelievers.

The lifestyle of unbelievers is then sketched in with a vice list. Such vice lists are common in the New Testament (cf. Mark 7:22; Rom 13:13; 1 Cor 5:10–11; 6:9–10; 2 Cor 12:20; Gal 5:19–21; Eph 4:31; 5:3–5; Col 3:5,8; Titus 3:3). The words "debauchery" *(aselgeia)* and "lust" *(epithymia)* may refer to sexual sin here (see Rom 13:13; 2 Cor 12:21; Gal 5:19; Eph 4:19 for the former and Rom 1:24; 1 Thess 4:5; 2 Pet 2:18 for the latter), but

---

[361] Rightly Achtemeier, *1 Peter,* 280; Bigg, *Epistles of Peter and Jude,* 167. Cf. HCSB "in order to live."

[362] Kelly, *Peter and Jude,* 169; Achtemeier, *1 Peter,* 281.

[363] Nor is there any basis for understanding the word σαρκὶ here to be one's sinful inclinations. The text refers to the life in the body here (rightly Davids, *First Peter,* 150; Selwyn, *First Peter,* 210; Achtemeier, *1 Peter,* 281). Still, as Davids remarks, "Since the flesh is weak and fallen, it is the mode of existence in which the evil impulse in human beings operates" (p. 150).

[364] The reference to the past life of the readers demonstrates that they were mainly Gentiles. Nor do the allusions and citations from the OT in 1 Peter suggest otherwise (against Hillyer, *1 and 2 Peter, Jude,* 121). Frequent reference to the OT is found in 1 Corinthians, which was written mainly to Gentiles.

they could also be general terms for sin.[365] The combination of sexual sin, drinking, and parties apparently was common in the Greco-Roman world, as it is today. The next three words all focus on drunkenness and carousing. The particular word for "drunkenness" *(oinophlygia)* occurs only here in the New Testament (but cf. Rom 13:13; Gal 5:21; Eph 5:18). Deuteronomy 21:20 uses a verbal form of the word to describe a drunkard *(oinophlygeō)*. "Orgies" *(kōmoi)* are also condemned in Rom 13:13 and Gal 5:21, and in both, these texts are also linked with drunkenness. Achtemeier says that the reference is to "festal gatherings, whether private and domestic or public and religious."[366] The term for "carousing" *(potoi)* occurs only here in the New Testament (see also Prov 23:30; Josephus, *Ant.* 5.289), referring probably to "social drinking parties."[367] It is evident that these people lived a dissolute life before their conversion. The last item mentioned is their "detestable idolatry." The reference to idolatry indicates that the readers were not Jews but Gentiles, for overt idolatry did not characterize Jewish communities. The word "lawless" does not focus on lack of conformity to the law but to an unholy and profane lifestyle (cf. Acts 10:28; *2 Mac* 6:5–6; 7:1; 10:34).[368] In addition, the sins listed in v. 3, though not absent from Jewish people, were not typical among religiously devout Jews.

4:4 The initial words of the text, deleted by the NIV ("in all this," NASB, *en hō*) should be understood as inferential and translated "therefore."[369] Because the Petrine readers no longer participate in the activities listed in v. 3, their neighbors "are surprised" (NRSV, *xenizontai*) or "think it strange" that Christians have forsaken their past lifestyle. In this verse we are reminded in what sense Christians are sojourners and exiles. They do not share the values and aspirations of the surrounding society, not fitting into the social fabric. What surprises unbelievers is that Christians do not "plunge" *(syntrechontōn)* into or participate in their immoral way of living—"the flood of dissipation" *(tēs asōtias anachysin)* that characterized life in Asia Minor. The participle *blasphēmountes,* translated "and they heap abuse on you," is connected by some commentators with v. 5, so that it provides the reason for the judgment pronounced there.[370] More likely the participle should be understood as designating the result or consequence of

---

[365] Michaels supports a reference to sexual sin (*1 Peter,* 231).

[366] Achtemeier, *1 Peter,* 282, n. 84. Elliott suggests a possible reference to Dionysian feasts (*1 Peter,* 724).

[367] Achtemeier, *1 Peter,* 282, n. 84.

[368] So Elliott, *1 Peter,* 724.

[369] So Michaels, *1 Peter,* 232–33; Fink, "Use of *en hō* in I Peter," 35. Reicke takes it as causal (*The Disobedient Spirits and Christian Baptism,* 111). Elliott thinks it is circumstantial (*1 Peter,* 725).

[370] So Michaels, *1 Peter,* 233; Achtemeier, *1 Peter,* 284.

the first clause in v. 4.[371] Pagans are surprised that believers do not participate in what they consider to be normal cultural activities; in response they criticize, defame, and revile believers and thereby also the God they worship.[372]

This verse is important for understanding the nature of the persecution in 1 Peter. There is little evidence of state-sponsored persecution that robbed early believers of their lives. Instead, unbelievers were at first puzzled and then outraged by the failure of believers to participate in activities that were a normal part of Greco-Roman culture. We see such a reaction in Tacitus when he says Christians have a "hatred of the human race" (*Ann.* 15.44). Pagans would feel this way because idolatry was woven into almost every dimension of their lives, from life in the home to public festivals to religious observances and even social occasions.[373] In the Western world we take for granted the segregation of private and public spheres, but public festivals, in which the gods were venerated, were considered a civic duty in the Greco-Roman world. In particular veneration of the emperor was simply a mark of good citizenship, and the deifying of the emperor was especially pronounced in Asia Minor.[374] Those who failed to participate would be social outcasts, just as today American citizens would look with suspicion on those who refused to take the Pledge of Allegiance to the flag. We can imagine that those who did not fit in with the mores of society would be discriminated against in daily life and that they would be the object of abuse. Identifying the specific lineaments of persecution in 1 Peter is important, for modern readers in the West tend to restrict persecution to imprisonment, physical deprivation, torture, and execution. As we noted, there is little evidence in 1 Peter for these things. The readers were mistreated by being socially ostracized. We should not overlook that criticism and social ostracism often lead to more severe action, that sharp words can easily turn into sharp swords. If Revelation was written around A.D. 95, it is evident that in Asia Minor at least some believers were losing their lives for their devotion to Christ. When 1 Peter was written, however, the penalties were not yet that severe, though Peter wrote to prepare his readers for whatever might come.

4:5 As is so often the case in the letter, Peter turned the readers' eyes toward the *eschaton*. Currently unbelievers may have been enjoying the favor and privileges of Greco-Roman society. They may have been experi-

---

[371] Rightly Elliott, who notes that the other interpretation does not fit with how Peter used participles elsewhere (*1 Peter,* 727).

[372] The focus is on reviling believers, not God, though God himself is reviled when his people are criticized (so Kelly, *Peter and Jude,* 170–71).

[373] See the excellent discussion in Achtemeier, *1 Peter,* 284–85.

[374] See S. R. F. Price, *Rituals and Power* (New York: Cambridge University Press, 1986), 78.

encing social advancement and the praise of their peers. They may have been the consummate "insiders," while the Petrine readers were on the outside. Present circumstances, however, are not the last word. Those who live now "for evil human desires" (v. 2), who live in debauchery and the "flood of dissipation" (vv. 3–4) and revile believers (v. 4), will be judged by God on the last day. They will need to "give account" to God. The phrase "give account" *(apodōsousin logon)* is courtroom language (cf. Matt 12:36; Luke 16:2; Acts 19:40; Heb 13:17; cf. Rom 2:6; 2 Tim 4:8,14; Rev 22:12), referring to the final judgment here.[375] That the final judgment is in view is evident from the words "the living and the dead" (cf. 1 Thess 4:16–17; 1 Cor 15:52). It is hardly credible to define the "dead" here as the spiritually dead, for when combined with the word "living" it refers to all people who have ever lived. The judge in view could quite possibly be Christ (cf. Matt 25:31–46; Mark 8:38; Acts 10:42; 17:31; Rom 14:9; 2 Tim 4:1).[376] It also is possible that the judge is God himself (cf. Rom 2:6; 3:6; 14:10), for in 1 Pet 1:17 and 2:23 God functions as the judge.[377] Perhaps Christ is to be favored slightly since he is typically designated as the judge of the living and the dead.[378] The main point of the verse is affirmed in either instance. Believers should not succumb to the temptation to renounce their faith so they can enjoy the approbation of society. Such approval is short-lived, and those who mistreat believers now will be judged in the future. We should note that Peter did not mention the final judgment of unbelievers to encourage vindictiveness (cf. 1 Pet 2:21–23). Nor did he address these words to unbelievers. He reminded *believers* of the final judgment of all, assuring them that their perseverance in the faith matters and that those who practice evil will be assessed and condemned on the final day. Hence, they must not align themselves with the oppressors to escape discrimination, for soon the tables will be turned.

4:6 Verse 6 is joined to the preceding by the word "for" *(gar),* and we will return in due course to how this verse relates to the preceding. The words "this is the reason" *(eis touto)* do not point backward to v. 5 in this case (cf. 1 Pet 2:21; 3:9) but ahead to the purpose clause ("so that," *hina*).[379] The reason the gospel was preached to the dead is articulated in the last clause of the verse. Before we examine the purpose, we must inves-

---

[375] Perhaps we have a reversal of 1 Pet 3:15–16 here (so Michaels, *1 Peter,* 234).

[376] So Beare, *First Peter,* 155–56; Best, *1 Peter,* 154; Selwyn, *First Peter,* 213–14; Kelly, *Peter and Jude,* 172.

[377] Michaels, *1 Peter,* 235; Goppelt, *I Peter,* 287–88; Achtemeier, *1 Peter,* 286; Richard, *Reading 1 Peter, Jude, and 2 Peter,* 172; Elliott, *1 Peter,* 730.

[378] Davids, *First Peter,* 153.

[379] Rightly Selwyn, *First Peter,* 214; Michaels, *1 Peter,* 238; Schweizer, "1. Petrus 4,6," 153; Elliott, *1 Peter,* 732.

tigate what Peter meant by preaching the gospel to the dead. The NIV translation reads, "The gospel was preached even to those who are now dead." The word "now" represents an interpretation of the text, one to which we will return. It should be noted at this juncture, however, that the word "now" is not in the Greek text. The NIV translators supply it in order to interpret the text. A more literal translation is supplied by the NRSV, "For this is the reason the gospel was proclaimed even to the dead." The NRSV translation, which renders the original text well, raises a question: What did Peter mean by the word "dead" *(nekrois)* here? Various answers have been given.[380] Some scholars argue that the term means "spiritually dead" (cf. John 5:25; Eph 2:1,5; Col 2:13).[381] This interpretation avoids the problem of the gospel being proclaimed to people who are physically dead and fits with Paul's notion that unbelievers are spiritually dead. The solution should be rejected, however, because Peter nowhere used the term "dead" *(nekros)* to refer to spiritual death.[382] Moreover, the word "dead" *(nekrous)* in the previous verse clearly refers to those who are physically dead.[383] Peter gave no contextual clues that he shifted the meaning of the term in this verse, though I will argue below that he did give contextual clues that alter the meaning of the term "judge."

Others maintain that the verse speaks of the preaching of the gospel to those who have died physically. This interpretation is often connected with 1 Pet 3:19, where the spirits are understood to be human beings and the gospel was proclaimed to them after their death (see commentary on 3:19). According to this view, however, 4:6 is an elaboration of what was communicated in 3:19, for now all those who have died have the gospel proclaimed to them.[384] Some limit this to those who died before Christ's coming; oth-

---

[380] See the summary of views and critique of Dalton, *Proclamation to Spirits,* 42–51.

[381] Cf. McCartney, "The Use of the Old Testament in the First Epistle of Peter," 172. This view was held by some of the church fathers. See Augustine, *James, 1–2 Peter, 1–3 John, Jude,* ACCS (Downers Grove: InterVarsity, 2000), 113. Others taught that Jesus preached to those in hell. See Oecumenius and Theophylact in *James, 1–2 Peter, 1–3 John, Jude,* ACCS (Downers Grove: InterVarsity, 2000), 114.

[382] Rightly Reicke, *The Disobedient Spirits and Christian Baptism,* 205.

[383] McCartney points to the shift in the meaning of the word νεκρός from one verse to another in Col 2:12–13 ("The Use of the Old Testament in the First Epistle of Peter," 172). The change of meaning is clearer in Col 2:12–13, however, since in the first instance the reference is to Christ's resurrection and the second is to the spiritual state of believers.

[384] Cf. Bigg, *Epistles of Peter and Jude,* 170–71; Beare, *First Peter,* 156; Cranfield, *I & II Peter and Jude,* 110; "1 Peter iii.19 and iv.6," 371–72; Goppelt, *I Peter,* 289; Schweizer, "1. Petrus 4,6," 152–54. For a variant view see Reicke, *The Disobedient Spirits and Christian Baptism*, 205, 209. For a recent defense of this view see D. J. Horrell, "Who Are 'The Dead' and When Was the Gospel Preached to Them?: The Interpretation of 1 Pet 4.6," *NTS* 49 (2003): 70–89. Against Horrell, it is quite possible that Petrine believers worried about the fate of dead believers in a context in which they were persecuted and reviled by unbelievers.

ers, to all those who died without hearing the gospel; and others, to all those who died without exception. The advantage of this interpretation is that it understands the "dead" in vv. 5–6 to refer to those who are physically dead, so that there is no shift in meaning. Nevertheless, this interpretation should be rejected for several reasons. First, we argued earlier that 1 Pet 3:19 does not refer to the preaching of the gospel at all but to a proclamation of triumph over demonic powers. Elliott rightly remarks, "The interest in a possible correspondence between 3:19 and 4:6 appears motivated more by dogmatic than by exegetical concerns; namely, a desire to find here a biblical expression of the universality of salvation."[385] Second, the passive verb phrase "the gospel was preached" *(euēngelisthē)* does not refer to preaching done *by Christ* but the preaching *of Christ* (cf. the passive verb from *kēryssō,* "announce, proclaim," in 1 Cor 15:12; 2 Cor 1:19; 1 Tim 3:16).[386] We should understand this to refer to preaching by human beings, therefore, not Christ himself. Hence, the verbal form provides no support for the preaching of the gospel by Christ after human beings have died. Third, there is no basis in the text for limiting the dead to those who preceded the incarnation, to Old Testament saints, or even to those who have not had the opportunity to hear the gospel. Peter did not even give a hint that he addressed any of these people specifically. We are left, then, with the notion that the gospel was preached to all of the dead after their demise. But this view can be confidently rejected. The New Testament nowhere else envisions the possibility of repentance and salvation after death, quite the contrary (cf. Luke 16:26; Heb 9:27). Furthermore, if v. 6 refers to all the dead, then it follows from the rest of the verse that all of the dead will be saved, for Peter said the gospel was preached to the dead so that they should "live according to God in regard to the spirit." Nothing is said in this verse about any being condemned, but the notion that all will respond positively to the gospel is ruled out by the rest of the New Testament, where the final judgment of the wicked is taught consistently (cf. Matt 25:31–46). Fourth, there is an insuperable problem contextually with this interpretation. In the entire letter Peter exhorted the readers to endure persecution, knowing that they have the future reward of eternal life. Even in this paragraph he presented that very argument, urging them to persevere because God will judge those who are sinners (v. 5). It would make no sense at all if he were to shift gears suddenly and promise a second chance to those who have rejected the gospel during this life. If Peter were promising a second chance, the Petrine readers could not be faulted for concluding that they could deny the faith now and then embrace it after death. Apostasy, in any

---

[385] Elliott, *1 Peter,* 731.

[386] So Kelly, *Peter and Jude,* 173–74; Achtemeier, *1 Peter,* 287; Elliott, *1 Peter,* 730.

case, would not be the last word, for they would have another opportunity after death to believe the gospel. This interpretation should be rejected, then, because it veers away from the purpose of the entire letter and even contradicts the teaching of 4:1–6.[387] Elliott rightly concludes that any notion of Christ's universal redemption or of a second chance "to those who died before Christ . . . is thoroughly inconsistent with the theology, ethics, and aim of 1 Peter as a whole."[388]

The interpretation that makes the best sense is reflected in the NIV.[389] Peter considered the case of believers who had died physically.[390] These people heard and believed the gospel when they were alive but had subsequently died.[391] Unbelievers viewed the death of believers as proof that there is no advantage in becoming a believer, for all without exception die. Peter indicated, however, that unbelievers do not understand the whole picture. Even though from a human perspective believers seem to gain no benefits from their faith since they die, from God's perspective (which is normative), they live according to the Spirit.[392] Elliott understands the phrase a little more precisely, so that the Gentiles did not merely observe the judgment on believers but, according to the context, with their slander "actively faulted the Christians according to their own God-opposed norms."[393] In any case, death is not the last word for believers. They will be

---

[387] Best argues that a second opportunity is not promised to persecutors but to others who have died without hearing the gospel. I have already noted that restricting the "dead" to such a category has no contextual basis. But there is another problem with this interpretation. It is difficult to see why Peter would suddenly bring up the fate of those who died without hearing the gospel and then just as quickly leave the subject. We would have a lightning bolt from out of the blue on the subject, and then just as suddenly the matter would be left behind. No plausible reason can be adduced as to why the matter is even addressed. Against Best see Elliott, *1 Peter,* 731.

[388] Elliott, *1 Peter,* 731.

[389] For this interpretation see Fitzmyer, "First Peter," 367; Grudem, *1 Peter,* 170–71; Selwyn, *First Peter,* 354; Dalton, *Proclamation to Spirits,* 270–72; Achtemeier, *1 Peter,* 290–91; Kelly, *Peter and Jude,* 174–75; Davids, *First Peter,* 153–55; France, "Exegesis in Practice," 265; Richard, *Reading 1 Peter, Jude, and 2 Peter,* 173–74; Elliott, *1 Peter,* 733–34.

[390] But it is unclear that their death was due to martyrdom (contra France, "Exegesis in Practice," 265). The language is too vague to yield this conclusion.

[391] Michaels adds a twist to this interpretation, arguing that it refers to all believers who have died throughout history (*1 Peter,* 236–37). This interpretation is possible, but it is more likely that Peter reflected on those who died in the Petrine community, addressing the specific concern of believers in Asia Minor. Further, the preaching of the gospel probably is restricted to the time after Christ's death and resurrection (1:12; 4:17). Michaels unconvincingly appeals to Hebrews (4:2,6) to solve the problem, but what is necessary is evidence from 1 Peter.

[392] The two κατὰ phrases refer to the standpoint of human beings and God. So Selwyn, *First Peter,* 215–16; Dalton, *Proclamation to Spirits,* 274–75; Michaels, *1 Peter,* 238; Achtemeier, *1 Peter,* 288.

[393] Elliott, *1 Peter,* 737–38.

raised from the dead.[394] The contrast between the "flesh" and "spirit" here is parallel to 1 Pet 3:18, for Christ also died in terms of his flesh, but he was raised to life by the Holy Spirit. A similar destiny awaits believers. They die physically but will be raised to life by the Holy Spirit. I am suggesting, therefore, that Peter did not consider the intermediate state here but the resurrection of the dead. He used the present tense because the future will certainly come to pass. This interpretation makes the best sense contextually, for it gives the readers encouragement to continue to endure the social ostracism they are facing from their contemporaries. Peter reminded his readers that even if they die physically, death is not the last word. The resurrection awaits them.

It could be objected against this view that the "dead" in v. 6 is restricted only to the believing dead, but such a limitation is derived from the context since Peter only spoke of those who live according to God by means of the Spirit. The limitation of the dead to believers, then, is not an arbitrary imposition on the text but is demanded by the verse itself. Another objection is similar, for judgment in v. 6 cannot be identical with the judgment in v. 5; v. 5 points to the condemnation of unbelievers, but the judgment in v. 6 refers to the death of *believers*. Once again the difference between the two parts of the verse is contextually grounded, since the verse tells us that the judgment is "according to men" and that they will "live" according to God. If they will live, it is evident that final condemnation is not in view here and that the judgment in v. 6 does not involve final condemnation as the judgment in v. 5 does.[395] Nor are we required to understand the datives "flesh" *(sarki,* NIV "body") and "spirit" *(pneumati)* identically.[396] As I argued in 3:18, the datives can be construed differently. Here the "Spirit" is likely a reference to the Holy Spirit and the resurrection. Believers died "in the sphere of the flesh," but they will live by means of the Holy Spirit.

We find an interesting parallel to what Peter taught here in *Wisdom of Solomon* (3:1–6):[397]

> But the souls of the righteous are in the hand of God, and no torment will ever touch them. In the eyes of the foolish they seemed to have died, and their departure was thought to be a disaster, and their going from us to be their destruction; but they are at peace. For though in the sight of others they were punished, their hope is full of immortality. Having been disciplined a little, they will receive great good, because God tested them and found them worthy

---

[394] Rightly Elliott, *1 Peter,* 738.

[395] Rightly Achtemeier, *1 Peter,* 287–88.

[396] Most commentators argue to the contrary here and see them as datives of sphere or reference (Best, *1 Peter,* 158; Goppelt, *1 Peter,* 289; Achtemeier, *1 Peter,* 288).

[397] Cf. Michaels, *1 Peter,* 239.

of himself; like gold in the furnace he tried them, and like a sacrificial burnt offering he accepted them.

The parallels should be noted: (1) the wicked think the death of the righteous is disaster and punishment; (2) the difficulties of the present are temporary; (3) believers have a future hope of life. The hope of the resurrection is explicit in Peter, while the author of *Wisdom* focuses more on immortality, which fits with his Greek point of view.

(4) Living in Light of the End (4:7–11)

[7]The end of all things is near. Therefore be clear minded and self-controlled so that you can pray. [8]Above all, love each other deeply, because love covers over a multitude of sins. [9]Offer hospitality to one another without grumbling. [10]Each one should use whatever gift he has received to serve others, faithfully administering God's grace in its various forms. [11]If anyone speaks, he should do it as one speaking the very words of God. If anyone serves, he should do it with the strength God provides, so that in all things God may be praised through Jesus Christ. To him be the glory and the power for ever and ever. Amen.

Verses 5–6 conclude with a reference to the final judgment, and Peter reprised that theme in v. 7a with a reminder that the end is near. Hence, he returned to the main theme of the previous paragraph. Since the end is near, believers should live according to God's will. What this means in practice is that believers should be alert and sober for prayer, that they should live in sacrificial love that includes hospitality, and that they should use their gifts, whether speaking or serving, to help others. Their aim and motivation in all they do is to see God glorified through Jesus Christ.

4:7 The previous paragraph ended with a reference to the final judgment (v. 5), death, and the resurrection (v. 6). Hence, it is not surprising that v. 7 opens with a reference to the end of history. The words "all things" *(pantōn)* could be translated "all people," but in this context "all things" makes better sense, being placed at the beginning of the sentence for emphasis.[398] The reason the end is near is that the ministry, death, and resurrection of Jesus Christ have inaugurated the last days (cf. 1 Cor 10:11; 1 John 2:18). In the New Testament the theme that the end of history is imminent is often sounded (Rom 13:11–12; Phil 4:5; Heb 10:23–25; Jas 5:7–8; Rev 1:3; 22:10). All the following exhortations in this paragraph draw an inference from the coming of the end. See the "therefore" *(oun)* in the middle of v. 7. Because the end is near, believers should live in the following way.

We have a typical feature of New Testament eschatology here. Nowhere does the New Testament encourage the setting of dates or of any other kinds

[398] Rightly D. E. Hiebert, "Living in Light of Christ's Return: An Exposition of 1 Peter 4:7–11," *BSac* 139 (1982): 244; contra Martin, *Metaphor and Composition in 1 Peter,* 235–36.

of charts. Eschatology is invariably used to encourage believers to live in a godly way (cf. Matt 24:36–25:46; Rom 13:11–14; 1 Cor 15:58; Phil 4:4–9; 1 Thess 5:1–11; 2 Pet 3:11–16). Nor does the New Testament ever invite believers to withdraw from the world because the end is near and to gaze at the skies, hoping that the Lord will return soon. The imminence of the end should function as a stimulus to action in this world. The knowledge that believers are sojourners and exiles, whose time is short, should galvanize them to make their lives count now.

We might expect a call for extraordinary behavior, thinking something unusual would be demanded in light of the arrival of the end. Peter exhorted his readers, however, to pursue virtues that are a normal part of New Testament paraenesis. We are reminded of what Martin Luther said when asked what he would do if the end would come today. He replied that he would plant a tree and pay his taxes. What Luther meant, of course, was that he lived every day in light of the end, and hence he would do the appointed task of that day. What is striking in the paragraph is how Peter shifted from a focus on relationship with outsiders to how believers should relate to one another.[399] Peter summoned his readers to "be clear minded and self-controlled." The two verbs "be clear minded" *(sōphronēsate)* and "be self-controlled" *(nēpsate)* are virtually synonymous and should be understood together. Indeed, the word "pray" (lit., "prayers," *proseuchas*) is attached to both verbs.[400] The nearness of the end has led some believers to lose their heads and act irrationally. On the contrary, believers should think sensibly as they contemplate the brevity of life in this world. Those who know the contours of history are able to assess the significance of the present. Their sensible and alert thinking is to be used for prayer, for entreating God to act and move in the time that still remains. The realization that God is bringing history to a close should provoke believers to depend on him, and this dependence is manifested in prayer, for in prayer believers recognize that any good that occurs in the world is due to God's grace.

4:8 The imminence of the end should also provoke believers to love. In the Greek the participle "having" *(echontes),* which is not translated at all in the NIV, is rendered by "keep" (NASB, HCSB), "maintain" (NRSV), and "hold" (RSV) in other translations. Many scholars understand the participle as an imperative, and this is reflected in the various translations, even in the idiomatic translation of the NIV.[401] Achtemeier understands the participle as dependent upon the imperatives in v. 7,[402] but even in this

---

[399] Cf. Michaels, *1 Peter,* 244.

[400] The preposition εἰς designates purpose here (so Elliott, *1 Peter,* 749).

[401] E.g., Michaels, *1 Peter*, 246; Goppelt, *I Peter*, 296–97; so Daube, "Participle," 484.

[402] Achtemeier, *1 Peter,* 295; so also Snyder, "Participles and Imperatives in 1 Peter," 196.

instance the construction functionally ends up being an imperative. Peter did not merely exhort believers to love one another in light of the *eschaton.*[403] He said that such love is "above all," and he exhorted his readers to "constant love" (NRSV, *agapēn ektenē*).[404] The importance of such constancy in love has already been underlined in 1 Pet 1:22, and the theme is broached again because love is central in the Christian life. Indeed, Jesus himself warned that love is apt to grow cold at the end of the age (Matt 24:12). Hence, the need is to continue to stoke the fires of love, so that it is displayed to others. The centrality of love is evident from 1 Cor 13:1–7, from the teaching of Jesus (Matt 22:34–40), and from Johannine teaching (e.g., John 13:34–35; 1 John 2:7–11). When believers contemplate how to spend their lives in light of the Lord's coming, in their few days as sojourners, they should remind themselves of the priority of love.

In the second half of the verse the reason love should be pursued is explicated, as the word "because" *(hoti)* indicates. The reason given is that love "covers over a multitude of sins."[405] The proverbial saying here also is found in Jas 5:20, though the future rather than the present tense is used in James. Two interpretations have been prominent. Did Peter mean that love covers over or atones for one's own sins?[406] It could be argued that such teaching is also present in Luke 7:47 and Matt 6:14–15. This interpretation should be rejected. It flies in the face of the rest of the New Testament and even 1 Peter (1:18–19; 2:24–25; 3:18) to see the love of believers as somehow atoning for their own sins. Nor do Luke 7:47 and Matt 6:14–15, rightly interpreted, teach that the love or forgiveness of believers somehow atones for their sins.[407] The second interpretation is preferable. When believers

---

[403] The reflexive pronoun ἑαυτοὺς here means "one another," and the latter meaning usually is communicated with the reciprocal pronoun ἀλλήλους.

[404] Possibly both constancy and fervency are in view (so Goppelt, *I Peter,* 297), but more likely it is only the former. See M. Evang, "Ἐκ καρδίας ἀλλήλους ἀγαπήσατε ἐκτενῶς: Zum Verständnis der Aufforderung und ihrer Begründungen in 1 Petr 1,22f.," *ZNW* 80 (1989): 122.

[405] Some manuscripts (𝔓[72], ℵ, P, 049, and the Majority text) support the future καλύψει instead of the present καλύπτει (e.g., A, B, K, Ψ, 33, 81, 323, 614, 630, 1241, 1505, 1739). The former may have crept in from Jas 5:20, and it also may have occurred to scribes that the truth enunciated here fits well with the final judgment. The present tense should be accepted as original.

[406] So Spicq, *Les Épîtres de Saint Pierre,* 150; Kelly, *Peter and Jude,* 178; Richard, *Reading 1 Peter, Jude, and 2 Peter,* 179–80; Brox, *Der erste Petrusbrief,* 205. Michaels thinks the question is beside the point, arguing that Peter was thinking in community terms of "the giving and forgiving love that binds them together as a community in Christ" (*1 Peter,* 247).

[407] L. Kline adopts this meaning but understands Peter to have been saying that the one who shows mercy to others is also able to receive mercy from God ("Ethics for the End Time: An Exegesis of I Peter 4:7–11," *RestQ* 7 [1963]: 117).

lavish love on others, the sins and offenses of others are overlooked.[408] Four arguments support this interpretation. First, it fits with the emphasis on mutuality in the immediate context. Love is directed to others, not oneself (v. 8). Genuine love is displayed to others through hospitality (v. 9), and gifts are employed to serve others, not oneself (v. 10). Second, the interpretation proposed here fits with Prov 10:12, which is alluded to here: "Hatred stirs up dissension, but love covers over all wrongs."[409] The clear meaning is that love covers over the wrongs of others, while those who are full of hatred use the sins of others as a springboard to attack them. Third, though Jas 5:20 is also disputed, it is quite likely that the one who restores the sinner from his errant way covers over the sins of the one who went astray.[410] Fourth, the notion that love overlooks the sins of others is clearly taught elsewhere in the New Testament (Matt 18:21–22; 1 Cor 13:4–7).

4:9 The theme of love continues in v. 9. We need to recall that these exhortations are all shaped by the nearness of the end (v. 7). No imperative or participle is actually present in the verse, but an imperative is surely implied and is reflected in all translations.[411] Hospitality was one of the marks of the Christian community (cf. Rom 12:13; 1 Tim 3:2; Titus 1:8; Heb 13:2). Hospitality was particularly crucial for the Christian mission in a day when lodging could not be afforded, and hence the advance of the mission depended on the willingness of believers to provide bed and board for those visiting (Matt 10:11,40; Acts 16:15; 3 John 7–11).[412] The early church was aware that such hospitality could be abused (cf. *Did.* 11:3–6). Furthermore, hospitality was necessary in order for the church to meet in various homes (cf. Rom 16:3–5,23; 1 Cor 16:19; Col 4:15; Phlm 2). The words "without grumbling" acknowledge that those who open their homes may grow tired of the service. Hence, they are exhorted to be hospitable gladly, not caving in to the temptation to begrudge their charity to others.

4:10 The theme of ministering to one another continues, but the emphasis shifts to gifts believers have received by God's grace. The word "gift" *(charisma)* implies that the gifts believers have are the result of God's grace, and the word "received" confirms this judgment. Paul used

---

[408] So most interpreters; e.g., Luther, *Commentary on Peter & Jude,* 179; Cranfield, *I & II Peter and Jude,* 114; Goppelt, *I Peter,* 298–99; Wand, *Epistles of Peter and Jude,* 114; Michaels, *1 Peter,* 247; Best, *1 Peter,* 159; Achtemeier, *1 Peter,* 296; van Unnik, "Good Works in I Peter," 107–8; Marshall, *1 Peter,* 143.

[409] Peter must have been depending on the MT of Prov 10:12, for the meaning is changed significantly in the LXX.

[410] Cf. Moo, *The Letter of James,* 250–51.

[411] The participle ὄντες may be implied (so Achtemeier, *1 Peter,* 296; Snyder, "Participles and Imperatives in 1 Peter," 196).

[412] For the importance of hospitality in Jesus' ministry, see Kline, "Ethics for the End Times," 118.

the term "gift" *(charisma)* quite often to designate spiritual gifts (Rom 12:6; 1 Cor 1:7; 12:4,9,28,30–31; 1 Tim 4:14; 2 Tim 1:6). Believers cannot boast about the gift they have, for otherwise they contradict its gracious character, thinking that somehow they merit its bestowal. The gifts are manifestations of "God's grace in its various forms." It is also implied that each believer has received at least one spiritual gift, for Peter addressed his words to "each one" *(hekastos)*. The notion that God has granted charismatic gifts to each believer is also Pauline (1 Cor 12:7). Even though every believer possesses at least one gift, the gifts are not necessarily the same. God's grace manifests itself "in its various forms," so that the diversity of gifts reveals the multifaceted character of God's grace. What is most important, of course, is the purpose for having gifts. Gifts are not given so that believers can congratulate themselves on their abilities. They are bestowed "to serve others." The word used here can be translated "ministering" *(diakonountes)*.[413] The term "serving" can be used in a variety of ways—of providing meals (Matt 8:15; Mark 1:31; Luke 4:39; 10:40; 12:37; 17:8; John 12:2; Acts 6:2), of visiting those in prison (Matt 25:44; 2 Tim 1:18), of providing financial support (Luke 8:3; Rom 15:25; 2 Cor 8:19,20), and in more general terms as well (Matt 20:28; Mark 10:45; Luke 22:26–27; John 12:26; Acts 19:22; 2 Cor 3:3; 1 Tim 3:10,13; Phlm 13; Heb 6:10).[414] The point is that spiritual gifts are given to serve and to help others, to strengthen others in the faith. They are bestowed for ministry, not to enhance self-esteem. Paul emphasized the same theme, reminding believers that gifts are given to build up and edify others, not to edify oneself (1 Cor 12:7,25–26; 14:1–19,26; Eph 4:11–12). When believers use their gifts to strengthen others, they are functioning as "good stewards" (NRSV, *kaloi oikonomoi*) of God's grace. The word translated "stewards" could also be translated as "managers" (cf. Luke 12:42; 16:1,3,8; 1 Cor 4:1–2; cf. Gal 4:2; Titus 1:7), as long as it is clear that believers hold these gifts in trust since they are gifts of God. Spiritual gifts are not fundamentally a privilege but a responsibility, a call to be faithful to what God has bestowed.

4:11 The gifts are divided into two categories, speaking and serving gifts.[415] It must be said immediately, from v. 10, that all gifts involve serving and edifying others, and Peter was not denying that emphasis here. Now he examines the gifts functionally, observing that some involve speaking and others serve fellow believers in a variety of ways. In placing

---

[413] The Greek participle functions as an imperative here (Michaels, *1 Peter,* 249; Elliott, *1 Peter,* 755).

[414] Elliott rightly argues, over against Collins, that the notion of humble service is found in the term (Elliott, *1 Peter,* 755; J. N. Collins, *Diakonia: Re-interpreting the Ancient Sources* [New York: Oxford University Press, 1990]).

[415] So Goppelt, *I Peter,* 302; Best, *1 Peter,* 160; Achtemeier, *1 Peter,* 298.

the gifts into the two categories of speaking and serving, all the spiritual gifts are included under these two classes. In his listing of the gifts Paul provided more detail, so that we have some idea which gifts would fall under speaking and which would fall under serving. The gifts of apostleship, prophecy, teaching, tongues, and exhortation are comprehended under speaking (Rom 12:6–7; 1 Cor 12:10,28–30; Eph 4:11), whereas gifts like giving, leading, mercy, helps, healing, and miracles (Rom 12:8; 1 Cor 12:9–10,28–30) fall under serving. It is not as if Peter did not know about the particular gifts. His purpose was to speak of them generally instead of discussing the gifts in particular.

Those who speak should endeavor to speak "the very words of God." The expression used is "oracles of God" (RSV, *logia theou*). The "oracles of God" refer to the words God has given his people (cf. Acts 7:38; Rom 3:2; Heb 5:12). The phrase is rooted in the Old Testament, where we have both "oracles of God" (LXX Num 24:4,16; Ps 106:11 and "oracles of the LORD," *logia kyriou,* LXX Pss 11:7; 17:31) and "your oracles" (LXX Pss 118:11,103, 148,158; 162; cf. *Wis* 16:11). Using speaking gifts to minister to others means that the one speaking endeavors to speak God's words.[416] How easy it is to think that we can assist others with our own wisdom, but those who are entrusted with the ministry of speaking should be careful to speak God's words, to be faithful to the gospel (cf. 1 Cor 4:1–2; 2 Tim 4:1–5). Goppelt correctly argues that the injunction to speak God's words constitutes an exhortation to the speaker. Hence, the phrase does not suggest that somehow the words spoken in church constitute revelation from God.[417] Peter wrote so that those who speak will do so in accord with the gospel, not to suggest that the words spoken become part of the revelational deposit for believers. Similarly, those who minister and serve others must not rely on their own strength. They must minister "with the strength God provides," relying on his power to carry out their tasks. Presumably they rely on his power through prayer. When those who speak utter God's words rather than their own and those who serve do so in God's strength rather than their own, God through Jesus Christ receives the glory. God receives the glory because he is the one who has provided the wisdom and strength for ministry. The provider is always the one who is praised. If human beings are the source of wisdom and strength for ministry, they deserve to be complimented. But if understanding and energy come from the Lord, he gets the glory as the one who empowers his people. We should note that God receives the glory "through Jesus Christ," for the

[416] I understand λόγια θεοῦ to be the direct object here (so Beare, *First Peter,* 160; Selwyn, *First Peter,* 219; Goppelt, *I Peter,* 302; Achtemeier, *1 Peter,* 298–99).

[417] Goppelt, *I Peter,* 303–4.

glory that redounds to God comes through the gospel the Petrine readers received (1:3,10–12,18–19; 2:21–25; 3:18). This gospel focuses on Jesus Christ as the crucified and risen Lord, and hence God is praised for what he has done in and through Jesus the Christ.

Peter concluded this section with a doxology, which some have seen as an indication that the letter ends here. Many letters, however, have doxologies before the conclusion (Rom 11:36; Gal 1:5; Eph 3:21; Phil 4:20; cf. Rev 1:6; 5:13; 7:12), though letters may indeed conclude with a doxology (Rom 16:25–27; 2 Pet 3:18; Jude 24–25). There is no basis, therefore, for thinking a doxology demonstrates that the letter concludes here. Instead the doxology signals the end of this major section of the letter, from 2:11–4:11. It is difficult to determine whether the doxology is addressed to God the Father or Jesus Christ. Supporting the latter is the fact that Jesus Christ is the nearest antecedent to "him."[418] On the other hand, most doxologies are addressed to the Father,[419] and God is said to be the one who receives the glory earlier in the verse.[420] Further, it seems strange to some to say that the glory is both "through" Christ and also "for" him (cf. *1 Clem.* 20:12; 50:7). But we probably should understand the last phrase to refer to Jesus Christ, for Christ is the nearest antecedent. Further, since the preceding clause speaks of glory belonging to God, it seems likely that here we have a reference to Jesus Christ. Nor is it difficult to think of the glory being effected "through" Jesus Christ and also being intended "for" him. We can think here of Rom 11:36, where "all things" are "through" God but they are also "for" him. The goal of the Christian faith is that glory belongs to God and Christ, and here Peter also added "power" *(kratos;* cf. also Rev 1:6). The word "amen" signifies an affirmation, indicating that the writer agreed with the sentiment expressed, here in the doxology (cf. also Rom 11:36; 16:27; Gal 1:5; Phil 4:20; 1 Tim 1:17; 6:16; 2 Tim 4:8; Heb 13:21; 1 Pet 5:11; 2 Pet 3:18; Jude 25; Rev 1:6; 5:14; 7:12; 19:4).

---

[418] So Bigg, *Epistles of Peter and Jude,* 176; Michaels, *1 Peter,* 253; Schweizer, "1. Petrus 4,6," 91.

[419] Luke 2:14; Rom 1:25; 11:36; 16:27; 2 Cor 11:31; Eph 3:21; Phil 4:20; 1 Tim 1:17; 2 Tim 4:18; Heb 13:21; Jude 25.

[420] See Best, *1 Peter,* 161; Hiebert, "Living," 252; Kelly, *Peter and Jude,* 181–82; Goppelt, *1 Peter,* 306, n. 57; Achtemeier, *1 Peter,* 299; Elliott, *1 Peter,* 762.

SECTION OUTLINE

IV. PERSEVERING IN SUFFERING (4:12–5:11)
  1. Suffer Joyfully in Accord with God's Will (4:12–19)
  2. Exhortations to Elders and the Community (5:1–11)
    (1) Exhortations for Elders and Younger Ones (5:1–5)
    (2) Closing Exhortations and Assurance (5:6–11)

IV. PERSEVERING IN SUFFERING (4:12–5:11)

1. Suffer Joyfully in Accord with God's Will (4:12–19)

**12Dear friends, do not be surprised at the painful trial you are suffering, as
though something strange were happening to you. 13But rejoice that you participate in the sufferings of Christ, so that you may be overjoyed when his glory is
revealed. 14If you are insulted because of the name of Christ, you are blessed, for
the Spirit of glory and of God rests on you. 15If you suffer, it should not be as a
murderer or thief or any other kind of criminal, or even as a meddler. 16However,
if you suffer as a Christian, do not be ashamed, but praise God that you bear that
name. 17For it is time for judgment to begin with the family of God; and if it
begins with us, what will the outcome be for those who do not obey the gospel of
God? 18And,**

> **"If it is hard for the righteous to be saved,**
> **what will become of the ungodly and the sinner?"**

**19So then, those who suffer according to God's will should commit themselves
to their faithful Creator and continue to do good.**

A new section of the letter commences with "dear friends" and the imperative not to be surprised at the fiery testing. We have no evidence that fresh news reached Peter about the increase of suffering in Asia Minor.[1] The language used in this paragraph is not remarkably different from what

---

[1] M. Dubis argues that the conception of Messianic woes plays a major role in 1 Peter as a whole and 4:12–19 in particular (*Messianic Woes in 1 Peter: Suffering and Eschatology in 1 Peter 4:12–19, SBL* 33 [New York: Peter Lang, 2002]). At times he overstates his case, but it does seem correct to say that Peter had in mind the distress and suffering that must precede the time of the end, and hence he may have been influenced by the tradition of the Messianic woes.

we have seen already in 1:6–7.[2] Peter reminded his readers again that the fiery ordeal was for the purpose of testing and refining their faith, and hence they ought not to conceive of their suffering as something strange or unexpected. Indeed, instead of being surprised at their sufferings, they should rejoice and be glad (v. 13), for such suffering indicates that they will exult with remarkable joy when Jesus Christ is revealed in all his glory. Verse 14 explicates the purpose clause from v. 13. Being reproached for the sake of Christ is an indication that the readers stand under God's blessing even now, indicating that the eschatological glory of v. 13 and the Holy Spirit rest on believers. In v. 15 Peter reverted to a theme we saw earlier (2:19–20; 3:17), that believers should not suffer because they practice evil. Rather they must suffer as those who are called Christians, that is, followers of Christ. For such suffering they should not be ashamed but glorify God by suffering with Jesus Christ. Verses 17–18 explain why believers were suffering. Suffering represents God's judgment of his house. By "house of God" here Peter meant the church of Jesus Christ. Peter did not mean by this that God was punishing believers for their sins. Rather suffering purifies the church, and God uses it (cf. 4:1) to provoke believers to make a clean break with sin. The judgment begins with the church and purifies it, but if God purifies the church by his judgment, then his judgment of those who disobey the gospel will have terrible consequences. In v. 18 the same point is restated and explained. If the righteous are saved by means of a purifying suffering, if they need such a refining work, then the judgment of the ungodly and the sinner will be terrible indeed. Verse 19 functions as the conclusion to the entire paragraph. We learn from vv. 12 and 17–18 that the suffering that strikes believers is according to God's will. It passes through his loving hands for the purification of believers. Hence, those who belong to God should entrust their lives to their faithful Creator, just as Jesus entrusted his life to God when he suffered (2:23). "Faithful Creator" signifies that God is sovereign and true. He is sovereign, and so no suffering occurs apart from his will. He is faithful, and so he will see to it that the suffering does not exceed what we can bear (cf. 1 Cor 10:13). Hence, believers should persist in doing good, for entrusting themselves to God always manifests itself in a changed life, in the pursuit of goodness.

4:12 A new section of the letter begins here. This is evident because the previous section closes with a doxology, and the new section is introduced by "dear friends" *(agapētoi)* and an imperative as was the new sec-

[2] P. A. Holloway argues that 1 Pet 4:12 and following develops the consolation topos that nothing accidental has happened in the lives of the readers ("*Nihil inopinati accidisse* – 'Nothing Unexpected Has Happened': A Cyrenaic Consolatory *Topos* in 1 Pet 4.12ff.," *NTS* 43 [2002]: 433–48).

tion in 2:11.[3] In addition, Peter again took up the subject of suffering, tackling it from a fresh and final angle, giving another perspective on what has been discussed earlier. The view that Peter recently heard news of suffering and so penned this section should be rejected.[4] There is no evidence that the suffering contemplated here was any more intense than that contemplated in 1:6–8. Peter began here by admonishing them not to "be surprised *[xenizesthe]* at the fiery ordeal" (NRSV) they were enduring. If they were astonished at the suffering that occurred, they may have been overwhelmed, concluding that God did not love them. An advance warning of suffering helps the readers to be prepared for suffering, so that their faith is not threatened when difficulties arise.

Some interpret the "fiery ordeal" as designating actual physical persecution,[5] but Peter said nothing different here from what had already been communicated in 1:6–7. We must beware of overreading the metaphor.[6] Johnson demonstrates that the metaphor should be interpreted in light of the Old Testament background, particularly Prov 27:21; Ps 66:10; Zech 13:9; and Mal 3:1–4.[7] The text in Ps 66:10 (65:10, LXX) is instructive, "For you, O God, tested *[edokimasas]* us; you refined *[epyrōsas]* us like silver." Zechariah used the verbs "refine" *(pyroō)* and "test" *(dokimazō)* in describing the Lord's testing and refining of his people. We know from 1 Pet 1:7 that Peter also spoke of testing *(dokimazō)* through fire, and in this verse the noun "fiery trial" *(pyrosis),* related to the verb *pyroō,* is used. Malachi 3:1–4 is especially important, for, although the wording does not match 1 Pet 4:12 as closely, the Lord in Malachi comes to his temple to purify his people. The echo is striking since Peter proceeded to say that God uses suffering as the means to purify his house (i.e., the church of God as his temple). Hence, Johnson rightly remarks that their sufferings are not a sign of God's absence but his purifying presence. Their unbelieving contemporaries may be "surprised" (*xenizontai,* 4:4) that Christians are not participating in their

---

[3] It might be objected that 2:11 does not formally have an imperative, but the verb παρακαλῶ and the infinitive constitute a command.

[4] Rightly L. Goppelt, *A Commentary on I Peter* (Grand Rapids: Eerdmans, 1993), 311; J. R. Michaels, *1 Peter,* WBC (Waco: Word, 1998), 258; J. N. D. Kelly, *A Commentary on the Epistles of Peter and Jude,* Thornapple Commentaries (Grand Rapids: Baker, 1981), 185; J. H. Elliott, *1 Peter: A New Translation with Introduction and Commentary,* AB (New York: Doubleday, 2000), 769–70. Contrary to F. W. Beare, *The First Epistle of Peter: The Greek Text with Introduction and Notes* (Oxford: Blackwell, 1947), 162–64.

[5] Beare, *First Peter,* 162–64.

[6] D. E. Johnson, "Fire in God's House: Imagery from Malachi 3 in Peter's Theology of Suffering (1 Peter 4:12–19)," *JETS* 29 (1986): 287; cf. also the comments of N. Brox, *Der erste Petrusbrief,* EKKNT, 2d ed. (Zürich: Benziger/Neukirchen-Vluyn: Neukirchener Verlag, 1986), 213.

[7] Johnson, "Fire in God's House," 287–89. It is not as clear that the term is technical, designating the end-time tribulation (contra Dubis, *1 Peter 4:12–19,* 76–85).

evil, and yet believers should not be astonished (same verb) that suffering strikes them. They should not consider it as if "something strange were happening." Such suffering is to be expected because its purpose is "to test you" *(pros peirasmon)*.[8] The NIV, unfortunately, leaves out the purpose altogether and hence fails to communicate why the readers should not be astonished. Peter returned here to the theology of 1:6–7, where suffering is allowed by God to refine the faith of believers.[9] This notion is standard in New Testament paraenesis, for God uses the trials of life to strengthen the character of believers and to make them fit for his presence (cf. Rom 5:3–5; Jas 1:2–4). The use of the word "test" *(peirasmon)* links this verse back to the same word translated "trials" *(peirasmois)* in 1:6.[10]

4:13 Verse 13 functions as a contrast to v. 12, as is indicated by the word "but" *(alla)* introducing the verse. Instead of being shocked that they were suffering, they should "rejoice" *(chairete)* at the privilege, to the degree that they "participate in the sufferings of Christ."[11] The "sufferings of Christ" refer to sufferings that come because of their allegiance to Christ.[12] Peter anticipated here what would be explained in the subsequent verses. Suffering for Christ is a cause for joy, but being mistreated because of one's own sins is nothing to brag about. The notion that suffering for Christ's sake is a cause for joy is reflected in Acts 5:41, "The apostles left the Sanhedrin, rejoicing because they had been counted worthy of suffering disgrace for the Name." The first part of the verse emphasizes that the believers should *rejoice now* if they suffer for Christ's sake. The purpose clause (introduced by "so that," *hina*) points readers to a future joy. Believers should rejoice even now in suffering "so that you may be overjoyed" in the future.[13] Rejoicing in their present suffering is mandated, precisely so that believers will have joy in God's presence at the day of judgment. How believers respond to suffering, in other words, is an indication of whether they truly belong to God at all. The promise of future joy, in fact, energizes

---

[8] I understand the preposition πρός to designate purpose. So also Michaels, *1 Peter,* 261; P. J. Achtemeier, *1 Peter: A Commentary on First Peter,* Her (Minneapolis: Fortress, 1996), 306.

[9] Satan may also be testing believers in their suffering, but he does so not to refine them but to destroy them (1 Pet 5:8; Achtemeier, *1 Peter,* 306).

[10] Dubis argues that testing is part of the Messianic woes (*1 Peter 4:12–19,* 85–95).

[11] The term καθὸ seems to refer to degree (W. Grudem, *The First Epistle of Peter,* TNTC [Grand Rapids: Eerdmans, 1988], 178) rather than being causal (against Elliott, *1 Peter,* 774).

[12] The idea is that believers are imitating Christ in their suffering (P. H. Davids, *The First Epistle of Peter,* NICNT [Grand Rapids: Eerdmans, 1990], 166; Michaels, *1 Peter,* 262). Hence, Peter was not referring to participating in Christ's sufferings sacramentally, mystically, or by sharing in the Messianic woes. Dubis thinks a reference to Messianic woes is in view (*1 Peter 4:12–19,* 97–117).

[13] So also Michaels, *1 Peter,* 262; Achtemeier, *1 Peter,* 306; contra D. C. Parker, who also sees a reference to the present ("The Eschatology of 1 Peter," *BTB* 24 [1994]: 30).

the joy that will be theirs in the future. The intensity of joy in the future is reflected in the two words that are used for joy, "rejoice and be glad" (RSV, *charēte agalliōmenoi*). The two terms used reflect the teaching of Jesus himself, for he exhorted his disciples to "rejoice and be glad" *(chairete kai agalliasthe)* when persecuted (Matt 5:12). This future joy will belong to believers "when his glory is revealed" (lit., "at the revelation of his glory, *en tē apokalypsei tēs doxēs autou*). The revelation of his glory almost certainly refers to the second coming of Christ. This is confirmed by 1:7, where, in a context that also discusses suffering and the final reward, reference is made to "the revelation of Jesus Christ" (RSV, *apokalypsei Iēsou Christou*). The same expression is used to describe the coming of Jesus Christ in 1:13. Indeed, such an expression describes the future coming of Christ in the Pauline letters (1 Cor 1:7; 2 Thess 1:7). Peter exhorted readers to rejoice in their present sufferings so that they will be able to rejoice and exult forever when Christ returns. By implication those who do not rejoice in their sufferings do not truly belong to Jesus Christ. If they groan about sufferings now, they will presumably be disappointed on the future day.

4:14 In v. 13 believers are commanded to rejoice in their present sufferings, but v. 14 adds a distinct point, emphasizing that believers are blessed by God if they are insulted because of their allegiance to Jesus Christ. The sufferings of believers are described here as being "insulted because of the name of Christ."[14] The word "insulted" *(oneidizesthe)* is important and helps us understand the "fiery ordeal" (NRSV; *pyrōsei*) in v. 12. The latter term might suggest that believers were being put to death and were experiencing some kind of physical torture for their faith. Peter certainly wanted the readers to be prepared for such experiences. The evidence of the letter does not support the idea that suffering had yet reached such an intense state. The opposition was mainly verbal at this stage.[15] They were "insulted" by others for their devotion to Christ.[16] We saw previously in 4:4 that they were abused by unbelievers for not participating in their former activities. Even the persecution in Rome under Nero (ca. A.D. 64) did not represent a concentrated empirewide campaign against Christians. It probably was a temporary response to the fire at Rome and designed to deflect responsibility from Nero (Tacitus, *Ann.* 15:44; Suetonius, *Vit.* 6.16.2). Pliny's correspondence with the emperor Trajan (ca. A.D.

---

[14] The "if" (εἰ) constitutes a real condition and should not be translated "since" or "when," for Peter wanted them to reflect on the condition, even if he expected it to become a reality (contra Achtemeier, *1 Peter,* 307).

[15] Cf. Kelly, *Peter and Jude*, 186; J. Moffatt, *The General Epistles: James, Peter, and Jude,* MNTC (New York: Harper & Brothers, 1928), 157; Achtemeier, *1 Peter,* 307; Elliott, *1 Peter,* 779.

[16] As some commentators point out, the preposition ἐν is causal here (Elliott, *1 Peter,* 778–79; Kelly, *Peter and Jude,* 186; Goppelt, *I Peter,* 323).

112–114) reveals that no official policy had been established to respond to Christians, nor do Trajan's responses suggest a policy throughout the empire in which believers were sought out and punished (*Ep.* 10.96). We do see in the Book of Revelation that some believers were being killed for their faith (cf. 2:13; 6:9–11; 13:7; 16:6; 17:6; 18:24; 19:2; 20:4), but even in this case the persecution probably did not represent an empirewide and official persecution. What we have are sporadic instances of intense persecution that threatened believers.[17]

The main point of the verse emerges in the second clause. Those who are insulted as Christians are actually "blessed" (*makarioi,* cf. 3:14). They may be insulted by human beings, but they are blessed by God himself. Peter was almost certainly recalling the words of Jesus here, for Matt 5:11 says "Blessed are you when people insult you" *(makarioi este hotan oneidisōsin hymas).* The words "blessed" and "insult" are in both texts. Christians may be reproached by human beings, but they are blessed by God.

The last clause in v. 14 explains why believers are blessed, "for the Spirit of glory and of God rests on you."[18] The NIV smooths out the Greek syntax, which is quite awkward. It is possible that the clause should be interpreted quite differently and could be paraphrased "for the eschatological glory promised in v. 13 and the Spirit of God rest upon you."[19] Achtemeier adduces a number of other examples in which the kind of construction found here *(to tēs doxēs)* would support the latter interpretation (LXX Lev 7:7; 1 Sam 6:4; Matt 21:21; 1 Cor 10:24; Jas 4:14; 2 Pet 2:22).[20] This interpretation also explains why the word "Spirit" *(pneuma)* is found only in the second phrase "the Spirit of God." If this interpretation is correct, Peter's point was that they were blessed because they possessed even now the glory that would be theirs at the end time and also that the eschatological gift of the Spirit even now rested upon them.[21] Davids, on the other hand, argues

---

[17] "That the letter assumes Christians had already been condemned to death, however, whether on the charge of murder or on the charge of being a Christian, seems highly unlikely. It is simply inconceivable that so grave a situation would not have been more clearly reflected in the letter" (S. R. Bechtler, *Following in His Steps: Suffering, Community, and Christology in 1 Peter,* SBLDS 162 [Atlanta: Scholars Press, 1998], 93–94).

[18] Some manuscripts add καὶ δυναμέως, so that the text reads "the spirit of glory and the spirit of power and the spirit of God" (א*, A, P, 33, 81, 323, 945, 1241, 1739, pm), but the shorter reading that deletes the phrase is to be preferred ($\mathfrak{P}^{72}$, B, K, L, Ψ, 049, 330, pm).

[19] According to this interpretation the τό preceding τῆς δόξης refers back to the glory mentioned in v. 13.

[20] Achtemeier, *1 Peter,* 309, n. 66.

[21] Cf. also Goppelt, who understands the καὶ as ascensive, the Spirit of glory is the Spirit of God (*1 Peter,* 323; so also Kelly, *Peter and Jude,* 187). By the Spirit they now experience the glory that will be theirs eschatologically (so E. J. Richard, "The Functional Christology of First Peter," in *Perspectives on 1 Peter,* ed. C. H. Talbert [Macon: Mercer University Press, 1986], 137). Goppelt thinks the text echoes Num 11:25–26, where the Spirit rested on the seventy elders (cf. Exod 24:17; 29:43).

that the reference is to the Spirit of glory and the Spirit of God as translated in the NIV.[22] First, he thinks the phrase "Spirit of God" is "stereotyped" and would not be broken up. Second, "glory" is placed first to contrast it with the "insult" of the first part of the verse. Finally, the use of the article to refer to glory would only work if we had a "stereotyped" phrase as in Matt 21:21; 1 Cor 10:24; Jas 4:14; 2 Pet 2:2. Davids maintains that such a stereotyped phrase is not evident here. The arguments Davids suggests fail to convince. First, the phrase "Spirit of God" on any reading is broken up in some sense, which is why scholars debate whether the first use of the article *(to)* refers to the Spirit. The second argument is not distinctive to the interpretation proposed by Davids. Since it can apply to both interpretations, it is not determinative. Third, it is unclear what Davids means by "stereotyped phrases," since the examples adduced seem to be parallel to what we have in 1 Pet 4:14.

The wording of the verse hearkens back to Isa 11:1–3, where the branch of Jesse, obviously Jesus himself for Peter, will be endowed with the Holy Spirit.[23] The wording of v. 2 in the Septuagint is especially important. Isaiah said about Jesse's branch that "the Spirit of the Lord will rest on him" *(anapausetai ep auton pneuma tou theou).*[24] The main difference is that Isaiah used a future tense verb, while in Peter we have a present tense, probably to emphasize that the prophecy uttered in Isaiah has now been fulfilled and that the Spirit that was upon Jesus now also rests on Christians. Believers who suffer are blessed because they are now enjoying God's favor, tasting even now the wonder of the glory to come and experiencing the promised Holy Spirit.[25]

4:15 The "for" introducing v. 15, deleted by the NIV, explains that believers' joy and blessing is conditioned upon truly suffering as Christians. Not all suffering qualifies one for God's blessing and joy, for human beings

---

[22] P. H. Davids, *The First Epistle of Peter,* NICNT (Grand Rapids: Eerdmans, 1990), 167–68, n. 10. See also Elliott, *1 Peter,* 782, who thinks it should be translated "the divine Spirit of glory."

[23] Johnson suggests that there is also an allusion to the temple as Yahweh's resting place, where God's glory and Spirit dwell ("Fire in God's House," 289–90).

[24] The LXX says "the *Spirit of God*" (emphasis mine). J. W. Pryor is quite unconvincing when he dismisses the clear allusion to Isaiah 11 and forges a link to the descent of God's glory upon Mount Sinai instead ("First Peter and the New Covenant [II]," *RTR* 45 [1986]: 49). At this point he forces the evidence in trying to sustain an exodus motif in 1 Peter.

[25] Some manuscripts have the intriguing addition κατὰ μὲν αὐτοὺς βλασφημεῖται, κατὰ δὲ ὑμᾶς δοξάζεται (in their eyes it is blasphemy, but in your eyes it is glory; Majority text, K, L, P, Ψ). Some scholars defend their authenticity, arguing that (1) the words were accidentally deleted because of the –ται ending, (2) that the μέν-δέ construction fits Petrine style, (3) that the addition does not contribute much to the passage, and (4) that abrupt use of αὐτοὺς parallels αὐτῶν in 3:14 (cf. P. R. Rodgers, "The Longer Reading of 1 Peter 4:14," *CBQ* 43 [1981]: 94; Michaels, *1 Peter,* 265). But external evidence favors its omission, and we probably have a gloss by an early scribe (see *TCGNT,* 625; Davids, *First Peter,* 168, n. 11).

also suffer when they do what is evil. The realism of Peter and of the early Christian movement manifests itself here. He knew how easily people can rationalize punishments that are deserved and explain them as "Christian" suffering. The admonition also reminds us that the early Christian churches were imperfect. Believers were still prone to sin, and hence they needed exhortations to encourage them to walk in godly pathways. The first two sins listed are blatant examples of falling short of God's standards. Indeed, murder and stealing are not only sins but also crimes in society. We should not discern from this that believers in the Petrine churches were actually committing such crimes, nor is it clear from this that Christians were being taken to court.[26] Blatant sins are listed for rhetorical reasons, so that believers will distinguish between genuine Christian suffering and suffering that is a consequence of misbehavior.[27] In any case, we see elsewhere in paraenesis prohibitions or warnings against murder (Matt 5:21; 19:18; Mark 10:19; Luke 18:20; Rom 1:29; 13:9; Jas 2:11; 4:2; Rev 9:21; 21:8; 22:15). Stealing is also regularly condemned (Matt 19:18; Mark 10:19; Luke 18:20; Rom 2:21; 13:9; 1 Cor 6:10; Eph 4:28). The third sin is defined by the NIV as "criminal" *(kakopoios)*. Peter used the same word on two other occasions, and in both those cases it refers to doing wrong in general and cannot be limited to criminal acts (1 Pet 2:12,14). The verbal form also seems to bear this same meaning and is invariably contrasted with doing good (Mark 3:4; Luke 6:9; 1 Pet 3:17; 3 John 11). Hence, the term probably should be translated as "wrongdoer" (RSV) rather than "criminal."[28] Some evidence suggests that the word could mean "sorcerer" or "magician,"[29] but no evidence for this can be sustained from the Petrine usage, which regularly contrasts doing good in general with doing evil in general.

The fourth word represents one of the most difficult interpretive problems in the New Testament. This word, translated "meddler" *(allotriepiskopos)* by the NIV, occurs nowhere else in the New Testament, nowhere in the Septuagint, and nowhere in other Greek literature before 1 Peter. When we examine the word's parts, we could define it as "watching over another's affairs." From this we can glean the interpretation that is represented in most English translations, "mischief-maker" (RSV, also NRSV), "busy-

---

[26] Contra Goppelt, *I Peter*, 39; Dubis, *1 Peter 4:12–19,* 134. I am not denying that Christians *may* have been hauled into court. The point is that this text does not clearly indicate that they were taken to court. Peter's language is rhetorical here (cf. Bechtler, *Following in His Steps,* 92).

[27] Nor is it clear that the admonitions against lawlessness signal the onset of the Messianic woes (contra Dubis, *1 Peter 4:12–19,* 134–35).

[28] So Michaels, *1 Peter,* 267; Achtemeier, *1 Peter,* 310; Elliott, *1 Peter,* 784–85. But K. Erbes thinks the parallels in 1 Pet 2:12; 3:16; John 18:30 suggest that criminal activity is in view ("Was *bedeutet* ἀλλοτριοεπίσκοπος 1 Pt 4,15?" *ZNW* 19 [1919–20]: 39).

[29] One of the suggestions of BDAG, 501.

body" (KJV, NKJV), "troublesome meddler" (NASB).[30] Others have suggested that the term means "revolutionary" or "embezzler."[31] The latter, especially, is promoted by quite a few scholars. Certainty is impossible because of the lack of data, but it is argued by some that "embezzler" makes the best sense contextually.[32] They claim that meddling is annoying, but the context demands actions that are seriously wrong, and meddling does not fit in such a context. Warnings against defrauding others are found elsewhere in the New Testament (Mark 10:19; 1 Cor 6:7–8; 1 Tim 3:8; Titus 1:7; 1 Pet 5:2). Yet the words "even as" *(ē hōs)* preceding the word in question suggest that Peter did think of something less serious than murder or thievery here.[33] Peter realized that most Christians will not be guilty of obvious sins like murder and stealing, and so he concluded by encouraging believers to even refrain from annoying others.[34] If believers act like busybodies, they would be considered to be pests who deserve ostracism and mistreatment. Hence, though certainty is impossible, a reference to being a busybody seems most probable. Peter wanted believers to refrain from acting tactlessly and without social graces.

4:16 Verse 16 now examines the other side. The word "if" as in v. 14 should not be translated as "since" or "when." It is not as though Peter was saying that Christians may escape suffering. The condition is used so the readers will consider the condition, focusing on the reason for suffering, namely, if someone suffers as a "Christian." Early believers did not typically call themselves "Christians." The name was first given to believers by outsiders in Antioch (Acts 11:26). Agrippa also used the term when Paul

---

[30] So E. G. Selwyn, *The First Epistle of St. Peter,* 2d ed. (Grand Rapids: Baker, 1981), 225; Goppelt, *I Peter,* 326; E. Schweizer, "1. Petrus 4,6," *TZ* 8 (1952): 94; E. Best, *1 Peter,* NCB (Grand Rapids: Eerdmans, 1971), 165; Michaels, *1 Peter,* 267–68; Kelly, *Peter and Jude,* 188–89; Davids, *First Peter,* 169; J. H. Elliott, *A Home for the Homeless: A Sociological Exegesis of 1 Peter, Its Situation and Strategy* (Philadelphia: Fortress, 1981), 141–42; id., *1 Peter,* 785–88.

[31] For the former see Moffatt, *James, Peter, and Jude,* 158; Beare, *First Peter,* 167; and for the latter Achtemeier, *1 Peter,* 310–13; Erbes, "Was *bedeutet?*" 40–44; J. Calvin, *Commentaries on the Catholic Epistles* (Grand Rapids: Eerdmans, 1948), 137; Brox, *Der erste Petrusbrief,* 219–20.

[32] Elliott shows that when ἀλλότριος is used in compounds, the "other" refers to the object, not the subject of the word (*1 Peter,* 786). Hence, ἀλλοτριοπραγέω refers to meddling in another's affairs, so also ἀλλοτριοπραγία. The term ἀλλοτριοφαγέω means "to eat another's food," while ἀλλοτριοφρονέω means "to be ill-disposed to another" (for these definitions see LSJ, 70–71). This evidence suggests that ἀλλοτριεπίσκοπος refers to meddling in or overseeing another's affairs.

[33] Rightly Bechtler, *Following in His Steps,* 92. For an earlier interpretation defending "meddler," see Theophylact in *James, 1–2 Peter, 1–3 John, Jude,* ACCS (Downers Grove: InterVarsity, 2000), 119.

[34] Cf. E. J. Richard, who points out that Peter in other places in the epistle may have been warning believers about annoying unbelievers (*Reading 1 Peter, Jude, and 2 Peter: A Literary and Theological Commentary,* RNT [Macon: Smith & Helwys, 2000], 192–93).

was making his defense in Caesarea (Acts 26:28). The usage here fits thc paradigm, for the label "Christian" is ascribed to believers by those looking at the community from the outside (cf. Tacitus, *Ann.* 15.44). The word "Christians" *(Christianoi)* means "followers of Christ," just as "Herodians" (*Hērōdianoi;* Mark 3:6; 12:13) means "partisans of Herod the Great and his family."[35] Even though we saw in v. 14 that the Christian faith was not officially declared to be illegal in Peter's day, the threat of persecution was constant, for as Christians emerged as a distinct entity from Judaism, they had no legal status as a religion. On the other hand, the term "Christian" does not indicate that being a Christian was a punishable offense per se when the letter was written. Even when Pliny wrote Trajan (ca. A.D. 112–114), the status of Christians was uncertain. It reflects instead sporadic and occasional persecution.[36]

The call to renounce shame focuses on actions that are shameful. Specifically, Christians would act shamefully by denying Christ before unbelievers or by failing to persevere in the faith (cf. Mark 8:38; 2 Tim 1:8,12,16; 2:15). Hence, those who are ashamed would be guilty of apostasy.[37] By way of contrast believers glorify God by confessing and praising his name publicly (cf. Rom 15:6; 2 Cor 9:13). They glorify God in the name "Christian" by enduring such suffering with joy (v. 13), pleased that they are privileged to suffer because of their allegiance to Jesus Christ. The final phrase of the verse, "in that name" (NASB, *en tō onomati toutō*), probably is a dative of sphere,[38] signifying that believers suffer for the epithet "Christian."[39]

4:17 The "for" *(hoti)* beginning this verse reaches back to the idea of suffering in v. 16. The suffering of believers is the beginning of God's judgment from "the household of God" *(tou oikou tou theou).* The NIV interprets the phrase as "family of God," but this obscures the Old Testament background of the term. The phrase "house of God" (translated literally) refers back to the Old Testament, where God's house is almost invariably

---

[35] BDAG, 440, 1090. For a helpful discussion of "Christian," see Elliott, *1 Peter,* 789–91.

[36] J. Knox's attempt to link the charges specifically with Pliny and Trajan's correspondence must be judged as unsuccessful ("Pliny and I Peter: A Note on I Pet 4:14–16 and 3:15," *JBL* 72 [1953]: 187–89). Rightly Elliott, *1 Peter,* 792–93.

[37] Rightly Dubis, *1 Peter 4:12–19,* 135–36.

[38] Achtemeier, *1 Peter,* 314–15; Selwyn, *First Peter,* 225. Kelly argues that sphere when linked with "name" signifies cause (*Peter and Jude,* 190–91). Others take it to be instrumental (Davids, *First Peter,* 170, n. 17; Elliott, *1 Peter,* 796). A number of manuscripts read ἐν τῷ μέρει τούτῳ (P, 049, Majority text) instead of ἐν τῷ ὀνόματι τούτῳ (𝔓[72], ℵ, A, B, Ψ, 33, 81, 323, 614, 1241, 1505, 1739). The external evidence supports the reading in the text, though the variant is surely the harder reading. In this case the external evidence is decisive enough to justify the inclusion of what we find in NA27. In favor of the variant, see Richard, *Reading 1 Peter, Jude, and 2 Peter,* 194–95.

[39] Cf. Goppelt, *I Peter,* 328; Kelly, *Peter and Jude,* 190–91; Elliott, *1 Peter,* 796.

his temple.[40] Many more examples could be adduced. The Old Testament background stems especially from Ezekiel 9 and Malachi 3. In Ezekiel 9 the Lord judges the sinners within Israel and begins from his sanctuary, the temple.[41] The language of Ezek 9:6 is similar to Peter's in that the Lord said, "Begin at my sanctuary" *(apo tōn hagiōn mou arxasthe),* while Peter wrote, "For the time has come for judgment to begin with the household of God" (NRSV; *arxasthai to krima apo tou oikou tou theou;* cf. Isa 10:11–12). The language is similar, but the theology is actually quite different, for in Ezekiel rebellious sinners are being destroyed, but in Peter the judgment does not involve the destruction of the godly but their refinement and purification.[42] The background of Malachi 3 is closer conceptually to Peter's message in this respect, for the Lord will come to his temple and refine and purify his people, and then the offerings of his people will be acceptable (Mal 3:1–4). That the judgment in Peter does not involve destruction is clear from the parallel statement in v. 18, where the godly are "saved." We have already seen in 1:6–7 that the trials and difficulties of the righteous are designed to purify and refine believers so that they will receive their final reward (cf. also 4:12). Even though God's household is the temple in the Old Testament, we see here that Peter, in concert with other New Testament writers (1 Cor 3:16; 2 Cor 6:16; Eph 2:19; 1 Tim 3:15; Heb 3:6), now conceives of the church, God's people, as his temple.[43] Such a move is not surprising in Peter, for he already had identified the church as God's priesthood, his chosen people, and his holy nation, so that blessings belonging to Israel now belong to the church (1 Pet 2:9). In Ezekiel 9 the judgment literally begins at the temple, but now God's judgment begins not at a building but with his people. The judgment that begins with God's people purifies those who truly belong to God, and that purification comes through suffering, making believers morally fit for their inheritance.

The judgment here is the final judgment (cf. 1:17; 2:23; 4:5), but this

---

[40] E.g., LXX 1 Kgs 5:14,17,19; 7:31,34,37; 8:1,17,18; 12:27; 14:26; 1 Chr 5:36; 6:16; 9:23, 26,27; 10:10; 22:1,2,6,7,11; 26:27; 28:21; 29:2,3; 2 Chr 3:3; 4:11; 5:14; 7:5; Ezra 1:3,4; 3:8,9; 4:3; 6:5; Neh 8:16; 10:33,34,35; Pss 41:5; 54:15; Mic 4:2; Joel 1:13,14,16; Isa 2:2,3; 38:20). Supporting the notion of family is Bechtler, *Following in His Steps,* 144–46.

[41] See here Johnson, "Fire in God's House," 291–93; I. H. Marshall, *1 Peter,* NTC (Downers Grove: InterVarsity, 1991), 156. Supporting Ezekiel 9 as the background is W. L. Schutter, *Hermeneutic and Composition in I Peter,* WUNT 2/30 (Tübingen: Mohr, 1989), 276–84. Dubis argues that Ezekiel 9 is the primary text, but references to Malachi 3 cannot be excluded (*1 Peter 4:12–19,* 148–54).

[42] Because of the differences Elliott disputes an allusion to Ezekiel 9 (*1 Peter,* 798–800), but the texts do not need to match in every respect for an allusion to be present.

[43] The temple language is bound up with the notion that the people of God are his temple. So Johnson, "Fire in God's House," 292–93; Michaels, *1 Peter,* 271; Achtemeier, *1 Peter,* 316.

judgment begins even now, in the present evil age.[44] The judgment "begins with us," which means that it commences with Christians. In the present age believers experience suffering, and this is the purifying judgment that begins with believers. Peter proceeded to argue from the lesser to the greater. If even those who are going to be saved are purified and judged by suffering, then the "outcome" *(telos)* or result of those who reject the gospel will surely be a greater punishment. Unbelievers are described here as "those who do not obey the gospel of God." Peter could have written about judgment falling on those who disbelieved the gospel, but here he wanted to focus on the failure to obey, for all unbelief leads to disobedience. On three other occasions those who will be judged (or are being judged) are described as disobeying (*apeitheō,* 1 Pet 2:8; 3:1,20). In 2:8 and 3:1 such disobedience is described as disobedience to the word *(logos),* and the "word" in these texts is simply another expression for the gospel. Believers, on the other hand, are characterized by obedience (1:2,14; 3:10–12; 4:3–4). Peter did not specify what judgment awaits unbelievers, but he already had indicated in 4:5 that they await final judgment. We should also observe that the order of Malachi 3 is preserved here. When the Lord comes to his temple, he refines and purifies his people (3:1–4), but those who are unrepentant sinners will be destroyed (3:5).

4:18 Verse 18 restates the truth of v. 17 in proverbial form. Indeed, Peter virtually quoted Prov 11:31 from the Septuagint. The Hebrew text is quite similar to the Septuagint in some respects, but it has the words "on earth" instead of "with difficulty" *(molis).* The text form indicates that Peter drew from the Septuagint.[45] The meaning of the proverb must be discerned from the context in which Peter used it, and it clearly functions as a restatement of the previous idea in v. 17. The word *molis* can mean "scarcely" (Rom 5:7) or "with difficulty" (Acts 14:18; 27:7–8,16), but context here favors the latter. Peter was not saying that the righteous are scarcely saved, as if they were almost consigned to destruction and were just pulled from the flames. What he meant was that the righteous are saved "with difficulty." The difficulty envisioned is the suffering believers must endure in order to be saved. God saves his people by refining and purifying them

---

[44] So Best, *1 Peter,* 165; Achtemeier, *1 Peter,* 315.

[45] For a suggestion about how the LXX translator developed this translation, see J. Barr, "בארץ~μόλις: Prov. xi.31, I Pet. iv.18," *JSS* 20 (1975): 149–64. In agreement with Barr is D. G. McCartney, "The Use of the Old Testament in the First Epistle of Peter" (Ph.D. diss., Westminster Theological Seminary, 1989), 97–98. Dubis, on the other hand, argues that the MT and the LXX are compatible (*1 Peter 4:12–19,* 164–67). According to Dubis, the MT refers to God punishing his people even when they are in the land of promise. Hence, μόλις in his view is parallel to בארץ. Just as God punishes his people even when they are in the land, so too he saves the righteous with difficulty in that he saves them through a purifying judgment. The main difference Dubis sees between the MT and the LXX is that the latter focuses on the eschatological future.

through suffering. It is implied here that salvation is eschatological, a gift that believers will receive after enduring suffering (cf. 1:5,9). If the godly are saved through the purification of suffering, then the judgment of the "ungodly and sinner" must be horrific indeed.[46] The verb "will become" *(phaneitai)* refers to the eschatological judgment of unbelievers.[47] Peter wrote this to motivate believers to endure in suffering, and we have seen a similar argument in 4:3–6. Suffering may be difficult now, but by participating in the pain of following Christ believers escape the condemnation coming upon the wicked.[48]

4:19 A conclusion from all of vv. 12–18 is now drawn.[49] Those who suffer according to God's will are those who share in Christ's sufferings (v. 12), who are insulted in Christ's name (v. 14), and who suffer as Christians rather than for doing something evil (vv. 15–16). The reference to God's will here as in 3:17 indicates that all suffering passes through his hands (cf. 3:17), that nothing strikes a believer apart from God's loving and sovereign control.[50] When suffering strikes, believers should "commit themselves to their faithful Creator." Christ modeled what Peter enjoined, for when he was suffering, he entrusted himself to God (1 Pet 2:23). Jesus used the same word *(paratithēmi)* when he entrusted his spirit to God at his death (Luke 23:46). In Acts the word is used when Paul entrusted his converts to God (Acts 14:23; 20:32), and in the Pastorals the word designates the entrusting of God's truth to faithful men (1 Tim 1:18; 2 Tim 2:2). Similarly, believers should entrust their lives to God as Creator.[51] The reference to God as Creator *(ktistēs)* implies his sovereignty, for the Creator of the world is also sovereign over it.[52] Therefore believers can be confident that he will not allow them to suffer beyond their capacity and that he will provide the strength needed to endure. Such confidence can be theirs because he is a "faithful" Creator, faithful to his promises and faithful to his people,

[46] Contra Elliott, Peter was not leaving open in this context the prospect that the wicked may repent in the future (*1 Peter,* 804).

[47] Dubis, *1 Peter 4:12–19,* 167.

[48] So C. E. B. Cranfield, *I & II Peter and Jude: Introduction and Commentary,* TBC (London: SCM, 1960), 122; Goppelt, *I Peter,* 333; Achtemeier, *1 Peter,* 316.

[49] The word ὥστε is an inferential conjunction, and καὶ modifies ὥστε (so Selwyn, *First Peter,* 226; Michaels, *1 Peter,* 272–73; Achtemeier, *1 Peter,* 317) rather than modifying οἱ πάσχοντες (Goppelt, *I Peter,* 334; Kelly, *Peter and Jude,* 194) or παρατιθέσθωσαν (C. Bigg, *The Epistles of St. Peter and St. Jude,* ICC [Edinburgh: T & T Clark, 1901], 181).

[50] Dubis agrees but also connects this to the Messianic woes that precede the end (*1 Peter 4:12–19,* 176–77).

[51] As we have seen elsewhere in Peter, the word "souls" (τὰς ψυχὰς) refers to the "lives" of believers, not the immaterial part of their being (see 1:9,22; 2:11,25; 3:20).

[52] Dubis overreads the text in seeing a reference to the new creation here (*1 Peter 4:12–19,* 174–75).

never abandoning them in their time of need, always vindicating the righteous and condemning the wicked (cf. 4:17–18). The way believers will reveal that they are trusting in God is by continuing "to do good" *(agathopoiia)*.[53]

2. Exhortations to Elders and the Community (5:1–11)

(1) Exhortations for Elders and Younger Ones (5:1–5)

[1]To the elders among you, I appeal as a fellow elder, a witness of Christ's sufferings and one who also will share in the glory to be revealed: [2]Be shepherds of God's flock that is under your care, serving as overseers—not because you must, but because you are willing, as God wants you to be; not greedy for money, but eager to serve; [3]not lording it over those entrusted to you, but being examples to the flock. [4]And when the Chief Shepherd appears, you will receive the crown of glory that will never fade away.

[5]Young men, in the same way be submissive to those who are older. All of you, clothe yourselves with humility toward one another, because,

"God opposes the proud
but gives grace to the humble."

The elders are now addressed because as leaders they may face the brunt of persecution first. Perhaps there is even an echo of Ezek 9:6, for the judgment that commences in God's temple begins with the elders.[54] Or it may be that the elders are addressed first simply because they are leaders of God's flock.[55] Peter as a coelder reminded the readers of the sufferings of Christ and the glories to follow, suggesting the paradigmatic function of Christ's sufferings. Three exhortations are given to the elders. They are to shepherd and oversee God's flock, doing so because it is God's will, not because they feel compelled to serve. Further, they are to be eager in fulfilling their task and should not serve for financial gain. Finally, they are to live as examples of the flock instead of using their authority to domineer the church. The motivation for the leadership of elders is explained in v. 4. When Jesus as the Chief Shepherd of the church returns, they will receive a glorious crown that never fades. If elders are to shepherd the church in a godly manner, the younger members of the congregation are to submit to the leadership of the elders. And every member of the church is to live in humility since God is opposed to the proud but grants grace to the humble.

5:1 The content shifts from suffering imposed from outsiders to mat-

---

[53] Cf. Michaels, *1 Peter,* 274.
[54] Cf. Schutter, *Hermeneutic and Composition in I Peter,* 156–65.
[55] So Elliott, *1 Peter,* 812.

ters within the community. The text actually begins with a conjunction *(oun)* that could be translated as "therefore," "then," or "so" (RSV).[56] The NIV omits it entirely, probably because it is difficult to see how it relates to the preceding verses. We probably should explain the logical relationship as follows. The suffering and persecution faced by believers (4:12–19) puts a strain on the entire community. Both leaders and those who are younger must, in such a situation, respond appropriately to others in the church. More specifically, since judgment begins with God's household (vv. 17–18), those in the church are exhorted to live in a way that pleases God, so that they can avoid the judgment that will be imposed on the ungodly.[57]

In vv. 1–4 Peter addressed the elders in the church. The word "elders" *(presbyteroi)* is often used in the New Testament to refer to those who had leadership positions in the church.[58] The church or churches in Jerusalem had elders (Acts 11:30; 15:2,4,6,22–23; 16:4; 21:18).[59] According to Acts 14:23 Paul and Barnabas appointed elders in all the churches visited during their first missionary journey. When a contingent of leaders visited Paul from Ephesus, they were called "elders" (Acts 20:17). The person who is sick and needs prayer is encouraged to summon the elders of the church for prayer and anointing according to James (Jas 5:14). The Pastoral Epistles show that elders functioned in Ephesus (1 Tim 5:17) and were to be appointed in Crete (Titus 1:5). Every piece of evidence we have shows that elders were widespread in the early church. They are mentioned by different authors: Luke, Paul, Peter, and James. They stretch over a wide region of the Greco-Roman world: from Jerusalem, Palestine, the whole of Asia Minor, and Crete. It is also likely that elders functioned as a plurality in the churches since the term is always plural, and Acts 14:23 says elders were appointed "for them in each church." Further, the elders who visited the sick in James were plural, but the elders who visited were almost certainly from one local church. Most scholars believe that the term was borrowed

---

[56] The conjunction is omitted in a few manuscripts, but the external evidence demonstrates that it is original. It probably was deleted because it was difficult to see how it connected with the preceding context.

[57] For a view similar to mine, see Davids, *First Peter*, 174–75. Conversely, Goppelt argues that οὖν is not inferential here, and it signals a loose transition best translated as "now" (*I Peter*, 340, n. 4). Kelly says that godly leadership and "respect between members" is crucial in the midst of suffering (*Peter and Jude*, 196).

[58] Supporting an official use here is Selwyn, *First Peter*, 228; Bigg, *Epistles of Peter and Jude*, 183; Goppelt, *I Peter*, 340; Kelly, *Peter and Jude*, 196; Achtemeier, *1 Peter*, 321–22; J. H. Elliott, "Ministry and Church Order in the NT: A Traditio-Historical Analysis (1 Pt 5,1–5 & plls.)," *CBQ* 32 (1970): 371. Richard thinks the emphasis here is on the age of the elders instead of office (*Reading 1 Peter, Jude, and 2 Peter*, 202).

[59] Calvin says that elders are equivalent to pastors and presbyters and that it designates office, not necessarily old age (*Catholic Epistles*, 143, 145).

from Jewish usage, for the term "elders" is quite common in the Old Testament and the Jewish tradition.[60]

In giving an exhortation to the elders, Peter referred to himself in a threefold way: (1) a fellow elder, (2) a witness of Christ's sufferings, and (3) a sharer of the glory to come. We will take up each of these in order. The term "fellow elder" *(sympresbyteros)* occurs first here in Greek literature and probably was Peter's coinage. Peter identified with the leaders of the churches by using the same title as theirs instead of appealing to the term "apostle" to emphasize his authority.[61] We already noted that the leaders in the Jerusalem church were also called elders. Nevertheless, it is also the case that Peter's authority shines through.[62] He was the one giving instructions as a fellow elder, and it has already been noted that he was an apostle (1:1). Second, Peter reminded them that he was a witness of Christ's sufferings. The reference to Christ's sufferings is obviously intentional, for as the letter has made clear, suffering is the pathway to glory. Jesus Christ himself traveled the same road, and hence believers should not be surprised (4:12) that they are called to do the same. Scholars debate whether Peter claimed to be an eyewitness of Christ's sufferings here. Some argue that the point is that he was a recipient of the early tradition that transmitted Christ's sufferings and observe that Peter was not an actual witness since he fled the scene.[63] This latter point should not be used against Petrine authorship, as some scholars have done, for Peter was not insisting that he observed every moment when Christ suffered.[64] Peter did actually observe Christ in his ministry, saw the opposition mount against him, was present when he was arrested, and may have found his way to the cross after denying him. Even if he was not present at the crucifixion, he would have received the tradition incredibly early from John the Apostle, the Lord's mother, and other witnesses.[65]

Lastly, Peter identified himself again with the other elders, saying that he would also "share in the glory to be revealed." Some scholars see here a ref-

---

[60] For the background of the term see B. Merkle, *The Elder and Overseer: One Office in the Early Church* (Ph.D. diss., The Southern Baptist Theological Seminary, 2000), 27–68.

[61] Selwyn rightly notes that Peter did not emphasize his humility here but instead revealed his empathy for their task (*First Peter*, 228). Cf. also Elliott, *Home for the Homeless,* 137.

[62] Brox understands the reference to Peter to be a fictional device (*Der erste Petrusbrief,* 228).

[63] E.g., Michaels, *1 Peter,* 280–81. Kelly thinks the author was a witness in the sense that he also suffered for his allegiance to Christ (*Peter and Jude,* 198–99; so already Calvin, *Catholic Epistles*, 144), but he fails to read the expression in its most natural sense.

[64] Rightly D. Guthrie, *New Testament Introduction*, 4th ed. (Downers Grove: InterVarsity, 1990), 774. For arguments supporting the notion that Peter was an eyewitness, see Dubis, *1 Peter 4:12–19,* 104–6.

[65] Others think the purpose is to emphasize that all leaders are witnesses to the gospel because of their allegiance to and experience of the crucified and risen Lord (Davids, *First Peter,* 176–77).

erence to the transfiguration (cf. Matt 17:1–8 par.; 2 Pet 1:16–18), and others detect an allusion to the resurrection.[66] Both of these explanations can be rejected, for Peter spoke of a *future* glory here, not something observed in the past. The glory to be revealed therefore is at the second coming of Christ.[67] Elsewhere in 1 Peter "glory" *(doxa)* is usually the future reward either believers will receive or that Christ received after his sufferings (1:7,11,21; 4:13–14; 5:4,10). Words from the "revelation" word group also point toward the second coming of Christ in the letter (1:5,7,13). Two verses in particular show that revelation and glory refer to the future coming of Christ. In 1:7 the testing of faith will "result in praise, glory and honor when Jesus Christ is revealed," and in 4:13, "Rejoice that you participate in the sufferings of Christ, so that you may be overjoyed when his glory is revealed." Further, in 1:11 the "sufferings" of Christ precede the "glories" that follow, which matches the suffering and glory in 5:2. All of the parallels here make it quite certain that the glory promised in 5:1 is the eschatological reward that will be given when Christ returns. Peter encouraged the elders to follow Christ's example, enduring suffering in the present so that they will receive the eschatological reward in the future.

5:2 The task of the elders is now explained. They are to function as shepherds of God's flock. They are not to be like the shepherds indicted in Ezekiel 34 who treated their flock "harshly and brutally" (34:4), who cared only for themselves (34:8). The words "God's flock" remind the elders that the congregation does not belong to them. It is God's church, and they are given the privilege and responsibility of shepherding it.[68] The verb *poimainō,* "shepherd," is used in Acts 20:28 to describe the responsibility of the elders in the church. We are also reminded of Jesus' words to Peter in John 21:16, where Jesus exhorted Peter to "shepherd my sheep" (literal translation).[69] Luther rightly argues that we shepherd God's flock by preaching the gospel.[70] The participle "serving as overseers" *(episkopountes)* specifies another function of the elders. As God's shepherds and

---

[66] E.g., Selwyn thinks the Transfiguration is in view (*First Peter,* 228–29).

[67] There is no suggestion here that the glory is partially experienced in the present (Parker, "The Eschatology of 1 Peter," 30–31).

[68] Rightly M. Luther, *Commentary on Peter & Jude* (Grand Rapids: Kregel, 1990), 205.

[69] The evidence is insufficient to establish dependence on gospel tradition (contra R. H. Gundry, "'*Verba Christi*' in I Peter: Their Implications concerning the Authorship of I Peter and the Authenticity of the Gospel Tradition," *NTS* 13 [1967]: 341–42; "Further *Verba* on *Verba Christi* in First Peter," *Bib* 55 [1974]: 216–18; Elliott, "Ministry and Church Order," 383–84; M. C. Tenney, "Some Possible Parallels between 1 Peter and John," in *New Dimensions in New Testament Study* [Grand Rapids: Zondervan, 1974], 375; rightly Best, "Gospel Tradition," 97–98).

[70] Luther, *Commentary on Peter & Jude,* 205.

leaders they are to oversee the church and superintend it.[71] We have a hint here that in the New Testament the offices of elder and overseer were the same. This conclusion is a matter of some debate in New Testament scholarship and has been seriously questioned in the recent work by Campbell.[72] A recent dissertation by B. Merkle establishes, however, that overseer and elder were indeed one office.[73] This is the most plausible way of reading the New Testament evidence. In Acts 20:17 Paul summoned the elders *(presbyteroi)* of the Ephesian church, but in v. 28 they are identified as "overseers" *(episkopoi),* demonstrating that two different terms are used for one office. Paul charged Titus to appoint "elders" in Titus 1:5, but in v. 7 he shifts to "overseer." The "since" *(gar)* connecting vv. 6–7 suggests that a new office is not in view, and hence we should understand the singular "overseer" as generic here. We should draw the same conclusion from 1 Timothy. The singular "overseer" of 1 Tim 3:2 is another way of describing the elders mentioned in 5:17 (cf. 1 Tim 3:1). In Phil 1:1 the officers of the church are listed as "overseers and deacons." It is quite likely that these two offices could also be described as elders and deacons.

In the remainder of vv. 2–3 three contrasts are drawn explaining the way elders should not behave as opposed to a way they should conduct themselves. These instructions are always apropos, but they take on a particular urgency in a situation where the church faces persecution. First, those who serve as elders are not to serve under compulsion but with a whole-hearted desire *(hekousiōs),* which is God's will for them. A similar thought is found in 1 Tim 3:1, where the desire to be an overseer is commended, though we need to balance this with the instruction from James, who reminds us that teachers have a great responsibility and face a stricter judgment (Jas 3:1). Those who serve only because they feel they must will lose their joy, and the church will suffer as a consequence. Davids observes that elders would presumably work long hours and be the first targets of persecution, both of which could quench their desire to continue.[74] Second, elders must not take a leadership position out of greed. The danger exists that they will resort to dishonest gain and embezzle funds in some fashion. The same term is used in Titus 1:7 *(aischrokerdōs),* where Paul instructed Titus not to appoint

[71] The participle ἐπισκοποῦντες is missing in some early manuscripts (א*, B, 323), but the majority of witnesses include it, and we should not put much confidence in B, which also wrongly omits v. 3. The corrector of Sinaiticus includes the participle, and it may have been omitted by some scribes because they distinguished the offices of elder and overseer and thought the text was mistaken in correlating them. Supporting omission is Richard, *Reading 1 Peter, Jude, and 2 Peter,* 206. In support of inclusion see Elliott, *1 Peter,* 824, n. 665.

[72] R. A. Campbell, *The Elders: Seniority with Earliest Christianity* (Edinburgh: T & T Clark, 1998).

[73] Merkle, *The Elder and Overseer.* So already Luther, *Commentary on Peter & Jude,* 206.

[74] Davids, *First Peter,* 177–78.

elders who desire dishonest gain (cf. also 1 Tim 3:3). In the New Testament false teachers are often indicted because of their love of money (cf. 2 Cor 2:17; 11:7–15; 1 Tim 6:5–10; 2 Pet 2:3,14–15; Jude 11). Genuine leaders, on the other hand, have an eagerness *(prothymōs)* in doing the work. The word "eagerly" (NRSV) here is another way of stating the word "willingly" (NRSV, *hekousiōs*).[75] The leaders of God's flock do not serve because they have to, as if it were simply another job, nor do they serve to skim off money for themselves.

5:3 The third contrast indicates that elders are not to use their positions of authority as an opportunity to oppress those under them. They are not to function as oppressors but as examples. The term "lording it over" *(katakyrieuō)* may allude to the teaching of Jesus, where he instructed his disciples not to imitate the Gentiles, who use their authority to rule over others and advance their own interests (Matt 20:25; Mark 10:42).[76] Followers of Jesus are to use their authority to serve, and in that way they imitate the example of Jesus himself (Matt 20:28; Mark 10:45). The words "those entrusted to you" *(klērōn)* have been interpreted in various ways. Some argue that the meaning is that elders should not be dictatorial in assigning offices or positions to those below them in ministry or that they should not be autocratic when dealing with ministers who possess less power.[77] The NIV, however, is almost certainly correct here. Peter referred to God's people here, not to those who are in positions of ministry.[78] We are uncertain whether the plural refers to the part of the congregation an elder superintends or whether the reference is to the various congregations from the different cities addressed in 1 Peter. In any case, the "flock" of v. 2 is what Peter had in mind. Elders are not to enter the ministry so they can boss others around but so they can exemplify the character of Christ to those under their charge.

5:4 We have already seen in v. 1 that the instructions to elders is introduced with the notion of suffering and then glory, implying that those who serve well now will receive a great reward later. Peter did not call on leaders "to sacrifice" with no thought of reward. He reminded them that their labor for others will have a great reward and will bring remarkable joy.

---

[75] So Achtemeier, *1 Peter,* 326.

[76] So Gundry, "*Verba Christi,*" 344; cf. G. Maier, "Jesustradition im 1. Petrusbrief," in *Gospel Perspectives: The Jesus Tradition outside the Gospels* (Sheffield: JSOT Press, 1984), 93–95; contra Best, "Gospel Tradition," 100. Elliott also sees the tradition in the Gospels reflected here and argues that the evidence is insufficient for any literary relationship to Qumran literature ("Ministry and Church Order," 372–74).

[77] Cf. Kelly for a survey of interpretations (*Peter and Jude,* 202–3).

[78] So Calvin, *Catholic Epistles,* 145–46; Beare, *First Peter,* 174; Goppelt, *I Peter,* 347; Michaels, *1 Peter,* 285–86; Achtemeier, *1 Peter,* 328; Elliott, *1 Peter,* 831.

Such a theme comes to the forefront specifically in v. 4. Jesus here is called "the Chief Shepherd" *(archipoimenos)*, a rare term that occurs nowhere else in the New Testament or in the Septuagint. The designation of Jesus as the Chief Shepherd reminds the leaders that they are fundamentally servants, not autocrats. Their positions of leadership are a responsibility, not a privilege by which they advance their own status. As shepherds they serve under the authority of the Chief Shepherd, doing his will rather than theirs. The appearance of Christ refers, of course, to his second coming (cf. 1:7,13; cf. also 1 John 2:28; 3:2; Col 3:4), reminding the leaders that their positions of leadership are temporary. Clearly Peter preserved an eschatological urgency. He did not focus on when leaders die but on the coming of the Lord. When the Lord comes, those elders who have served in accordance with the instructions in vv. 2–3 will receive a reward, "the crown of glory that will never fade away." The word translated "will receive" *(komieisthe)* is also used elsewhere to designate either reward or punishment on the last day (2 Cor 5:10; Eph 6:8; Col 3:25; Heb 10:36; 1 Pet 1:9). Peter contrasted the crown elders will receive with the leafy crowns bestowed in the Greco-Roman world. Such crowns were given after athletic victories or military conquests (Martial, *Epig.* 2.2; Pliny, *Hist. nat.* 15.5; Dio Chrysostom, *Or.* 8.15). Such crowns faded as time elapsed, but the crown given by God (cf. 1 Pet 5:10) will never fade. The word "glory" is appositional to "crown."[79] It is difficult to know if the crown is equivalent to eternal life itself or if it is a special reward for elders. In the other "crown" *(stephanos)* texts the reward is entrance into heaven itself (cf. 1 Cor 9:25; 2 Tim 4:8; Jas 1:12; Rev 2:10; 3:11). The usage in the rest of the New Testament slightly favors the latter notion. Elders can be confident that they will receive the greatest reward conceivable when the *eschaton* arrives.

5:5 The texts shifts from "elders" to those who are "younger" (NRSV, *neōteroi*), perhaps echoing Ezek 9:6.[80] The use of the word "younger" might cause us to doubt that elders in the previous verses referred to a position of leadership, concluding instead that those who are advancing in age are described.[81] This interpretation can be ruled out since the descriptions of their activities in vv. 2–3 make clear that they were also leaders, and we saw that the term was commonly used to designate an office in the New Testament. It is also possible that the word "elders" shifts meaning in this verse, so that in vv. 1–4 the reference is to those who are in an official posi-

---

[79] Michaels, *1 Peter,* 287; Kelly, *Peter and Jude,* 204; Elliott, *1 Peter,* 835.

[80] Campbell, *Honor, Shame, and the Rhetoric of 1 Peter,* 216. Ezekiel 9:6 uses both the term πρεσβύτερον and νεανίσκον.

[81] So Bigg, *Epistles of Peter and Jude,* 190; Selwyn, *First Peter,* 233; Cranfield, *I & II Peter and Jude,* 131–32.

tion of authority, but now Peter turned to those who are older.[82] This solution is possible, but it seems unlikely, for the interpretation that does not require a change in definition for the term "elders" should be preferred.[83] And the verse is tied quite closely to the previous section with the term "likewise" (*homoiōs,* deleted in the NIV). We have seen in 3:1 and 3:7 that the term "likewise" binds paragraphs together when complementary entities are addressed (e.g., husbands and wives). Another possibility is to limit the "younger" to a part of the congregation. Perhaps the young are those who are young in faith, neophytes who have been recently baptized,[84] or perhaps as in Titus 2:6–8 those who are young are given a particular exhortation, especially since young people may tend to be more independent and less inclined to submit to those in authority.[85] The former notion is quite unlikely, for the evidence is insufficient to indicate that the term "younger" refers to those who are recent converts. Further, the argument depends upon alleged parallels to the Qumran literature, and such parallels are not firmly established. Nor is it likely that we have a reference to young people recently appointed as elders.[86] It is possible that "younger" refers to the entire congregation, which is contrasted to the elders. If this interpretation is correct, the term "younger" is used because generally speaking the remaining believers are younger in contrast to the elders.[87] The designation "younger" is a suitable "formal counterpart" to "elders."[88] A decision is difficult, but we probably should understand Peter to refer to those who are literally younger, perhaps because younger people would be more apt to act rebelliously. This view is suggested by the address to "all" *(pantes)* that follows the younger—introduced by "and" (NRSV, *de*—unfortunately deleted by the NIV). The "and all" (NRSV) could imply that now the entire congregation is addressed instead of merely the "elders" and the "younger."

The younger in particular, then, should submit *(hypotagēte)* to the leadership of the elders. We have seen elsewhere that Peter understood submission as the responsibility of believers to those in positions of authority (cf.

---

[82] So Calvin, *Catholic Epistles,* 147.

[83] Rightly Brox, *Der erste Petrusbrief,* 233.

[84] Elliott, "Ministry and Church Order," 375–86; id., *1 Peter,* 836–40.

[85] Cf. Best, *1 Peter,* 171; Grudem, *1 Peter,* 192–93; C. Spicq, *Les Épîtres de Saint Pierre,* SB (Paris: Gabalda, 1966), 170–71; Davids, *First Peter,* 183–84; Richard, *Reading 1 Peter, Jude, and 2 Peter,* 209; Schelke, *Der Petrusbriefe—Der Judasbrief,* 130; Marshall, *1 Peter,* 164–65. Marshall says that people could be considered young up to the age of forty.

[86] Against N. Hillyer, *1 and 2 Peter, Jude,* NIBC (Peabody: Hendrickson, 1992), 141.

[87] So Michaels, *1 Peter,* 288–89; Goppelt, *I Peter,* 350–51; Reicke, *The Epistles of James, Peter, and Jude,* 130; Achtemeier, *1 Peter,* 331–32; S. McKnight, *1 Peter,* NIVAC (Grand Rapids: Zondervan, 1996), 263.

[88] So Goppelt, *I Peter,* 339. Brox thinks Peter drew on traditional formulations here (*Der erste Petrusbrief,* 234).

2:13,18; 3:1,5). The purpose is not to encourage obedience no matter what leaders might say, for if leaders give counsel that contravenes God's moral standards or violates the gospel, then they should not be followed. Nor is the verse suggesting that leaders are exempt from accountability before the congregation. We have already observed that elders are admonished not to use their authority as dictatorial rulers but are to serve those under their charge. Conversely, those who are under leadership should be inclined to follow and submit to their leaders. They should not be resisting the initiatives of leaders and complaining about the direction of the church.

Smooth relations in the church can be preserved if the entire congregation adorns itself with humility. When believers recognize that they are creatures and sinners, they are less apt to be offended by others. Humility is the oil that allows relationships in the church to run smoothly and lovingly. Pride gets upset when another does not follow our own suggestions. Peter grounded this admonition with a citation from Prov 3:34, which is also quoted in Jas 4:6. The citation is closer to the Septuagint than it is to the Hebrew text, but the meaning in both cases is essentially the same.[89] Believers should heed the injunction to be humble because God sets his face against the proud, but he lavishes his grace upon the humble. Those who submit to God's sovereignty in humility will find that he will lift them up and reward them.

(2) Closing Exhortations and Assurance (5:6–11)

[6]Humble yourselves, therefore, under God's mighty hand, that he may lift you up in due time. [7]Cast all your anxiety on him because he cares for you.

[8]Be self-controlled and alert. Your enemy the devil prowls around like a roaring lion looking for someone to devour. [9]Resist him, standing firm in the faith, because you know that your brothers throughout the world are undergoing the same kind of sufferings.

[10]And the God of all grace, who called you to his eternal glory in Christ, after you have suffered a little while, will himself restore you and make you strong, firm and steadfast. [11]To him be the power for ever and ever. Amen.

The paragraph division is somewhat artificial since the admonition in v. 6 is an inference from v. 5. Since God resists the proud and gives grace to the humble (v. 5), believers should humble themselves under God's mighty and sovereign hand in their suffering. They are to humble themselves so that God will exalt them and give them the reward of eternal life on the last day (v. 6). Humility also manifests itself in handing over our worries to God (v. 7a), and hence it follows that worry is a form of pride. Worry constitutes

---

[89] Both James and Peter used the term θεός instead of κυριός from Prov 3:34 (LXX).

pride since it denies the care of a sovereign God. The antidote to worry is believing in and resting in God's care for believers (v. 7b). Suffering does not only call for humility but also believers are enjoined to be sober and alert (v. 8). Alertness is necessary because the devil is prowling about and is using suffering to roar at believers, hoping to frighten them into apostasy and hence to destroy their faith. Because the devil is on the loose, believers must resist him, and such resistance is maintained by continuing strong in faith (v. 9). Believers should be encouraged when they realize that fellow believers throughout the world are experiencing the same suffering. Peter concluded in vv. 10–11 by reflecting on the grace and sovereignty of God. He prayed in v. 10 that the God who gives all grace and who effectually called believers to himself will give them strength to endure the sufferings of this age and that the sovereignty will belong to him forever.

5:6 The "therefore" in v. 6 demonstrates that the call to humility reaches back to v. 5. The logic of the verse is as follows. Since God resists the proud and pours his grace upon the humble, "therefore" believers should humble themselves. By humbling themselves they will experience God's grace, for God bestows his favor on those who acknowledge their need of him. The humbling enjoined probably means that they are to accept the suffering God has ordained as his will instead of resisting and chafing against his will while suffering.[90] They should realize that the purification of God's house has begun (1 Pet 4:17). When Peter said they are to humble themselves under God's "mighty hand" *(krataian cheira),* he used an expression that is associated particularly with God's delivering Israel out of Egypt (e.g., Exod 3:19; 32:11; Deut 4:34; 5:15; 6:21; 7:8,19; 9:26; 11:2; 26:8; Dan 9:15). Just as the Lord delivered his people from Egypt, so he would vindicate his people in Asia Minor who suffered. The image of a mighty hand emphasizes the power of God. Believers humble themselves before a mighty God, the all-powerful one. Humility should not be seen as the ultimate goal here. Those who humble themselves before the Lord will be exalted. The theme that the humble will be exalted can be traced back to the teaching of Jesus (Matt 23:12; Luke 14:11; 18:14), and there is no reason to doubt that Peter recalled the teaching of his Lord here. The verse promises exaltation "in due time" *(en kairō).* Peter was not promising vindication and exaltation in this life. The point is not, against Grudem, that such vindication occurs occasionally in this life.[91] The time in view is the day of judgment and salvation, what Peter called "the last time" *(en kairō eschatō)* in v. 6, or "the day of visitation" (RSV, *en hemera episkopēs*) in

[90] So F. V. Filson, "Partakers with Christ: Suffering in First Peter," *Int* 9 (1955): 405.

[91] Grudem, *1 Peter,* 194–95. Richard's view is similar to Grudem's (*Reading 1 Peter, Jude, and 2 Peter,* 216).

2:12.[92] That the exaltation would occur on the last day fits with the eschatological focus of 1 Peter and draws us back into the orbit of the first verses of the letter (1:3–12), where the salvation envisioned is an end-time salvation. The day of humiliation is limited to this world, but the readers will be lifted on high by God's grace forever.

The words of Peter here are remarkably similar to Jas 4:10. Indeed, the parallels with James are striking in this section since both also cite Prov 3:34 as noted above (Jas 4:6; 1 Pet 5:5), and both also call on believers to resist the devil (Jas 4:7; 1 Pet 5:9). These commonalities have led some to think that James and 1 Peter draw on common tradition.[93] The use of common tradition is possible, but the evidence for such a conclusion is by no means clear. James and 1 Peter have remarkably different purposes in the texts in question. James warned complacent believers, while Peter encouraged those who are suffering. The content of Jas 4:6–10 and 1 Pet 5:5–9 also diverges in remarkable ways, so that the texts when read side by side have notable similarities and notable differences. The themes of humiliation and exaltation are a staple of Christian tradition and hence do not clearly show dependence on a common tradition. The reference to resisting the devil probably is not distinctive enough to warrant the conclusion that the same source lies behind both Peter and James. If they did use the same tradition, Peter and James applied it in very different ways.

5:7 The NIV begins v. 7 with a command, "cast all your anxiety." The Greek text, however, uses the participle "casting" *(epiripsantes),* and hence the NASB represents a better translation, "casting all your anxiety upon him." The participle should be understood as an instrumental participle,[94] and it explains *how* believers can humble themselves under God's strong hand. Seeing the relationship between the main verb ("humble yourselves," v. 6) and the participle ("casting all your anxiety upon him," NASB) is important because it shows that giving in to worry is an example of pride. The logical relationship between the two clauses is as follows: believers humble themselves *by casting* their worries on God. Conversely, if believers continue to worry, then they are caving in to pride. How can anxiety and worry be criticized as pride? We can see that it might be a lack of faith, but

---

[92] So Michaels, *1 Peter,* 296; Kelly, *Peter and Jude,* 208; Goppelt, *I Peter,* 357; Achtemeier, *1 Peter,* 339; Schelke, *Der Petrusbriefe—Der Judasbrief,* 131. The parallel from 2:12 probably is the reason some manuscripts add the word ἐπισκοπῆς in v. 12 (A, P, [Ψ], 33, 623, and a few other manuscripts). The addition represents an accurate interpretation but probably is secondary.

[93] Cf. Best, *1 Peter,* 172; Goppelt, *I Peter,* 356; Michaels, *1 Peter,* 294–95.

[94] Rightly Kelly, *Peter and Jude,* 208; Michaels, *1 Peter,* 296; Achtemeier, *1 Peter,* 339; So S. Snyder, "Participles and Imperatives in 1 Peter: A Re-examination in the Light of Recent Scholarly Trends," *FNT* 8 (1995): 196. Against Elliott, *1 Peter,* 851, who sees it as an independent imperative.

does it make sense to identify worry as pride? Worry is a form of pride because when believers are filled with anxiety, they are convinced that they must solve all the problems in their lives in their own strength. The only god they trust in is themselves. When believers throw their worries upon God, they express their trust in his mighty hand, acknowledging that he is Lord and Sovereign over all of life. As Goppelt says, "Affliction either drives one into the arms of God or severs one from God."[95]

Peter wrote this to a church afflicted by suffering and distress, and hence he realized that they faced anxiety.[96] Casting one's worries on God would not bring comfort if he were unable to afford assistance in times of distress.[97] Nor would anyone tell his worries to those who are cruel or apathetic, for those who are hateful and indifferent mock our worries by their lack of concern. Giving our anxiety to God makes eminent sense "because he cares for you." God is not indifferent, nor is he cruel. He has compassion on his children and will sustain them in every distress. Peter's words here remind us of Jesus' exhortation to avoid anxiety (Matt 6:25–34), and some even see an allusion to Jesus' words.[98] More probably, the allusion is to Ps 55:22. Psalm 55 fits nicely with Peter's theme, for the psalmist implored God to help him because the wicked were attempting to destroy him, and even his close friend had turned against him. Verses 4–8 express the anguish and torment he felt in the midst of such opposition. Again we see evidence that Peter considered the thematic context of the Old Testament when he alluded to it. We find the allusion in v. 22 (Ps 54:23, LXX), "Cast your anxiety upon the Lord, and he will sustain you" *(epiripson epi kyrion tēn merimnan sou, kai autos se diathrepsei).*

5:8 As Peter drew the letter to a close, he continued to give final exhortations to his readers. With two aorist imperatives he summoned them to be vigilant: "Be self-controlled and alert." The first imperative could be translated literally as "be sober" *(nēpsate).* The same verb is used in 1:13 and 4:7, and both contexts address the need for alertness since the end is impending (cf. also 1 Thess 5:6,8; 2 Tim 4:5). Similarly, the second imperative, which can be translated "watch" *(grēgorēsate)* is also used in eschatological contexts (Matt 24:42–43; 25:13; Mark 13:34–35,37; Luke 12:37; 1 Thess 5:6; Rev 3:2–3; 16:15). The call for vigilance hearkens back to the beginning of the letter (1:13) and functions as an inclusio.

---

[95] Goppelt, *I Peter,* 359.

[96] Cf. Brox, *Der erste Petrusbrief,* 236.

[97] Calvin remarks: "For all those who recumb not on God's providence must necessarily be on constant turmoil and violently assail others. We ought the more to dwell on this thought, that God cares for us, in order, first, that we may have peace within; and, secondly, that we may be humble and meek towards men" (*Catholic Epistles*, 149).

[98] Cranfield, *I & II Peter and Jude*, 134; Maier, "1. Petrusbrief," 102.

Vigilance is needed because the devil is on the prowl. A number of manuscripts add the word "because" *(hoti)* to explain the relationship between the imperatives and the latter part of the verse. Even though the word "because" is secondary, it reveals an early and accurate interpretation of the verse. Believers must remain vigilant and alert until the very end because the devil seeks to destroy their faith. The devil inflicts persecution on believers so that they will deny Christ and lose their eschatological reward. Peter identified the devil as an "enemy" *(antidikos)*. The term is not used elsewhere for the devil, but the same idea is found in the word "Satan," which means "adversary." The word "devil" means "slanderer" or "accuser," and we are reminded of his accusations against Job (Job 1:9–11; 2:4–5) and Joshua, the high priest, in the Old Testament (Zech 3:1–2; cf. also Rev 12:10).

Peter portrayed the devil here as a roaring lion seeking to devour its prey.[99] The devil roars like a lion to induce fear in the people of God. In other words, persecution is the roar by which he tries to intimidate believers in the hope that they will capitulate at the prospect of suffering. If believers deny their faith, then the devil has devoured them, bringing them back into his fold.[100] The contrast between God and the devil is quite striking. God tenderly cares for his children (5:6–7), inviting them to bring their worries to him so that he can sustain them. God promises to protect his flock (v. 2) in all their distress. Conversely, the devil's aim is not to comfort but to terrify believers. He does not want to deliver them from fear but to devour their faith. Peter warned believers to be vigilant. The roaring of the devil is the crazed anger of a defeated enemy, and if they do not fear his ferocious bark, they will never be consumed by his bite.

5:9 Verse 9 continues the exhortation to stand against the devil. In v. 8 Peter called for vigilance and alertness, so that believers will not droop with sleep and be captured unawares by their enemy. In this verse he summoned them to resist actively the devil. The word for "resist" *(antistēte)* is used of Elymas's resistance to the gospel (Acts 13:10), of Paul's opposition to Peter in Antioch (Gal 2:11), of Jannes' and Jambres' stance against Moses (2 Tim 3:8), and of Alexander the coppersmith's response to Paul (2 Tim 4:5). Resistance, then, is not passive but represents active engagement against a foe. Believers will not triumph over the devil if they remain passive.

The NIV renders the next line "standing firm in the faith." In Greek there is no verb, and the word "steadfast" is an adjective; hence it could be under-

---

[99] The textual tradition is quite complicated here, with some manuscripts deleting τινα and some substituting καταπίῃ for καταπιεῖν. See *TCGNT*, 626–27, for the whole discussion. The reading in the NA27 is likely original.

[100] For the notion that the devil is trying to induce God's people into apostasy, see Goppelt, *I Peter*, 361; Kelly, *Peter and Jude*, 210.

stood as if it were in apposition to the first clause, "You who are steadfast in faith, should resist the devil." It is much more likely, however, that the NIV is correct and that an imperative idea is implied in the text.[101] Peter was not simply saying that believers are firm in their faith. He explained what resistance to the devil truly means. The call to resistance does not summon believers to do Herculean acts on God's behalf. Believers are not encouraged to gather all their resources to do great works for God. No, resisting the devil means that believers remain firm in their faith, that is, in their trust in God.[102] Believers triumph over the devil as they continue to trust God, believing that he truly cares for them and will sustain them until the end. Perseverance until the last day is accomplished from first to last by faith.

In the last clause of the verse motivation for standing firm in the faith and resisting the devil is given. The NIV introduces this clause with the words "because you know that." The Greek word used here is merely the word "knowing" *(eidotes),* and some commentators maintain that it should be translated "knowing how" rather than "knowing that."[103] It seems more likely, however, that Peter was explaining *that* believers suffer worldwide instead of communicating *how* they suffer.[104]

What encouragement did Peter provide to the readers here? He remarked that believers elsewhere experience suffering in the same way as his readers.[105] Believers in Asia Minor should not fear that they are singled out specially for torment. They are simply experiencing the same opposition Christians face throughout the world.[106] The "world" *(kosmos)* here does not refer to the world in enmity against God, as John regularly used the term.[107] Such an idea may be implied, but Peter's point was that such sufferings are inflicted on believers throughout the Greco-Roman world.[108] Not everyone in the world faces such opposition; it is directed against those who believe in Jesus Christ. It is noted that the sufferings are experienced "by your brotherhood" (NKJV, *adelphotēti*).

---

[101] So Michaels, *1 Peter,* 300.

[102] So also Goppelt, *I Peter,* 362; Kelly, *Peter and Jude,* 210; Davids, *First Peter,* 191–92.

[103] E.g., Bigg, *Epistles of Peter and Jude,* 194; Beare, *First Peter,* 180; Best, *1 Peter,* 175.

[104] For this interpretation see Kelly, *Peter and Jude,* 211; J. W. C. Wand, *The General Epistles of St. Peter and St. Jude,* WC (London: Methuen, 1934), 125; Achtemeier, *1 Peter,* 342; Michaels, *1 Peter,* 300–301; Elliott, *1 Peter,* 861–62.

[105] Achtemeier provides a survey of interpretation for the phrase τὰ αὐτὰ παθημάτων, but in the end various interpretations proposed are not remarkably different (*1 Peter,* 342–43).

[106] I understand the infinitive ἐπιτελεῖσθαι to be passive rather than middle (see Wand, *Epistles of Peter and Jude,* 125; Goppelt, *1 Peter,* 363, n. 22; Achtemeier, *1 Peter,* 343; Elliott, *1 Peter,* 862). Some manuscripts have the indicative here ἐπιτελεῖσθε (א, A, B, K, 0206, 33, 614, 630, 1505, 2495, *al*). Even though the external evidence is quite strong for the variant, in context an infinitive seems more likely.

[107] Against Calvin, *Catholic Epistles,* 151; Beare, *First Peter,* 180.

[108] Goppelt, *I Peter,* 363; Kelly, *Peter and Jude,* 212; Michaels, *1 Peter,* 301; Achtemeier, *1 Peter,* 343; Elliott, *1 Peter,* 863.

In other words, everyone in the Christian family faces the same rejection and discrimination. It is a mark, indeed, of being part of the same family. As Goppelt says, their sufferings "are not the personal misfortune of individuals, but belong to the essence of faith and are signs of its power against evil. Even more, they are signs that faith is sustained through grace."[109]

Here we have further evidence that the persecution in 1 Peter was not an officially enforced policy from Rome. No evidence exists that Nero (or Domitian for that matter) systematically and officially persecuted Christians. What Peter had in mind instead was the pattern of discrimination and abuse experienced by Christians in the Greco-Roman world.[110] Believers stood out as social outcasts because they would not participate in any activities devoted to foreign deities and refused to live as they did formerly (1 Pet 4:3–4). Their life as spiritual exiles explains why believers were mistreated on an informal and regular basis throughout the empire.

5:10 Verses 10–11 together constitute the conclusion to the body of the letter and contain the message of the letter as a whole.[111] The conjunction *de* loosely connects vv. 10–11 to vv. 6–8. It is likely that Peter now focused on God's strength as the means by which believers obtain their eternal reward. The one who called believers by his grace will also enable them to persevere until the end. He begins by designating God as "the God of all grace." "Grace" is a favorite word of Peter's (1:2,13; 2:19,20; 3:7; 4:10; 5:5,12), and here it means that God is both the possessor and giver of all grace. The sufferings of believers are intense, but God's grace is stronger still. This grace is expressed particularly in God's calling of believers to eternal glory.[112] The word "calling" *(kalesas)* has occurred previously in Peter (1:15; 2:9,21; 3:9) with the same meaning it has here. We have another indication that as the letter concludes, crucial terms used previously are reprised to remind readers of the letter's central themes. Here it should simply be said (see esp. 2:9) that "calling" refers to God's effective work by which he inducts believers into a saving relationship with himself. That the calling is to salvation is clear since believers are called to God's "eternal glory." The eschatological character of the glory is apparent from earlier Petrine usage (1:7,11,21; 4:13; 5:1,4). The words "in Christ" could be understood as modifying the entire clause, "eternal glory" or "called."[113]

---

[109] Goppelt, *I Peter,* 364.

[110] Rightly Goppelt, id., 363, n. 25.

[111] Goppelt says the verse "summarizes the intention of the entire letter" (id., 364).

[112] The Majority text replaces ὑμᾶς with ἡμᾶς. The external evidence clearly favors the former, and the substitution would naturally occur because the two words sounded similar.

[113] A number of manuscripts support ἐν Χριστῷ 'Ιησοῦ (𝔓[72], A, P, Ψ, 33, 1739, Majority text, etc). Still, 'Ιησοῦ is missing in B, ℵ, 614, 630, 1505, pc). The NIV probably is correct in preferring the shorter text.

Each interpretation is possible, but on balance the latter is preferable.[114] Peter thereby emphasized that God's saving calling is effectual in and through Christ. The theme of calling to glory reminds the readers that end-time salvation is sure, for God himself is the one who initiated and secured their salvation. As the rest of the verse will demonstrate, God will certainly complete what he has inaugurated. Their calling to glory is not questionable but sure.

Before glory arrives, however, believers must suffer. Still, the suffering is for a short while *(oligon).* The echo to 1:6 is quite noticeable since there believers are said "for a little while *[oligon]* . . . to suffer grief in all kinds of trials."[115] Saying that the suffering will last a short time does not mean that it will only last for a brief interval during the earthly sojourn of believers.[116] The short time period refers to the entire interval before eternal glory commences. The sufferings of this life will seem as if they lasted a little while when compared to the eternal glory that endures forever (cf. 2 Cor 4:16–18).

Four different verbs are used to describe God's promise for believers.[117] There is no need to distinguish carefully between the meanings of the verbs, for together they emphatically make the same point.[118] The God who has called believers to eternal glory will strengthen and fortify them, so that they are able to endure until the end.[119] He will fulfill his promise to save and deliver them. We understand from this that the exhortations to vigilance and resistance are not intended to raise questions about whether believers will receive the eschatological promise. Peter instead conceived of his exhortations as means by which believers will persevere and receive the promise of salvation on the last day. The God who has given such promises also uses exhortations to provoke his people to be faithful until the last day. The exhortations and promises, therefore, should not be played off against each other, as if the exhortations introduce an element of uncertainty to the promises. The exhortations are the very means by which God's promises are secured, and indeed God in his grace grants believers the strength to

---

[114] Those who defend the interpretation adopted here are Kelly, *Peter and Jude,* 212; Michaels, *1 Peter,* 302; Achtemeier, *1 Peter,* 345; Goppelt, *1 Peter,* 365, n. 29. Davids argues that both are intended and that Peter did not intend such precision (*First Peter,* 195).

[115] For the connection to 1:6, see Schutter, *Hermeneutic and Composition in I Peter,* 29.

[116] Contra Richard, *Reading 1 Peter, Jude, and 2 Peter,* 222.

[117] The verb σθενώσει probably was accidentally deleted by 𝔓[72] and 𝔓[81], for the similar ending could have led to the deletion. The attempt to substitute optatives for futures reflects a misunderstanding of the text by early scribes, in which they turned promises into prayers.

[118] Rightly Calvin, *Catholic Epistles,* 153; Elliott, *1 Peter,* 867.

[119] Dubis emphasizes the eschatological character of these verbs (*1 Peter 4:12–19,* 54) but concedes that they may relate also to the present and culminate in the *eschaton.* He overreads the text, however, in seeing a reference to the rebuilding of God's eschatological temple (pp. 55–56).

carry out the exhortations. Still, such grace can never be used to cancel out the need for responding to the exhortations.

5:11 After emphasizing the power of God's sustaining grace, even in the midst of suffering, it is not surprising that Peter concluded with a doxology. Some manuscripts add the word "glory" *(doxa)* here, but this is almost surely due the word's presence in other doxologies, and it should be rejected as secondary.[120] Rather, Peter emphasized here the sovereignty and power of God, and hence he used the term *kratos*. The God who permits suffering in the lives of his children, and even allows the devil to rage at them (cf. Job 1–2), is the sovereign God and the God who cares (5:7). The dominion belongs to him—forever. He wields a "mighty hand" (5:6) on behalf of his people. Hence, believers should be full of comfort, knowing that they are on the side of victory and celebration. The NIV is possibly correct in understanding the verb to be an implied optative or imperative, so that we have a prayer, "To him be the power"; but the parallel in 4:11 suggests that the indicative verb "is" *(estin)* is more likely. We should then translate "dominion belongs to him."[121] The doxology, as is typical, concludes with "amen," signifying that Peter longed for the day when God's rule will be evident to all, that he anticipated the day when suffering is past and glory and peace and joy reign forevermore.

---

[120] So *TCGNT* 627.

[121] So Achtemeier, *1 Peter,* 346; cf. also Selwyn, *1 Peter,* 241; Michaels, *1 Peter,* 304; Elliott, *1 Peter,* 867.

SECTION OUTLINE

V. CONCLUDING WORDS (5:12–14)

V. CONCLUDING WORDS (5:12–14)

[12]With the help of Silas, whom I regard as a faithful brother, I have written to you briefly, encouraging you and testifying that this is the true grace of God. Stand fast in it.

[13]She who is in Babylon, chosen together with you, sends you her greetings, and so does my son Mark. [14]Greet one another with a kiss of love.

Peace to all of you who are in Christ.

Verse 12 summarizes the letter as a whole. Peter wrote the letter to exhort believers and to testify to God's grace. The grace of God consists of what God has done for believers in Christ. In 1 Peter the gracious work of God in Christ is communicated in 1:1–12 and 2:4–10. God's foundational saving work is also explicated in the reference to the work of Christ in 1:18–19; 2:21–25 and 3:18–22, showing that the imperatives and exhortations in the letter are based on the indicative of God's work in Christ. The summons to stand in the grace God has given summarizes the message of the entire letter. Suffering is at hand, but believers must stand in the grace God has given and resist apostasy. The letter concludes with a commendation of Silvanus, greetings from Peter's church in Rome, greetings from Mark, and the call to greet one another with a kiss of love. The final words are a benediction of peace for all believers.

5:12 The closing begins with a reference to Silvanus. The NIV introduces two changes in the text. First, it translates "Silvanus" as "Silas." Silas is mentioned often in Acts as Paul's partner in ministry (Acts 15:22,27, 32,40; 16:19,25,29; 17:4,10,14–15; 18:5). He most likely was the same person as the Silvanus mentioned in 2 Cor 1:19; 1 Thess 1:1; 2 Thess 1:1 and here. Hence, the NIV translation is defensible here. The problem with the theory of pseudepigraphy arises here, for those who adopt such a theory argue that Peter was not the real author, and so they also raise the question of whether Silvanus is a real person or simply a fictive device. Hence, Achtemeier concludes with the awkward solution that a real person is intended, but Silvanus was too old to carry out the task of taking the letters to Asia

Minor.[1] If the realism of the text is accepted, it is more economical to argue that Silvanus really and truly carried the letter to the various churches.[2]

Second, the NIV translation suggests that Silvanus helped author the letter. "With the help of Silas . . . I have written to you briefly." A number of scholars have supported such a view, understanding Silvanus to be the amanuensis or secretary of 1 Peter.[3] As we noted in the introduction, ascribing the letter to Silvanus possibly could solve the problem of the excellent Greek found in the letter. Nevertheless, contrary to the NIV, the wording used here cannot and should not be used to defend the theory that Silvanus functioned as the amanuensis in 1 Peter. The NRSV is therefore more cautious and accurate in translating the phrase, "Through Silvanus . . . I have written this short letter." The phrase to "write through someone" *(graphein dia tinos)* during the time the New Testament was written does not identify the amanuensis but the carrier of the letter. Hence, Peter did not specify the amanuensis but informed the readers that Silvanus was the one designated to carry the letter to them. For example, the letter containing the decision of the apostolic meeting in Jerusalem was sent "through" Silas and Barsabbas (*grapsantes dia cheiros autōn,* Acts 15:23). In some manuscripts Romans contains a subscription that says the letter was written "through Phoebe" *(dia Phoibēs)*. This certainly does not mean that she served as the secretary since Rom 16:22 clearly demonstrates that Tertius filled that role. What we have here is a formula designating the bearer of the letter (cf. Ignatius, *Rom.* 10:1; *Phld.* 11:2; *Smyrn.* 12:1; *Pol.* 8:1; Polycarp, *Phil.* 14:1).[4] Such an observation does not rule out conclusively Silvanus as a secretary since it is possible that Silvanus functioned as Peter's secretary and Peter failed to

---

[1] P. J. Achtemeier, *1 Peter: A Commentary on First Peter,* Her (Minneapolis: Fortress, 1996), 351.

[2] It is unpersuasive to argue that Peter is fictional but Silvanus is the real carrier (contra J. H. Elliott, *1 Peter: A New Translation with Introduction and Commentary,* AB [New York: Doubleday, 2000], 873–74). N. Brox maintains that Silvanus is also fictional (*Der erste Petrusbrief,* EKKNT, 2d ed. [Zürich: Benziger/Neukirchen-Vluyn: Neukirchener Verlag, 1986], 241–42).

[3] E.g., L. Goppelt, *A Commentary on I Peter* (Grand Rapids: Eerdmans, 1993), 369–71; E. G. Selwyn, *The First Epistle of St. Peter,* 2d ed. (Grand Rapids: Baker, 1981), 11, 241; J. N. D. Kelly, *A Commentary on the Epistles of Peter and Jude,* Thornapple Commentaries (Grand Rapids: Baker, 1981), 215. Selwyn believes he was both the secretary and bearer of the letter. P. H. Davids argues that Silvanus is the primary author behind the letter and its contents derive from him (*The First Epistle of Peter,* NICNT [Grand Rapids: Eerdmans, 1990], 198).

[4] See especially the thorough discussion in E. R. Richards, "Silvanus Was Not Peter's Secretary: Theological Bias in Interpreting διά Σιλουανοῦ . . . ἔγραψα," *JETS* 43 (2000): 417–32. Richards also includes some important examples from secular papyri. Cf. also J. R. Michaels, *1 Peter,* WBC (Waco: Word, 1998), 306–7; Achtemeier, *1 Peter,* 349–50; Elliott, *1 Peter,* 124, 872; Brox, *Der erste Petrusbrief,* 242–43; J. A. T. Robinson, *Redating the New Testament* (Philadelphia: Westminster, 1976), 168–69.

mention that fact. It does show, however, that the formula used here does not constitute evidence that he served as Peter's amanuensis.

Peter also remarked that he "regard[s]" Silvanus as a "faithful brother." We have here the typical commendation of the person who bears the letter (Rom 16:1–2; Eph 6:21–22; Col 4:7–8). Those who carried letters would also convey news from the letter writer and presumably could function as the first interpreter of the letter if the recipients had questions about its meaning. The words "I regard" *(logizomai)* represent Peter's apostolic judgment on the matter of Silvanus's credibility, indicating that Silvanus delivered the letter with Peter's imprimatur (cf. Rom 3:28; 8:18; 2 Cor 11:5).[5]

Peter followed convention in describing his letter as brief (e.g., Heb 13:22). He then identified the purpose of the letter, saying that he had written to encourage and bear witness to the true grace of God. The word "this" *(tautēn)* in the phrase "this is the true grace of God" refers to the letter as a whole and should not be traced back to a specific antecedent.[6] The grace of God has been manifested in Jesus the Christ, who suffered on the cross and then was exalted to glory. Similarly, Peter called on his readers to suffer faithfully as Christians as a prelude to entering into glory. In the interval before the consummation of all things, believers are exhorted to "stand fast" in such grace.[7] Failure to stand constitutes apostasy, and those who apostatize will face destruction on the last day. Peter could summarize his message, therefore, as a call to stand in grace. The delicate balance between the indicative and imperative is preserved here. Grace has grasped every believer in Jesus Christ, and believers have been begotten by God's grace (1:3). Still, they must stand in the grace that has secured them. Grace does

---

[5] E.g., Michaels, *1 Peter*, 307.

[6] So C. Bigg, *The Epistles of St. Peter and St. Jude,* ICC (Edinburgh: T & T Clark, 1901), 196; J. W. C. Wand, *The General Epistles of St. Peter and St. Jude,* WC (London: Methuen, 1934), 128–29; Michaels, *1 Peter*, 308–10; Achtemeier, *1 Peter*, 352; cf. the comments of Brox, *Der erste Petrusbrief,* 245–46. Elliot thinks the antecedent is the word "grace" in v. 10 (*1 Peter*, 878). E. R. Wendland argues that the aim of the entire letter is summed up here ("'Stand Fast in the True Grace of God!' A Study of 1 Peter," *JOTT* 13 (2000): 25–26. See also D. G. Horrell, "The Product of a Petrine Circle? A Reassessment of the Origin and Character of 1 Peter," *JSNT* 86 (2002): 29–60.

[7] The word εἰς usually means "into," but the distinction between εἰς and ἐν was diluted during the era of the NT (A. T. Robertson, *A Grammar of the Greek New Testament in the Light of Historical Research* (Nashville: Broadman, 1934), 591–93; BDF §205. In this instance εἰς should be translated as "in" (so Kelly, *Peter and Jude,* 217; Achtemeier, *1 Peter,* 352–53). Michaels retains the sense of the preposition, translating the clause, "For it you must stand" (*1 Peter,* 305, 310). Contra E. J. Richard the verb in context should be read as an imperative, not a subjunctive (*Reading 1 Peter, Jude, and 2 Peter: A Literary and Theological Commentary*, RNTS [Macon: Smith & Helwys, 2000], 228; rightly Elliott, *1 Peter,* 879). We should also note that some manuscripts supply an indicative (ἑστήκατε) instead of the imperative. But the weight of the evidence supports the imperative. Goppelt mistakenly interprets the text to contain an indicative and an imperative (*1 Peter,* 373), but we must allow the imperative of the text to stand with its bracing quality.

not cancel out the imperative but establishes it.[8]

5:13 The letter now closes with greetings and a benediction, which is characteristic of letter closings. The greeting in v. 13 comes from the one who is chosen in Babylon *(hē syneklektē)* and from Mark. Hence, the notion of election functions as an inclusio framing the letter (cf. 1:1).[9] It is unlikely that the fellow elect should be identified as an individual woman.[10] It is quite unlikely that readers in Asia Minor would know the identity of this unnamed woman. Some have even seen a reference to Peter's wife. But this is quite improbable.[11] Early manuscripts add the word "church," and even though the addition is secondary, we see an early and accurate interpretation of the identity of the chosen woman.[12] The fellow elect one represents the church in Babylon, which sends her greeting to those who are elect pilgrims from Asia Minor. Such an interpretation is confirmed by 2 John, where the church is described as "the chosen lady and her children" (v. 1), and John closes by saying, "The children of your chosen sister send their greetings" (v. 13). A reference to the church is also suggested by the teaching that the church is Christ's bride (cf. Eph 5:22–33; Rev 19:7–9).

The interpretation proposed above is strengthened when we recognize that Peter wrote symbolically about the church in Babylon. There would be no need for Peter to specify his wife was in Babylon.[13] The historical Babylon of the Old Testament was a city in ruins, and so Peter could not have been referring to that city.[14] Moreover, no evidence exists that Peter ministered in such a locale. Some scholars have noted a place called Babylon on the Nile Delta (cf. Josephus, *Ant.* 2.315), but it is doubtful that this military

---

[8] Brox mistakenly defines "grace" here to be equivalent to the usage in 2:19–20, but as explained in this commentary the term "grace" has a different meaning in 2:19–20 (*Der erste Petrusbrief,* 244–45).

[9] So W. L. Schutter, *Hermeneutic and Composition in I Peter,* WUNT 2/30 (Tübingen: Mohr, 1989), 28.

[10] Contra J. K. Applegate, "The Co-elect Woman of 1 Peter," *NTS* 38 (1992): 587–604. Applegate argues that this woman was a leader known to the churches in Asia Minor. She is mentioned because women leaders in Asia Minor would have resisted the household code, where they are enjoined to submit to unbelieving husbands. By mentioning this woman, the author provides support for the household code, which would have been questionable to women leaders in the churches addressed. Applegate's theory should be rejected as speculative. We have no evidence that women functioned as leaders in the Petrine churches, nor is there any clear evidence that the household code was questioned. For rejection of Applegate's view see also Elliott, *1 Peter,* 881.

[11] Rightly Brox, *Der erste Petrusbrief,* 247.

[12] So Michaels, *1 Peter,* 310. Similarly, some manuscripts betray the same interpretive tendency in replacing "Babylon" with "Rome." The interpretation is correct, but the manuscript evidence for "Rome" is inferior. The word "church" should be preferred over "brotherhood" (contra Elliott, *1 Peter*, 882).

[13] So E. Best, *1 Peter*, NCB (Grand Rapids: Eerdmans, 1971), 178.

[14] For the evidence see Achtemeier, *1 Peter,* 353, n. 73.

outpost is in view. Peter drew on Old Testament tradition, where Babylon represents those opposed to God (cf. Isaiah 13–14; 46–47; Jeremiah 50–51). In this instance, as in Revelation (17–18), Babylon designates Rome itself, the enemy of God.[15] The mention of Babylon constitutes another reminder that believers are exiles in their present situation, and the allusion to exile under the dominion of Babylon constitutes a bookend between the beginning and end of the letter.[16]

The greeting from Mark comes from John Mark, who accompanied Paul on his first missionary journey.[17] He subsequently left Paul and Barnabas, and Barnabas recruited him for further missionary work after Paul rejected him (cf. Acts 12:25; 13:4,13; 15:35–39). Paul later spoke highly of Mark (Col 4:10; 2 Tim 4:11; Phlm 24). Peter, of course, would have known Mark from the earliest experience of the early church, where meetings were held in the home of Mark's mother (Acts 12:12). The early tradition that Mark wrote under Peter's influence is also historically credible (see Eusebius, *Hist. eccl.* 2.15.1–2; 3.39.15; 6.25.5). Calling Mark his "son" is not literal but designates the fatherly love Peter had for the younger Mark.[18] We have already seen that the closing is full of symbolic language, and the phrase should be read as symbolical here as well.

5:14 The injunction to "greet one another with a kiss of love" is similar to the Pauline letters, where the holy kiss is enjoined (Rom 16:16; 1 Cor 16:20; 2 Cor 13:12; 1 Thess 5:26).[19] Peter's language differs since he spoke of "a kiss of love" instead of a "holy kiss." The love between members should be comparable to the love that exists in a healthy family, though the greetings with a kiss were, of course, to be pure and unstained by any kind of sexual lust. The kiss of love probably was practiced during worship, since it would naturally occur when believers met together as a community. The letter concludes with a peace wish. Paul, in contrast, closed his letters with grace benedictions (e.g., Rom 16:20; 1 Cor 16:23; 2 Cor 13:14; Gal

---

[15] So most scholars. So already M. Luther, *Commentary on Peter & Jude* (Grand Rapids: Kregel, 1990), 226. Cf. the discussion in Kelly, *Peter and Jude*, 218–20; Elliott, *1 Peter*, 882–87. Brox thinks the reference to Rome may be part of the fictional device in the letter (*Der erste Petrusbrief*, 247), but as I. H. Marshall observes the reference to Rome as "Babylon" may have come from the time of Nero (*1 Peter*, NTC [Downers Grove: InterVarsity, 1991], 175).

[16] Rightly Michaels, *1 Peter*, 311; Achtemeier, *1 Peter*, 354; D. G. McCartney, "The Use of the Old Testament in the First Epistle of Peter" (Ph.D. diss., Westminster Theological Seminary, 1989), 114.

[17] Once again Brox suggests the reference to Mark may be part of the pseudepigraphical nature of the letter (*Der erste Petrusbrief*, 247).

[18] Cf. Michaels, *1 Peter*, 312; Elliott, *1 Peter*, 887–89.

[19] Some manuscripts read "holy kiss," but surely this is a case of Pauline influence and is hence secondary.

6:18, etc.). The reference to peace recalls 1:2 and in that sense functions as yet another inclusio. The phrase "in Christ" simply means "Christian" here, with the result that Peter prayed that peace would be the portion for all those who are believers.[20] Closing the letter with a peace wish is significant. Believers in the Petrine churches were buffeted by trials and persecutions. The stress of life was significant. What believers need in such a situation is God's peace and strength, a peace that will enable them to stand (5:12) amidst the pressures of the present evil age. Such peace will fortify believers so they can endure opposition and persevere to the end, so that they will receive an eschatological reward.

---

[20] A number of manuscripts add "Jesus" and "amen," but the words are missing in other manuscripts, and scribes would be prone to make an ending more liturgical; therefore the additions should be rejected.

2 Peter

INTRODUCTION OUTLINE

1. Authorship
   (1) Arguments against Authenticity
   (2) Arguments Defending Authenticity
   (3) Pseudepigraphal Letters
   (4) Testament Genre
2. Date and Destination
3. Opponents
4. Structure

INTRODUCTION

Second Peter is often ignored because of its brevity and because scholars question its authenticity.[1] For example, the value of the book is questioned severely by Käsemann in a famous essay.[2] Käsemann identifies the letter as "early Catholic" and criticizes it for departing from the center of the gospel—justification by faith. He dates it in the second century and argues that the writer works from a canon of Scripture, perhaps even from a completed canon of Scripture. The church has become an institution that dispenses salvation, and doctrine is a fixed entity that is passed on by the apostles. The church is now the interpreter of tradition, and the Spirit is confined to churchly authority. The Spirit is subordinated to the letter, so that doctrinal rigidity limits the freedom of the Spirit. The Christology of the letter is superficial, fixed only on Christ's return but lacking any full-orbed view of Christ. The view of salvation is Hellenistic, so that it is conceived in 1:4 as an escape from the material world and sensual desires. Indeed, salvation is understood in ontological terms as participation in the divine nature, and this explains why Peter included the account of the transfiguration. The

[1] For a survey of recent scholarship on 2 Peter, see P. Müller, "Der 2. Petrusbrief," *TRu* 66 (2001): 310–37.

[2] E. Käsemann, "An Apologia for Primitive Christian Eschatology," in *Essays on New Testament Themes* (Philadelphia: Fortress, 1964), 169–95. For a summary of some common criticisms of 2 Peter, see Müller, "Der 2. Petrusbrief," 310.

focus has become anthropological—the piety of the individual person. A mechanical view of reward and punishment is substituted for the new obedience of the gospel. We have a new law, and life is grasped as a matter of religion.[3] Käsemann concludes his essay as follows: "What have we to say about a Church, which is so concerned to defend herself against heretics, that she no longer distinguishes between Spirit and letter; that she identifies the Gospel with her own tradition, and further, with a particular religious world-view; that she regulates exegesis according to her system of teaching authority and makes faith into a mere assent to the dogmas of orthodoxy?"[4]

G. Klein's assessment is no more positive: "The author does a miserable job of presenting his case. . . . In spite of how vigorously he asserts himself he is basically helpless."[5] He proceeds to say that it is unfortunate the letter was even included in the canon. Dunn remarks that some of the writings of Luther and Wesley are equal to, or even better than, what we find in 2 Peter.[6]

I will argue in this commentary that such assessments misread 2 Peter dramatically or that they contain an extreme bias against tradition and orthodoxy. In our postmodern world we realize that all of us have presuppositions, that none of us has a God's eye view of reality. The negative views of some relative to 2 Peter tell us more about these scholars than they tell us about 2 Peter. For instance, the commencement of the letter communicates powerfully the grace of God in Christ, a grace that is the foundation for and the securing of a new life in Christ. One would think from the scholarly comments made above that the message of grace is completely lacking in 2 Peter. When we actually read the letter, however, we see that it is the first theme introduced.[7]

We must also recognize that 2 Peter does not include the whole of Petrine theology. The letter is, after all, comprised of only three short chapters. Still, one wonders if an extreme form of Lutheranism fails to see that life in the Spirit leads to a changed life, a life that is morally beautiful. Peter never even considered the notion that the salvation bestowed in Christ

---

[3] R. Martin, though not as negative as Käsemann, complains about the letter's "rigidity and somewhat mechanical reaction to innovation and theological enterprise." He also worries that "2 Peter represents a Christianity that is on the road to becoming tradition-bound, authoritarian, and inward-looking" ("2 Peter," in *The Theology of the Letters of James, Peter, and Jude* [Cambridge: University Press, 1994], 163).

[4] Käsemann, "Apologia for Primitive Christian Eschatology," 195.

[5] The translation of Klein is by J. D. Charles, *Virtue amidst Vice: The Catalog of Virtues in 2 Peter 1,* JSNTSup 150 (Sheffield: Academic Press, 1997), 19–20. The citations from Klein derive from G. Klein, "Der Zweite Petrusbrief und der neutestamenliche Kanon," in *Ärgernisse: Konfrontationen mit dem Neuen Testament* (Munich: Chr. Kaiser, 1970), 111–12.

[6] J. D. G. Dunn, *Unity and Diversity in the New Testament: An Inquiry into the Character of Earliest Christianity,* 2d ed. (Philadelphia: Westminster, 1990), 386.

[7] R. W. Wall maintains that 2 Peter is complementary to 1 Peter when viewed from a canonical perspective ("The Canonical Function of 2 Peter," *Biblical Interpretation* 9 [2001]: 64–81).

could be untethered from moral transformation. He wrote to a situation in which antinomian opponents threatened the church, and hence he naturally stressed the life-changing work of Jesus Christ.

The eschatological enthusiasm of the early church still pulsates in 2 Peter. Peter continued to expect the return of Jesus Christ, but he did not anticipate settling down in the world for thousands of years. He merely acknowledged that the day of Christ's coming was not revealed and that the apparent delay should not trouble believers. Nor is there any basis for the view that Peter had a deficient Christology. It will be argued in the commentary that in the very first verse Peter identified Jesus Christ as God.

The charge that 2 Peter collapses into traditionalism also veers off course. Again, such a claim appears to come from Protestants who worry that any vestige of tradition or "early catholicism" diverges from the gospel. The Spirit and tradition are not necessarily at loggerheads. The Spirit may even inspire that which becomes tradition. In any case, Peter did not maintain that the church is the inspired interpreter of the tradition. Rather, he emphasized that God's revelation in Christ, particularly at the transfiguration, demonstrated that the apostles rightly interpreted the Old Testament Scriptures about the day of the Lord to refer to the judgment and salvation that will commence at Christ's coming.[8] Finally, we actually see Peter's creativity in the letter, for he recast his message in Hellenistic idiom to speak to his contemporaries. The letter does not represent a hardened traditionalism but the proclamation of the gospel to a new situation.

1. Authorship

The burning question in 2 Peter is whether it is authentic, that is, was the letter truly written by Peter, the apostle of Jesus Christ? Most scholars are now convinced that the letter was not written by Peter. They identify it as a pseudonymous writing, composed in Peter's name to convey his authority to the next generation (or generations). In his outstanding commentary Bauckham readjusts this view by arguing that 2 Peter belongs to the testament genre.[9] It was a "transparent fiction" written in Peter's name, repre-

---

[8] See the discussion of 2 Pet 1:19–21 below.

[9] R. Bauckham, *Jude, 2 Peter* (Waco: Word, 1983). Many argue 2 Peter is a testament. W. G. Kümmel, *Introduction to the New Testament,* rev. ed. (Nashville: Abingdon, 1975), 433; B. Reicke, *The Epistles of James, Peter, and Jude,* AB (Garden City: Doubleday, 1964), 146; T. V. Smith, *Petrine Controversies in Early Christianity: Attitudes toward Peter in Christian Writings of the First Two Centuries,* WUNT 2/15 (Tübingen: Mohr, 1985), 67; T. Fornberg, *An Early Church in a Pluralistic Society: A Study of 2 Peter,* ConBNT 9 (Lund: Gleerup, 1977), 10–12; Müller, "Der 2. Petrusbrief," 329–30; E. Fuchs and P. Reymond, *La Deuxième Épître de Saint Pierre, L'Épître de Saint Jude,* CNT (Neuchâtel–Paris: Delachaux & Niestlé, 1980), 25–26. T. S. Caulley, "The Idea of 'Inspiration' in 2 Peter 1:16–21" (Ph.D. diss., Eberhard-Karls Universität zu Tübingen, 1982), 83–105.

senting a farewell discourse from Peter for the next generation. Bauckham's view differs from those who think the author intentionally deceived his readers by writing pseudonymously. According to Bauckham, it was evident to all that the letter was not genuinely from Peter.[10] We will begin by considering arguments against the authenticity of the letter.

(1) Arguments against Authenticity

Various arguments have been used to contest Petrine authorship, some of which are stronger than others. I will include a representative sampling of the arguments, so that readers will understand clearly the nature of the debate.[11]

First, many scholars believe that 2 Peter is dependent upon Jude as a source. In many instances Jude is reckoned to be postapostolic. It follows, then, that 2 Peter could not have been written by Peter, for if Jude was written after the time of the apostles and 2 Peter used Jude, then Peter was deceased when 2 Peter was written. Others present a different argument. Even if Jude was written in apostolic times, they reject the idea that Peter would have used a nonapostolic writer like Jude as a source.

Second, the Hellenistic concepts and language used in the letter testify against Petrine authorship. The idea that a Galilean fisherman would use so many words and concepts from Greek culture seems quite improbable, especially when 2 Peter is compared to 1 Peter, for the latter does not betray

---

[10] D. Farkasfalvy suggests that the writer chose Peter's name because writing in Paul's name would not solve the problems facing his readers. The author desired to provide a "normative context" for interpreting both Pauline and other apostolic teachings ("The Ecclesial Setting of Pseudepigraphy in Second Peter and Its Role in the Formation of the Canon," *SecCent* 5 [1985–86]: 12–13, 26–27). This solution is only persuasive if one had already adopted pseudonymity for the letter. Indeed, one can imagine an objection to the author's attempt to write authoritatively in Peter's name, in which it is said that the author has no right to claim the mantle of Peter's authority since he is not Peter. W. R. Farmer suggests that the term "pseudepigraphic" should be avoided, even though another wrote the book in Peter's name, for the term suggests an unethical practice ("Some Critical Reflections on Second Peter: A Response to a Paper on Second Peter by Denis Farkasfalvy," *SecCent* 5 [1985–86]: 40–45).

[11] For standard arguments against Petrine authorship, see J. N. D. Kelly, *A Commentary on the Epistles of Peter and Jude,* Thornapple Commentaries (Grand Rapids: Baker, 1981), 235–37; Kümmel, *Introduction to the New Testament*, 430–34; Reicke, *James, Peter, and Jude,* 143–44; C. E. B. Cranfield, *I and II Peter and Jude: Introduction and Commentary,* TBC (London: SCM, 1960), 148–49; J. W. C. Wand, *The General Epistles of Peter and Jude,* WC (London: Methuen, 1934), 143–44; K. H. Schelke, *Der Petrusbrief—Der Judasbrief,* HTKNT (Freiburg: Herder, 1980), 179–81; H. Paulsen, *Der Zweite Petrusbrief und der Judasbrief,* KEK (Göttingen; Vandenhoeck & Ruprecht, 1992), 93–95; A. Vögtle, *Der Judasbrief, Der 2 Petrusbrief,* EKKNT (Neukirchen-Vluyn: Neukirchener Verlag, 1994), 122–27; Fuchs and Reymond, *2 Pierre, Jude,* 30–34. J. B. Mayor, *The Epistle of St. Jude and the Second Epistle of St. Peter* (1907; reprint, Grand Rapids: Baker, 1965), cxv–cxxxiv.

the same Hellenistic flavor. Many scholars think 2 Peter is grandiose and bombastic when compared to 1 Peter. Some scholars who are persuaded that 1 Peter is genuine observe the differences between 1 and 2 Peter and confidently declare that 2 Peter is inauthentic. Second Peter has fifty-seven words that occur nowhere else in the New Testament, and thirty-two of these words do not appear in the Septuagint either.[12] Of these thirty-two words fifteen of them are also used in other Jewish sources. Thirteen words occur only in 2 Peter, and the latter has more synonyms and triplets than 1 Peter. Indeed, when we compare 1 and 2 Peter, what stand out are the differences between them. The favorite terms of 2 Peter are not found in 1 Peter and vice versa. Bauckham notes that in 2 Peter we have terms like "knowledge" *(epignōsis,* 1:2–3,8; 2:20), "godliness," (*eusebeia* and *eusebēs,* 1:3,6; 2:9; 3:11), "diligence" (*spoudazein* and *spoudē,* 1:5,10,15: 3:14), "way" (*hodos,* 2:2,15,21), "to establish" (*stērizein, stērigmos,* and *astēriktos,* 1:12; 2:14: 3:16–17), "savior" *(sōter)* for Christ combined with "our Lord" (*kyrios hēmōn,* 1:8,11,14,16; 3:18), and "divine" (*theios,* 1:3–4).[13] None of these terms is found in 1 Peter, except for *stērizein* in 1 Pet 5:10. Moreover, 2 Peter describes Jesus' second coming as a "coming" *(parousia),* while 1 Peter prefers the term "revelation" *(apokalypsis).*

The Greek character of 2 Peter is indicated by the use of the word "goodness" (*aretē,* 1:3,5), which is the typical term for virtue in Greek writings. The phrase "divine nature" (*theias physeōs,* 1:4) would be expected from a Greek philosopher, but we would expect Peter to speak of the Holy Spirit instead of using a philosophical phrase. Some scholars argue that the term "eyewitnesses" (*epoptai,* 1:16) hails from the mystery religions, providing firm proof that Peter could not be the author.

Käsemann argues that the conception of evil is not in accord with the earliest Christian writings.[14] Evil is attributed to material existence, and salvation becomes ours when liberated from the material world (1:4).[15] He also contends that the view of Jesus Christ is inferior in the letter and that the eschatology advanced is not centered on Jesus Christ. Indeed, the delay of the parousia is seen as evidence of early catholicism, as proof that the imminent hope of the second coming was fading.

Third, a late date is postulated on the basis of the opponents. The false teachers are identified as second-century Gnostics who questioned the second coming of Christ, spiritualized the second coming, and led libertine lives.[16]

---

[12] See Bauckham for a thorough discussion on this matter (*Jude, 2 Peter,* 135–36).

[13] So Bauckham, *Jude, 2 Peter,* 144.

[14] Käsemann, "Apologia for Primitive Christian Eschatology," 179–80.

[15] Ibid., 179–80; see also Smith, *Petrine Controversies,* 95.

[16] E.g., Kümmel, *Introduction to the New Testament,* 432. Fuchs and Reymond argue for proto-Gnosticism (*2 Pierre, Jude,* 28–29).

Fourth, the appeal to the Pauline letters as Scripture shows that they have been collected together and are now considered to be canonical (3:15–16). Any such collection or canonization, of course, was impossible in Peter's lifetime. Second Peter reveals that church authorities are now the interpreters of Scripture (1:20–21; cf. also 2:2).[17] Ecclesiastical officials now dispense and interpret acceptable doctrine to congregations.

Fifth, Bauckham thinks there is commonality between *1–2 Clement, Shepherd of Hermas,* and 2 Peter.[18] They all have their roots in Roman Christianity. In terms of date, most of them hail from the last part of the first century A.D. Similarly, Peter should be located in that time frame.

Sixth, 2 Peter lacks external attestation in the second century, and even in the fourth century the letter was unknown by some and its canonicity questioned by others. All of this leads Kümmel to the conclusion that the letter was written between A.D. 125 and 150.[19]

We now turn to Bauckham and his testament thesis.[20] Bauckham does not endorse many of the objections raised against Petrine authorship, but he agrees that the Hellenistic language casts significant doubt on its authenticity. He does not, however, think the evidence necessitates dating it as late as is often proposed. Second Peter, according to Bauckham, is a testament or farewell speech. Hence, it is not addressed to all Christians everywhere but written to a particular community struggling with specific problems. Testaments have two characteristics: they contain (1) ethical exhortations and (2) revelations of what will occur in the future.

Bauckham believes that 2 Peter fits the testament genre for several reasons. The first paragraph of the letter (1:3–11) summarizes Peter's ethical and religious teaching, and the content is characteristic of testaments intended for readers after the death of the writer. The wording of 1:12–15 resonates with farewell themes inasmuch as Peter instructed his readers in light of his imminent departure. The testament theme emerges clearly in 2:1–3 and 3:1–4, where the incursion of false teachers is predicted. In fact, such teachers were already present, showing that Peter is not the author. Their arrival, however, is described as future to preserve the testament genre. Bauckham notes that testaments need not be pseudepigraphal, though virtually all of them are fictional. In one instance we have a testamentary letter, and in that case the testament is also clearly pseudepigraphal (cf. *2 Baruch* 78–86). Jewish readers recognized testaments as fictional, and Bauckham concludes that readers would have recognized 2 Peter similarly. Hence, one of the keys of Bauckham's view emerges. The letter would have been recognized as "transparent fiction." No one would have

[17] Käsemann, "Apologia for Primitive Christian Eschatology," 174–75.

[18] Bauckham, *Jude, 2 Peter,* 149–51.

[19] Kümmel, *Introduction to the New Testament,* 434.

[20] Bauckham, *Jude, 2 Peter,* 131–35.

thought that Peter actually wrote the letter. It was patently obvious that he did not. The shift from the future to the present tense is crucial for Bauckham's hypothesis, for it reveals to the readers that the future predictions have already become a reality. Therefore the use of the future is a literary device. Predictions are put into the mouth of Peter to demonstrate that the apostolic predictions are now being fulfilled.

Some have tried to explain the differences between 1 and 2 Peter on the basis of different secretaries being used. Bauckham rejects this solution, arguing that the differences between the two letters are too fundamental for such a view to be accepted. Second Peter does not merely differ from 1 Peter stylistically. Its theology and terminology reveal that a different person stands behind the two letters.[21] Indeed, Bauckham thinks the differences are so significant that we can rule out a member of the Petrine school or any theory that posits significant dependence on 1 Peter.[22] The author is neither a disciple of Peter nor a second-century pseudepigrapher distantly removed from Peter. Instead, the author was one of Peter's colleagues, who considered his writings and message to be in harmony with Peter's. Since the author knew Paul's letters but did not use them in detail, we have further evidence to confirm a late first century date—before Paul's letters became the common property of the church.

Bauckham concludes that we should consider the letter as a testament written after Peter's death. The letter purports to be written by Peter—though the original readers would have recognized easily enough that Peter was not the genuine author. In the history of the church the letter has often been accepted as authentic, precisely because the literary genre has eluded us. In the early church the same phenomenon occurred. Gentiles failed to recognize the testamentary genre and hence assigned the letter to Peter.[23] The authentic opening, "Simeon Peter" (NRSV, *Symeōn Petros*), demonstrates that the author was acquainted with Peter, and he felt confident writing in Peter's name. This is apparent because he does not cite other Petrine writings. We should not dismiss the work as fraudulent but should understand that the author wanted to mediate apostolic teaching to a new generation.[24]

(2) Arguments Defending Authenticity

If one were inclined to doubt the authenticity of any letter in the New Testament, it would be 2 Peter. Schlatter defended the authenticity of every

---

[21] Bauckham, *Jude, 2 Peter,* 145–47.

[22] Against a Petrine school see also Vögtle, *Judasbrief, 2 Petrusbrief,* 125.

[23] Bauckham, *Jude, 2 Peter,* 162.

[24] Ibid., 161–62.

epistle in the New Testament, except for 2 Peter.[25] Nevertheless, good reasons still exist to support the authenticity of 2 Peter. One is not sacrificing one's intellect in believing that 2 Peter is authentically Petrine. Indeed, Petrine authorship is still the most credible position for the following reasons.[26]

I begin with the most important evidence for the authenticity of 2 Peter—the internal evidence.[27] The book opens with the claim that it was written by Peter himself. Indeed, Peter used a Hebraic form of his name "Simeon Peter" (NRSV, *Symeōn Petros,* 1:1), which is a touch of authenticity, for this form only occurs elsewhere in Acts 15:14.[28] If the letter were pseudepigraphic, we would expect him either to copy the form of address in 1 Peter or to employ one of the common expressions used to denote Peter in the New Testament.[29] The fact that he chose an original form is a mark of

---

[25] A. Schlatter, *The Theology of the Apostles: The Development of New Testament Theology* (Grand Rapids: Baker, 1999), 356.

[26] Supporting authenticity are M. J. Kruger, "The Authenticity of 2 Peter," *JETS* 42 (1999): 645–71; C. Bigg, *The Epistles of St. Peter and St. Jude,* ICC (Edinburgh: T & T Clark, 1901), 199–247; M. Green, *The Second Epistle General of Peter and the General Epistle of Jude,* 2d ed., TNTC (Grand Rapids: Eerdmans, 1988), 13–39; D. J. Moo, *2 Peter, Jude,* NIVAC (Grand Rapids: Zondervan, 1997), 21–26. See also the arguments of various scholars noted below.

[27] In a stimulating article M. J. Gilmour maintains that the evidence supporting both authenticity and inauthenticity is ambiguous and does not support clearly either position ("Reflections on the Authorship of 2 Peter," *EvQ* 73 [2001]: 291–309). Many of Gilmour's arguments are correct. Often the arguments on both sides are not decisive in establishing the view defended. Nevertheless, there are several weaknesses with Gilmour's view. First, he should acknowledge more clearly that historical work involves plausibility, not absolute proof. It is true that many of the arguments adduced on both sides are not compelling. Still, some arguments are more plausible than others, and it is the task of the historian to indicate such. Second, Gilmour wrongly concludes that neither position is more likely than the other from a historical standpoint. He ignores entirely the internal evidence of the letter, viewing it only in terms of presuppositions. The self-claim of the letter cannot be dismissed merely as presuppositional. We must remember that the letter itself represents historical evidence containing documentary claims about the author. Third, Gilmour fails to recognize clearly enough that those who support authenticity do not think that all of the arguments are decisive in and of themselves. But the arguments do demonstrate that the letter's own claim is defensible and plausible. Fourth, Gilmour does not perceive the historical weakness of the testament hypothesis (see below). The notion that 2 Peter was a transparent fiction is historically flawed since there is no evidence that anyone in the early history of the church identified the letter as transparent fiction. Finally, Gilmour rightly notes that presuppositions play a role in establishing authorship, but he does not explain clearly the relationship between presuppositions and evidence and thus appears to suggest that the former is in an airtight compartment that is hermetically sealed off from the latter.

[28] So B. B. Warfield, "The Canonicity of Second Peter," in *Selected Shorter Writings,* 2 vols. (Phillipsburg, N.J.; Presbyterian & Reformed, 1973), 2:69; Kruger, "The Authenticity of 2 Peter," 662.

[29] Rightly D. Guthrie, *New Testament Introduction*, 4th ed. (Downers Grove: InterVarsity, 1990), 820–21.

genuineness—unless one adopts the view that the writer was consciously and cleverly trying to deceive his readers, but even this seems improbable since this form of Peter's name is never used in the Apostolic Fathers or psuedepigraphic Petrine literature. Not only did Peter claim to be the author, he also said that he would die soon (1:14). This is most naturally interpreted to say that Peter was older and realized his death was imminent. Such a statement is quite awkward on the lips of a pseudonymous writer.

Even more powerful, perhaps, is the claim to be an eyewitness of the transfiguration (1:16–18). The truth of the second coming is anticipated in the event of the transfiguration. Peter emphasized that he was present on the holy mountain, that he was not inventing what happened, that he was an eyewitness of what occurred, and that he also heard the words transmitted from heaven. It is difficult to see how a pseudepigraphal author could write such words with any credibility.[30] A footnote would seem to be required by any other author to say: "Well, actually, I did not see or hear what happened on the mountain. I am speaking of what happened to Peter." Those who support pseudonymity are hard pressed to explain how such statements are not fundamentally deceptive. Furthermore, why would a pseudepigrapher appeal to the transfiguration? Guthrie observes that the account is not used to verify further revelation, nor does it match precisely any of the Synoptic accounts.[31] Hence, what we have here is an independent account of the event. Moreover, a pseudepigrapher would likely have embellished the account, and yet such embellishment is lacking in 2 Peter.[32]

The above facts are best accounted for if Peter himself was the author. The reference to Paul as a "beloved brother" (3:15) is fitting for Peter. It would seem writers in successive generations would not put themselves on the same plane as the apostle Paul.[33] Peter recognized that God had granted Paul wisdom (3:15–16), and such a statement accords with Gal 2:9. The manner in which he referred to Paul is just the right touch if Peter himself was the author—respectful, and yet no sense of inferiority is communicated.[34] We think by contrast of later writers who make it clear they are not on the same level as the apostles (cf. Ign., *Trall.* 3:3; *Rom.* 4:3). Finally, the letter claims to be the second one written by Peter (3:1). Wallace rightly

---

[30] Charles rightly remarks, "Such requires too much from the reader" (*Virtue amidst Vice,* 97).

[31] Guthrie, *New Testament Introduction,* 823.

[32] Rightly D. B. Wallace, "Second Peter: Introduction, Argument, and Outline," at http://www.bible.org/studies/soapbox/2petotl.htm.

[33] J. A. T. Robinson notes that the term points to a coworker who was still living (*Redating the New Testament* [Philadelphia: Westminster, 1976], 181).

[34] So also Robinson. Cf. R. Riesner, "Der Zweite-Petrus Brief und die Eschatologie," in *Zukunftserwartung in biblischer Sicht: Beiträge zur Eschatologie* (Giessen: Brunnen, 1984), 132–33; Kruger, "The Authenticity of 2 Peter," 664–65.

remarks that the claim here does not fit with pseudepigraphy since the second letter does not depend in a clear fashion on 1 Peter.[35] A forger would be disposed to borrow more extensively from 1 Peter, whereas the independence of 2 Peter reveals that the same author addresses a new situation.

We turn next to the external evidence for 2 Peter.[36] It is admittedly not as strong as for other New Testament writings. The Muratorian Canon does not mention 2 Peter, but neither does it mention 1 Peter. The text of the Canon is incomplete in any case, and so definite conclusions should not be gleaned from its omission. In a careful study Picirilli investigates allusions to 2 Peter in the Apostolic Fathers.[37] He concludes that there is a strong possibility that 2 Peter is alluded to (though Peter is not mentioned by name) in *1 Clement, 2 Clement, Barnabas,* and *Shepherd of Hermas*. He thinks such allusions may also exist in the Ignatian letters and *Martyrdom of Polycarp*. The evidence Picirilli compiles suggests that the letter was used in the second century and perhaps even in the first.[38] These allusions cast doubt on a second-century date but do not speak directly to the issue of authorship.[39] On the other hand, Picirilli notes that the Apostolic Fathers[40] cite Paul thirty-one times but never name him.[41] Hence, the failure to name Peter is hardly decisive. Entirely different solutions could be posited, of course. It could be argued that the similarities in the tradition demonstrate that the author of 2 Peter used some of the Apostolic Fathers. Others may posit a common source as the explanation for the similar material.[42] Resolving this issue definitively is impossible, but in considering the cumulative case for Petrine authorship, it is also quite possible, and in my mind probable, that the Apostolic Fathers used 2 Peter. Two allusions seem very likely. In *Epistle of Barnabas* there seems to be an allusion to 2 Pet 3:8

---

[35] Wallace, "Second Peter: Introduction, Argument, and Outline."

[36] For citations and assessment of the evidence, see Bigg, *Peter and Jude,* 199–215.

[37] R. E. Picirilli, "Allusions to 2 Peter in the Apostolic Fathers," *JSNT* 33 (1988): 57–83. See also C. P. Thiede, "A Pagan Reader of 2 Peter: Cosmic Conflagration in 2 Peter 3 and the *Octavius* of Minucius Felix," *JSNT* 26 (1986): 79–96. Thiede argues that Minucius Felix knew 2 Peter and used his notion of the conflagration in his dialogue *Octavius*. Thiede also thinks there are "unmistakable allusions to 2 Peter" in Justin Martyr (so also Warfield, "The Canonicity of Second Peter," 55) and Minucius (p. 80). He dates Minucius's *Octavius* in the 140s and concludes from the evidence presented that 2 Peter was written in the first century.

[38] For an older study that draws similar conclusions to those of Picirilli, see Warfield, "The Canonicity of Second Peter," 49–68. Cf. also Kruger, "The Authenticity of 2 Peter," 655.

[39] Gilmour rightly observes that Picirilli's arguments do not establish authenticity ("Reflections on the Authorship of 2 Peter," 298–99).

[40] Mayor, *Jude and Second Peter,* cxxvii.

[41] Picirilli, "Allusions to 2 Peter," 74.

[42] So K. P. Donfried, *The Setting of Second Clement in Early Christianity* (Leiden: Brill, 1974), 91, 93; Bauckham, *Jude, 2 Peter,* 149–51.

(*Barn.* 15:4).[43] *Second Clement* 16:3 may also depend upon 2 Pet 3:7, 10,12.[44] There is also good reason to think Justin Martyr alluded to 2 Pet 2:1 (*Dial.* 82:1).[45] The citations in Hippolytus may also indicate that he used 2 Peter.[46]

Origen noted that some doubted the authenticity of 2 Peter (Eusebius, *Hist. eccl.* 6.25.11), but in his own writings he cited it six times, and we can conclude from this that the doubts of others were not compelling to him.[47] It is also likely that Irenaeus knew and used 2 Peter, though the matter is disputed.[48] The phrase "With the Lord a day is like a thousand years, and a thousand years are like a day" (2 Pet 3:8) matches quite closely with the wording of Irenaeus (*Haer.* 5.23.2). It is instructive to note that what Irenaeus wrote is much closer to 2 Pet 3:10 than to Ps 90:4 (LXX).[49] Eusebius also mentions that it was disputed, but he adds, significantly, that most accepted it (*Hist. eccl.* 3.3.1,4; 3.25.3–4). He does not place it in the spurious classification, though personally he has doubts about its canonicity. The evidence is disputed, but it seems likely that Clement of Alexandria wrote a commentary on 2 Peter (*Hist. eccl.* 6.14.1). Such a commentary would indicate a high estimation of the letter and would also cast doubt on a late forgery since it is unlikely that Clement would have no information about its pseudonymity if the letter were written in the second century.[50]

Jerome anticipated modern scholarship in suggesting two different secretaries for 1 and 2 Peter, acknowledging a difference in style (*Ep.* 120.11). It is also quite likely that *Apocalypse of Peter* was dependent upon 2 Peter.[51] If so, 2 Peter was in circulation in the early part of the second century. Calvin's view on 2 Peter is quite interesting, indicating his careful critical judgment.[52] He thinks the style is quite unlike 1 Peter and ques-

[43] So also Warfield, "The Canonicity of Second Peter," 56.

[44] Warfield thinks the evidence is sufficient to indicate that the *Shepherd of Hermas* used 2 Peter ("The Canonicity of Second Peter," 55), but the parallels are not as clear as he suggests.

[45] Kruger, "The Authenticity of 2 Peter," 654. See also my comments under 2:1.

[46] See the evidence in Bigg, *Peter and Jude,* 203; Kruger, "The Authenticity of 2 Peter," 653–54, n. 52.

[47] Cf. Guthrie, *New Testament Introduction,* 806; Warfield, "The Canonicity of Second Peter," 49–50; Kruger, "The Authenticity of 2 Peter," 649–50.

[48] See the argument of Warfield, "The Canonicity of Second Peter," 52–54. Warfield also presents evidence that Theophilus of Antioch and Melito of Sardis seem to depend on 2 Peter (p. 54).

[49] Kruger deduces from this that Irenaeus had access to 2 Peter, that it was known to many others, that he recognized its authenticity and probably considered it to be authentic ("The Authenticity of 2 Peter," 653).

[50] See the discussion in Kruger, "The Authenticity of 2 Peter," 652–53.

[51] See Kruger, "The Authenticity of 2 Peter," 654; Bauckham, *Jude, 2 Peter,* 162; Robinson, *Redating,* 178; Smith, *Petrine Controversies,* 52–53.

[52] J. Calvin, *Commentaries on the Catholic Epistles* (Grand Rapids: Eerdmans, 1948), 363–64, 423.

tions, therefore, whether Peter was genuinely the author. Still, he rejects pseudonymity since "it would have been a fiction unworthy of a minister of Christ, to have personated another individual."[53] Hence, he suggests that a Petrine disciple wrote it for him since he was old and near death. It is clear from the above survey that scholars in previous eras were not oblivious to the differences between 1 and 2 Peter, and yet they still accepted the authenticity of the latter.

Other evidence also points to the authenticity of the letter: "2 Peter was recognized as fully canonical by the Canons of Laodicea and by the time of the church councils of Hippo and Carthage of the fourth century."[54] Kruger goes on to say that these bodies rejected *1 Clement* and *Epistle of Barnabas,* showing that they discriminated carefully between authoritative documents and those that were merely edifying. Textual evidence also points to the authenticity of 2 Peter, for it is included in the Bodmer papyrus ($\mathfrak{P}^{72}$) from the third century and also in Codexes Sinaiticus, Vaticanus, and Alexandrinus.[55]

Guthrie has an interesting insight that needs to be mixed into the discussion.[56] Other pseudo-Petrine literature circulated in the early church, creating confusion about what was authentically Petrine. The church went through a process by which it sifted the authentic from the spurious. When the decision was made, 2 Peter was accepted, but other alleged Petrine writings were rejected. The early church was not inclined, therefore, to include a document just because it had Peter's name on it. Many other "Petrine" writings were excluded, but the church recognized the legitimacy of 2 Peter. Hence, the acceptance of 2 Peter witnesses to the discrimination of the church, to their conviction that this writing, in contrast to many other alleged Petrine writings, was authentic. Kruger rightly maintains that the conclusion of the early church should not be set aside easily.[57]

Scholars often point to the linguistic differences between the two letters, and the differences are not to be denied. And yet they can also be overemphasized. We have noted above that 2 Peter is called Hellenistic because he used terms like "goodness" *(aretē)* and "eyewitnesses" *(epoptai).* And yet 1 Peter used the term "goodness" as well, even if it is in the plural (1 Pet 2:9). And the verbal form of "eyewitnesses" *(epoptō)* is used in both

---

[53] Calvin, *Catholic Epistles,* 363. T. L. Wilder rightly points out that Calvin does not accept pseudonymity but argues that "the letter had been written by a secretary under Peter's direction" ("Pseudonymity and the New Testament," in *Interpreting the New Testament: Essays on Methods and Issues* [Nashville: Broadman & Holman, 2001], 310).

[54] Kruger, "The Authenticity of 2 Peter," 651.

[55] Ibid., 651.

[56] Guthrie, *New Testament Introduction,* 809.

[57] Kruger, "The Authenticity of 2 Peter," 651.

1 Pet 2:12 and 3:2.[58] We can agree that 2 Peter has a certain Hellenistic dress, but the question is whether the language used is unlikely for a Palestinian fishermen. We must remind ourselves that we should conceive of Peter as a businessman who engaged in physical labor and commerce. When we add to this the fact that Galilee was influenced by Hellenism and Greek culture, it is not astonishing that he would be familiar with Greek philosophical terms.[59] The terms he used would not require a thorough study of Greek philosophy or classics, nor did Peter use the terms in a technical sense. Indeed, Peter likely used Hellenistic terms to speak to the culture of his day.[60]

Green rightly observes that the differences between 1 and 2 Peter reflect the specific pastoral situations addressed in each.[61] The different style may in part be explained by the problem addressed. We know, for example, that 2 Peter was written in response to false teachers who denied the second coming, while 1 Peter addressed a suffering church. Moreover, it is quite possible that different secretaries were employed. Perhaps Silas or someone else assisted Peter in the composition of 1 Peter (1 Pet 5:12), and there is no reason to doubt that another person may have played a similar role in 2 Peter.[62] We do not know how much freedom Peter granted to secretaries in the composition of the letter.

The style of the two letters is not identical, and yet arguments from style are hardly conclusive when the corpus is so small.[63] Guthrie wisely remarks: "It is notoriously difficult to devise any certain criteria for the examination of style and this is particularly true where comparison is made between two short epistles. The area of comparison is so restricted that the results may well be misleading. Moreover, subjective impressions are likely to receive greater stress than is justified."[64] Analyses of style lack a scientific foundation when we are dealing with just a few pages. Some differences between the two letters may be observed, and yet we must be cautious about drawing definite conclusions when our database is so limited. It has been noted, for example, that both letters repeat words for effect.[65] In 2 Peter such words connect the various parts of the argument,

---

[58] For other links to 1 Peter, see Guthrie, *New Testament Introduction,* 850–52; Mayor, *Jude and Second Peter,* lxviii–cv.

[59] In his work Fornberg points out the Hellenistic flavor of 2 Peter (*An Early Church in a Pluralistic Society*), but he minimizes the Jewish and OT background in the letter.

[60] Cf. Guthrie, *New Testament Introduction,* 837.

[61] Green, *2 Peter and Jude,* 20–21; cf. Kruger, "The Authenticity of 2 Peter," 658.

[62] Bigg, *Peter and Jude,* 247; Guthrie, *New Testament Introduction*, 833; Charles, *Virtue amidst Vice,* 60–63.

[63] See the discussion in Kruger, "The Authenticity of 2 Peter," 656–59.

[64] Guthrie, *New Testament Introduction,* 832.

[65] Cf. Bigg, *Peter and Jude,* 224–32.

revealing that the letter was composed thoughtfully. A number of scholars also have argued that 2 Peter deliberately adopts a more expansive and florid Asiatic style that was pleasing to the ear.[66] And yet the letter also provides evidence of Semitic influence, and so one cannot argue that the expansive language rules out a Galilean author (cf. 2:2,10,12,14,22; 3:3). Wallace argues that the florid style and inferior Greek is evidence that Peter himself composed the letter, whereas 1 Peter was written by a secretary.[67] Certainty on these matters is impossible, but an appeal to a different style does not rule out Petrine authorship.[68] Furthermore, we should note that 2 Peter is similar to 1 Peter in some remarkable ways.[69] The parallels may point to a common author. At the very least they cast some doubt on those who insist that the letters cannot be from the same hand.

Some who doubt the authenticity of the letter view arguments defending its authenticity as special pleading. They object that, on the one hand, we say that perhaps different secretaries were used. And then we say, on the other hand, that the corpus of the two letters is too small to establish stylistic variation. Is it the case that conservatives tack this way and then that, searching desperately for any answer to preserve their preformed theory? It may seem that way, but in reality suggesting more than one answer to a problem often represents good scholarship. When we examine historical documents, we are not granted comprehensive knowledge of the circumstances in which the document was birthed. Hence, we must postulate probabilities, and in some cases, of course, more than one scenario is probable. Furthermore, in some instances the probable scenarios are not internally contradictory but both constitute plausible answers to the problem posed. Suggesting more than one solution is not necessarily a resort to desperation but may be an indication of humility—a recognition that the evidence only takes us so far. And most significantly the letter itself claims to have been written by Peter himself, and the self-claim of the letter should be accepted unless clear evidence exists to overturn such a judgment.

Others, as we have noted, think Peter cannot be genuine since it borrows from Jude. I refer readers to the introduction to Jude, where the literary relationship between Jude and 2 Peter is discussed. Some argue that neither letter is dependent upon the other, at least in terms of documentary dependence.[70] It is difficult to be sure, but it is argued in the introduction to Jude

[66] So, e.g., Green, *2 Peter and Jude,* 18–19.

[67] Wallace, "Second Peter: Introduction, Argument, and Outline."

[68] Riesner remarks that if 2 Peter were truly pseudonymous, we would expect an author to copy the style of 1 Peter. Hence, the argument from style also could pose a problem for pseudonymity ("Der Zweite-Petrus Brief," 131).

[69] For a convenient summary see Kruger, "The Authenticity of 2 Peter," 659–61.

[70] See Green, who thinks both are dependent on a common source (*2 Peter and Jude,* 58–64).

that 2 Peter likely was familiar with Jude. Even in this instance the objection against Petrine authorship does not stand. First, it is just possible that Jude drew from Peter.[71] If that is the case, the objection collapses. Second, even if Peter used Jude as a source, arguments against Petrine authorship are not conclusive.[72] In the introduction to Jude reasons are given for thinking that Jude is genuinely from the brother of Jesus and hence a late date is unnecessary.[73] The real objection is that Peter as an apostle would not have used a nonapostolic writing as a source. The reply to this is simple. How do we know this is the case? We must beware of assuming what an apostle would do. Those from another century may think and act differently from us. We know that Paul cited pagan poets (Acts 17:28; Titus 1:12), and Peter may well have quoted Jude if he found its content fitting. There is some evidence that early Christian creeds and hymns were used in other writings (e.g., Eph 5:14; 1 Tim 3:16), and there is no credible reason why an author would refuse to cite at some length a source that was considered helpful.

The Hellenistic character of 2 Peter can be overemphasized, for he could simply have used terminology that spoke effectively to his readers. Modern-day evangelists and writers commonly follow the same procedure. The importance of knowledge is emphasized constantly in the New Testament. We think here of the Letter to the Colossians, where knowledge of Christ is fundamental (Col 1:9–11,28–2:8). Sharing in the divine nature is merely another way of speaking of the indwelling of the Holy Spirit. Green remarks that Peter used Greek terminology to communicate with his readers.[74] Josephus and other writers speak of sharing in the divine nature, and the fundamental Jewishness of their writings is not thereby sacrificed.[75] Käsemann's claim that the Christology is inferior is a stunning mistake, for there are convincing grounds for claiming that Jesus Christ is called God himself in 1:2.[76] The letter ends with an ascription of glory to Jesus Christ (3:18), and doxologies are usually directed to God instead of Jesus Christ (but cf. 2 Tim 4:18; Rev 1:5–6). One of Peter's favorite designations for Jesus Christ was Lord and Savior (cf. 1:1–2,8,11,14,16; 2:1,20; 3:2,18). Furthermore, Peter reported the words spoken to Jesus at the transfiguration, where as God's elect Son he is given honor and glory (1:17–18). Christ's work on the cross

---

[71] So Bigg, *Peter and Jude,* 216–24.

[72] So Fornberg, though he rejects Petrine authorship on other grounds (*An Early Church in a Pluralistic Society,* 59).

[73] Robinson postulates that Jude wrote 2 Peter as his secretary (*Redating,* 193–95). This is improbable as the distinct vocabulary and the failure to mention Jude as a cosender in 2 Peter show (cf. Riesner, "Der Zweite-Petrus Brief," 133).

[74] Green, *2 Peter and Jude,* 26.

[75] See the work of J. M. Starr, *Sharers in Divine Nature: 2 Peter 1:4 in Its Hellenistic Context,* ConBNT 33 (Stockholm: Almqvist &: Wiksell, 2000).

[76] Note also the helpful observations of Kruger, "The Authenticity of 2 Peter," 667.

in purchasing human beings (2:1) and the cleansing of sins by Christ's death (1:9) are noted. Peter did not unpack his Christology or a theology of the cross, but evidence of a defective Christology is lacking.

Some scholars think the letter commends self-effort and thereby betrays early catholicism.[77] But again they misinterpret the letter. All the virtues commended in Peter (1:5–11) are grounded in God's gracious work in Christ (1:3–4), in the gift of divine righteousness given by grace to believers (1:1). Unfortunately, some scholars dismiss as early catholic any New Testament letter that emphasizes moral norms. Such views demonstrate more about the critic than the New Testament. Typically these scholars have adopted a one-sided view of Paul, failing to see that grace in Paul grants power for a godly life. Peter did not sunder the connection between Christ's coming and ethics. Eschatology is one of the foundations for ethics. This is precisely what Paul argued in 1 Corinthians 15 (see the conclusion drawn from eschatology in 1 Cor 15:58). Or we can compare the eschatological grounding for the exhortations in Rom 13:11–14. The relationship between eschatology and ethics in Peter looks similar to Paul's view in his major epistles.

It is also said that the hope for the second coming is fading, but the case is unpersuasive.[78] Even in 1, 2 Thessalonians questions arose about the resurrection and the Lord's coming. Moreover, Peter did not necessarily teach that a long time would elapse before the Lord comes. He simply asserted that the Lord did not reckon time as we do (3:8–10), that we should not dismiss the Lord's coming simply because it appears to be delayed. The eschatological hope is still lively, for believers await entrance into God's kingdom (1:10–11) and should not surrender the hope of Christ's coming, despite the scoffing of opponents. Furthermore, Charles rightly points out that an interval of time before the return of Christ is present in the teaching of Jesus himself.[79] Green points out that by the second century A.D. the delay of the parousia was not the subject of discussion, and so one can scarcely place Peter at a late date for this reason. Nor does the reference to

---

[77] In an instructive essay J. H. Elliott criticizes those who reject some writings as early catholic. He notes that Käsemann's own view is reductionistic, that it arbitrarily erects a canon within the canon, and that he himself turns the gospel into a doctrine ("A Catholic Gospel: Reflections on 'Early Catholicism' in the New Testament," *CBQ* 36 [1969]: 213–23). Fornberg also argues that the term "early catholicism" is "an artificial category which cannot do justice to a document such as 2 Peter" (*An Early Church in a Pluralistic Society,* 4–5). See also the effective critique of the label "early catholicism" in Charles, *Virtue amidst Vice,* 11–37.

[78] Even though C. H. Talbert denies authenticity, he agrees that the alleged delay of the parousia does not constitute a serious problem for the readers of 2 Peter. The objection is raised by the opponents and fits with what we find in letters such as 1 Corinthians and *1 Clement* ("2 Peter and the Delay of the Parousia," *VC* 20 [1966]: 137–45). So also Bauckham, *Jude, 2 Peter,* 151.

[79] Charles, *Virtue amidst Vice,* 29–30. See his discussion of this issue on pp. 26–32.

the "fathers" in 3:4 signal the decease of the apostolic generation.[80] I point out in the commentary that the word "fathers" nowhere clearly refers to the first generation of Christians but invariably refers to the Old Testament patriarchs.[81] Hence, the verse does not constitute evidence that Peter or the apostolic generation was deceased. Furthermore, it is noticeable that the saying about one day being as a thousand years is not used in a chiliastic sense in Peter.[82] If Peter were written in the second century, we might expect a millennial allusion, and the lack of such may point to the early date for the letter.

Many scholars think the high estimate of Paul's letters is impossible for the genuine Peter (3:15–16) and suggests a collection or even canon of Paul's letters that cannot be placed into Peter's lifetime. The reader is again referred to my commentary on these verses, but it must be noted here that the verses do not suggest a complete canon of Paul's letters, nor do they suggest that Peter was acquainted with all of Paul's letters. All the verses require is that Peter thought highly of the letters of Paul with which he was familiar. The authority he assigns to the Pauline letters harmonizes with Paul's own estimate of his apostolic authority (cf. 1 Cor 2:16; 14:37; Col 4:16; 1 Thess 2:13; 5:27; 2 Thess 3:14).[83] The Tübingen view that Paul and Peter were fundamentally opposed to each other needs to be laid to rest once and for all. They were not, of course, carbon copies of each other. They did have different circles of ministry. And their confrontation at Antioch is famous in the annals of New Testament study (Gal 2:11–14). Too many scholars, however, impose their own reading upon this text, arguing, contrary to Paul's explicit words, that Peter acted from conviction instead of hypocritically. Scholars are free, naturally, to suggest that the text deviates from what actually occurred, but they are distant from the event, and we should be clear that such theories deviate from what the text says. Furthermore, it is unnecessary to conclude from the reference here that Paul personally wrote to all of the Petrine churches. It may be the case that some of the churches in the Petrine circle had received Pauline letters. Or perhaps the churches had read some of the Pauline letters that were circulating (such as Colossians and Ephesians).[84]

Nor is it clear that interpretation is reserved for church officials, contrary

---

[80] See the trenchant comments of Kruger, "The Authenticity of 2 Peter," 665.

[81] Contrary to Robinson, who thinks 1 John 2:13–14 refers to "fathers" of the first generation in contrast to second and third generation Christians (*Redating,* 180). But it is quite unlikely that John was speaking of different *generations* of believers in 1 John. The reference is to older and younger believers or believers who are more or less mature.

[82] Bigg, *Peter and Jude,* 213–14; Riesner, "Der Zweite-Petrus Brief," 134.

[83] Rightly Fornberg, *An Early Church in a Pluralistic Society,* 21–22; Robinson, *Redating,* 182.

[84] For this point see Wallace, "Second Peter: Introduction, Argument, and Outline."

to Käsemann. Such a view misrepresents 1:20–21, for the latter do not restrict interpretation to church officials but insists rather that all interpretation must match the apostolic standard.[85] Indeed, 2 Peter does not show any signs of a monarchial episcopate and the more developed church structure of the second century.[86] Surely leaders existed in the Petrine churches addressed, but Peter said nothing about such leaders in the letter. Instead, his injunctions were directed to the congregation as a whole.[87]

(3) Pseudepigraphal Letters

It should also be noted that evidence for accepting pseudepigraphic letters as authoritative is not strong.[88] Paul specifically criticized false writings in his name in 2 Thess 2:2 and ensured the authenticity of the letter in 2 Thess 3:17.[89] The author of *Acts of Paul and Thecla* was defrocked as bishop even though he wrote out of love for Paul (Tertullian, *De Bapt.* 17).[90] In addition, *Gospel of Peter* was rejected in A.D. 180 in Antioch because the author claimed to be Peter and was not. Serapion the bishop said, "For our part, brethren, we both receive Peter and the other apostles as Christ, but the writings which falsely bear their names we reject, as men of experience, knowing that such were not handed down to us" (Eusebius, *Hist. Eccl.* 6.12.1–6). Evidence that early Christians accepted psuedepigraphic documents as authoritative Scripture is completely lacking. Some argue that *Acts of Paul and Thecla* and *Gospel of Peter* were only rejected

[85] Bauckham proposes another interpretation, saying that these verses "have nothing to do with the exegesis of Scripture, and therefore do not insist on an authoritative interpretation of Scripture by officeholders who alone possess the Spirit" (*Jude, 2 Peter,* 152).

[86] Rightly Bigg, *Peter and Jude,* 233.

[87] So Charles, *Virtue amidst Vice,* 33. He argues that Käsemann fails to see the centrality of the Spirit in 2 Peter (pp. 34–35).

[88] So Guthrie, *New Testament Introduction,* 1012–18; cf. also E. E. Ellis, "Pseudonymity and Canonicity of New Testament Documents," in *Worship, Theology and Ministry in the Early Church: Essays in Honor of Ralph P. Martin,* JSNTSup 87 (Sheffield: JSOT, 1992), 212–24. S. E Porter remarks, "The general, if not invariable, pattern was that, if a work was known to be pseudonymous, it was excluded from any group of authoritative writings" ("Exegesis of the Pauline Letters, Including the Deutero-Pauline Letters," in *Handbook to Exegesis of the New Testament* [Leiden: Brill, 1997], 533). His whole discussion is illuminating (see pp. 531–39).

[89] Wilder argues that pseudonymity does not square with the early Christian virtue of truthfulness. Furthermore, some have argued for pseudonymity by seeing a parallel with Greco-Roman writings. E.g., pseudonymity was common among the disciples of Pythagoras. The parallel is not apt, as Wilder observes, since pseudonymity was not common in Jewish epistolary literature ("Pseudonymity and the New Testament," 297–303). Some argue, of course, that 2 Thessalonians itself is pseudonymous, and hence they would reject any reference to 2 Thessalonians.

[90] Wilder points out that *Shepherd of Hermas* was excluded by the Muratorian Canon because it was not from the apostolic era. He concludes from this that pseudonymous works from postapostolic times were rejected (ibid., 304).

for deviant teaching, not for pseudepigraphy.[91] But both of the texts say otherwise, specifically indicting the writers for falsely ascribing the writing to another.[92] Bauckham sees a parallel in Hebrews where the theology derives from Paul but a disciple wrote it. The parallel is not apt, for no author is named in Hebrews.[93] The Muratorian Canon rejected *Letter to the Laodiceans* and *Letter to the Alexandrians* because they were suspected to be forgeries. Origen says that he rejects *Doctrine of Peter* since it was "not included among the books of the Church and . . . not a writing of Peter nor of any one else inspired by the Spirit of God."[94] Many pseudonymous works in Jewish literature borrow the name of a famous person from the ancient past (Enoch, Moses, Solomon, etc.), but such documents were never included in the Jewish canon, even if some of the material in the book was considered to be valuable. Furthermore, it is difficult to see what would have motivated the author to use a pseudonym in 2 Peter. The letter does not advance any new or esoteric teaching, for pseudonymous writings often support novel teachings under the name of a respected person.[95]

The practice of pseudonymity is defended in Meade's *Pseudonymity and Canon*.[96] The fundamental problem with Meade is that he assumes pseud-

---

[91] Bauckham, *Jude, 2 Peter,* 162; Farkasfalvy, "Ecclesial Setting," 28; Fornberg, *An Early Church in a Pluralistic Society,* 15–19. So also Farmer, "Some Critical Reflections on Second Peter," 40–45. Farmer calls attention to a pseudonymous letter written by Salvian to his bishop Salonius (ca. A.D. 440), in which the latter detected from the substance of the letter that it was authored by his former teacher (pp. 43–45). Salvian wrote a letter to his former student, explaining why he wrote pseudonymously. He argued that he did so to avoid human glory. He also wrote in the name of Timothy because he was honored and people might not pay attention to the contents of the work since Salvian himself was an obscure person. The example Farmer adduces is interesting indeed. It demonstrates that Salvian intended to deceive his readers in referring to a famous personage rather than himself in order to secure a hearing for his letter. The response of the bishop indicates that the authority of the letter was questioned when the device of pseudonymity was recognized. The bishop does not respond to Salvian by saying that writing under false pretences is a venerable tradition, including even canonical writings. He questions the ethics of Salvian. In my judgment the same problem obtained during the time of the writing of 2 Peter, and writing under false pretenses would have raised severe questions about his credibility.

[92] Rightly Wilder, "Pseudonymity and the New Testament," 304–5; Green, *2 Peter and Jude,* 33–34; Guthrie, *New Testament Introduction,* 1019–20; Kruger, "The Authenticity of 2 Peter," 647–48. See pp. 306–9 in Wilder for further support of this thesis.

[93] Wilder also shows that Tertullian's apparent support of disciples writing works that belong to their masters does not support the notion of pseudonymity ("Pseudonymity and the New Testament," 305).

[94] I owe this reference to Wilder, "Pseudonymity and the New Testament," 305. It derives from *On Principles,* Preface 8.

[95] So Guthrie, *New Testament Introduction,* 839–40.

[96] D. G. Meade, *Pseudonymity and Canon: An Investigation into the Relationship of Authorship and Authority in Jewish and Earliest Christian Tradition* (Tübingen: Mohr, 1986). J. D. G. Dunn (Meade's doctoral supervisor) presents the same case (see "Pseudepigraphy," *Dictionary of the Later New Testament and Its Developments* [Downers Grove: InterVarsity, 1997], 977–84).

onymity was practiced and accepted. In that sense his work begs the question.[97] Meade argues that pseudonymous writers employed tradition and contemporarized it *(Vergegenwärtigung)* for a new generation. But Meade's claim that naming the author is not intended to convey who wrote the book in question but only transmits the tradition of the alleged author is unpersuasive.[98] The lack of parallels for such a practice is striking, and no real explanation is given about why the practice was discontinued.[99]

At this point we need to discuss the stimulating work of Donelson on the Pastoral Epistles.[100] What Donelson says about the Pastorals also applies in principle to 2 Peter. Ultimately Donelson draws very different conclusions from my own, but his perspective overlaps with mine in some significant ways. He argues that no evidence exists that pseudonymous letters were accepted as authoritative. Pseudonymity was practiced, however, and hence one was compelled to deceive to carry it off. People in the ancient world believed it was legitimate to deceive if the cause was important enough to justify the lie.[101] He remarks, "No one ever seems to have accepted a document as religiously and philosophically prescriptive which was known to be forged. I do not know a single example."[102] Similarly, "We are forced to admit that in Christian circles pseudonymity was considered a dishonorable device and, if discovered, the document was rejected and the author, if known, was excoriated."[103] Writers used a "noble lie" because they believed that the end justified the means. Some even may have written in the name of an apostle, believing that they transmitted what apostles would say to a new generation. And yet "they were still consciously employing a

[97] J. Zmijewski's solution is rather similar ("Apostolische Paradosis und Pseudepigraphie im Neuen Testament: 'Durch Erinnerung wachhalten' [2 Petr 1,13; 3,1]," *BZ* 33 [1979]: 161–71). Zmijewski argues that pseudepigraphy does not involve deception or falsity as long as the writer's purpose is to transmit authentic apostolic tradition, so that it will be remembered by coming generations. The church criticized those who conveyed teaching that was not in accord with apostolic tradition but was not opposed to pseudepigraphy itself. Zmijewski certainly puts the best face on pseudepigraphy, but it is not apparent that he has explained how the device of pseudonymity is spared from deception in his scheme. It would seem that his solution would work only if one also accepts Bauckham's view that the pseudonymity in the case of 2 Peter is a "transparent fiction."

[98] Guthrie, *New Testament Introduction,* 1026–28.

[99] Against Meade, see Wilder, "Pseudonymity and the New Testament," 317–18. For a very helpful summary of the history of scholarship relative to pseudonymity, see ibid., 310–22. Wilder remarks on the work of past scholars who defended pseudonymity, "With little or no supporting documentation, the scholars highlighted in the foregoing discussion defended the view that the early church readily accepted the practice of pseudonymity" (ibid., 313).

[100] L. R. Donelson, *Pseudepigraphy and Ethical Argument in the Pastoral Epistles* (Tübingen: Mohr, 1986).

[101] Ibid., 19–20.

[102] Ibid., 11.

[103] Ibid., 16.

lie which they knew was potentially damaging if discovered. Thus we cannot conclude that forgery was ever innocently or naively done."[104] Indeed, Donelson argues that the personal touches and allusions in the Pastoral letters, and by the same token 2 Peter, were inserted deliberately to provide authenticity to the letters and are therefore an integral part of the author's attempt to mislead his readers.[105] Donelson concludes that New Testament writers employed pseudonymity, even though it was fundamentally deceptive, because they believed the end justified the means.

I am persuaded that evidence is lacking that any canonical document is actually pseudonymous. But Donelson is correct that there is no evidence that pseudonymous documents were ever accepted as authoritative. He also rightly argues that pseudonymous letters involved an attempt to deceive. Aland's view that pseudonymity was justified since the crucial matter for writers was the influence of the Spirit is not borne out by the evidence.[106] As Guthrie remarks, if Aland is correct, then one wonders why any inspired documents name the author.[107] It would seem to follow that all the documents were originally anonymous and later became pseudonymous since the original anonymity was designed to feature the work of the Spirit. Furthermore, no evidence exists that any pseudepigraphic letters were originally anonymous. Finally, Aland's theory does not explain why a pseudonym was used if all that mattered was the Spirit's inspiration. Naming a notable author would be superfluous if the Spirit's authority is decisive. It is hard to escape the conclusion that pseudonyms were used to support the authority of what was written. But this demonstrates the implausibility of Aland's thesis. Apparently those who used pseudonyms did not merely appeal to the Spirit's inspiration. They also introduced a pseudonym to impress readers with the stature of the writer. We should note again that no one has yet shown that pseudonymous documents were embraced as authoritative and canonical.[108] Employing pseudonymity contradicts the early Christian desire to be truthful.[109]

Others argue that "your apostles" in 3:2 indicates that the letter cannot be Petrine, since the apostles now belong to all the churches. We have an example here of two different ways of reading a text. "Your apostles" could

---

[104] Donelson, *Pseudepigraphy and Ethical Argument,* 62.

[105] Ibid., 24–42.

[106] K. Aland, "The Problem of Anonymity and Pseudonymity in Christian Literature of the First Two Centuries," *JTS* 12 (1961): 39–49.

[107] Guthrie, *New Testament Introduction,* 1025–26.

[108] Guthrie states that 2 Peter is either authentic or "a forgery" (*New Testament Introduction,* 812).

[109] Ibid., 1021–22; Charles, *Virtue amidst Vice,* 64–66. See his whole discussion of the issue and especially his critique of Bauckham's view on pp. 49–75.

indicate that the apostles now belong to all the churches. Such a conception, in my opinion, does not necessarily rule out apostolic authorship. The Book of Acts, for instance, implies that the apostles functioned as leaders of all the churches (Acts 1:15–26; 15:6–35). And yet Peter probably did not have in mind the notion that all the apostles served the Petrine churches in 3:2. More likely, he referred to the particular apostles who had played a role in planting and nurturing the churches addressed. Peter, then, was not referring to the apostles as a whole, and so the verse cannot be used to point to an ecclesiastical structure that was allegedly established after Peter's death.

(4) Testament Genre

We should examine briefly Bauckham's testament theory. His view is more acceptable to evangelicals because, according to him, Peter did not write to deceive. The testament genre was well established, and it was apparent to all that the letter was a "transparent fiction."[110] It should be said at the outset that Bauckham's view is possible. If we could establish that testaments were written in the name of another (pseudepigraphy), that the convention was recognized by all, and that such documents could still be confirmed as canonical, then there would be no objection. We would simply recognize a cultural practice that seems foreign to us today.

It seems to be the case, however, that Bauckham's theory fails. It does not necessarily fail because it contradicts the inspiration of Scripture, for there could have been a convention in which testaments were accepted as transparent fictions. Rather, it fails because hard evidence to support the theory is lacking. The most damaging piece of evidence against Bauckham's theory is this: If the testament genre and the pseudepigraphal device in it were transparent, it is curious that no intimation of this idea has come down to us historically.[111] No evidence exists that the early church accepted 2 Peter while recognizing its pseudepigraphal character. How could a "transparent fiction" vanish from the historical scene, so that we have no evidence whatsoever that anyone ever recognized it as such? Starr makes the following comment on Bauckham's thesis, "While this is appealing, the fiction which Bauckham asserts was transparent has in fact been opaque for every reader apart from his first generation of readers (who left no record other than their preservation of the text) and himself."[112] Bauckham replies that the Jews would have recognized the device, but not Gen-

---

[110] C. Gempf rightly says, "We must conclude that if pseudonymous works got into the canon, the church fathers were *fooled* by a transparent literary device that was originally intended *not* to fool anyone" ("Pseudonymity and the New Testament," *Them* 17 [1992]: 9).

[111] So also Green, *2 Peter and Jude,* 36–37, and Müller (who rejects authenticity), "Der 2. Petrusbrief," 335.

[112] Starr, *Sharers in Divine Nature,* 51.

tiles. This is curious indeed, for evidence that the letter was written to Jews is lacking. It is likely that 2 Peter was written to Gentiles in the same way as 1 Peter.[113] In any case, Bauckham's theory is still implausible. It is quite unlikely that the "transparent fiction" would vanish without a trace simply because of Gentile ignorance. We are faced then, of course, with a document that is fundamentally deceptive, and the objections we raised to such an idea above could be repeated here. Furthermore, if everyone knew that the writing was pseudonymous, what is the purpose of pseudonymity?[114] The device seems superfluous.[115]

Nor is it clear that testaments must be fictional.[116] One's views on a host of critical questions are involved here, and there is simply not space to defend every critical judgment at this juncture. Paul's speech in Acts 20:17–38 could be described as a last testament, and yet there is no reason to describe it as fictional. Similarly, the final testaments of Jacob (Gen 49:1–28), Moses, and David in the Old Testament need not be fictional. There are also good grounds for accepting the authenticity of Jesus' farewell discourse in John 13–17 and Paul's final words in 2 Timothy. It does not follow, then, that all farewell discourses were recognized as fictional. Nor is there any clear evidence that any work in the canon of Scripture is pseudepigraphic. Jewish testaments that were pseudepigraphal were clearly written (e.g., *Testaments of the Twelve Patriarchs*), but none of these were ever accepted as authoritative documents. They may have been considered to be edifying, but they were not approved as part of the sacred writings of Judaism.

Moreover, we should also ask whether it is clear that 2 Peter is in the testament genre.[117] Perhaps it is. But such a notion was not clear to previous generations of scholars.[118] The section in 2 Pet 1:3–15 could be taken as final advice and instruction from a man whose death is imminent. If such comprises a testament, then 2 Peter is aptly named. But it should be noted

---

[113] But cf. Mayor, who thinks the letter was addressed to Jews and Gentiles (*Jude and Second Peter,* 181).

[114] Kruger, "The Authenticity of 2 Peter," 646.

[115] Kruger also points out that most pseudonymous writings advance a distinctive view not accepted in the church, such as defending Gnosticism, Docetism, etc. No such distinct contribution is evident in 2 Peter, casting further doubt on the theory of pseudonymity (ibid., 669–70).

[116] So Green, *2 Peter and Jude,* 37; Charles, *Virtue amidst Vice,* 57; Wallace, "Second Peter: Introduction, Argument, and Outline."

[117] See especially the questions posed by Charles, *Virtue amidst Vice,* 49–75; cf. also Green, *2 Peter and Jude,* 37–38. Charles thinks the letter does not clearly belong to the testament genre but is "apostolic paraenesis that is urgently needed in a local situation" (p. 75, n. 123).

[118] Guthrie raises doubts about whether 2 Peter truly belongs to the testament genre (*New Testament Introduction,* 822).

that 2 Peter is remarkably brief in terms of reviewing the past and predicting the future, and letters containing testaments are rare.[119]

Finally, perhaps Guthrie is correct in suggesting that Peter was not received widely because of its limited circulation.[120] Still, we have seen that the evidence for Peter's early reception is stronger than most scholars think. We conclude that 2 Peter is authentic and that such a conclusion is more persuasive than competing theories.

2. Date and Destination

The date of 2 Peter depends on authorship. If the letter is authentically Petrine, as I have argued, it will be dated shortly before Peter's death, anywhere from A.D. 60 to 68. If 2 Peter used Jude, then one would also be required to argue that Jude was composed before 2 Peter (see introduction to Jude). Moo argues that Peter died in A.D. 65 and dates it shortly before his death.[121] Guthrie thinks it was written after Paul's death in A.D. 68.[122] Robinson dates it earlier, from A.D. 60 to 62.[123] Those who see the letter as authentic usually follow the tradition that Peter was at Rome at the end of his life (cf. Ignatius, *Rom.* 4:3; *1 Clem.* 5:4). Perhaps the Neronian persecution had even begun when the letter was written. For those who see the letter as pseudonymous, it is dated between A.D. 80 and 150. Bauckham, for example, dates the letter between A.D. 80 and 90, arguing that at least this much time had to pass to explain the scoffing because of the delay of the parousia.[124] Kelly dates it between A.D. 100 and 110.[125] Knowing where the letter was sent is even more difficult. If one understands the first letter to refer to 1 Peter (2 Pet 3:1), as I do, then the letter was sent to churches in

---

[119] So J. H. Neyrey, *2 Peter, Jude,* AB (Garden City: Doubleday, 1993), 112.

[120] Guthrie, *New Testament Introduction,* 840–41.

[121] For Peter dying in 65 see Robinson, *Redating,* 149; Moo, *2 Peter, Jude,* 24. Wallace dates it in A.D. 64 or 65 ("Second Peter: Introduction, Argument, and Outline." But whether Paul had already died, as Wallace avers, is less clear though certainly possible.

[122] Guthrie, *New Testament Introduction,* 843–44. Warfield dates it in A.D. 67 ("The Canonicity of Second Peter," 78).

[123] Robinson, *Redating,* 197–98. Green suggests from A.D. 61 to 68 (*2 Peter and Jude,* 41).

[124] Bauckham, *Jude, 2 Peter,* 158–59. Reicke thinks the letter was written ca. A.D. 90 (*James, Peter, and Jude,* 144).

[125] Kelly, *Peter and Jude,* 237. Cranfield dates it between A.D. 120 and 125 (*Peter and Jude,* 149; cf. also Wand, *Epistles of Peter and Jude,* 144; Mayor opts for 125 (*Jude and Second Peter,* cxxvii). D. G. Horrell dates it between A.D. 90 and 110 (*The Epistles of Peter and Jude,* EC [Peterborough: Epworth, 1998], 138). Fuchs and Reymond place the letter between A.D. 100 and 125 (*2 Pierre, Jude,* 40).

Asia Minor, churches that were mainly Gentile.[126] If the first letter refers to a lost letter, it is much more difficult to establish a destination. It could still have been sent to Asia Minor, while other scholars suggest Egypt. If it was sent to Asia Minor, there are clues that Peter wrote to a church facing syncretism and that he used the language of their culture to address the church (or churches).[127]

3. Opponents

Identifying the opponents in 2 Peter is quite difficult.[128] It is evident from 2:1–3,14,18 that they were from the church, claiming to be Christians. Peter viewed them as false teachers who had emerged from within the congregation.[129] Apparently they initially gave evidence of being converted and subsequently began to live and teach in a way that revealed their apostasy. Their central teaching was eschatological skepticism, for they denied a future coming of Christ (1:16–18; 3:4–7) and along with it any future judgment (2:3–10). The denial of a future judgment opened the door for a libertine lifestyle (2:1–3,11–16). Or perhaps they began by living licentiously and then defended their lifestyle theologically by denying a future judgment. They probably used Paul's writings in defense of their licentiousness, perhaps arguing that God's grace released believers from ethical obligation. In any case they viewed their own agenda as the pathway to freedom (2:19). Their argument seems to have been rationalistic, contending that the world functions normally and regularly without any interruption. Perhaps they claimed that the apostles invented the idea of Christ's coming (1:16), and they also rejected the wording of prophetic texts that taught the parousia (1:20–21).[130]

---

[126] Guthrie admits that we can have no certainty about the recipients (*New Testament Introduction,* 842–43). It is possible that the letter was sent to the same churches (or some of the same churches) that received 1 Peter and yet lacked the same wide circulation (cf. here the view of Wallace, "Second Peter: Introduction, Argument, and Outline." The problem of attestation, however, indicates that the recipients of the letter cannot be identified with certainty.

[127] So Fornberg, *An Early Church in a Pluralistic Society,* passim; Charles, *Virtue amidst Vice,* 80–83.

[128] It can be argued that the rhetorical language eliminates the possibility of identifying the opponents. So T. A. Miller, "Dogs, Adulterers, and the Way of Balaam: The Forms and Socio-Rhetorical Function of the Polemical Rhetoric in 2 Peter (Part I)," *IBS* 22 (2000): 123–44. Certainly the language used is emotional and defamatory. It does not follow logically, however, that the opponents are thereby misrepresented. The preservation of the letter may suggest that Peter described accurately the adversaries.

[129] So also Caulley, "Inspiration in 2 Peter 1:16–21," 33.

[130] Smith notes that it is not that the opponents argued for the delay of the parousia. What they argued was that the second coming would not occur at all, and the argument regarding its delay was utilized to defend their view (*Petrine Controversies,* 85).

Scholars have often identified the opponents as Gnostics or proto-Gnostics for the following reasons:[131] (1) the emphasis on knowledge in 2 Peter was a response to the *gnosis* of the opponents; (2) the lifestyle of the adversaries demonstrated that they were Gnostic libertines; (3) such a libertine lifestyle can perhaps be traced to a rejection of the material world; (4) similarly, their rejection of the last judgment may be linked to a refusal to believe in a bodily resurrection; (5) the interpretation of Paul reflects Gnostic exegesis; (6) their denial of the Lord (2 Pet 2:1) may indicate a denial of his incarnation, showing a Docetic theology; (7) they taught "myths" to their adherents (1:16).[132] Identifying the opponents as Gnostic in any form is increasingly and rightly questioned today.[133] We can sketch quickly why the Gnostic thesis is unpersuasive.[134] We see no evidence of cosmological dualism in 2 Peter, nor is it clear that the false teachers propounded a realized eschatology or even that their ethical libertinism stemmed from such dualism. Peter said nothing about the resurrection, and so it is unclear that they rejected the "material" world. Indeed, it is possible that they embraced the material world, arguing that it is the only world we will ever experience. The word "myths" hardly points to Gnosticism in 1:16, for Peter did not even use the word "myths" to refer to the views of the opponents. Instead, the adversaries threw the word "myths" in the face of those supporting the parousia. Peter did not accuse the opponents of propounding myths. On the contrary, the false teachers charged the apostles with spreading myths.[135] Gnosticism as we know emphasized knowledge

[131] E.g., Talbert, "2 Peter and the Delay of the Parousia," 141–43; Smith, *Petrine Controversies,* 93–100.

[132] A number of scholars support some form of the Gnostic hypothesis. See Schelke, *Der Petrusbrief—Der Judasbrief,* 232; Kelly, *Peter and Jude,* 231; Käsemann, "Apologia for Primitive Christian Eschatology," 170–72; T. S. Caulley, "The False Teachers in Second Peter," *SBT* 12 (1982): 27–42; id., "Inspiration in 2 Peter 1:16–21," 50–82.

[133] See Fornberg, *An Early Church in a Pluralistic Society,* 31; J. H. Neyrey, "The Form and Background of the Polemic in 2 Peter," *JBL* 99 (1980): 407–31; Guthrie, *New Testament Introduction,* 815, 828, 848–50; Vögtle, *Judasbrief, 2 Petrusbrief,* 266–72. For rejection of a Gnostic polemic from a scholar of a past era, see Bigg, *Peter and Jude,* 239.

[134] Bauckham, *Jude, 2 Peter,* 156–57; J. Kahmann, "Second Peter and Jude," in *The New Testament in Early Christianity: La réception des écrits néotestamentaires dans le christianisme primitif,* BETL 86 (Leuven: University Press, 1989), 114–15; M. Desjardins, "The Portrayal of the Dissidents in 2 Peter and Jude: Does It Tell Us More about the 'Godly' than the 'Ungodly'?" *JSNT* 30 (1987): 93–95; J. H. Neyrey, "The Apologetic Use of the Transfiguration in 2 Peter 1:16–21," *CBQ* 42 (1980): 506–7. See also Neyrey's essay in which he subjects Käsemann's denigration of 2 Peter to evaluation, concluding that Käsemann missed the point in his analysis of the letter ("Polemic in 2 Peter," 407–31). Rightly Müller, "Der 2. Petrusbrief," 327; contra Guthrie, *New Testament Introduction,* 847; Miller, "Polemical Rhetoric in 2 Peter (Part I)," 137.

[135] Rightly Müller, "Der 2. Petrusbrief," 327; contra Guthrie, *New Testament Introduction,* 847; Miller, "Polemical Rhetoric in 2 Peter (Part I)," 137.

for the elite, and it is evident that the word "knowledge" was important in 2 Peter. Peter's use of the word "knowledge," however, is not directed in any clear way against the adversaries. A licentious lifestyle is not unique to Gnosticism, and hence by itself it does not tell us anything about the worldview of the opponents. To conclude from 2 Pet 2:1 that the adversaries embraced Docetism misreads the verse, for nothing in particular is said about their Christology.[136] In context (see commentary) the denial probably relates to their lifestyle, not a discernible Christological heresy. The Gnostic hypothesis has survived on bits and pieces of evidence and the view that 2 Peter is a second-century document.[137] It does not genuinely explain what 2 Peter said about the false teachers, representing an imposition of data collected elsewhere on 2 Peter. Nor, contrary to Käsemann, is there any evidence Peter embraced Gnosticism.[138] He expected a new heaven and a new earth, not deliverance from the material world. He did not dismiss the body per se in 1:4 but the lusts of this world that make people prize something more than God.

Neyrey has noticed some parallels between Epicurean teaching and the worldview of the opponents, suggesting that the opponents were either Epicureans or "scoffers."[139] Epicureans denied God's providential rule over the world, maintaining that the world operated without God's intervention.[140] In such a world God would not pronounce judgment, nor would there be a parousia. Human beings are free to choose their own way, and after death

---

[136] Riesner notes that there are actually many parallels between the false teaching in 2 Peter and the problems Paul encountered in Corinth, suggesting a possible early date ("Der Zweite-Petrus Brief," 135).

[137] The patchwork nature of the evidence is obvious from Caulley's essay, where he stitches together a few clues to support a Gnostic hypothesis ("The False Teachers in Second Peter"). Reading Caulley's work is instructive, for it clarifies that determinative evidence for Gnosticism is lacking.

[138] Käsemann, "Apologia for Primitive Christian Eschatology," 179–80.

[139] Neyrey, *2 Peter, Jude,* 122–28; cf. id., "Polemic in 2 Peter," 407–31. In the latter essay Neyrey notes his purpose is not to demonstrate that the opponents were Epicurean but merely to indicate where analogies exist. In his commentary, however, he says, "It is the hypothesis of this commentary that the opponents were either Epicureans, who rejected traditional theodicy, or 'scoffers' *(Apikoros),* who espoused a similar deviant theology" (p. 122).

[140] K. Berger is in substantial agreement with Neyrey's thesis, exploring the matter further by investigating some texts in Philo. He also argues that the author of 2 Peter responded to the opponents' slander of angels by resorting to the Pharisaic tradition, where regard for angels is linked with cultic purity ("Streit um Gottes Vorsehung: Zur Position der Gegner im 2. Petrusbrief," in Tradition and Re-interpretation in Jewish and Early Christian Literature: Essays in Honour of Jürgen H. Lebram, SPB 36 [Leiden: Brill, 1986], 121–35). There is no evidence in the letter, however, that Peter espoused cultic purity (rightly Kahmann ["Second Peter and Jude," 121]). Hence, the appeal to Pharisaic tradition is not substantiated by the evidence.

the body returns to the elements from which it is composed. Hence, in the Epicurean worldview humans cannot look forward to a future judgment in which rights and wrongs would be recompensed (2 Pet 2:1,3; 3:9). It is here that we could place the promise of freedom heralded by the opponents (2 Pet 2:19). Even though Epicurus himself did not espouse an immoral lifestyle, one could easily see how such a conclusion could be drawn from his teaching. Neyrey also sees an analogy to Epicurean thinking in the dismissal of the parousia as a myth since Epicureans often derided judgments in the future as mythical. Furthermore, they rejected prophecy since any definite predictions of the future would cancel out human freedom. We can certainly see some areas of commonality between the opponents and Epicurean thought, but it is unlikely that the opponents were full-fledged Epicureans. It is difficult to see how the false teachers could be Christian in any sense of the word if they embraced Epicurean thought. Any notion of Jesus as the Christ would be precluded by Epicureanism, and it is unclear that the opponents rejected Jesus as the Messiah. Epicureans believed God was completely inactive in the world, but the opponents simply may have argued that there would not be a future judgment or second coming of Christ.[141] They could have maintained, therefore, that God was working in the world currently and only denied future cataclysms. The latter makes better sense of their claim to be Christians. The promise of freedom represents the kind of distortions we see in Pauline opponents, without any suggestion of Epicureanism.[142] Neyrey illustrates some areas where the opponents' thinking may have intersected with Epicureanism, but we would go too far to identify or even associate them with Epicureans.

Instead of identifying the opponents precisely, we must be content, historically, with the limited information available to us regarding the false teachers. We know that they denied the parousia and that they were antinomians. Perhaps they drew upon Paul's letters to justify their libertinism. Their denial of the future coming of Christ probably was linked with the rejection of the future judgment. New Testament scholars have a penchant for attaching a name and a full-fledged theology to opponents so that they can be classified precisely. But in this instance we are limited to a rather sketchy outline of the theology of the false teachers. We face our distance from the original events here since the letter was written to Peter's churches, who knew the false teachers very well, and not to us.

---

[141] Kahmann thinks it is unclear that they even rejected a future judgment ("Second Peter and Jude," 119).

[142] Ibid., 119.

4. Structure

The structure of the letter is reflected in the following outline. No compelling reasons have been offered to doubt the unity of the letter.[143] Watson has analyzed the letter in terms of Greek rhetoric, seeing an Epistolary Prescript (1:1–2), an Exordium (1:3–15), the Probatio (1:6–3:13), and the Peroratio (3:14–18).[144] We noted in Jude that Watson's analysis reminds us that that letter was structured carefully, even though there are reasons to doubt that Jude or any New Testament letter writer followed the canons of Greek rhetoric. Watson's case for 2 Peter is much less convincing.[145] It is unclear that the analysis conforms to the letter as it is actually written. For instance, Watson identifies 2:10b–22 as a digression, and such a long digression calls into question whether the proposed analysis fits. It will be more helpful to examine the structure of the letter as it unfolds, so that we can avoid the error of imposing an alien structure upon it. The problem with many rhetorical analyses of New Testament letters is that they tend to force the data to fit the proposed outline. At some points rhetorical analyses are helpful because New Testament writers were effective communicators, and hence they inevitably used elements of Greek rhetoric. Nevertheless, it is quite another thing to argue that the letters were consciously structured in accord with such rhetoric.[146]

[143] Contra M. McNamara, "The Unity of Second Peter: A Reconsideration," *Scr* 12 (1960): 13–19. McNamara argues that 2 Peter 1 and 3 originally circulated independently, but no clear evidence can be adduced to support such a conclusion.

[144] D. F. Watson, *Invention, Arrangement, and Style: Rhetorical Criticism of Jude and 2 Peter,* SBLDS 104 (Atlanta: Scholars Press, 1988), 81–146. For an acceptance of Watson's argument with some adjustments, see Starr, *Sharers in Divine Nature,* 53–58. For another attempt to analyze the structure of 2 Peter, see G. K. Barr, "The Structure of Hebrews and of 1st and 2nd Peter," *IBS* 19 (1997): 17–31.

[145] See also the criticisms of Müller, "Der 2. Petrusbrief," 315–16.

[146] For instructive evaluations of the role of rhetoric in NT epistles, see S. E. Porter and T. H. Olbricht, *Rhetoric and the New Testament: Essays from the 1992 Heidelberg Conference* (Sheffield: JSOT Press, 1993); J. A. D. Weima, "What Does Aristotle Have to Do with Paul? An Evaluation of Rhetorical Criticism," *CTJ* 32 (1997): 458–68.

OUTLINE OF 2 PETER

I. Greeting (1:1–2)
II. God's Grace the Foundation for a Life of Godliness (1:3–11)
  1. Divine Provision (1:3–4)
  2. Pursue a Godly Life Diligently (1:5–7)
  3. Godly Virtues Necessary for Entrance into the Kingdom (1:8–11)
III. Peter's Apostolic Reminder (1:12–21)
  1. The Function of the Reminder: To Stir Them for Action (1:12–15)
  2. The Truth of Jesus' Coming Is Based on Eyewitness Testimony (1:16–18)
  3. The Truth of Jesus' Coming Is Based on the Prophetic Word (1:19–21)
IV. The Arrival, Character, and Judgment of False Teachers (2:1–22)
  1. The Impact of False Teachers (2:1–3)
  2. The Certain Judgment of the Ungodly and the Preservation of the Godly (2:4–10a)
  3. False Teachers Judged for Their Rebellion and Sensuality (2:10b–16)
  4. The Adverse Impact of the False Teachers on Others (2:17–22)
V. Reminder: The Day of the Lord Will Come (3:1–18)
  1. Scoffers Doubt the Coming Day (3:1–7)
  2. The Lord's Timing Is Different from Ours (3:8–10)
  3. Living Righteously because of the Future Day (3:11–18)

SECTION OUTLINE

I. GREETING (1:1–2)

I. GREETING (1:1–2)

[1]Simon Peter, a servant and apostle of Jesus Christ,

To those who through the righteousness of our God and Savior Jesus Christ have received a faith as precious as ours:

[2]Grace and peace be yours in abundance through the knowledge of God and of Jesus our Lord.

As in most other New Testament letters, Peter began by naming the sender, the recipients, and adding a greeting. The sender, "Simon Peter," is identified in the first words of the letter and the recipients by the phrase "to those who . . . have received a faith as precious as ours." The greeting is communicated in v. 2. Virtually all New Testament letters contain greetings that are more weighty than what is typical in Greco-Roman culture. Peter not only identified himself but explained why he was qualified to write to his readers. He was a slave and apostle of Jesus Christ. The recipients are described in terms of their faith in God, which is theirs by virtue of the righteousness of their God and Savior, Jesus Christ. Peter did not restrict himself to the usual "greetings" *(chairein)* of the Greco-Roman world, but he prayed that God's grace and peace would abound in their lives through the knowledge of God and the Lord Jesus. Some of the central themes of the letter appear in the greeting: the centrality of faith in the Christian life, the saving righteousness of God, the primacy of Jesus Christ, and the importance of knowing God and the Lord Jesus Christ. Indeed, the themes of grace and knowledge form an inclusio since the letter ends with an admonition to grow in the grace and knowledge of Jesus Christ (3:18).

1:1 The first unusual feature appears in the first word in the letter. Peter did not use the usual Greek term "Simon" (*Simōn)* to describe himself (as in, e.g., Matt 4:18; 10:2; 16:16–17; 17:25; John 1:40,42; Acts 10:5) but *Simeōn*—still translated "Simon" by English versions. The latter term is Semitic and would only be used in a Palestinian setting. The only other occasion in which Peter was called *Simeōn* was at the Jerusalem Council (Acts 15:14), where James appealed to Peter's testimony regarding Cornelius. The Palestinian flavor of the Council may explain the use of the term. The name *Simeōn* is also used of the Simon who pronounced a blessing on and prophesied about the infant Jesus (Luke 2:25,34). The Semitic flavor of Luke 1–2 is acknowledged by virtually all. Luke used the name in Jesus' genealogy (Luke 3:30), and one of the prophets bears the name *Simeōn* (Acts 13:1; cf. also *1 Macc* 2:65). The term *Simeōn* is an indication of an early date since it was not used in the second century.[1] Some scholars suggest that the pseudonymous author used the Semitic name to communicate "verisimilitude."[2] If this theory is true, it is difficult to see how "the author" was not engaging in deception. Bauckham tries to evade this conclusion by suggesting that the writer may have been "an associate of Peter's who belonged to Peter's circle in Rome."[3] This theory is more difficult to believe than the one that posits deliberate pseudonymity since it is quite improbable that someone in Rome would use Peter's Semitic name. Indeed, the terms "Peter" and "apostle" in this verse show that the letter claims to be from Peter himself, the apostle of Jesus Christ. I conclude that the Semitic *Simeōn* comes from Peter himself, and further it represents an authentic touch from the apostle Peter.

Peter designated himself as a "servant and apostle of Jesus Christ." The term "servant" *(doulos)* is better translated "slave." It demonstrates that Peter was under the authority of Jesus Christ, that he submitted to his lordship, and that he had no inherent authority. It is also the case, however, that the term *doulos* suggests honor. Peter was honored because he was a servant of Jesus Christ. In the Old Testament prominent men who served Yahweh were called his "servants": Abraham, Isaac, and Jacob (Exod 32:13; Deut 9:27); Moses (Deut 34:5; Josh 1:1–2; 1 Kgs 8:53,56); Samuel (1 Sam 3:9–10), and David (1 Sam 17:32; 2 Sam 3:18; 7:5,8,19–21,25–29).[4] In the New Testament, Paul (Rom 1:1; Gal 1:10; Phil 1:1; Titus 1:1), James (Jas 1:1), and Jude (Jude 1) are also called *douloi*. The term, then, not only suggests humility but the honor of serving Jesus Christ.[5]

Peter not only called himself a slave but also an "apostle of Jesus Christ." The term "apostle" in some contexts may refer to missionaries or messengers (Rom 16:7; 2 Cor 8:23; Phil 2:25), but neither of those meanings fits here. Peter was speaking more technically of those whom Jesus Christ specially called and appointed to serve as apostles (Matt 10:1–11:1; Mark 3:13–19; cf. Acts 1:21–26). The authority of the apostles is communicated in 2 Pet 3:2 and the high estimate of Paul (2 Pet 3:15–16). Peter,

---

[1] So C. Bigg, *The Epistles of St. Peter and St. Jude,* ICC (Edinburgh: T & T Clark, 1901), 248.

[2] See J. N. D. Kelly, *A Commentary on the Epistles of Peter and Jude,* Thornapple Commentaries (Grand Rapids: Baker, 1981), 296. Cf. B. Reicke, *The Epistles of James, Peter, and Jude,* AB (Garden City: Doubleday, 1964), 150.

[3] R. Bauckham, *Jude, 2 Peter* (Waco: Word, 1983), 167.

[4] See R. Rengstorf, *TDNT* 2.268, 276–77.

[5] See esp. J. H. Neyrey, *2 Peter, Jude,* AB (Garden City: Doubleday, 1993), 144–45.

therefore, was not merely sharing his opinion in his letter. He wrote as a commissioned slave of Jesus Christ and his appointed apostle. He wrote authoritatively to a church threatened by false teachers.

Peter did not identify the recipients geographically, though they probably were Gentiles.[6] He described them as receiving a faith that has equal privileges. The word "received" *(lanchousin)* connotes the receiving of something by lot. Zechariah obtained by lot the privilege of offering incense in the temple (Luke 1:9). Roman soldiers cast lots to see who would get Jesus' garment (John 19:24). Judas was appointed to serve in an apostolic ministry (Acts 1:17). In each instance receiving something by lot is a gift that one receives.[7] According to Peter, what was received was "faith" in God or Jesus Christ. Most scholars maintain that faith refers here to a body of teaching or doctrine (cf. Jude 3,20).[8] One would expect Peter, however, to speak of faith being "handed down" or "transmitted" rather than received if it refers to doctrine. Hence, Peter likely referred to personal and subjective faith in God and/or Jesus Christ.[9] The statement is remarkable indeed. Faith, which is necessary for salvation, is a divine gift. It cannot be produced by the mere will of human beings but must be received from God himself. He appointed, as it were by lot, that Peter's readers would receive such faith.

It is difficult to know whom Peter had in mind in saying that theirs was "a faith as precious as ours." The word "precious" *(isotimon)* signifies that they had equal privileges and honor as others. The translation "equal standing" in the RSV communicates more precisely what Peter intended than the NIV's "precious," since the latter focuses unduly on the emotional value of the gift. Josephus used the term to refer to civic equality (*Ant.* 12.119). Some scholars maintain that Peter compared the privileges of the apostles with that of the readers.[10] It is difficult to see, however, why Peter would make this particular point to the readers. Others argue that Peter referred to

---

[6] So A. Vögtle, *Der Judasbrief, Der 2 Petrusbrief,* EKKNT (Neukirchen-Vluyn: Neukirchener Verlag, 1994), 127.

[7] "In this sentence the point of λαγχάνειν is that faith has come to them from God with no co-operation on their part" (H. Hanse, "λαγχάνω," *TDNT* 4.2).

[8] E.g., Kelly, *Peter and Jude*, 296; K. H. Schelke, *Der Petrusbrief—Der Judasbrief,* HTKNT (Freiburg: Herder, 1980), 185; H. Paulsen, *Der Zweite Petrusbrief und der Judasbrief,* KEK (Göttingen; Vandenhoeck & Ruprecht, 1992), 104.

[9] Rightly M. Green, *The Second Epistle General of Peter and the General Epistle of Jude,* 2d ed., TNTC (Grand Rapids: Eerdmans, 1988), 68; Bauckham, *Jude, 2 Peter,* 168; D. J. Moo, *2 Peter, Jude,* NIVAC (Grand Rapids: Zondervan, 1997), 34–35; J. D. Charles, "The Language and Logic of Virtue in 2 Peter 1:5–7," *BBR* 8 (1998): 66.

[10] J. Calvin, *Commentaries on the Catholic Epistles* (Grand Rapids: Eerdmans, 1948), 366; Bigg, *Peter and Jude,* 250; Kelly, *Peter and Jude,* 297; Bauckham, *Jude, 2 Peter,* 167; E. Fuchs and P. Reymond, *La Deuxième Épître de Saint Pierre, L'Épître de Saint Jude,* CNT (Neuchâtel–Paris: Delachaux & Niestlé, 1980), 44–46. This interpretation is ancient. See Andreas and Oecumenius in *James, 1–2 Peter, 1–3 John, Jude,* ACCS (Downers Grove: InterVarsity, 2000), 130.

the historical contrast between Jews and Gentiles.[11] Etched in the mind of every Jew was their special place as God's chosen people. The inclusion of the Gentiles on an equal basis with the Jews was stunning to the early Jewish Christians (cf. Acts 10:1–11:18; Eph 2:11–3:13), a truth that sunk in slowly. Still, there is no clear indication that Jew-Gentile tensions inform 2 Peter, and hence Peter likely made the general point that all believers of all places, classes, and ethnic backgrounds share the same blessings.[12]

Since Peter emphasized the equality of privilege among believers, it is not surprising that many think the "righteousness of God" *(dikaiosynē tou theou)* refers to God's fairness and equity in granting equal salvation.[13] Despite the popularity of this interpretation, I think it is mistaken. The phrase "through the righteousness of our God and Savior" modifies the participle "received." The emphasis on God's grace and gift in the context (cf. 1:3–4) suggests that fairness is not the most natural meaning in context. The gift of faith given by God is not understood in the New Testament to be "fair" but entirely of grace. Hence, God's righteousness here does not denote his fairness but his saving righteousness.[14] This accords with the Old Testament, where God's righteousness is parallel to his "salvation" (Pss 22:31; 31:1; 35:24,28; 40:10; Isa 42:6; 45:8,13; 51:5–8; Mic 6:5; 7:9). The faith received, then, is rooted in God's saving righteousness, his free gift of salvation, which is in accord with his steadfast love and mercy.[15] The interpretation favored here may also be supported by the reference to the Pauline writings (3:15–16), indicating that Peter knew and agreed with Paul's theology of God's saving righteousness.

The source of God's saving righteousness is Jesus Christ. The Greek construction here is particularly interesting. It literally reads "the righteousness of our God and Savior Jesus Christ" *(dikaiosynē tou theou hēmōn kai sōtēros Iēsou Christou)*. The grammar clearly indicates that Jesus Christ is called "God" in this verse.[16] The structure of the clause accords with the

---

[11] So J. B. Mayor, *The Epistle of St. Jude and the Second Epistle of St. Peter* (1907; reprint, Grand Rapids: Baker, 1965), 81; Moo, *2 Peter, Jude*, 34. Against this Fuchs and Reymond object that the Jew/Gentile conflict is over (*2 Pierre, Jude*, 44).

[12] N. Hillyer, *1 and 2 Peter, Jude,* NIBC (Peabody: Hendrickson, 1992), 157.

[13] Mayor, *Jude and Second Peter,* 81; Bigg, *Peter and Jude*, 250; Kelly, *Peter and Jude*, 297; Bauckham, *Jude, 2 Peter*, 168; G. Schrenk, "δικαιοσυνη," *TDNT* 2.198; J. M. Starr, *Sharers in Divine Nature: 2 Peter 1:4 in Its Hellenistic Context,* ConBNT 33 (Stockholm: Almqvist &: Wiksell, 2000), 41–42; Vögtle, *Judasbrief, 2 Petrusbrief,* 133.

[14] So M. Luther, *Commentary on Peter & Jude* (Grand Rapids: Kregel, 1990), 232; Calvin, *Catholic Epistles*, 366; Moo, *2 Peter, Jude*, 35; J. D. Charles, *Virtue amidst Vice: The Catalog of Virtues in 2 Peter 1,* JSNTSup 150 (Sheffield: Academic Press, 1997), 160. Cf. C. Spicq, *Les Épîtres de Saint Pierre,* SB (Paris: Gabalda, 1966), 208.

[15] This interpretation is supported by the NLT, which translates the last clause "who makes us right with God."

[16] See Bigg's excellent discussion (*Peter and Jude,* 250–52). Cf. T. Callan, "The Christology of the Second Letter of Peter," *Bib* 82 (2001): 253; Kelly, *Peter and Jude,* 298; Bauckham, *Jude, 2 Peter,* 168–69; Starr, *Sharers in Divine Nature,* 29; Paulsen, *Petrusbrief und Judasbrief,* 104–5.

famous rule of G. Sharp, that when two singular nouns, which are not proper nouns, fall under the same article, they refer to the same entity.[17] The phrase used here fits every part of this definition. If Peter wanted to distinguish Jesus Christ from the Father, he would have inserted an article before the noun "Savior." The pronoun "our" also indicates that only one person is referred to here. Moreover, in four parallel texts "Lord and Savior" refers in every case to the same person, Jesus Christ (2 Pet 1:11; 2:20; 3:2,18). The primary reason some scholars doubt this interpretation is that the New Testament writers rarely use "God" explicitly in reference to Jesus Christ.[18] Nonetheless, in a number of texts Jesus Christ is surely called God (John 1:1,18; 20:28; Rom 9:5; Titus 2:13; Heb 1:8),[19] though the intention is never to teach a form of modalism. To deny such a reading here would be to violate the clear sense of the grammar. Bigg rightly remarks, "Yet the first and sovereign duty of the commentator is to ascertain, and to guide himself by the grammatical sense."[20] The glory of Jesus Christ is emphasized as well at the conclusion of the letter in the doxology (3:18), so that the letter is bounded by the theme of Christ's supremacy. Jesus Christ is both God and Savior. The term "Savior" often was used of divine rulers in the Caesar cult, but there is no evidence that Peter countered such views in the letter.[21] Finally, Callan effectively argues that the attribution of "Lord" with reference to Jesus Christ implies his deity since the same title also refers to God.[22] He thinks that Jesus Christ received the title "Lord" in 1:2,8,11,14,16; 2:20; 3:18, and the Father is called "Lord" in 2:9,11; 3:8,10,12. Even though scholars debate whether the Father or Christ is called "Lord" in some of these verses (see commentary on the relevant verses), Callan's point still stands, for there is no doubt that both the Father and Christ are called "Lord." He is also correct in suggesting that such a title for Christ points to Jesus' divinity.

1:2 The first words of the greeting are in exact agreement with 1 Pet 1:2. Peter infused the greeting with Christian content by using the word "grace" *(charis)*. The term is not perfunctory, for we have already seen in

---

[17] D. B. Wallace restates Sharp's rule in the following way: "In the TSKS construction, the second noun refers to the same person mentioned with the first noun" (*Greek Grammar Beyond the Basics* [Grand Rapids: Zondervan, 1996], 271–72). Wallace is also careful to note that Sharp's rule applied only with "personal, singular, and non-proper nouns." See also discussion on pp. 276–77.

[18] See the hesitation in Neyrey (*2 Peter, Jude,* 147–48).

[19] For a careful analysis of these texts, see M. J. Harris, *Jesus as God: The New Testament Use of Theos in Reference to Jesus* (Grand Rapids: Baker, 1992).

[20] Bigg, *Peter and Jude,* 251. See also Fornberg, *An Early Church in a Pluralistic Society,* 83, 142–43.

[21] Fuchs and Reymond suggest the term may have been used to counter the emperor cult or incipient Gnosticism (*2 Pierre, Jude,* 45). For background on the term, see W. Foerster, "σωτήρ," *TDNT* 7.1004–12.

[22] Callan, "Christology of Second Peter," 254–55; cf. also Schelke, *Der Petrusbrief—Der Judasbrief,* 185.

v. 1 that God has granted faith to the readers through his saving righteousness. Verses 3–4 continue in this vein, reminding us that God has given his people everything so that they may be like him. The term "peace" represents a typical Jewish greeting, and the order may be significant. Those upon whom God has bestowed his grace experience his peace. Peter prayed that God would multiply his grace and peace in the lives of the readers, for he knew that their progress in the Christian life depended upon God alone.

The greeting in 2 Peter does not merely conform to what is written in 1 Peter, which we would expect if the letter were pseudonymous. Peter added a distinctive wrinkle, praying that God's grace and peace would abound "through the knowledge of God and of Jesus our Lord." English readers may wonder if Peter identified Jesus as God as he did in v. 1. The answer is no. The construction is quite different, for "Jesus" is a proper name, and therefore Sharp's rule does not apply in this instance. God the Father and Jesus Christ as distinct persons are in view, which is typical in greetings (e.g., Rom 1:7; 1 Cor 1:3; 2 Cor 1:2; Gal 1:3; 2 John 3). Grace and peace are multiplied through knowing God and Jesus Christ our Lord. Such knowledge of God is personal and relational, but it also involves intellectual content.[23] Biblical writers never divorce the head and the heart in terms of spiritual growth. Grace and peace abound when believers know more about God and come to know God in a deeper way in the crucible of experience. "Knowledge" was a key word for Peter. It is probable that the term *epignōsis* focuses on conversion (1:3,8; 2:20).[24] It is doubtful, though, that we should separate *epignōsis* from *gnōsis* (1:5,6; 3:18).[25] The two terms are closely related in Hos 4:6. Knowledge of God and Christ begins, of course, at conversion, but it is difficult to sustain the view that Peter confined *epignōsis* to conversion and *gnōsis* to postconversion growth.[26] It is common for Greek terms to overlap in meaning, and the prepositional prefix *epi* often adds nothing distinctive to a word. In this verse knowledge refers both to the knowledge of God they had at conversion and for its increase in their lives. It follows, therefore, that we have an inclusio since the book ends with an exhortation to grow in grace and knowledge *(gnōsis)* of Jesus Christ. Nor should we read into this a polemic against Gnosticism since the opponents do not clearly fit into such a mold.[27]

---

[23] Charles says on this subject, "Not the philosophic reflection of contemporary ethicists and moral philosophers, not the protognostic speculation of pseudo-Christian mystics, but the knowledge 'of God and of our Lord Jesus Christ'" (*Virtue amidst Vice,* 134).

[24] R. E. Picirilli, "The Meaning of 'Epignosis,'" *EvQ* 47 (1975): 85–93; Bauckham, *Jude, 2 Peter,* 169–70; Fornberg, *An Early Church in a Pluralistic Society,* 14.

[25] Rightly Bigg, *Peter and Jude,* 253; Starr, *Sharers in Divine Nature,* 136–38; Vögtle, *Judasbrief, 2 Petrusbrief,* 134.

[26] For the view that the two terms cannot be distinguished sharply, see Fuchs and Reymond, *2 Pierre, Jude,* 127–31, esp. 129–30.

[27] Against Kelly, *Peter and Jude,* 299; Reicke, *James, Peter, and Jude,* 151.

II. GOD'S GRACE: THE FOUNDATION FOR A LIFE OF GODLINESS (1:3–11)

1. Divine Provision (1:3–4)

3His divine power has given us everything we need for life and godliness through our knowledge of him who called us by his own glory and goodness. 4Through these he has given us his very great and precious promises, so that through them you may participate in the divine nature and escape the corruption in the world caused by evil desires.

The grammar of vv. 3–4 is complicated and difficult, and the NIV has smoothed it out for English readers.[1] Verse 3 begins with the word *hōs* ("as"). Most likely the "as" clause that introduces vv. 3–4 introduces the exhortation that follows in vv. 5–7.[2] This yields good sense, for God's power and grace are the foundation for the call to a life of godliness in vv. 5–7. Others argue that the "as" in v. 3 loosely connects vv. 3–4 with v. 2. If this is the case, *hōs* could be translated as "seeing that."[3] The logical rela-

[1] F. W. Danker argues that 2 Pet 1:3–11 is modeled on decretal forms of honor, which were well known in the Hellenistic world ("2 Peter 1: A Solemn Decree," *CBQ* 40 [1978]: 64–82). Danker's evidence indicates that the language of 2 Peter would have been familiar to Hellenistic readers. The parallels are not close enough, however, to conclude that 2 Peter 1 is modeled after Hellenistic decrees (rightly R. Bauckham, *Jude, 2 Peter* [Waco: Word, 1983], 174).

[2] So J. M. Starr, *Sharers in Divine Nature: 2 Peter 1:4 in Its Hellenistic Context,* ConBNT 33 (Stockholm: Almqvist &: Wiksell, 2000), 24–26; J. H. Neyrey, *2 Peter, Jude,* AB (Garden City: Doubleday, 1993), 150; J. D. Charles, *Virtue amidst Vice: The Catalog of Virtues in 2 Peter 1,* JSNTSup 150 (Sheffield: Academic Press, 1997), 84.

[3] So C. Bigg, *The Epistles of St. Peter and St. Jude,* ICC (Edinburgh: T & T Clark, 1901), 253; J. N. D. Kelly, *A Commentary on the Epistles of Peter and Jude,* Thornapple Commentaries (Grand Rapids: Baker, 1981), 299; Bauckham, *Jude, 2 Peter,* 173; T. Fornberg, *An Early Church in a Pluralistic Society: A Study of 2 Peter,* ConBNT 9 (Lund: Gleerup, 1977), 86.

tionship between the verses if we follow this latter interpretation would be as follows. In v. 2 Peter prayed that grace and peace would abound in the knowledge of God and of Jesus Christ. Verse 3 explains the resources believers have through knowing God. Those who know God have everything they need for life and godliness. A decision is difficult here since the grammar is rather awkward. We probably should see vv. 3–4 as linked with vv. 5–7, for the salutation would be unusually long if vv. 3–4 were joined with vv. 1–2.[4] Furthermore, it seems to make the most sense to see vv. 3–4 as the presupposition for the exhortation in vv. 5–7.[5] The contents of vv. 3–4 are crucial in interpreting the imperatives that follow in vv. 5–7. Peter did not fall prey to moralism or synergism. The call to godliness is rooted in and secured by God's grace; his gracious power supplies what he demands.

Unraveling the logic within vv. 3–4 is not easy. I understand the flow of thought as follows. Those who know God have everything they need for life and godliness, that is, they have everything they need for eternal life—the eschatological gift of life that has been inaugurated in the present age through the death and resurrection of Christ.[6] The reason they have everything they need for eternal life is explained in the last part of v. 3, namely, Christ has called believers by means of his moral excellence and glory. Christ's call, as Peter understood it, is an effective one, so that believers understand the glory of Christ when they are called to salvation. When God calls or speaks, it is so, as when he said, "Let there be light" (Gen 1:3). The call of Christ, then, is effective and performative.

Understanding the connection between vv. 3 and 4 is, if anything, more difficult. Identifying the antecedent of the pronoun "these" *(hōn)* is the subject of debate. It probably refers back to "his own glory and goodness" (v. 3). We could say that Christ has given precious and very great promises to his people as they perceive his glory and moral beauty. The glory of Christ is not limited to his moral excellence, but his moral excellence and goodness are what Peter emphasized here. And through these promises (*toutōn* in Greek) believers participate even now in the divine nature, since they have escaped the corruption that is in the world, a corruption that has its roots in evil desire. Peter was not saying, of course, that believers are sinless now. In one sense believers have already escaped the corruption of the world and are like God even now, but the process will not be completed until the day of the Lord. Only on the last day will believ-

---

[4] So Starr, *Sharers in Divine Nature,* 24.

[5] One of the problems with this interpretation is that the words καὶ αὐτὸ τοῦτο δὲ in v. 5 often point forward in the text instead of backward. Still, a backward reference is not impossible here (see Starr, *Sharers in Divine Nature*, 25).

[6] Fornberg argues that "life" is closely related to "godliness," so that "life" here has an ethical meaning (*An Early Church in a Pluralistic Society,* 90).

ers be free from sin and fully like God.

1:3 When Peter referred to "his divine power," it is difficult to know whether he referred to God or Christ. Some commentators think Christ is in view since he is actually called God in v. 1.[7] Others think it is more likely that Peter would refer to the Father as the one possessing "divine power."[8] The immediate antecedent in v. 2 is Christ rather than God, and hence a reference to Christ would be natural. In addition, the word "power" *(dynamis)* is also used in v. 16, where it clearly refers to Christ, suggesting that the same conclusion should be drawn here. Even though Peter likely referred to Christ, the language is ambiguous and hence certainty is precluded.[9] The ambiguity in the text indicates that Peter did not clearly distinguish between God and Christ. We can conclude from this that God and Christ were venerated equally.

The same question arises with the word "called." Does it refer to Christ or the Father? Typically in the New Testament calling is attributed to God (cf. though Rom 1:6), and hence a reference to the Father is certainly fitting. If we understand "his divine power" to refer to Christ, then Christ is the immediate antecedent.[10] A decision is again remarkably difficult. Perhaps it is slightly preferable, given the antecedent, to identify Christ as the one who calls.[11]

The main point of the first clause is that Christ has provided everything believers need for "life and godliness." The word "us" refers to all believers, not merely the apostles or Jewish Christians. It is unlikely that Peter restricted what he said to any particular group of believers.[12] When Peter referred to "life"

---

[7] Bigg, *Peter and Jude,* 253; Bauckham, *Jude, 2 Peter,* 177; D. J. Moo, *2 Peter, Jude,* NIVAC (Grand Rapids: Zondervan, 1997), 41; A. Vögtle, *Der Judasbrief, Der 2 Petrusbrief,* EKKNT (Neukirchen-Vluyn: Neukirchener Verlag, 1994), 138.

[8] So Kelly, *Peter and Jude,* 300; D. G. Horrell, *The Epistles of Peter and Jude,* EC [Peterborough: Epworth, 1998), 149.

[9] Starr wisely remarks: "Where 2 Peter could easily have specified Christ's agency in 1:3–4, then, he is content to imply it, leaving open the possibility of understanding God as the agent. This is not especially surprising, since 2 Peter would have assumed that behind Christ stands God as the one who prompts the Christ event" (*Sharers in Divine Nature,* 34).

[10] So Fornberg, *An Early Church in a Pluralistic Society,* 81, 144; T. Callan, "The Christology of the Second Letter of Peter," *Bib* 82 (2001): 253; Starr, *Sharers in Divine Nature,* 32; Kelly, *Peter and Jude,* 300–301.

[11] For another view see Vögtle, *Judasbrief, 2 Petrusbrief,* 138. E. Fuchs and P. Reymond argue that God and Jesus are mentioned respectively, so that, in their view, we have a reference to God's power and Christ's calling (*La Deuxième Épître de Saint Pierre, L' Épître de Saint Jude,* CNT [Neuchâtel–Paris: Delachaux & Niestlé, 1980], 50, n. 2). The diversity among commentators demonstrates how difficult it is to make a decision, indicating again that Peter himself did not unambiguously resolve the matter for readers. The problem is complicated further because Peter already had called Jesus Christ "God" in v. 1.

[12] Rightly Bauckham, *Jude, 2 Peter,* 177; Vögtle, *Judasbrief, 2 Petrusbrief,* 138–39. Vögtle observes that all Christians are called in 1:10.

(zōen), eternal life is intended. Believers have eternal life even now and yet await the day when such life will be consummated at the eschaton. "Godliness" *(eusebeian)* is linked to life because the latter is not gained without the former. Eternal life is not merely the experience of bliss but also involves transformation, so that believers are morally perfected and made like God.[13] Hence, believers should live in a godly way even now, though perfection in godliness will not be ours until the day Christ returns. The word "godliness" anticipates 3:11, where the coming of the Lord should be an incentive to godliness (cf. 1:6). The teaching of the opponents is insidious because their denial of the Lord's coming impedes the quest for godliness. Only those who are godly will experience eternal life, and hence it is fitting that Christ's "divine power" is the source of godliness. Only God can make people godly.

The church must not conclude that godliness comes from their own inherent abilities since the gifts given to believers are rooted in the knowledge of Christ.[14] Everything needed for eternal life is mediated through the knowledge of the Christ, who calls believers to himself. The word for knowledge is again *epignōsis* (cf. 1:2), referring to the encounter with Jesus Christ that began in conversion and continues thereafter. The focus is on conversion since Peter referred to God's calling *(kalesantos).* English readers are apt to understand calling in terms of an invitation that can be accepted or rejected. Peter had something deeper in mind. God's call is effective, awakening and creating faith. Paul referred to calling in this way regularly (e.g., Rom 4:17; 8:30; 9:12,24–26; 1 Cor 1:9; 7:15; Gal 1:6,15; 5:8,13; 1 Thess 2:12; 4:7; 5:24; 2 Thess 2:14; 1 Tim 6:12; 2 Tim 1:9). More significantly, the word "called" also has this meaning in 1 Peter (1:15; 2:9,21; 3:9; 5:10). First Peter 2:9 indicates that conversion is in view, for God called believers out of darkness into his marvelous light. The terminology reminds us that God is the one who called light out of darkness (Gen 1:3). Some scholars maintain that the calling of the apostles is in view,[15] but it is not likely that Peter restricted such to the apostles.

Christ calls believers "by his own glory and goodness."[16] "Glory" *(doxa)*

---

[13] Bauckham fails to see that eternal life here is linked with godliness and hence misconstrues the relationship (*Jude, 2 Peter,* 178).

[14] Cf. also Charles, *Virtue amidst Vice,* 161.

[15] Kelly, *Peter and Jude,* 301.

[16] Bauckham, *Jude, 2 Peter,* 178; Moo, *2 Peter, Jude*, 42; Starr, *Sharers in Divine Nature,* 40, n. 59. Bauckham argues that κάλεω εἰς would be more likely if the translation "called *to*" were intended rather than "called *through*" (cf. Col 3:15; 1 Thess 2:12; 1 Tim 6:12). Second Timothy 1:9 may indicate that the dative can be translated "called to." Still, such an interpretation seems less likely. The variant reading διά, though clearly secondary, may indicate that some scribes support the interpretation suggested here. Bigg thinks that ἰδίᾳ δόξῃ καὶ ἀρετῇ are linked with the verb δεδωρημένης (*Peter and Jude*, 254). But the word order suggests that they should be attached to the participle καλέσαντος.

here refers to Christ's splendor and majesty as a divine being, not his "fame or honor."[17] The word "goodness" *(aretē)* refers to the moral life of believers in 1:5. Peter used the term (RSV "excellence") that was commonly used in Greek literature for moral virtue.[18] When combined with "glory," "goodness" refers to the divine moral excellence of Christ, focusing especially on the beauty of his goodness.[19] Some scholars think Peter's use of this term, along with "divine" *(theias)*—another term uncommon in the New Testament—indicates pseudonymity. Would a Palestinian fisherman write like this? But Peter also used the term *aretē* in 1 Pet 2:9, and his use of Hellenistic terms reveals that he wanted to communicate in the idiom of his readers. This could merely indicate that Peter was not closeted off from the rest of the world, and he was familiar with Hellenistic culture.

The terms "glory" and "goodness" together point to the same reality.[20] Those whom God saves are called by Christ, and this calling is accomplished through the knowledge of Christ's glory and goodness. In other words, when Christ calls people to himself, they perceive the beauty and loveliness of his moral character. His character becomes exceedingly attractive to them, and they trust God for their salvation. One of the central themes of Peter's letter emerges in this verse. Believers will be morally transformed, but the foundation for their transformation is God's grace. Peter here indirectly criticized the false teachers of chap. 2, for their lives were marked by moral anarchy, but those whom Christ calls have seen Christ's goodness and glory and will live a godly life.

1:4 The connection between vv. 3 and 4 is difficult to trace. The prepositional phrase "through these" *(di hōn)* joins the verses. What is the antecedent? Most scholars agree it is God's "glory and goodness."[21] What Peter was saying was that believers inherit God's promises as they come to know Christ, as they experience his moral excellence and glorious radiance in conversion. Great and precious promises have been given to God's people through the gospel, a gospel that provides everything believers need. What "promises" did Peter have in mind? Probably he had participation in "the divine nature" (1:4) particularly in mind. Such likeness to God will be the

---

[17] Similarly, Starr, *Sharers in Divine Nature,* 42.

[18] Charles emphasizes that Peter drew on Stoic vocabulary in these verses but incorporated the terms into a Christian worldview (*Virtue amidst Vice,* 134–38).

[19] Cf. Starr, *Sharers in Divine Nature,* 43–44.

[20] Bauckham agrees, but he thinks they point to divine power rather than to virtue (*Jude, 2 Peter,* 178–79).

[21] J. B. Mayor, *The Epistle of St. Jude and the Second Epistle of St. Peter* (1907; reprint, Grand Rapids: Baker, 1965), 87; Bigg, *Peter and Jude,* 255; Kelly, *Peter and Jude,* 301; M. Green, *The Second Epistle General of Peter and the General Epistle of Jude,* 2d ed., TNTC (Grand Rapids: Eerdmans, 1988), 72; Bauckham, *Jude, 2 Peter,* 179; Moo, *2 Peter, Jude*, 43; Starr, *Sharers in Divine Nature*, 26; N. Hillyer, *1 and 2 Peter, Jude,* NIBC (Peabody: Hendrickson, 1992), 161.

portion of believers fully when the Lord returns. And the word "promises" *(epangelmata)* directs our attention to the Lord's coming since there is a verbal connection to 2 Peter 3. We learn from chap. 3 that the false teachers deny Christ's future coming. They reject "the promise of his coming" (*hē epangelia tēs parousias autou,* 3:4). Even though the Lord's "promise" seems slow (3:9), it will become a reality. It is when the Lord comes, after all, that believers will experience fully likeness to Christ (1 John 3:2). Peter anticipated here later criticisms of the false teachers, for by denying the coming of the Lord they undercut the gospel that promises moral perfection when Christ returns. If there is no future coming of Christ, their salvation does not include the promise of likeness to God, and the gospel is a sham.

God's promises have been given to us "so that through them you may participate in the divine nature." The words "through them" *(dia toutōn)* almost certainly refer to God's promises and the reality these promises guarantee.[22] Again we see Peter's preference for Hellenistic terms since he spoke of "the divine nature" *(theias physeōs),* and presumably he wrote this way to speak to the cultural situation of his readers.[23] The other use of "divine" *(theios)* in the New Testament is found in Acts 17:29, where Paul spoke to those in Athens influenced by Greek culture.[24] What Peter meant by this is that believers are promised that they will be like God. The notion of sharing in the divine nature has exerted a tremendous influence in Eastern Christianity, where the doctrine of *theiōsis* (i.e., deification) has been emphasized.[25] Peter was not saying (nor did Eastern Christianity) that human beings will actually become divine or that they will share in the divine nature in every respect. Believers will share in the divine nature in that they will be morally perfected; they will share in the moral excellence that belongs to God (1:3).[26] Believers will "participate" *(koinōnoi)* in the divine nature, but they will not become gods.[27] This conclusion is borne out

[22] Rightly Bigg, *Peter and Jude,* 255; Kelly, *Peter and Jude,* 301; Bauckham, *Jude, 2 Peter,* 179; Fuchs and Reymond, *2 Pierre, Jude,* 52.

[23] For concept of divine nature in the Greco-Roman world, see Neyrey, *2 Peter, Jude,* 157–58.

[24] So Charles, *Virtue amidst Vice,* 137.

[25] See R. Rakestraw, "Becoming Like God: An Evangelical Doctrine of Theosis," *JETS* 40 (1997): 257–69; D. B. Clendenin, *Eastern Orthodox Christianity: A Western Perspective* (Grand Rapids: Baker, 1994), 117–37, 157–59.

[26] So Vögtle, *Judasbrief, 2 Petrusbrief,* 141. Fornberg rightly argues that the Stoic notion of the divine being inherent in humanity is not what Peter intended here (*An Early Church in a Pluralistic Society,* 86). He thinks the idea is that believers will obtain immortality (p. 88), but it is unclear, contra Fornberg, that the letter speaks to those influenced by mystery religions.

[27] A. Wolters argues that the phrase should be translated "partners of deity," not "sharers in the divine nature" ("'Partners of the Deity': A Covenantal Reading of 2 Peter 1:4," *CTJ* 25 [1990]: 28–44; id., "Postscript to 'Partners of the Deity,'" *CTJ* 26 [1991]: 418–20). Wolters has demonstrated the possibility, but not the probability, of his interpretation. But the word φύσις most naturally refers to God's nature. Wolters rightly notes that it can be glossed as "deity" in some instances.

by the careful study of Starr, where he investigates the terminology used by Peter with reference to his social world.[28] He analyzes the language Peter used here and compares it with similar notions in the Old Testament, Josephus, Philo, Plutarch, Stoicism, Pauline Christianity, and non-Pauline Christianity. He concludes from his comparative study that sharing in the divine nature does not mean "deified." Instead Peter maintained that believers will share in the moral qualities of Christ.[29]

Do believers share in the divine nature now, or is such participation exclusively future? Certainly the process will reach its consummation in the future, for only then will all of God's promises be fulfilled. Believers will not be morally perfected until Christ returns. Nevertheless, it is doubtful that Peter referred *only* to the future.[30] Even now believers are indwelt by the Holy Spirit and are like God to some extent.[31] Believers begin to know God and to be changed by him at their conversion. The last clause in v. 4 supports this interpretation as well. The NIV masks the function of the clause by turning it into a purpose clause that is parallel with "you may participate in the divine nature." In fact, the last clause is introduced by a participle *(apophygontes),* which can be translated as "having escaped." The logical relationship in the verse should be explained as follows: God has given saving promises to his people, so that they will become like God. They will become like God and are becoming like God because they have escaped "the corruption in the world caused by evil desires." Once again, some scholars argue that believers will escape the corruption of the world at death or when the Lord returns.[32] It is more likely, however, that Peter operated with an already-but-not-yet schema. Believers have already escaped the world's corruption in that they belong to God,[33] but the full realization of such a liberation will be theirs on the day of resurrection.[34] The parallel expression in 2 Pet 2:20 supports this interpretation. Peter, speaking of the lapse of the false teachers, said, "If they have escaped the corruption of the world by knowing our Lord and Savior Jesus Christ." The participle "escaped" is exactly the same word *(apophygontes)* and the same

---

[28] Starr, *Sharers in Divine Nature.*

[29] Perhaps, as my editor R. Clendenen suggests, we have an allusion to Gen 3:5,22, which refers to becoming like God.

[30] Rightly Starr, *Sharers in Divine Nature,* 47–48; against Bauckham, *Jude, 2 Peter,* 181–82; H. Paulsen, *Der Zweite Petrusbrief und der Judasbrief,* KEK (Göttingen; Vandenhoeck & Ruprecht, 1992), 108.

[31] For the notion that sharers of the divine nature refers to the Holy Spirit, see Bigg, *Peter and Jude*, 256).

[32] See especially Bauckham, *Jude, 2 Peter,* 182–83; Vögtle, *Judasbrief, 2 Petrusbrief,* 141–42.

[33] Rightly Kelly, *Peter and Jude,* 302; M. J. Kruger, "The Authenticity of 2 Peter," *JETS* 42 (1999): 668–69.

[34] Charles sees only a present fulfillment (*Virtue amidst Vice*, 161).

form (an aorist participle) as in 1:4. A different word for corruption is used—*phthora* in 1:4 and *miasma* in 2:20—but the idea is the same. Most important, Peter spoke of them as having escaped already the corruption of the world in coming to know Jesus Christ. We should interpret 1:4 similarly. Believers have already escaped the corruption of the world, but the completion of that process will occur on the day of the Lord.

The word "corruption" *(phthora)* refers to that which is perishing because it is part of the present world order. The natural world is corrupted because of the sin of human beings (Rom 8:21). Foods are corruptible and pass through the body after being consumed (Col 2:22). Human bodies are corruptible in the sense that they will die and are not immortal (1 Cor 15:42,50). Those who sow to the flesh will experience corruption forever, while those who sow to the Spirit will reap eternal life (Gal 6:8). The false teachers are slaves of corruption (2 Pet 2:19), and they are compared to animals that will experience dissolution (2 Pet 2:12). The "corruption" Peter had in mind is death and the coming judgment. Those who believe in Jesus Christ have escaped that future judgment even now.[35] The corruption in the world is rooted in evil desires. The NIV rightly interprets the Greek phrase (*en epithumia,* "in desire") to say "caused by evil desires." The root of corruption lies in desires for what is evil and wicked. In other words, Peter did not see the material world itself as evil; what corrupts is the selfish desire that dominates human beings.[36] Hence, there is no call to asceticism here. Those who have come to know Jesus Christ have had their desires transformed. Now they love goodness and holiness, whereas those ensnared in the world love what is evil.

2. Pursue a Godly Life Diligently (1:5–7)

[5]For this very reason, make every effort to add to your faith goodness; and to goodness, knowledge; [6]and to knowledge, self-control; and to self-control, perseverance; and to perseverance, godliness; [7]and to godliness, brotherly kindness; and to brotherly kindness, love.

The logical relationship between vv. 3–4 and vv. 5–7 is crucial. Verses 5–7 summon the readers to a life of virtue, but vv. 3–4 remind us that a life of godliness is rooted in and dependent upon God's grace. Believers should live in a way that pleases God *because* Christ has given them everything they need for life and godliness. The indicative of God's gift precedes and undergirds the imperative that calls for human exertion. Peter did not lapse,

[35] Rightly Mayor, *Jude and Second Peter,* 88; Moo, *2 Peter, Jude,* 44.

[36] So Fornberg, *An Early Church in a Pluralistic Society,* 89; Vögtle, *Judasbrief, 2 Petrusbrief,* 142.

therefore, into works righteousness here since he grounded his exhortations in God's merciful gifts.

The striking feature in these verses is the chain of eight virtues. It is doubtful, contrary to some commentators, that the number eight is selected because it is the perfect number.[37] Nor should we conclude that there are only eight virtues to be pursued. We make a mistake in detecting any significance in the number of virtues listed. Peter used a literary form here that is called *sorites,* in which we have a step-by-step chain that culminates in a climax. We see an example of this in *Wis* 6:17–20: "The beginning of wisdom is the most sincere desire for instruction, and concern for instruction is love of her, and love of her is the keeping of her laws, and giving heed to her laws is assurance of immortality, and immortality brings one near to God; so the desire for wisdom leads to a kingdom" (RSV). An example that is even closer appears in the Mishnah: "Heedfulness leads to cleanliness, and cleanliness leads to purity, and purity leads to abstinence, and abstinence leads to holiness, and holiness leads to humility, and humility leads to the shunning of sin, and the shunning of sin leads to saintliness, and saintliness leads to the gift of the Holy Spirit, and the Holy Spirit leads to the resurrection of the dead (*m. Sotah* 9:15).[38] When we examine the chain of virtues in 2 Peter, it is doubtful that we should understand each virtue as actually building on the previous one.[39] Charles insists that there is a logical progression.[40] He explains the order as follows: Faith is the root of all moral virtue, and such virtue is linked with what we do with our knowledge of God.[41] If we use this knowledge well, we will exercise self-control. Such self-control will give us ability to endure difficulties. Endurance will then lead to godliness in our relationships, and these relationships will be governed by brotherly affection and Christian love.

Even in Charles's analysis he seems to intertwine virtue and knowledge by implying that the former is somehow dependent on the latter.[42] It is difficult to see how goodness literally precedes knowledge. One could just as easily argue that we need knowledge in order to pursue what is good. Or, at

---

[37] Against Kelly, *Peter and Jude,* 305; Neyrey, *2 Peter, Jude,* 155.

[38] *The Mishnah,* trans. H. Danby (New York: Oxford University Press, 1933), 306–7. For other parallels see Bauckham, *Jude, 2 Peter,* 174–76.

[39] Rightly Bauckham, *Jude, 2 Peter,* 184–85; Vögtle, *Judasbrief, 2 Petrusbrief,* 150. Mayor observes that the relationship between each virtue is unclear (*Jude and Second Peter,* 91).

[40] Charles, *Virtue amidst Vice,* 145–46, 156–57; id., "The Language and Logic of Virtue in 2 Peter 1:5–7," *BBR* 8 (1998): 70–71.

[41] "First of all comes faith, which is the foundation and source of all good works." So Theophylact in *James, 1–2 Peter, 1–3 John, Jude,* ACCS (Downers Grove: InterVarsity, 2000), 133.

[42] Charles notes the common language between 1:5–7 and a first-century inscription in Asia Minor ("The Language and Logic of Virtue in 2 Peter 1:5–7," 71–72). Any literary dependence, however, is unlikely in my view.

the very least, we can conceive of how the two are mutually interrelated. Neither is it evident that one will only have self-control when one has knowledge. And, is it clear that self-control must precede endurance? The ethical chain of virtues, therefore, is more likely a literary device, and it would be a mistake to read anything into the order in which the virtues are listed. Practically, the matter is important, for the other interpretation could possibly lead one to work on one virtue at a time, thinking that one virtue must be "mastered" before moving on to another. Such a view of the Christian life smacks of moralism and a Ben Franklin approach to the Christian life, where we concentrate for a period of time on a particular virtue. Such a view is an invitation to self-effort instead of dependence upon God. There could be two exceptions to what has just been said. It does seem significant that the chain begins with faith and ends with love. Faith is the root of all the virtues, and love is the goal and climax of the Christian life.[43] Otherwise, we should not press the order of the virtues listed, nor should we think Peter encouraged his readers to work first on one virtue before moving to the next one.[44]

1:5 The phrase "for this very reason" links vv. 5–7 to vv. 3–4. Peter exhorted his readers to a godly life (vv. 5–7) because Christ has given them everything they need for a godly life, and they possess magnificent promises of future perfection. It would be a serious mistake, therefore, to dismiss the call to virtue as legalism or moralism. The exhortation to holiness is grounded in God's work of salvation as it has been accomplished in Jesus Christ.[45] As is typical in the New Testament, grace precedes demand. The priority of grace, however, does not cancel out strenuous moral effort. Believers are to "make every effort" or apply "all diligence" (NASB) in carrying out Peter's commands. A godly character does not emerge from passivity or lassitude. As Luther says, "They should prove their faith by their good works."[46]

The chain of virtues begins with "faith" *(pistis)*.[47] Some commentators maintain that Peter referred to "the faith" here, so that he meant by "faith" Christian doctrine.[48] It has already been argued that "faith" in 1:1 refers to

---

[43] Rightly Fuchs and Reymond, *2 Pierre, Jude,* 56. On the priority of faith see Charles, *Virtue amidst Vice,* 162.

[44] I am not suggesting, incidentally, that Charles falls into such an error, only that some might deduce such from the interpretation offered.

[45] Fornberg fails to clarify this crucial point in his explanation of the relationship between vv. 3–4 and vv. 5–7 (*An Early Church in a Pluralistic Society,* 97).

[46] M. Luther, *Commentary on Peter & Jude* (Grand Rapids: Kregel, 1990), 237.

[47] Charles discusses an inscription from first-century Asia Minor that lists many of the same virtues (*Virtue amidst Vice,* 139). Cf. also discussion of an inscription on pp. 146–47.

[48] E.g., Bigg, *Peter and Jude,* 257.

personal faith or trust.[49] The same is likely here. Trusting God is the root from which all the other virtues spring. Those who rely on God and his promises begin to live a new way. Peter's theology here is in accord with Paul's, who said that faith expresses itself in love (Gal 5:6). All the godly virtues in the Christian life find their source in faith, in trusting God for everything, and the culmination and climax of such faith is love. We should note that some of the virtues featured here are common in Greco-Roman culture, providing another indication that Peter drew some connections with the social world of his readers.[50]

Believers are to "add to" or supply with *(epichorēgēsate)* their faith "goodness" *(aretē)*. In Greek culture a benefactor *(chorēgos)* furnished what was necessary for choruses. Those who did such were known as generous and lavish benefactors.[51] The word *aretē,* probably best translated "moral excellence," was used in 1:3 to designate by what God has called believers. God's call, we argued, is effective. He creates the moral excellence he demands. Hence, it follows that the moral excellence of believers can only be attributed to God's grace. And yet New Testament writers never polarize divine sovereignty and human responsibility. Those whom God has effectively called to virtue are also to practice virtue with energy and intensity.

The term *aretē* is often used in Greek literature to describe those who are morally virtuous. Once again Peter used a term that would speak to the culture he addressed (cf. Phil 4:8). Believers are not only to pursue moral excellence but also "knowledge" *(gnōsis)*. Peter probably referred to the knowledge of God's will and ways that are necessary for every Christian. Indeed, the letter concludes with an exhortation to grow in the grace and "knowledge" of Jesus Christ (2 Pet 3:18). "Goodness" *(aretē)* and "knowledge" were closely allied in Stoic thought, but Charles notes that "knowledge" is distinct from the Stoic conception because it is not conceived as the foundation of one's ethical life.[52] True knowledge is rooted in God's grace. Bauckham separates too neatly *epignōsis* from *gnōsis,* saying that the former relates to conversion and the latter relates to progress in discernment for Christian living.[53] There is some truth in this characterization, but it should be noted that progress in all these moral virtues is necessary for

---

[49] Danker mistakenly sees a link to benefaction here and translates the term as "faithfulness" ("2 Peter 1," 460; so also Neyrey, *2 Peter, Jude,* 158–59). For a convincing explication of faith here, see Charles, *Virtue amidst Vice,* 140. Charles also argues that faith denotes trust instead of focusing on creedal belief.

[50] See discussion in Fornberg, *An Early Church in a Pluralistic Society,* 97–101; Charles, *Virtue amidst Vice,* 139–40. Fornberg observes that love is not commonly featured in Greek literature.

[51] See the discussion in Charles, *Virtue amidst Vice,* 148, though he probably goes too far in explaining the parallel.

[52] Ibid., 141.

[53] Bauckham, *Jude, 2 Peter,* 186.

one's heavenly inheritance, and hence progress in knowledge is necessary, ultimately, for eternal life.

1:6 Those who add knowledge to their lives should also be ardently seeking self-control *(enkrateia).* Paul identified self-control as one of the fruits of the Spirit (Gal 5:23; cf. 1 Cor 7:9; 9:25; Titus 1:8). Genuine knowledge can never exist apart from self-control (cf. 1 Pet 1:14). Self-restraint was one of the prized virtues in Hellenistic culture.[54] A sideways glance is cast here at the false teachers, for their lives are marked by dissolution and licentiousness.[55] They are characterized by sensuality (2:2), inflamed by sinful desires (2:10); they live for soft and comforting pleasures (2:13), never cease thinking of adultery (2:14), and are enslaved to corruption (2:19). Those who live a godly life exercise self-discipline and are able to restrain themselves so that they do not capitulate to sinful desires.

Believers should also add "endurance" *(hypomonē)* to self-restraint. The word "endurance" often describes the desired character of believers (Rom 5:3–4; 8:25; Col 1:11; 1 Thess 1:3–4; 1 Tim 6:11; 2 Tim 3:10; Titus 2:2; Heb 12:1; Jas 1:3–4; 5:11; Rev 2:2–3,19). The need to persevere is particularly important in the situation Peter addressed, for the opponents were threatening the church, attracting others to follow them (2:2), so that some who began in the way of the gospel had since abandoned it (2:20–22). Moral restraint must be combined with endurance and steadfastness for those who hope to win the eschatological prize.

The readers are also called to "godliness" *(eusebeia).* Another connection is forged with vv. 3–4 because believers have, by God's grace, already been given everything they need "for life and godliness" (1:3). Here we see that the imperative stands on the indicative. Christ has given believers everything to be godly, and yet believers must pursue godliness. The term godliness refers to piety or, more simply, to living a life that is like God.[56] Believers should live in a holy and "godly" way since Jesus is going to return (2 Pet 3:11). The word "godliness" is especially common in the Pastoral Epistles for living the kind of life that pleases God (1 Tim 2:2; 3:16; 4:7–8; 6:3,5–6,11; 2 Tim 3:5; Titus 1:1). Once again it was a virtue prized in Hellenistic society, indicating that Peter appropriated and recast a cultural ideal in a Christian framework.

1:7 The last two virtues focus on love. It is fitting, as already noted, that love should climax the chain since love is the supreme Christian virtue. Peter exhorted his readers first to pursue "brotherly kindness" *(philadel-*

---

[54] See W. Grundmann, "ἐγκράτεια," *TDNT* 2.340–41.

[55] See especially Neyrey, *2 Peter, Jude,* 159–60.

[56] Cf. W. Foerster, "εὐσέβεια," *TDNT* 7.175–85.

phia). The term is used elsewhere in biblical exhortations (Rom 12:10; 1 Thess 4:9; Heb 13:1; 1 Pet 1:22; cf. 1 Pet 3:8). The focus is on the love between fellow believers, on the family-like devotion that should characterize the Christian community. Here Peter used a word that is distinctive of the Christian community in the sense that all believers are brothers and sisters.[57] The opponents surely do not display such love (2:13–14,17). The chain climaxes with Christian love, the supreme evidence that one is a believer.[58] Paul said love is the goal of Christian instruction (1 Tim 1:5). It is the most excellent way (1 Cor 12:31–13:13), the virtue that sums up all other virtues (Col 3:14). Anyone who loves will possess the other qualities Peter mentioned. The false teachers are lacking in faith and love and hence are not genuine believers at all.

3. Godly Virtues Necessary for Entrance into the Kingdom (1:8–11)

8For if you possess these qualities in increasing measure, they will keep you from being ineffective and unproductive in your knowledge of our Lord Jesus Christ. 9But if anyone does not have them, he is nearsighted and blind, and has forgotten that he has been cleansed from his past sins.

10Therefore, my brothers, be all the more eager to make your calling and election sure. For if you do these things, you will never fall, 11and you will receive a rich welcome into the eternal kingdom of our Lord and Savior Jesus Christ.

The word "for" *(gar)* connects vv. 8–11 with vv. 5–7. If the virtues listed in vv. 5–7 are abounding in the lives of believers, their knowledge of Jesus Christ is fruitful and effective (v. 8). On the other hand, if these qualities are lacking, such persons are blind, and they have forgotten about their forgiveness of sins (v. 9). What precisely was Peter saying in such statements? Verses 10–11 help us clarify what he had in mind. Believers are enjoined to confirm their calling and election *by practicing the virtues* described in vv. 5–7. It is only by practicing these virtues that the readers will avoid stumbling. That is, the readers will escape apostasy if they put into practice such godly qualities. In this way, that is, by living a godly life, they will enter into the eternal kingdom on the day of the Lord. It would be tempting for some who are familiar with Paul to dismiss this theology as a form of works righteousness. But Paul himself insisted that those who practice the works of the flesh will not inherit God's kingdom (Gal 5:21). He taught the

---

[57] Cf. Neyrey, *2 Peter, Jude,* 161; Fornberg, *An Early Church in a Pluralistic Society,* 100. Charles thinks it is equivalent to φιλανθρωπία in paganism (*Virtue amidst Vice*, 144), but he ignores the familial dimension of the word Peter used.

[58] Seeing love as the supreme virtue distinguishes Peter from Stoicism (Charles, *Virtue amidst Vice*, 145).

unrighteous that they would be excluded from the kingdom (1 Cor 6:9–11). Moreover, Peter had not abandoned the fundamental character of God's grace. We have already seen in 1:3–4 that everything needed for life and godliness has been given to us. Christ's call is so powerful that we are promised that we will obtain glory and moral virtue. Even now believers have escaped the world's corruption in the sense that their desires have been changed, though the consummation of that process will only occur on the day of the Lord.

1:8 The word *tauta* is rightly rendered by the NIV as "these qualities," pointing back to the chain of virtues in vv. 5–7. Peter said two things about these qualities. First, they must exist in the lives of his readers *(hyparchonta)*. The NIV obscures this by translating the phrase "if you possess these qualities in increasing measure." The NIV merges the two participles "existing" and "increasing" *(pleonazonta)*. The NRSV keeps them distinct, "If these things are yours and are increasing among you."[59] The second requirement is evident already from what has just been said. The qualities must abound" *(pleonazonta)* in believers. Most translations use the word "increasing," and this rendering is certainly defensible. However, it could possibly suggest to English readers that we are able to calculate our improvement in godliness as each year passes, as if we become five percent more loving each year. What Peter wanted to emphasize was not that precise. His point was that godly qualities must both exist and overflow in the lives of his readers. Surprisingly, Bigg rejects the interpretation proposed here on the grounds that it would squelch the difference between *hyparchonta* and *pleonazonta*.[60] But if *pleonazonta* means "abounding," that is hardly the same thing as saying that certain qualities "exist" in one's life. The latter idea says that the virtues are discernible in a person's life, but the former means that they are overflowing. The two ideas are scarcely the same.

If the godly qualities of vv. 5–7 exist and abound in the lives of believers, they are neither "ineffective" *(argous)* nor "unfruitful" *(akarpous)* in their knowledge of Christ.[61] Peter made the point negatively. It could be restated as follows: When the virtues both exist and abound in believers, believers are effective and fruitful with respect to their knowledge of Christ. The word "ineffective" is used of idle workers who are wasting their day in the marketplace instead of working (Matt 20:3,6). James said that faith without works is "idle" or "ineffective" (Jas 2:20). Being without fruit reminds us of the parable of the soils, where the seed sown among thorns is unfruitful because it is choked by the worries of the world and the deceitfulness of money (Matt 13:22; cf. Jude 12 and by contrast Col 1:10). Peter

---

[59] The participles are conditional (Fuchs and Reymond, *2 Pierre, Jude,* 57).

[60] Bigg, *Peter and Jude,* 258.

[61] The word εἰς means "in." The use of εις for ἐν is typical of Hellenistic Greek.

thought that believers must practice godly virtues to receive the eschatological blessing of eternal life. But he also was saying that those who lack godly virtues and are not abounding with them give no indication that they are believers. Or, as Fuchs and Reymond say, there is no virtue without knowledge, but also there is no knowledge without ethics.[62] The ineffectiveness and unfruitfulness relate to their knowledge *(epignōsis)* of the Lord Jesus Christ. Perhaps the opponents are particularly in view, for their libertine lifestyle contradicts their profession of faith. Peter likely meant that they give no evidence that their conversion is genuine.[63]

1:9 Verse 9 elaborates (*gar,* usually translated "for"; see NRSV, ESV) on v. 8. If the virtues *(tauta)* are lacking, such people are "blind" *(tuphlos).* The NIV actually reverses the order of the Greek in translating "nearsighted and blind," for the Greek says "blind" and "nearsighted" *(myōpazōn).* This latter word is rare and has provoked some discussion. Perhaps the idea is that those who are nearsighted actually shut their eyes, so that they cannot see anything at all.[64] If this is the case, then the second term emphasizes their decision to shut their eyes. Bauckham objects that people who are nearsighted screw their eyes nearly shut to see more clearly and are therefore not blind.[65] Perhaps it is best to understand the participle as "shortsighted," that is, as clarifying in what sense people become blind.[66] They are blind in that they fail to see what they should see. They have become so shortsighted that they have forgotten the most important reality of all. The metaphor, then, could be used for rhetorical effect, not to convey a new thought. This may fit with the next clause, which says that such a person has "forgotten that he has been cleansed from his past sins." The cleansing *(katharismou)* from past sins refers to baptism, where the baptismal waters symbolize the washing away of sins and hence the forgiveness of sins.[67] Moo thinks that forgiveness of sins is intended without any clear reference to baptism.[68] There is no need to divorce forgiveness and baptism since in the early church virtually all converted believers were baptized immediately.[69] They would naturally recall their baptism when they thought about

---

[62] Fuchs and Reymond, *2 Pierre, Jude,* 57.

[63] So Kelly, *Peter and Jude,* 307; Bauckham, *Jude, 2 Peter,* 188–89. In this context Peter was not speaking of growing more in one's knowledge of Christ but conceived of knowing Christ as the foundation for growth (contra B. Reicke, *The Epistles of James, Peter, and Jude,* AB [Garden City: Doubleday, 1964], 154; Green, *2 Peter and Jude,* 81).

[64] Kelly, *Peter and Jude,* 308; Charles, *Virtue amidst Vice,* 149–50.

[65] Bauckham, *Jude, 2 Peter,* 189.

[66] Cf. Horrell, *The Epistles of Peter and Jude,* 152.

[67] So Mayor, *Jude and Second Peter,* 97.

[68] Moo, *2 Peter, Jude,* 48.

[69] But neither should we conclude that the expression used here points to second-century Christianity (contra Paulsen, *Petrusbrief und Judasbrief,* 112).

being "cleansed" from sin, and the water of baptism would remind them that they were cleansed from their sins through the death and resurrection of Jesus Christ (cf. Acts 22:16; 1 Cor 6:11; Eph 5:26; Titus 3:5). The terminology used here is rooted in the cultic language of the Old Testament (Lev 16:30; Job 7:21; Ps 51:2; cf. *Sir* 23:10; 38:10). Peter observed that those who are not practicing these virtues have forgotten their baptism and their forgiveness of sins. In other words, they are not living as forgiven sinners. They are behaving like unconverted people. In Peter's theology the priority of grace is maintained since forgiveness of sins comes first, and a godly life is *evidence* that they are truly forgiven.[70] If members of the church are living immoral lives, they bear witness that forgiveness of sins means little to them. Those who treasure being forgiven live in a way that pleases God.[71]

1:10 The "therefore" *(dio)* links v. 10 to v. 9.[72] Those who live ungodly lives show no evidence that they truly belong to God, that they have genuinely received forgiveness. Hence, Peter exhorted his readers to exercise diligence *(spoudasate)* to confirm their calling and election. Bigg wrongly concludes from the aorist that a single and definite action is intended.[73] Recent study on the tenses calls such a conclusion into question. The aorist does not necessarily signify once-for-all action, and here it may be used to stress that decisive action must be taken, and yet it is a decisive action that must be repeated again and again in the Christian life. The word *spoudasate* ("be all the more eager," NIV) recalls *spoudēn* ("effort") in v. 5. God's grace should not lead to moral relaxation but intense effort.[74] The word translated "sure" *(bebaian)* is often a legal term in Greek literature, denoting that which is valid, ratified, or confirmed. In this instance believers are to confirm their "calling and election" *(klēsin kai eklogēn)*. These two words are very close in meaning. Perhaps we should translate them as one—"elective call." We saw in v. 3 that Christ's call is an effective one, one that creates faith. God's effective call occurs in history when the gospel is preached. If this is the case, the term "election" is distinct, referring to God's pretemporal decision to save some. The reference to "calling and election" highlights God's grace. He is the one who saves.

The emphasis here, however, is not on what God has done but on the

---

[70] So against Kelly, Peter did not emphasize works more than Paul (*Peter and Jude*, 309).

[71] Luther remarks that those who do not have "the fruits of faith" lack genuine faith (*Commentary on Peter & Jude*, 239).

[72] Moo thinks it reaches back to vv. 3–9 (*2 Peter, Jude*, 48).

[73] Bigg, *Peter and Jude*, 258.

[74] Some have questioned whether Peter overemphasized human effort, but Fornberg rightly remarks that Peter's comment here is akin to what Paul said in Phil 2:12–13 (*An Early Church in a Pluralistic Society*, 27).

responsibility of human beings.[75] Believers are "to make your calling and election sure." Calvin understood this verse subjectively, saying that believers should satisfy themselves mentally about their calling and election.[76] On this reading, Peter was only referring to believers' subjective consciousness of their right-standing before God. This interpretation is not entirely satisfying, for Peter was also speaking of *objective* reality.[77] Believers confirm their calling and election by concretely practicing the virtues detailed in vv. 5–7. Still, Calvin was not completely mistaken. Those who practice such virtues will also experience subjective assurance, but we should note that their objective obedience is the foundation for subjective assurance.[78] Peter did not tolerate those who claimed to be Christians but contradicted the claim by their behavior.[79] We learn from chap. 2 that the false teachers did not confirm their call and election.

I understand the "for" *(gar)* in v. 10b to explain further the idea in v. 10a. When Peter said "for if you do these things you will never fall," the word *tauta* ("these things") probably refers to the godly qualities of vv. 5–7.[80] The word "fall" *(ptaisēte)* possibly could mean "sin."[81] The verb clearly has this meaning in James (Jas 2:10; 3:2). And yet such a notion is difficult to defend in the Petrine context both theologically and contextually. It is quite improbable that Peter thought Christians can actually live without sin. If so, he would contradict the Lord's Prayer, which enjoins Christians to ask for forgiveness often (Matt 6:12). Another meaning makes much better sense in context. Believers who confirm their call and election by living in a godly manner will not "stumble," that is, they will not forsake God, abandon him, and commit apostasy (cf. Rom 11:11; Jude 24).[82] Believers who abound in the qualities described in vv. 5–7 will never fall away from God. They are cultivating their relationship with him daily. Those seduced by the false teachers reveal that the problem is a moral one. They have forsaken goodness, allowed their wills to be captivated by evil,

---

[75] Fuchs and Reymond remark that an emphasis on human responsibility is surprising when the subject is calling and election (*2 Pierre, Jude,* 60).

[76] J. Calvin, *Commentaries on the Catholic Epistles* (Grand Rapids: Eerdmans, 1948), 376–77.

[77] Rightly Reicke, *James, Peter, and Jude,* 153; Bauckham, *Jude, 2 Peter,* 190.

[78] Note the agreement with Calvin by Charles, *Virtue amidst Vice,* 151.

[79] "Those who go back to their crimes after they have been called and who die in their sins make it clear to everyone that they are damned" (Bede in *James, 1–2 Peter, 1–3 John, Jude,* ACCS [Downers Grove: InterVarsity, 2000], 135).

[80] The participle ποιοῦντες is conditional (Fuchs and Reymond, *2 Pierre, Jude,* 60).

[81] So Fornberg, *An Early Church in a Pluralistic Society,* 95. Nevertheless, he proceeds to say, "The author regarded good deeds as essential for salvation" (p. 96). He argues such a perspective does not necessarily contradict the Pauline claim that good works are a consequence of salvation.

[82] So most commentators. See, e.g., Bigg, *Peter and Jude,* 261; Kelly, *Peter and Jude,* 309; Bauckham, *Jude, 2 Peter,* 191; Moo, *2 Peter, Jude,* 49; Fuchs and Reymond, *2 Pierre, Jude,* 60.

and are now easy prey for deception.

1:11 The NIV omits the connecting words "for thus" *(houtōs gar)*. The NRSV's "for in this way" is far superior to the NIV rendering. The "way," of course, is the pathway of virtue, the keeping of the qualities in vv. 5–7, which were mentioned again in v. 10. Those who have such virtues and abound in them will find that their entrance into the kingdom is "richly provided for" (NRSV).[83] Some scholars suggest that Peter contemplated a reward above and beyond eternal life, but we should note that he was speaking of "entrance" *(eisodos)* into the kingdom. Unfortunately, the NIV completely changes the reading of the Greek text here, so that readers cannot appreciate precisely what Peter said. Note the NRSV's use of the term "entry." This fits what Peter just said in v. 10, where those who practice the virtues are assured that they will never commit apostasy. Conversely, v. 11 says that those who continue in such godly qualities will enter into heaven. Furthermore, the interpretation proposed here makes sense of the book as a whole. Peter warned his readers, lest they succumb to the influence of the false teachers and abandon the church. In 2:20–22 those who have come to know the way of truth and turn back Peter likened to a dog that returns to its vomit and a pig to its mud pile. Peter was not concerned here about rewards but whether people will *enter* the kingdom at all. He insisted that people cannot enter it without living in a godly way, but this is not salvation *by* works but salvation *with* works.[84] These are the works that God, after all, accomplishes in his people. Identifying the "eternal kingdom" as that of the Lord Jesus Christ is unusual. Usually the kingdom is God's in the New Testament (but cf. Luke 22:30; John 18:36; Eph 5:5; Col 1:13; 2 Tim 4:1; Heb 1:8; Rev 11:15). The kingdom is clearly eschatological here, designating what believers will enter on the day of the Lord. Since the kingdom here is Christ's, he is the one who will provide entrance into the kingdom for believers.[85] Furthermore, believers will have a "rich welcome," and the word "rich" *(plousiōs)* indicates that the eschatological reward is gracious, that believers receive much more than they ever deserved.[86]

---

[83] Again the NRSV rendering is superior.

[84] Cf. the helpful comments of Charles, *Virtue amidst Vice,* 152.

[85] Starr, *Sharers in Divine Nature,* 32.

[86] Ibid., 49.

SECTION OUTLINE

III. PETER'S APOSTOLIC REMINDER (1:12–21)
   1. The Function of the Reminder: To Stir Them for Action (1:12–15)
   2. The Truth of Jesus' Coming Is Based on Eyewitness Testimony (1:16–18)
   3. The Truth of Jesus' Coming Is Based on the Prophetic Word (1:19–21)

III. PETER'S APOSTOLIC REMINDER (1:12–21)

1. The Function of the Reminder: To Stir Them for Action (1:12–15)

[12]So I will always remind you of these things, even though you know them and are firmly established in the truth you now have. [13]I think it is right to refresh your memory as long as I live in the tent of this body, [14]because I know that I will soon put it aside, as our Lord Jesus Christ has made clear to me. [15]And I will make every effort to see that after my departure you will always be able to remember these things.

Perhaps Peter used a literary form of a farewell address or a testament (see introduction).[1] Scholars have identified various elements in such farewell addresses. Neyrey sees five formal elements: (1) prediction of death, (2) prophecy of future crises, (3) exhortations to virtue, (4) a commission, and (5) the legacy of the author.[2] In a general sense we could say that nearly every element is present in 2 Peter, except that a commission is not really in the text. The fundamental element of a farewell address is that the person giving the address is dying and wants to pass on his teaching to those who remain behind. Farewell addresses like this are common in the Scriptures: the final words of Jacob (Gen 49:1–33), of Moses (Deut 33:1–29), of Joshua (Josh 24:1–28), of Jesus (John 13:1–17:26), and of Paul at Miletus (Acts 20:17–35). The testament genre was common in second-temple Judaism as well, with books such as *Testaments of the Twelve Patriachs, Testament of*

---

[1] Cf. E. Fuchs and P. Reymond, *La Deuxième Épître de Saint Pierre, L'Épître de Saint Jude,* CNT (Neuchâtel–Paris: Delachaux & Niestlé, 1980), 62.

[2] J. H. Neyrey, *2 Peter, Jude,* AB (Garden City: Doubleday, 1993), 164.

Job, Testament of Moses. The latter books were clearly pseudonymous, and some draw the same conclusion regarding 2 Peter. I would argue, however, that the canonical accounts all represent *authentic* testaments, and there is no reason to draw a different conclusion about 2 Peter. Peter wrote so that his readers would be able to remember and apply his teaching in the days when he had departed and was no longer with them. What we have here, therefore, is an apostolic reminder. Peter put himself in the same role as Moses, Joshua, and even Jesus. As an apostle of Jesus Christ, he reminded the church of the truth to which they should remain devoted. Peter, by appealing to his death and the words of Jesus, invoked his authority.

The "therefore" (*dio*, v. 12, NRSV) points back to all of vv. 3–11.[3] Christ has given believers everything they need for life and godliness and has called them by his powerful grace (vv. 3–4). Such grace serves as an incentive for a godly life of virtue (vv. 5–7), and a life of godliness is necessary for entering the eternal kingdom (vv. 8–11). Such a godly life is not the earning of salvation but evidence that salvation truly belongs to the readers. But it also is the human means by which salvation is realized. Peter felt constrained, therefore, to remind the readers (vv. 12–15) of his teaching because eternal life was at stake. False teachers had crept into the community (2:1), and Peter admonished the church so that they would not forget the faithful teaching they heard when they first believed. The paragraph has one basic point: to remind believers to keep pursuing a virtuous life.

1:12 Peter began by saying he wanted to remind believers of "these things" *(toutōn)*. Probably by "these things" he refers to all of vv. 3–11.[4] But if that is the case, why did Peter use the future tense? Some scholars have deduced from this that Peter referred to future reminders and excluded 2 Peter. The construction is difficult, but perhaps we should conceive of Peter as he actually wrote or dictated the letter. What he had already written was in his mind, and what was still to come in the letter was also intended.[5] Peter resolved to remind believers as long as life lasts, and the primary vehicle is the letter he now wrote, though future reminders were not necessarily excluded.

In one sense the believers do not need any reminder because they already "know" and "are firmly established in the truth." The idea is quite similar to Jude 3, where the faith is described as transmitted once for all to the saints. The readers should not be swayed by the false teachers because they already know

---

[3] Fuchs and Reymond, *2 Pierre, Jude*, 62.

[4] So Fuchs and Reymond, *2 Pierre, Jude*, 63; R. Bauckham, *Jude, 2 Peter* (Waco: Word, 1983), 195.

[5] Bauckham questions whether Peter could have been referring to the remainder of the letter since he did not remind the readers of 1:3–11 in what follows (*Jude, 2 Peter,* 195). Peter may, however, have been thinking of the letter as a whole, in which 1:3–11 is the foundation for what is to come.

the truth, and they are strengthened by it even now. The reference to "strengthening" reminds the readers of the power of the gospel. The truth they know cannot be limited to mental comprehension, for the truth grasps and strengthens them; it grants them the power to live in a way that is pleasing to God. The truth "has come" *(parousē)* to them and belongs to them (cf. Col 1:5–6). The innovations suggested by the false teachers are superfluous and dangerous. The church has been taught and fortified by the gospel.

1:13 Peter now reflected on why he felt a responsibility to remind the church. He thought it was fitting and right for him, as an authoritative apostle, to prompt the church with the truth of the gospel as long as he lived. This responsibility was incumbent upon him as long as he lived "in the tent of this body" (the Greek actually does not have "of this body").[6] Similarly, Paul compared our present bodies to a tent (2 Cor 5:1,4). Some think there is a connection to the transfiguration, where Peter suggested building three tents (Matt 17:4), but the link does not fit the present context and is quite implausible.[7] What the word "tent" signifies here is actually quite different, for, as in 2 Cor 5:1–10, the weakness and inadequacy of the present body is featured. Reminding the readers is urgent because Peter's body was subject to death, and he would soon die. We are not surprised, therefore, that the focus is on the function of reminders. Even though believers are already firmly established in the truth, they need to be "stirred up" or "aroused" *(diegeirein)* by reminders. The NIV's "refresh" is too tame. Reminders arouse and provoke believers, prompting them to prize the gospel afresh. Peter hoped that his words would stab the believers awake so they would reject what the opponents taught. Believers know the gospel, and yet they must, in a sense, relearn it every day.

1:14 Peter's urgency to remind the believers finds its rationale in the shortness of his life. He again refers to his body as a "tent" ("it," NIV), stressing again its weakness and transience. Commentators debate whether the idea is that Peter would die "suddenly" or "soon" *(tachinē)*. The rendering "soon" is contextually more likely.[8] As Peter grew older, he knew that the days of his life on earth were numbered, that the time of his death was near. Unfortunately, we do not know the precise circumstances of Peter's

---

[6] Contra to T. Fornberg it is not at all likely that there is any allusion to the soul being imprisoned in the body (*An Early Church in a Pluralistic Society: A Study of 2 Peter,* ConBNT 9 [Lund: Gleerup, 1977], 124).

[7] Rightly Bauckham, *Jude, 2 Peter,* 198. Against M. Green, *The Second Epistle General of Peter and the General Epistle of Jude,* 2d ed., TNTC (Grand Rapids: Eerdmans, 1988).

[8] See Bauckham, *Jude, 2 Peter,* 199; Fuchs and Reymond, *2 Pierre, Jude,* 65, n. 11. D. Guthrie thinks "swift" is possible (*New Testament Introduction*, 4th ed. [Downers Grove: InterVarsity, 1990], 821).

life when he wrote the letter, and so we cannot determine if some event in his life elicited this comment.

What Peter did say was that the Lord Jesus revealed to him that he would die. Scholars have investigated thoroughly what Peter had in mind.[9] Some have detected a reference to John 13:36, but the prophecy here is rather vague. Others point to *Apocalypse of Peter,* where Jesus appears to Peter and commands him to die in Rome; still others, to the famous "Quo Vadis" story in *Acts of Peter* (ca. A.D. 180). In this account Peter met Jesus as the former was leaving Rome. Peter asked the Lord where he was going, and the Lord replied he was going to Rome to be crucified again. Peter responded by returning to Rome to be crucified. Others see a reference to the tradition in chap. 2 of *Epistle of Clement to James*. The last three sources are all dated after 2 Peter and hence cannot be the source of Peter's story if the letter is authentic. The "Quo Vadis" story is likely legendary. Since Peter was writing, he could have been referring to an oral saying of Jesus that was not codified anywhere. It is most likely, however, that he referred to the tradition found in John 21:18–19, where Jesus informed Peter that his hands would be stretched out in a way he did not choose. Of course, an allusion to John 21:18–19 does not demand that 2 Peter was written after the Gospel of John, for if Peter was the author of the letter, he recalled the prophecy that was uttered by the Lord Jesus, and subsequently John wrote down the account.[10] The prophecy itself does not say that Peter would die "soon," but if Peter was now an older man, he knew that the prophecy would come to pass soon.[11] Perhaps, if he was in Rome when the letter was written, he could have seen that events were now shaping up that would lead to his death. If the Neronic persecutions had begun, perhaps Peter thought that the end of his life was near with the advent of intense persecution.

1:15 This verse basically restates v. 12, though now Peter stressed that he would be diligent ("I will make every effort," *spoudasō*) to remind believers before his departure. The future tense is again puzzling, but perhaps Bauckham is correct in saying that Peter thought of the future usefulness of what he wrote.[12] Or it may be, as suggested in v. 12, that the remainder of the letter and the short time Peter had on earth were both in mind. We should note that in 2 Pet 2:1 the arrival of the false teachers was described in the

---

[9] See the excellent discussion in Bauckham, *Jude, 2 Peter,* 200–201.

[10] So also D. B. Wallace, "Second Peter: Introduction, Argument, and Outline," at http://www.bible.org/studies/soapbox/2petotl.htm.

[11] This would answer the objection of J. B. Mayor (*The Epistle of St. Jude and the Second Epistle of St. Peter* [1907; reprint, Grand Rapids: Baker, 1965], cxliv) and A. Vögtle (*Der Judasbrief, Der 2 Petrusbrief,* EKKNT [Neukirchen-Vluyn: Neukirchener Verlag, 1994], 160) that no date is given in John 21.

[12] Bauckham, *Jude, 2 Peter,* 201.

future tense, but it is evident that they were already present. Another alternative is that the future tense was used to denote certainty. It seems most likely that Peter thought especially of his letter, which would continue to remind believers after Peter's death. Others argue that we have a reference here to the Gospel of Mark, which, according to tradition, was written by Mark as Peter's disciple.[13] McNamara argues that we have evidence here that chaps. 1 and 3 were not originally part of the same letter but circulated independently and were later combined into the same letter.[14] Neither of these latter theories is persuasive. It is not evident in 2 Peter that we have any reference to the Gospel, which was written after all by Mark and not Peter. Nor is there any compelling reason to maintain that chaps. 1 and 3 originally circulated independently. No clear evidence of different documents patched together exists.[15] Scholars now rightly emphasize that the letters were written as wholes and what we have here is an anticipation of what Peter communicated in 2 Pet 3:1–2. The word "departure" *(exodos)* is used elsewhere to refer to death (*Wis* 3:2; *T. Naph.* 1:1). It is far-fetched to see any allusion to the transfiguration simply because Jesus mentioned his exodus in Luke 9:31. Such a reading superimposes the next paragraph in 2 Peter upon this one.

2. The Truth of Jesus' Coming Is Based on Eyewitness Testimony (1:16–18)

16We did not follow cleverly invented stories when we told you about the power and coming of our Lord Jesus Christ, but we were eyewitnesses of his majesty. 17For he received honor and glory from God the Father when the voice came to him from the Majestic Glory, saying, "This is my Son, whom I love; with him I am well pleased." 18We ourselves heard this voice that came from heaven when we were with him on the sacred mountain.

In the previous paragraph (vv. 12–15) Peter resolved before his death to remind his readers of the truth of the gospel, focusing especially on the need to live virtuously, so that they would enter the heavenly kingdom (vv. 5–11). The call to virtue is grounded in God's saving work and should not, therefore, be dismissed as works righteousness. In vv. 16–21 he began to respond to those who were deflecting his readers from their eternal reward.[16] The false teachers doubted the future coming of Jesus Christ, apparently maintaining that life will go on as it always has (3:3–7). If there is no second coming or judgment, Peter's emphasis on pursuing godliness

---

[13] Cf. Mayor, *Jude and Second Peter,* 102–3.

[14] M. McNamara, "The Unity of Second Peter: A Reconsideration," *Scr* 12 (1960): 13–19.

[15] Guthrie, *New Testament Introduction,* 846.

[16] Neyrey rightly says that what Peter reminded his readers of included this section and what followed (*2 Peter, Jude,* 169).

diligently to receive an eternal reward collapses. Living a godly life is optional, to say the least, if one's heavenly destiny is not involved. We see from v. 16 that the false teachers rejected the idea of a future coming of Jesus Christ as a fable.[17] Peter defended the truth of the coming of Christ in a surprising manner. He appealed to his eyewitness testimony of what occurred at the transfiguration. Apparently he conceived of the transfiguration as a proleptic and prophetic indication of the glory and power of Christ that would be displayed at his future coming. Peter combated the idea that the coming of Christ is a fable by appealing to history, to what was seen and heard, and the historical event of the transfiguration anticipates a later event in history—the coming of Jesus Christ.

1:16 The main verb in v. 16 is "we made known" *(egnōrisamen),* which the NIV renders as a temporal clause ("when we told"). The "we" here stands for the apostles generally.[18] Peter probably was not claiming that he personally established the churches addressed. His point was that the churches were founded on apostolic tradition and teaching. These early Christians were instructed about "the power and coming of our Lord Jesus Christ." The terms *dynamis* ("power") and *parousia* ("coming") should be interpreted together.[19] They do not designate two different things but speak of the "powerful coming" of Jesus Christ. When Jesus returns, he will return in power (cf. Matt 25:31; 2 Thess 1:7–10). The word *parousia* can simply mean "presence" (2 Cor 10:10; Phil 2:12), and a few scholars have seen a reference to Jesus' incarnation here.[20] But in the New Testament it becomes virtually a technical term for the arrival or future coming of Jesus Christ (Matt 24:3,27,37,39; 1 Cor 15:23; 1 Thess 2:19; 3:13; 4:15; 5:23; 2 Thess 2:1,8; Jas 5:7–8; 2 Pet 3:4,12; 1 John 2:28).[21] In the Hellenistic world the word is also used for the arrival of a ruler or a god.[22] In 2 Pet 3:4,12 the term is used of the Lord's coming, where Peter refuted the skepticism of the false teachers. Peter foreshadowed here his refutation of the opponents in chap. 3.

What the apostles preached, then, was the powerful future coming of the Lord. On that day it will be decided who will enter Christ's eternal kingdom (1:11), and it is reserved only for those who have lived godly lives (1:5–10). Peter informed them with two contrasting participles about the nature of the

---

[17] For a history of interpretation of 1:16–21, see T. S. Caulley, "The Idea of 'Inspiration' in 2 Peter 1:16–21" (Ph.D. diss., Eberhard-Karls Universität zu Tübingen, 1982), 3–16.

[18] In defense of the apostolic "we," see Fuchs and Reymond, *2 Pierre, Jude,* 67.

[19] So Bauckham, *Jude, 2 Peter,* 215.

[20] See, e.g., C. Spicq, *Les Épîtres de Saint Pierre,* SB (Paris: Gabalda, 1966), 219–20.

[21] Rightly Fornberg, *An Early Church in a Pluralistic Society,* 79–80; Vögtle, *Judasbrief, 2 Petrusbrief,* 165. A reference to both comings is not plausible (contra Fuchs and Reymond, *2 Pierre, Jude,* 68).

[22] See A. Oepke, "παρουσία," *TDNT* 5.859–61.

apostolic knowledge that was conveyed to them. He told them what it was *not* and then what it *was*. First, the apostles "did not follow cleverly invented stories." The word "stories" is from the Greek word *mythos* from which we derive the English word "myth." We should note first of all that Peter did not describe the teaching of his opponents as "myths." On the contrary, the false teachers insisted that the apostolic teaching was a myth, in particular the notion that Jesus Christ would return.[23] They likely appealed to the stability of the world, arguing against sudden interventions and holding to the constancy of the natural order. The word "myth" was often used in Greek culture to convey stories about the Greek gods. The stories were not literally true, but they conveyed a message that was still instructive for the day.[24] D. F. Strauss and R. Bultmann used the term in a similar way to communicate their understanding of gospels.[25] The term "myth," however, could also designate something that is a "fable." In Greek literature the word is also used with that meaning. In the latter instance myths stand for teachings or stories that have no basis in reality and are fantasies. Such stories have no value whatsoever. Paul likely used the term with this meaning in describing the false teachers in the Pastoral Epistles (1 Tim 1:4; 4:7; 2 Tim 4:4; Titus 1:14). The false teachers in 2 Peter describe the apostolic teaching as mythical in this derogatory sense. The adjectival participle *sesophismenois* ("cleverly devised") supports this interpretation. They see no kernel of truth in the preaching of the second coming of Christ but ridicule it as a fable. Some suggest the opponents were influenced by an Epicurean type of teaching that rejected any notion of God's

---

[23] Contra Guthrie, *New Testament Introduction,* 847; K. H. Schelke, *Der Petrusbrief—Der Judasbrief,* HTKNT (Freiburg: Herder, 1980), 197. J. N. D. Kelly rightly perceives this but then, somewhat inconsistently, opts for a both-and view (*A Commentary on the Epistles of Peter and Jude,* Thornapple Commentaries [Grand Rapids: Baker, 1981], 316). Rightly Mayor, *Jude and Second Peter,* 103; Bauckham, *Jude, 2 Peter,* 213. Caulley argues that the term "myths" refers primarily to the opponents, noting that the author reverses the charges against his own teaching and applies them to the opponents. According to Caulley, the Gnostic creation myth of the false teachers is criticized by the author ("Inspiration in 2 Peter 1:16–21," 61, 109–12). Contra Caulley the term cannot refer primarily to the opponents, for the text clearly indicates that the label "myths" was applied to apostolic teaching. Nor is there any clear evidence that Peter characterized the opponents' teaching as mythical by turning their own accusations against them, for nowhere did he identify the opponents' teaching as mythical. Caulley relies on evidence from the Pastorals and Irenaeus to identify the opponents, but such a procedure is methodologically unconvincing since it is questionable whether the adversaries in the Pastorals should be identified as Gnostic or that data from the Pastorals should be used to delineate the false teaching in 2 Peter. Moreover, the evidence from Irenaeus is too late to be helpful in establishing the nature of the heresy in 2 Peter.

[24] On myths see Neyrey's helpful comments (*2 Peter, Jude,* 175–76).

[25] J. D. G. Dunn, "Demythologizing—The Problem of Myth in the New Testament," in *New Testament Interpretation: Essays on Principles and Methods* (Grand Rapids: Eerdmans, 1977), 289–90, 294–96.

providence or of punishment after death.[26] Others believe they may have held to some form of overrealized eschatology, like the opponents in the Pastoral Epistles (2 Tim 2:18), so that they concluded there was no future resurrection; the only resurrection is a spiritual one.[27] As I argued in the introduction, the Epicurean hypothesis is too specific in identifying the opponents; it is also not clear that the false teachers argued for a realized eschatology.[28] In any case, we do know that they ridiculed the notion that Jesus would come again.

Peter insisted, however, that the apostles did not trade in myths. On the contrary, they were "eyewitnesses of his majesty." The apostolic teaching is anchored in history. Presumably, Peter could have replied that it is irrelevant whether Jesus would return physically. What matters is the spiritual truth that God controls the future. But Peter was concerned about historical facticity. The Christian faith teaches that the Lord's coming will occur in the space-time order of this world and cannot be reduced to a "spiritual" truth sundered from history. The word "eyewitnesses" *(epoptai)* could possibly derive from Hellenistic religion, especially the mystery religions. If so, Peter again used a term familiar to his hearers, though it is likely the term did not carry such specific associations for his readers.[29] The use of the verb in 1 Pet 2:12 and 3:2 indicates that a technical sense should not be given to the verb. The word "majesty" *(megaleiotēs)* in this context points to the deity of Jesus Christ (cf. 1:1; of God—Luke 9:43; Jer 40:9 LXX; *1 Esdr* 4:40), though the term "majesty" does not necessarily signify deity (*1 Esdr* 1:4). We learn from the next verse that the majesty of Christ was observed at the transfiguration.

1:17 The syntax of this verse is quite difficult since we have an ungrammatical construction. The NIV clarifies the Greek for English readers. The emphasis of the verse is on God's imprimatur of approval upon his Son. The Son received honor and glory from the Father.[30] The Father signified his approval with a divine voice that came from heaven itself (cf. Dan 4:31; Rev 11:12; 16:1).[31] The words spoken demonstrated that God was

---

[26] See J. H. Neyrey, "The Form and Background of the Polemic in 2 Peter," *JBL* 99 (1980): 94–195, 185. Concerning Epicurus's dismissal of providence see also G. Stahlin, "μῦθος," *TDNT* 4.779, n. 102.

[27] For a proto-Gnostic view of the opponents, see Fuchs and Reymond, *2 Pierre, Jude,* 28, 67.

[28] Bauckham, *Jude, 2 Peter,* 332.

[29] Contra Fornberg, *An Early Church in a Pluralistic Society,* 114; J. D. Charles, *Virtue amidst Vice: The Catalog of Virtues in 2 Peter 1,* JSNTSup 150 (Sheffield: Academic Press, 1997), 84. Cf. W. Michaelis, "ἐπόπτης," *TDNT* 5.373–75.

[30] T. Callan says that such honor and glory are an indication of Christ's divinity ("The Christology of the Second Letter of Peter," *Bib* 82 [2001]: 255; so also Caulley, "Inspiration in 2 Peter 1:16–21," 116).

[31] Cf. the tradition of the divine voice in Judaism (O. Betz, "φωνή," *TDNT* 9.288–90).

pleased with his Son, Jesus. Peter likely mentioned that God is "Father" because he pronounced that Jesus is his "Son." He then described God as "the Majestic Glory" *(tēs megaloprepous doxēs)*. Sirach speaks of "the glory of his voice" (*Sir* 17:3). In v. 17 the Greek word for "majestic" differs from the word used for Christ in v. 17, but the idea is the same. Peter implied that the majesty of the one and only God was shared by his Son. Furthermore, the glory that belongs to God also belongs to Jesus, for the Son received glory from the Father, the one who is majestic in glory.[32]

It is obvious that Peter referred to the transfiguration, which was a theophany that occurred on a mountain, as did the theophanies on Sinai or Horeb (Exodus 19–20; 34; 1 Kgs 19:8–18). Neyrey thinks the transfiguration is utilized differently from the Synoptics, where it "authorizes his way to Jerusalem, his cross and vindication."[33] A different use of the tradition can be acknowledged, though in both the Synoptics and 2 Peter the transfiguration authorizes Jesus as God's Son. In any case, Peter focused on his "vindication" at the second coming, on his glory that will be revealed to all. Some scholars think the terms "honor and glory" denote one concept, like "power and coming" in v. 16.[34] Such an interpretation is certainly possible, but the reference to the transfiguration points to two separate parts of the one event.[35] Glory refers to the transformation of his face and clothing (cf. Luke 9:29,32). Honor refers to the words of commendation that came from heaven. The actual words, of course, are also found in Matt 17:5; Mark 9:7; Luke 9:35.[36] Peter's words here do not correspond exactly with any of them. The NIV translates Matt 17:5 and 2 Pet 1:17 exactly the same, but there are some minor differences between the accounts in Greek. For example, "this is" *(houtos estin)* is placed first in the sentence in Matthew, Peter has *eis hon* instead of Matthew's *en hō*, and only Peter has *egō*. Mark and Luke do not have the statement about God being well pleased, and so they differ even more dramatically from 2 Peter.[37] Some scholars argue that Peter's tradition is independent here.[38] Such a view is not surprising if Peter was truly the author. He could remember the event without consulting any other sources. On the other

---

[32] Hence, we have a reference to Christ's deity here (Fuchs and Reymond, *2 Pierre, Jude,* 69).

[33] Neyrey, *2 Peter, Jude,* 173.

[34] E.g., Bauckham, *Jude, 2 Peter,* 217.

[35] Rightly Kelly, *Peter and Jude,* 319; D. J. Moo, *2 Peter, Jude,* NIVAC (Grand Rapids: Zondervan, 1997), 72.

[36] For a careful sifting of the tradition, see Bauckham, *Jude, 2 Peter,* 204–10.

[37] P. Dschulnigg argues that Peter was closest to and most dependent on Matthew of the three Synoptics ("Der theologische Ort des Zweiten Petrusbriefes," *BZ* 33 [1989]: 168–76). Dschulnigg exaggerates to some degree the closeness of Peter to Matthew, but he does show that in some texts Peter may depend upon Matthean tradition.

[38] E.g., Bauckham, *Jude, 2 Peter,* 205–10. H. Paulsen argues that Peter is dependent on general traditional material (*Der Zweite Petrusbrief und der Judasbrief,* KEK [Göttingen: Vandenhoeck & Ruprecht, 1992], 119).

hand, the differences between the Petrine and Matthean accounts are relatively insignificant, and Miller makes a good case for Petrine dependence upon Matthew.[39] Still, it is also possible that Peter recalled the event from memory.[40] The minor differences do not cast doubt on the historical authenticity of any of the accounts, for the authors select what part of the event is significant for their purposes. Hence, Peter omitted "listen to him," which is in all the Synoptic accounts, since he was not emphasizing that Jesus is superior to the law and the prophets. What Peter emphasized is the honor and glory given to Jesus at the transfiguration because such honor and glory looks forward to and will be replicated at the second coming.

The words spoken at the transfiguration recall Jesus' baptism, where he was anointed for ministry and commissioned as God's Son (Matt 3:17 par.). The acclamation of sonship recalls Ps 2:7 ("You are my Son; today I have become your Father"), where the Davidic king is acclaimed and appointed as Yahweh's anointed. Likewise, an allusion to Isa 42:1 is also present ("Here is my servant, whom I uphold, my chosen one in whom I delight"). We should remember that Peter recorded the words God spoke and that these words were recalled because of their theological import. Jesus is the Servant-Son par excellence, who fulfills the promises to David and the prophecies about the Servant of the Lord. He is the Son in a way David was not, for he also shares in God's majesty (1:16). To say that God is "well pleased" *(eudokēsa)* with Jesus denotes God's electing pleasure (cf. Luke 12:32; 1 Cor 1:21; Gal 1:15; see also the noun *eudokia* in Matt 11:26; Luke 10:21; Eph 1:5,9).[41]

The transfiguration seems at first glance to be a strange event to verify the truth of Christ's future coming. We should note, however, that in all three of the Synoptic Gospels the transfiguration immediately follows the declaration that God's kingdom will come with power, suggesting that the transfiguration represents and anticipates Christ's powerful coming (Matt 16:28–17:13; Mark 9:1–13; Luke 9:27–36). The transfiguration, then, is a manifestation of the coming of the kingdom. Peter recalled the event because it anticipates Christ's glory when he returns.[42] Moreover, the eyewitness character of the event demonstrates that Peter was not dreaming or propounding some myth. He saw Jesus transformed, and he heard God's very words.[43]

---

[39] R. J. Miller, "Is There Independent Attestation for the Transfiguration in 2 Peter?" *NTS* 42 (1996): 620–25.

[40] M. J. Kruger, "The Authenticity of 2 Peter," *JETS* 42 (1999): 663.

[41] Cf. G. Schrenk, "εὐδοκέω," *TDNT* 2.739–41.

[42] So Fornberg, *An Early Church in a Pluralistic Society,* 80.

[43] T. V. Smith argues that the event verifies Peter's authority but does not point to the parousia (*Petrine Controversies in Early Christianity: Attitudes Toward Peter in Christian Writings of the First Two Centuries,* WUNT 2/15 [Tübingen: Mohr, 1985], 79). He introduces a false disjunction here, for Peter's witness of the transfiguration in history demonstrates his authority and anchors the second coming in a historical event that functions as a prelude of the parousia.

1:18 Peter confirmed again that he heard the divine voice while he was on the holy mountain. Bauckham's view that the author wrote a transparent fiction in Peter's name as a testament is difficult to square with these verses.[44] The author emphasized that he was an eyewitness and actually heard what was said on the mountain. If Bauckham is correct, it was clear to the readers that Peter himself did not write this. Evidence that this is a transparent fiction is lacking in church history, since readers in the early centuries did not detect the literary device Bauckham thinks is apparent.[45] A more natural reading takes the text at face value. Peter himself claimed to have seen and heard these things. The only other credible option is that the author wrote to deceive his readers, trying to pass himself off as Peter. As I argue in the introduction, Peter himself either wrote or dictated these words, and he spoke of his own experience.

Some scholars think a late date is indicated by the words "sacred mountain," showing that the place on which the transfiguration occurred is now venerated. Interestingly, Sinai is never called the "holy mountain." And if the purpose was to venerate the mount of transfiguration, it is curious that its location eludes us. Venerating specific places was the result of later church history. Bauckham probably is correct in seeing an allusion to Ps 2:6, where the king is appointed "on Zion, my holy hill."[46] This is strengthened by the allusion to Ps 2:7 in v. 17. The main purpose, however, is to locate the event in history. Peter did not refer to an ethereal or ineffable event. The mountain in which Jesus was glorified and where God spoke really exists, and it is holy because God revealed himself there.[47]

Some scholars have suggested that the transfiguration is actually an account of the resurrection that has been inserted into a different place in the gospel narratives. This theory has been soundly debunked by Stein.[48] We also have noted

---

[44] Bauckham thinks the author adheres to the literary form of a testament in recounting eyewitness testimony (*Jude, 2 Peter,* 216).

[45] "There used to be many people who thought that this letter was not written by Peter. But it is enough to read this verse, and you will soon see that it was Peter who stood with Jesus on the mount of transfiguration. It is therefore the same Peter who heard the voice testifying to the Lord who wrote this letter" (Gregory the Great in *James, 1–2 Peter, 1–3 John, Jude,* ACCS [Downers Grove: InterVarsity, 2000], 139–40). Cf. also Bede, "Those who doubt that Peter wrote this letter need to pay careful attention to this verse and to the one which follows, because the eyewitness testimony makes it clear that no one else could have written it" (ibid., 140).

[46] Bauckham, *Jude, 2 Peter,* 221.

[47] So Vögtle, *Judasbrief, 2 Petrusbrief,* 169. For the genuineness of what Peter said here, see Guthrie, *New Testament Introduction*, 824.

[48] R. H. Stein, "Is the Transfiguration (Mark 9:2–8) a Misplaced Resurrection-Account?" *JBL* 95 (1976): 79–96; cf. also Bauckham, *Jude, 2 Peter,* 210–11; Fuchs and Reymond, *2 Pierre, Jude,* 69–70.

above that the transfiguration in all three Synoptic Gospels is associated with the coming of the kingdom in power. Even in the Synoptic Gospels the purpose of the transfiguration cannot be restricted to a temporary glorification of Jesus that vanishes forever. While Jesus goes to the cross, God reveals the future glory that will belong to Jesus, a prophecy of what is to come. This glory will be manifested publicly at his future coming, and so Peter rightly appealed to it to defend the powerful coming of the Lord Jesus.

3. The Truth of Jesus' Coming Is Based on the Prophetic Word (1:19–21)

19 And we have the word of the prophets made more certain, and you will do well to pay attention to it, as to a light shining in a dark place, until the day dawns and the morning star rises in your hearts. 20 Above all, you must understand that no prophecy of Scripture came about by the prophet's own interpretation. 21 For prophecy never had its origin in the will of man, but men spoke from God as they were carried along by the Holy Spirit.

Peter reminded (cf. 1:12–15) the readers in vv. 16–18 that the powerful coming of Jesus Christ is not a myth but a certain reality, for it is rooted in his own eyewitness testimony. Peter saw the Lord's glory when he was transfigured before him, and he heard God's words that pronounced Jesus as the Son of his good pleasure. The transfiguration anticipates the second coming, for it unveils the glory that will belong to Jesus at his coming. In vv. 19–21 Peter employed a second argument supporting the future coming of the Lord. The apostolic interpretation of the prophetic word (i.e., the OT Scriptures) confirmed at the transfiguration verifies that the Lord will come in salvation and judgment. Verse 19b contains the main point of the argument and the central point of the entire letter thus far. Since the transfiguration indicates the proper interpretation and verification of the prophetic word, believers should pay careful attention to that word, for it is like a lamp illumining the darkness. Believers will need that word for direction until the day of the Lord comes. When Jesus returns, the prophetic word will be fulfilled, for he will illumine our hearts with his light, and the prophetic word will be eclipsed forever by the living Word. The logical relationship between vv. 19 and 20 is that we must pay attention to the prophetic word and use it as the criterion of our thinking because prophecy is not a matter of private interpretation. The reason for this is stated in v. 21. Prophecy is not rooted in the will of human beings, but men spoke from God as they were inspired by the Holy Spirit.

1:19 The "we" in the text continues to refer to the apostles, as is the case in vv. 16–18. This is confirmed by the contrast between "we" and "you" in the verse, for the apostles had the more sure prophetic word to which the church needs to pay attention.[49] What did Peter mean by "the prophetic word" *(ton prophētikon logon),* translated by the NIV "the word of the prophets"? Neyrey argues that the prophetic word is the transfiguration.[50] This is attractive in that it joins vv. 16–18 and 19–21 closely together. An insuperable difficulty arises, however, that makes this interpretation quite unlikely. The prophetic word almost certainly refers to the Old Testament Scriptures, not to an event in Jesus' life nor to any other text that is now codified in the New Testament.[51] Verses 20–21 support this view in that they refer to "prophecy of Scripture." The word "Scripture" *(graphē)* reveals that *writings* are in view, not an event like the transfiguration. Some scholars conclude that the Old Testament Scriptures as a whole are in view here.[52] Such a judgment, however, does not account well for the emphasis on prophecy in the text, and so it is preferable to see a reference to Old Testament prophecies related to the day of judgment and salvation, that is, the day of the Lord.[53] Caulley's work is especially instructive at this juncture, for he identifies the prophetic word with Isaiah 42 and Psalm 2, and there are allusions to both of these texts in the wording of the divine voice—"This is my beloved Son, with whom I am well pleased" (Ps 2:7; Isa 42:1).[54] He remarks that both of these chapters also contain the theme of judgment and hence would refute the eschatological skepticism of the opponents.[55] It may be that Caulley unduly limits the prophetic word to these two texts and that the reference is to Old Testament prophetic texts as a whole.[56] But Caulley's interpretation puts us on the right track in interpreting the text. The prophetic word of Scripture is made more sure by the transfiguration, for the transfiguration confirms the proper interpretation of Old Testament Scripture, that is, that there is a future coming of Christ for judgment and salvation.

Another difficult question relates to the meaning of the term *bebaioteron*

---

[49] For support of the notion that the "we" refers to the apostles, see Caulley, "Inspiration in 2 Peter 1:16–21," 126; B. P. Wolfe, "The Prophets' Understanding or Understanding the Prophets?: 2 Peter 1:20 Reconsidered," *BRT/RBT* 8 (1998): 96–97; Bauckham, *Jude, 2 Peter,* 224–25; Fuchs and Reymond, *2 Pierre, Jude,* 72. For a reference to all believers, see Kelly, *Peter and Jude,* 320.

[50] Neyrey, "2 Peter 1:16–21," 514–16; id., *2 Peter, Jude,* 178–79.

[51] Rightly Bauckham, *Jude, 2 Peter,* 224; Vögtle, *Judasbrief, 2 Petrusbrief,* 170; D. Farkasfalvy, "The Ecclesial Setting of Pseudepigraphy in Second Peter and Its Role in the Formation of the Canon," *SecCent* 5 (1985–86): 8, n. 12.

[52] Kelly, *Peter and Jude,* 321; Schelke, *Die Petrusbrief—Die Judasbrief,* 200; Paulsen, *Petrusbrief und Judasbrief,* 120; Fuchs and Reymond, *2 Pierre, Jude,* 72.

[53] So Wolfe, "2 Peter 1:20 Reconsidered," 96. Moo thinks the reference is to OT prophecies about the establishing of the Messianic kingdom (*2 Peter, Jude,* 75).

[54] Caulley, "Inspiration in 2 Peter 1:16–21," 128–30. Caulley argues that the reference is to Messianic texts uttered during the event of the transfiguration (pp. 129–30).

[55] In citing the OT, Peter did not limit himself merely to the words cited but the entire context drawn upon. Supporting the notion that NT writers drew upon the wider context from which they quoted is the classic work by C. H. Dodd, *According to the Scriptures* (New York: Scribners, 1952).

[56] So Wolfe, "2 Peter 1:20 Reconsidered," 96, n. 23.

("made more certain"). Some suggest that the written prophecies of the Old Testament are more certain than an event like the transfiguration because the transfiguration was subjectively experienced.[57] It is difficult to believe that Peter would say this. According to this interpretation, Peter would be pitting the transfiguration against the Scriptures, arguing that the latter are more certain than the former. But this would subvert the argument in vv. 16–18, for Peter then would be suggesting that his appeal to the transfiguration is not quite convincing, so he needed something better, namely, the Old Testament Scriptures. But vv. 16–18 demonstrate that Peter believed that the transfiguration was decisive proof for his view, not questionable in the least. He was not suggesting its deficiency in contrast to the Old Testament Scriptures but was simply giving another argument for the validity of his view.

Another possibility is that the word *bebaioteron* should be translated as "most reliable"[58] or "very certain."[59] On this view Peter was not actually engaging in a comparison at all. He was simply saying that believers have a word from God that is entirely reliable. Peter was not suggesting, then, that the prophetic word is more reliable than the transfiguration, but he was saying that we can say with certainty that the prophetic word of the Old Testament refers to the coming of Christ.

A decision is difficult, but it is preferable to conclude that the transfiguration renders more certain the interpretation of the prophetic word.[60] The word *bebaioteron* should be taken in context as signifying a comparison, so that the transfiguration provides confirmation of the interpretation of the prophetic word. The transfiguration, then, is not conceived as more or less reliable than the prophetic word. It provides a confirmatory interpretation of that word, and this interpretation was granted to Peter and the other apostles. The transfiguration shows that the promise of the Lord's coming should be taken literally and cannot be dismissed as a "spiritual" truth.[61] The advantage of this interpretation is that it holds tightly together the prophetic word and the transfiguration without identifying the transfiguration as the prophetic word.

Verses 16–19a, then, function as the ground or reason for v. 19b. Since believers have in the Old Testament Scriptures a prophetic word that is more

---

[57] Cf. C. Bigg, *The Epistles of St. Peter and St. Jude,* ICC (Edinburgh: T & T Clark, 1901), 268; Green, *2 Peter and Jude,* 97–98.

[58] B. Reicke, *The Epistles of James, Peter, and Jude,* AB (Garden City: Doubleday, 1964), 158.

[59] Neyrey, *2 Peter, Jude,* 183; cf. also Bauckham, *Jude, 2 Peter,* 223; N. Hillyer, *1 and 2 Peter, Jude,* NIBC (Peabody: Hendrickson, 1992), 179.

[60] Kelly, *Peter and Jude,* 320–21; Moo, *2 Peter, Jude,* 75–76; Fornberg, *An Early Church in a Pluralistic Society,* 82, n. 1; Horrell, *The Epistles of Peter and Jude,* 158; Caulley, "Inspiration in 2 Peter 1:16–21," 130–34; Wolfe, "2 Peter 1:20 Reconsidered," 96–97.

[61] G. L. Green maintains that the discussion about prophecy must be set against the canvas of skepticism about the validity of prophecies in the Greco-Roman world ("'As for Prophecies, They Will Come to an End': 2 Peter, Paul and Plutarch on 'the Obsolescence of Oracles,'" *JSNT* 82 [2001]: 107–22).

reliable because of the interpretive confirmation of the transfiguration, they should pay close attention to the word and heed what it says. Peter's call to pay heed to the word is the main point of the text, for the entire letter up to this point has been pointing to this command. The readers are to pay attention to the prophetic word, as it has been apostolically interpreted. Caulley remarks, "By virtue of their witness to the transfiguration, and specifically to the divine voice, the apostles have confirmation of the prophetic word in its affirmation of Jesus as exalted Son of God who will return in judgment."[62] The prophetic word functions as a light. The image is a common one. "Your word is a lamp to my feet and a light for my path" (Ps 119:105; cf. Prov 6:23; *Wis* 18:4). In other words, the prophetic word illumines people with the truth about the end of history. The false teachers had deviated from the truth.

The last clauses in v. 19 inform the readers how long they will need to pay heed to prophetic Scriptures. The prophetic word points forward to the day of the Lord, and obviously it will not be needed when "the day dawns." The day here is almost certainly the day of the Lord. In the Old Testament the day of the Lord is a day of judgment and salvation, when those who oppose God will be punished and those who love him will be delivered (Isa 13:6,9; Ezek 13:5; 30:3; Joel 1:15; 2:1,11,31; 3:14; Amos 5:18,20; Obad 15; Zeph 1:7,14; Mal 4:5). In the Old Testament there are days of the Lord in history, when he defeats his enemies and vindicates his own. Such days of the Lord foreshadow the final day of the Lord, when the Lord will bring to a consummation his purposes (cf. Acts 2:20; 2 Cor 1:14; 1 Thess 5:2; 2 Thess 2:2). In the New Testament the day of the Lord is also the day of Christ (2 Cor 1:14; Phil 1:6,10; 2:16). It is clear in 2 Peter that this day is the eschatological day, when the present world order ceases (2 Pet 3:10,12). The opponents denied that there would be any day of the Lord, but the prophetic word as confirmed by the transfiguration promises it will come.

The day of the Lord is also described as the time when "the morning star rises in your hearts." The "morning star" *(phōsphoros)* was a name for Venus in the ancient world. The reference here is almost certainly to the coming of Jesus Christ. Perhaps Peter alluded to Num 24:17, "A star will come out of Jacob; a scepter will rise out of Israel."[63] The text goes on to say that God's enemies will be crushed, which fits the eschatological cast of Peter's writing and the judgment awaiting the opponents. Peter said that the morning star "rises" *(anateilē),* while Num 24:17 in the Septuagint says a "star will arise" *(astron anatelei)* from Jacob (cf. Rev 22:16; *T. Levi* 18:3; *T. Jud.* 24:1–5; 1QM 11:6–7; CD 7:18–20). Some have detected an inconsistency within v. 19 since Venus as the morning star appears before the dawn,[64] but we should not press the language into such a firm mold. Peter

[62] Caulley, "Inspiration in 2 Peter 1:16–21," 133.

[63] Ibid., 136.

[64] Kelly, *Peter and Jude,* 322.

clearly saw the day of the Lord and the coming of the Lord as one event. It also seems strange that he spoke of the morning star that "rises in your hearts." How could Jesus Christ arise in one's heart? The objective event and the subjective experience seem to be confused. Bigg says that it refers to the joy that will be ours when the Lord returns.[65] The language of illumination in the verse suggests another interpretation. When Jesus comes, we will not need the prophetic word to shine in a dark place—this sinful world. Then our hearts will be enlightened by the Morning Star himself, and that to which prophecy points will have arrived.[66] It is not incompatible to speak of an eschatological event and its interior impact.[67] Caulley rightly emphasizes that the knowledge of God that shines upon us in conversion (2 Cor 4:6) will reach its consummation at the second coming.[68]

1:20 This verse can be interpreted in two plausible ways, and hence as interpreters we must discern which of the two is most probable.[69] In either case v. 20 provides a reason for the admonition to pay heed to the word in v. 19. The issue is whether Peter focused on the origin of prophecy or its interpretation. Before introducing the two different views, a word should be said about "interpretation" *(epilysis)*. Despite the suggestions by some exegetes, the term almost certainly refers to "interpretation" (cf. Mark 4:34). In a version of the Septuagint translated by Aquila, both the noun and the verb are used of Joseph interpreting dreams (Gen 40:8; 41:8,12; cf. also Josephus, *Ant.* 8.167; Herm. *Sim.* 5:3:1–2). We are now prepared to examine the two main approaches to the verse.

The first view is represented by the NIV (cf. also NET, NLT), "No prophecy of Scripture came about by the prophet's own interpretation," and its most sophisticated defense today is found in Bauckham.[70] In this instance Peter responded to the opponents, who claimed that the prophets misinterpreted their revelations from God. Peter insisted that the revelation and the interpretation are of one piece. Both the revelation and the interpretation of what is revealed do not originate from the prophet. The vision and the explanation of the vision both come from God.[71] A genuine prophetic word does not simply consist of the content of the dream but an accurate interpretation of what the dream says. The same could be said about visions (cf. Jer 1:11–14; Dan 7:2; 8:1; Amos 7:1; Zech 1:8–11). Peter defended, then, both the revelation given and the interpretation of the revelation provided by the

---

[65] Bigg, *Peter and Jude,* 269.

[66] Cf. Bauckham, *Jude, 2 Peter,* 226; Fornberg, *An Early Church in a Pluralistic Society,* 85.

[67] Rightly Fuchs and Reymond, *2 Pierre, Jude,* 73.

[68] Caulley, "Inspiration in 2 Peter 1:16–21," 140–41.

[69] For a detailed discussion of this verse see Bauckham, *Jude, 2 Peter,* 229–33.

[70] Bauckham, *Jude, 2 Peter,* 229–33.

[71] "They were fully aware that the message had been given to them, and they made no attempt to put their own interpretation on it" (Oecumenius in *James, 1–2 Peter, 1–3 John, Jude,* ACCS [Downers Grove: InterVarsity, 2000], 141).

prophets. Here he followed an Old Testament precedent. Bauckham argues that Peter did not criticize the opponents here but defended himself against some of their charges.[72] Criticism of the opponents commences in chap. 2.

Despite the strengths of the first view, it seems likely that the second is preferable. This view is represented by the ESV (cf. HCSB, NKJV, NRSV), "No prophecy of Scripture comes from someone's own interpretation." Peter likely was attacking the opponents, arguing that they interpreted prophecy to support their own views.[73] In doing so they resisted the proper interpretation given by the apostles. Presumably the opponents interpreted the Scriptures in such a way that the return of Christ is denied and proceeded to argue that history will go on as it always has (cf. 2 Pet 3:4–7).[74] We have already seen in previous verses that the transfiguration verifies the apostolic interpretation of Old Testament prophecy (vv. 16–19).[75] Verses 16–21 fit together well as an argument if in v. 20 the opponents questioned the apostolic interpretation of prophecy, so that they rejected the parousia of Christ.[76] This may explain why the opponents are designated as "false teachers" (2:1) and not as "false prophets" (2:1), in that their error manifested itself in their interpretation of prophecy, not their claim to be the recipients thereof.[77] The initial comments made about the word "interpretation" *(epilysis)* above also support this interpretation, for this term does not focus on the origination of prophecy but its proper interpretation after the prophecy was given.[78] This interpretation also finds support in 2 Pet 3:16, where we see that the opponents misuse and distort the Scriptures.[79] Peter's argument, then, is that the readers must pay attention to the prophetic word as it is interpreted by the apostles, for the Old Testament prophecies are not a matter of personal interpretation but have been authoritatively interpreted by the apostles.[80]

1:21 Verse 21 provides the ground for the statement in v. 20.[81] The mean-

---

[72] Bauckham, *Jude, 2 Peter,* 232.

[73] Bigg, *Peter and Jude,* 269–70; Kelly, *Peter and Jude,* 323–24; Reicke, *James, Peter, and Jude,* 158–59; Guthrie, *New Testament Introduction,* 847. Vögtle rightly says that no polemic against Gnosticism can be read out of this verse (*Judasbrief, 2 Petrusbrief,* 173–74; contra Fuchs and Reymond, *2 Pierre, Jude,* 74–75).

[74] Caulley, "Inspiration in 2 Peter 1:16–21," 142–48. Neyrey argues that opponents charge the author with arbitrary interpretations, and hence the author defends the legitimacy of his interpretation ("2 Peter 1:16–21," 516–19).

[75] Wolfe rightly observes that Bauckham does not integrate vv. 16–19 into his interpretation and concentrates mainly on vv. 20–21 ("2 Peter 1:20 Reconsidered," 99).

[76] Ibid., 102–3.

[77] Caulley, "Inspiration in 2 Peter 1:16–21," 147–48.

[78] Wolfe, "2 Peter 1:20 Reconsidered," 103.

[79] Wolfe rightly argues that the passage should not be read as a defense of early catholicism, as if the point of the passage is the rejection of any attempt to interpret Scripture. Rather, Peter insisted that all interpretation must measure up to the apostolic standard (see ibid., 104–6). The interpretation proposed here should not be confused with the historic Roman Catholic view that individuals cannot interpret the Bible without the magisterium. Rather, Peter insists that valid interpretations must square with the apostolic meaning.

[80] Caulley confirms v. 20 functions as a ground to v. 19 ("Inspiration in 2 Peter 1:16–21," 142).

[81] Ibid., 146.

ing of v. 20, then, is that the interpretation by the apostles does not come from them but ultimately has a divine source, for prophecy comes from God. In this verse, then, Peter brings together two themes: both the origin of prophecy and its subsequent interpretation stem from God himself.[82] Peter stated the main point in v. 21 both negatively and positively. Negatively, prophecy does not originate in the will of human beings. By definition prophecy is a divine work and cannot be attributed to the ingenuity or native gifts of human beings. Positively, prophecy hails from God himself. Peter stated it baldly, "Men spoke from God." Human beings spoke, and they spoke with their own personalities and literary styles; hence inspiration does not require a dictation theory of inspiration. The words the prophets spoke, however, ultimately came from God. They were inspired, or "carried along," by the Holy Spirit. Hence, Peter defended the accuracy of the prophecies in the Scriptures. Note that v. 20 speaks of "prophecy of Scripture," so Peter's words cannot be limited to oral prophecies.

We have strong biblical support here for what B. B. Warfield called concursus. Both human beings and God were fully involved in the process of inspiration.[83] The personality and gifts of the human authors were not squelched or suppressed. We can detect their different literary styles even today. And yet the words they spoke do not cancel out the truth that they spoke the word of God. Concursus means that both God and human beings contributed to the prophetic word. Ultimately, however, and most significantly, these human words are God's words. The prophets were "carried along by the Holy Spirit." The verb for "carry" is used twice in this verse (the aorist passive *ēnechthē,* "had its origin," and the present passive participle *pheromenoi,* "were carried along"). The verb is also used twice in participial form in vv. 17–18 (translated "came" in the NIV) to designate the divine voice that came from God during the transfiguration. In Acts 27:15,17 the term is used to refer to a ship that is carried by the wind (cf. Acts 2:2; John 3:8). Perhaps we cannot press the analogy of the prophets being carried as a ship's sails are caught up by the wind. But the word certainly conveys the idea that the prophets were inspired by the Holy Spirit. Peter, of course, referred only to the prophets here, but by extension we are justified in concluding that what Peter said about the prophets is also true of the New Testament canon. These writers also spoke from God and were carried along by the Holy Spirit. Evangelical theology rightly infers from this that the Scriptures are authoritative, infallible, and inerrant, for God's words must be true.

---

[82] Verse 20, however, does not emphasize the origin of prophecy but its interpretation.

[83] B. B. Warfield, *The Inspiration and Authority of the Bible* (Philadelphia: Presbyterian & Reformed, 1948), 83–96. S. Voorwinde says: "Thus he draws our attention to a profound mystery. The words of Scripture are divine words, and yet they are also the words of human writers. We cannot explain this antinomy. All we can do is observe the evidence there is for it" ("Old Testament Quotations in Peter's Epistles," *VR* 49 [1987]: 3–16). He also says there is no evidence for the theory of dictation (p. 6) and argues that Peter respected the OT context in his citations (in both letters), that his interpretation is Christologically centered (following the example of Jesus himself), and that he uses a grammatical historical approach that is integrated with redemptive history.

IV. THE ARRIVAL, CHARACTER, AND JUDGMENT OF FALSE TEACHERS (2:1–22)
1. The Impact of False Teachers (2:1–3)
2. The Certain Judgment of the Ungodly and the Preservation of the Godly (2:4–10a)
3. False Teachers Judged for Their Rebellion and Sensuality (2:10b–16)
4. The Adverse Impact of the False Teachers on Others (2:17–22)

IV. THE ARRIVAL, CHARACTER, AND JUDGMENT OF FALSE TEACHERS (2:1–22)

1. The Impact of False Teachers (2:1–3)

[1]But there were also false prophets among the people, just as there will be false teachers among you. They will secretly introduce destructive heresies, even denying the sovereign Lord who bought them—bringing swift destruction on themselves. [2]Many will follow their shameful ways and will bring the way of truth into disrepute. [3]In their greed these teachers will exploit you with stories they have made up. Their condemnation has long been hanging over them, and their destruction has not been sleeping.

It now becomes evident why the readers needed to be reminded about the importance of a godly life and why they needed to maintain the truth of Jesus' future coming. False teachers had arisen within the church who denied the former and questioned the latter. If there is no future coming of the Lord, the foundation for ethics vanishes, and the way is opened for a dissolute lifestyle. The words in chap. 1 do not represent an abstract thesis on Christian growth. Peter urgently responded to a threat to the churches, to false teaching that was inevitably accompanied by an evil lifestyle.

The connection between the end of chap. 1 and the beginning of chap. 2 is prophecy. Peter concluded the first chapter by emphasizing that his readers should pay heed to the prophetic word as their source of illumination and teaching. The prophetic Scriptures should be trusted because both the revelation and its interpretation are from God, since the Holy Spirit inspired the prophets. Now in chap. 2 he remarked that not all prophets were from God. As the Old Testament amply demonstrates, false prophets also existed among God's people. Indeed, it was prophesied that false teachers would also arise in the church. The prediction about the arrival of false teachers, according to Peter, had now been fulfilled. Errant teachers were in the midst of God's people, and they were introducing teachings that would lead people to eternal destruction. People would suffer judgment because they denied the Lord Jesus Christ by both their behavior and teaching, despite the fact that as their master he bought them and made them his servants. When Peter thought of denying the Lord, he considered the penalty that comes from such denial—swift destruction. In vv. 2–3 the influence of the false teachers is sketched in. Many would be attracted to their antinomian sensual teaching, and their dissolute lifestyle would bring criticism upon the gospel of truth. The false teachers were motivated by covetousness, and they would exploit others with their rhetorical artistry. Nonetheless, though judgment seemed to be far off, it would come. They would not escape forever.

2:1 Peter had just emphasized in vv. 19–21 that his readers should apply themselves to the prophetic word, since the prophetic Scriptures are wholly from God both in terms of the vision given and the interpretation of the vision. He did not want his readers to draw the conclusion that everyone who claims to be a prophet speaks God's words. False prophets were in Israel as well. Many texts in the Old Testament warn Israel about the danger of false prophets (Deut 13:1–5; 1 Kgs 22:5–28; Isa 9:15; 28:7–8; 29:9–12; Jer 2:8,26; 5:31; 14:13–15; 23:9–40; 27:9–18; 28:1–29:8; Ezek 13:1–23; Mic 3:5–12; Zeph 3:4). The pattern has not changed, though surprisingly the opponents are described as "false teachers" instead of "false prophets." Justin Martyr, probably depending on Peter, used similar words: "And just as there were false prophets contemporaneous with your holy prophets, so are there now many false teachers amongst us" (*Dial.* 82:1).[1] The appellation "teachers" may stem from their refusal to be called prophets, perhaps because they rejected any notion of prophetic inspiration at all.[2] Peter, nonetheless, thought they were like the false prophets of old in that they were promulgating a message contrary to God's truth. Bauckham nicely summarizes three characteristics of false prophets: (1) they lack divine

[1] Note R. Bauckham's careful discussion, where he draws a similar conclusion (*Jude, 2 Peter* [Waco: Word, 1983], 237).

[2] H. C. C. Cavallin surmises that perhaps the reference to teaching indicates that they claimed the ability to teach and interpret prophecy rather than possessing the gift of prophesy itself ("The False Teachers of 2 Pt as Pseudo-Prophets," *NovT* 21 [1979]: 269–70; cf. also A. Vögtle, *Der Judasbrief, Der 2 Petrusbrief,* EKKNT [Neukirchen-Vluyn: Neukirchener Verlag, 1994], 184). E. Fuchs and P. Reymond also observe that the opponents were teachers, not prophets (*La Deuxième Épître de Saint Pierre, L'Épître de Saint Jude,* CNT [Neuchâtel–Paris: Delachaux & Niestlé, 1980], 77).

authority, (2) they promise the people peace when God threatens judgment, and (3) they will certainly be judged by God.[3] Each of these applies nicely to the false teachers in 2 Peter. In particular, they denied divine judgment since they did not foresee the culmination of history with the coming of Jesus Christ.

One of the puzzling elements of the text is how Peter consistently used the future tense in vv. 1–3 with reference to the false teachers. Some interpret this to say that the false teachers had not yet arrived in the church.[4] They were wreaking havoc elsewhere, and Peter warned that they would arrive soon. This view fails to persuade because the rest of the letter plainly demonstrates that the opponents were already affecting the church. In 2:13 they are described as eating even now in the love feasts held in the churches. The present tense is used in 2:17 and in 3:5, indicating that the opponents were already present. The adversaries are also described with the aorist tense in 2:15, "they wandered off" *(eplanēthēsan),* but this should not be interpreted to say that the opponents had departed. We can be quite sure that Peter spoke of people who were already on the scene and continued to threaten the church. Others explain the change in tense as a device in a pseudonymous letter. The predictions made by Peter and the other apostles were being fulfilled after the death of the apostles.[5] This theory is only convincing to those who think the letter is pseudonymous, and it has already been argued in the introduction that there are good reasons to accept its authenticity. It is more likely that Peter alluded to prophecies uttered in the early church, predicting the coming of false prophets (cf. Matt 24:11,24; Mark 13:22; cf. also Deut 13:2–6).[6] He reminded his hearers that the advent of the false teachers was foreknown beforehand and hence that God reigns even in such perilous times. It is instructive to note that in 1 Tim 4:1 and 2 Tim 3:1 the future tense is also used to predict the arrival of opponents, though it is evident their false teaching was already subverting the churches addressed.

The verb *pareisagō* is interpreted by the NIV in a negative sense, "They will secretly introduce destructive heresies." The verb does not necessarily have a negative connotation, and we could retranslate the NIV to say "will

---

[3] Bauckham, *Jude, 2 Peter,* 238.

[4] J. D. Charles, *Virtue amidst Vice: The Catalog of Virtues in 2 Peter 1,* JSNTSup 150 (Sheffield: Academic Press, 1997), 86; C. Bigg, *The Epistles of St. Peter and St. Jude,* ICC (Edinburgh: T & T Clark, 1901), 271. Alternatively, Bigg says they may appear at various times.

[5] Bauckham, *Jude, 2 Peter,* 239. Hence, it fits with the testament hypothesis (so also H. Paulsen, *Der Zweite Petrusbrief und der Judasbrief,* KEK [Göttingen; Vandenhoeck & Ruprecht, 1992], 127).

[6] D. J. Moo, *2 Peter, Jude,* NIVAC (Grand Rapids: Zondervan, 1997), 92; M. Green, *The Second Epistle General of Peter and the General Epistle of Jude,* 2d ed., TNTC (Grand Rapids: Eerdmans, 1988), 104.

introduce destructive heresies." Nonetheless, the context suggests a nefarious purpose, so that the NIV reading is preferable.[7] A parallel term in Gal 2:4 has a similar sense: "But because of false believers secretly brought in *[pareisaktous]*, who slipped in to spy on the freedom we have in Christ Jesus" (NRSV). Similarly, Jude refers to opponents who "infiltrated" *(pareiseduēsan)* the church (Jude 4). The difference between Peter and Jude is significant. In the latter instance the opponents came from outside and were intruders and interlopers. In Peter's case it seems that the resistance sprang up within the church and surreptitiously introduced false teaching.[8]

The word translated "heresies" *(haireseis)* is also disputed. The singular form of the noun may refer to a sect, without any suggestion of false teaching. For instance, Acts refers to the sects of the Sadducees (5:17) and Pharisees (15:5; 26:5). Josephus also uses the term for various Jewish sects, such as the Essenes, Pharisees, and Sadducees, and perhaps Zealots (*Life* 12; *J.W.* 2.118; *Ant.* 13.171, 293). In Acts the term is used to describe the Christian "sect," and it does not clearly mean "heresy" in these texts, though the accounts in Acts indicate that serious questions were being raised about the messianic sect (24:5,14; 28:22). The word can also refer to factions or dissensions in a church (Gal 5:20; 1 Cor 11:18). Hence, many scholars think Peter did not refer to false teaching here but the introduction of factions into the church. The word *hairesis* clearly refers to false teaching by the beginning of the second century when Ignatius wrote his letters (*Eph.* 6:2; *Trall.* 6:1). In this instance, in accord with the NIV translation, the context supports the idea that false teaching is in view. The opponents are called "false teachers," and hence it makes sense to say that they introduced "false teaching," that is, heresies into the church.[9] They insinuated themselves into the church and under the cover of the church's blessing were introducing wrong doctrines. These doctrines are "destructive heresies." The word "destructive" indicates that they led to destruction or eschatological punishment presumably because they encouraged people to lead immoral lives.[10]

The root problem with these false teachers is conveyed in the phrase "even denying the sovereign Lord who bought them." The NIV captures precisely the meaning of *kai* by translating it "even."[11] The Greek word *despotēs* is not the usual one for "Lord," and again the NIV's rendering is

---

[7] See especially J. H. Neyrey, *2 Peter, Jude,* AB (Garden City: Doubleday, 1993), 190; contra Charles, *Virtue amidst Vice,* 86.

[8] Rightly Bauckham, *Jude, 2 Peter,* 239.

[9] So Bauckham, *Jude, 2 Peter,* 239; D. G. Horrell, *The Epistles of Peter and Jude,* EC (Peterborough: Epworth, 1998), 161; Fuchs and Reymond, *2 Pierre, Jude,* 78–79.

[10] Charles rightly sees that libertinism rather than false doctrine is the focus in 2 Peter, though he downplays unduly the presence of doctrinal aberrations (*Virtue amidst Vice,* 48–49, 86–87).

[11] Rightly Bigg, *Peter and Jude,* 273.

felicitous ("sovereign Lord"). The word designates earthly masters of slaves in several texts (1 Tim 6:1–2; Titus 2:9; 1 Pet 2:18), or it emphasizes God's lordship (Luke 2:29; Acts 4:24; 2 Tim 2:21; Jude 4; Rev 6:10; cf. Gen 15:2,8; Isa 1:24; 3:1; 10:33). This verse may be the only text in the New Testament where the term refers to Jesus Christ, though Jude 4 may be another instance. A reference to Jesus Christ is likely in the phrase he "bought them" (cf. Rev 5:9). The verb for "bought" *(agorazō)* is part of the redemption word group in the New Testament.[12] Jesus as Lord bought them as his slaves, and he purchased them through his atoning death on the cross. Peter would not speak of the false teachers as bought by the death of the Lord if they were pagan outsiders. The expression indicates that the false teachers were part of the church Peter addressed, that they professed faith in Jesus Christ. At one time they were loyal servants of Jesus Christ, but now they denied the Lord who spilled his blood for them.

The language of denial alludes to Jesus' words, "Whoever denies me before others, I also will deny before my Father in heaven" (Matt 10:33, NRSV). Those who deny Jesus will experience eschatological judgment when he denies them forever before his Father. From the remainder of 2 Peter it is evident that the denial of Jesus' lordship was practical, in that they rejected his moral authority over their lives. It is harder to discern whether specific Christological errors were part of the denial.[13] Probably the denial of the second coming of Christ should be included here, for in doing so they in effect rejected his lordship (cf. 2 Pet 3:4–7).[14] Those who introduce false teaching and deny the Lord Jesus Christ will bring "swift destruction on themselves." Peter used the same word for "destruction" *(apōleia)* that was appended to the word "heresies" in this verse. The word is a common one in the New Testament for the eschatological punishment to come. We already noted that those who deny Jesus will be denied before the Father. Peter clarified here that the false teachers were not guilty of minor defections but that judgment awaited them if they did not repent. The word "swift" *(tachinēn)*

---

[12] See I. H. Marshall, "The Development of the Concept of Redemption in the New Testament," in *Reconciliation and Hope: New Testament Essays on Atonement and Eschatology Presented to L. L. Morris on His Sixtieth Birthday* (Grand Rapids: Eerdmans, 1974), 153–69.

[13] Bauckham thinks the denial is only moral (*Jude, 2 Peter,* 241). D. Guthrie suggests that they denied Christ's redemptive work (*New Testament Introduction,* 4th ed. [Downers Grove: InterVarsity, 1990], 847). B. Reicke, very implausibly, thinks the author addressed masters who wanted to foment a political revolt (*The Epistles of James, Peter, and Jude,* AB [Garden City: Doubleday, 1964], 145, 161). T. V. Smith argues that they denied "the redemptive meaning and significance of Jesus' crucifixion" (*Petrine Controversies in Early Christianity: Attitudes Toward Peter in Christian Writings of the First Two Centuries,* WUNT 2/15 [Tübingen: Mohr, 1985], 87). This latter interpretation reads more into the text than is warranted.

[14] So J. N. D. Kelly, *A Commentary on the Epistles of Peter and Jude,* Thornapple Commentaries (Grand Rapids: Baker, 1981), 328.

could also be translated "sudden."[15] We do not need to choose between these ideas. The judgment will be sudden, and it will be soon. Bauckham rightly remarks that Peter did not repudiate an imminent eschatology, even though he refused to calculate when the end would arrive.[16]

In the history of theology two issues have arisen in the interpretation of this verse, and they are related. Was Peter teaching that believers can commit apostasy and lose their salvation? Furthermore, did he teach what is called "unlimited atonement," that is, the idea that Christ died for all people, but only those who believe in Christ receive the benefit of the atonement that was offered to all? We should reject the interpretation defended by J. Owen, for he argued that the "buying" done by Christ was nonsoteriological in this text, so that Peter did not even have spiritual salvation in mind.[17] The problem with this view is that the New Testament nowhere else uses the word for redemption in association with Christ in a nonsoteriological sense (cf. 1 Cor 6:20; 7:23; 1 Pet 1:18–19; Rev 5:9; 14:3–4).[18] The interpretation suffers from special pleading since redemption is invariably soteriological.

We should note that many scholars who defend "unlimited atonement" also think that believers cannot lose their salvation. But a problem also arises for their interpretation. The verse seems to say that eschatological judgment will be the destiny of those who were bought by the Lord, who were members of the church, who, apparently, acknowledged Jesus Christ at some point as their Lord and Savior. The verse does not refer to people in general who are the *potential* beneficiaries of Christ's death. It speaks of false teachers who were part of Peter's church and had now rejected the gospel they first embraced. The entire discussion on limited atonement in this verse cannot be segregated from the issue of whether believers can truly apostatize. That is an issue we will face again in this chapter since

---

[15] Vögtle rejects the notion that the reference is to a sudden judgment (*Judasbrief, 2 Petrusbrief,* 185).

[16] Bauckham, *Jude, 2 Peter,* 241.

[17] J. Owen, *The Death of Death in the Death of Christ* (1852; reprint, Carlisle, Pa.: Banner of Truth, 1995), 250–52. Cf. also G. D. Long, *Definite Atonement* (Rochester: Backus, 1988), 67–84. A. D. Chang rightly argues that attempts to understand ἀγοράζω nonsoteriologically constitute special pleading ("Second Peter 2:1 and the Extent of the Atonement," *BSac* 142 [1985]: 54–56).

[18] D. W. Kennard agrees that redemption is a soteriological term. His view is distinctive in that he argues that one may be genuinely redeemed and yet one may not obtain eschatological salvation on the last day. Kennard argues that some of those who are redeemed are not elect, and hence the redeemed and elect are not necessarily coterminus ("Petrine Redemption: Its Meaning and Extent," *JETS* 39 [1987]: 399–405). At the end of the day this view is a more nuanced explanation of the notion that one can lose salvation, although it could be labeled more precisely as "the loss of redemption" view. Kennard's attempt to segregate redemption, salvation, and election does not square with the rest of the NT, nor is it evident that Peter desired his readers to distinguish an irrevocable election from a revocable redemption.

Peter spoke of those who "have left the straight way" (2:15), of those who have escaped the clutches of the world through knowing Christ but have subsequently been entangled and conquered by the world again (2:20), of those who have known the way of righteousness but have now turned from it (2:21). The issue raised by these verses will be discussed in 2:17–22. We must see, however, that 2:1 raises fundamentally the same question.

The easiest solution, in some ways, would be to take the verse straightforwardly. Some who submit to Christ's lordship subsequently deny him and are therefore damned forever.[19] This is now the view of most commentators, and it has the virtue of providing a lucid and uncomplicated understanding of the text. At one level the proposed interpretation is correct. Some members of the Christian community had departed from the Christian faith. The issue is whether those who are genuinely Christians can commit apostasy. Peter taught elsewhere that those who are called by God's grace are effectually called by his own glory and excellence (2 Pet 1:3), and 1 Pet 1:5 clearly says that those who belong to God will be preserved by his power through faith so that they will possess eschatological salvation.[20] When we add to this many other texts that teach that those whom God has called will never perish (e.g., Rom 8:28–39; 1 Cor 1:8–9; Phil 1:6; 1 Thess 5:23–24), it suggests that we should consider another interpretation. I would suggest that Peter used phenomenological language. In other words, he described the false teachers as believers because they made a profession of faith and gave every appearance initially of being genuine believers. Peter did not refer to those who had been outside the community of faith but to those who were part of the church and perhaps even leaders among God's people. Their denial of Jesus Christ reveals that they did not truly belong to God, even though they professed faith. Peter said that they were bought by Jesus Christ, in the sense that they gave every indication initially of genuine faith. In every church there are members who appear to be believers and who should be accepted as believers according to the judgment of charity. As time elapses and difficulties arise, it becomes apparent that they are wolves in the flock (Acts 20:29–30), that though they called on Jesus as Lord their disobedience shows that he *never* knew them (Matt

---

[19] Cf. Bauckham, "Thus 2 Peter does not deny that the false teachers are Christians, but sees them as apostate Christians who have disowned their Master" (*Jude, 2 Peter,* 240). Chang adopts what he calls the "spiritual redemption" view in which he embraces unlimited atonement and then argues that the problem with the false teachers was that they did not embrace the salvation purchased for them ("Extent of the Atonement," 52–63). What Chang does not explain thoroughly, however, is the remaining context of 2 Peter, where it is clear that the false teachers claimed to be part of the Christian community, were recognized as Christians by others in the church (at least initially), and made a profession of faith in Jesus as Messiah. Hence, to be consistent he should argue that those who initially submit to the lordship of Christ may in fact apostatize.

[20] See my comments on that verse.

7:21–23), that they are like the seed sown on rocky or thorny ground that initially bears fruit but dries up and dies when hard times come (Matt 13:20–22).

2:2 Peter turned in this verse to the impact the false teachers have on others and the consequence of that influence. He did not expect their influence to be minimal, so that everyone would recognize how inauthentic they are. Instead "many" will become devoted to them, following their unethical example. The word translated "shameful ways" by the NIV *(aselgeiais)* often refers to sexual sin in the New Testament (Rom 13:13; 2 Cor 12:21; Gal 5:19; Eph 4:19; probably 1 Pet 4:3; Jude 4; cf. *Wis* 14:26).[21] The same is likely true here as well. What attracts people to these false teachers is that they advocate a licentious lifestyle, and therefore many people are only too glad to follow their example.[22]

The infection from the false teachers spreads to others, but it does not stop there. The unbelieving world sees the impact on the church and responds by maligning and ridiculing "the way of truth." "The way of truth" is a reference to the gospel. The term "way" *(hodos)* was popular in the early church. According to Acts the early Christian movement was designated "the Way" (Acts 9:2; 19:9,23; 22:4; 24:14,22). The gospel is also described as "the way to be saved" (Acts 16:17), "the way of the Lord" (Acts 18:25), and "the way of God" (Acts 18:26). Peter said that the false teachers "have left the straight way . . . to follow the way of Balaam" (2 Pet 2:15). He remarked in 2:21 that it "would have been better for them not to have known the way of righteousness." The language of the two ways also was prominent in the writings that succeeded the New Testament (e.g., *Barn.*18:1–21:9; *Did.* 1:1–6:3). Peter's main point was that the gospel, which he designated as the way of truth, would be maligned because of the impact of the false teachers. When unbelievers see the moral effect produced by the opponents in the lives of their followers, they will conclude that the way of truth is a way of error. They will think that any message that leads to dissolute behavior cannot be from God. Paul indicted the Jews similarly in Rom 2:24, quoting Isa 52:5. The Gentiles maligned God's name because of the disobedience of the Jews. Christian slaves were to honor their masters so that God's name and Christian teaching would not be criticized (1 Tim 6:1). Young believing wives were to live in a godly way so that people would not revile God's word (Titus 2:5; cf. also 1 Thess 4:12; 1 Pet 2:12,15; 3:16).

---

[21] So Paulsen, *Petrusbrief und Judasbrief,* 129; Fuchs and Reymond, *2 Pierre, Jude,* 80.

[22] T. Fornberg suggests that in context the term may refer to doctrinal deviation rather than sexual immorality (*An Early Church in a Pluralistic Society*: *A Study of 2 Peter,* ConBNT 9 [Lund: Gleerup, 1977], 37). Quite unlikely as well is the view of T. A. Miller that the author did not refer literally to sexual immorality ("Dogs, Adulterers, and the Way of Balaam: The Forms and Socio-Rhetorical Function of the Polemical Rhetoric in 2 Peter [Part I]," *IBS* 22 [2000]: 133).

2:3 We saw in v. 2 that the false teachers would captivate many and thereby bring criticism on the gospel. Peter pounced on their central motive in v. 3. They were not disinterested teachers of truth, impartially and sacrificially seeking to help others. They were motivated by greed, a desire for the comforts of this life. The word translated "exploit" *(emporeuomai)* often in Greek literature refers to engaging in business (cf. Jas 4:13). The NIV rightly renders it "exploit" here since it is associated with the words "in greed." These teachers were not selling a product to help their hearers. They were hawking defective goods (morally speaking) for their own financial advantage. As 2:14 says, "They are experts in greed." We have seen two characteristics of the false teachers in vv. 2–3. They were sexually licentious and motivated by greed. These two vices often appear in the lives of false teachers. Peter said that they would exploit others with "stories they have made up." Literally the phrase means "fabricated words" *(plastois logois)*. The reference probably is to their teaching about the future, in which they denied the coming of the Lord and the future judgment (3:3–7). The false teachers charged the apostles with devising myths to support the Lord's coming (1:16), but the opponents themselves distorted the truth.[23] Such teaching paves the way for an immoral lifestyle that the false teachers allege will face no consequences.

What people think about judgment, of course, does not necessarily square up with reality. Peter assured his readers that the judgment would come. Probably the point is that the judgment has been planned for them for a long time (cf. Jude 4). Literally Peter said "it is not idle" *(ouk argei)*. The false teachers should not conclude from the elapse of a long period of time that the judgment would never come (3:3–4). The next line expresses the same truth in a complementary way. The word for "destruction" *(apōleia)* is a common word for the consequences of the future judgment. To say that their destruction is not sleeping is to say that it will certainly come.[24] The "fabricated words" will be exposed in all their hollowness on the day of judgment.

2. The Certain Judgment of the Ungodly and the Preservation of the Godly (2:4–10a)

[4]For if God did not spare angels when they sinned, but sent them to hell, putting them into gloomy dungeons to be held for judgment; [5]if he did not spare the ancient world when he brought the flood on its ungodly people, but protected Noah, a preacher of righteousness, and seven others; [6]if he condemned the cities of Sodom and Gomorrah by burning them to ashes, and made them an example

[23] Cf. Bauckham, *Jude, 2 Peter,* 243.

[24] Note Ps 121:3–4, where we are told that God does not sleep.

of what is going to happen to the ungodly; [7]and if he rescued Lot, a righteous man, who was distressed by the filthy lives of lawless men [8](for that righteous man, living among them day after day, was tormented in his righteous soul by the lawless deeds he saw and heard)— [9]if this is so, then the Lord knows how to rescue godly men from trials and to hold the unrighteous for the day of judgment, while continuing their punishment. [10]This is especially true of those who follow the corrupt desire of the sinful nature and despise authority.

Verse 3b is a transitional verse, and hence some commentators link it with this section; but since the verse is transitional, it fits well with either paragraph.[25] The logic of vv. 1–3 functions like this: Because the false teachers both lived wickedly and disseminated their wickedness to others (vv. 1–3a), *therefore* God would certainly judge them (v. 3b). The theme of God's judgment in v. 3b also informs vv. 4–10. God's future judgment of the wicked is certain (v. 3b) because God has consistently judged the wicked throughout history. Three examples of the judgment of the wicked are adduced: (1) the judgment of the angels of Gen 6:1–4, (2) the destruction of the world during the time of the flood, and (3) the razing of Sodom and Gomorrah. We know that the false teachers in 2 Peter were skeptical about the Lord's coming and hence about the future judgment (3:3–7). Three representative and typological examples of God's judgment demonstrate that God's character has not changed. Previous judgments in history point toward and anticipate the final judgment, which is the climax of all other judgments. In the summary of Jude 5–7 the Jewish tradition on which both Jude and 2 Peter drew is sketched in, and readers should consult the discussion there for important antecedents to Peter's thought.

The parallels with Jude (vv. 5–7) are significant, though Peter departed from Jude in terms of exact wording. Peter and Jude both mentioned the judgment on angels and Sodom and Gomorrah. Peter, however, included a reference to the flood, while Jude drew attention to the judgment of Israel after their liberation from Egypt. Jude did not present the incidents in canonical order, placing Israel at the beginning of his list. Peter, on the other hand, followed the canonical order of the judgment of the angels of Genesis 6, the flood, and Sodom and Gomorrah. Can we detect any reason for the difference? We know from 2 Pet 3:6 that the flood functions as a particularly vivid example and type of God's future judgment. Nothing prepared the people of Noah's day for such a calamity. It was unexpected, and Peter suggested that Noah was mocked by his contemporaries for proclaiming its imminence. The completeness of the destruction also prefigures the final judgment. Only Noah and his family were left. The rest of the world was swept away. Recalling the flood is apt indeed in the situation addressed

[25] Rightly Moo, *2 Peter, Jude,* 100.

by 2 Peter since the false teachers denied future judgment and ridiculed believers who continued to believe in the future coming of Christ.

Peter wove in another theme lacking in Jude, namely, the preservation of the righteous, in which Noah and Lot were presented as key examples. The future judgment does not only consist of the condemnation of the wicked, but it will also involve the vindication of the righteous, whom God is able to preserve in the midst of difficulties. Perhaps Peter included this theme because the faithful were a small minority in the church, needing encouragement with the onslaught of the false teachers. The false teachers had emerged from within the church (2:1), in contrast to Jude, where the opponents were intruders from the outside (Jude 4). Believers are encouraged with the grace of God, for if God strengthened Noah and Lot in situations where evil dominated, then he would also preserve the believers who were confronting the deception posed by false teachers.

We should also notice the structure of the text. Peter began with a protasis, an "if" clause in v. 4, and the apodosis (a "then" clause) is delayed until v. 9. He gave a series of three examples of God's judgment and two examples of his preservation in vv. 4–8, leading up to his conclusion in v. 9.[26] The structure of the text helps us to see clearly Peter's main themes: the judgment of the wicked and the preservation of the godly. We can set forth the text like this:

If God judged the angels (v. 4), and

if he judged the flood generation (v. 5),	while at the same time sparing Noah (v. 5),
and if he judged Sodom and Gomorrah, (v. 6)	while at the same time preserving Lot (vv. 7–8),

then it follows that the Lord will preserve the godly in the midst of their trials (drawing this conclusion from the examples of Noah and Lot),

and it also follows that the Lord will punish the ungodly on the day of judgment (drawing this conclusion from the three examples of the angels, the flood, and Sodom and Gomorrah).

2:4 The "for" *(gar)* links v. 4 with v. 3b and introduces the first of three examples that illustrate God's judgment in the past and guarantee it for the future. Hence, the judgment functions typologically. The first judgment relates to the angels whom God did not spare when they sinned. Peter differed from Jude in that he emphasized the judgment without giving specifics of the

---

[26] It could be argued that we do not have a second example here since angels and human beings were judged at the same time, and seeing two examples would fit nicely with the preservation of both Noah and Lot. Still, the parallel with Jude (vv. 5–7) suggests three examples of judgment.

angels' sin.[27] Some scholars in the history of interpretation have identified this as the prehistoric fall of angels. It is doubtful, however, that Peter referred to this event in this particular text, even if it is a legitimate deduction theologically. Instead, we can be almost certain that Peter followed Jewish tradition at this point and referred to the sin angels committed with women in Gen 6:1–4 (*1 Enoch* 6–19,21,86–88; 106:13–17; *Jub.* 4:15, 22; 5:1; CD 2:17–19; 1QapGen 2:1; *T. Reu.* 5:6–7; *T. Naph.* 3:5; *2 Bar.* 56:10–14; cf. Josephus, *Ant.* 1.73).[28] Under Jude v. 5 I have summarized more completely the Jewish tradition that identifies the sons of God in Gen 6:1–4 with angels, and I also briefly explain there why such a view is a plausible reading of Genesis 6. The sin committed by angels was sexual intercourse with the daughters of men. Three reasons support the view that Peter thought of angels who committed sexual sin in Gen 6:1–4. First, such an interpretation, as the texts above indicate, was widespread in Jewish tradition. Peter's readers would naturally have understood the account in terms of such a tradition unless Peter indicated clearly that he was departing from the common understanding of his day. Peter gave no indication, however, that he differed from the tradition. Second, nor would such an understanding be difficult for Peter's readers. The Greeks also had the story of the Titans, which is similar in some respects to Gen 6:1–4 (Hesiod, *Theogony* [713–35]). Third, Jude almost certainly understood the story of Gen 6:1–4 to refer to angels who sinned, given that he was influenced by *1 Enoch,* and the account is more prominent in *1 Enoch* than any other work. It is quite unlikely that Peter veered off in another direction from Jude, for regardless of the question of literary dependence, it is obvious that Jude and 2 Peter both drew from common tradition in some form.

The second half of the verse conveys the judgment experienced by the angels. The NIV says that the angels were sent to "hell." But Peter did not use the word *gehenna* here, the usual word for "hell," but the Greek verbal participle *tartarōsas,* from which we get our word "Tartarus." Tartarus in Greek literature refers to the underworld, and here we have another indication that Peter desired to communicate with his readers in terms of their own idiom. The word "hell" is misleading if it suggests final punishment since the verse makes clear that the climactic judgment still awaits the angels.[29] Nor does the use of the term indicate that Peter was familiar with Greek literature, for he simply employed the common currency of the day, and hence we should not conclude that Peter was necessarily familiar with

---

[27] So J. Kahmann, "Second Peter and Jude," in *The New Testament in Early Christianity: La réception des écrits néotestamentaires dans le christianisme primitif,* BETL 86 (Leuven: University Press, 1989), 108; cf. Fornberg, *An Early Church in a Pluralistic Society,* 48 (though he may underemphasize the presence of sexual sin in 2 Peter).

[28] Another possibility is that Gen 6:1–4 itself represents the fall of angels from righteousness. If this is the case, then the angels fell from righteousness after Adam and not at the same time as Satan.

[29] Rightly Moo, *2 Peter, Jude,* 103.

Greek classics simply from the use of this word. Indeed, the word is used by other Jewish writers, so that it was even available from the Septuagint (Job 40:20; 41:24; Prov 3:16; cf. *1 Enoch* 20:2; *Sib. Or.* 2:303; 4:186; Josephus, *C. Ap.* 2.240; Philo, *Rewards,* 152; *Embassy,* 103).[30]

The angels confined to Tartarus were confined to "gloomy dungeons." A significant textual variant exists here between the Greek words *sirois* and *seirais*. Nestle-Aland[27] prefers the latter, which could be translated "chains" or "cords." This reading is reflected in the NRSV, which says God "committed them to chains of deepest darkness" (cf. KJV, NKJV, HCSB).[31] The NIV translation favors *sirois,* translating it as "dungeons" (cf. RSV, NASB). The textual evidence is evenly divided, so internal evidence probably is more important. Some scholars think Peter substituted a more elegant term for Jude's *desmois* ("chains").[32] But it is more likely that scribes conformed Peter's wording to Jude's since the texts are parallel, and seeing *sirois* ("pits") they altered it to *seirais* ("chains").[33] In any case, the term Tartarus suggests that the angels are both confined and restrained because of their sin. The language of confinement could be interpreted literally, as if the angels are restricted to a physical locality. More likely the language is symbolic, conveying the idea that the angels who sinned are now restrained in some way because of their sin, that God has now limited their sphere of operation.[34] The last phrase in the verse, "held for judgment," conveys a similar idea. The future judgment of these angels is certain, and presently they are being kept by God for their punishment on the eschatological day. In the case of the angels, then, the punishment has two dimensions—the restriction imposed immediately as a result of their sin and the punishment they will receive on the day of the Lord's return.

2:5 The second example of judgment is the flood that deluged the world in the time of Noah (Gen 6:5–7:24).[35] The words "did not spare" are repeated from v. 4, emphasizing that the judgment was a reality and at the

---

[30] Rightly Paulsen, *Petrusbrief und Judasbrief,* 133.

[31] But note that the datives modify ταρταρώσας in my judgment. The difference in meaning is not significant either way.

[32] Cf. *TCGNT* 632.

[33] So Mayor, *Jude and Second Peter,* 121; Fornberg, *An Early Church in a Pluralistic Society,* 52; Moo, *2 Peter, Jude,* 102; Fuchs and Reymond, *2 Pierre, Jude,* 83. Fornberg notes that σιρός was used for storage rooms for seed. The word also was used for hell since it denoted "the underground silos at Eleusis, where the firstfruits were stored as a symbol of Kore's descent to, and sojourn in Hades" (pp. 52–53).

[34] Rightly Moo, *2 Peter, Jude,* 116.

[35] M. Luther says about this verse: "This is also a fearful example, the most horrible one in the Scriptures. One might almost despair in view of it, even if he were strong in faith. For when such language and judgment of God go to man's heart, and he thinks of it, that he too shall die. He must tremble and fear if he is not well armed, since among so many in the whole world no one but these eight only were saved" (*Commentary on Peter & Jude* [Grand Rapids: Kregel, 1990], 261).

same time eliminating any hope that God might show mercy and relent from judging the world. Peter also referred to the judgment of the flood in 3:6, when he countered the false teachers who denied the second coming. It is evident, therefore, that the deluge was crucial for Peter's argument against the opponents since it provided concrete evidence that God judges sin and functions as a type of the future judgment.[36] One of the reasons the flood functions well as a type is that it includes the whole world. Peter used the word "world" *(kosmos)* twice in the verse (it is translated "people" in the second instance by the NIV). The universality of the judgment in Noah's day functions well as a preview of the universal judgment at the end of the age. No one will be spared, or, more precisely, none of the ungodly *(asebōn)* will escape. The reference to the ungodly indicates that the focus is on the *people* who were destroyed rather than focusing on the flood as embracing the entire world.[37] Perhaps, though, both ideas are intended.[38]

Peter did not focus only on the judgment of the wicked but also the preservation of the righteous. God is the one who preserved and protected *(ephylaxen)* Noah from the judgment. Peter's lesson for his readers is evident. God will protect those who resist the enticements of the false teachers. The faithful will be vindicated by God. Noah was not alone in his righteousness, but he was preserved along with seven others—his wife, his three sons, and their wives. The Greek text actually uses the word "eighth" *(ogdoon),* which is conveyed in the KJV translation he "saved Noah the eighth *person.*" Why did Peter use the word "eighth"?[39] In early church writings the number eight was considered the number of perfection since Jesus was raised on the eighth day—Sunday.[40] Hence, it may be that Noah is portrayed here as the beginning of a new creation after the flood, and similarly believers are a new creation in Christ. It is unclear, however, that any New Testament writer used the number eight symbolically, nor does the context indicate such a use here.[41] In 1 Pet 3:20 we see that the number eight was used to convey the idea that God's people, though few in number, were saved by God during the flood. Since we have the same author and even the same subject, a similar conclusion should be drawn here. Even if the righteous are completely outnumbered, they will prevail

---

[36] Note the link between the judgment at the time of the flood (ἐπάξας, v. 5) and the future judgment (ἐπάγοντες, v. 1). I owe this insight to Fornberg, *An Early Church in a Pluralistic Society,* 42.

[37] So Kelly, *Peter and Jude,* 332, but cf. Vögtle, *Judasbrief, 2 Petrusbrief,* 190.

[38] So Bauckham, *Jude, 2 Peter,* 250.

[39] Bigg adopts the view that Noah is the eighth from Adam chronologically (*Peter and Jude,* 276), but the parallel with 1 Pet 3:20 suggests otherwise, nor is there any suggestion that Peter began with Adam.

[40] Cf. Reicke, *James, Peter, and Jude,* 165; Bauckham, *Jude, 2 Peter,* 250.

[41] Rightly Paulsen, *Petrusbrief und Judasbrief,* 133.

because God is faithful to his people.

We are also told that Noah was "a preacher of righteousness." The description here elicits interest because the Old Testament never informs us that Noah preached to his contemporaries. The idea that Noah entreated his generation to repent, however, is common in Jewish tradition (Josephus, *Ant.* 1.74; *Jub.* 7:20–29; *Sib. Or.* 1:128–29, 150–98; cf. *1 Clem* 7:6; 9:4). As Josephus said, "But Noah, indignant at their conduct and viewing their counsels with displeasure, urged them to come to a better frame of mind and amend their ways" (*Ant.* 1.74). That Noah proclaimed God's righteousness is a fair deduction from the Old Testament itself, since it is quite unlikely that he did not share with his contemporaries why he was building the ark. The verse is marked by duality. God did not spare the ancient world, but he protected Noah. He destroyed many people but saved a few. Noah was preserved as a preacher of *righteousness*, but the world of the *ungodly* was destroyed. Most commentators understand "righteousness" to refer to God's justice in judging the ungodly,[42] and certainly Noah proclaimed such a standard. But we have already noted that Jewish tradition also taught that Noah preached repentance. I think such an idea is implicit in "righteousness" as well. In emphasizing God's righteous judgment of sinners, Noah also invited the people of his age to repent and to enjoy God's forgiveness, his saving righteousness. This fits with what Peter said about God's righteousness in 1:1, which is a gift received by believers. Those who enjoy God's saving righteousness repented of their sins and turned to God, acknowledging his righteous judgment against them. The ungodly refuse to hear God's word of judgment against them, insisting, as Noah's contemporaries did, that any notion of a future condemnation is laughable. Similarly, the false teachers in the Petrine churches rejected a future judgment, maintaining that the world will continue to follow the same course (3:4). Thereby they abandoned God's righteous standards and refused to accept his saving righteousness.

2:6 The third example of God's judgment focuses on the cities of Sodom and Gomorrah. Unlike Jude (v. 7), Peter did not identify the sin of the cities but directed attention to their judgment. Probably there was no need to highlight the sin since it was well known both from the Scriptures and postbiblical tradition.[43] In any case, Peter emphasized the result of God's judgment in that the cities were reduced "to ashes" *(teprōsas)*. The Old Testament itself does not say the cities were burned to ashes, though it is a fair deduction from the fire that leveled the cities (Gen 19:23–29). It was likely a common idea that the cities turned to ashes, for Philo attests

[42] E.g., Fuchs and Reymond, *2 Pierre, Jude,* 85.

[43] See the more extensive discussion on Jude 7.

this very idea (*Drunkenness* 223; *On the Life of Moses* 2.56). Perhaps Peter brought attention to this phenomenon since it functioned as hard evidence in his day that the cities were indeed destroyed, for this theme emerged in postbiblical writings. "Evidence of their wickedness still remains: a continually smoking wasteland, plants bearing fruit that does not ripen" (*Wis* 10:7). Josephus said: "In fact, vestiges of the divine fire and faint traces of five cities are still visible. Still, too, may one see ashes reproduced in the fruits, which from their outward appearance would be thought edible, but on being plucked with the hand dissolve into smoke and ashes. So far are the legends about the land of Sodom borne out by ocular evidence" (*J.W.* 4.484–85).[44] Philo made similar remarks (*Abraham* 141): "Even to this day there are seen in Syria monuments of the unprecedented destruction that fell upon them, in the ruins, and ashes, and sulphur, and smoke, and the dusky flame which still is sent up from the ground as of a fire smouldering beneath" (*Moses* 2.56).

It is difficult to know whether the word *katastrophē* is part of the original text. It is omitted in the NIV, but it appears in the NASB, "condemned . . . to destruction" (cf. also KJV, RSV, NRSV).[45] Once again the textual evidence is finely balanced.[46] I suspect that Metzger's suggestion that some scribes overlooked the word *katastrophē* since the next word "condemned" *(katekrinen)* begins with the same letters *(kat)* is correct.[47] The inclusion of the word fits with Peter's emphasis on the *results* of the judgment. Perhaps Peter alluded here to the Septuagint, for Gen 19:29 says that God sent Lot away from the middle of "the destruction" *(tēs katastrophēs).*

Jude emphasized that the judgment of the cities forecast the fiery nature of the future judgment, but Peter stressed that God appointed the cities as an example for the ungodly still to come. The words translated "made them" probably designate God's appointment since the verb *tithēmi* often has this sense in the New Testament (Matt 22:14 par.; Acts 1:7; 13:47; 20:28; Rom 4:17; 1 Cor 12:18,28; 1 Thess 5:9; 1 Tim 2:7; 2 Tim 1:11; Heb 1:2; 1 Pet 2:8), and it makes good sense here since Peter emphasized that God appointed the judgment of these cities to provide a picture of what is to come for the ungodly. The judgment of Sodom and Gomorrah is not merely a historical curiosity but functions as a type of what God will do in the future.[48] It previews the condemnation of the false teachers of Peter's day and those who succumbed to the influence of these teachers. The word

[44] Josephus claims to have seen the pillar of salt that was Lot's wife (*Ant.* 1.203).

[45] Against Mayor, who reads the dative of καταστροφῇ as instrumental (*Jude and Second Peter,* 124).

[46] Against its inclusion see Fuchs and Reymond, *2 Pierre, Jude,* 83.

[47] *TCGNT* 632

[48] Cf. Fornberg, *An Early Church in a Pluralistic Society,* 43.

"example" (*hypodeigma;* cf. Jude's *deigma* in v. 6) is rightly translated "example" here instead of "pattern" or "model" (cf. Heb 8:5; 9:23).[49] The word clearly means "example" in a number of texts (John 13:15; Heb 4:11; Jas 5:10), and the latter makes better sense in the context of 2 Peter.

The verse closes with another difficult textual problem. The NIV translates "an example of what is going to happen to the ungodly" *(hypodeigma mellontōn asebesin).* Alternatively, the Greek could be rendered "an example for those who will live in an ungodly way" *(hypodeigma mellontōn asebein).*[50] Once again the textual evidence is evenly divided, so making a decision on external grounds is quite difficult. The reading in the NIV is preferred on internal grounds because it is slightly more likely that Peter would emphasize the *judgment to come* rather than the *ungodly who will come.* The former theme fits with the entire letter, where the certainty of the second coming and as a corollary the future judgment are taught.

2:7 Not everyone was destroyed at Sodom and Gomorrah. Just as Noah and his family were preserved during the flood, so God delivered Lot from the judgment imposed on Sodom and Gomorrah. Many readers of Genesis have wondered why Peter described Lot as righteous, for they find fault with him for living in Sodom, for being hesitant to leave, and for getting drunk with the result that his daughters had sexual relations with him (see Genesis 19).[51] Writers in the postbiblical tradition thought of Lot as righteous (e.g., *Wis* 10:6). *First Clement* 11:1 confirms such an interpretation: "Because of his hospitality and godliness Lot was saved from Sodom, when the entire region was judged by fire and brimstone." Neither was Peter violating the meaning of the Old Testament. Abraham prayed in Genesis 18 that the Lord would preserve Sodom if there were even ten righteous within it. The Lord more than answered Abraham's prayer, for he rescued from the city the one person who was righteous.[52] The Judge of all the earth does not destroy the righteous along with the wicked (Gen 18:25). The narrator of Genesis, by recording the rescue of Lot, intimates

---

[49] See E. K. Lee, "Words Denoting 'Pattern' in the New Testament," *NTS* 8 (1961): 167–69.

[50] Cf. Fuchs and Reymond, *2 Pierre, Jude,* 85.

[51] Supporting the argument here is T. D. Alexander, "Lot's Hospitality: A Clue to His Righteousness," *JBL* 104 (1995): 289–91. Alexander concludes his article with these words (p. 191): "The portrait of Lot as 'righteous' represents an accurate interpretation of the author's intention in Genesis 18–19."

[52] Moo rightly notes that "righteous" can denote one's status before God (*2 Peter, Jude,* 105), but it is unlikely that Peter suggests that notion here. His point is that Lot lived a righteous life in comparison to the inhabitants of Sodom and Gomorrah. Hence, Charles is incorrect to say that Lot functions as a contrast to Noah, nor is he on target when he claims that Lot is not presented as righteous in the OT (*Virtue amidst Vice,* 88–89).

that he was righteous.[53] And other hints are in the narrative as well. Only Lot showed the angels hospitality when they arrived in the city (Gen 19:1–3). Lot remonstrated with the men who wanted to have sexual relations with the visitors, when he could have spared himself trouble by abandoning the angels (Gen 19:5–9). Modern readers, of course, are struck by the fact that he offered his daughters, and clearly Lot was not without fault. Nonetheless, ancient readers would have saluted his courage in trying to protect those who were in his house, a matter of great danger when the whole city was at his doorstep. Indeed, Lot's godliness was all the more remarkable given the context in which he lived. We are prone, from the safe offices and homes in which we write and read, to criticize Lot, but most of us have never been even close to death in a conflict with others. Nor have any of us ever lived in a city like Sodom with no comrades to strengthen us in the faith. Lot wavered and doubted, but Peter addressed readers who also were wavering because of the appearance of false teachers. Just as Peter was confident that the believers he addressed would resist the opponents, so too Lot *was different* from the rest of Sodom. That is why the Lord rescued him. Peter informs us that Lot was oppressed by living in Sodom, that their ungodly conduct took a toll on him psychologically. The word translated "filthy" by the NIV renders the Greek word *aselgeia,* which often designates sexual sin (note the NASB "sensual conduct").[54]

2:8 The oppression Lot experienced is expanded on in v. 8, which is connected to v. 7 by "for" *(gar)*. Hence, the parenthesis in the NIV is justified in that v. 8 elaborates on Lot's distress from v. 7. Peter repeated that Lot was "righteous" *(dikaios),* standing in stark contrast to the inhabitants of Sodom and Gomorrah. The emphasis on his righteousness is also communicated by the phrase "his righteous soul." One indication of righteousness is torment and distress over those who live unrighteously, and the main point of this verse is that Lot was so tormented. Since he lived in the midst of them, he experienced daily the distress of their "lawless deeds." How was he aware on a regular basis of the antinomian lifestyle of such

---

[53] N. Hillyer remarks that "Lot's heart was clearly still somewhat responsive to God, even after having his permanent home in such an environment" (*1 and 2 Peter, Jude,* NIBC [Peabody: Hendrickson, 1992], 190).

[54] For a reference to sexual sin, see Fuchs and Reymond, *2 Pierre, Jude,* 86. J. Makujina appeals to Jewish tradition and a textual variant represented by the LXX in Gen 19:16 (which reads "and they were troubled" instead of "he hesitated") to explain the positive reference to Lot here ("The 'Trouble' with Lot in 2 Peter: Locating Peter's Source for Lot's Torment," *WTJ* 60 [1998]: 255–69). Doubtless Peter may have referred to extrabiblical tradition when referring to Lot, though it seems to me that one can appeal to the biblical material itself to explain the positive reference to Lot. Furthermore, it is difficult to sustain the notion that Peter was using the LXX of Gen 19:16 in 2 Peter. The evidence is insufficient to warrant such a conclusion.

sinners? Peter informs us that he was confronted with their evil by what he saw and heard.

2:9 The long protasis, beginning with the "if" in 2:4, finally reaches its conclusion in the apodosis in this verse. Having given three examples of divine judgment (angels, flood, and Sodom and Gomorrah) and two of divine preservation (Noah and Lot), Peter now draws the threads together and presents a conclusion from the particular examples. The conclusion has two distinct parts. First, the Lord knows how to preserve the godly in their trials. Second, he knows how to keep the unrighteous for the future day of judgment. We will examine both of these points in order. The word "rescue" *(rhyesthai)* picks up the same verb that was used with reference to Lot in v. 7, and it overlaps in meaning with "protected" *(ephylaxen)* with reference to Noah in v. 5. The NIV uses the plural "trials," but the external evidence supports the singular "trial" *(peirasmou),* though the singular is generic and thus includes the idea of many trials. The NRSV renders the original text more accurately "the Lord knows how to rescue the godly from trials." The word *peirasmou* could be rendered "temptation" (cf. Jas 1:13–14), but in this context the focus is not on internal inclinations to sin (as in James) but on external situations that are difficult and could lead to sin. In this instance the difficulty comes from the false teachers. The line between the English "temptation" and "trials" is a slender one, for they represent the same Greek word. The external situation ("trials") may become the occasion in which believers are "tempted" internally, so perhaps we should not press the difference between the two.[55] There probably is an allusion to the Lord's Prayer, in which believers are urged to pray that the Lord would deliver them from temptation (Matt 6:13; cf. Luke 11:4; Matt 26:41). The danger in a time of trial is apostasy (Luke 8:13; 22:28). God is faithful and promises to keep his people in a time of trial (1 Cor 10:13; Rev 3:10; cf. *Sir* 33:1). Hence, some scholars detect a reference to the test of faith that will conclude history.[56] We should not separate the final test, however, from the tests oppressing Peter's readers at the time the letter was written, for any trial becomes an occasion in which one's faithfulness to the Lord is tested. Thus Moo rightly says that "trial" refers to "all those challenges to faith that Christians experience in this world."[57]

The parallel texts noted above are important because Peter could be understood to say that believers will not have to experience times of trial, in the sense that God will exempt them from facing any trials at all. This is most emphatically not what the text means. Both Noah and Lot lived in the

---

[55] Kelly thinks the focus is on "temptation" (*Peter and Jude,* 334).

[56] Green, *2 Peter and Jude,* 113; Bauckham, *Jude, 2 Peter,* 253.

[57] Moo, *2 Peter, Jude,* 106.

midst of the wicked and were confronted by a great majority of evil people. Similarly, Peter's readers were oppressed and tormented (like Lot) by the false teachers of their day. Peter was not promising that such teachers would be removed immediately from the scene. Nor was Peter communicating the idea that true believers never sin. His point was that those who are godly and righteous will be prevented from committing apostasy. God will guard them so that in the end they will not forsake him. We should not read this to say that the Lord knows how to rescue the godly from trial, but some actually fall anyway. Instead, all the godly *will be preserved* by the Lord. He will keep them from apostasy, just as he guarded Noah and Lot so that they did not depart from him.

The second point is derived from the three examples of judgment in history. If the Lord judged the angels who sinned, the flood generation, and Sodom and Gomorrah, he will also "hold the unrighteous for the day of judgment." The angels, the flood generation, and Sodom and Gomorrah were not judged immediately. They pursued their sin for some time before the fateful day of judgment. Hence, Peter's readers were not to be discouraged or wonder if God is faithful simply because the false teachers were prospering. God was granting them time to repent before the end arrives (3:9). For those who do not repent, the eschatological judgment is certain. The one difficulty here is the present participle *kolazomenous*. The present participle might suggest that the wicked are being punished even now.[58] This would fit with the example of angels who are confined before their future punishment (2:4). Intermediate punishment also seems to be taught in Luke 16:23–24 (cf. *1 Enoch* 22:10–11; *4 Ezra* 7:79–87). The NIV adopts this interpretation by translating the participle as a present reality: the Lord keeps "the unrighteous for the day of judgment *while continuing their punishment*." The wicked, on this view, are suffering punishment even now while awaiting the judgment of the final day. Though this interpretation is possible, present participles do not necessarily denote present time (cf. 2 Pet 3:11).[59] Context is the decisive criterion. I think it is quite unlikely that Peter depicted the present judgment of the wicked. The false teachers in the letter gave every appearance of current prosperity.[60] They may have influenced some for this very reason, for they mocked the coming of the Lord without suffering any ill consequences. Hence, it seems more likely

[58] So Kelly, *Peter and Jude*, 335; Moo, *2 Peter, Jude*, 107; Fornberg, *An Early Church in a Pluralistic Society*, 45; Hillyer, *1 and 2 Peter, Jude*, 191.

[59] Cf. N. Turner, *A Grammar of New Testament Greek*, Volume 3: Syntax (Edinburgh: T & T Clark, 1964), 87; D. B. Wallace, *Greek Grammar Beyond the Basics: An Exegetical Syntax of the New Testament* (Grand Rapids: Zondervan, 1996), 626; A. T. Robertson, *A Grammar of the Greek New Testament in the Light of Historical Research* (Nashville: Broadman, 1934), 891, 1115.

[60] So also Bauckham, *Jude, 2 Peter*, 254.

that Peter reminded his readers of the final judgment, the day when the opponents will experience condemnation.[61]

2:10a The paragraph ends with two reasons that explain why the future judgment is fitting. The NIV, as usual, renders the word "flesh" *(sarx)* by "sinful nature." The "corrupt desire" of the flesh followed by these men likely refers to sexual sin.[62] We have already seen a reference to their sexual sin in 2:2. The sin of the angels (2:4) and Sodom and Gomorrah (2:6) included sexual deviation, and 2:7 indicates that Lot was oppressed in part by their sensual perversity. Since the opponents repudiated any future judgment, they lived dissolute lives sexually, without any thought of a reckoning on the last day.[63] The second sin of the teachers is that they "despise authority," which is close to Jude's statement that they "reject authority" (v. 8). The word for "authority" here is *kyriotēs.* Some see a reference to angels (Eph 1:21; Col 1:16), but the singular indicates that angels probably were not intended. Even less likely is the idea that the reference is human authorities, whether leaders in the churches or governmental officials.[64] Probably the focus is on Christ's sovereignty and authority that is rejected by the adversaries, but by refusing to submit to Christ, they reveal their insubordination and rebelliousness in general.[65] These people will not submit to anyone, being supremely confident of their intellectual ability.

3. False Teachers Judged for Their Rebellion and Sensuality (2:10b–16)

Bold and arrogant, these men are not afraid to slander celestial beings; [11]yet even angels, although they are stronger and more powerful, do not bring slanderous accusations against such beings in the presence of the Lord. [12]But these men blaspheme in matters they do not understand. They are like brute beasts, creatures of instinct, born only to be caught and destroyed, and like beasts they too will perish.

[13]They will be paid back with harm for the harm they have done. Their idea of pleasure is to carouse in broad daylight. They are blots and blemishes, reveling in their pleasures while they feast with you. [14]With eyes full of adultery, they never stop sinning; they seduce the unstable; they are experts in greed—an accursed

[61] So already J. Calvin, *Commentaries on the Catholic Epistles* (Grand Rapids: Eerdmans, 1948), 400; cf. Fuchs and Reymond, *2 Pierre, Jude,* 88.

[62] See Neyrey, *2 Peter, Jude,* 201.

[63] Perhaps Peter had homosexuality specifically in mind (so Green, *2 Peter and Jude,* 114; Moo, *2 Peter, Jude,* 107).

[64] Supporting church officials are Luther, *Commentary on Peter & Jude,* 265–66; Calvin, *Catholic Epistles*, 401; Smith, *Petrine Controversies,* 89–91.

[65] Most scholars see a reference to Christ's authority (Bigg, *Peter and Jude,* 279; Kelly, *Peter and Jude*, 336; Bauckham, *Jude, 2 Peter,* 255; J. M. Starr, *Sharers in Divine Nature: 2 Peter 1:4 in Its Hellenistic Context,* ConBNT 33 [Stockholm: Almqvist & Wiksell, 2000], 28). But Moo is also correct in seeing a general rejection of authority (*2 Peter, Jude,* 108).

brood! [15]They have left the straight way and wandered off to follow the way of Balaam son of Beor, who loved the wages of wickedness. [16]But he was rebuked for his wrongdoing by a donkey—a beast without speech—who spoke with a man's voice and restrained the prophet's madness.

Verse 10a functions as a transition to these verses, and two *reasons* for the judgment declared in vv. 4–9 are identified: the sexual sin and rebelliousness of the false teachers. Moo is correct in suggesting that vv. 10b–16 unpack these two themes in reverse order—the arrogance of the teachers in vv. 10b–13a and their sensuality in vv. 13b–16.[66] Actually, we should specify a third reason for the judgment: their greed for money. All three of these themes were mentioned in vv. 1–3, where the teachers denied the Lord who purchased them (v. 1), seduced others with their sensual teaching (v. 2), and exploited others with their covetousness (v. 3). The focus on the same three sins in 2:10–16 demonstrates that the argument of 2:1–16 falls into an A B A pattern.

A The sins of the false teachers recounted: 2:1–3
  B Therefore the teachers will be judged: 2:4–10
A′ The sins of the false teachers elaborated: 2:10–16

The detailing of the false teachers' sins provides reasons why the judgment of 2:4–10 is justified. Neither should we collapse 2:1–3 and 2:10b–16 as if the arguments are identical in every respect. Second Peter 2:1–3 focuses on the adverse affect the false teachers had on others, while 2:10b–16 zeroes in on the evil of the teachers, without noting their influence on others. Verses 10b–16 are more graphic and descriptive, so that the readers had no doubt of the evil of the false teachers.

The verses are also effective rhetorically, something that is more difficult to detect in English. The argument of vv. 10–12 is carried along by the words *blasphēmountes* ("slander," v. 10), *blasphēmon* ("slanderous," v. 11), and *blasphēmountes* ("blaspheme," v. 12). In v. 12 words of destruction are featured: *phthoran* ("destroyed"), *phthora* (omitted in NIV), *phtharēsontai* ("perish"). The parallels are easily missed since the NIV translates the first use of the noun *phthora* as "killed." In v. 13 we see another play on words, which the NIV captures quite nicely, *adikoumenoi misthon adikias* ("They will be paid back with harm for the harm they have done"). The next line contains alliteration: *hēdonen hēgoumenoi tēn en hēmera* ("their idea of pleasure . . . in broad daylight"). The word *tryphēn* ("carouse") has a cognate later in the verse, *entryphōntes* ("reveling," v. 13). The exact phrase *misthon adikias* is used in vv. 13,15 ("wages of wickedness"), but the duplication is missed by the NIV in v. 15 precisely because the NIV aptly translates the expression in

[66] Moo, *2 Peter, Jude,* 120.

v. 13 with a play on words in English, demonstrating that it is impossible for any English translation to communicate every nuance of the text. Finally, in v. 16 the term *paraphronian* ("madness") probably plays off the term *paranomias* ("wrongdoing").

2:10b The rebelliousness of the false teachers is communicated with the two terms: "bold" *(tolmētai)* and "arrogant" *(authadeis)*.[67] The two words overlap in meaning—the former occurring in both Philo (*Joseph*, 222) and Josephus (*J.W.* 3.475), while the latter is a bit more common in the literature (Gen 49:3,7; Prov 21:24; Titus 1:7; cf. Josephus, *Ant.* 1.189; 4.263; *1 Clem* 1:1). Together they could be translated "boldly arrogant."[68] The false teachers were blessed with an extraordinary confidence, but unfortunately this confidence was not leavened with wisdom or humility.

The arrogance of the false teachers is reflected in that they were "not afraid to slander celestial beings." Literally, "they do not tremble" *(tremousin)* in slandering "glories" *(doxas)*. The NIV provides an interpretation here since the word "glories" could refer to human beings—either church leaders or civil authorities (cf. Ps 149:8; Isa 3:5; 23:8; Nah 3:10; 1QpHab 4:2; 4QpNah 2:9; 3:9; 4:4; 1QM 14:11).[69] It seems more likely that angels are designated as glorious beings (Exod 15:11, LXX; *T. Jud.* 25:2; *T. Levi* 18:5; 1QH 10:8). We might also think that the reference is to good angels since describing evil angels as "glories" seems inappropriate. Nevertheless, the context suggests that evil angels are indeed in view, as will be argued from the next verse.[70]

2:11 Verse 11 functions as a contrast with v. 10. The false teachers, as suggested above, had no fear in reviling evil angels. But good angels, on the other hand, even though they were "stronger and more powerful" than evil angels, did not venture to utter a negative judgment from the Lord against these evil angels. The verse could be construed quite differently. We could read it to say that angels that are "stronger and more powerful" than the false teachers do not presume to pronounce a reviling judgment against these false teachers before the Lord. But this latter interpretation is improb-

---

[67] Fuchs and Reymond understand αὐθάδεις to be an adjective modifying τολμηταὶ (*2 Pierre, Jude,* 90).

[68] I am not suggesting by this that αὐθάδεις is an adjective (see previous note), only that such a translation renders the Greek in a dynamic way.

[69] For a reference to church leaders see Bigg, *Peter and Jude,* 279–80; Green, *2 Peter and Jude,* 116–17; Smith, *Petrine Controversies,* 89–91; for political leaders see Reicke, *James, Peter, and Jude,* 167.

[70] So also Kelly, *Peter and Jude,* 337; Bauckham, *Jude, 2 Peter,* 261–62; Moo, *2 Peter, Jude,* 121; K. H. Schelke, *Der Petrusbrief—Der Judasbrief,* HTKNT (Freiburg: Herder, 1980), 210.

able for several reasons.[71] First, it is obvious that angels are stronger than false teachers, and so this scarcely needs to be said in this instance. Conversely, we can understand why Peter might have wanted to say that good angels are superior in strength to evil angels since the latter share angelic status. Second, the idea of angels pronouncing a judgment against the false teachers does not seem to fit well in the context. Why would the angels have any role whatsoever in a judgment against the false teachers? Nothing in the context prepares us for this notion. Indeed, the Scriptures teach that human beings will judge angels, not vice versa (1 Cor 6:3). Third, the most natural antecedent from v. 10 is "glories." It seems most sensible if we are told that angels are stronger than the glories just mentioned at the end of v. 10 instead of the antecedent being the false teachers who sneer at the "glories."[72] Fourth, the parallel from Jude points us in the same direction. There Michael did not dare to pronounce judgment against the devil on his own authority. Similarly, Peter argued the same thesis, though he broadened the point. Good angels do not venture to announce judgment over evil angels. They leave such judgment to the Lord. It is difficult to believe that Peter and Jude, since their texts are so similar here, would communicate different ideas. Finally, an interesting, though inexact, parallel exists in *1 Enoch* 9, where human beings lament the evil brought on them by fallen angels. The good angels in response do not act directly to assist humans but commend the matter to the Lord.[73]

In conclusion, the false teachers did not fear demonic powers. Peter called them "glories," not because they were good but simply because they were created by God himself, even though subsequently they fell into sin. Perhaps the teachers did not tremble before them because they disbelieved in their existence. This would fit nicely with the skeptical worldview they adopted about the coming of the Lord (3:3–7). Or they may have ridiculed any idea that human beings should be frightened about the power of spiritual beings. Bauckham and Moo suggest that the teachers ridiculed the notion that their sins would make them the prey of evil angels.[74] By way of con-

---

[71] So Mayor, *Jude and Second Peter,* 129. Cf. here the discussion of Vögtle, *Judasbrief, 2 Petrusbrief,* 199–200; Fuchs and Reymond, *2 Pierre, Jude,* 90.

[72] Incidentally, the observation made above strengthens the view that the "glories" are not church leaders. Verse 11 suggests, after all, that the angels restrain themselves from making a judgment that is deserved. But Peter would scarcely be saying that the church leaders deserve rebuke from good angels! Such an idea would seem to play right into the hands of the false teachers.

[73] Perhaps Peter, in contrast to Jude, omits any direct reference to *1 Enoch* or *Assumption of Moses* to preclude any suggestion that these works should be considered as authoritative Scripture, on the same level as the OT or Pauline writings (1:19–21; 3:15–16). So D. Farkasfalvy, "The Ecclesial Setting of Pseudepigraphy in Second Peter and Its Role in the Formation of the Canon," *SecCent* 5 (1985–86): 15. Fornberg thinks pseudepigraphal books were omitted because such Jewish traditions would not be meaningful to Gentiles (*An Early Church in a Pluralistic Society,* 58).

[74] Bauckham, *Jude, 2 Peter,* 262; Moo, *2 Peter, Jude,* 123.

trast, good angels do not even declare God's judgment against evil angels. They leave it with the Lord. The prepositional phrase in Greek may mean, as the NIV translates, "in the presence of the Lord."[75] In this case, however, the NRSV has a more fitting translation, "from the Lord." The angels do not venture to declare a judgment from the Lord, but they entrust the fate of demons to the Lord's judgment.

2:12 The false teachers prided themselves on their insight and wisdom, thinking that not trembling before evil angels is one manifestation of their understanding (v. 10b). In contrast (*de,* "But," NIV) to their high estimate of themselves, Peter compared them to "irrational animals" (NRSV, *aloga zōa*), rendered by the NIV "brute beasts." In the Greek text Peter began the verse by stressing their irrationality, but the NIV reverses the order and places the statement on blaspheming first. I will follow the order of the Greek here. The irrationality of the teachers is emphasized in the phrase "creatures of instinct" *(zōa . . . physika).*[76] Like animals, the opponents operated on the basis of desires and feelings instead of reason. Peter considered the fate of animals that are hunted. They are born to be captured and destroyed by human beings. The false teachers were comparable to animals since the latter are bereft of rationality. The teachers believed they were reasonable, but they displayed their foolishness in criticizing what they did not comprehend. The phrase *en hois* is translated by the NIV as "in matters," referring to the things the opponents did not grasp. Bauckham suggests that *en hois* refers to the "glories" of v. 10, so that Peter continued to emphasize their incomprehension of demonic powers.[77] This seems unlikely. The *autōn* ("their") in v. 11 is the last reference to the "glories," and it is quite distant from *en hois*. Furthermore, we would expect an accusative if the reference were to angels, and *en hois* is used elsewhere in a general sense (e.g., Phil 4:11; 2 Tim 3:14). In saying that the adversaries reviled what they did not comprehend, demons, of course, are included. The statement is general, however, and applies to other matters as well.

[75] The words παράν κυρίῳ and παρὰ κυρίου are both represented in the textual tradition. Other texts omit the words altogether. The omission of the words altogether is likely due to the influence of Jude 9, where in a similar context the words are lacking. It is much more difficult to decide between the dative and the genitive, but παρὰ κυρίῳ is the more difficult reading and enjoys Alexandrian support; it is thus probably original. See T. J. Kraus, "Παρὰ κυρίου, παρὰ κυρίῳ oder *omit* in 2Petr 2,11: Textkritik und Interpretation vor dem Hintergrund juristischer Diktion und der Verwendung von παρά," *ZNW* 91 (2000): 265–73; Fuchs and Reymond, *2 Pierre, Jude,* 88–89; *TCGNT* 633.

[76] Most English translations attach φυσικα to ζῷα.

[77] Bauckham, *Jude, 2 Peter,* 263. This interpretation is also reflected in the NLT, "They laugh at the terrifying powers they know so little about."

The verse concludes by identifying the fate of the opponents with the fate of animals. The NIV translates this "and like beasts they too will perish." The idea is correct, but the repetition of the noun *phthora* ("destruction") is omitted, so that its connection with *phtharēsontai* ("will perish") is lacking. The NRSV, in this respect, is preferable in its rendering, "When those creatures are destroyed, they also will be destroyed."[78] Bauckham understands the verse differently, arguing that the false teachers would be destroyed and judged when demons perish.[79] He understands the pronoun "their" *(autōn)* to refer back to *hois,* which in turn he relates to the noun "glories" *(doxas).* We have already seen, however, that the NIV rightly renders *en hois* "in matters." Furthermore, the most natural antecedent of "their" *(autōn)* is "beasts" *(zōa),* not the angelic glories. So the NIV has the basic meaning correct. The false teachers would experience destruction, just as animals are eventually captured and destroyed.[80] The fate of hunted animals is a picture of the fate of the wicked. When we analyze the destiny of animals and the false teachers more closely, we see that the NIV is preferable to the NRSV on another point. It is possible that the verse means that the opponents will perish "when" (NRSV) animals do. But this is an unlikely reading, for Peter thought of the final judgment, which has not yet occurred and will not happen until the second coming. The NIV captures the sense of the verse in comparing the fate of the teachers and animals. Their destiny is similar, but not at the same time.[81] Peter could not go long without emphasizing that the opponents will be judged for their ungodliness.

2:13 Verse 12 concludes with an assertion that the opponents would face judgment and destruction. A string of participles and adjectives explain why they will be judged—the NIV smooths out the Greek here by using a number of brief sentences. Peter began with a wordplay, "They will be paid back with harm for the harm they have done" *(adikoumenoi misthon adikias).* Literally the phrase can be translated "being harmed for an unrighteous wage." It is difficult to make sense out of the phrase, and we are not surprised to learn that a number of manuscripts, especially the majority text, read "receiving" *(komioumenoi)* instead of "being injured" *(adikoumenoi).*[82] The variant reading is attractive because the meaning of the

---

[78] The term φθορᾷ could refer to moral corruption, but the parallel term φθαρήσονται shows that destruction at the end of the age is intended.

[79] Bauckham, *Jude, 2 Peter,* 264; Horrell, *The Epistles of Peter and Jude,* 168.

[80] Reicke thinks the destruction here is inflicted by political authorities, but there is no basis for seeing such authorities as the subject of the verb (*James, Peter, and Jude,* 167). The divine passive (φθαρήσονται) points to God as the one who brings destruction.

[81] Rightly Kelly, *Peter and Jude,* 339; Moo, *2 Peter, Jude,* 124. Peter was not saying, then, that animals will be judged (rightly Vögtle, *Judasbrief, 2 Petrusbrief,* 203).

[82] Bigg says that the term in the text does not yield any sense and believes the text has been corrupted (*Peter and Jude,* 281).

phrase is clarified. Nevertheless, the reading represented in the NIV is to be preferred as the difficult reading, and scribes who changed the text failed to see the play on words.[83] We could understand Peter to have been saying that the teachers would not enjoy the profits gained by their evil actions.[84] But the pun suggests another interpretation. Peter simply said in a colorful way that the teachers would reap what they sowed.[85] Those who live unrighteously will be injured by God at the last judgment. We have here the standard Jewish teaching that judgment is according to works, that people will get what they deserve.

The theme of sensuality emerges in the next clause. The opponents were so consumed by and fascinated with evil that they could not even wait until dark, the time when evil is typically practiced (cf. Rom 13:12–13). Ecclesiastes 10:16 says, "Woe to you, O land whose king was a servant and whose princes feast in the morning." Similarly, we read in Isa 5:11, "Woe to those who rise early in the morning to run after their drinks, who stay up late at night till they are inflamed with wine." They make evil an all day affair and even use the daytime, the period when ordinary people work, to indulge in their pleasures (see also *T. Mos.* 7:4). As members of the church the opponents were "blots and blemishes" *(spiloi kai moμmoi)*. Jude said the intruders were "hidden reefs" *(spilades,* Jude 12*)* in the congregation, whereas Peter emphasized that they stained and defiled the church. At the conclusion of the letter Peter exhorted his readers to be precisely the opposite of the teachers; instead of being "blots and blemishes," they should be "spotless" *(aspiloi)* and "blameless" *(amōmētoi)* before God (2 Pet 3:14). Apparently the opponents were blemishes in terms of their sensuality. For Peter returned to their passion for pleasure, framing "blots and blemishes" (2:13) with "carouse" *(tryphēn)* on one side and "reveling" *(entryphōntes)* on the other. The NIV translates the text "reveling in their pleasures while they feast with you." Literally, the Greek reads "reveling in their deceitfulness *[apatais]* while they feast with you." The NIV understands "deceitfulness" probably in terms of deceitful pleasures. The word "deceitfulness" is somewhat surprising, especially when we compare Peter with Jude, for the latter referred to hidden reefs "in your love feasts" (*agapais,* Jude 12). Furthermore, both Peter and Jude immediately referred to eating with other believers *(syneuōchoumenoi)*.[86] A number of manuscripts in Peter, in fact, have the term

[83] P. W. Skehan suggests that a colon should be inserted after ἀδικούμενοι and that ἀδικούμενοι should be connected to φθαρήσονται in v. 12 (*Bib* 41 [1960]: 69–71). Thus μισθὸν ἀδικίας should be attached to φθαρήσονται.

[84] So Green, *2 Peter and Jude,* 120; Reicke, *James, Peter, and Jude,* 167–68.

[85] So Bauckham, *Jude, 2 Peter,* 265.

[86] The same verb is used of Noah feasting with his house after the flood and also of eating during the three Jewish feasts each year (see Josephus, *Ant.* 1.92 and 4.203 respectively).

"love feasts" instead of "deceitfulness." The insertion of "love feasts" is clearly an example of assimilation from Jude. Peter engaged again in word-play, since he did not believe the behavior of the teachers was worthy of the appellation "love feasts." Hence, he identified their participation as "deceitfulness." When they ate together with other believers, presumably in meals that culminate in the Lord's Supper, they were deceitfully pursuing their own pleasures rather than seeking the good of others.

2:14 As we come to v. 14, we should remember that Peter continued to give reasons the teachers deserved judgment and continued to support the main clause in 2:12, "they too will perish." The focus on sensuality also remains. The NIV translates the first clause "with eyes full of adultery," but the Greek literally reads "having eyes full of an adulteress" *(moichalidos).* Because the reading is unusual, one manuscript substituted "adultery" *(moicheias).* Other manuscripts introduce a word that occurs nowhere else and whose meaning is unknown *(moichalias).* Peter's language is vivid and arresting. These people looked at every woman, considering them as a potential candidate for adultery. How different from Job, who covenanted not to look lustfully at virgins (Job 31:1; cf. Matt 5:28).[87] There was a pun in Greek literature that a man with no shame does not have "maidens" *(koras)* in his eyes but "harlots" (*pornas,* Plutarch, *Mor.* 528E). The next clause, "they never stop sinning," is connected with the phrase "with eyes," and the NIV severs the connection here. The idea is that they had eyes that never ceased from sin. Presumably their lust for other women was still intended, though perhaps their greed for material things was also included.

The adverse affect the teachers had on others is expressed in the words "they seduce the unstable." The word "seduce" *(deleazō)* hails from the world of fishing and hunting, where bait is used to snare an unsuspecting fish or animal (cf. Jas 1:14). In v. 18 the word occurs again, translated "entice" by the NIV to indicate the influence of the false teachers on others. Here we are told that it was the "unstable" *(astēriktous)* who were seduced. The related verb appears in 1:12, referring to those "firmly established *(estērigmenous)* in the truth." In 3:16 we are warned that the "unstable" *(astēriktoi)* distorted Paul's writings and the rest of the Scriptures. Since the verse directs our attention to sexual sin and greed, perhaps the teachers enticed people to sin by promising them that they could live for sexual pleasure and the material comforts of this life without any thought of judgment. Such a theology seemed too good to pass up for the unstable, and they swallowed the bait quite eagerly.

The sins of the false teachers take center stage in the next phrase, though

---

[87] P. Dschulnigg detects a reference to Matthean tradition here ("Der theologische Ort des Zweiten Petrusbriefes," *BZ* 33 [1989]: 169).

Peter shifted from sexual sin to covetousness. They were "experts in greed." The NRSV translation is preferable, "They have hearts trained in greed." The word translated "trained" comes from the Greek term *gegymnasmenēn,* from which we derive our word "gymnasium" (cf. 1 Tim 4:7; Heb 5:12; 12:11; cf. Josephus, *Ant.* 3.15). These people devoted energy and practice to greed, and now it was a fully developed habit. In that sense the NIV's "experts" is quite fitting. Having listed all of these sins, Peter returned to the consequence of such behavior. They were "an accursed brood," literally, "accursed children."[88] In other words, they were under God's curse. Again and again the theme of judgment surfaces, for this is the reality the teachers denied, and Peter wanted to arouse his readers so they would take it seriously and repudiate the teachers.

2:15 Those who were the cursed children were like Israel of old, in that they were, at least formally, part of the people of God.[89] "They have left the straight way" and wandered astray from it. Leaving the way implies that they were once part of the people of God (cf. 2:1,20–21).[90] They had gone astray like Israel of old. We have already commented on the importance of "the way" in v. 2, and the word is used twice in this verse. We noted in v. 2 the tradition of the two ways, the way of righteousness and the way of wickedness (cf. Prov 2:15). No other ways exist, and those who have strayed from "the straight way" are now following a new way, "the way of Balaam."[91] Balaam is a curious character in the Old Testament, and the interpretation of Numbers 22–24 is difficult enough that some think he was portrayed in a positive light in those chapters. This interpretation, however, does not read Numbers 22–24 with a keen enough eye and ignores the rest of the canonical witness. In fact, Peter detected one of the key features of the narrative in v. 16. Balaam's donkey protected Balaam from death and rebuked him (Num 22:21–35). The donkey's speaking to Balaam indicates that Balaam had less insight into what God was doing than his animals.[92] The narrator in Numbers suggested that Balaam's intentions in going were impure, that he desired financial reward (Num 21:15–20). The point of the story is that the Lord sovereignly spoke through Balaam to bless Israel, even though the prophet desired to curse God's people (cf. Deut 23:4–5;

---

[88] In the phrase κατάρας τέκνα the genitive κατάρας is Semitic.

[89] Fornberg points to Deut 11:26–28 as background where the blessing and curse are set before Israel, and Moses spoke of Israel forsaking the straight way and going astray (*An Early Church in a Pluralistic Society,* 102–3).

[90] So ibid., 102.

[91] With some alterations my discussion here matches the discussion in Jude 11.

[92] So Fuchs and Reymond, *2 Pierre, Jude,* 98. Mayor engages in rationalization, arguing that Balaam heard the voice in his own conscience, not from the donkey (*Jude and Second Peter,* 203). Such a comment reveals Mayor's worldview, but it hardly constitutes a valid reading of what Peter intended.

Josh 24:9–10; Neh 13:2; cf. Josephus, *Ant.* 4.118–22; Philo, *On the Life of Moses* 1.277, 281, 283, 286; *On the Migration of Abraham* 114). The account in Numbers testifies to Balaam's true character since he was slain fighting against Israel (Num 31:8), and the sexual sin at Baal Peor in which the Midianites snared Israel was attributed to Balaam's advice (Num 31:16; cf. Rev 2:14; Josephus, *Ant.* 4.129–30; Philo, *On the Life of Moses* 1.295–300).[93]

Surprisingly, Peter did not designate Balaam as the "son of Beor" (contra NIV, NASB, RSV, NKJV), who actually was his father in the Old Testament (Num 22:5; 24:3,15). Instead Peter wrote "son of Bosor" (rightly KJV, NRSV, HCSB). The attribution perplexes us because the name appears nowhere else. Some commentators assume that Peter made a mistake here.[94] We have already noted, however, Peter's penchant for playing on words. He continued to do so here. The word "Bosor" likely derives from a pun on the word "flesh" *(basar)* in Hebrew.[95] Balaam was not a man of the Spirit but a man of the flesh. The false teachers, like Balaam, were not leading God's people in the righteous way but in the way of the flesh.[96] I have already noted that Balaam was motivated by greed, and the verse closes with this charge: He "loved the wages of wickedness." The phrase *misthon adikias,* translated by the NIV "wages of wickedness," was previously used in v. 13. Peter's point here was that Balaam loved money, that a desire for material gain governed and motivated his prophetic ministry. Similarly, the false teachers were driven by greed (2:3,14). A soft life can only be pursued if one has the requisite finances. The false teachers, like Balaam, were unprincipled purveyors of teachings that would ensure their own comfort and security.[97]

2:16 The most humorous dimension of Balaam's story is featured by Peter. While he was traveling to meet Balak, under the cloak of false piety and motivated by greed, his donkey instead of Balaam perceived the threat from God's angel and complained about Balaam's mistreatment (Num 22:21–35). Some commentators remark that the donkey did not really rebuke Balaam but simply complained about his beatings. This observation fails to read the story at a deep enough level. The donkey's complaints were

---

[93] R. Eliezer of Modiim (ca. A.D. 135) reports how certain rulers responded to Balaam, who promised that God would not bring another flood. "Perhaps He may not bring a flood of water, but He may bring a flood of fire" (*Mek.* Exod 18:1). I owe this reference to Fornberg, *An Early Church in a Pluralistic Society,* 40, n. 3.

[94] Cf. Bigg, *Peter and Jude,* 283; Kelly, *Peter and Jude,* 342–43.

[95] Rightly Bauckham, *Jude, 2 Peter,* 267–68; Moo, *2 Peter, Jude,* 128.

[96] Reicke again overreads the text, seeing the teachers as hired agents of foreign employers (*James, Peter, and Jude,* 169).

[97] But Charles takes the point too far in seeing Balaam as an example of apostasy (*Virtue amidst Vice,* 90). There is no evidence that Balaam was ever a believer in Yahweh.

a rebuke because he perceived the spiritual reality (the threat of death), while Balaam, the prophet, was oblivious to the danger. The prophet who presumably read the entrails of animals to prophesy was bested by one of his own animals, who discerned the things of God better than he. We have another play on words in the words "wrongdoing" *(paranomias)* and "madness" *(paraphronian)*. Balaam, of course, was not literally insane. But anyone who pursues "wrongdoing" is really out of his mind, for unrighteousness always leads to judgment. The only sane way to respond to the teachers is to reject their lawless course because every Bible reader knows what finally happened to Balaam. He was ignominously slain while fighting against Israel (Num 31:8). A similar destiny awaited the teachers, and hence Peter's readers should repudiate their teaching.

4. The Adverse Impact of the False Teachers on Others (2:17–22)

[17]These men are springs without water and mists driven by a storm. Blackest darkness is reserved for them. [18]For they mouth empty, boastful words and, by appealing to the lustful desires of sinful human nature, they entice people who are just escaping from those who live in error. [19]They promise them freedom, while they themselves are slaves of depravity—for a man is a slave to whatever has mastered him. [20]If they have escaped the corruption of the world by knowing our Lord and Savior Jesus Christ and are again entangled in it and overcome, they are worse off at the end than they were at the beginning. [21]It would have been better for them not to have known the way of righteousness, than to have known it and then to turn their backs on the sacred command that was passed on to them. [22]Of them the proverbs are true: "A dog returns to its vomit," and, "A sow that is washed goes back to her wallowing in the mud."

The emphasis shifts from the character of the false teachers to their effect on others. Peter began by emphasizing how deceptive they were. They promised water and clarity to those who were thirsty and confused, but instead they left them parched and confused. Hence, their judgment (v. 17c) is just. Verses 18–19 explain more specifically how they seduced recent converts. We are told three things: (1) They spoke with a kind of assertive confidence that made the weak think they must have known what they were talking about. (2) They appealed to sinful human desires, arguing that it made no difference at all if we indulge our sexual appetites to the full. (3) They maintained that their teaching was the pathway to freedom, arguing that the gospel originally received is nothing other than bondage. Peter (v. 19) saw the promise of freedom as highly ironic since the teachers themselves were captivated by sin. It is difficult to know if Peter referred to the teachers or those seduced by them in vv. 20–22. In either case he explained that apostasy is dangerous because once one embraces the gospel and then turns back, it is even harder to reclaim them afresh for the truth.

The last state has become worse than the first. It is better not to have known the righteous way than it is to repudiate it, probably because those who have known it will not be inclined to consider the truth again. Those who have fallen reveal themselves to be like dogs and pigs. Their true nature emerges in that they return to vomit or the mud pile. Peter warned his readers, therefore, that they should not travel the road of those who had been seduced, for it is a road that descends steeply and quickly, and climbing upwards again is virtually impossible, probably because those who have descended no longer desire to return.

2:17 Peter now turned to the effect the false teachers had on others, especially recent converts to the gospel. The language continues to be very close to Jude's. Peter wrote of "springs without water," while Jude referred to "clouds without rain" (Jude 12). The idea in both instances is similar. In the intense heat of the Middle East a spring would be a haven for the thirsty traveler. He would experience frustration and disappointment upon seeing that the spring that promised water was dried up. Peter reflected on the teaching of the false teachers. They promised satisfaction for thirsty souls, but in the end they left people parched and in need. We think here of the parallel in Jer 2:13, "They have forsaken me, the spring of living water, and have dug their own cisterns, broken cisterns that cannot hold water." Water elsewhere refers to teaching that sustains one's spiritual life (cf. Prov 10:11; 13:14; 14:27; *Sir* 24:23–31).[98] Green rightly remarks, "Heterodoxy is all very novel in the classroom; it is extremely unsatisfying in the parish."[99]

For Jude the rainless clouds were driven along by the wind, while Peter reflected on "mists driven by a storm." The "mists" *(homichlai)* could signify a storm in which vision is obscured.[100] On this reading the false teachers sowed confusion by their teaching.[101] Most commentators, however, see the expression as parallel to the first one in the verse. The mists promise water that is so desperately needed in a dry climate, but the wind sweeps through and drives the hazy mists away, leaving the land parched.[102] In both instances the teachers did not deliver on what they promised. They pledged harmony and produced dissonance. Peter then returned to the theme of judgment. False teaching was not a light matter. "Blackest darkness is reserved" for those who propagate error. Peter continued to press home the future judgment of the teachers. Commentators often remark that the imagery of darkness being reserved does not fit with the imagery of waterless springs and hazy mists. The language of mists, however, may fit

[98] Vögtle, *Judasbrief, 2 Petrusbrief,* 205; Fuchs and Reymond, *2 Pierre, Jude,* 98.

[99] Green, *2 Peter and Jude,* 126.

[100] Bigg, *Peter and Jude,* 284.

[101] So Hillyer, *1 and 2 Peter, Jude,* 207.

[102] So Kelly, *Peter and Jude,* 345; Bauckham, *Jude, 2 Peter,* 274.

rather well with darkness since a heavy mist can obscure vision.[103] Even if the imagery is inconsistent, authors often mix metaphors, and so we should not be surprised if that is what Peter did here.[104]

2:18 The main clause in v. 18 is obscured by the NIV, but in the original text it is, "They entice people who are just escaping from those who live in error." The false teachers were attempting to seduce recent believers so that the latter renounced their devotion to the gospel. The "for" *(gar)* gives another reason the teachers would be consigned to the gloom of darkness (v. 17b), namely, because they maximized their evil by including others in their evil ways. The teachers were waterless springs and a hazy mist because they did not lead people to truth but into error. Instead of providing people with the water of life, they gave them "broken cisterns that cannot hold water" (Jer 2:13). Instead of giving them an inclination for the truth, they gave recent converts a delight in error. The word "entice" *(deleazousin)* repeats the same term used in 2:14. We noted there its association with bait for hunting and fishing. The English verb "entice" expresses aptly the meaning of the term. The false teachers were as misleading and seductive as the hunter who attempts to catch his prey.

A textual issue emerges with the word *oligōs,* translated "just" in the NIV. This term refers to those who have recently or "barely" (NAB, CEV; "scarcely," NJB) escaped from error. Many manuscripts say "really" *(ontōs)* instead of *oligōs* (NKJV), and when these words are in caps, as they are in the earliest manuscripts, it would be difficult to distinguish them. We can be almost certain, however, that *oligōs* is original. The term "recently" is supported by both the Alexandrian and Western text types. Furthermore, the word *oligōs* is used rarely in Greek literature, and so scribes could mistakenly have inserted a more common term. Contextually, "recently" or "just" makes better sense. We understand that the false teachers would influence recent converts who were still unstable in their faith. Conversely, it seems quite improbable that Peter would say that they seduced those who "really escaped from those living in error."[105] Another textual variant intrudes in the verse. Should we read the present tense "those escaping" *(apopheugontas)* or the aorist *(apophygontas)?* The external evidence favors the former, and scribes would be likely to insert an aorist tense instead of the present since in two other instances Peter used the aorist form *apophygontes* (1:4; 2:20). The present tense combined with *oligōs* may emphasize the recency of the events narrated. The NIV captures nicely the nuance. They were "just escaping from those who live in error." It is likely, then, that Peter was not

[103] So Calvin, *Catholic Epistles,* 407; Green, *2 Peter and Jude,* 126.

[104] Rightly Moo, *2 Peter, Jude,* 141.

[105] See the helpful comments here in *TCGNT* 635.

saying that they "barely" escaped the clutches of the world but that they had recently escaped it. The word "error" *(planē)* designates unbelievers (cf. Rom 1:27; Eph 4:14; 1 Thess 2:3; 2 Thess 2:11; Jas 5:20; 2 Pet 3:17; 1 John 4:6; Jude 11). The false teachers were crafty. They targeted those who were unstable and liable to be taken in by their schemes.

The two modifying clauses are both instrumental, explaining *how* the teachers baited their hook to lure away recent converts. The NIV turns the first participle into an independent clause, translating it "they mouth empty, boastful words." If it were translated as an instrumental participle, it would read "by mouthing empty, boastful words." The NIV renders well the prepositional phrase, "by appealing to the lustful desires of sinful human nature." So we see that the false teachers enticed recent converts in two ways: (1) with boastful speech and (2) with invitations to indulge the flesh. Bigg expresses aptly the significance of the two phrases: "Grandiose sophistry is the hook, filthy lust is the bait, with which these men catch those whom the Lord had delivered or was delivering."[106] We will look at each of the phrases in more detail. Their speech apparently was full of confidence *(hyperonka),* which Peter considered to be nothing other than arrogant vanity. Those who are weak are often susceptible to the assertive confidence of others, even if such confidence flows from arrogance and sin. Ultimately their arrogant speech is futile *(mataiotēs)* since anything that deviates from the truth is destined to fail. The words of the teachers breathe confidence, but in the end they will rue their own prescriptions.

I have already noted that the NIV correctly identifies the prepositional phrase as instrumental, "by appealing to the lustful desires of sinful human nature." Its translation of the verse masks some of its difficulties. Literally Peter wrote, "They entice with desires of the flesh, sensualities." The word "sensualities" *(aselgeiais)* is awkward in Greek. We would expect a genitive instead of a dative, and some scribes made this substitution, but there is no doubt that Peter used the dative. We could translate the noun as an adjective, "sensual desires," or, more likely, we should take it as appositional, "desires of the flesh—sensual ones." The word *aselgeiais* identifies what kind of fleshly desires Peter had in mind, and the term typically refers to sexual sin.[107] Peter had already used the word twice in chap. 2 (vv. 2,7), and we noted in both instances that sexual sin was in view. The word "flesh" *(sarkos)* is translated by the NIV as "sinful nature." The phrase "sinful nature" is not so much wrong as misleading since the term does not focus on the ontological nature of human beings. Peter wrote in redemptive historical categories, referring to what human beings are apart from salvation. The teachers

[106] Bigg, *Peter and Jude,* 284.
[107] Fuchs and Reymond, *2 Pierre, Jude,* 99.

probably lured recent converts by teaching that no judgment was forthcoming (3:3–7). And if there was no judgment, it followed that morality was irrelevant. People could live however they wished since judgment is an illusion. The door was opened, then, to sexual sin at every level.

2:19 The participial clause in this verse gives the third means by which the teachers seduced those who had recently joined the church. Again the NIV uses a main clause, "they promise them freedom," for what is a participle in Greek, "promising them freedom." Certainly this participial clause is related to the previous one. They promised freedom, particularly by removing moral restraints—especially, it seems, in the realm of sexuality. Such teaching may have arisen through a distortion of Paul's gospel of freedom, since we know from 3:15–16 that some were perverting his teaching.[108] Freedom from any moral constraints also fits nicely with the notion that there was no future judgment.[109] Their promise of freedom is highly ironic since the teachers were "slaves of depravity." Peter, by way of contrast, was a "slave of Jesus Christ" (1:1, lit. translation). The word "depravity" is more literally rendered "corruption," and some commentators maintain that the word should not be restricted to moral corruption since it also includes the notion of destruction, as we saw with the term in 2:12.[110] Moral depravity and eschatological destruction, of course, are logically related. And yet it seems doubtful to me that the latter idea is included here. The collocation of the word "slaves" *(douloi)* with "corruption" suggests that Peter indicted the teachers for their moral corruption.[111] Seeing a reference to destruction introduces more complexity in the phrase than is warranted. The teachers were hardly free when they could not liberate themselves from sin. Those who cannot look at a woman without contemplating adultery and have hearts exercised and trained in greed are truly slaves (2:14). The freedom they promised others was an illusion.

The verse closes with an explanation of why they were slaves: "For a man is a slave to whatever has mastered him." Some commentators think the proverbial saying should be translated, "For a man becomes the slave of him who overpowers him."[112] Even though the proverb originally derives from the slave trade, its proverbial nature suggests that the neuter "whatever" is fitting.[113] Peter's meaning is clear. If people cannot overcome cer-

---

[108] So also Kelly, *Peter and Jude,* 346; Fornberg, *An Early Church in a Pluralistic Society,* 106–7. Hence, the appeal to freedom does not constitute evidence of a Gnostic threat (rightly Vögtle, *Judasbrief, 2 Petrusbrief,* 218–19).

[109] Contra to Smith, who understands their freedom to consist of their knowledge (*Petrine Controversies,* 92).

[110] E.g., Kelly, *Peter and Jude,* 346; Bauckham, *Jude, 2 Peter,* 276.

[111] Cf. also Bigg, *Peter and Jude,* 287; Moo, *2 Peter, Jude,* 144.

[112] Bauckham, *Jude, 2 Peter,* 277; Schelke, *Der Petrusbrief—Der Judasbrief,* 217.

tain habits and sins, they are slaves to such things. How could the teachers proclaim a message of freedom when they were unable to extricate themselves from sin? Their lifestyle contradicted their message.

2:20 The first question we need to pose for vv. 20–22 is whether Peter referred to the false teachers or the recent converts they were enticing. Reasons favoring a reference to recent converts who had been seduced are as follows.[114] (1) The "for" *(gar)* introducing v. 20 (omitted by the NIV) refers back to v. 18, explaining the consequences of being snared by the opponents. (2) The repetition of the same word, "escaping" *(apopheugontas)* and "escaped" *(apophygontes)* in vv. 18,20, indicates that recent converts were the subject. In v. 18 they escaped from those entrapped in error, while in v. 20 they escaped from "the pollutions of the world." (3) Kelly argues that vv. 20–21 are a warning to those about to succumb, while Peter held out no hope at all for the false teachers, concluding that they would never return to the faith.[115] Others are convinced that the false teachers are in view.[116] (1) The chapter as a whole is directed against the opponents, and hence these verses address them as well (2) The word "mastered" is repeated in vv. 19 and 20. In v. 19 it is clearly the false teachers who were "mastered" *(hēttētai)* by evil, and the same word ("overcome," NIV *[hēttōntai]*) in v. 20 is, therefore, most naturally applied to them as well. (3) The teachers had definitely committed apostasy, which these verses portray, but Peter hoped those recently seduced would still be rescued.[117]

A decision is difficult precisely because the text is vague. Perhaps it is mistaken to opt for either view because what Peter said applies to both the false teachers and all those who were seduced by them and who renounced the Christian faith.[118] Kelly is incorrect when he says that the text is a warning. Peter described what "has happened" (NRSV, *symbebēken,* v. 22)

---

[113] Rightly Moo, *2 Peter, Jude,* 144–45.

[114] See especially Kelly, *Peter and Jude,* 347–48; Fuchs and Reymond, *2 Pierre, Jude,* 100–101; cf. also D. A. Dunham, "An Exegetical Study of 2 Peter 2:18–22," *BSac* 140 (1983): 41–42.

[115] Kelly, *Peter and Jude,* 347–48.

[116] See, e.g., Bauckham, *Jude, 2 Peter,* 277. Bauckham wrongly, though, argues that Kelly advances such a view, when it is clear that Kelly holds a different view from Bauckham. Seeing a reference to the false teachers is the majority view. See Vögtle, *Judasbrief, 2 Petrusbrief,* 207; Bigg, *Peter and Jude,* 285; Reicke, *James, Peter, and Jude,* 172; Green, *2 Peter and Jude,* 129; Moo, *2 Peter, Jude,* 145; R. A. Peterson, "Apostasy," *Presbyterion* 19 (1993): 18; Fornberg, *An Early Church in a Pluralistic Society,* 106; Mayor, *Jude and Second Peter,* 142.

[117] Dunham argues that the verses relate to new converts, and the sin in view is not apostasy ("2 Peter 2:18–22," 40–54). On the contrary, the entire letter shows that the danger is apostasy. The epithets "dog" and "sow" point to unclean animals, i.e., those who are not in the realm of the sacred. Dunham's comments on the fastidiousness and cleanness of dogs and pigs (p. 50) misses the Jewish background of the proverbial saying, where such animals were conceived of as unclean. Also his view that the imperfect tense in 2:21 is a desiderative imperfect is quite improbable (p. 49).

[118] Note here the comments of Fornberg, *An Early Church in a Pluralistic Society,* 106.

to some who had abandoned the church. In one sense, however, we should construe the text as a warning. The fate of those who had apostatized stands as a warning to those wavering under the influence of the teachers. Peter wanted his readers to see that those who commit apostasy are very unlikely to return to the truth. The decision is of great consequence, and those who are wavering must see that heaven and hell are at stake. Nevertheless, the verses before us refer to those who had become entangled in the ways of the world after having escaped from its pollutions, of those who had turned away from the holy commandment, of those who had returned to their old ways, like dogs and pigs return to vomit and dirt. At the conclusion of this section, some comments will be made about whether these verses teach that believers can lose their salvation.

Verse 20 refers to conversion, noting those who had "escaped the corruption of the world by knowing our Lord and Savior Jesus Christ." We have already seen in v. 18 that those who had just escaped "from those who live in error" speaks of those who had recently turned away from the error of unbelief. Similarly, in 2 Pet 1:4 the same term is used of conversion, of those who "escape from the corruption that is in the world because of lust." In v. 20 conversion is from "the corruption of the world" (translated better "defilements of the world," NRSV). This is parallel to escaping the error of unbelief in v. 18 and the lust of the world in 1:4. Conversion also is signaled when the text speaks of "knowledge" *(epignōsis)*. This term was one of Peter's favorites, for grace and peace come through knowing God and Jesus Christ (1:2). Those who know God have everything they need for a godly life (1:3; cf. 1:8). Here Peter focused on knowledge of Jesus Christ as Lord and Savior. We see again two Greek nouns that are joined by one article *(tou)*, indicating that Jesus is both Lord and Savior and that those entering into the church confess him as such.

Although these people had escaped the pollutions of the world, they had returned again to its snares. They had been "overcome" *(hēttōntai)* by its power and "entangled" again by its delights. The gospel they initially confessed they had now repudiated. The Lord and Savior they had embraced they now rejected. The world they had escaped recaptured them afresh. Peter concluded from this that their last state was worse than their former one. The former state, of course, refers to their lives before conversion, when they were still enthralled by the desires of the world. The last state designates their recent rejection of the Christian faith. Why was the last state worse than the first? It was worse because those who had experienced the Christian faith and then rejected it were unlikely to return to it again. They would not grant a fresh hearing to the gospel, concluding that they had already been through "that phase." Peter employed a number of proverbs in this section, and here he seemed to draw on a proverb uttered by

Jesus.[119] Jesus told a parable of an evil spirit evicted from a man that wanders looking for a dwelling place. Finding none it returns to its original habitation, but seven other spirits join it in reclaiming the lost possession (Matt 12:43–45). He concludes, "The last state of that person is worse than the first" (Matt 12:45, NRSV). This aphorism applies nicely to those who had acknowledged Jesus as their Lord and Savior and now rejected him.

2:21 Verse 21 explains why (*gar,* "for"—but omitted by the NIV) the last state is worse than the first. Peter used a proverbial statement, with the "better than" formula (cf. e.g., Matt 5:29–30; 18:6,8–9; 1 Cor 7:9; 1 Pet 3:17). The verb "known" *(epiginōskō)* links back to the noun of the previous verse (*epignōsei,* "knowing," NIV). Again it refers to one's entrance into the Christian church. Such entrance here is described as knowing "the way of righteousness" *(tēn hodon tēs dikaiosynēs).* The way of righteousness is the moral life demanded of those who belong to God (cf. Prov 8:20; 12:28; 16:31; Matt 21:32).[120] We saw in the first verse of the letter that righteousness denoted God's saving power, but for Peter this saving power leads to a transformed life. The emphasis here is on the new kind of life lived by one who is a member of God's people. Noah was a preacher of this righteousness (2:5), and righteousness will characterize the new heaven and new earth (3:13). The "sacred command" is another way of describing "the way of righteousness." The Christian life can be viewed in singular terms as a command to live a new quality of life. This commandment "was passed on to them" *(paradotheisēs),* the same term Jude used for the faith handed down once and for all to the saints (Jude 3). Peter emphasized thereby the reliability and faithfulness of the tradition, as he did in the word "sacred," where we see that the commandment came from God himself.[121] Nonetheless, these people had turned away from it and repudiated what they once embraced. We can say again that it would have been better for them not to have known because it is so difficult to reclaim apostates.

2:22 Verse 22 is a closing proverb reflecting on those who had apostatized. The NIV speaks of "proverbs" in the plural, but the Greek text actually uses the singular, suggesting that both proverbs are to be interpreted together as making *one* point. We need to recall in reading this that both dogs (Exod 22:31; 1 Kgs 14:11; 16:4; Matt 7:6; 15:26,31; Luke 16:21; Phil 3:2; Rev 22:15) and pigs (Lev 11:7; Deut 14:8) were unclean animals for the Jews. Dogs often roamed in packs, scavenged from garbage, and were

[119] Supporting the idea that Jesus tradition is used here is Farkasfalvy, "Ecclesial Setting," 7.

[120] There may be dependence on Matthean tradition here (cf. Dschulnigg, "Der theologische Ort des Zweiten Petrusbriefes," 169). But Dschulnigg probably goes beyond the evidence in seeing the Matthean emphasis on the law in 2 Peter (pp. 174–75).

[121] Fuchs and Reymond rightly observe that there is no basis to see legalism in the reference to "command[ment]" (*2 Pierre, Jude,* 102).

definitely not considered lovely pets. The proverb regarding dogs hails from Prov 26:11, "As a dog returns to its vomit, so a fool repeats his folly." The point of the proverb is easy to see. Dogs return to what is disgusting and unclean, sniffing even at their own vomit. Similarly, those who have renounced the Christian faith have returned to what is disgusting, finding it more attractive than the "way of righteousness" and "the sacred command." The origin of the second proverb is unknown. A common view is that it stems from Heraclitus,[122] but others suggest that it derives from *The Story of Ahikar.*[123] In the Syriac the latter reads, "You were to me, my son, like a swine which had had a bath, and when it saw a slimy pit, went down and bathed in it."[124] We must admit that we do not know the origin of the proverb used in 2 Peter. Some, seeing a connection to Heraclitus and noting that the participle "returns" *(epistrepsas)* is not repeated in the second line (the NIV supplies the verb "goes back"), think the point of the proverb is that pigs delight to wash in the mud.[125] But the primary issue for interpreting the saying is context, and in proverbs the second verb is often omitted but clearly implied. That is the case in this instance. Hence, most commentators rightly understand the second line to be parallel with the first. Pigs, after washing themselves clean, spy the mud and wallow in it. Similarly, those who confess faith in Jesus Christ as Lord and Savior and then deny him are like pigs who are washed clean and then return to their original filth. We probably should not overread the proverb and see an allusion to baptism in the original washing, since it refers to the washing of a pig.[126]

What do these verses say about apostasy? Can a genuine believer forsake his or her salvation? We can certainly see why most commentators draw such a conclusion after reading these verses in 2 Peter, for they are not merely a warning about apostasy but reflect on those who have abandoned the church, who were previously members of it.[127] They remind us that walking the aisle, making a profession of faith, making a decision for Christ, or Christian baptism do not ensure a future destiny in heaven. Perseverance is the mark of genuineness, as Peter taught throughout the letter. Only those who continue to live a life of godliness will receive the reward of eternal life (1:5–11). Those who teach that genuine Christians can and do

---

[122] See G. S. Kirk, *Heraclitus: The Cosmic Fragments* (Cambridge: University Press, 1954), 76–80.

[123] Kelly, *Peter and Jude,* 350; Bauckham, *Jude, 2 Peter,* 279–80.

[124] The translation of the proverb is cited as quoted in Kelly, *Peter and Jude,* 350.

[125] So Bigg, *Peter and Jude,* 287.

[126] For this possibility see, e.g., Fuchs and Reymond, *2 Pierre, Jude,* 103; Fornberg, *An Early Church in a Pluralistic Society,* 107.

[127] So, e.g., I. H. Marshall, *Kept by the Power of God: A Study of Perseverance and Falling Away* (Minneapolis: Bethany, 1969), 169–70; Green, *2 Peter and Jude,* 131.

apostatize are taking these verses seriously, and sometimes believers who deny such a possibility brush them off without serious reflection.[128]

Nevertheless, I think it is a mistake to conclude that genuine believers can apostatize. The God who calls believers will see to it that they will reach their destination, participation in the divine nature (see the comment on 2 Pet 1:3).[129] Furthermore, we saw in 1 Pet 1:5, from the same author (see the commentary there), that God guards believers so that they will *certainly,* not probably, obtain eschatological salvation. Peter did not contradict himself, teaching in one place that believers can fall away and in another that they cannot. Some might try to explain the tension by saying that Peter was not actually saying that these people were headed for eternal destruction, and he spoke only of the loss of rewards. This view flies in the face of the entire argument in chap. 2, and really the whole letter. We have seen in many individual verses that eschatological judgment is promised to those who fall away. For example, three times in 2:1–3 Peter used the word "destruction" *(apōleia),* a term that regularly denotes eschatological condemnation in the New Testament. The judgment of the flood and Sodom and Gomorrah are types of eternal judgment, not merely the loss of rewards, while Noah and Lot are a type of those who were preserved under adversity (2:5–9). The term "perish" in 2:12 also signifies the last judgment and eschatological corruption. In the same way the errorists are compared to Balaam, who wandered from the truth, a man who did not merely lose rewards but faced eternal judgment (2:15–16). Finally, it does not make much sense to say the last state is worse than the first (2:20) and it is better not to have known God's righteous way if the people described will ultimately be saved. If they will experience salvation, then the last stage *is better than the first* since previously they were bound for hell, and now they are destined for heaven. Furthermore, *it is better to know the righteous way* if one will experience eschatological life, even though one will lose one's rewards. These strong statements signify that Peter did not merely criticize the loss of rewards. Heaven and hell are at stake in this instance.

The best solution is to say that the language used in 2 Peter is phenomenological. In other words, Peter used the language of "Christians" to describe those who fell away because they gave every appearance of being Christians. They confessed Christ as Lord and Savior, were baptized, and joined the church. But the false teachers and some of those they seduced,

---

[128] Charles argues that the examples of the fallen angels and Balaam show that apostasy can and does happen (*Virtue amidst Vice,* 166–67, 169–73). See also the remarks of Hillyer, *1 and 2 Peter, Jude,* 208.

[129] Charles, e.g., reduces predestination to God's future judgment when he says, "One perseveres, one persists in the faith, precisely because the sovereign Lord has predestined all humans to give account of themselves" (*Virtue amidst Vice,* 168).

though still present physically in the church, were no longer considered to be genuine believers by Peter. Nonetheless, he used "Christian" language to describe them, precisely because of their participation in the church, because they gave some evidence initially of genuine faith. Those who had apostatized revealed that they were never truly part of the people of God, for remaining true to the faith is one sign that one truly belongs to God. The words of 1 John apply well to what has happened in 2 Peter: "They went out from us, but they did not really belong to us. For if they had belonged to us, they would have remained with us; but their going showed that none of them belonged to us" (1 John 2:19). Peter pointed in the same direction in the illustration of the dog and pig. In the final analysis, those who fell away never really changed their nature.[130] They remained dogs and pigs inside. They may have washed up on the outside and appeared to be different, but fundamentally they were dogs and pigs. In other words, they were always unclean; they only seemed to have changed. Perseverance, therefore, is the test of authenticity. Scholars will continue to disagree on whether believers can apostatize, but it is hoped that all will agree that believers must persevere to the end to be saved.[131] In this respect there is a remarkable agreement between Arminians and Calvinists.

---

[130] So E. A. Blum, *2 Peter,* EBC 12 (Grand Rapids: Zondervan, 1981), 283; Peterson, "Apostasy," 19–20.

[131] For a full examination of the issues of perseverance and assurance, see T. R. Schreiner and A. B. Caneday, *The Race Set Before Us: A Biblical Theology of Perseverance and Assurance* (Downers Grove: InterVarsity, 2001).

V. REMINDER: THE DAY OF THE LORD WILL COME (3:1–18)

1. Scoffers Doubt the Coming Day (3:1–7)

1Dear friends, this is now my second letter to you. I have written both of them as reminders to stimulate you to wholesome thinking. 2I want you to recall the words spoken in the past by the holy prophets and the command given by our Lord and Savior through your apostles.

**3First of all, you must understand that in the last days scoffers will come, scoffing and following their own evil desires. 4They will say, "Where is this 'coming' he promised? Ever since our fathers died, everything goes on as it has since the beginning of creation." 5But they deliberately forget that long ago by God's word the heavens existed and the earth was formed out of water and by water.
6By these waters also the world of that time was deluged and destroyed. 7By the same word the present heavens and earth are reserved for fire, being kept for the day of judgment and destruction of ungodly men.**

A new section is clearly marked in terms of both content and structure. Peter's long discussion on the false teachers (chap. 2) concludes, and he turns afresh to his readers. The new section is introduced with the affectionate words "dear friends" *(agapētoi),* better rendered "beloved." The purpose of the second letter is to arouse the readers from lethargic thinking and to remind them of the words of the Old Testament prophets and the command, that is, the moral requirements of Jesus Christ—as these commands have been transmitted by the apostles. The particular reason the readers were to remember such teachings is explained in vv. 3–4. Peter reminded them that the arrival of mockers in the last days was prophesied. Hence, their immoral lifestyle and their rejection of the Lord's coming should occasion no surprise. The arrival of the false teachers fulfilled predictions that must come to pass before the Lord returns. The opponents rejected the second coming, arguing that from the beginning of time (i.e., since the time of the patriarchs) history continues without cosmic interventions from God. Peter had a three-pronged argument against this view in vv. 5–7. First, the very creation of the world represents God's intervention in the world. The opponents had failed to see the implications of their own view, for by appealing to creation they concurred that there was a beginning, a time when God brought the world into being. Second, the opponents might object that God set the world in motion but did not intervene cosmologically thereafter. But such a view does not account for the flood, which involved a cataclysm for the entire world. Third, history will end with a great conflagration, when the present heavens and earth will be burned, and the ungodly will be judged.[1]

3:1 The words "dear friends" mark a transition in the letter. The NIV translation is too weak since the term is "beloved" (*agapētoi,* cf. also 3:14,17). "Beloved" signifies that the readers were the recipients of God's saving love and perhaps also communicates Peter's tender concern for his readers. Peter remarked that he wrote his second letter to the readers. Scholars have postulated at least four different possibilities regarding the first letter. (1) Some think 2 Peter is not a unity, that its present composition stitches together more than one letter. McNamara, for example, argues that chap. 1 is the first letter, and chap. 3 is subsequent to the letter composed in chap. 1.[2] There is no textual evidence, however, for any partition theory in 2 Peter. The letter has come down to us as a unity. The transition in chap. 3 to a new subject is not surprising in a letter; in fact, chap. 3 continues to refer to the opponents criticized in chap. 2. (2) Other scholars have suggested that the first letter was Jude and the second one is 2 Peter.[3] Such a view would hardly be apparent to the readers since Peter wrote *in his name,* while Jude wrote under his.[4] How could the readers possibly recognize both letters as Peter's when they have different names on them? Furthermore, it is difficult to explain, if this theory is correct, why Peter would change the wording of Jude. (3) More plausible is the idea that Peter wrote another letter that has since been lost.[5] We know that Paul wrote letters that were lost (cf. 1 Cor 5:9), and most scholars believe that he wrote a severe letter that also has been lost (2 Cor 7:8). Furthermore, Paul wrote a letter to the Laodiceans (Col 4:16) that has perished. Peter may have written other letters that

---

[1] R. Bauckham argues that the parallels between 2 Peter 3 and *1 Clem* 23:3–4; 27:4, *2 Clem* 11:2–4 and 16:3 indicate dependence upon a common source (*Jude, 2 Peter* [Waco: Word, 1983], 284, 296–97). The discussion is a complex one. It seems that the evidence is insufficient to draw such a conclusion.

[2] M. McNamara, "The Unity of Second Peter: A Reconsideration," *Scr* 12 (1960): 13–19.

[3] J. A. T. Robinson, *Redating the New Testament* (Philadelphia: Westminster, 1976), 193–95.

[4] Rightly Bauckham, *Jude, 2 Peter,* 285.

[5] So M. Green, *The Second Epistle General of Peter and the General Epistle of Jude,* 2d ed., TNTC (Grand Rapids: Eerdmans, 1988), 134.

have not survived as well.[6] This theory is certainly a possibility, and it may be the best answer. It appeals, however, to correspondence that has never been found and isn't mentioned elsewhere. Hence, I think the fourth option is still preferable. (4) Peter referred to 1 Peter. This is still the majority view among commentators.[7] The main objection to this view is the content of 1 Peter. Peter seems to have known his readers well in 2 Peter, but the same kind of knowledge is not apparent in 1 Peter. This argument is not particularly compelling. In fact, the degree of Peter's experience with the readers is not readily apparent from either letter. A more significant objection is that 1 Peter does not seem to be a call for "pure thinking." But perhaps we have failed to see the parallel with 1 Peter here. In his first exhortation to his readers he said, "Therefore, prepare your minds for action; be self-controlled; set your hope fully on the grace to be given you when Jesus Christ is revealed" (1 Pet 1:13). Peter used the same word for "mind" *(dianoia)* as we find in 2 Pet 3:1. In addition, from our commentary on 1 Peter in the first part of this volume, it is evident that eschatology is central for the entire book, and the adversaries in 2 Peter denied the eschatological judgment and the coming of the Lord. But in 1 Peter the readers were exhorted to fix their hope on the eschatological coming of Christ. Indeed, all of the exhortations in 1 Peter flow from 1:3–12, where eschatology takes center stage. So we could summarize the argument of 1 Peter in such a way that he encouraged his readers to right thinking in light of the *eschaton.* The parallels between 1 and 2 Peter are closer than many scholars

---

[6] D. J. Moo is particularly attracted to this option, though he remains undecided (*2 Peter, Jude,* NIVAC [Grand Rapids: Zondervan, 1997], 162–163).

[7] See C. Bigg, *The Epistles of St. Peter and St. Jude,* ICC (Edinburgh: T & T Clark, 1901), 288–89; B. Reicke, *The Epistles of James, Peter, and Jude,* AB (Garden City: Doubleday, 1964), 173; J. N. D. Kelly, *A Commentary on the Epistles of Peter and Jude,* Thornapple Commentaries (Grand Rapids: Baker, 1981), 352–53; J. H. Neyrey, *2 Peter, Jude,* AB (Garden City: Doubleday, 1993), 229; T. V. Smith, *Petrine Controversies in Early Christianity: Attitudes Toward Peter in Christian Writings of the First Two Centuries,* WUNT 2/15 (Tübingen: Mohr, 1985), 70–74; T. Fornberg, *An Early Church in a Pluralistic Society: A Study of 2 Peter,* ConBNT 9 (Lund: Gleerup, 1977), 12; H. Paulsen, *Der Zweite Petrusbrief und der Judasbrief,* KEK (Göttingen: Vandenhoeck & Ruprecht, 1992), 150. G. H. Boobyer presents evidence that the author of 2 Peter referred to the first letter ("The Indebtedness of 2 Peter to 1 Peter," in *New Testament Essays: Studies in Memory of Thomas Walter Manson* [Manchester: University Press, 1959], 34–53). Not all of Boobyer's arguments are compelling, but he does demonstrate that the author referred to 1 Peter here. For further evidence that 2 Peter knew and used 1 Peter, see W. J. Dalton, "The Interpretation of 1 Peter 3:19 and 4:6: Light from 2 Peter," *Bib* 60 (1979): 547–55; D. Farkasfalvy, "The Ecclesial Setting of Pseudepigraphy in Second Peter and Its Role in the Formation of the Canon," *SecCent* 5 (1985–86): 16–20. B. Witherington argues that the author of 2 Peter used a Petrine source for 2 Pet 1:12–2:3a and 3:1–3 ("A Petrine Source in Second Peter," SBLSP [Atlanta: Scholars, 1985], 187–92). The argument is not that 2 Peter used 1 Peter per se, but he "had access to another source by the same person who was responsible for 1 Peter" (p. 188). Though the evidence presented by Witherington shows that 2 Peter probably knew 1 Peter, it is more likely that 2 Peter refers to 1 Peter as a whole.

concede. I conclude that 1 Peter is the letter referred to here.

Peter returned to the theme of 1:12–15, namely, that he wrote to arouse the readers' "wholesome thinking" by means of reminders. The adjective "wholesome" *(eilikrinē)* signifies that which is pure, right, and good. Believers need reminders about the truths they already know and accept precisely because such reminders, though including the mind, address the whole person. In biblical thinking reminders grip the whole person, so that we are possessed again by the gospel and its truth, so that we are energized to live for the glory of God.

3:2 In v. 2 Peter specified what he wanted them to remember. The NIV actually masks the relationship between the two verses, for the verb "recall" in v. 2 is a purpose infinitive *(mnēsthēnai),* modifying the verb "stimulate" in v. 1. The NRSV translates the connection well, "I am trying to arouse . . . that you should remember." Peter wanted to stimulate their thinking so that they would recall what they were previously taught and not fall prey to the new-fangled ideas of the false teachers. More specifically, he wanted them to remember the words of the prophets and the apostles. Jude (v. 17) had a similar idea, but he omitted any mention of the prophets. What Peter said here, however, reaches back to the conclusion of chap. 1. There Peter appealed to apostolic (1:16–18) and prophetic (1:19–21) testimony to verify the future coming of the Lord. He circled back to the prophets and the apostles, reversing the order here, and picked up his argument from the end of chap. 1. We saw in chap. 2 the false path and teaching promulgated by the opponents, which Peter exhorted them to avoid. Here the readers were reminded to return to the teaching of the prophets and the apostles so that their teaching, especially about the culmination of history, would not be forgotten. The parallel with 1:16–21 and the order in which prophets and apostles occur indicate that Old Testament prophets were in view here, not New Testament prophets.[8] What words from the Old Testament prophets did Peter have in mind? In light of 2 Peter as a whole, he likely thought of those prophecies that referred to the end of history, the day of judgment and salvation.[9] The Old Testament prophets often spoke of the day of the Lord, and because of the arrival of that day, they exhorted readers to live godly lives.

The syntax of the part of the verse relating to the apostles is quite difficult in Greek. Genitives are piled up, but they are not easy to disentangle, so that the Greek is rather rough. The NIV smooths out the text and captures its meaning well: "The command given by our Lord and Savior

---

[8] So also Bauckham, *Jude, 2 Peter,* 287.

[9] For a reference to the whole OT, see E. Fuchs and P. Reymond, *La Deuxième Épître de Saint Pierre, L'Épître de Saint Jude,* CNT (Neuchâtel–Paris: Delachaux & Niestlé, 1980), 106.

through your apostles."[10] Peter wanted to emphasize that the commands of the apostles actually represented the words of Jesus Christ as Lord and Savior.[11] The point is that the words of Jesus Christ had been transmitted by the apostles. The word "command" (*entolēs;* cf. 2:21) probably is collective, using a singular to denote the moral norms incumbent upon believers.[12] The moral standard for believers, according to Peter, was summed up in the teaching of Jesus Christ himself. The false teachers, on the other hand, were notorious for their dissolute lifestyle. The terms "Lord and Savior" *(tou kyriou kai sōtēros)* have one Greek article, indicating (cf. 1:1) that the same person, Jesus Christ, is in view.

The phrase "your apostles" has elicited discussion. Some scholars argue that this is clear evidence that the letter is not by Peter.[13] The author, according to this view, saw all of the apostles as belonging to the church addressed. It is unlikely, however, that the phrase should be read in such a way. Second Peter is not a general letter that lacks specific recipients. Peter addressed the particular circumstances of his readers. The phrase "your apostles," therefore, represents the particular apostles who evangelized and taught the churches receiving this letter.[14] Neither did Peter necessarily exclude himself from their number. He may have been included in the plural "apostles."

3:3 Verses 3–4 explain why the readers were to remember the words of the prophets and the commands of the apostles. The nominative participle "knowing" (NKJV, *ginōskontes,* NIV "you must understand") is awkward in Greek, for we expect an accusative.[15] It probably should be understood as giving a reason why the readers should remember what they were taught. They should have known, after all, that the arrival of mockers was prophesied for the last days. The presence of those who doubt the coming of Christ functions as evidence that his coming is near.[16] The phrase "the last days" *(eschatōn tōn hēmerōn)* is rather common in the Scriptures (LXX Gen 49:1; Isa 2:2; Jer 23:20; 25:19; 37:24; Ezek 38:16; Dan 2:28; Hos 3:5; Mic 4:1; Acts 2:17; 2 Tim 3:1; Heb 1:2; Jas 5:3; cf. Jude 18). New Testament writers emphasized that the last days had arrived in the death and res-

---

[10] See F. Blass and A. Debrunner, *A Greek Grammar of the New Testament and Other Early Christian Literature* (Chicago: University of Chicago Press, 1961), 168.

[11] The reference to the apostles and prophets does not necessarily indicate a postapostolic situation (contra A. Vögtle, *Der Judasbrief, Der 2 Petrusbrief,* EKKNT [Neukirchen–Vluyn: Neukirchener Verlag, 1994], 215).

[12] Rightly Moo, *2 Peter, Jude,* 164.

[13] E.g., Kelly, *Peter and Jude,* 354.

[14] Cf. Bauckham, *Jude, 2 Peter,* 287; Moo, *2 Peter, Jude,* 164–65.

[15] The words τοῦτο πρῶτον γινώσκοντες are exactly repeated from 1:20.

[16] Fornberg rightly notes that we have an example of irony here since the skepticism of the false teachers is a sign of the imminence of the end (*An Early Church in a Pluralistic Society,* 61).

urrection of Jesus Christ (see esp. Acts 2:17; Heb 1:2). Hence, there is no suggestion that the prophecy recorded here was still unfulfilled. Peter believed it was fulfilled in the false teachers that had arrived in the churches he addressed. We see the same phenomenon in 1 Tim 4:1–5; 2 Tim 3:1–9; and Jude 18. Paul himself prophesied that false shepherds would arise among the flock (Acts 20:29–30). Jesus also predicted that false prophets would emerge (Matt 24:3–4,11).[17] The future form does not rule out Petrine authorship of the letter, nor does it constitute a clear hint that the letter was not written by Peter. The words "scoffers . . . scoffing" represent the Greek *(en empaigmonē empaiktai),* and the construction is a semitism (cf. Luke 22:15). The reference to their scoffing elicits the negative things said about the teachers in chap. 2. When Peter noted that they followed their own desires, we are again reminded of the criticisms of chap. 2. The false teachers were not constrained by any moral standards. They were libertines who lived to satisfy their own selfish desires; and so before we hear the content of their teaching in v. 4, we are prepared to dismiss their perspective, since the false teachers were mockers and licentious.[18]

3:4 The content of the scoffers' teaching is now recorded. Presumably Peter put in his own words their teaching, "Where is this 'coming' he promised?" The term "coming" *(parousia)* refers (see commentary under 1:16) to the future coming of Jesus Christ. Expressions with the phrase "Where is . . ." reflect skepticism about the content contained in the question. Jeremiah's critics mocked him by saying: "Where is the word of the Lord? Let it now be fulfilled!" (Jer 17:15). The Israelites in Malachi's day fatigued the Lord when they said, "Where is the God of justice?" (Mal 2:17; cf. also Pss 79:10; 115:2; Joel 2:17; Mic 7:10). Their skepticism parallels God's people in Ezekiel's day, for they doubted that the judgment promised would come, saying, "The days go by and every vision comes to nothing" (Ezek 12:22).

Verse 4b records the reason ("for," omitted by NIV) they doubted the future coming of Christ. They argued that since the death of the patriarchs, God had not intervened in the world. Indeed, from the beginning of creation the world has progressed with an order and regularity that forbids us to look for something dramatic like a future coming of Christ. We can add another thought to the previous one. If Christ will not come in the future, neither will there be a future judgment.

We have summarized the basic meaning of the verse, but controversy

---

[17] E. Lövestam points out the remarkable similarities between 2 Peter 3 and Matt 24:34–51 ("Eschatologie und Tradition im 2. Petrusbrief," in *The New Testament Age: Essays in Honor of Bo Reicke* [Macon: Mercer University Press, 1984], 2:297–99).

[18] Fornberg thinks the reference to "desires" may refer to their false teaching rather than their licentiousness (*An Early Church in a Pluralistic Society,* 39), but the latter probably is in view.

exists over some of the details. The NIV rightly translates the Greek phrase *aph hēs* temporally ("ever since," cf. Luke 7:45; Acts 20:18; 24:11). The NIV says the fathers "died," but the literal word is "slept" *(ekoimēthēsan)*. Surely the word "sleep" is a metaphor for death here, but Moo interestingly observes that the term is reserved only for believers who die (Matt 27:52; John 11:11–12; Acts 7:60; 13:36; 1 Cor 7:39; 11:30; 15:6,18,20,51; 1 Thess 4:13–15). Perhaps this is an indication that the metaphor was not a dead one, that it signaled to the readers not soul sleep but the notion that death is temporary.[19] The most important word in this verse is "fathers" *(pateres)*. Many commentators argue that it refers to Christian believers of the first generations, and if this is the case, then the author could not be Peter since he was a member of the first generation.[20] But there is a decisive objection against this interpretation.[21] The plural "fathers" never refers to the first generations of Christians in the New Testament, but it always refers to the patriarchs of the Old Testament (e.g., Matt 23:30,32; Luke 1:55,72; 6:23,26; 11:47; John 4:20; 6:31,49,58; 7:22; Acts 3:13,25; 5:30; 7:2,11–12,15,19,32,38–39,44–45,51–52; 13:17,32,36; 15:10; 22:1,14; 26:6; 28:25; Rom 11:28; 15:8; 1 Cor 10:1; Heb 1:1; 3:9; 8:9).[22] Furthermore, there are hundreds of verses in the Old Testament where "fathers" refers to the patriarchs. Another piece of evidence points toward fathers referring to the Old Testament patriarchs. The term "fathers" overlaps with the phrase "since the beginning of creation." The two phrases are not synonymous of course. But both phrases point to the regularity of life for a long time, whether from the time God created the world or from the time the patriarchs walked the earth.

Bauckham argues that Peter referred to the first Christian generation, but he admits that defining the "fathers" as the first Christian generation "is unattested elsewhere" and that "2 Peter seems to be unique in the literature of the first two Christian centuries in referring to the first Christian generation as 'the fathers.'"[23] I would simply respond by saying that these comments demonstrate that his view flies in the face of the lexical evidence and strengthens the idea that Peter referred to the Old Testament patriarchs.[24]

---

[19] See esp. Moo, *2 Peter, Jude,* 173–74.

[20] Reicke, *James, Peter, and Jude,* 174; Kelly, *Peter and Jude,* 355–56; Bauckham, *Jude, 2 Peter,* 291–92; Smith, *Petrine Controversies,* 86; D. G. Horrell, *The Epistles of Peter and Jude,* EC (Peterborough: Epworth, 1998), 176; Vögtle, *Judasbrief, 2 Petrusbrief,* 216.

[21] Cf. also Green, *2 Peter and Jude,* 139–40.

[22] Rightly D. Guthrie, *New Testament Introduction,* 4th ed. (Downers Grove: InterVarsity, 1990), 829. I am excluding, of course, texts in which physical fathers are addressed (e.g., Eph 6:4; Col 3:21). In Fornberg's objection to the interpretation proposed here he cannot point to a single example in the NT where "fathers" refers to the first Christian generation (*An Early Church in a Pluralistic Society,* 62–63).

[23] Bauckham, *Jude, 2 Peter,* 291–92.

[24] Rightly Bigg, *Peter and Jude,* 291.

Bauckham objects that the opponents could not have said that all things remain from the time of the patriarchs since Jesus Christ's arrival fulfills many Old Testament prophecies.[25] Hence, they must have said that all things have remained the same since the coming of Christ. The objection is not compelling.[26] First, we must beware of overconfidence in sketching in what the false teachers said. Unfortunately, our knowledge of them, despite the contents of 2 Peter, is rather scanty. Second, the opponents may have accepted the fulfillment of prophecy but argued for continuity in this world. It is possible that they saw fulfillments soteriologically while denying that there had ever been any changes cosmologically. Third, the phrase "since the beginning of creation" indicates that their argument did reach back past the first generation of Christians to the beginning of the world. This confirms the suggestion that they argued against cosmological changes.

In saying that "everything goes on as it has since the beginning of creation," Peter paraphrased the cosmological worldview of the teachers.[27] Soteriological prophesies may have been fulfilled in Jesus Christ, but the physical world had been stable from the time the world was created. Scholars sometimes have seen in the view of the scoffers the Aristotelian view that the world is eternal.[28] But all the text demands is that they argue against any divine intervention in the world, that the regularity of the world's order is such that postulating sudden irruptions is fanciful.[29]

3:5 The basic meaning of this verse is clear, but the details become murky because the syntax is complicated and unclear. We will begin, therefore, by summarizing how the verse contributes to the argument. Peter gave three arguments against the scoffers, refuting their notion that God does not intervene in the world. His first argument shows an internal flaw in the scoffers' worldview. They claimed continuity since creation, but the creation of the world itself represents divine intervention. When they spoke of "creation," they referred to a new work of God. Further, when we read Genesis carefully, it is apparent that the world was chaotic (Gen 1:2) before

---

[25] Bauckham, *Jude, 2 Peter,* 290.

[26] Cf. Guthrie's response (*New Testament Introduction,* 829, n. 2).

[27] S. Meier contends that the author shared the same worldview of the opponents, arguing that uniformity in history demands divine judgment instead of all things proceeding as usual ("2 Peter 3:3–7—An Early Jewish and Christian Response to Eschatological Skepticism," *BZ* 32 [1988]: 255–57). Contrary to Meier the short description of the worldview of the opponents does not indicate a shared conception, for it seems more probable that the opponents envisioned a world without cataclysmic interventions. It seems unlikely that Peter merely reminded them that in the usual course of history we find divine judgments and interventions.

[28] Bigg, *Peter and Jude,* 292.

[29] Fornberg thinks it is possible that the author misconstrued the teaching of the opponents, but he rightly observes that the letter probably would not have been preserved if it did not address accurately the concerns of his readers (*An Early Church in a Pluralistic Society,* 65).

God made it habitable for human life. The present stability of the world can be traced back to God's intervention, and hence there is no reason to doubt that he will intervene again.

Now some of the details in the verse will be examined. The first phrase "they deliberately forget" *(lanthanei gar autous touto thelontas)* stresses the self-will of the mockers if we follow the NIV. The translation proposed by the NIV (cf. also KJV, NKJV, RSV, NRSV), however, is unlikely. Syntactically, it makes more sense if the word "this" *(touto)* is the object of *theolontas*. The term *thelō* can be translated "maintain."[30] Hence, the translation of the NASB should be accepted here, "For when they maintain this, it escapes their notice." The word "this" refers back to the contents of v. 4, showing that they forgot something crucial when they maintained that God does not intervene cosmologically. Peter emphasized in vv. 1–2 that his readers should remember God's words transmitted by the prophets and apostles. Now we are told that one of the major problems with the scoffers was that they forgot some important truths in defending their own view.

Peter likely taught in this verse both that the heavens came into existence long ago and that the earth coheres by God's word. Such an interpretation is attractive syntactically, for in reading the Greek we could place the word "heavens" with the verb "existed" *(ēsan)* and "earth" with the participle "formed" *(synestōsa)*. The NIV represents this view, "Long ago by God's word the heavens existed and the earth was formed out of water and by water."[31] The initial creation of the universe was in Peter's purview, showing that God has intervened in the world. Even though the scoffers apparently concurred with creation (see v. 4), they had not drawn the right conclusions from it. The world God created was initially watery chaos, unformed and undeveloped (Gen 1:2). Human life could not have existed if the world were left as it was. The world, however, was "formed" *(synestōsa)*, that is, it took shape, "by God's word." Colossians 1:17 is a parallel text in some respects, for there we are told that "all things hold together" *(synestēken)* in Christ. The physical universe is preserved and maintained by Christ himself (cf. Heb 1:3). Peter emphasized here that the original creation was formed and took shape by God's word. Dependence on Genesis is obvious since again and again the creation is due to what "God said" (Gen 1:3,6,9,11,14,20,24,26,29). The theme is common elsewhere in the Old Testament as well. "By the word of the LORD were the heavens made, their starry host by the breath of his mouth" (Ps 33:6; cf. Prov 8:27–29; Heb 11:3; and in the postbiblical tradition, *Sir* 39:17; *Wis* 9:1; *4 Ezra* 6:38,43).

What is most puzzling about the verse is the statement that the world

[30] BDAG, 448; Bauckham, *Jude, 2 Peter,* 297.

[31] So Fuchs and Reymond, *2 Pierre, Jude,* 112–13.

"was formed out of water and by water." We could interpret this as if Peter were reflecting on the basic stuff out of which the world is made, as if, like Thales, he were saying that water is the basic element in the world.[32] We need to remind ourselves, however, that Peter drew upon Genesis 1 and was not giving a philosophical answer regarding the "stuff" of the universe. We have already noted that in Genesis 1 a watery chaos covers the earth, making life impossible for human beings. In creating the world, God separated the waters by making the expanse of the sky so that the waters were above and below the expanse (Gen 1:6–8). Furthermore, the waters on earth were collected so that dry ground would also exist (Gen 1:9–10). Hence, when Peter said that the world was created "out of water" *(ex hydatos),* he probably had in mind the emergence of the earth and sky from these waters. Discerning what he meant by the world being formed "by water" *(di hydatos)* is more difficult. Some think he referred to the rain by which the earth is sustained.[33] Peter, however, referred to the creation of the world, not how it keeps going, and so we should reject this idea. Others understand *dia* locally, so that the idea is that the world was formed in the midst of the waters.[34] This is a possibility but represents an unusual definition for the preposition. We should settle, then, for the third option, which is that God used the water as an instrument in forming the world.[35] Perhaps Peter stressed water for rhetorical purposes since it is the agent of judgment in the next verse.

3:6 Peter shifted to his second argument supporting God's intervention in the world. If at creation God introduced stability into the world by separating the waters, during the flood the chaos returned. For the waters were unleashed and the world was destroyed. The false teachers could hardly maintain that the world is marked by regularity, when a flood destroyed human beings. Once again the syntax is puzzling. We begin with the phrase *di' hōn,* translated "by these waters" in the NIV. What the NIV offers is a possible interpretation. The two singular uses of the word "water" in v. 6 function as the antecedent of the plural pronoun according to the NIV. Despite the possibility of this view, it is questionable for two reasons. First, it seems strange that Peter would use the plural since in both instances in v. 5 the term "water" is in the singular. Second, if this view is correct, the verse could be translated literally as follows, "The former world was destroyed through water, being deluged by water." The repetition of "water" is superfluous in the second instance, suggesting that Peter meant something different in the first clause. Reicke suggests that the antecedent is "the

---

[32] See here the discussion of Bigg, *Peter and Jude,* 293.

[33] Bigg, *Peter and Jude,* 293; Green, *2 Peter and Jude,* 141.

[34] J. W. C. Wand, *The General Epistles of Peter and Jude,* WC (London: Methuen, 1934), 178.

[35] Bauckham, *Jude, 2 Peter,* 297–98; Moo, *2 Peter, Jude,* 170.

heavens and the earth."[36] Against this it is not evident how the world could be destroyed by the heavens and the earth, unless one sees these as the repository of water. The allusion is so indirect, however, that one doubts whether the readers would make the connection. The view with the least problems is that the plural relative pronoun refers to water and to the word of God, both of which are mentioned in v. 5.[37] Peter wanted to emphasize, it seems, that the very same agents that brought order to the world—water and God's word—were also responsible for its destruction. The flood, according to Peter, was not merely a natural disaster. It was God's judgment on the world, appointed by his word and effected through water. Some scholars understand "world" *(kosmos)* here to refer to the heavens and the earth, so that the parallel between the future destruction of the heavens and earth is paralleled here.[38] This interpretation is not compelling.[39] First, it does not solve the problem to say that the waters "poured through the windows of the firmament to inundate the earth" (see Gen 7:11).[40] Water gushing through the windows of the firmament says nothing about the heavens being destroyed. Second, the shift of words from "heavens and earth" to "world" is significant. Peter signaled to us a new referent, less inclusive than the heavens and earth. Third, the argument constructed is analogous, not exact. Peter was not arguing that the destruction in the flood is the same in scope as the future judgment by fire. His point was that the judgment at the flood was comprehensive enough to include the world and functioned as an anticipation of an even greater judgment to come. Fourth, we have already seen in 2:5 that "the ancient world" *(archaiou kosmou)* and the "world of the ungodly" (*kosmō asebōn,* both NRSV) refer to the human beings destroyed during the flood. Bauckham is likely correct that "world" here refers to a judgment that affects more than people,[41] but it does not follow that it includes the heavens. A judgment of the earth is "cosmic" enough.

3:7 Verse 7 contains Peter's third argument against the regularity of the world. God intervened at creation (v. 5), at the flood (v. 6), and he will intervene again in the future. The future catastrophe will be like the original creation in that it will include the heavens and the earth. Furthermore, it will parallel God's work in creation and flood in that it will be accom-

[36] Reicke, *James, Peter, and Jude,* 174.

[37] So Bigg, *Peter and Jude,* 293–94; Kelly, *Peter and Jude,* 359–60; Bauckham, *Jude, 2 Peter,* 298; Moo, *2 Peter, Jude,* 170–71; Vögtle, *Judasbrief, 2 Petrusbrief,* 226; Fuchs and Reymond, *2 Pierre, Jude,* 113.

[38] Kelly, *Peter and Jude,* 359; Bauckham, *Jude, 2 Peter,* 298–99.

[39] Cf. also Moo, *2 Peter, Jude,* 171.

[40] Bauckham, *Jude, 2 Peter,* 299.

[41] Ibid.

plished by his word. The instrument of destruction is different in one respect. Instead of using water, God will employ fire. Water cannot be the instrument since God pledged not to destroy the world by means of it again (Gen 9:11–17). The reference to fire is surprising since nowhere else are we told that the world will be destroyed by fire. Some detect Stoic or Iranian influence, but if there is any dependence, it is very indirect. Stoicism expected the world conflagration to be repeated again and again. Peter expected the end to come once.[42] Furthermore, the Old Testament itself associates fire with judgment, sometimes at the end of history (Deut 32:22; Ps 97:3; Isa 30:30; 66:15–16; Ezek 38:22; Amos 7:4; Zeph 1:18; Mal 4:1). We should note that the fiery judgments in the Old Testament refer to the judgment of people, not the cosmos. And yet that the world would be destroyed by fire is found in the postbiblical tradition (1QH 3:29–36; *Sib. Or.* 3:54–90, 4:173–92; 5:211–13, 531; *Apoc. Adam* 49:3; Josephus, *Ant.* 1.70). The future destruction of the world was inseparable, in Peter's mind, from judgment. That day, recalling the day of the Lord of the Old Testament, will be the day of judgment. It will also involve the day of destruction for the ungodly. The false teachers, unless they repented, would realize too late that the judgment was no myth and that God does intervene in the world.

2. The Lord's Timing Is Different from Ours (3:8–10)

[8]But do not forget this one thing, dear friends: With the Lord a day is like a thousand years, and a thousand years are like a day. [9]The Lord is not slow in keeping his promise, as some understand slowness. He is patient with you, not wanting anyone to perish, but everyone to come to repentance.

[10]But the day of the Lord will come like a thief. The heavens will disappear with a roar; the elements will be destroyed by fire, and the earth and everything in it will be laid bare.

The importance of remembering continues in the present paragraph. In vv. 1–2 the readers were exhorted to remember the words of the prophets and the commands of the apostles. Such remembrance was crucial because scoffers had emerged who doubted the future coming of Jesus Christ. Indeed, these scoffers had forgotten (v. 5) and not perceived the significance of God's works in history. They had forgotten these things because they had strayed from God and repudiated the gospel. Peter feared that they could influence his readers. But he also was concerned that the faithful might for-

[42] Rightly Green, *2 Peter and Jude,* 29; Vögtle, *Judasbrief, 2 Petrusbrief,* 228; cf. R. Riesner, "Der Zweite-Petrus Brief und die Eschatologie," in *Zukunftserwartung in biblischer Sicht: Beiträge zur Eschatologie* (Giessen: Brunnen, 1984), 140.

get (v. 8) important truths, not because they were rebelling but simply because the false teachers might sow confusion in their minds. Hence, he gave them two further arguments about the coming of the Lord. First, the apparent failure of the Lord to appear within a certain time frame should not dampen their faith. The Lord does not reckon time as we do (v. 8). A thousand years is like one day to him. What seems like a long time to us is not long to him. The fact that he has not arrived, therefore, says nothing about whether he will come in the future. Second, the Lord is not slow in fulfilling his promise to return (v. 9). He delays his coming to give opportunity for all to repent. Finally, in v. 10 Peter reiterated with confidence that the day of the Lord will arrive. It will come suddenly, and when it does, the world as we know it will be dissolved.

3:8 The next section of the letter is marked by "dear friends" *(agapētoi),* as in 3:1,14,17. For the significance of this term see the comments under 3:1. The verb "forget" *(lanthanō)* is repeated from v. 5. There we saw that the opponents had forgotten about the implications of God's work at creation. The world has not always been marked by regularity and order. God in his creative work shaped the chaotic world so that it was habitable for human beings. Peter exhorted the beloved believers not to forget a crucial truth about God, a truth they were liable to forget since they were under pressure from the teachers, who quite likely argued that too much time had elapsed for the promise of Christ's return to be credible. Peter reminded them of the truth that "with the Lord a day is like a thousand years, and a thousand years are like a day."[43] Peter alluded to Ps 90:4, where the psalmist said, "A thousand years in your sight are like a day that has just gone by, or like a watch in the night." In Psalm 90 the eternity of God is contrasted with the temporality of human beings (cf. also *Sir* 18:9–11; *2 Apoc. Bar.* 48:12–13). The lives of human beings are short and frail, but God does not weaken or fail with the passage of time. In one sense the marking of time is irrelevant to God because he transcends it. Peter applied this insight to the coming of the Lord. If the passing of time does not diminish God in any way and if he transcends time so that its passing does not affect his being, then believers should not be concerned about the so-called delay of Christ's coming. The passing of a thousand years, after all, is like the passing of a single day to him. Bigg nicely captures the idea: "The desire of the Psalmist is to contrast the eternity of God with the short span of human life. What St. Peter wishes is to contrast the eternity of God with the impatience of human expectations."[44] Peter had not surrendered

---

[43] The "Lord" here is a reference to God and not Christ (so Fuchs and Reymond, *2 Pierre, Jude,* 115).

[44] Bigg, *Peter and Jude,* 295.

the imminence of Christ's coming here.[45] He was scarcely arguing that Christ would not come until a great amount of time had elapsed. Second Peter 3:12 indicates an expectation that Christ would return soon. But Peter, like all the New Testament writers, did not prescribe when Christ returns or set a certain date. He preserved the tension between the imminence of Christ's coming and the uncertainty about when he will come.[46]

The phrase also could be interpreted literally to say a day with the Lord is a thousand years. This interpretation was occasionally used in interpreting Genesis to say that human history would last six days (i.e., six thousand years), which would culminate in the millennium (the last thousand years—cf. *Barn.* 15:4; Irenaeus, *Adv. Haer.* 5.28.3). Such an interpretation fails on two grounds. First, the text does not say that one day with the Lord is a thousand years. It says one day with the Lord is *like* a thousand years.[47] We do not have a literal statement here but a comparison, an analogy. Second, the proposed interpretation does not make sense in context. Peter would then have been saying that the day of judgment lasts one thousand years, which is a rather strange notion. Finally, such an interpretation does not fit well with Peter's response to the false teachers.[48] What Peter did say cogently responds to the teachers. Even though the Lord has not returned yet, one should not conclude from this that he will never arrive.[49] The Lord does not reckon time as humans do. What seems agonizingly long to us is a whisker of time to him.

3:9 The first part of v. 9 draws an implication from v. 8. If God does not reckon or indeed experience time as we do, then it follows that he is not slow about keeping his promise (cf. Hab 2:3). The promise *(epangelia),* of course, hearkens back to v. 4 and refers to the promise of the Lord's coming. God, that is, the Father, is not dilatory in fulfilling the promise uttered about his Son's coming again. The Son will come as promised, but the apparent slowness should not be misunderstood. The phrase "as some understand slowness" could possibly refer to those in the churches wavering under the influence of the false teachers.[50] More likely the reference is to the false teachers themselves, referring to them negatively as "some"

---

[45] So also Bauckham, *Jude, 2 Peter,* 310.

[46] For the tradition history in Jewish thought in this verse, see W. Schrage, "'Ein Tag ist beim Herrn wie tausend Jahre, und tausend Jahre sind wie ein Tag,'" in *Glaube und Eschatologie: Festschrift für Werner Georg Kümmel zum 80. Geburtstag* (Tübingen: Mohr, 1985), 267–75.

[47] Rightly Moo, *2 Peter, Jude,* 186; cf. also Fornberg, *An Early Church in a Pluralistic Society,* 69–70.

[48] Rightly Bauckham, *Jude, 2 Peter,* 307.

[49] Fornberg argues that the contemporary writers have overemphasized the problem of the delay of the parousia, noting that many passages in the Gospels indicate that a temporal interval will obtain before Christ returns (*An Early Church in a Pluralistic Society,* 69).

[50] Kelly, *Peter and Jude,* 362.

who lack an understanding of God's ways.[51] The verse may be highly ironic. The false teachers use God's patience as an argument against God, when it should lead them to repentance.[52]

Peter explained why the coming is delayed. God is patient with his people. Notice that the verse says "patient with you" *(eis hymas).* The reason for his patience is then explicated. He does not want "anyone to perish, but everyone to come to repentance." The idea that God is patient so that people will repent is common in the Scriptures (Joel 2:12–13; Rom 2:4). That he is "slow to anger" is a refrain repeated often (Exod 34:6; Num 14:18; Neh 9:17; Pss 86:15; 103:8 145:8; Joel 2:13; Jonah 3:10; 4:2; Nah 1:3), but he will not delay forever (see esp. *Sir* 35:18). We should note at the outset that perishing *(apolesthai)* refers to eternal judgment, as is typical with the term. Repentance *(metanoia),* correspondingly, involves the repentance that is necessary for eternal life. Peter did not merely discuss rewards that some would receive if they lived faithfully. He directed his attention to whether people would be saved from God's wrath. We must also ask who was in view when he spoke of "anyone" *(tinas)* perishing and "all" *(pantas)* coming to repentance. One option is that he considered every person without exception. Some understand 1 Tim 2:4 similarly, "God . . . wants all men to be saved and to come to the knowledge of the truth."[53] We do not have space to comment on the text in 1 Timothy here, but we should note that debate exists over the meaning of "all men" in 1 Tim 2:4 as well. Or we can think of Ezek 18:32: "For I take no pleasure in the death of anyone, declares the Sovereign LORD. Repent and live!" (cf. also 18:23). In this latter instance God's regret over the perishing of anyone is clear. Nevertheless, we have to ask whether the verse in 2 Peter has the same meaning as the texts in Ezekiel. If it does, how does this fit with the teaching that God has ordained and decreed that only some will be saved? Many scholars, of course, doubt that the Scripture teaches that God ordains that only some will be saved, but in my estimation the Scriptures do clearly teach such an idea (cf. John 6:37,44–45,65; 10:16,26; Acts 13:48; Rom 8:29–30; 9:1–23; Eph 1:4–5,11, etc.).[54] Space does not permit a full answer to this question, but an answer that has a long pedigree in church history suffices. We must distinguish between two different senses in God's will. There is a decretive will of God and a desired will of God. God desires the salvation of all in one sense, but he does not ultimately ordain that all will be saved. Many

---

[51] Bigg, *Peter and Jude,* 296; Moo, *2 Peter, Jude,* 187.

[52] I owe this insight to my research assistant, Jason Meyer.

[53] Vögtle remarks that this verse rules out Calvinist theology (*Judasbrief, 2 Petrusbrief,* 231–32). Cf. also the comments of Fuchs and Reymond, *2 Pierre, Jude,* 116.

[54] For a defense of this view see T. R. Schreiner and B. A. Ware, eds., *Still Sovereign* (Grand Rapids: Baker, 2000).

think this approach is double-talk and outright nonsense.[55] Again, space forbids us from answering this question in detail, but this view has been recently and convincingly argued by J. Piper.[56] He demonstrates that such distinctions in God's will are not the result of philosophical sleight of hand but careful biblical exegesis.

Having said all this, 2 Pet 3:9 may not relate to this issue directly anyway. The "anyone" and "all" in the verse may be an expansion of "you" *(hymas)* earlier in the verse.[57] Peter did not reflect, according to this view, on the fate of all people in the world without exception. He considered those in the church who had wavered under the influence of the false teachers. God desires every one of them to repent. But even if this solution is correct, it does not solve the issue theologically, for Peter probably reflected on God's desired will instead of decreed will in this instance. That is, he was not teaching that all of those in the church whom God desires to repent will actually repent. Even if the verse is restricted to those influenced by the false teachers, Peter referred to what God desires, not to what he ordains. At the end of the day, restricting "anyone" to church members is not the most satisfying solution in this text. By extension we should understand 2 Pet 3:9 in the same way as Ezek 18:32. It refers to God's desire that everyone without exception be saved. It follows, then, that Peter spoke of the desired rather than the decreed will of God. God has not ordained that all will be saved since many will perish forever.[58] Still, God genuinely desires in one sense that all will be saved, even if he has not ultimately decreed that all will be saved. Many object that a desire that is not decreed is nonsense and theological double-talk. I would reply that such a view is rooted in biblical exegesis, that the Scriptures themselves, if accepted as a harmonious whole, compel us to make such distinctions. Such complexity is not all that surprising since God is an infinite and complex being, one who exceeds our understanding. In other words, such exegesis is not a rationalistic expedient but an acknowledgment of the mystery and depth of God's revelation. Neither dimension of the biblical text should be denied. God really and truly desires that every person repent and turn to him. We should not retreat to God's decreed will to nullify and negate what the text says. Nor should we use this verse to cancel out God's ordained will. Better to live with the ten-

---

[55] This view is suggested already by J. Calvin (*Commentaries on the Catholic Epistles* [Grand Rapids: Eerdmans, 1948], 419–20).

[56] J. Piper, "Are There Two Wills in God?" in *Still Sovereign,* 107–31.

[57] Bauckham, *Jude, 2 Peter,* 313; Moo, *2 Peter, Jude,* 188; Horrell, *The Epistles of Peter and Jude,* 180 (though he thinks all people can be included by extension). Fornberg argues, on the other hand, that the adversaries are included in God's desire for all to repent (*An Early Church in a Pluralistic Society,* 71).

[58] We cannot adduce the evidence here, but universalism is ruled out by many biblical texts.

sion and mystery of the text than to swallow it up in a philosophical system that pretends to understand all of God's ways. God's patience and his love are not illusions, but neither do they remove his sovereignty.

3:10 Peter did not want to give the impression that there was any hesitation about the coming of the Lord.[59] Hence, he asserted that "the day of the Lord will come." The verb "will come" *(hēxei)* is first in the Greek text, emphasizing that the day will certainly come. The day of the Lord is familiar from the Old Testament, where it often is used to refer to God's judgment and salvation. In the Old Testament such days occur in history, but ultimately the day of the Lord points to the final day, when God will definitively judge his enemies and vindicate the righteous.[60] In the New Testament the day of the Lord also is the day of Christ (1 Cor 1:8; 2 Cor 1:14; Phil 1:6,10; 2:16). Peter emphasized that the day of the Lord will arrive "like a thief." He depended on tradition here, and we know from 3:15–16 that he was familiar with the Pauline letters. In 1 Thess 5:2 Paul informed his readers, "For you know very well that the day of the Lord will come like a thief in the night." Indeed, the Lord will come, according to 1 Thess 5:3, when people least expect it, thinking that they are safe from all harm. Paul most likely derived his image from the historical Jesus, for Jesus warned his hearers to be ready for his coming, noting that he would arrive when people were not anticipating his coming, as a thief breaks in at night (Matt 24:42–44; cf. Rev 3:3; 16:15). The image of the day coming like a thief is notable in Peter, for the readers are reminded to be ready. Circumstances may suggest that the day will not arrive. The false teachers may have scorned the notion of a sudden change in history. The day of the Lord, however, will arrive suddenly, and so no definite signs of its coming can be trumpeted. The signs that precede it, apparently, are ambiguous enough to lead to other conclusions. The teachers will be humiliated and judged when it comes, and Peter implored his readers to be ready.

Three things will occur when the day arrives, and all of them together indicate that the physical world as we know it will be destroyed. It is much more difficult, however, to understand the details. We will look at each in turn. First, we are told that the heavens "will disappear with a roar." The "heavens" reverts back to vv. 5 and 7, where in tandem with the earth it refers to all that God has created in the universe. The word "roar" *(rhoizēdon)* refers to a rushing sound, whether the whizzing of an arrow, the rush of wings, or the hissing of snakes.[61] In this context we should think of

---

[59] Fuchs and Reymond argue that the author refers to God here and not Christ (*2 Pierre, Jude,* 117).

[60] Isa 13:6,9; Ezek 13:5; 30:3; Joel 1:15; 2:1,11,31; 3:14; Amos 5:18,20; Obad 15; Zeph 1:7,14; Mal 4:5; cf. Acts 2:20; 1 Cor 5:5; 2 Cor 1:14; 1 Thess 5:2; 2 Thess 2:2.

[61] Bigg, *Peter and Jude,* 296.

the crackling sound of fire, destroying the heavens. Bauckham thinks it could possibly refer to "the thunder of the divine voice,"[62] but the term seems to be associated with physical phenomena. Jesus himself, using the same verb, *parerchomai* ("pass away"), said that heaven and earth would "disappear" (Matt 5:18; 24:35; Mark 13:31; Luke 16:17; 21:33). Isaiah 34:4 pictures the sky being rolled up like a scroll, and John in Revelation picks up this picture (Rev 6:14; cf. also Heb 1:10–12).

The second part of the picture is that "the elements will be destroyed by fire." The word "elements" *(stoicheia)* refers to the building blocks or basic stuff of which things are made. It can refer to the ABC's or the notes of a musical scale or often to the (presumed) basic elements of the world—earth, air, fire, and water. In post New Testament times the term also began to refer to spiritual beings, and scholars debate whether Paul used the term with such a meaning in Gal 4:3,9 and Col 2:8,20. In Heb 5:12 it refers to the basic elements or teachings of the Christian faith. Three different interpretations have been proposed for the meaning here. First, the "elements" may be angels or spirits that rule over the natural world.[63] This view has not been accepted by many commentators, for it does not fit well in the context. Peter referred to the dissolution of the physical universe and betrayed no interest in whether spiritual powers inhabit stars or planets. Second, he may have referred to the heavenly bodies, that is, the sun, moon and stars.[64] This meaning for the term is attested in the second century.[65] Bauckham thinks Peter may have been depending on a text from the Septuagint, which says that "all the powers of the heavens will melt."[66] This is certainly a possible reading of the text, and it fits the context well. Third, "elements" refers to the stuff of which the physical things in the world are made. I think this view is the most likely, for it represents the common meaning of the term "elements."[67] Such a meaning also seems to be attested in the Sibylline Oracles (3:80–81; cf. 2:206–7; 8:337–39). Some wonder if this fits since Peter proceeded to speak of the earth and the works done in the earth as "found." We will discuss the meaning of this controversial and difficult phrase below. Here the focus is on the consequences of the destruction of the heavens and the elements of the world. When they are burned up, the result is that the earth and all the works performed on the earth will be, as the NIV says, "laid bare." Verse 12 supports the notion that the heavens

---

[62] Bauckham, *Jude, 2 Peter,* 315.

[63] E.g., Paulsen, *Petrusbrief und Judasbrief,* 167.

[64] Bigg, *Peter and Jude,* 297; Kelly, *Peter and Jude,* 364; Vögtle, *Judasbrief, 2 Petrusbrief,* 234. Fornberg thinks stars are in view (*An Early Church in a Pluralistic Society,* 74).

[65] G. Delling, "στοιχέω," *TDNT* 7.681–82.

[66] Cf. Vaticanus, Lucian; cf. *2 Clem.* 16:3.

[67] Ibid., 7:672–79; Neyrey, *2 Peter, Jude,* 243; Moo, *2 Peter, Jude,* 190.

and elements together comprehend all that exists.[68] Together they will be destroyed by fire. It is difficult to know if Peter thought of the purification and renovation of this world by fire or if he had in mind the complete destruction of this present world and the creation of a new one.

The last phrase in the verse is the most difficult, which the NIV translates, "And the earth and everything in it will be laid bare." A literal translation is, "And the earth and the works in it shall be found." But what does it mean to say the earth and its works "shall be found" *(heurethēsetai)?* Some scholars despair of finding any meaning.[69] We are not surprised to discover that textual variations and even conjectural emendations exist, as scholars try to discern the meaning of this last phrase. We can say immediately that the external evidence decisively favors "shall be found," but alternates have been pursued because, as Metzger notes, the text as it reads "seems to be devoid of meaning."[70] We will canvass other options to note the difficulty.

1. One version (Sahidic) adds the negative so that the text reads that the earth and its works "shall not be found." This yields better sense but lacks adequate textual support.[71]

2. An early papyrus (𝔓[72]) adds the word "destroyed" *(luomena),* so that the verse says that the earth and its works will be destroyed.[72] Again the meaning is clear, and one wonders why it is, therefore, so poorly attested. A scribe more likely inserted a form of the verb *luō* ("destroy") to clarify the text.

3. The Majority text reads "shall be burned" *(katakaēsetai),* and this reading is found in many English versions, "The earth also and the works that are therein shall be burned up" (KJV; cf. also NKJV, RSV, NASB). If this reading were original, it is difficult to see how "will be found" would have come to be in its place.

4. Another text (C) reads "will vanish" *(aphanisthēsontai).* The meager external evidence betrays that it is a scribe's conjecture.

5. Scholars also have conjectured a number of possibilities, suggesting the verbs "will run" (*rhyēsetai,* Westcott/Hort), "will run together" (*syrryēsetai,* Naber), "will be burned in fire" (*ekpyrōthēsetai,* Olivier), "will be taken away" (*arthēsetai,* Mayor),[73] and "will be judged" (*krithēsetai,*

---

[68] For this view see also C. P. Thiede, "A Pagan Reader of 2 Peter: Cosmic Conflagration in 2 Peter 3 and the *Octavius* of Minucius Felix," *JSNT* 26 (1986): 82–83.

[69] G. van den Heever concludes that the text is corrupt and no solution has been plausibly advanced to explain its meaning ("In Purifying Fire: World View and 2 Peter 3:10," *Neot* 27 [1993]: 107–18).

[70] *TCGNT* 636.

[71] For this view see Fornberg, *An Early Church in a Pluralistic Society,* 74–76.

[72] Fornberg observes that this reading fits with his interpretation (ibid., 76–77).

[73] J. B. Mayor, *The Epistle of St. Jude and the Second Epistle of St. Peter* (1907; reprint, Grand Rapids: Baker, 1965), 160.

Nestle). Other suggestions have been made, but none have commended widespread support.

We return to the most likely idea, which is that Peter wrote "will be found," and we must try to discover what he meant by it. Kelly thinks we must understand the text as a question, "and the earth and the works it contains—will they be found?"[74] It is hardly evident, however, that a question is intended, and hence this solution must be rejected. Fornberg sees a reference to what was created by God, including all that is in heaven and on earth.[75] It is not evident, however, what it means for such to be found, and hence we are not surprised to see that Fornberg amends the text. More promising is the notion that human beings will be found before God at the judgment.[76] This could be the meaning of the NIV and of the NRSV's "will be disclosed." The word "found" in Hebrew *(māṣāʾ)* has judicial overtones (Exod 22:8; Deut 22:28; Ezra 10:18), and the Greek word "found" *(heuriskō)* is used to depict one's relationship before God (*Sir* 44:17,20; Dan 5:27; Theodotion; cf. Acts 5:39; 24:5; 1 Cor 4:2; 15:15; Gal 2:17; Phil 3:9; 1 Pet 1:7; Rev 5:4). We also are told whether someone is found out as a sinner or righteous before God (1 Sam 25:28; 26:18; 1 Kgs 1:52; Ps 17:3; Jer 2:34; 50:20; Ezek 28:15; Zeph 3:13; Mal 2:6). Bauckham rightly says that the verb could be construed as roughly synonymous with "will be made manifest" (*phanerōthēsetai* and *phanera genēsetai*—Mark 4:22; John 3:21; 1 Cor 3:13; 14:25; Eph 5:13).[77] Perhaps *2 Clem.* 16:3 represents an early interpretation of 2 Peter: "But you know that the day of judgment is already coming as a blazing furnace, and some of the heavens will dissolve, and the whole earth will be like lead melting in a fire, and then the works of men, the secret and the public will appear *[phanēsetai]*." If Clement was alluding to 2 Peter, which seems likely, he understood it as referring to divine judgment.[78] The phrase refers, then, to the consequence of the burning of the heavens and the earth in the first part of v. 10. The earth and the works performed in it will be laid bare before God, and so the NIV translation effectively communicates the notion of divine judgment in the divine passive verb "will be found." We should observe that in v. 7 the same pattern exists. The heavens and earth will be burned, and judgment will come upon the ungodly. The problem with this interpretation is that "earth" *(gē)* in the con-

---

[74] Kelly, *Peter and Jude,* 364–66; so also R. L. Overstreet, "A Study of 2 Peter 3:10–13," *BSac* 137 (1980): 358.

[75] Fornberg, *An Early Church in a Pluralistic Society,* 74–76.

[76] Bauckham, *Jude, 2 Peter,* 319–20; Moo, *2 Peter, Jude,* 191; cf. also Fuchs and Reymond, *2 Pierre, Jude,* 118–19.

[77] Bauckham, *Jude, 2 Peter,* 319; see also Neyrey, *2 Peter, Jude,* 243–44.

[78] So also R. E. Picirilli, "Allusions to 2 Peter in the Apostolic Fathers," *JSNT* 33 (1988): 64; A. Wolters, "Worldview and Textual Criticism in 2 Peter 3:10," *WTJ* 49 (1987): 411.

text is physical and does not refer to human beings. But again Bauckham rightly interprets the verse, suggesting that "it can easily mean the physical earth as the scene of human history, the earth as the dwelling place of humanity."[79] It seems that this is the most satisfying way to explicate this remarkably difficult phrase.

Wolters understands the term in light of "the day of judgment," which is portrayed "as a smelting process from which the world will emerge purified."[80] The world that emerges from the fiery judgment will be one purified by fire.[81] As background he posits Mal 3:2–4, where the Levites will be purified and refined on the day of the Lord (cf. also Mal 4:1–2). Hence, he understands "to be found" to refer to the eschatological world that survives the smelting process. The advantage of this interpretation is its explanation of the meaning of the word "earth." It is less clear, however, how this interpretation integrates the term "works." Nor does the Malachi background provide evidence for his interpretation since it does not refer to the purification of the cosmos but the refining of human beings. Furthermore, Wolters' view does not explain as adequately the parallel in 2 Pet 3:14. Therefore the interpretation presented by Bauckham should be preferred.

3. Living Righteously because of the Future Day (3:11–18)

[11]Since everything will be destroyed in this way, what kind of people ought you to be? You ought to live holy and godly lives [12]as you look forward to the day of God and speed its coming. That day will bring about the destruction of the heavens by fire, and the elements will melt in the heat. [13]But in keeping with his promise we are looking forward to a new heaven and a new earth, the home of righteousness.

[14]So then, dear friends, since you are looking forward to this, make every effort to be found spotless, blameless and at peace with him. [15]Bear in mind that our Lord's patience means salvation, just as our dear brother Paul also wrote you with the wisdom that God gave him. [16]He writes the same way in all his letters,

---

[79] Bauckham, *Jude, 2 Peter,* 320. For similar interpretations see W. E. Wilson, "Εὑρεθήσεται in 2 Pet. iii.10," *ExpTim* 32 (1920–21): 44–45; J. W. Roberts, "A Note on the Meaning of II Peter 3:10d," *ResQ* 6 (1962): 32–33; Thiede, "A Pagan Reader of 2 Peter," 82; D. Wenham, "Being 'Found' on the Last Day: New Light on 2 Peter 3:10 and 2 Corinthians 5:3," *NTS* 33 (1987): 477–79. Wenham detects allusions to Jesus' eschatological parables, where the Lord "finds" his servants to be faithful or unfaithful (Matt 24:46 par.). He also sees a parallel in 2 Cor 5:3, where some are "being found naked," understanding that to refer to evil works (cf. Luke 12:36–38; Mark 13:34–36; Rev 16:15). F. W. Danker proposes a similar interpretation, but he conjectures that the words κατὰ τὰ ἔργα are original, seeing a parallel in *Pss. Sol.* 17:10. ("II Peter 3:10 and Psalm of Solomon 17:10," *ZNW* 53 [1962]: 82–86). It is unlikely, however, that the phrase would have dropped out if it were original.

[80] Wolters, "2 Peter 3:10," 408.

[81] Ibid., 408–12.

speaking in them of these matters. His letters contain some things that are hard to understand, which ignorant and unstable people distort, as they do the other Scriptures, to their own destruction.

[17]Therefore, dear friends, since you already know this, be on your guard so that you may not be carried away by the error of lawless men and fall from your secure position. [18]But grow in the grace and knowledge of our Lord and Savior Jesus Christ. To him be glory both now and forever! Amen.

The section here could easily be split into three sections (3:11–13,14–16,17–18). I have chosen to combine them for thematic reasons. The end is coming, and the present heavens and earth will be destroyed (3:7,10,11a). Since this world is temporary, Peter exhorted the readers to live godly lives (v. 11). Not only should they look forward to that day, but they can also hasten its arrival (v. 12). And Peter reminded them again that a fire will burn in that day that will consume the present world (v. 12b). Language of destruction may imply utter dissolution, but this is not the ultimate end. A new heavens and earth will arrive, and righteousness will dwell in that world (v. 13). By implication, then, the false teachers will be excluded, and only those who heed Peter's message will be included. Hence, this leads naturally to the exhortation to be diligent (cf. 1:5–7) and to be spotless and blameless and at peace with God on the day of judgment (v. 14). The exhortation here is parallel to the one in v. 11, and both are grounded on the eschatological future.

Eschatology and ethics are firmly wed in 2 Peter. The apparent delay of the future, after all, is only meant to give people an opportunity to be saved. This, Peter explains, is in accord with what Paul himself taught in his letters. In other words, Paul himself exhorted people to holiness and salvation in light of the end of history. Apparently some were misusing and distorting what Paul wrote in his letters, probably to advance an antinomian and licentious agenda. We see, therefore, that such misunderstandings were not innocent mistakes, nor did they relate to inconsequential matters. Those who hoist Paul's writings (and other Scriptures) to support license are destined for destruction, that is, eternal judgment. Thinking of those who twist Paul's writings and other Scriptures led Peter to an exhortation that aptly sums up the entire letter. We could understand the "therefore" *(oun)* in v. 17 to introduce an inference from all of 1:1–3:16. Given all that Peter had taught, the readers should have been on their guard and alert. Given the fact that those who ignored his teaching would be destroyed (3:16), that only those who were holy would experience God's saving peace (3:14), and that Peter had warned them in advance of the danger of such teachers (3:17), they must be alert. Otherwise, they could be carried away from their firm standing in Christ by the false teachers and commit apostasy. At the end of the letter, as at the beginning, Peter wrote so that his readers would not commit apostasy. The antidote to apostasy is not merely negative, that is, resisting the influence of the false teachers, but also positive. The readers were to grow in grace, just as Peter prayed that grace would be multiplied for them in 1:2. And they were also to grow in their knowledge of Jesus Christ. We have seen throughout this letter how important knowledge is (1:3), and believers will stay true to the gospel only if they continue to grow in their knowledge of Jesus Christ. Peter concluded with a doxology to Jesus Christ, praying that the glory will be his forever.

3:11 The NIV rightly understands the participle as giving a reason believers should live in a godly way ("since everything will be destroyed in this way"). The Greek participle *luomenōn* is actually present tense ("being destroyed") instead of future ("will be destroyed"). Some commentators conclude from this that the world is in the process of dissolution even now, culminating in its final destruction.[82] It is more likely, however, that the NIV is correct and the present participle designates the future (cf. also Matt 26:25; Luke 1:35; John 17:20; Acts 21:2–3).[83] The destruction described is total and complete, involving a burning of the present elements of the world. Any wearing down of the world now is trivial and unnoticeable in comparison, and hence the future consumption of the world is intended. The destruction Peter spoke of refers back to vv. 7 and 10. In the former verse the heavens and earth are reserved for a fire. In the latter verse we are told that the heavens will pass away and that the elements of the world will be destroyed by burning.

The destruction of the world is not relayed to satisfy curiosity. Knowing the outcome of this world should motivate believers to live a new quality of life. The Greek literally reads "in holy behaviors and godliness [godly acts]" *(en hagiais anastrophais kai eusebeiais).* A similar call to holy "conduct" *(anastrophē)* occurs in 1 Pet 1:15. The importance of godliness in 2 Peter is reflected in its use in 1:3,6–7. From the beginning of the letter, Peter emphasized that God has given everything we need for life and godliness and that it is a prime Christian virtue that should be ardently pursued. The plural of the terms for "behavior" and "godliness" is unusual and may emphasize numerous acts of goodness. Or perhaps the plurals are used abstractly and should not be pressed. The meaning of the verse is not greatly affected in either case.

3:12 The focus on the future continues. Godly lives are related to and grounded in eschatology. Those who disregard the future cosmos will not live well in the present one. Hence, believers live in a way that pleases God as they "look forward to" *(prosdokōntos)* and "speed" *(speudontos)* the

[82] So Kelly, *Peter and Jude,* 366; Moo, *2 Peter, Jude,* 196–97.
[83] Bigg, *Peter and Jude,* 298; Bauckham, *Jude, 2 Peter,* 323.

coming of God's day. The term "look forward to" *(prosdokaō)* occurs three times in the space of three verses (3:12–14), designating the eager expectation believers should have for the coming of Christ and the fulfillment of God's future promises. An eschatological hope is signified by the term elsewhere (Matt 11:3; Luke 7:29–30; cf. *2 Macc* 7:14; 12:44). We are surprised to see Peter speak of the coming of "the day of God," since that expression is unusual in the New Testament (Rev 16:14; cf. Jer 46:10). The word "coming" *(parousia)* in 1:16 and 3:4 refers to the coming of Christ, but the day of God refers to the day of the Father, not the Son. Nonetheless, the coming of God's day is inseparable from the future coming of Christ. When Christ comes, the day of God will commence, this world will be destroyed, and a new one will be instituted. Peter therefore continued to direct his readers to the coming of Christ.

We may be surprised to see that Peter spoke of hastening the day of God.[84] Some understand this to say that we should be diligent to prepare for the day,[85] but this is not the most natural sense of the verb (cf. Luke 2:16; 19:5–6; Acts 20:16; 22:18). Peter clearly taught that believers can advance or hasten the arrival of God's day by living godly lives.[86] We think here of the prayer, "Your kingdom come" (Matt 6:10). Surely the idea is that our prayer has some impact on when the kingdom arrives. Such an idea was current in Judaism as well, for some rabbis taught that God would fulfill his promises if Israel would repent (cf. *b. Sanh.* 98a).[87] Acts 3:19–21 appears to teach a similar idea.[88] God would send his Christ and restore all things if Israel repented fully. But does not such an idea threaten divine sovereignty, his control over history? Was Peter suggesting that God himself does not know when the end will be, since he does not know if his people will live in a godly way? We can dismiss the idea that the future is obscured from God, for if that were true, how could we know that history would ever end? After two thousand years of history, how could we be sure that Christians would ever live righteously enough to bring about God's day? Divine sovereignty is not threatened, for God himself foreknows what his people will do.[89] Indeed, he even foreordains what we will do (e.g., Prov 16:33; Isa 46:9–11; Lam 3:37–38; Eph 1:11). Nevertheless, such teaching must never cancel out the call to live godly lives and the teaching

---

[84] The collocation of "day of the Lord" and "day of God" with the coming of Christ implies Christ's deity (so J. M. Starr, *Sharers in Divine Nature: 2 Peter 1:4 in Its Hellenistic Context,* ConBNT 33 [Stockholm: Almqvist &: Wiksell, 2000], 30).

[85] E.g., Overstreet, "2 Peter 3:10–13," 366–67.

[86] Kelly, *Peter and Jude,* 367; Moo, *2 Peter, Jude,* 198.

[87] For further discussion of this theme, see Bauckham, *Jude, 2 Peter,* 325.

[88] Cf. also *2 Clem.* 12:6.

[89] Cf. the comments of Bauckham, *Jude, 2 Peter,* 313, 325.

that our prayers and godliness can speed his coming. We must not fall prey to rationalism that either squeezes out divine sovereignty or ignores human responsibility. Both of these must be held in tension, and here the accent falls on what human beings can do to hasten the day of God.

Peter returned to what will occur when God's day arrives. Literally he said that "the heavens will be destroyed by burning."[90] In v. 7 the heavens are said to be reserved for fire; and in v. 10, that they will pass away with a roar. We argued in the latter case that the roar designated a crackling fire, and so what v. 12 says coheres with v. 10. The heavens will be destroyed by a great conflagration. The elements of the world (earth, air, fire, and water—as we argued in v. 10) "will melt in the heat." The description is quite similar to v. 10, where the elements are predicted to be destroyed by burning. The verb "melt" *(tēketai)* is in the present tense in Greek, but it surely describes a future event. Isaiah 63:19–64:1 (LXX) portrays the mountains melting when the Lord manifests himself (cf. Mic 1:4). An interesting parallel emerges in Isa 34:4, "All the powers of the heavens will melt" *(takesontai pasai hai dynameis tōn ouranon).*[91] The command to live holy lives in the middle of v. 11 is framed on each side by the assertion that the present world will be destroyed by fire. The false teachers had badly miscalculated. Unfortunately, they had made the kind of mistake in which they would know they were wrong only when it was too late.

3:13 Believers, of course, are not merely waiting for the destruction of the present world. Such destruction, however, is crucial because it is bound up with the judgment of the ungodly (3:7). Nevertheless, if the future offered only destruction, believers would be miserable indeed. The day of God, the day of the Lord (i.e., the coming of Christ) involves both judgment and salvation. This salvation is not merely spiritual, an ethereal out-of-body experience with God. God promises a new world for believers, a transformed world, a new heavens and a new earth. Hence, the Petrine view should be distinguished from Stoicism that does not look forward to a new world.[92] The word "promise" was important for Peter, focusing especially on the coming of Christ (3:4,9; cf. also 1:4). The coming of Christ is inseparable from the arrival of the day of God and the new heavens and new earth. The promise of a new heavens and new earth reaches back to Isaiah (65:17; 66:22), and often in postbiblical literature writers reflect on the new creation that God will institute (*Jub.* 1:29; *1 Enoch* 45:4–5; 72:1; 91:16; *Sib. Or.* 5:211–213; *2 Apoc. Bar.* 32:6; 44:12; 57:2; *4 Ezra* 7:25). In Peter, therefore, we see two themes juxtaposed. On one hand, the old world will be

[90] It is unclear to me, contra Moo (*2 Peter, Jude,* 199), that the heavens refer to the invisible "spiritual dimension of the universe."

[91] Cf. LXX—Vaticanus, Lucian.

[92] So Thiede, "A Pagan Reader of 2 Peter," 79, 81.

destroyed, and on the other, there will be a new heavens and new earth—a new universe created by God. Revelation teaches us that the new heavens and new earth will become a reality with the coming of the New Jerusalem (Rev 21:1–22:5). At the same time we are told that "every island fled away and the mountains could not be found" (Rev 16:20). And, "Earth and sky fled from his presence, and there was no place for them" (Rev 20:11). The first verse of Revelation 21 brings both themes together, "Then I saw a new heaven and a new earth, for the first heaven and the first earth had passed away, and there was no longer any sea" (Rev 21:1; cf. Matt 19:28).[93] Did Peter teach that the old heavens and earth will be annihilated and that God will create something brand new?[94] Or is the idea that God will purify the old world and create out of the same elements a new one?[95] It is difficult to be sure, and we would do well to be cautious in postulating how God will fulfill his promises. Thiede points out that the debate is a very old one, with Justin Martyr and Minucius Felix endorsing annihilation, whereas Irenaeus and Origen argued for purification and renovation.[96] In either case, it seems that we can fairly say that the future world is physical, that a new universe will be born. Believers "are looking forward" *(prosdokōmen)* to this world, to the day of God (3:12), to the fulfillment of God's promises.

In that future world righteousness will dwell (cf. Isa 32:16, LXX).[97] The righteousness here is God's righteousness (cf. 1:1), which fills the future world with his glory and beauty. And Peter had clarified throughout the letter that only the righteous will participate in that world. The antinomian teachers will be excluded, as will all their disciples. Only those who heeded Peter's message will inherit the promises and enjoy the new world. We should remind ourselves that no notion of works righteousness is involved here, for as Peter had already taught (1:3–4), those who live righteously have been transformed by God himself. They do what is right as a consequence of God's gracious work in their lives.

3:14 The arrival of the new heavens and new earth is the hope of believers, awaited eagerly *(prosdokaō)* by all who truly know God. Then God's righteousness will be all in all (cf. 1 Cor 15:28). Verse 14 is stitched to v. 13 by the repetition of the verb "looking forward" *(prosdokaō)*. It is

---

[93] Perhaps Peter drew on Matthean tradition here (cf. P. Dschulnigg, "Der theologische Ort des Zweiten Petrusbriefes," *BZ* 33 [1989]: 170).

[94] So, e.g., Overstreet, "2 Peter 3:10–13," 362–65.

[95] So, e.g., Wolters, "2 Peter 3:10," 405–13; Thiede, "A Pagan Reader of 2 Peter," 79–91.

[96] Thiede, "A Pagan Reader of 2 Peter," 83–91. Supporting renovation is G. Z. Heide, "What Is New about the New Heaven and the New Earth? A Theology of Creation from Revelation 21 and 2 Peter 3," *JETS* 40 (1997): 37–56.

[97] Fornberg rightly rejects Vögtle's view that the text only refers to personal salvation and does not relate to cosmic, eschatological events (*An Early Church in a Pluralistic Society,* 78).

the new heavens and earth that believers long for, the realization of God's righteousness. The false teachers, of course, repudiated the very idea of such a future world. Once again, as in vv. 11–13, the eschatological future becomes the basis for ethical exhortation. Indeed, the exhortation in v. 14 restates in different terms the summons to a godly life in v. 11, and in both instances the exhortation flows from God's promise that the present world will be destroyed and a new world is coming. The teachers' libertine lifestyle and ethic was inseparable from their eschatology. They rejected the future coming of Christ and therefore lived however they pleased. Peter realized that he must convince his readers of Christ's coming if they were going to live in a way that pleases God. Peter's argument is not pragmatic. That is, he did not invent the idea of a future judgment to foster ethical living now. On the contrary, the day of the Lord, consisting of both judgment and salvation, was bedrock reality for him. On the basis of this reality, believers are exhorted to godliness.

As we come to the end of the letter, many themes from its beginning reappear. Here Peter summoned his readers to diligence—"make every effort" *(spoudasate)* in light of the destruction and renovation of the heavens and earth. We are reminded of 1:5, where believers are to apply "all diligence" (NASB, *spoudēn pasan*) in pursuing the virtues detailed in 1:5–7. And in 1:10 Peter said, "Be all the more diligent *[spoudasate]* to make certain about His calling and choosing you" (NASB). In this instance the verb is the exact form that we find in 1:10. Nor has the subject changed. Diligently pursuing godly virtues is necessary for the final reward, that is, eternal life in 1:5–11. Similarly, in 3:14 diligence in godliness is requisite for enjoying the new heavens and new earth. In this verse diligence is to be exercised to live a "spotless and blameless" life before God. The words "spotless" *(aspiloi)* and "blameless" *(amōmētoi)* contrast with the opponents, who were "blots" *(spiloi)* and "blemishes" *(mōmoi)* in the church (2:13).[98] When we examine texts where a similar idea is found (Eph 1:4; 5:27; Phil 2:15; Col 1:22; Jude 24; Rev 14:5), it is apparent that being "spotless and blameless" is necessary for eternal life. We should not confuse this, then, with moral perfection, at least in this life. The New Testament does teach, however, that those who belong to God's people will live godly lives and that they will be perfected on the last day. The false teachers, in other words, will not be saved on the last day since their blemished lives will condemn them. Indeed, the terminology "be found" *(eurethēnai)* is judicial, anticipating the judgment before God (see esp. 2 Pet 3:10; cf. 1 Cor 4:2; 15:15; Gal 2:17; Phil 3:9; 1 Pet 1:7; Rev 5:4). Hence, there is little doubt that believers need to be "spotless and blameless" to be saved.

[98] Cf. 1 Pet 1:19 on Christ as a sacrifice without blemish or spot.

Evangelicals are disposed to emphasize at this point the imputed righteousness of Christ as the basis of our righteousness, and, of course, Christ's righteousness is the basis for all our righteousness. We should simply observe, however, that this is not what Peter emphasized here. In this context spotless and blameless behavior of believers is required to inherit the eternal reward. Thereby we will "be found" to be "at peace with him." Peace *(eirēnē)* designates being right with God, entering into his presence with joy rather than experiencing his wrath.[99]

3:15 On the one hand, believers should not fall prey to laxity, thinking that there will be no judgment and that they can live however they wish. They must live spotless and blameless lives to receive the reward of eternal life. They must diligently pursue godliness and resist the libertinism of the false teachers. On the other hand, those who are straying from God are not automatically excluded from eternal life. God does not count up good works as it were. Those who repent and turn to him will receive his mercy and reward, be it ever so late in their lives. Hence, Peter said, "Regard the patience of our Lord as salvation" (NRSV). He meant by this that we should consider the Lord's patience, that is, his delay in coming, as an opportunity to repent and be saved.[100] The NIV misses the connection with 3:9 by translating the verb *hēgeisthe* "bear in mind" instead of "regard" (NRSV, NASB) or "count" (RSV). The RSV is most satisfying because it preserves the echo of 3:9, "The Lord is not slow about his promise as some count slowness, but is forbearing toward you, not wishing that any should perish, but that all should reach repentance." In both instances the RSV renders the verb *hēgeomai* as "count." Furthermore, the central idea in each verse is similar. The adversaries in 3:9 counted the failure of the Lord to come as slowness, so slow that they thought he would never arrive. And yet what they called slowness grants believers the opportunity to repent. That thought is reiterated in 3:15. The alleged "slowness" of the Lord is really his patience, granting time for sinners to repent and to experience his favor. When the requisite number of sinners repents—and only God knows that number—then the end will arrive (cf. 3:12).

In the midst of such exhortations Peter suddenly brought Paul into the discussion. The reference to Paul, of course, has provoked much discussion; but before we launch into that subject, we should note the main idea communicated. The logic of vv. 14–15 can be summed up as follows: "Because you are waiting for God to destroy the present world and to form a new one, you should do two things. First, be diligent to live godly lives so that you

---

[99] Rightly Bauckham, *Jude, 2 Peter,* 327; Moo, *2 Peter, Jude,* 208; Fuchs and Reymond, *2 Pierre, Jude,* 122.

[100] The "Lord" here probably is not Christ (Bigg, *Peter and Jude,* 299) but the Father (Kelly, *Peter and Jude,* 370; Moo, *2 Peter, Jude,* 208; Paulsen, *Petrusbrief und Judasbrief,* 172–73).

will receive your eternal reward. Second, consider the Lord's patience, or apparent delay in coming, as an opportunity for salvation. Both of these notions, that is, that we should live godly lives to receive salvation and that the Lord has exercised patience so that sinners can repent, are also taught by Paul." Why did Peter emphasize that Paul also taught these two truths? Presumably because the opponents had seized on Paul's writings to advance their own agenda. Some scholars think they distorted Paul's writings (v. 16) by appealing to statements about a spiritual resurrection to support an overrealized eschatology (Eph 2:5–6; Col 2:12; 3:1; 2 Tim 2:17–18).[101] Such a scenario is a possibility, but evidence is lacking that the opponents promulgated an overrealized eschatology.[102] More likely the opponents latched on to Paul's statements about freedom from law to advance libertinism (cf. Rom 3:20,28; 4:15; 5:20; 7:5,7; 1 Cor 15:56; Gal 5:1).[103] This fits with the licentiousness of the false teachers, which is amply attested in 2 Peter. It also accords with the context since Peter emphasized that Paul also taught that believers must live in a godly way to experience God's promise and that in the interval before Christ's coming God grants people an opportunity to repent. We may also have an allusion to Rom 2:4 (cf. Rom 3:25–26; 9:22), where God's patience with sinners is featured.[104]

Peter referred to Paul, then, to reclaim him and to explain that Paul was not on the side of the opponents. He was Peter's "beloved brother," that is, coworker in the gospel and fellow believer. The "our," then, designates Paul as fellow worker with other apostles, not as a fellow believer with all other Christians.[105] Paul's letters are a manifestation of divine wisdom. Paul himself often emphasized that his apostolic calling was given by God (Rom 12:3; 15:15; 1 Cor 3:10; Gal 2:9; Eph 3:2,7; Col 1:25). The word "given" *(dotheisan)* is a divine passive, emphasizing that Paul's ability was not to be traced to his native gifts but God's grace.[106] The other question that arises is what it means to say that Paul wrote "to you." Many scholars take this as evidence that Peter and Paul had both died and that the letters of Paul were now the common property of all the churches. But if 2 Peter is an authentic letter, as I have argued in the introduction, then Peter referred to letters that

---

[101] Cf. Bigg, *Peter and Jude,* 301.

[102] Rightly Bauckham, *Jude, 2 Peter,* 332. Overrealized eschatology posits that perfection and full glorification that will be ours in the age to come belongs to us now. Hence, it sees no need for a future physical resurrection or a second coming of Christ.

[103] Many scholars agree that this was part of the opponents' teaching (Bigg, *Peter and Jude,* 301; Reicke, *James, Peter, and Jude,* 183).

[104] So Mayor, *Jude and Second Peter,* cxxxvii.

[105] Bauckham, *Jude, 2 Peter,* 327–28.

[106] Fornberg thinks that Peter may have been drawing on 1 Cor 3:10 here (*An Early Church in a Pluralistic Society,* 26).

Paul actually wrote to the churches in Asia Minor.[107] Or, possibly, some of the letters of Paul had been circulated so that readers had access to some of the letters that had been preserved. There is no need to conclude that the full corpus of Pauline letters had been collected, nor is there any firm evidence to suggest such here.[108] Given the content of vv. 14–15, scholars have tried to discern what letters the readers might have had access to. If the letters were written in Asia Minor, Ephesians and Colossians are possibilities. We must admit, however, that ultimately we do not know. Paul encouraged a wider distribution of his letters in Col 4:16, and hence it is possible that they had received some of his other letters. Moreover, the necessity of living a godly life and God's patience is widespread enough to include a number of Pauline letters.

3:16 Verse 16 continues the discussion on Paul's letters with the remark that Paul spoke "of these matters," that is, of the importance of holiness (v. 14) and the patience of the Lord. The reference to "all his letters" indicates that Peter saw both these themes in all the Pauline letters with which he was acquainted. We would be overreading the text to deduce from "all his letters" that a Pauline corpus of letters was officially established or even that Peter was personally familiar with all of Paul's letters.[109] Peter referred to the particular Pauline letters with which he was acquainted. How many letters are in view is impossible to say, but it is obvious that a number of Pauline letters were known to Peter. This indicates that at quite an early stage the Pauline letters were valued enough to be read on a fairly wide scale, though any notion of a canon of letters is anachronistic at this stage.

The Pauline letters arose as a subject only because they were being distorted by the false teachers, and perhaps the converts of the false teachers as well. This explains why we are told that some things are "hard to understand" in them. The term *dysnoētos* is used of matters that are difficult to interpret.[110] Misinterpretation, however, is inexcusable. The "ignorant" and "unstable" twist the Scriptures, but it is clear that such ignorance and instability were not merely due to lack of instruction. Elsewhere Peter spoke of believers as "firmly established" *(estērigmenous)* in the truth (1:12). Furthermore, we are informed that the teachers enticed "the unstable" (*astēriktous,* 2:14). Now we are told that the "unstable" *(astēriktoi)* distorted the

---

[107] So Bauckham, *Jude, 2 Peter,* 329–30.

[108] Rightly Guthrie, *New Testament Introduction,* 824.

[109] Kelly, e.g., thinks Paul's letters were beginning to be collected and that the canonical process was underway (*Peter and Jude,* 370–71). See D. Trobisch, *Paul's Letter Collection: Tracing the Origins* (Minneapolis: Fortress, 1994). For a view similar to my own, see Moo, *2 Peter, Jude,* 210–11.

[110] See Bauckham, *Jude, 2 Peter,* 331.

Pauline writings.[111] Their culpability is evident, for Peter went on to say that they did so "to their own destruction." "Destruction" *(apōleia)* is a typical term for eschatological punishment. The verbal and noun form of the term are used quite often in 2 Peter to designate God's judgment on the wicked (2:1,3; 3:6–7,9). Their errant use of Paul's writings landed them in hell—hardly an innocent peccadillo. Bauckham says, "It was therefore not a question of minor doctrinal errors, but of using their misinterpretations to justify immorality, for it is 2 Peter's consistent teaching that eschatological judgment . . . is coming on the false teachers because of their ungodly lives."[112] Those who were twisting and distorting Paul's writings lacked the humility to learn from others, but they were perverting what Paul wrote to justify their licentious lifestyles.[113] Luther plausibly suggests that they were abusing Paul's teaching on justification by faith and freedom from the law to enjoy a life of moral laxity.[114] It is quite reasonable to think that James responded to at least an oral distortion of Paul's teaching about justification by faith in Jas 2:14–26. We know from Paul's own letters that occasionally what he wrote was misconstrued. The famous lost letter to Corinth noted in 1 Cor 5:9–11 was misinterpreted by the Corinthians so that they thought Paul excluded all contact with unbelievers. Perhaps the Corinthians also misunderstood Pauline teaching on the law and cited one of his own formulations ("all things are lawful") in a way he did not intend (1 Cor 6:12; 10:23, RSV).

When the false teachers misused Paul's writings, they were hardly innovative. They distorted "the other Scriptures" *(tas loipas graphas)* as well. What is particularly interesting is that Paul's writings appear to have been identified as Scripture. This could be disputed if one argued that "other" *(loipas)* refers to writings that are in a different category from Paul's. But this view cannot be sustained, for the Greek word "other" refers to "other" of the same kind. This is evident where "other" *(loipos)* functions as an adjective. In each instance the "other" refers to others of the same kind: "other virgins" (Matt 25:11, NASB, ESV), "other apostles" (Acts 2:37), "other churches" (2 Cor 12:13), "other Jews" (Gal 2:13; cf. also Rom 1:13;

---

[111] Possibly the verb "distort" is future, "They will distort" (so J. D. Charles, *Virtue amidst Vice: The Catalog of Virtues in 2 Peter 1,* JSNTSup 150 [Sheffield: Academic Press, 1997], 36; J. Crehan, "New Light on 2 Peter from the Bodmer Papyrus," *SE* (Berlin: Akademie, 1982), VII, 145–49.

[112] Bauckham, *Jude, 2 Peter,* 334.

[113] Perhaps Bauckham is correct in seeing a reference to both the false teachers and their disciples (*Jude, 2 Peter,* 331). Fuchs and Reymond wrongly see a reference to Gnosticism here (*2 Pierre, Jude,* 124).

[114] M. Luther, *Commentary on Peter & Jude* (Grand Rapids: Kregel, 1990), 286.

1 Cor 9:5; Phil 4:3). Peter clearly identified Paul's writing as Scripture.[115] And yet it may be objected that calling something "Scripture" does not necessarily place it on the same level of authority as the Old Testament Scriptures.[116] But the term "scripture" *(graphē)* occurs fifty times in the New Testament and invariably refers to the Old Testament Scriptures, even in Jas 4:5.[117] Hence, we have good grounds for concluding that Peter classed Paul's writings as Scripture, on the same level as the Old Testament Scriptures.[118] Many think that such a statement reveals that 2 Peter is a post-apostolic document, that the Peter who was rebuked by Paul (Gal 2:11–14) would never classify Paul's writings as Scripture. Furthermore, the statement could indicate that a completed corpus of Paul's writings had been collected, something impossibly early for Peter's lifetime.

Substantive responses can be given to each of the objections raised. First, New Testament scholars overinterpret the significance of Gal 2:11–14. Many subscribe to the view that Peter and Paul went separate ways after the incident at Antioch and that Paul was divided from the Jerusalem apostles henceforth. I am not suggesting that Peter and Paul were carbon copies of each other, but the differences between them are overestimated.[119] Galatians 2:11–14 does not suggest that Paul and Peter adopted different theologies. The text says that Peter acted hypocritically, meaning that he agreed with Paul and acted contrary to his own convictions—because he feared what other Jews might think and do. Many New Testament scholars, of course, disagree with this assessment, but we ought to note that they depart from the text at this very juncture and insert their guess about what Peter really thought. Second, the Book of Acts—whose historical accuracy is doubted by some (perhaps many)—does not portray Paul as if he had severed ties with Jerusalem. When he returned to Jerusalem in Acts 21, he was well received according to Luke. Again, many scholars doubt the credibility of Luke's account, but they lack textual evidence for their theories.[120] Third, the recounting of one disagreement between Peter and Paul should not become the lens by which we interpret their entire relationship. Other evidence exists in the Pauline letters and Petrine corpus (including here) that their relationship was one of mutual admiration and respect (Gal 1:18;

---

[115] There is no basis for Bigg's view that Peter actually disagrees with some of what Paul has written (*Peter and Jude,* 234).

[116] So Bauckham, *Jude, 2 Peter,* 333.

[117] That Peter referred to authoritative writings when he referred to the Scriptures is supported by Bigg, *Peter and Jude,* 302.

[118] So Moo, *2 Peter, Jude,* 212.

[119] Rightly Bauckham, *Jude, 2 Peter,* 328.

[120] For a defense of the historical accuracy of Acts, see C. J. Hemer, *The Book of Acts in the Setting of Hellenistic History,* WUNT 49 (Tübingen: Mohr, 1989).

2:1–10; 1 Cor 15:1–11). Fourth, I have already observed that a reference to Paul's letters does not indicate that an entire corpus was collected or that his letters were part of a canon of Scripture.[121] Paul himself taught that his words were authoritative (cf. 1 Cor 14:37), and this is evident because he enjoined public reading of his letters in the churches (Col 4:16; 1 Thess 5:27). Presumably from the strong words in 2 Peter, Peter saw his letter as authoritative as well. We conclude that Peter included the Pauline writings as authoritative for the churches and placed them on the same level as the Old Testament Scriptures. The implications for what belongs in the New Testament canon and for the authority of the Pauline writings today are, of course, immense. Finally, the fact that Peter addressed Paul as "brother" implies a partnership and equality with him that is not apparent in later church writers. Guthrie points out that the Apostolic Fathers speak of Paul in more exalted terms (e.g., "the blessed Paul").[122] The appellation "brother" is a genuine touch from the hand of Peter himself. In addition, Peter implied that Paul was not easy to understand even for himself. Such an admission likely would not be from a later writer.[123]

3:17 Verses 17–18 could be divided from the previous verses, for the "therefore" *(oun)* introducing them really functions as the conclusion of the entire letter. The two imperatives in these verses summarize the entire letter well. On the one hand, the readers must be on their guard *(phylassesthe),* so that they do not fall prey to the false teachers and lose their eschatological reward. On the other hand, they will only remain vigilant if they "grow" *(auxanete)* in grace and in the knowledge of Jesus Christ. The "you" *(hymeis)* is emphatic, and "dear friends" *(agapētoi)* signals a new section and God's love for the readers.

They were to be on their guard because they knew in advance *(proginōskontes)* the danger at hand. Bigg maintains that the participle "knowing in advance" is synonymous with "knowing this first of all" (*touto prōton ginōskontes;* 1:20; 3:3).[124] But the meanings are different.[125] In the latter case the idea is that something is of primary importance, while in the former the idea is that they knew in advance what is coming. The advance warning for the readers comes both from the Old Testament, the teaching of

[121] Cf. Bigg, *Peter and Jude,* 302–3. Note, e.g., K. H. Schelke, who speaks of a canon (*Der Petrusbrief—Der Judasbrief,* HTKNT [Freiburg: Herder, 1980], 236–37). Mayor agrees that the writer need not know of all Pauline letters but then proceeds to say that the verse must refer to a collection of the letters after Paul's death (*Jude and Second Peter,* 165).

[122] Guthrie, *New Testament Introduction,* 826–27.

[123] Ibid., 827.

[124] Bigg, *Peter and Jude,* 303.

[125] Rightly Bauckham, *Jude, 2 Peter,* 337.

the apostles (3:2), and what Peter had written in his letter.[126] Hence, they had no excuse for falling away—any plea of ignorance would be rejected. All that Peter had written, all that he had warned them of, was so that they would be vigilant. Elsewhere in the New Testament we are told that the Lord will "guard" *(phylassō)* those who are his, ensuring that they will not fall away irretrievably (2 Thess 3:3; Jude 24). Such promises, however, should never cancel out the injunction to watch ourselves so that we do not apostatize. And this latter thought is precisely what Peter relayed here. He desired his readers to be on guard "so that you may not . . . fall from your secure position." The word "fall" *(ekpesēte)* refers to apostasy (cf. Rom 11:11,22; 14:4; 1 Cor 10:12; Heb 4:11; Rev 2:5), to departing from the Christian faith. Peter had clarified in the entire letter that those who fall away, like the teachers, are destined for eternal destruction. Believers maintain their secure position, in other words, by heeding warnings, not by ignoring them. Experienced mountain climbers ensure their safety by studying their climb, taking necessary precautions, and knowing their climbing partners. Paying attention to warnings does not quench confidence but is the means to it. So also Peter was not putting a damper on the assurance of his readers. He knew that assurance becomes a reality by heeding warnings. Those who are on their guard will not fall from their secure position, while those who are careless are apt to slip away because they ignored warning signals. We should add here that any who finally do turn aside and fall away reveal that they were never part of the people of God (1 Cor 11:19; 1 John 2:19). But Peter's purpose in a warning was not to handle that question. The warning is prophylactic and prospective, not a restrospective analysis of those who have departed.

The NIV turns the participle "carried away" into a finite verb, so that it is parallel with the verb "fall." But the relationship between the two verbs is captured better if we translate the Greek as follows, "Be on your guard, so that you do not fall away by being carried away by the error of lawless men." The participle "carried away" *(synapachthentes)* delineates how the readers could possibly apostatize. They might be swept away by the influence of the false teachers. The verb "carried away" is used in Gal 2:13 to describe how Barnabas was swayed by Peter and those from James and ceased eating with Gentiles in Antioch. Peter warned that the "error" *(planē)* of lawless false teachers could affect his readers (cf. 2:18). It is difficult to discern whether "error" here is active or passive; perhaps it is both. If passive, it would denote their false doctrine. If active, it would refer to the promulgation of that false teaching to others. That the adversaries were "lawless" *(athesmos)* has been suggested by the parallel to Sodom in 2:7.

---

[126] Cf. Moo, *2 Peter, Jude,* 213.

3:18 Peter now turned from the negative to the positive. It is insufficient to be prepared to ward off the false teaching of the opponents. Believers will only persevere to the end and receive their eternal reward if they "grow in the grace and knowledge of our Lord and Savior Jesus Christ." The nouns "grace" and "knowledge" could be construed as parallel, so that they are both connected to Jesus Christ. Christ could be understood to be the source of both grace and knowledge.[127] Or Jesus Christ could be the source of grace in the first instance and the object of knowledge in the second. The third option is the most likely, that grace is not connected to Jesus Christ in the sentence.[128] The first admonition is simply to "grow in grace." At the inception of the book the grace of God in Jesus Christ was primary. His grace was expressed in his saving righteousness that gave faith to believers (1:1), and Peter prayed that grace would be multiplied in the lives of believers (1:2). Furthermore, his grace has granted believers everything they need to live a godly life (1:3–4), so that they will experience in full God's saving promises. Grace is the foundation of the lives of believers and is entirely God's gift, and yet believers are exhorted to grow in it, to be nurtured in it, and to be strengthened by it. Grace is not a static reality. Believers are to grow in it until the day they die. Otherwise they might be carried away by the lawlessness of the false teachers. Second, believers are to grow in the knowledge of Jesus Christ. Jesus Christ is clearly an objective genitive here; he is the one whom believers know. Again a theme that has been prominent in the entire letter is echoed at the end. In 1:2 grace and peace will be amplified in knowing Jesus Christ as God and Savior. Everything needed for life and godliness is available through knowing God (1:3). Growing in knowledge is necessary for living the Christian life (1:5–6). Only those who progress in godly virtues reveal that their knowledge of Jesus Christ is fruitful (1:8). Conversely, those who renounce Christ after coming to know him are worse off than those who never professed faith in Christ (2:20–21). Growing in the knowledge of Jesus Christ, then, is not optional. It is essential for eternal life, and Peter fittingly placed this theme at the conclusion of the letter.

Doxologies that are clearly directed to Jesus Christ seldom occur in the New Testament, though 2 Tim 4:18 and Rev 1:5–6 are doxologies to Christ. A doxology to Christ constitutes another way that the letter is framed, for we already saw in 1:2 that Peter identified Jesus Christ as God and Savior. Doxologies, of course, are only directed to God himself, and so the deity of

[127] Vögtle, *Judasbrief, 2 Petrusbrief,* 265; Fuchs and Reymond, *2 Pierre, Jude,* 127.

[128] See Kelly, *Peter and Jude,* 375; Bauckham, *Jude, 2 Peter,* 337; Moo, *2 Peter, Jude,* 214.

Jesus Christ is communicated in the doxology.[129] Glory should be attributed to Christ because the salvation and perseverance of believers is ultimately his work, and the one who does the work deserves the glory. We are reminded of the transfiguration, where glory and honor are given Jesus Christ (1:17). Peter did not call on believers to exercise incredible self-effort and be saved. God grants grace so that believers can grow in the knowledge of himself. The glory belongs to Jesus Christ both in the present age and "forever." The Greek literally says "to the day of eternity" (NRSV, *eis hēmeran aiōnos*). The expression is unusual (cf. *Sir* 18:10), but it designates the age to come. The false teachers denied the accession of such an age, but Peter reminded his readers again that it will surely come, and that age will be characterized by glory to Jesus Christ forever and ever. It is difficult to know whether "Amen" is original. The external evidence clearly supports its inclusion, but on the other hand some manuscripts (such as Vaticanus) do omit it. Scribes would tend to insert "amen" after a doxology, but they would not be disposed to omit "amen" if it were originally present in the text.[130] I incline, therefore, to the view that "Amen" is secondary and a later insertion.

---

[129] Rightly Calvin, *Catholic Epistles,* 426; T. Callan, "The Christology of the Second Letter of Peter," *Bib* 82 (2001): 255. Callan goes on to argue that the author of 2 Peter was a monotheist, and yet he also distinguished Jesus from God (pp. 256–63).

[130] Cf. *TCGNT* 637–38.

Jude

INTRODUCTION OUTLINE

1. Author
2. Recipients and Date
3. Opponents
4. Relation to 2 Peter
5. Structure

INTRODUCTION

D. J. Rowston begins an article on Jude with the sentence, "The most neglected book in the New Testament is probably the book of Jude."[1] His assessment probably is accurate, although 2 John and 3 John are close competitors. Jude is often overlooked because of its brevity, consisting of only twenty-five verses. The book is also neglected because of its strangeness, in that he quotes *1 Enoch* and alludes to *Assumption of Moses*. Some may wonder how a canonical book can cite writings that have never been considered canonical. Furthermore, the message of Jude is alien to many in today's world, for Jude emphasized that the Lord will certainly judge evil intruders who are attempting to corrupt the church.[2] The message of judgment strikes many in our world as intolerant, unloving, and contrary to the message of love proclaimed elsewhere in the New Testament. Nevertheless, this short letter should not be ignored. Some of the most beautiful statements about God's sustaining grace are found in Jude (vv. 1,24–25), and they shine with a greater brilliance when contrasted with the false teachers who had departed from the Christian faith.

We can also say that the message of judgment is especially relevant to people today, for our churches are prone to sentimentality, suffer from moral breakdown, and too often fail to pronounce a definitive word of judgment because of an inadequate definition of love. Jude's letter reminds us that errant teaching

[1] D. J. Rowston, "The Most Neglected Book in the New Testament," *NTS* 21 (1974–75): 554–63.

[2] I will use the singular "church" in the commentary, even though Jude may have written to a number of churches.

and dissolute living have dire consequences. Hence, we should not relegate his words to a crabby temperament that threatens with judgment those he dislikes but as a warning to beloved believers (vv. 3,17) to escape a deadly peril. Jude was written so that believers would contend for the faith that was transmitted to them (v. 3) and so that they would not abandon God's love at a crucial time in the life of their church. Such a message must still be proclaimed today, for moral degradation is the pathway to destruction.

1. Author

The author of the letter is named in the first verse, "Jude, a servant of Jesus Christ and a brother of James."[3] The James mentioned here was almost certainly James the brother of Jesus.[4] It would follow, then, that Jude was the brother of this James and also the brother of Jesus Christ.[5] The designation points to a Jude who is well known and to a James who is well known. The author felt no need to identify himself further, suggesting a well-established reputation in the community. If we examine others with the name "Jude" in early Christianity, it is clear that no other candidate fits the authorship of this letter. "Judas of James" *(Ioudas Iakōbou)* is listed as one of the twelve apostles (Luke 6:16; Acts 1:13). Calvin believed that he was the author of this letter.[6] "Judas of James," however, does not mean "Judas brother of James" but "Judas son of James," and so the apostle Jude is not a likely candidate.[7] Furthermore, we would expect in this case that Jude would call himself an apostle. Another possibility is that Jude was

---

[3] For a helpful survey on recent work on Jude, see R. Heiligenthal, "Der Judasbrief: Aspekte der Forschung in den letzen Jahrzehten," *TRu* 51 (1986): 117–29; P. Müller, "Der Judasbrief," *TRu* 63 (1998): 267–89.

[4] See commentary on v. 1.

[5] In this commentary I am adopting a historical approach. R. A. Reese, on the other hand, adopts a literary approach to Jude. She does not pursue the author's intention but explores the literary ambiguity and creativity of the letter (*Writing Jude: The Reader, the Text, and the Author in Constructs of Power and Desire,* Biblical Interpretation Series 51 [Leiden: Brill, 2000]). Contrary to Reese, I believe that the goal of interpretation is to pursue the author's intention. I am unpersuaded that works like Reese's contribute in a helpful way to biblical interpretation since the text is separated from the author's intention. For a defense of authorial intention and a historical approach, see E. D. Hirsch, *Validity in Interpretation* (New Haven: Yale University Press, 1967), and K. J. Vanhoozer, *Is There a Meaning in This Text?* (Grand Rapids: Zondervan, 1998).

[6] J. Calvin, *Commentaries on the Catholic Epistles* (Grand Rapids: Eerdmans, 1948), 428–29. This was the traditional view before the nineteenth century, though R. Bauckham notes that most who defended this view also believed that the apostle James was the same person as the relative of Jesus listed in Mark 6:3. See Bauckham's *Jude and the Relatives of Jesus in the Early Church* (Edinburgh: T & T Clark, 1990), 172.

[7] Rightly C. Bigg, *The Epistles of St. Peter and St. Jude,* ICC (Edinburgh: T & T Clark, 1901), 319.

"Judas Barsabbas" (Acts 15:22,27,32). There is no indication, however, that "Judas Barsabbas" was the brother of the James who is so prominent in Acts. Nevertheless, Ellis suggests that he is the author of the letter, arguing that the word "brother" *(adelphos)* does not refer to a relative but to a coworker in the gospel.[8] Ellis's proposal is stimulating, but it is doubtful that the word "brother" refers to coworkers in the gospel. Contrary to Ellis the term does not denote a ministry position but refers either to genealogical relationships or inclusion in God's family. When we read the New Testament letters, it is clear that the term "brother" typically refers to a fellow believer, not to a partner in ministry (e.g., Rom 14:10,13,15,21; 16:23; 1 Cor 5:4; 6:5–6; 7:12,14–15; 8:11; Jas 1:9; 2:5; 4:11; 1 John 2:9–11; 3:10). Philemon is an interesting test case. His participation in ministry (Phlm 1) is indicated by the term "coworker" (NRSV, *synergos*), not the term "brother" (NASB, *adelphos*). So too in Jude the designation "brother of James" does not itself demonstrate that Jude was in a formal ministry. Here it indicates that Jude was the physical brother of James. Hence, the notion that Judas Barsabbas was the author of the letter should be rejected.

Other theories are even more speculative and unlikely. Some scholars find some plausibility in the view that Jude in the epistle refers to the apostle Thomas since Thomas was likely a surname instead of a personal name.[9] This view is based on Syrian tradition where we have the name "Judas Thomas" or Judas "the twin." Several pieces of evidence render this view improbable.[10] We would expect the author of the Epistle of Jude to identify himself as "Thomas" or "the twin" if "Judas Thomas" were the author, for these designations identify Thomas in the Syrian traditions. Without such identification any reference to Thomas is scarcely evident. Hence, we are not surprised to learn that no one in the early church identified Thomas as the author of the letter. The view also founders because we would expect the author to identify himself as an apostle. Finally, if the author desired to identify himself with Thomas, it would be quite confusing for him to identify himself as the brother of James, for there is no evidence that Thomas identified himself as James's brother.

Another theory is suggested by Streeter, who opts for a late date and identifies the author as "Judas of James," the third bishop of Jerusalem (*Apostolic Constitutions* 7:46).[11] He can only sustain this theory by arguing that "brother" is a later insertion to the text, a desperate expedient to fortify his

[8] E. E. Ellis, "Prophecy and Hermeneutic in Jude," in *Prophecy and Hermeneutic in Early Christianity: New Testament Essays* (Grand Rapids: Eerdmans, 1978), 226–30; see also in the same volume his essay "Paul and His Co-Workers," 13–22.

[9] See H. Koester, "GNOMAI DIAPHOROI," *HTR* 58 [1965]: 296–97.

[10] For a helpful assessment of the evidence see Bauckham, *Relatives of Jesus,* 32–37.

[11] B. H. Streeter, *The Primitive Church* (London: Macmillan, 1930), 178–80.

theory. Moffatt thinks that both Jude and James are unknown, but such a theory suffers from the difficulty of explaining why Jude would call himself the brother of James when it was customary to refer to oneself as the son of someone.[12] It makes better sense to say that Jude called himself James's brother because James was well known as the brother of Jesus. More credible than Moffatt's suggestion is that the letter is deliberately pseudonymous and that the author wanted to pass himself off as Jude the brother of James.[13] The theory of pseudonymity, however, does not furnish a convincing explanation for attributing the work to Jude since the latter was not well known in early Christianity.[14] We would expect a pseudonymous writer to invest his writing with dignity by choosing someone other than the rather obscure Jude as the author. Nevertheless, some think that Jude was honored and well known in Palestinian Christianity.[15] But if one desired to select a famous person in Palestine, James would have been a better candidate, for even the author of Jude locates himself in relation to James. Furthermore, a pseudonymous author, if he desired to impress readers with his credentials, would have introduced himself as "Jude the brother of Jesus."[16] The writer did not try to impress the reader with Jude's relationship to Jesus but simply stated his relation to James. It is most likely, then, that the author was genuinely Jude the brother of James, both of whom were brothers of Jesus Christ.[17]

Unfortunately, our knowledge of Jude is scanty, which, as we noted, argues for the letter's authenticity. He was one of the four brothers of Jesus

---

[12] J. Moffatt, *The General Epistles: James, Peter, and Jude* (New York: Harper & Brothers, 1928), 224–26. Rightly R. Bauckham, *Jude, 2 Peter* (Waco: Word, 1983), 23.

[13] So J. N. D. Kelly, *A Commentary on the Epistles of Peter and Jude,* Thornapple Commentaries (Grand Rapids: Baker, 1981), 234; B. Reicke, *The Epistles of James, Peter, and Jude,* AB (Garden City: Doubleday, 1964), 9; D. J. Rowston, "The Most Neglected Book in the New Testament," *NTS* 21 (1974–75): 559–61; Müller, "Der Judasbrief," 286; H. Paulsen, *Der Zweite Petrusbrief und der Judasbrief,* KEK (Göttingen: Vandenhoeck & Ruprecht, 1992), 44–45; E. Fuchs and P. Reymond, *La Deuxième Épître de Saint Pierre, L'Épître de Saint Jude,* CNT (Neuchâtel–Paris: Delachaux & Niestlé, 1980), 148. For a list of others who see the attribution as a reference to the brother of Jesus or as pseudonymous, see Bauckham, *Relatives of Jesus,* 174.

[14] So J. W. C. Wand, *The General Epistles of Peter and Jude,* WC (London: Methuen, 1934), 188. A. Vögtle suggests that the author desired to counter the antinomianism of the opponents by appealing to the circle of the Lord's brothers. Since James was already known to be dead, he selected Jude, who was still known at the end of the first century (*Der Judasbrief, der 2 Petrusbrief,* EKKNT [Neukirchen-Vluyn: Neukirchener Verlag, 1994], 11). Such a view suggests that the author deliberately intended to deceive the readers.

[15] Rowston, "Most Neglected Book," 560.

[16] Bauckham, *Jude, 2 Peter,* 14; id., *Relatives of Jesus,* 176.

[17] So also C. E. B. Cranfield, *I and II Peter and Jude: Introduction and Commentary,* TBC (London: SCM, 1960), 146–48 (A.D. 70–80); D. Guthrie, *New Testament Introduction*, 4th ed. (Downers Grove: InterVarsity, 1990), 902–5; M. Green, *The Second Epistle General of Peter and the General Epistle of Jude,* 2d ed., TNTC (Grand Rapids: Eerdmans, 1987), 48–52.

(Matt 13:55; Mark 6:3).[18] The order of the names varies in the two accounts, though James is named first in both texts. Perhaps we are justified in concluding that James was older than Jude, though he could have been listed first because of his reputation. The evidence we have suggests that Jude did not believe that Jesus was the Messiah during the latter's ministry (Mark 3:21,31; John 7:5). He likely became a believer after the resurrection since Acts 1:14 says the Lord's brothers were part of the prayer meetings prior to Pentecost. We learn from 1 Cor 9:5 that the Lord's brothers were itinerant missionaries, and Jude probably was included here. His missionary work would explain his writing to the church in an authoritative manner. Hegesippus (Eusebius, *Hist. Eccl.* 3.19.1–20.8) provides a fascinating account in which two grandsons of Jude were brought before the emperor Domitian (A.D. 81–96) and questioned about their loyalty since they were from the royal family of David. They were released when they explained that they were farmers, waiting for the kingdom to come in the next world. The accuracy of the account is debated, and we will not linger over that question here. But it is at least likely that Jude had grandsons during the era of Domitian, suggesting perhaps that Jude was dead by the time the incident occurred. Such an observation does not rule out necessarily the writing of Jude during the reign of Domitian since he could have composed the letter during the first part of Domitian's reign, and Jude's grandsons may have been hailed before the emperor during the last years of his tenure.

Many scholars cast doubt on the authenticity of Jude because the Greek in the letter seems too polished to come from a rural Jew like Jude.[19] A number of studies have shown, however, that Greek was common in Palestine, especially in Galilee. The influence of Hellenistic culture on Palestine was significant during the New Testament era. Moreover, if Jude traveled as a missionary, he could have acquired greater facility in Greek to foster his ministry.[20] Palestinians probably had a greater ability in the Greek language than many New Testament scholars have thought, and so assigning the letter to Jude is not improbable. As Bauckham says about Jude: "It could easily be among the earliest of the New Testament documents, as well as being rare and valuable firsthand evidence of the character of the Christian devo-

[18] J. P. Meier demonstrates conclusively that the references to the brothers of Jesus in the Gospels refer to the biological sons of Joseph and Mary ("The Brothers and Sisters of Jesus in Ecumenical Perspective," *CBQ* 54 [1992]: 1–28). Hence, if we are correct in our identification of Jude, he was the biological son of Joseph and Mary. Bauckham thinks the view that the brothers were sons of Joseph by a previous marriage is also quite possible (*Relatives of Jesus,* 19–32), but Meier's assessment of the evidence is more persuasive.

[19] E.g., Kelly, *Peter and Jude,* 233; W. G. Kümmel, *Introduction to the New Testament,* rev. ed. (Nashville: Abingdon, 1975), 428; Vögtle, *Judasbrief, 2 Petrusbrief,* 4–11.

[20] So Bauckham, *Jude, 2 Peter,* 15.

tion and developing theology of those original Palestinian circles in which Jesus' own relatives were leaders."[21]

It is also argued that the letter is pseudonymous because the apostolic age is considered to be a past era (v. 17), and a body of doctrine is established (v. 3).[22] As we argue in v. 17, it is unnecessary to conclude that the writings of the apostolic age were collected together or that all the apostles had died when Jude wrote.[23] Indeed, v. 18 could mean that the apostles actually wrote personally to those addressed by Jude.[24] Furthermore, predictions of future apostasy belong to the earliest oral stage of Christian preaching (Acts 20:29–30). Nor does the reference to the faith transmitted to the saints once for all necessarily point to a late date. The transmission of tradition is important in the Pauline letters that all acknowledge to be authentic (Rom 6:17; 1 Cor 11:23–26; 15:1–4).[25] Hebrews also teaches that the revelation given in the last days through Christ is definitive and final (Heb 1:2).

The external evidence for Jude is actually quite strong, given that the letter is brief and circumscribed in purpose.[26] Some scholars have detected references to Jude in some of the Apostolic Fathers, but the allusions are not considered by most to be clear enough to be definite. Jude is attested as Scripture by the Muratorian Canon (ca. A.D. 200). Tertullian (*De cult. fem.* i. 3) and Clement of Alexandria both refer to it (see Eusebius, *Hist. Eccl.* vi.14.1). Later Jude came to be doubted by some. Origen accepted it but suggested that others questioned its authority (*In Matt.* x.17). Eusebius relayed that some questioned it (*Hist. eccl.* vi.13.6; 14.1). Apparently it was questioned because of the citation of *1 Enoch* (so Jerome, *De vir. ill.* iv). The earliest external evidence, then, witnesses to the letter's authenticity.[27] It probably was only doubted later because of the use of pseudepigraphical books,[28] which actually is an indirect support of its authenticity, for an author concerned about the appearance of authenticity would not have cited them.

2. Recipients and Date

Locating the recipients and assigning a date to Jude is quite difficult. Unfortunately, we have little evidence on which to base conclusions, so the

[21] Bauckham, *Relatives of Jesus,* 178.

[22] So, e.g., Kümmel, *Introduction to the New Testament,* 428.

[23] Rightly, Guthrie, *New Testament Introduction,* 906–7.

[24] D. B. Wallace, "Jude: Introduction, Argument, and Outline," at http://www.bible.org/studies/soapbox/jude.htm.

[25] Cf. Guthrie, *New Testament Introduction,* 906.

[26] See the primary sources in Bigg, *Peter and Jude,* 305–8.

[27] For older defenses of authenticity, see Bigg, *Peter and Jude,* 305–22; J. B. Mayor, *The Epistle of St. Jude and the Second Epistle of St. Peter* (1907; reprint, Grand Rapids: Baker, 1965), cxlvi–clii.

[28] Kümmel, *Introduction to the New Testament,* 428; Kelly, *Epistles of Peter and Jude,* 223–24.

recipients and date are typically decided on the basis of other conclusions, such as whether the letter is authentic, its relationship to 2 Peter, its early catholic character, and the identity of the opponents. Dates for Jude between A.D. 50 and 160 have been proposed.[29] I have argued that the letter is authentic, so a second-century date is ruled out. Some identify the opponents as Gnostics and assign a late date. But it is unclear that the opponents were Gnostics since the evidence for Gnosticism in the letter is scanty, and full-fledged Gnosticism is restricted to the second century.[30] More promising is the relationship between Jude and 2 Peter. I will argue, however, that Jude precedes 2 Peter. If this is the case, 2 Peter furnishes little assistance in determining the date, though dependence upon 2 Peter would mean that the letter could not have been written until the mid 60s at the earliest.[31] Most scholars, however, who see dependence, claim that 2 Peter used Jude, and in this instance the date of 2 Peter is not determinative for Jude. In any case, the interpretation of the letter is not affected dramatically whether we date the letter in the 60s or the 80s. It seems most likely that a date in the 60s is closest to the truth.

Labeling Jude as a form of early catholicism is unconvincing.[32] The notion that some writings in the New Testament reflect early catholicism suffers from historical anachronism and the forcing of evidence to fit a thesis. Scholars are still prone to read debates in later church history in some form into the New Testament. Even if one were to agree that early catholicism was budding during the New Testament era, no sprouts are evident in Jude. A vigorous hope for the Lord's return animates the letter (vv. 1,14,21,24), which is contrary to

---

[29] See the full list in Bauckham, *Relatives of Jesus,* 168–69. E. M. Sidebottom suggests a date between A.D. 100 and 120 (*James, Jude and 2 Peter,* NCB [London: Thomas Nelson, 1967], 78). For a date ca. A.D. 100, see Kümmel, *Introduction to the New Testament,* 429. Reicke suggests A.D. 90 (*James, Peter, and Jude,* 192). D. G. Horrell suggests A.D. 75–90 (*The Epistles of Peter and Jude,* EC [Peterborough: Epworth, 1998], 107). Fuchs and Reymond suggest A.D. 80–100 (*2 Pierre, Jude,* 152). Paulsen postulates A.D. 80–120 (*Petrusbrief und Judasbrief,* 45). Cranfield suggests A.D. 70–80 (*I and II Peter and Jude*), 146–48. Vögtle suggests either the 90s or the turn of the century (*Judasbrief, 2 Petrusbrief,* 12).

[30] Against a Gnostic background, see J. Kahmann, "Second Peter and Jude," in *The New Testament in Early Christianity: La réception des écrits néotestamentaires dans le christianisme primitif,* BETL 86 (Leuven: University Press, 1989), 114–15; I. H. Eybers, "Aspects of the Background of the Letter of Jude," *Neot* 9 (1975): 117–19; Bauckham, *Relatives of Jesus,* 162–65; Guthrie, *New Testament Introduction,* 911.

[31] Ellis suggests A.D. 55–65 ("Prophecy and Hermeneutic in Jude," 235–36); J. A. T. Robinson, A.D. 60–62 (*Redating the New Testament* [Philadelphia: Westminster, 1976], 197–98); Bigg, ca. A.D. 61–62 (*Peter and Jude,* 318); Wallace, A.D. 66–67 ("Jude: Introduction, Argument, and Outline"); Guthrie, A.D. 65–80 (*New Testament Introduction,* 908); Green, A.D. 65–80 (*2 Peter and Jude,* 55–56); Kelly, A.D. 70s (*Peter and Jude,* 233); Eybers, A.D. 80 ("Aspects of the Background of the Letter of Jude," 113–23). Bauckham seems to be open to any date between A.D. 60 and 90 (*Jude, 2 Peter,* 13–14). Mayor opts for near 80 (*Jude and Second Peter,* cxlv).

[32] Rightly Bauckham, *Relatives of Jesus,* 158–62; Kümmel, *Introduction to the New Testament,* 426–27.

so-called early catholicism where the church settles down for a long stay in the world. Nor is there any evidence of the institutionalization of offices in Jude, a reputed indication of early catholicism. Jude nowhere appealed to church leaders or something like a monarchial bishop to suppress the opponents. Some detect evidence of early catholicism in the emphasis on preserving the faith that was handed down once for all (vv. 3,20). Often New Testament scholars think that any reference to a body of codified belief has the odor of early catholicism. On the contrary, the importance of orthodoxy informs even the earliest letters (cf. Rom 6:17; 1 Cor 15:1–11; Gal 1:23; 1 Thess 4:1–2). In any case, Jude did not have in mind an articulated and detailed confession or a fully developed catechetical instrument. He referred here to the gospel, a gospel that includes doctrinal content and definition. Of course, the gospel includes the demand to live a godly life, and it is precisely here that the opponents disagree.

Most scholars believe that the recipients had some kind of Jewish background, given Jude's predilection for Jewish apocalyptic tradition (*1 Enoch* and *Testament of Moses*).[33] Indeed, the use of apocalyptic literature is another indication that Jude wrote the letter.[34] It is possible that Gentiles attracted to Judaism were in view since Jewish antinomianism was not a common phenomenon, and the intruders were clearly licentious in their lifestyle.[35] Still, the emphasis on Jewish traditions points to Jewish rather than Gentile readers. It is also possible that we have a mixed audience composed of both Jews and Gentiles.[36] Suggestions for a destination include Palestine, Syria, Asia Minor, and Egypt.[37] We must admit that we really have no way of knowing the letter's destination. Nothing in the interpretation of the letter is based on its destination, nor do we know whether Jude wrote to one church or churches. In the commentary I will refer to Jude's "church," but I do not mean to imply thereby that only one church is addressed. The terminology is used to avoid the awkwardness of oscillating between "church" and "churches" in the commentary.

---

[33] E.g., Eybers, "Background of the Letter of Jude," 114. For the pervasiveness of Jewish traditions in Jude, see T. Wolthuis, "Jude and Jewish Traditions," *CTJ* 22 (1987): 21–41; J. D. Charles, "Jude's Use of Pseudepigraphical Source-Material as Part of a Literary Strategy," *NTS* 37 (1991): 130–45. See also id., *Literary Strategy in the Epistle of Jude* (London and Toronto: Associated University Presses, 1993).

[34] So Wand, *Epistles of Peter and Jude,* 189.

[35] Kelly, *Peter and Jude,* 233–34; Wallace, "Jude: Introduction, Argument, and Outline"; cf. also Bigg, *Peter and Jude,* 321; Vögtle, *Judasbrief, 2 Petrusbrief,* 10.

[36] Fuchs and Reymond, *2 Pierre, Jude,* 144.

[37] See the discussion in Bauckham, *Jude, 2 Peter,* 16. J. J. Gunther argues that Jude was written for Alexandrian believers ("The Alexandrian Epistle of Jude," *NTS* 30 [1984]: 549–62). Gunther's argument is particularly dependent upon the notion that Jude was written against a Gnostic heresy. It will be argued below that evidence for such a view is lacking. Hence, the main argument for an Egyptian destination (or origin) fails. Wallace suggests Ephesus ("Jude: Introduction, Argument, and Outline"). Vögtle suggests Asia Minor (*Judasbrief, 2 Petrusbrief,* 12).

3. Opponents

Historically Jude has been classified as one of the catholic epistles. The designation is misleading since Jude was written to a particular situation, to counter opponents who introduced destructive teaching to the church. Jude did not write a letter in which he summed up his theology or sketched in his view of the Christian life. He addressed specific circumstances to assist the church in its response to intruders who had invaded the church.[38] The opponents likely came from the outside since they are said to have "secretly slipped in among you" (v. 4).[39] From this we can rightly call them "intruders" or "interlopers" or "infiltrators."[40] Jude did not give us a detailed portrait of the adversaries. Instead he compared them to notorious sinners from the Old Testament, showing that they were especially wicked.[41]

In the history of scholarship the opponents have typically been identified as Gnostics,[42] or as representing a form of incipient Gnosticism.[43] Some draw on the background of the Gnostic systems of the second century, seeing a libertine form of Gnosticism in the adversaries. According to this view, the adversaries reject the moral order of the creation, distinguish between pneumatics and psychics (v. 19), are individualistic (v. 12), and revile angelic powers (v. 8). Kelly is more guarded, seeing the heretics as involved in "the opening shots in the fateful struggle between the Church and Gnosticism."[44] He sees "Gnostic colouring" in their libertinism and

---

[38] F. Wisse argues for a contrary view. He maintains that the polemic against the opponents is not addressed to specific circumstances, that Jude borrows from Jewish apocalyptic to demonize heretics, and hence we learn nothing from Jude about the opponents ("The Epistle of Jude in the History of Heresiology," in *Essays on the Nag Hammadi Texts in Honour of Alexander Böhlig,* NHS 3 [Leiden: Brill, 1972], 133–43). The specific character of the letter suggests, on the contrary, that Jude describes real opponents. G. Sellin rightly notes that Wisse's position is extreme ("Die Häretiker des Judasbriefes," *ZNW* 77 [1986]: 207). Bauckham observes that reviling angels is a specific feature that calls into question the notion that we have a stock denunciation of opponents (*Relatives of Jesus,* 167; cf. also C. D. Osburn, "Discourse Analysis and Jewish Apocalyptic in the Epistle of Jude," in *Linguistics and New Testament Interpretation: Essays on Discourse Analysis* [Nashville: Broadman, 1992], 312).

[39] Contra Guthrie, *New Testament Introduction,* 910.

[40] For a sociological study of Jude, see S. J. Joubert, "Language, Ideology and the Social Context of the Letter of Jude," *Neot* 24 (1990): 335–49.

[41] Rightly S. J. Joubert, "Facing the Past: Transtextual Relationships and Historical Understanding in the Letter of Jude," *BZ* 42 (1998): 67.

[42] For a helpful listing of various identifications, see Osburn, "Discourse Analysis and Jewish Apocalyptic in the Epistle of Jude," 310.

[43] E.g., Kümmel, *Introduction to the New Testament,* 426. In support of an early form of Gnosticism, see Kelly, *Peter and Jude,* 231; Fuchs and Reymond, *2 Pierre, Jude,* 143.

[44] Kelly, *Peter and Jude,* 231.

suspects they embraced Christological heresy.[45] Their inclination to Gnosticism manifests itself in their reception of revelations by dreams (v. 8) and in their regard for themselves as pneumatics (v. 19). On the other hand, according to Kelly, no evidence exists for a polemic against an inferior God who created this world. So the Gnosticism found here cannot be equated with the developed systems of the second century. The Gnostic thesis is still advocated by most in German scholarship. The article by Seethaler is representative.[46] He sees a mixture of traditional beliefs and Gnostic conceptions. The opponents in Jude were libertines (vv. 4,18). Verse 19, in which the opponents are said to be "soulish" *(pyschikoi)* and are charged with not having the Spirit, indicates the use of technical terms from Gnosticism. The reference to dreaming (v. 8) shows that the opponents received Gnostic revelatory dreams and visions. Their reviling of angelic powers (v. 8) demonstrates a rejection of the material world created by God since such powers helped create the physical world. Jude's mention of Cain (v. 11) indicates they were part of the Gnostic Cainite sect that lived in a libertine way. Their rebellion signals their rejection of any church hierarchy (v. 11).

Alternatively, Sellin rejects any Gnostic identification of the opponents.[47] He thinks instead that they were pneumatics. They trumpeted moral autonomy and did not promote an immoral lifestyle. Nor, says Sellin, did they espouse the doctrine of the Demiurge. Instead, the heresy is close to what we see in Colossians 2. As ecstatic visionaries (v. 8) the opponents received heavenly visions, and thus they despised angels because they thought of themselves as part of the spiritual elite. Jude did not criticize them, according to Sellin, for sexual sin as is commonly argued in vv. 6–7. Instead, the problem with the opponents was that they transcended their proper sphere. The angels in v. 7 are not criticized for sexual sin but for leaving the realm of heaven and coming to earth. So too the opponents through ecstatic visions tried to transcend the sphere of this world and thus participate in the heavenly world. The opponents claimed to be spiritual, but they were like animals in that they did not have spiritual knowledge (v. 10). The "clothing" stained by the flesh (v. 23) does not refer to sexual sin but identifies the teachers as wandering charismatics. Hence, Sellin thinks the opponents were neither Gnostic nor libertine, but under the influence of hyper-Pauline antinomians they emphasized grace and the Spirit,

---

[45] Ibid., 230–31.

[46] P. A. Seethaler, "Kleine Bemerkungen zum Judasbrief," *BZ* 31 (1987): 261–64.

[47] Sellin, "Die Häretiker des Judasbriefes," 206–25.

seeing themselves as pneumatics who were exalted above angels.[48]

It will be argued here that both the Gnostic and pneumatic theses are incorrect. Those who see a primitive form of Gnosticism are more careful, but even in this case the terminology is unfortunate since it leads readers to see some kind of linear development between the teaching of Jude and later Gnostic systems. It is unclear, however, that there is any genealogical relationship between the opponents in Jude and later Gnostic teaching. We exceed the evidence, then, in seeing some sort of continuity between the opponents in Jude and later Gnosticism. We must beware of the danger of labeling the opponents and then concluding that we understand their position.[49] Unfortunately, our grasp of the opponents is partial since we are restricted to what Jude said about them. Thurén maintains that we cannot identify the opponents historically since stock language was used to vilify opponents, and hence the descriptions employed are not objective.[50] Thurén is correct in saying that Jude used emotive and strong language to denounce the adversaries.[51] Furthermore, the difficulty of identifying the opponents precisely is evident by the various theories promulgated by scholars. Nevertheless, Thurén's thesis is questionable, in that he suggests that Jude's accusations do not represent the intruders. If this is the case, it is doubtful that Jude's letter would have convinced the recipients. The preservation of the letter indicates that the recipients found it to be persuasive and useful. The letter was effective precisely because it genuinely identified the nature of the opposi-

---

[48] Many other theories have been promulgated. Ellis identifies the opponents as Judaizers, and he appears to argue that the adversaries were the same faced by Paul in all his letters ("Prophecy and Hermeneutic in Jude," 230–35). Seeing the opponents as Judaizers does not seem to fit well with their libertinism. Furthermore, the method Ellis uses is unconvincing in that he does not distinguish the Pauline opponents in the various letters. Hence, he lumps all the opponents in the Pauline letters into one category and then sees the same set of adversaries in Jude. It is questionable in any case whether the opponents in Jude can be linked with those in any of the Pauline letters. To see all the Pauline adversaries through a single lens is quite improbable, and then Ellis cites various texts to show similarities to Jude. Before such a link can be established, a thorough inductive study is needed to establish the identity of the opponents in each Pauline letter and then in Jude. C. Daniel identifies them as Essenes ("La mention des Esséniens dans le texte grec de l'épître de S. Jude," *Mus* 81 [1968]: 503–21), but again the libertinism of the adversaries contradicts the attempt to see them as Essenes.

[49] Rowston rightly observes, "The refusal to attempt an exact identification of the opponents is judicious. One may go as far as listing their characteristics and visualizing a likely occasion during which the confrontation occurred. But putting a definite label on the heretics seems to be out of the question" ("Most Neglected Book," 555). However, Rowston immediately violates his own canon and too confidently identifies the opponents as "proto-gnostic" (pp. 555–56). Methodologically he makes the mistake of using Irenaeus to describe the opponents in Jude.

[50] L. Thurén, "Hey Jude! Asking for the Original Situation and Message of a Catholic Epistle," *NTS* 43 (1997): 451–65.

[51] Cf. R. L. Webb, who argues that Jude's rhetoric has a social function, and its intention is to influence the readers so that they separate themselves from the intruders ("The Eschatology of the Epistle of Jude and Its Rhetorical and Social Functions," *BBR* 6 [1996]: 139–51).

tion. In our postmodern world we know that no one inhabits "neutral space." We all view reality from a certain perspective. For those who subscribe to the inspiration and authority of Scripture, Jude's posture on the adversaries represents God's view of their beliefs and actions. We will proceed, then, by noting from the text itself what we can know about the opponents, commenting as we go on the weaknesses of the Gnostic and pneumatic hypotheses.

The most remarkable feature is the libertinism of the opponents. Jude's favorite designation for them is "godless" (*aseb-* word group, vv. 4,15,18). For instance, they rejected the lordship of Christ and lived licentiously (*aselgeia,* v. 4), and the latter is almost certainly a reference to sexual sin. Contrary to Sellin, vv. 6–7 clearly show that the adversaries indulged in sexual sin (see commentary below). Nor does the garment in v. 23 signify that they were wandering charismatics. It is much more probable that we have another reference here to libertine behavior. Since the emphasis is on their immoral lifestyle, it is likely that they did not deny any specific doctrine about Jesus Christ. There is no evidence, for example, that they promulgated a Gnostic Christology. They denied Christ's lordship by the way they lived, by their antinomian lifestyle.

Verse 8 suggests that they defended their "ethics" by appealing to revelations or dreams from the Lord,[52] and the reference to shepherding themselves in v. 12 suggests they were teachers.[53] It seems, then, that their charter for the Christian life had a charismatic foundation.[54] Apparently they were blessed with high self-esteem, for they confidently criticized angels (vv. 8,10), but it is unclear that they claimed to be exalted above angels by virtue of their visions. It probably is the case that they reviled angels because angels as mediators of the law upheld moral norms, the very norms that were shunned by the opponents.[55] Nor should we follow Sellin when he forces the opponents of Jude into the mold of the "philosophy" opposed in Colossians.[56] One of their chief characteristics

---

[52] For an analysis of ethical admonition in Jude that uses G. Stassen's model for evaluating Christian social ethics, see K. R. Lyle, Jr., *Ethical Admonition in the Epistle of Jude* (New York: Peter Lang, 1998).

[53] So Bauckham, *Relatives of Jesus,* 166.

[54] Bauckham thinks they were "itinerant charismatics" (ibid., 167).

[55] Bauckham, *Relatives of Jesus,* 167.

[56] Alternatively, R. Heiligenthal thinks the opponents promoted the theology advocated in the Letter to the Colossians. Jude did not counter Gnostic teaching, but he opposed the sort of teaching we find in the Letter to the Colossians. Heiligenthal locates the opponents' teaching in Pharisaism that hails from the diaspora (see *Zwischen Henoch und Paulus: Studien zum theologiegeschichtlichen Ort des Judasbriefes,* Texte und Arbeiten zum neutestamentlichen Zeitalter 6 [Tübingen: Francke, 1992]). Heiligenthal rightly sees the Jewish character of Jude, but evidence for a Pharisaic connection is not supported by clear evidence in his book. Nor is it clear that Jude opposed the sort of theology we find in Colossians (rightly Vögtle, *Judasbrief, 2 Petrusbrief,* 51). Heiligenthal lays the theology of Colossians on the opponents of Jude, but the specific features we find in Colossians (e.g., adherence to asceticism, Col 2:16–23) hardly fits with the libertine opponents of Jude.

seems to have been a stubborn self-righteousness and inflexibility to any correction. Hence, they are said to reject God's lordship over their lives (v. 8; cf. v. 4), and their rebellion is compared to Korah's (v. 11). They are deceptive, in that they do not produce what they promise (v. 12), and they show kindness to people only to gain their favor, probably financially (v. 16). Their lives are splendid examples of "doing it my way" (vv. 12,16,18). Like most people who live for themselves, they are deeply unhappy, grumbling and complaining about circumstances that disappoint them (v. 16). The fruit of their lives is disgusting and unpredictable, compared to the slimy foam that washes up on the seashore or to planets that wander off course (v. 13). After describing the opponents in such terms, Jude's conclusion is not surprising. These intruders in the community are divisive. Not only are they divisive, but they are also plainly unbelievers, people who do not have the Spirit (v. 19).

It is sometimes said that Jude only denounced his opponents and did not refute them. Such a judgment fails to perceive the accomplishment of the letter. Jude exposed the moral rootlessness and utter godlessness of the intruders. By revealing their character Jude stripped them of any authority in the congregation. No thinking Christian would follow people who are fundamentally selfish. Jude did not merely revile them. He unveiled who they truly were, removing any grounds for their influence in the church.

The actual content of the letter also indicates that we do not have any solid evidence for identifying the intruders as Gnostic. The reference to their licentious lifestyle at first glance could support the Gnostic thesis. But this is hardly sufficient evidence to call opponents Gnostic, for antinomianism is hardly limited to Gnosticism. Missing is Gnostic cosmology, Christology, and a clear denigration of the material world. Therefore no inductive grounds exist for identifying the opponents with the second century. Everything said here fits well into a first-century setting, before the more developed tenets of Gnosticism appeared. Indeed, it even exceeds the evidence to label the heresy "incipient Gnosticism," for we have no real evidence of any Gnostic influence at all.

4. Relation to 2 Peter

One of the most vexing issues when interpreting Jude and 2 Peter is how to explain the relationship between them. In a number of verses the two letters have remarkable parallels. The parallels would be even clearer if cited in Greek, but in this commentary I will cite the NIV for the sake of the English reader.

Jude	2 Peter
[4]For certain men whose condemnation was written about long ago have secretly slipped in among you. They . . . deny Jesus Christ our only Sovereign and Lord.	2:1 There will be false teachers among you. They will secretly introduce destructive heresies. even denying the sovereign Lord who bought them
[4]For certain men whose condemnation was written about long ago	2:3 Their condemnation has long been hanging over them, and their destruction has not been sleeping.
[6] And the angels who did not keep their positions of authority but abandoned their own home—these he has kept in darkness, bound with everlasting chains for judgment on the great Day.	2:4 For if God did not spare angels when they sinned, but sent them to hell, putting them into gloomy dungeons to be held for judgment.
[7] In a similar way, Sodom and Gomorrah and the surrounding towns gave themselves up to sexual immorality and perversion. They serve as an example of those who suffer the punishment of eternal fire.	2:6 if he condemned the cities of Sodom and Gomorrah by burning them to ashes, and made them an example of what is going to happen to the ungodly
[8] these dreamers pollute their own bodies, reject authority and slander celestial beings.	2:10 This is especially true of those who follow the corrupt desire of the sinful nature and despise authority. Bold and arrogant, these men are not afraid to slander celestial beings.
[9] But even the archangel Michael, when he was disputing with the devil about the body of Moses, did not dare to bring a slanderous accusation against him, but said, "The Lord rebuke you!"	2:11 yet even angels, although they are stronger and more powerful, do not bring slanderous accusations against such beings in the presence of the Lord.

Jude	2 Peter
[10] Yet these men speak abusively against whatever they do not understand; and what things they do understand by instinct, like unreasoning animals—these are the very things that destroy them.	2:12 But these men blaspheme in matters they do not understand. They are like brute beasts, creatures of instinct, born only to be caught and destroyed, and like beasts they too will perish.
[11] they have rushed for profit into Balaam's error.	2:15 They have left the straight way and wandered off to follow the way of Balaam son of Beor, who loved the wages of wickedness.
[12] These men are blemishes at your love feasts, eating with you without the slightest qualm—shepherds who feed only themselves.	2:13 They are blots and blemishes, reveling in their pleasures while they feast with you.
[12] They are clouds without rain	2:17 These men are springs without water
[13] for whom blackest darkness has been reserved forever	2:17 Blackest darkness is reserved for them.
[16] they boast about themselves	2:18 For they mouth empty, boastful words
[17–18] But, dear friends, remember what the apostles of our Lord Jesus Christ foretold. They said to you, "In the last times there will be scoffers who will follow their own ungodly desires."	3:2–3 I want you to recall the words spoken in the past by the holy prophets and the command given by our Lord and Savior through your apostles. First of all, you must understand that in the last days scoffers will come, scoffing and following their own evil desires.

Scholars have disputed for some time how to explain the parallels that exist between the two letters. Three plausible explanations have been offered: (1) Second Peter is dependent on Jude; (2) Jude is dependent on 2 Peter;[57] and (3) they are both dependent on either a written or oral source, or perhaps a combination thereof. Most scholars now believe that 2 Peter depends on Jude, ques-

[57] So Mayor, *Jude and Second Peter,* i–xxv; Bigg, *Peter and Jude,* 216–24. Guthrie has a fine summary of the evidence, and though he is undecided, he seems to favor slightly the priority of 2 Peter (*New Testament Introduction,* 916–25).

tioning whether Jude would have written his letter otherwise, since he restated much of 2 Peter.[58] On the other hand, a significant number of scholars still defend the view that Jude drew on 2 Peter. Wallace has an interesting recent defense of this thesis.[59] He argues that most scholars opt for the posteriority of 2 Peter because they assume its inauthenticity. In addition, the rougher grammar and style of 2 Peter suggest that Jude smoothed out and improved Peter's writing. Wallace suggests that a distinct motive for Jude still exists because his main purpose in writing and the crucial part of the letter is vv. 20–23, which is not contained in 2 Peter.[60]

Each of these theories is plausible. We should not, for instance, rule out the notion that both writers drew on a common source.[61] A shared written tradition would seem to be required if one defends this view, since the words and themes are strikingly the same. A teacher receiving Jude and 2 Peter would certainly wonder about the literary relationship between the two. Moreover, some of the themes touched on are rather unusual (the reviling of angels), suggesting that the authors were not drawing on the common stock of Christian preaching. We should note that the two letters rarely agree in the exact words used, and often the same themes are developed in different ways.[62] Still, the common source theory should be rejected because the simpler hypothesis should be preferred, and the simpler hypothesis is that one of the authors used the writing of the other. And yet it should be acknowledged that scholars are often too confident in declaring that some form of literary dependence exists.[63] The most probable solution, in my judgment, is that

[58] E.g., T. Fornberg, *An Early Church in a Pluralistic Society: A Study of 2 Peter,* ConBNT 9 (Lund: Gleerup, 1977), 33–59; Cranfield, *Peter and Jude,* 145–46; Kelly, *Peter and Jude,* 225–27; Paulsen, *Petrusbrief und Judasbrief,* 97–100.

[59] Wallace, "Jude: Introduction, Argument, and Outline."

[60] Less convincing is Wallace's claim that the apostolic age had ended according to Jude. Neither is it persuasive to say that the opponents were only predicted in 2 Peter, whereas in Jude they were already present. Another problem with Wallace's theory is that a denial of the second coming is nowhere mentioned in Jude. It seems like special pleading to say, as Wallace does, that the Petrine prophecy was "only *partially* fulfilled" when Jude was written.

[61] E.g., Green, *2 Peter and Jude,* 58–64; C. Spicq, *Les Épîtres de Saint Pierre,* SB (Paris: Gabalda, 1966], 197, n. 1). So also Reicke, *James, Peter, and Jude,* 190, who sees both as coming from a "sermon pattern."

[62] T. V. Smith rightly says: "In fact, verbal agreements between the two documents are slight. . . . There is nothing comparable to the close similarities one finds, for example, in the Synoptic relationships" (*Petrine Controversies in Early Christianity: Attitudes toward Peter in Christian Writings of the First Two Centuries,* WUNT 2/15 [Tübingen: Mohr, 1985], 76). Nevertheless, he comes to the conclusion that Jude is the source for 2 Peter (p. 77).

[63] "The traditional penchant for assuming a literary relationship between the two documents fails to account for the fact that the material Jude has in common with 2 Peter occurs in a different context and is deficient of the verbal precision one encounters, for instance, among the Synoptic Gospels. Accordingly, while recognizing a certain similarity, one must question the validity of assuming at the outset that one can reconstruct the ancient walls of Jude by using stones borrowed indiscriminately from 2 Peter" (Osburn, "Discourse Analysis and Jewish Apocalyptic," 311).

2 Peter used Jude. Wallace makes a good case for the priority of 2 Peter, but I remain unconvinced for several reasons. First, as we will see in the introduction to 2 Peter, the priority of Jude does not necessarily lead to the conclusion that 2 Peter is inauthentic. Second, smoothing out grammar does not clearly or necessarily indicate a later date. Finally, though Jude and 2 Peter are not identical, there does not seem to be enough distinctive material in Jude if he had 2 Peter before him. Evangelicals have occasionally worried that literary dependence would call into question inspiration and authority. But inspiration does not rule out the use of sources as if only direct messages from God were inspired. We can approach the issue of literary dependence asking what view is the most plausible and best supported by the evidence. Since the matter cannot be resolved definitively, though I incline to 2 Peter using Jude, I will not base my interpretation on any theory. Finally, we should reject the notion that Jude should be included in a Petrine school, which has been advocated by both Soards and Ward.[64] The letters are distinct enough to warrant separate treatment.[65]

5. Structure

The Epistle of Jude is a vigorous and pointed piece of writing.[66] Scholars have often remarked that the Greek is quite good and that Jude used imagery effectively.[67] The letter bears the marks of a careful and disciplined structure, even though it was directed to specific circumstances in the life of the church.[68] Watson argues that Jude used Greek rhetoric in structuring the letter.[69] Many letters in the New Testament are now being analyzed and explained on the basis of Greek rhetoric.[70] Watson outlines the letter as follows.[71]

---

[64] M. L. Soards, "1 Peter, 2 Peter, and Jude as Evidence for a Petrine School," in *Aufstieg und Niedergang der Romischen Welt* II.25 (New York: de Gruyter, 1988), 3827–49. See also the "Addenda" by V. O. Ward (1988:3844–49) in support of a Petrine school. For arguments against a Petrine school see D. G. Horrell, "The Product of a Petrine Circle? A Reassessment of the Origin and Character of 1 Peter," *JSNT* 86 (2002): 29–60.

[65] Cf. Fornberg, *An Early Church in a Pluralistic Society,* 33–59; Bauckham, *Relatives of Jesus,* 146–47.

[66] See J. D. Charles, "Literary Artifice in the Epistle of Jude," *ZNW* 82 (1991): 106–24.

[67] The structure of the text is dependent, of course, on what the text *is.* For a text critical study of Jude from the standpoint of thoroughgoing eclecticism, see C. Landon, *A Text-Critical Study of the Epistle of Jude,* JSNTSup 135 (Sheffield: Academic Press, 1996). Landon's study is useful, but rational eclecticism is a better approach to text criticism in my judgment.

[68] For the structure of Jude see also H. Harm, "Logic Line in Jude: The Search for Syllogisms in a Hortatory Text," *JOTT* 1 (1987): 147–72.

[69] D. F. Watson, *Invention, Arrangement, and Style: Rhetorical Criticism of Jude and 2 Peter,* SBLDS 104 (Atlanta: Scholars Press, 1988), 29–79.

[70] See the study by S. J. Joubert, "Persuasion in the Letter of Jude," *JSNT* 58 (1995): 75–87.

[71] Ibid., 77–78. Followed by Vögtle, *Judasbrief, 2 Petrusbrief,* 4.

I. Epistolary Prescript (1–2)
II. *Exordium* (3)
III. *Narratio* (4)
IV. *Probatio* (5–16)
  A. First Proof (5–10)
  B. Second Proof (11–13)
  C. Third Proof (14–16)
V. *Peroratio* (17–23)
VI. Doxology (24–25)

Contrary to Watson, it is doubtful that Jude consciously imitated the rhetorical handbooks in composing the letter.[72] Nor is Watson's analysis convincing at every point, since he sees a more detailed pattern of rhetoric than is plausible. Wolthuis rightly suggests, in an invented dialogue between Jude and Cicero, that a writer may follow some of the canons of rhetoric without consciously intending to do so.[73] Hence, Watson's analysis is helpful in understanding the structure of Jude's composition, even though it is doubtful that Jude deliberately wrote according to the pattern of Greek rhetoric.[74]

Many writers throughout history have used features of Greek rhetoric and have known nothing about it, for such rhetoric includes common sense rules that many skillful writers have followed. The rules of rhetoric were designed for *speeches,* not *letters,* and hence we must be careful about imposing the pattern of the former on the latter. Furthermore, it is interesting that the early church fathers who were familiar with Greek rhetoric did not identify the New Testament epistles as such.[75] Hence, the rhetorical character of the letter should be supplemented with the epistolary features evident in the epistle. Nevertheless, Watson's understanding of Jude provides a helpful inroad into its structure. Describing the letter as a piece of

---

[72] See especially the critique and analysis of Jude by E. R. Wendland, "A Comparative Study of 'Rhetorical Criticism,' Ancient and Modern—with Special Reference to the Larger Structure and Function of the Epistle of Jude," *Neot* 28 (1994): 193–228. He points out that Watson does not take into account sufficiently the midrashic and Jewish character of the letter, and hence Bauckham's structure is to be preferred over Watson's. For criticism of Watson's view, see also Müller, "Der Judasbrief," 272.

[73] T. R. Wolthuis, "Jude and the Rhetorician: A Dialogue on the Rhetorical Nature of the Epistle of Jude," *CTJ* 24 (1989): 126–34.

[74] Osburn points out that Watson's scheme incorrectly separates vv. 3–4, and hence the connection between these verses and vv. 20–23 is also missed (see "Discourse Analysis and Jewish Apocalyptic in the Epistle of Jude," 289).

[75] For instructive evaluations of the role of rhetoric in NT epistles, see S. E. Porter and T. H. Olbricht, *Rhetoric and the New Testament: Essays from the 1992 Heidelberg Conference* (Sheffield: JSOT Press, 1993); J. A. D. Weima, "What Does Aristotle Have to Do with Paul? An Evaluation of Rhetorical Criticism," *CTJ* 32 (1997): 458–68.

deliberative rhetoric helps us see that Jude's design was to persuade the readers to reject the opponents and remain faithful to the tradition transmitted to them. Jude did not write dispassionately. His aim was to persuade the church to adopt his point of view.

The "epistolary prescript" (vv. 1–2) does not fit as well with analyzing the letter rhetorically. The prescript (vv. 1–2) is understood better in terms of an epistolary analysis of the letter, in which there are three elements: sender, recipients, and greeting. Some of the themes expressed in the rest of the letter are mentioned in these verses, indicating that Jude composed the letter carefully and with a unified purpose. Watson designates v. 3 as the *exordium* where Jude introduced the letter and explained the purpose for which it was written.[76]

Jude reminded the readers that they shared a common salvation and alerted them to the need for vigilance in contending for the faith, disposing them to be receptive to what followed. Watson identifies v. 4 as *narratio,* which explains more concretely the introduction in v. 3. The reason the church must contend for the faith is that intruders were troubling the church. The danger of the opponents is brought to center stage here. Watson remarks that the "three qualities of brevity, clarity, and plausibility should especially characterize the *narratio*."[77] The content of v. 4 certainly fits this description, where Jude introduced his readers to the opponents, pronounced judgment upon them, and sketched in their vices. Unfortunately, however, Watson's analysis might suggest that vv. 3–4 are to be separated from each other (see further below), when in reality the verses are bound tightly together. In epistolary terms vv. 3–4 function as the "body opening" of the letter.

Verses 5–16 provide the evidence (called the *probatio* by Watson) for what is said in v. 4. In v. 4 Jude points out that intruders had infiltrated the church and that their intrusion was no idle matter since they were ungodly. In vv. 5–16 Jude demonstrated that the thesis in v. 4 is indeed the case. The beginning of a new section is marked by a "disclosure formula" in v. 5, "Though you already know all this, I want to remind you." Watson divides the proof section into three subsections: vv. 5–10, 11–13, and 14–16. These suggested subsections are helpful, but the particular structure of the verses is better explained by Bauckham, who notes the midrashic character of Jude's writing. Three examples of God's judgment in the past are relayed in

---

[76] Wallace argues that Jude was written after the death of both Paul and Peter to encourage the readers not to defect from the gospel they were taught ("Jude: Introduction, Argument, and Outline"). But clear evidence that Peter and Paul had died recently is lacking, and the scenario painted by Wallace is nowhere stated in the letter. Nor is it evident that the reference to "our common salvation" indicates that previously Jude had little contact with the readers. We must admit that we do not know the motive for the inclusion of the word "common."

[77] Watson, *Invention, Arrangement, and Style,* 46.

vv. 5–7, and in vv. 8–10 Jude clarified that the opponents deserved judgment as well because of their lifestyle. In v. 11 the opponents are compared to three men who went astray in the past: Cain, Balaam, and Korah. Verses 12–13 clarify that the character of the opponents placed them in the same category as these infamous figures. Jude closed this section with the prophecy of Enoch, which promises judgment on the ungodly (vv. 14–15). Once again Jude correlated the lives of the adversaries with those who will experience judgment (v. 16). We should notice that the examples of prophecy are always linked to the false teachers of Jude's day by the word "these" (*houtoi;* cf. Gal 4:24; 2 Tim 3:8).[78]

Jude regularly applied Old Testament types and texts to the interlopers who had invaded the church (vv. 8,12,16). Some have labeled this technique as midrash,[79] and it is evident that if one uses the term "midrash" in this loose sense (see further below), then identifying his approach as midrashic is suitable.[80] Jude was steeped in the Old Testament and Jewish tradition,[81] but his method of using the Old Testament is not precisely the same thing as Jewish midrash.

Verses 17–23 function as the *peroratio* according to Watson. The peroration summarizes the main themes of the letter and makes an emotional appeal for the author's case. Watson sees vv. 17–19 functioning as the summation where the words of the apostles are recalled and then sees v. 20 as introducing the body closing. In my outline I delineate three sections here: (1) vv. 17–19 focus on the outside threat of the false teachers, which was predicted by the apostles; (2) vv. 20–21 summon the readers to focus on their own spiritual lives, reminding them that they must not stray from God; (3) vv. 22–23 encourage the readers to reach out to those affected by the false teachers, warning them not to become ensnared in the process. Verses 17–18 contain an apostolic prophecy, where Jude recounted that the apostles predicted the rise of mockers. In v. 19 the term "these" *(houtoi)* is again used to draw a connection between the prediction of the apostles and the false teachers. Jude clarified that "these" false teachers were those whom the apostles foretold would arise.

The letter closes with an epistolary feature, a doxology (vv. 24–25). Missing is any grace benediction or greetings to any individuals. The emphasis on God and Jesus Christ and their ability to keep believers until the end reminds us of the first two verses of the letter. The doxology, then, forms an inclusio.

My outline is rather similar to Watson's in some respects, and it is

---

[78] See J. D. Charles, "'Those' and 'These': The Use of the Old Testament in the Epistle of Jude," *JSNT* 38 (1990): 110–11.

[79] Ellis, "Prophecy and Hermeneutic in Jude," 221–26.

[80] Ibid., 225.

[81] See Bauckham, *Relatives of Jesus,* 201–6.

instructive to compare Bauckham's structure with Watson's analysis. Bauckham sees the theme of the letter in vv. 3–4, in which v. 3 constitutes the appeal to the readers and v. 4 the background or reason for the appeal. The background is explicated in vv. 5–19, while the theme is unpacked in vv. 20–23. He notes that the catchwords that occur support the connections between the two sections.[82] Bauckham concludes from this that vv. 20–23 are not a "postscript" but "the climax of the letter to which all the rest leads up."[83] The most significant difference between Bauckham and Watson is the former divides the text at v. 20, whereas Watson posits a break at v. 17. It seems that the latter is more persuasive since the words "dear friends" mark out a new section.

Bauckham also argues that we should beware of identifying vv. 5–19 as a denunciation of opponents. We have here a scripturally shaped argument that criticizes the opponents for their libertinism, not their false doctrine.[84] Bauckham cautions that we must remember that Jude addressed believers about the opponents and did not confront the adversaries directly here.[85] Surely the invective is strong here, but Bauckham's words are salutary. Perhaps Jude would have spoken differently if he addressed the adversaries directly. Furthermore, we must remember that criticism was much more direct in the ancient world than is common in Western culture.

One of the disadvantages of Watson's focus on Greek rhetoric is that the Jewish character of the letter is slighted. Both Ellis and Bauckham rightly perceive that Jude's hermeneutic is shaped by Jewish practices. Ellis identifies vv. 5–19 as midrash, though he does not use the term in the technical sense found in the rabbinic midrashim. Bauckham finds Ellis's work persuasive as well.[86] According to his analysis we have citations (vv. 5–7,9,11,14–15,18) and then a commentary on the text (vv. 8,10,12–13,16,19). Both Ellis and Bauckham recognize that Jude often summarized or merely referred to Old Testament texts without actually quoting from them (5–7,9,14–15), though v. 18 constitutes a prophecy from the apostles. Both scholars see a relationship to the pesharim of Qumran, but they also acknowledge the differences. What is remarkable in Jude is his regular use of *houtoi* to comment on the text to which he referred. Verb tenses also change so that the texts referred to are found in the past or future, but the

---

[82] Ibid., 153–54, 179–80.

[83] Ibid., 154; so also Müller, "Der Judasbrief," 275; Osburn, "Discourse Analysis and Jewish Apocalyptic in the Epistle of Jude," 289.

[84] Bauckham, *Relatives of Jesus,* 157. Bauckham says that vv. 5–19 are "a very carefully composed piece of scriptural commentary which *argues* for the statement made in verse 4" (p. 181).

[85] Ibid., 157.

[86] Ibid., 150–54, 182.

interpretation is in the present tense.[87]

Bauckham's outline of the letter is as follows.[88]

1–2 Address and Greeting
3–4 Occasion and Theme of the Letter
  A The Appeal (summary, 3)
    B The Background to the Appeal (summary, 4)
5–19 **B′** The Background to the Appeal:
  A Midrash on the Prophecies of the Doom of the Ungodly
5–7 (a) Three Old Testament types
8–10 *plus* interpretation
9 (a′) Michael and the Devil
11 (b) Three More Old Testament Types
12–13 *plus* interpretation
14–15 (c) The Prophecy of Enoch
16 *plus* interpretation
17–18 (d) The Prophecy of the Apostles
19 *plus* interpretation
20–23 **A′** The Appeal (reiterated)
24–25 Closing Doxology

We conclude this section by considering two chiastic outlines of Jude. The most impressive work has been done by Wendland, as we will see shortly. Wendland argues that Bauckham's structure is to be preferred over Watson's.[89] He notes that it has a symmetry lacking in Watson's treatment. Furthermore, vv. 3–4 are separated in Watson's scheme, whereas they are tightly bound together in Bauckham's outline. Verses 3–4 together seem to constitute the theme of the letter, and this is not evident in Watson's analysis. Finally, Bauckham provides a more detailed explanation than Watson of the relationship between Old Testament examples and Jude's application of them to the opponents.

We begin with the chiastic structure of Osburn.[90]

---

[87] R. Bauckham, "James, 1 Peter and 2 Peter, Jude," in *It Is Written: Scripture Citing Scripture: Essays in Honour of Barnabas Lindars* (Cambridge: University Press, 1988), 304. J. T. Reed and R. A. Reese note that Jude alternates between the aorist and the present. Often Jude commences in the aorist tense and then follows with the present tense. It seems that their analysis of the tenses used supplements Bauckham's view ("Verbal Aspect, Discourse Prominence, and the Letter of Jude," *FNT* 9 [1996]: 191).

[88] Bauckham, *Jude, 2 Peter,* 5–6. I have adopted the modification of Bauckham's outline set forth by Wendland ("Structure of Jude," 207).

[89] Wendland, "Structure of Jude," 207–9.

[90] Osburn, "Discourse Analysis and Jewish Apocalyptic in the Epistle of Jude," 287–319, see esp. 309.

A Greeting (1–2)
  B Introduction (3–4)
    C Literary Warnings: Rebellion = Fate (5–7)
    C′ Link Rebellion = Fate of Eschatological Enemies of God to Rebellion = Fate of Intruders (8–16)
      D Apostolic Warnings (17–19)
  B′ Concluding Appeal. Specific of "Contend" in Verse 4 (20–23)
A′ Doxology (24–25)

Osburn's analysis has the advantage of simplicity, but it suffers from at least two defects. First, the outline is rather general and does not explain concretely specific features of the text. Second, the intrusion of point D also seems rather awkward.

Wendland presents another chiasm structure of the letter, and his outline seems to fit the contents of the letter quite well. I present an abbreviated outline of his structure below.[91]

A Epistolary Introduction: Participants and Threefold Characterization of Receptors (1)
  B Salutation—Threefold Benediction (2)
    C Purpose Introduced—Appeal (3)
      D Motivation, First Mention—False Teachers (4)
        E Reminder—Warning from Old Testament Times (5–7)
          F Description—Heretics: 3 Attributes (8)
            G Extracanonical example (Ancient)—Michael (9)
              H Description—Heretics: 3 Attributes (10)
                I Woe Oracle: 3 Archetypes from Old Testament (11)
              H′ Description—Heretics: 6 Attributes (12–13)
            G′ Extracanonical Prediction (Ancient)—Enoch (14–15)
          F′ Description—Heretics: 3 Attributes (16)
        E′ Reminder—Warning from New Testament Times (17–18)
      D′ Motivation, Final Mention—False Teachers (19)
    C′ Purpose Elaborated—Appeal (20–21)
  B′ Commission—A Threefold Assignment (22–23)
A′ Epistolary Conclusion (24–25)

Scholars often overplay chiastic schemes, and I admit that it is quite improbable that chiastic schemes exist in long pieces of literature, especially if they are quite detailed. Perhaps Jude himself did not consciously write chiastically, and hence too much should not be made of the presence of such in interpretation. Still, Wendland's analysis is impressive and does not appear to force the evidence. He shows that the letter fits together

[91] Wendland, "Structure of Jude," 211–12.

nicely. Furthermore, his analysis shows that Jude begins and ends on a positive note and so the letter should not be appraised as a negative tract but as a positive encouragement for the readers.

OUTLINE OF JUDE

I. Greeting (1–2)
II. The Purpose for Writing (3–4)
III. Judgment of the Intruders (5–16)
  1. God's Judgment (5–10)
  2. Woe Oracle (11–13)
  3. Enoch's Prophecy (14–16)
IV. Exhortations to Believers (17–25)
  1. Remember the Apostolic Predictions (17–19)
  2. Keep Yourselves in God's Love (20–21)
  3. Show Mercy to Those Affected by Opponents (22–23)
  4. Doxology (24–25)

SECTION OUTLINE

I. GREETING (1–2)

I. GREETING (1–2)

1 Jude, a servant of Jesus Christ and a brother of James,

To those who have been called, who are loved by God the Father and kept by Jesus Christ:

2 Mercy, peace and love be yours in abundance.

Most ancient letters begin with the sender, the recipients, and a greeting. In the Epistle of Jude the sender and recipients are identified in v. 1, and the greeting is found in v. 2. In most Greco-Roman letters the sender, recipients, and greeting are stated concisely. Acts 23:26 serves as a good example of the brevity of a typical greeting, "Claudius Lysias, to the most excellent governor Felix: Greetings." What distinguishes Jude, in particular, and New Testament epistles, in general, from such Greco-Roman letters is the theological substance of their greetings. Jude did not give a perfunctory or customary hello. He invested the greeting with the content of the gospel, anticipating the major themes of the letter from the outset. More specifically, we know from the rest of the letter that interlopers had intruded into the church, threatening the faith of believers. Significantly, Jude reminded his readers that the God who set his love upon them called them to faith and that Jesus Christ would preserve them to the end.

1 I will examine the elements of the first two verses in order: (1) the sender, (2) the recipients, and (3) the greeting. The sender is identified as "Jude" *(Ioudas)*. We saw in the introduction that a number of people with the name of Jude have been suggested as the author. We argued there that the traditional view, which identifies Jude as the brother of Jesus Christ, is still the most persuasive (cf. Matt 13:55 par.).[1] Jude identified himself as "a servant of Jesus Christ and a brother of James." The term Jude used is not *diakonos,* which can also mean "servant," but *doulos* ("slave"). He did not commence the letter by emphasizing the privilege of his brotherly relationship to Jesus Christ but his submission to Christ's lordship. In this sense Jude was like every other Christian. And yet the term *doulos* also designates the honor of serving as Jesus Christ's slave. Those called to special service in the Old Testament were identified as the "slave"

[1] A. Vögtle agrees that the Lord's brother is intended but argues for pseudonymity (*Der Judasbrief, Der 2 Petrusbrief,* EKKNT [Neukirchen–Vluyn: Neukirchener Verlag, 1994], 16).

(doulos) of the Lord: Abraham, Moses, Joshua, David, and the prophets (Josh 14:7; 24:29; 2 Kgs 17:23; Ps 89:4,20).[2] In the New Testament era Paul, Peter, and James also called themselves slaves of God and Jesus Christ (Rom 1:1; Gal 1:10; Phil 1:1; Titus 1:1; Jas 1:1; 2 Pet 1:1). With the same term Jude expressed his humility (since he was Jesus Christ's slave) and his authority (since he was an honored slave of the Lord as were those in the OT era).

Jude was not only the slave of Jesus Christ but he was also James's brother.[3] As we maintained in the introduction, this phrase identifies Jude clearly to the readers. Since James needed no further introduction, he probably was James, the brother of the Lord. James, like the rest of the Lord's brothers, did not believe in Jesus during the days of his earthly ministry (cf. Mark 3:21,31–35; John 7:2–5). James presumably came to faith when Jesus Christ appeared to him after his resurrection (1 Cor 15:7). James came to prominence as the leader of the church in Jerusalem (Acts 12:17; 15:13; 21:18), and Paul identified him as one of the pillars of the church (Gal 2:9; cf. Gal 1:19; 2:12). It is likely that the epistle that bears the name of James was written by James, the brother of the Lord.[4] Why did Jude describe himself as James's brother instead of the Lord's brother? Kelly thinks the failure to mention that he was the Lord's brother is an indication of pseudonymity.[5] This is a serious misreading of Jude's intention. James also did not identify himself as the Lord's brother, and neither did Jude since his relationship with the Lord, as I already stated, was one of slave to master, not brother to brother. Jude avoided saying that he was the Lord's brother because of his humility, and yet it would be a mistake to conclude that the only purpose was to communicate his humility. The reference to James as his brother is also honorific, designating Jude's authority. Neyrey rightly emphasizes the honor and status derived from Jude's blood relationship with an important person like James.[6] Jude did not merely transmit his opinion in this letter. He wrote authoritatively as Jesus Christ's slave and as the brother of James.

---

[2] See K. H. Rengstorf, "δοῦλος" *TDNT* 2:268, 276–77; E. Fuchs and P. Reymond, *La Deuxième Épître de Saint Pierre, L'Épître de Saint Jude,* CNT (Neuchâtel–Paris: Delachaux & Niestlé, 1980), 154.

[3] R. Bauckham observes that Jude has "a striking preference for the 'double-name'" Jesus Christ (*Jude and the Relatives of Jesus in the Early Church* [Edinburgh: T & T Clark, 1990], 285). He goes on to observe that Jewish Christians would have applied the epithet "Christ" to Jesus from the beginning to distinguish Jesus of Nazareth from others with the name Jesus. Nor is there any reason to doubt that the term "Christ" retained its Messianic import in Jude's letter.

[4] For this view of the authorship of James, see D. J. Moo, *The Letter of James,* PNTC (Grand Rapids: Eerdmans, 2000), 9–22; L. T. Johnson *The Letter of James,* AB (New York: Doubleday, 1995), 92–108.

[5] J. N. D. Kelly, *A Commentary on the Epistles of Peter and Jude,* Thornapple Commentaries (Grand Rapids: Baker, 1981), 242.

[6] J. Neyrey, *2 Peter, Jude,* AB (Garden City: Doubleday, 1993), 45, 47–48. But he engages in speculation in saying that the opponents claimed "achieved authority" in contrast to Jude's claim to status by kinship. We have no evidence that the opponents even criticized Jude or contrasted themselves specifically with him.

We should note as well that Jude did not identify himself as an apostle. We can compare this to 2 Pet 1:1, where Peter called himself a slave *(doulos)* and apostle *(apostolos)* of Jesus Christ. Jude did refer to the apostles in v. 17, "Remember what the apostles of our Lord Jesus Christ foretold." Some scholars believe Jude separated himself from the apostles in this verse. But Jude 17 does not in and of itself demonstrate that Jude was not an apostle. The comparison with 2 Peter is instructive. We have already seen that Peter designated himself as an apostle in 2 Pet 1:1. But in 2 Pet 3:2 he said, "I want you to recall the words spoken in the past by the holy prophets and the command given by our Lord and Savior through your apostles." The language is remarkably similar to Jude's, and yet Peter's words do not exclude him from the apostolic circle. We cannot conclude from Jude 17 alone that Jude was not an apostle. What is important is to note that Jude, contrary to Peter, did not identify himself as an apostle in the introduction to the letter. His authority stemmed from his being a slave of Jesus Christ and a brother of James.

After identifying himself as the author, Jude addressed the recipients of the letter. Perhaps we should note first what he did not say. Many letters in the New Testament specify the church or churches addressed, so that we know the geographical destination of the letter (e.g., Rom 1:7; 1 Cor 1:1–2; Gal 1:2; 1 Pet 1:1). Jude, however, did not identify the recipients, and therefore it has been called one of the catholic epistles. It is likely, however, that Jude was addressed to a specific church or churches since he spoke against interlopers troubling the church (see introduction). Even though we cannot locate with certainty the destination of the letter, it is clear that Jude addressed particular circumstances in the life of his churches.

Jude addressed his readers as the "called" *(klētois)*. Two attributive participles modify the term "called," and these participles are translated as "loved" and "kept" by the NIV. We will begin with the term "called." English readers, when asked to define the word "called," might give the definition "invited." Such a definition would misunderstand radically what Jude intended. The term "called" does not merely mean that God invited believers to be his own.[7] Those whom God calls are powerfully and inevitably brought to faith in Jesus Christ through the proclamation of the gospel. The call of God is extended only to some and is always successful, so that all those who are called become believers. Such an understanding of "called" is clearly attested in the Pauline writings (Rom 1:1,6–7; 8:28,30; 1 Cor 1:1–2,9,24; Gal 1:15; 1 Thess 2:12; 5:24; 2 Thess 2:14; 2 Tim 1:9; cf. 1 Pet 2:9; 5:10; 2 Pet 1:3; Rev 17:14). Why did Jude emphasize such an idea here? We need to recall that intruders threatened the faith of the church. Jude, in the course of his letter, will give some sharp warnings to his readers. Such warnings, however, could give the impression that the

[7] Rightly D. J. Moo, *2 Peter, Jude,* NIVAC (Grand Rapids: Zondervan, 1997), 222.

focus is on human effort and endurance. Jude, by stressing God's supernatural calling, reminds the readers of the efficacy of God's grace.

Those who are called are described as those "who are loved by God the Father and kept by Jesus Christ."[8] The NIV translation does not represent the view of many commentators in its translation of this verse. The KJV and NKJV reflect a different textual tradition in the first phrase and read "sanctified by God the Father" rather than "loved by God the Father." The KJV tradition depends on the Majority text, but the textual tradition overwhelmingly supports "loved" rather than "sanctified." The variant reading in the KJV signals to the reader the difficulty of the expression used by Jude. Some scholars and translations understand the first participle phrase *(en theō patri ēgapēmenois)* to say "beloved in God the Father" (RSV, NASB, NRSV).[9] Such a rendering is attractive because often the verb "love" *(agapaō)* is linked with the preposition "by" *(hypo)* if agency is intended. The preposition *en,* on this reading, suggests the sphere in which God's love is exercised. Such an interpretation of the phrase is certainly possible, but I think it is unlikely because the participle "loved" is passive, and God is the agent of the passive verb.[10] Hence, it seems that the NIV rightly captures the meaning here. Believers have been loved by God the Father, and his effective love is the reason they belong to the people of God.

A translation difficulty also arises with the phrase "kept by Jesus Christ." The consensus among commentators and most modern translators is that the phrase should be translated "kept for Jesus Christ," that is, kept until the day of redemption for Jesus Christ (cf. RSV, NASB, NRSV). The syntax is again difficult, and certainty is impossible. Those who support this rendering argue that if the agency of Jesus Christ were in view, we would expect the preposition "by" to be inserted with either the words *en* or *hypo*. Furthermore, it makes sense to say that Jude emphasized God the Father as the one who both loves and keeps (cf. v. 24). Finally, such an interpretation fits with the eschatological flavor of the text, emphasizing that believers are preserved "for Jesus Christ" until the final judgment.[11] Despite the arguments supporting "kept for Jesus Christ," the inter-

---

[8] Bauckham argues that the Christology of Jude can be summed up to say "that Jesus is the eschatological agent of God's salvation and judgment," that he is God's Messiah, and that as such he bears God's authority relative to both judgment and salvation (*Relatives of Jesus,* 312–13).

[9] So also N. Turner, *A Grammar of New Testament Greek,* Vol. III, *Syntax* (Edinburgh: T & T Clark, 1963), 264. Cf. also C. Bigg, *The Epistles of St. Peter and St. Jude,* ICC (Edinburgh: T & T Clark, 1901), 324; R. Bauckham, *Jude, 2 Peter* (Waco: Word, 1983), 25.

[10] Rightly Moo, *2 Peter, Jude,* 223. BDAG also demonstrates that the preposition *en* can denote personal agency (p. 329).

[11] Fuchs and Reymond, *2 Pierre, Jude,* 155; N. Hillyer, *1 and 2 Peter, Jude,* NIBC (Peabody: Hendrickson, 1992), 233. D. B. Wallace thinks the dative should be translated "kept for Jesus Christ" and thinks that it is very unlikely it denotes agency (*Greek Grammar Beyond the Basics: An Exegetical Syntax of the New Testament* [Grand Rapids: Zondervan, 1996], 144, 165).

pretation proposed by the NIV ("kept by Jesus Christ") is preferable. According to this view, the words "Jesus Christ" *(Iēsou Christou)* denote agency,[12] the notion of being kept by Jesus Christ. If Jesus Christ is the agent, then the two clauses are symmetrical: "loved by God the Father and kept by Jesus Christ." Seeing the dative as one of agency is reasonable and fits with Wallace's own description of a dative of agency:[13] (1) the dative noun must be personal; (2) the person specified by the dative must be portrayed as exercising volition; (3) a perfect passive verb is present; and (4) the agent of the passive verb can also function as the subject of an active verb, while the dative of means normally cannot.[14] Verse 1 fulfills all of these requirements. The dative is personal (Jesus Christ), he exercises volition, we have a perfect passive (participle), and the agent also could function as the subject (Jesus Christ keeps).

Whatever interpretation one adopts, the main emphasis of the two participial clauses is clear. Those whom God has called to himself are loved by him and kept until the day of salvation. The grace of God that called believers to faith will sustain them until the end. The emphasis on God's grace does not cancel out human responsibility. In v. 21 the readers are exhorted, "Keep yourselves in God's love." God's grace does not promote human passivity and laxity. It should stir the readers to concerted action. Nonetheless, the ultimate reason believers will persevere against the inroads of the intruders is the grace of God by which he set his love upon believers, called them to be his people, and pledged to preserve them until the end.[15]

When Jude spoke of "being loved" *(ēgapēmenois),* he referred to the unique love God grants to his elect. Often in the Scriptures God's love and calling are closely associated (cf. Isa 41:8–9; Hos 11:1). By identifying his recipients as loved ones, the privileges of Israel as God's people now belong to believers in Jesus Christ. Indeed, Israel was "called" by God to be his people (Isa 41:9; 42:6; 48:12,15; 49:1; 54:6; Hos 11:1). Now the chosen people of God are those who trust in Jesus Christ.[16] Neyrey reads into these designations the contrast between honor and shame, arguing that "God has deemed them worthy of his benefaction."[17] An overemphasis on the social scientific approach emerges here because Jude highlighted *God's grace,* not the worthiness or honor of the readers.

---

[12] Cf. J. B. Mayor, *The Epistle of St. Jude and the Second Epistle of St. Peter* (1907; reprint, Grand Rapids: Baker, 1965), 18. B. Reicke adopts this view but gives no supporting argumentation to defend it (*The Epistles of James, Peter, and Jude,* AB [Garden City: Doubleday, 1964], 194).

[13] I owe the following arguments and much of the wording to one of my Ph.D. students, Jason Meyer.

[14] Wallace, *Greek Grammar,* 75–76.

[15] Vögtle rightly sees the need for human agency but fails to see that God's grace secures a persevering response (*Judasbrief, 2 Petrusbrief,* 18).

[16] Cf. here Fuchs and Reymond, *2 Pierre, Jude,* 155.

[17] Neyrey, *2 Peter, Jude,* 48.

2 A greeting, as noted above, is typical in Greco-Roman letters, and a greeting that includes mercy and peace is found in *2 Bar.* 78:3. Jude's greeting is distinctive in that he prayed for mercy, peace, and love to be multiplied for his readers. Jude's love for triplets appears in this verse as well: mercy, peace, and love.[18] Remarkably, grace is omitted from the prayer wish. Virtually every other New Testament letter that contains a greeting mentions grace (but cf. Jas 1:1). Too much should not be made of this since mercy includes the idea of grace. Paul's letters usually convey the twofold prayer wish of grace and peace (Rom 1:7; 1 Cor 1:3; 2 Cor 1:2; Gal 1:3; Eph 1:2; Phlm 2; Col 1:2; 1 Thess 1:1; 2 Thess 1:2; Titus 1:4), though in both letters to Timothy he prayed for grace, mercy, and peace (1 Tim 1:2; 2 Tim 1:2). Both Petrine letters pray for grace and peace to *be multiplied* to the readers (1 Pet 1:2; 2 Pet 1:2). Fuchs and Reymond maintain that the order is significant in Jude.[19] Mercy and pardon are the foundation of one's relationship to God. Such forgiveness leads to peace with God, which in turn manifests itself in love.

It is also notable that the source of mercy, peace, and love is not specified, though God is surely in view (cf. also 1 Pet 1:2; 2 Pet 1:2).[20] This is no indication of a low Christology in Jude, for he had already noted in v. 1 that he was a slave of Jesus Christ. We saw in the Old Testament that Moses, David, and others were servants of Yahweh. Furthermore, v. 1 constructs a parallel between the love of God and being kept by Jesus Christ, suggesting that Jesus Christ deserves the same honor as the Father. Jude did not present an explicit doctrine of the Trinity, and yet he provided the data from which such a doctrine was constructed. Interestingly, a Trinitarian formula is found in vv. 20–21. The prayer wish anticipates themes developed in the rest of the letter. Jude prayed for mercy because his readers would resist the opponents only by God's mercy and because they needed to experience God's mercy so that they could extend the same to those captivated by the false teachers (vv. 22–23). They needed peace because the interlopers caused division (v. 19) and introduced strife and grumbling wherever they went (vv. 10,16). They needed love because the intruders cared only for themselves and abused the very purpose of the love feasts (v. 12). Jude prayed that mercy, peace, and love would be multiplied because an abundance of these qualities was needed at a stressful time in the church's life. He also prayed because he knew that only God can produce these virtues in the lives of his people.

[18] For a discussion and listing of triads in Jude, see J. D. Charles, "Literary Artifice in the Epistle of Jude," *ZNW* 82 (1991): 122–23. It has long been recognized that Jude loved triplets (Mayor, *Jude and Second Peter,* lvi).

[19] Fuchs and Reymond, *2 Pierre, Jude,* 155.

[20] The source also is lacking in 1 Thess 1:1.

SECTION OUTLINE

II. THE PURPOSE OF WRITING (3–4)

I. THE PURPOSE OF WRITING (3–4)

[3]Dear friends, although I was very eager to write to you about the salvation we share, I felt I had to write and urge you to contend for the faith that was once for all entrusted to the saints. [4]For certain men whose condemnation was written about long ago have secretly slipped in among you. They are godless men, who change the grace of our God into a license for immorality and deny Jesus Christ our only Sovereign and Lord.

The transition to the purpose of the letter, and in this case the "body opening" of the letter, commences in v. 3.[1] The marker introducing the body is the term "beloved" *(agapētoi),* translated as "dear friends" in the NIV, which is a remarkably weak translation, for the term likely emphasizes that the readers are loved by God. The same term is found in vv. 17 and 20, emphasizing again that believers are specially loved by God. In v. 1 the readers are said to be loved by God the Father, v. 2 concludes with a prayer wish for love to be multiplied, and we noted that the adversaries were indicted for their lack of love in the rest of the letter. The purpose of the letter is communicated in v. 3. The readers were to contend for the faith that was transmitted to them. Verse 4 provides the reason the admonition in v. 3 was needed. Intruders had entered into the church and threatened the purity of its faith.

3 Jude explained the circumstances that led to his writing. He wrote so that the readers would strive for the faith that was handed down to the saints. Scholars debate the meaning of the first clause of the sentence. The difference in interpretation can be observed by contrasting the NIV with the NRSV. The NIV translates the first clause "although I was very eager to write to you about the salvation we share." The NRSV renders it "while eagerly preparing to write to you about the salvation we share" (cf. also KJV, NKJV, NASB). The interpretive issue rests on our understanding of the participle *poioumenos* ("making"). Should it be understood as a concessive participle ("although" per the NIV) or as temporal ("while" per the NRSV)? What is the difference between the two interpretations? If we follow the

[1] Cf. J. L. White, *The Form and Function of the Body of the Greek Letter,* SBLDS 2 (Missoula: Scholars Press, 1972), 18.

NIV, Jude explained that he wished to write *another letter* about the salvation believers share. He was prevented from doing so, however, by the sudden intrusion of the opponents; and so he had to write a very different letter, one that took issue with the adversaries who had infiltrated the church. If we follow the NRSV, Jude's attack on the opponents represents the letter about salvation that he desired to write. Jude was not hindered from writing a letter about salvation by the intrusion of the opponents because the letter we have is the very letter about salvation that he intended to write. It seems to me that the NIV is on target here. A number of arguments have been set forth in defense of both views, but most of the arguments adduced are inconclusive.[2] What inclines me to the NIV translation are the words "I had necessity" (*anagkēn eschon grapsai*—"I felt I had to write," NIV). These words seem to indicate a change of plan, a sudden interruption of Jude's intended course of action. The first clause seems superfluous if the reading proposed by the NRSV is correct. Jude could simply have written, "I had necessity to write to you about our common salvation, urging you to strive for the faith that was once delivered to the saints." It is not the change in the verb tense of "write," then, that supports the NIV reading. What supports it is the repetition of the term "write." Confirming the interpretation presented here is the content of v. 4 since Jude explained that the intrusion of adversaries precipitated the writing of the letter.

Jude was eager to write about "the salvation we share." Kelly argues that Jude diverged from both Paul and 1 Peter since salvation is conceived of as a present possession in Jude instead of an eschatological reality.[3] This judgment badly misreads Jude.[4] The very example of Israel being "saved" (*sōsas*) out of Egypt demonstrates that genuine salvation involves perseverance until the end (v. 5). The exhortation to keep themselves in God's love is given because only those who do so will experience "eternal life" on the last day (v. 21). We have already seen that the letter begins and ends with promises of preservation (vv. 1,24–25), indicating that the "not yet" of Christian experience informed Jude's worldview. Finally, even Paul spoke of salvation as a present gift since the end time had invaded the present time (Eph 2:5,8). Referring to salvation as a present possession does not nullify

---

[2] Cf. the discussion in A. Vögtle, *Der Judasbrief, der 2 Petrusbrief,* EKKNT (Neukirchen–Vluyn: Neukirchener Verlag, 1994), 21–23. E.g., some defend the view I support by the shift from the present infinitive γράφειν to the aorist infinitive γράψαι. But it is difficult to see how the change in verb tense establishes one view or the other.

[3] J. N. D. Kelly, *A Commentary on the Epistles of Peter and Jude,* Thornapple Commentaries (Grand Rapids: Baker, 1981), 246. Contra E. Fuchs and P. Reymond, there is not a polemic here against mystery cults that restricted salvation to some (*La Deuxième Épître de Saint Pierre, L'Épître de Saint Jude,* CNT [Neuchâtel–Paris: Delachaux & Niestlé, 1980], 157). Rightly Vögtle, *Judasbrief, 2 Petrusbrief,* 23, n. 12.

[4] Rightly R. Bauckham, *Jude, 2 Peter* (Waco: Word, 1983), 31.

or contradict its eschatological character. Salvation in Jude, as in Paul, was both an end-time gift and a present reality, for the eschatological gift had invaded this present evil age.

The purpose for the letter is conveyed in the exhortation "to contend for the faith that was once for all entrusted to the saints." The word group from which "contend" *(epagōnizesthai)* comes may designate a military (John 18:36; Eph 6:12; *2 Macc* 8:16) or athletic context (1 Cor 9:25; 2 Tim 4:7; Heb 12:1). The metaphor often cannot be pressed, and in such cases the word refers to a struggle or intense effort (Rom 15:30; Phil 1:30; Col 1:29; 2:1; 4:12; 1 Tim 6:12).[5] Jude exhorted his readers to strive intensely to preserve the faith once handed down to the saints.[6] In *Sirach* we find an interesting parallel, "Strive *[agōnisai]* even to death for the truth and the Lord God will fight for you" (*Sir* 4:28, RSV).

The term "entrusted" (lit., "handed down," *paradotheisē* along with the noun *paradosis*) is commonly used for the transmission of tradition (e.g., Mark 7:13; 1 Cor 11:2,23; 15:3; Gal 1:14; Col 2:8; 2 Thess 2:15; 3:6). Whether the tradition is laudable or lamentable must be derived from the context. Jude, obviously, used the term in a positive sense. There is also little doubt that the tradition was handed down from the apostles to "the saints," that is, to Christian believers.[7] That the apostles were the source of the tradition is suggested by v. 17, "Remember the words that were spoken beforehand by the apostles of our Lord Jesus Christ" (NASB). Of course, in vv. 17–18 a specific prophecy of the apostles is communicated, but such a prediction is part of the apostolic tradition that must be guarded.

The tradition believers must strive to preserve is designated as the "faith" *(pistei)*. Faith in this context does not refer to trusting God, as Paul typically used the term. In this context "faith" refers to the traditional teaching that was to be safeguarded. Even in Paul "faith" may refer to the message of the gospel (Gal 1:23; Eph 4:5; Col 1:23; 1 Tim 3:9; 4:1; 6:10, 12?,21; 2 Tim 3:8?; 4:7?; cf. Acts 6:7; 13:8).[8] Jude returned to the theme near the conclusion to the letter, saying believers must "build yourselves up in your most holy faith" (v. 20). Some scholars have dated Jude late and labeled it "early catholic" because they are convinced that an emphasis on

---

[5] For the motif see V. C. Pfitzner, *Paul and the Agon Motif: Traditional Athletic Imagery in the Pauline Literature,* NovTSup 16 (Leiden: Brill, 1967).

[6] Bauckham wrongly puts the emphasis on contending for the faith as a positive growth in the gospel instead of opposing the false teachers (*Jude, 2 Peter,* 32). Both ideas are present, and we should not exalt one over the other.

[7] Though D. B. Wallace thinks the agent is likely God (*Greek Grammar beyond the Basics: An Exegetical Syntax of the New Testament* [Grand Rapids: Zondervan, 1996], 436).

[8] Rightly J. Neyrey, *2 Peter, Jude,* AB (Garden City: Doubleday, 1993), 55; cf. R. Bauckham, *Jude and the Relatives of Jesus in the Early Church* (Edinburgh: T & T Clark, 1990), 159.

doctrinal preservation smacks of later church history. Of course, this same objection is raised to call into question the authenticity of the Pastoral Epistles. Bauckham rightly defends the genuineness of such a statement by Jude himself, the brother of Jesus.[9] He also rightly remarks that the focus is on the gospel rather than the detailed doctrinal formulas of later church history. And yet we must also acknowledge that the gospel itself involves doctrines that must be confessed. We have an early recognition here that the touchstone for the Christian faith is in the teaching of the apostles and that any deviation from their teaching is unorthodox (cf. Acts 2:42; Jude 17,20).[10] Jude did not merely say that the faith was handed down, but the NIV rightly translates *hapax* to say "once for all" handed down. No supplements or corrections will be tolerated. The gospel of Jesus Christ has received its full explication through the apostles. The author of Hebrews drew a similar conclusion when he said that God has spoken definitively and conclusively through his Son in the last days (Heb 1:2). From statements like these early Christians rightly concluded that the canon of Scripture should be restricted to those early writings that explicated the death and resurrection of Jesus Christ.[11]

4 Now Jude explains (note the "for" in the NIV) why his readers must strive to guard the faith that was handed down. Intruders had crept into the church, and apparently they were disturbing the congregation to such an extent that Jude felt compelled (v. 3) to respond. Jude described them as "certain men," which many commentators feel is a slightly disparaging reference to the interlopers.[12] The verbal form used of the opponents (they "have secretly slipped in") is certainly derogatory.[13] The verb implies that the adversaries had hidden their true character and motives. It also indicates that they were outsiders, perhaps wandering prophets or teachers.[14] They had been surreptitious and crafty, pretending to be godly members of the Christian church. Paul, similarly, criticized the Judaizers who had infiltrated the ranks of the church to spy out and destroy the liberty of those committed to the gospel (Gal 2:3–5). Peter indicted opponents who secretly intro-

---

[9] Bauckham, *Jude, 2 Peter,* 33.

[10] Bauckham, unfortunately, suggests that there was only a concern for moral probity and not doctrinal fidelity (*Jude, 2 Peter,* 34). The separation of the one from the other distorts the true character of the gospel Jude proclaimed, almost reducing it to a kind of moralism.

[11] I am not denying, of course, that many other factors must be considered when we think of canonicity.

[12] E.g., Fuchs and Reymond, *2 Pierre, Jude,* 158. It seems to me that Neyrey imposes his social scientific analysis on the text when he says that the major issue is that they challenged the honor of God and Jude (*2 Peter, Jude,* 52). A danger with the social scientific approach is that modern theories may be imposed on the text (cf. P. Müller, "Der Judasbrief," *TRu* 63 [1998]: 278–79).

[13] See W. Michaelis, "Παρεισάγω," *TDNT* 5.824–25.

[14] So Bauckham, *Jude, 2 Peter,* 35.

duced destructive factions (2 Pet 2:1).[15]

Jude proceeds to tell us four things about these intruders: (1) their judgment was predicted long ago, (2) they are ungodly, (3) they turn grace into an opportunity for license, and (4) they deny the Lord Jesus Christ. We should notice that the first statement tells us the opponents will be judged by God, and then items two through four inform us why they will be judged by God, namely, for their ungodly behavior. Jude began by saying that their "condemnation was written about long ago." Actually the NIV smooths out the Greek here, which can be translated "they were written about in advance long ago for this judgment." What Jude specifically meant has been the subject of considerable debate, but we can begin with the general meaning of the statement. The judgment that these intruders will face was "prescripted" *(progegrammenoi)* long ago. Jude reminded his readers at the outset that these adversaries had not taken God by surprise. Their judgment was prescripted from the beginning, and it followed as a corollary that God knew they would appear on the scene (cf. vv. 14,17).[16] We think here of Prov 16:4, "The Lord works out everything for his own ends — even the wicked for a day of disaster."[17] The reference to judgment indicates that the adversaries would not triumph. God will dispose of them ceremoniously and finally on the day of judgment. Jude encouraged his readers to persevere in the faith by assuring them that the intruders would ultimately fail and be judged by God.

At this juncture we need to examine the details of the phrase. Of what was Jude thinking when he said their judgment was prescripted long ago? Some think the reference is to the judgment of the false teachers predicted in 2 Pet 2:1–3:4. If Jude was not dependent on 2 Peter, this interpretation fails. Furthermore, it seems unlikely, unless we adopt a very late date for Jude, that he would refer to 2 Peter as something written "long ago." Some scholars maintain that *palai* does not always refer to ancient history, and hence a long interval is not demanded.[18] But the association of *palai* with the verb *progegrammenoi* suggests that prophecies from long ago were being fulfilled in Jude's day (cf. Isa 37:26; 48:5,7; Matt 11:21; Heb 1:1).

---

[15] Jude used the verb παρεισέδυσαν, while Paul used the terms παρεισάκτους and παρεισῆλθον in Gal 2:3. Peter used the term παρεισάξουσιν in 2 Pet 2:1.

[16] Contra C. D. Osburn, "Discourse Analysis and Jewish Apocalyptic in the Epistle of Jude," in *Linguistics and New Testament Interpretation: Essays on Discourse Analysis* (Nashville: Broadman, 1992), 289.

[17] S. J. Joubert remarks: "The actions of people, however contrary they seemed to appear to the divine will, were thus in no way outside the control of God. History has continued to run its predetermined course, in spite of various forms of evil and catastrophes. The false teachers in the midst of Jude's community will therefore also not interfere with the divine plan" ("Facing the Past: Transtextual Relationships and Historical Understanding of the Letter of Jude" *BZ* 42 [1998]: 68).

[18] Cf. N. Hillyer, *1 and 2 Peter, Jude,* NIBC (Peabody: Hendrickson, 1992), 239.

Others detect a reference here to the future judgment of opponents recorded in heavenly books.[19] Bauckham rightly points out that the evidence for this view is not persuasive and that most of the texts used to support this notion are wrongly interpreted.[20] Perhaps Jude referred to the arrival and judgment of the opponents prophesied by Enoch, foreshadowing the reference to Enoch in vv. 14–15. Osburn suggests that *1 Enoch* 67:10 is in view:[21] "So the judgment shall come upon them, because they believe in the debauchery of their bodies and deny the spirit of the Lord."[22] It is unclear, however, that this particular verse in *1 Enoch* was in view. Jude likely thought of the Old Testament since the judgment was anticipated, at least typologically, by the examples in vv. 5–7 and v. 11. Still, we should not exclude *1 Enoch* either, for the judgment of the ungodly was forecast by both the Old Testament and Enoch's prophecy in vv. 14–16.[23] The judgment of the ungodly is certain because that is the way God has always worked in history as the examples in vv. 5–7 and v. 11 show. If we understand vv. 5–16 to be one section, the judgments in vv. 5–7 and 14–16 constitute an inclusio, emphasizing that the opponents will be condemned. The middle section of the epistle, in other words, fleshes out the prescripted judgment mentioned in v. 4.

The judgment in Jude, then, refers to the judgment that was foreseen by God. The phrase "this judgment" *(touto to krima)* is puzzling since nothing in the previous context clearly refers to the judgment. Some have argued that the judgment alludes to 2 Pet 2:2,[24] but again this solution is satisfactory only if Jude used 2 Peter, which is doubtful. Others have suggested that the judgment refers to the opponents being ungodly, licentious, and denying Christ's lordship. But these sins do not constitute judgment but the *reason for* the judgment, and so we can reject this option as well. "This" *(touto)* could refer back to some word or concept, and yet there is no mention of judgment in the preceding verses.[25] It is best, therefore, to understand "this

---

[19] So Kelly, *Peter and Jude,* 250–51.

[20] Bauckham, *Jude, 2 Peter,* 35–36.

[21] Osburn, "Discourse Analysis and Jewish Apocalyptic in the Epistle of Jude," 290; id., "*1 Enoch* 80:2–8 (67:5–7) and Jude 12–13," *CBQ* 47 (1985): 300. For a reference to *1 Enoch* see also J. B. Mayor, *The Epistle of St. Jude and the Second Epistle of St. Peter* (1907; reprint, Grand Rapids: Baker, 1965), 24.

[22] J. H. Charlesworth, *OTP* (Garden City: Doubleday, 1983–85), 1:46.

[23] Cf. F. Maier, "Zur Erklärung des Judasbriefes (Jud 5)," *BZ* 2 (1904): 386; Vögtle, *Judasbrief, 2 Petrusbrief,* 26–27. Maier also sees a connection to vv. 14,17, as do Bauckham (*Jude, 2 Peter,* 36) and D. J. Moo (*2 Peter, Jude,* NIVAC [Grand Rapids: Zondervan, 1997], 230). It is doubtful, though, that the apostles (vv. 17–18) would be included in those who wrote "long ago."

[24] So C. Bigg, *The Epistles of St. Peter and St. Jude,* ICC (Edinburgh: T & T Clark, 1901), 326.

[25] The notion that we have a reference to Rom 3:8 is quite improbable and should be rejected (contra G. Sellin, "Die Häretiker des Judasbriefes," *ZNW* 77 [1986]: 209–11). Instead the antecedent or postcedent should be derived from Jude itself.

judgment" as anticipatory of the judgment explicated in vv. 5–16. Verses 5–16 refer to the texts from the Old Testament and *1 Enoch* that promise judgment for the wicked.

The remaining portion of v. 4 gives three reasons for the judgment: (1) ungodliness, (2) licentiousness, and (3) denial of Jesus' lordship. Jude often used words from the godless word group (*aseb-* in Greek). He used terms from the word group three times in the citation from *1 Enoch* in v. 15 and also in v. 18. Of course, the concept informed Jude's depiction of the intruders in all of vv. 5–16. We see again, then, that v. 4 functions as a preview of what is to come. To be "godless" is to commit the fundamental sin because of living without reckoning with God (e.g., Pss 1:1; 37:38; 51:13; Prov 1:32; Rom 1:18; 2 Pet 2:5–6; 3:7). The godless live as if God does not exist, so they do not honor him as their Lord and Master.[26]

The second reason for judgment is that the interlopers subverted God's grace and lived licentiously. The word "license" *(aselgeia)* often denotes sexual sin (*Wis* 14:26; Rom 13:13; 2 Cor 12:21; Gal 5:19; Eph 4:19) or some kind of gross debauchery in more general terms (*2 Macc* 2:26; Mark 7:22; 1 Pet 4:3; 2 Pet 2:2,7,18).[27] The context of the letter as a whole suggests that sexual sin is intended. The foundational character of v. 4 manifests itself again since sexual sin is featured as the reason for the judgment of the angels and Sodom and Gomorrah (vv. 6–7). Perhaps Jude also had this in mind when he spoke of defiling the flesh in v. 8 (cf. also vv. 13,16 possibly).

The third reason for judgment concludes the verse. The interlopers denied Jesus Christ as their Sovereign and Lord. Some scholars think the Father is designated by "Sovereign" *(despotēn)* and Jesus Christ by "Lord" *(kyrion)*. Since both titles are under the same Greek article *(ton),* they may both refer to Jesus Christ.[28] If 2 Peter and Jude have the same referent in view, then it is likely that both Jude and Peter (cf. 2 Pet 2:1) referred to Jesus Christ as *despotēs*. Against this view it is argued that elsewhere *despotēs* only refers to the Father (Luke 2:29; Acts 4:24; Rev 6:10; cf. also *1 Clem.* 59:4; 61:1–2; *Did.* 10:3).[29] Certainty eludes us, but the parallel to 2 Pet 2:1 suggests a reference to Jesus Christ.[30] Bauckham notes that the term used here *(despotēs)* is an indication that the Christology of Jude hails

[26] W. Foerster, "εὐσέβια," *TDNT* 7.185–91.

[27] See H. Paulsen, *Der Zweite Petrusbrief und der Judasbrief,* KEK (Göttingen: Vandenhoeck & Ruprecht, 1992), 55; O. Bauernfeind, "ἀσέλγεια," *TDNT* 1.490.

[28] Cf. Wallace, *Greek Grammar,* 270–90; see esp. 276 and his cautionary remarks there.

[29] So Kelly, *Peter and Jude,* 252; Fuchs and Reymond, *2 Pierre, Jude,* 160. The latter think the "only" in v. 25 supports this view as well.

[30] So also Osburn, "Jude 12–13," 301; Bauckham, *Relatives of Jesus,* 302–3.

from Palestinian circles.[31] Furthermore, the terms "Sovereign" and "Lord" do not point to two different functions for Jesus Christ. Both of them together focus on the lordship of Jesus Christ.[32] Indeed, as Bauckham argues, it appears that the phrase suggests the divinity of Jesus Christ (cf. the similar phrase in Josephus, *Ant.* 18.23). How were the opponents denying Jesus Christ as their Sovereign and Lord? Scholars in the past, seeing Jude as countering some form of Gnosticism, attempted to identify doctrinal deviations in the Christology of the intruders.[33] We now know that the developed Gnosticism of the second century A.D. was not present when the New Testament was written, though some antecedents to what was later called Gnosticism certainly existed. In any case we search in vain in Jude for any criticism of the opponents' doctrine of Christ. In comparison, John attacked the Christology of his opponents on several occasions (1 John 2:22–23; 4:2–3; 5:1,6–8; 2 John 7). It is likely, then, that Jude saw a denial of the sovereignty and lordship of Jesus Christ in the way the opponents lived.[34] Their evil lifestyle constituted a denial of Christ's lordship. A similar sentiment is reflected elsewhere in the New Testament (Matt 7:21–23; Titus 1:16). Verses 5–16, then, also reveal how the readers denied Christ's lordship, in that they had given their lives over to evil. More specifically examples of a rejection of lordship are also present. We see how the angels violated their apportioned place, rebelled, and committed sin (v. 6). Similarly, the intruders rejected lordship and reviled glories (v. 8). The opponents were like Korah in that they were guilty of rebellion (v. 11).

---

[31] Bauckham, *Relatives of Jesus,* 283–84. Bauckham argues that the term used here developed in the earliest Palestinian churches in the bilingual context of early Christianity.

[32] Ibid., 306–7.

[33] This is exceedingly common. For an example of this mistake, see D. J. Rowston, "The Most Neglected Book in the New Testament," *NTS* 21 (1974–75): 556; K. H. Schelke, *Der Petrusbrief—Der Judasbrief,* HTKNT (Freiburg: Herder, 1980), 152. Cf. also Mayor, *Jude and Second Peter,* 27.

[34] So already M. Luther, *Commentary on Peter & Jude* (Grand Rapids: Kregel, 1990), 232; cf. also Bauckham, *Relatives of Jesus,* 303; Osburn, "Discourse Analysis and Jewish Apocalyptic in the Epistle of Jude," 291; Vögtle, *Judasbrief, 2 Petrusbrief,* 29–32.

III. JUDGMENT OF THE INTRUDERS (5–16)
   1. God's Judgment (5–10)
      (1) Three Historical Examples of God's Judgment (5–7)
      (2) Application to Adversaries: Three Sins Warranting Judgment (8–10)
   2. Woe Oracle (11–13)
      (1) Three Types (11)
      (2) Application to Adversaries (12–13)
   3. Enoch's Prophecy (14–16)
      (1) The Prophecy: Judgment on the Ungodly (14–15)
      (2) Application to Adversaries (16)

III. JUDGMENT OF THE INTRUDERS (5–16)

Verses 5–16 unpack what is said in v. 4, demonstrating that the assertions made there correspond to reality. The section is bracketed by an inclusio in that the theme of judgment opens (vv. 5–7) and closes (vv. 14–16) the argument. The certainty of judgment is illustrated with three Old Testament examples (vv. 5–7): the punishment of Israel, the angels, and Sodom and Gomorrah. The section concludes with Enoch's prophecy that the Lord will judge the ungodly (vv. 14–15), and then Jude indicated in v. 16 that the opponents' character demonstrated that they were indeed ungodly. Verses 8–13 constitute the middle of the section. Verses 8–10 are linked back to vv. 5–7 in that they show that the intruders were deserving of judgment because of their sins. The woe in v. 11 functions as the inference of what is stated in vv. 8–10. The pronouncement of woe, however, is also supported by vv. 11b–13, for the adversaries deserved judgment because they had followed the paths of Cain, Balaam, and Korah. Verses 12–13 demonstrate that the woe oracle pronounced in v. 11 rightly applies to the opponents, providing further reasons for the judgment and using highly colorful language to castigate them for their ungodly ways.

1. God's Judgment (5–10)

(1) Three Historical Examples of God's Judgment (5–7)

5 Though you already know all this, I want to remind you that the Lord delivered his people out of Egypt, but later destroyed those who did not believe. 6 And

the angels who did not keep their positions of authority but abandoned their own home—these he has kept in darkness, bound with everlasting chains for judgment on the great Day. [7]In a similar way, Sodom and Gomorrah and the surrounding towns gave themselves up to sexual immorality and perversion. They serve as an example of those who suffer the punishment of eternal fire.

In v. 4 the judgment of the intruders is said to have been prescripted long ago. Verses 5–7 function as typological warnings, in which examples of judgment from the history of Israel, the angels, and Sodom and Gomorrah are presented.[1] All three function as illustrations of leaving their proper sphere contrary to God's will.[2] Jude's preference for triads emerges again. The order is not chronological, for then Israel would be last. Probably Jude began with Israel because they were God's people, the objects of his favor and redemption, and yet they experienced his judgment when they sinned. The parallel to the Christian community is obvious, since they too have experienced God's favor but are liable to his judgment if they stray from him.[3] Perhaps Sodom and Gomorrah are inserted last because the severity of the judgment stands as a warning to the church or churches Jude addressed. Emblazoned on their consciousness are the consequences of persisting in sin.

The examples cited here are often found in Jewish tradition (cf. *Sir* 16:7–10; *3 Macc* 2:4–7; *T. Naph.* 3:4–5; *Jub.* 20:2–7; CD 2:17–3:12; *m. Sanh.* 10:3; see also Luke 17:26–29). The parallels are instructive. *Sirach* notes the judgment of the giants (v. 7), which would be offspring of the angels in Gen 6:1–4, the judgment of Lot's neighbors for their ignorance (v. 8), and of Israel in the wilderness (v. 10). *Third Maccabees* 2 does not mention the judgment of Israel in the wilderness but describes the judgment of the giants at the flood (v. 4) and of Sodom and Gomorrah with sulfur and fire because of their arrogance and vices. *Testament of Napthali* also omits a reference to Israel but pronounces judgment on Sodom for abandoning the order of nature and of the Watchers of Genesis 6 for committing the same sin (*T. Naph.* 3:4–5). *Jubilees* proclaims God's judgment on the giants and Sodomites because of their fornication and impurity, also omitting the judgment of Israel (*Jub.* 20:5–6). The Damascus Document of the Dead Sea Scrolls indicts the Watchers and the wilderness generation for their stubbornness and failure to keep God's commands, and it omits any reference to Sodom and Gomorrah (CD 2:17–3:12). The Mishnah says there is no portion in the world to come for the flood generation, Sodom, and the wilder-

---

[1] On the importance of typology in Jude, see J. D. Charles, "'Those' and 'These': The Use of the Old Testament in the Epistle of Jude," *JSNT* 38 (1990): 109–24. R. Bauckham rightly notes that all three serve as "eschatological types" (*Jude and the Relatives of Jesus in the Early Church* [Edinburgh: T & T Clark, 1990], 187, 217–18).

[2] So ibid., 116.

[3] So R. Bauckham, *Jude, 2 Peter* (Waco: Word, 1983), 50.

ness generation (*m. Sanh.* 10:3), though a rabbinic debate on whether the wilderness generation will be saved is immediately noted. From the evidence cited above, we see that the tradition of appealing to the three examples of judgment was common in Jewish circles. Second Peter similarly pronounces judgment on the angels who sinned and Sodom and Gomorrah and leaves out the judgment of Israel. The variety in wording in the literature and the flexibility of the theme (e.g., Israel is often left out) points to an oral tradition, in which the theme of judgment was impressed on hearers through these three examples. Of course, the tradition also was written down in the documents before us, but evidence of literary dependence is lacking. I conclude that Jude was not dependent on any single source, but he drew on a tradition well known in Judaism.

5 The new section begins with a disclosure formula, "I want to remind you," signifying the beginning of a new section. Disclosure formulas are common in other letters as well (Rom 1:13; 11:25; 1 Cor 8:1; 10:1; 12:1; 2 Cor 1:8; Gal 1:11; Phil 1:12; 1 Thess 4:13), and here it functions as the transition to the next section of the letter.[4] The placement of the word "once for all" (omitted by the NIV) is textually uncertain. Some witnesses place it after "Lord," with the result that there is a parallelism between the Lord saving Israel out of Egypt the "first" time and then destroying them the "second" time. But the textual evidence actually favors placing the word *hapax* with the first clause, and in that case it would read as the NASB translates it, "Now I desire to remind you, though you know all things once for all."[5] On this reading, a connection is forged between Jude's readers knowing "all things once for all," and "the faith . . . once for all entrusted to the saints." Jude reminded them of the gospel message they already knew because it was preached to them when they heard the gospel. Hence, Jude was not claiming that his readers had comprehensive knowledge of everything but that they truly knew the gospel in contrast to the opponents. Knowing the truth of the gospel, of course, did not mean that reminders were superfluous. Reminders were needed so that believers experience afresh the power of the gospel. Jude reminded them because they were

[4] On disclosure formulas see J. L. White, *The Form and Function of the Body of the Greek Letter,* SBLDS 2 (Missoula: Scholars Press, 1972), 11–15.

[5] Supporting this view is Metzger, *TCGNT* 657–58; A. Wikgren, "Some Problems in Jude 5," *Studies in the History and Text of the New Testament in Honor of Kenneth Willis Clark, Ph.D.* (Salt Lake City: University of Utah Press, 1967), 147–48; C. D. Osburn, "The Text of Jude 5," *Bib* 62 (1981): 109–11; E. Fuchs and P. Reymond, *La Deuxième Épître de Saint Pierre, L'Épître de Saint Jude,* CNT (Neuchâtel–Paris: Delachaux & Niestlé, 1980), 162. For the former view see M. Black, "Critical and Exegetical Notes on Three New Testament Texts: Hebrews xi. 11, Jude 5, James i. 27," in *Apophoreta: Festschrift für Ernst Haenchen zu seinem siebzigsten Geburtstag* (Berlin: Töpelmann, 1964), 44–45; C. Landon, *A Text-Critical Study of the Epistle of Jude,* JSNTSup 135 (Sheffield: Academic Press, 1996), 77.

prone to forget the truth they had already embraced.

Jude began his reminder with the triad of judgments the Lord had inflicted in the past, beginning with the judgment of Israel. Another textual problem exists, for many manuscripts read "Jesus" instead of "Lord." Indeed, the external evidence suggests that "Jesus" rather than "Lord" is the correct reading.[6] Most scholars doubt that the reference could be to Jesus on internal grounds, arguing that God led Israel out of Egypt and destroyed the wicked angels.[7] A reference to Jesus Christ, however, is not as strange as some suggest.[8] Paul saw Christ as present with Israel in the wilderness (1 Cor 10:4,9), and so it is possible to think Jude believed that Jesus Christ delivered Israel out of Egypt. Moreover, since *1 Enoch* 69:26–29 describes the Son of Man as sitting in judgment over the bound angels, it is not unlikely, as Osburn notes, that the same could be applied to Jesus Christ.[9] Fossum supports the view that Jude referred to Jesus Christ, arguing that Jude understood Jesus to be the Angel of the Lord in the Old Testament.[10] Furthermore, New Testament writers identify Jesus Christ with texts that refer to Yahweh in the Old Testament. John said that Isaiah saw the glory of Jesus Christ (John 12:41), referring to the throne room vision of Isaiah 6. Isaiah said every knee will bow to Yahweh and confess allegiance to him (Isa 45:23), but Paul related this to Jesus Christ (Phil 2:10–11). Hence, it is not surprising that Jude could attribute the destruction of Israel, the angels, and Sodom and Gomorrah to Jesus Christ. Fossum rightly notes that in the

---

[6] The reading Ἰησους is supported by A, B, 33, 81, 1241, 1739, 1881, 2344. 𝔓[72] has the reading θεός Χριστός, which is certainly a corruption. Some scholars support κύριος (Bauckham, *Relatives of Jesus,* 308–9; Landon, *A Text-Critical Study of the Epistle of Jude*, 75–76), especially on internal grounds (אΨ, C*, 630, 1505, etc.). See the discussion in *TCGNT* 657, where the committee is itself divided. Supporting Ἰησους are Wikgren, 148–49; Osburn, "The Text of Jude 5," 111–15; C. Bigg, *The Epistles of St. Peter and St. Jude,* ICC (Edinburgh: T & T Clark, 1901), 328; Bauckham, *Jude, 2 Peter,* 49.

[7] Cf. J. N. D. Kelly, *A Commentary on the Epistles of Peter and Jude,* Thornapple Commentaries (Grand Rapids: Baker, 1981), 255; D. J. Moo, *2 Peter, Jude,* NIVAC (Grand Rapids: Zondervan, 1997), 239–40; A. Vögtle, *Der Judasbrief, Der 2 Petrusbrief,* EKKNT (Neukirchen–Vluyn: Neukirchener Verlag, 1994), 37–40; Fuchs and Reymond, *2 Pierre, Jude,* 162.

[8] E. E. Kellett agrees that Ἰησους is the superior reading but then argues that the reference is to Joshua ("Note on Jude 5," *ExpTim* 15 [1903–1904]: 381). Kellett's identification of Ἰησους with Joshua should be rejected. Joshua did not destroy those in the wilderness who failed to believe, and neither is it plausible that he judged the angels who sinned in Genesis 6. Rightly Osburn, "The Text of Jude 5," 111–12; J. Fossum, "Kyrios Jesus as the Angel of the Lord, in Jude 5–7" *NTS* 33 (1987): 226; cf. also H. Paulsen, *Der Zweite Petrusbrief und der Judasbrief,* KEK (Göttingen: Vandenhoeck & Ruprecht, 1992), 62–63.

[9] Osburn, "The Text of Jude 5," 112–13; cf. E. E. Ellis, "Prophecy and Hermeneutic in Jude," in *Prophecy and Hermeneutic in Early Christianity: New Testament Essays* (Grand Rapids: Eerdmans, 1978), 232, n. 49.

[10] Fossum, "Angel of the Lord," 226–43; so also R. Martin, "Jude," in *The Theology of the Letters of James, Peter, and Jude* (Cambridge: University Press, 1994), 77–78.

Old Testament account of the destruction of Sodom and Gomorrah, the annihilation of those cities is attributed to the Angel of the Lord (cf. Gen 18:1,13–14,17–33; 19:13–14,25,29).[11] Fossum indicates that intermediaries, such as the Logos or Wisdom, are also understood as the means by which the cities were destroyed in Philo and *Wisdom of Solomon*. The step of identifying Jesus as the Angel of the Lord is explicitly argued by Justin Martyr, and hence it is not impossible that Jude preceded Justin in drawing such a conclusion. Despite some plausible evidence supporting a reference to Jesus Christ, Jude likely referred to the Father rather than Christ. Fossum and others rightly show that references to Jesus Christ exist in other texts, and hence such a reading is not impossible.[12] But in many of the other texts a clear reference to Christ exists, and such is lacking here. It is more natural to think of the Father delivering Israel from Egypt and of the Father judging the angels who sinned in Genesis 6. Of course, we would have a clear reference to Jesus if "Jesus" is the superior reading in the manuscripts. The textual issue is as difficult as the interpretive debate, and so again we must admit that the reading "Jesus" is certainly possible. On the other hand, the inclusion of "Jesus" in some manuscripts could be due to scribal confusion of the *nomina sacra*. If a mistake arose in the *nomina sacra,* then a reference to the Father as "Lord" is preferable.

Israel was "delivered" (NIV), that is, "saved" *(sōsas),* out of Egypt by virtue of the Exodus (Exodus 6–14). But after liberating them from their bondage, the Lord "destroyed those who did not believe." The word "second time" *(deuteron)* is rightly translated "later" by the NIV, since the word emphasizes what occurred after Israel's liberation.[13] Jude had in mind the events of Numbers 14, where the spies returned (except for Caleb and

[11] The text attributes the destruction of the cities to God, the Angel of the Lord, and the other two angels. Such merging of activities is typical of the OT text and does not preclude what is being said here.

[12] For arguments against Fossum, see Bauckham, *Relatives of Jesus,* 310–11; Landon, *A Text-Critical Study of the Epistle of Jude,* 71–74. They raise the following objections to Fossum's view. Fossum depends on *1 Enoch* 10:4–6 and 10:11–12, but in *1 Enoch* two angels are referred to, and so it is difficult to see how the references can now be collapsed to refer to one person, Jesus. Furthermore, the reference to Michael in v. 9 shows that he rather than Jesus was identified as the angel of the Lord. References to Jesus as the preexistent Christ do not occur in the NT. Stylistically, Jude always refers to "Jesus Christ," never "Jesus" alone. To sum up, decisive arguments cannot be presented for either interpretive option, but it seems that the arguments supporting a reference to the Father are slightly stronger.

[13] Rightly J. P. Louw and E. A. Nida, *Greek-English Lexicon of the New Testament Based on Semantic Domains* (New York: United Bible Societies, 1988), 67.50; Fuchs and Reymond, *2 Pierre, Jude,* 163. Some scholars have postulated some strange interpretations based on the word δεύτερον. E.g., B. Reicke (*The Epistles of James, Peter, and Jude,* AB [Garden City: Doubleday, 1964], 199) and M. Green (*The Second Epistle General of Peter and the General Epistle of Jude,* 2d ed., TNTC [Grand Rapids: Eerdmans, 1987], 164) suggest a reference to the second coming of Christ here, which seems completely out of place in this context.

Joshua) with their disbelieving report, and the Israelites also disbelieved and were judged so that they were prevented from entering the land for forty years. Two words in particular link this verse to Numbers 14. Jude said that Israel "did not believe" *(pisteuō),* and the same term is used to depict Israel's unbelief in Num 14:11 *(ou pisteuousin).* Jude also said that the Lord "destroyed" *(apōlesen)* those who disbelieved, and the Lord threatens destruction *(apolō)* in Num 14:12.[14]

The main point Jude made is clear. No person in the believing community can presume on God's grace, thinking that an initial decision to follow Christ or baptism ensures their future salvation regardless of how they respond to the intruders. Israel's apostasy stands as a warning to all those who think that an initial commitment secures their future destiny without ongoing obedience. Those who are God's people demonstrate the genuineness of their salvation by responding to the warning given. The warnings are one of the means by which God preserves his people until the end. Those who ignore such warnings neglect the very means God has appointed for obtaining eschatological salvation. Nor should such a perspective be considered a form of works righteousness. Jude pinpointed the fundamental reason Israel was judged. They failed to "believe" in God. The call to perseverance is not a summons to something above and beyond faith. God summons his people to believe in his promises to the very end of their lives. Christians never get beyond the need to believe and trust, and all apostasy stems from a failure to trust in God's saving promises in Christ, just as the wilderness generation disbelieved that God would truly bring them into the land of Canaan, thinking instead that he had maliciously doomed them to die in the wilderness.

Another theological question is raised by what Jude said about Israel. The text says that God destroyed those whom he saved out of Egypt. This would seem to indicate that some of those who are genuinely saved may actually commit apostasy and forsake their salvation. Some might want to stave off this view by saying that the judgment was not eternal but temporal. But the use of the same tradition in 1 Cor 10:1–12 and Heb 3:7–4:13 indicates that the New Testament writers understood the judgment to be an eternal one.[15] As Hebrews says, those who sinned did not enter into God's heavenly "rest," which is another term for life in the age to come. Jude

---

[14] Some might object to the connection since the Lord did not carry out his threat to destroy the whole people because of Moses' intercession. The objection is not compelling. Yahweh did not destroy the entire nation (hence he responded to Moses' prayer), but he did destroy the adult generation that sinned.

[15] We saw earlier that in rabbinic circles (*m. Sanh.* 10:3) they debated whether the wilderness generation had a portion in the world to come. The debate is significant since it shows that Israel's behavior in the eyes of the rabbis had implications for their future destiny, not just temporal judgment. The NT perspective on this debate is clear from 1 Corinthians and Hebrews. The wilderness generation was cursed forever. This is a generalization, of course, and does not exclude the notion that some truly belonged to God.

understood it similarly, as the next two examples demonstrate. The angels who sinned and Sodom and Gomorrah were damned forever (vv. 6–7). Similarly, no hope existed for the unrepentant Israelites who sinned in the wilderness. It would seem to follow, then, that believers could be truly saved and apostatize.

I would like to suggest that the conclusion that true believers can lose their salvation is mistaken, even though it appears on first glance to be convincing. The central issue here is to discern the difference between the type and the fulfillment. The analogy drawn between Israel and the church of Jesus Christ does not stand at every point. We need to recall that Israel was both a political entity and also the people of God. The Lord was not merely calling out for himself a people, but he was also calling into existence a nation. It follows, therefore, that not every circumcised member of Israel was truly circumcised in heart (Deut 10:16; 30:6; Jer 4:4). Jude constructed an analogy between the saving of Israel out of Egypt (a physical act) and God's saving act in Jesus Christ, but we ought not necessarily to conclude from this that the Israelites liberated from Egypt were truly circumcised in heart, that they truly belonged to the people of God. Indeed, those who sinned in the wilderness and were then judged demonstrated that they did not truly belong to the Lord at all, that they did not have circumcised hearts in the first place. We ought not, then, construct a strict correspondence between the deliverance of Israel out of Egypt and the spiritual salvation of believers. Am I simply reading my theology into Jude? Some might think so. But I would contend that Jude himself promised that those whom God has called will be preserved to the end (vv. 1,24–25). Jude preserved the tension between warnings that are necessary for perseverance until the end and God's grace that ensures that those who belong to him will experience eschatological salvation.

There is another sense in which the situation of Israel and Jude's readers is likely the same. The Israelites destroyed in the wilderness probably believed they were truly part of God's people. Their disobedience demonstrated otherwise. Similarly, some in Jude's community may have thought they were genuinely part of God's people, but Jude insisted that continued faithfulness is the only way to demonstrate this. Those who "apostatize" reveal that they were not truly members of God's people (cf. 1 John 2:19). Responses to warnings reveal, retrospectively, who really belongs to the people of God.

6 The second example of judgment involves the angels who sinned. We have already noted that Jewish tradition linked together the sin of angels in Gen 6:1–4, the judgment of Sodom and Gomorrah, and the punishment of the wilderness generation. We can be almost certain that Jude referred here to the sin of the angels in Gen 6:1–4.[16] The sin the angels committed, according to the Jewish tradition, was sexual intercourse with the daughters of men. Apparently Jude also understood Gen 6:1–4 in the same way. Three reasons support such a conclusion. First, Jewish tradition consistently understood Gen 6:1–4 in this way (*1 En.* 6–19; 21; 86–88; 106:13–17; *Jub.* 4:15,22; 5:1; CD 2:17–19; 1QapGen 2:1; *T. Reu.* 5:6–7; *T. Naph.* 3:5; *2 Bar.* 56:10–14; cf. Josephus, *Ant.* 1.73). Second, we know from vv. 14–15 that Jude was influenced by *1 Enoch*, and *1 Enoch* goes into great detail about the sin and punishment of these angels. Jude almost certainly would need to explain that he departed from the customary Jewish view of Gen 6:1–4 if he disagreed with Jewish tradition. The brevity of the verse supports the idea that he concurred with Jewish tradition. Third, the text forges a parallel between the sin of Sodom and Gomorrah and the angels ("In a similar way," v. 7; *hōs* and *ton homoion tropon toutois*). The implication is that sexual sin was prominent in both instances.[17]

Before providing more detail on Jewish tradition, it would be helpful to explain what Jude said in v. 6. He charged the angels with not keeping "their positions of authority." The Greek word here is *archēn,* signifying the domain or rule or sphere of influence given to the angels. The angels abandoned "their own home" *(to idion oikētērion)* and transgressed proper bounds. The language is rather vague. What Jude meant, however, was that they left their proper sphere, came to the earth, became males, and had sexual relations with women. Jude used the language of retaliation here. Since the angels "did not keep" *(mē tērēsantas)* their proper sphere, God "has kept" *(tetērēken)* them "in darkness." Abandoning what is right has consequences because God is still Lord of the world. These angels experience punishment even now in that they are "bound with everlasting chains." We might think that literal chains are in view, but Hillyer rightly remarks: "We are not intended to imagine a literal dungeon in which fallen angels are fettered. Rather, Jude was vividly depicting the misery of their conditions. Free spirits and celestial powers, as once they were, are now shackled and

[16] Contra Osburn, who believes that only *1 Enoch,* and not Genesis 6, is the source for Jude's discussion ("Discourse Analysis and Jewish Apocalyptic in the Epistle of Jude," 296).

[17] A. F. J. Klijn understates the presence of sexual sin in his essay ("Jude 5 to 7," in *The New Testament Age: Essays in Honor of Bo Reicke* [Macon: Mercer University Press, 1984], 1:237–44). G. Sellin, unconvincingly, denies any reference to sexual sin at all ("Die Häretiker des Judasbriefes," *ZNW* 77 [1986]: 216–17), arguing that even in reference to Sodom and Gomorrah the sins should be understood metaphorically to designate denial of the true God and a turn toward idols. His interpretation fails to convince, for both the OT and Jewish tradition indicate that the sin of the angels and Sodom and Gomorrah included sexual deviance. Supporting a reference to sexual sin is F. Hand, "Randbemerkungen zum Judasbrief," *TZ* 37 (1981): 212. Nevertheless, Sellin rightly notes that the emphasis is on the angel's abandoning their allotted role (so also Charles, "The Use of the Old Testament in Jude," 114).

impotent. Shining ones, once enjoying the marvelous light of God's glorious presence, are now plunged in profound darkness."[18] Their current imprisonment, however, is not their final punishment. They are being preserved even now for the judgment on the day of the Lord. Now they are imprisoned, but they still await their final and definitive judgment on the last day.[19] The main point is that those who transgress and sin will experience judgment. The angels did not escape unscathed when they violated what was fitting. Neither will the opponents sin with impunity, and hence Jude encouraged the church to resist their teaching.[20]

At this juncture I want to sketch in briefly the Jewish tradition, so that we sense how pervasive it was. In *Testament of Naphtali* 3:4–5 the angels of Gen 6:1–4 are designated as "Watchers," and they are said to have "departed from nature's order" and hence are cursed with the flood. According to *T. Reu.* 5:6–7 women charmed the Watchers with their beauty, so that the Watchers lusted after them. They transformed themselves into males and gave birth to giants (cf. 1QapGen 2:1). *Jubilees* also teaches that the Watchers sinned with the daughters of men by mingling with them sexually (*Jub.* 4:22). The angels of the Lord saw the beauty of the daughters, took them to be their wives, the offspring were giants, and because of such wickedness the Lord brought the flood (*Jub.* 5:1–11). The Damascus Document is quite brief in its rendition of the story. The Watchers fell because they did not keep God's commands. The tradition of giants as offspring is preserved since their sons are said to be like cedar trees and their bodies are comparable to mountains (CD 2:17–19). God sent the flood as a result of such sin.

The tradition, as we said, is most extensive in *1 Enoch*. The angels desired the daughters of men (6:1–2) and took them as wives, who in turn gave birth to giants (7:1–2; 9:7–9; 106:14–15,17). As a result of their sin, God threatened to send a flood (10:2). The evil of the angels is quite clear when the author said they "fornicated" with women (10:11). Some of the language used bears remarkable parallels to Jude. The angel Raphael is ordered to "'Bind Azaz'el hand and foot (and) throw him into the darkness!' And he made a hole in the desert which was in Duda'el and cast him there; he threw on top of him rugged and sharp rocks. And he covered his face in order that he may not see light; and in order that he may be sent into the fire on the great day of judgment" (10:4–6).[21] Jude also taught that the

---

[18] N. Hillyer, *1 and 2 Peter, Jude,* NIBC (Peabody: Hendrickson, 1992), 242.

[19] J. B. Mayor observes that the bonds are said to be eternal, but they last only until the day of judgment (*The Epistle of St. Jude and the Second Epistle of St. Peter* [1907; reprint, Grand Rapids: Baker, 1965], 31).

[20] It is possible that Gen 6:1–4 records the original fall of angels, and hence their alignment with Satan was subsequent to the fall of Adam and Eve.

[21] J. H. Charlesworth, *OTP* (Garden City: Doubleday, 1983–85), 1.17.

angels who sinned were bound in darkness and await the day of judgment. That those who sinned will experience a temporary judgment before the final judgment is clearly communicated in *1 Enoch* 10:12–13: "Bind them for seventy generations underneath the rocks of the ground until the day of their judgment and of their consummation, until the eternal judgment is concluded. In those days they will lead them into the bottom of the fire—and in torment—in the prison (where) they will be locked up forever" (cf. 13:2).[22] Similarly, the Watchers are told, "You will not be able to ascend into heaven unto all eternity, but you shall remain inside the earth, imprisoned all the days of eternity" (14:5; cf. 21:1–4,10; 88:1,3). The idea that the Watchers abandoned their proper sphere, emphasized in Jude, is communicated in *1 Enoch* as well (along with a concise summary of the event): "For what reason have you abandoned the high, holy, and eternal heaven; and slept with women and defiled yourselves with the daughters of the people, taking wives, acting like the children of the earth, and begetting giant sons?" (15:3). Jude followed the tradition in pronouncing judgment on angels who violated their proper sphere.

We must be careful, however, to avoid saying that Jude necessarily agreed with everything found in *1 Enoch* or Jewish tradition in general. His own reference to the tradition is terse and avoids the kind of speculation we find in *1 Enoch* 6–8. Nor did Jude display any interest in the specific names of angels. A general appropriation of a tradition is not the same thing as accepting every detail of the tradition. We must remember that *1 Enoch* is the most detailed account, and elsewhere in Jewish tradition the story is communicated with brevity. We must beware of reading more into Jude than is warranted. Still, I think it is clear that Jude believed angels had sexual relations with women and that God judged the angels for violating their ordained sphere.

The story is certainly bizarre to modern readers, stemming from Gen 6:1–4. Unfortunately, this passage is the subject of considerable debate, and no consensus has been realized about its meaning. Many interpreters are convinced that the "sons of god" were not angels but divine beings or humans.[23] This is not the place to conduct an exegesis of this disputed text. I would only like to register my opinion that Jude interpreted Gen 6:1–4 correctly. In my judgment the "sons of god" *(bene elohim)* of Gen 6:1–4 are most plausibly identified as angels. The "sons of God" are clearly angels in

[22] Ibid., 1.18. All subsequent citations are from Charlesworth.

[23] For a reference to divine beings see C. Westermann, *Genesis I–II: A Commentary* (Minneapolis: Augsburg, 1984), 371–72. For a reference to human beings see C. F. Keil and F. Delitzsch, *Biblical Commentary on the Old Testament: Vol. 1. The Pentateuch* (Grand Rapids: Eerdmans, n.d.), 127–34; K. Mathews, *Genesis 1–11:26*, NAC (Nashville: Broadman & Holman, 1996), 323–32. For a reference to angels see G. Wenham, *Genesis 1–15*, WBC (Waco: Word, 1987), 139–40.

Job (1:6; 2:1; 38:7). One of the Qumran manuscripts of Deut 32:8, following the Septuagint, also reads "sons of god" *(bene elohim),* which the Septuagint renders *angelōn theou* ("angels of God"). It is possible, of course, that Jude alluded to a traditional story without believing it was historical, but this is problematic since the judgment of Israel in the wilderness and Sodom and Gomorrah are considered to be historical events. We must beware of a rationalistic worldview that dismisses such strange events as impossible. The objection most raise is that angels are asexual (Matt 22:30). Actually, Matthew did not say angels do not have sexuality, but they neither marry nor are given in marriage. There is no evidence that angels reproduce or engage in sexual intercourse. But when angels come to earth, they often come as human beings; and presumably the human form is genuine, not a charade, so that the sexuality of angels when they appear on earth is genuine. Nor is it plausible that Jude derived the account from Hesiod's account of the Titans in his *Theogony* (713–35), especially since it is clear that he was familiar with the book of *1 Enoch* and Jewish tradition. It is instructive, however, that many cultures have the story of the sexual union of angels and human beings. I would suggest that such accounts are distortions of an event that once occurred, an event that is accurately recorded in Gen 6:1–4. Nevertheless, the presence of such a story in so many cultures functions as evidence of a historical event that occurred. Do sexual unions between angels and human beings still happen today? I think the point of the imprisonment of angels and the flood narrative is that God now hinders any such unions from taking place.

7 The third example of judgment is the punishment of Sodom and Gomorrah. Jude was familiar with Jewish tradition, as we have seen, but he also knew well the biblical story from Genesis 19.[24] "The surrounding towns" were Admah, Zeboiim, and Zoar, though Zoar was spared the disaster (cf. Deut 29:23; Hos 11:8; Gen 19:19–22). The words "in the same manner as these"[25] *(ton homoion tropon toutois)*—the NIV translates the comparison by placing it at the beginning of the verse, "In a similar way"—establish a parallel between the sexual immorality of the angels and the sex-

[24] Against Osburn, who wrongly locates Jude's allusion to Jewish tradition and excludes Genesis 19 ("Discourse Analysis and Jewish Apocalyptic in the Epistle of Jude," 297).

[25] M. A. Kruger argues that τούτοις here refers back to the τινες ἄνθρωποι of v. 4, not to the angels of v. 6 or to the cities of Sodom and Gomorrah ("ΤΟΥΤΟΙΣ in Jude 7," *Neot* 27 [1993]: 119–32). The antecedent, however, is too distant to refer back to v. 4. Kruger also contends that οὗτοι in v. 8 refers back to v. 4. But οὗτοι is regularly used to denote the opponents as a stock term, and hence the fact that οὗτοι in v. 8 reaches back to τινες in v. 4 is not decisive. For a reference to the angels see Paulsen, *Petrusbrief und Judasbrief,* 64; Fuchs and Reymond, *2 Pierre, Jude,* 165.

ual immorality of Sodom.[26] Sexual sin was not the only sin for which Sodom and Gomorrah were punished. Ezekiel said they were also punished for their pride and lack of concern for the poor (Ezek 16:49). *Sirach* and *3 Maccabees* mention their arrogance, and the latter also mentions "injustice" (*Sir* 16:8; *3 Macc* 2:5). Josephus criticized Sodom for its pride and hatred of foreigners (*Ant.* 1.194). Some scholars, however, underestimate the extent to which homosexuality is listed in condemnations of Sodom.[27] The sin of homosexuality is featured prominently in the account in Genesis in that the men of Sodom desired to have sexual relations ("know" in Hebrew) with the angels who visited Lot (Gen 19:5–8). Bauckham neglects evidence from Josephus that Sodom also was punished for homosexual desires (*Ant.* 1.200–201). Philo specifically traced their sin to homosexuality, though he scored the cities for general moral debauchery as well (*T. Ab.* 134–36; *T. Mos.* 2.58). Homosexuality is certainly in view in *Testament of Naphtali,* where Israel is exhorted to avoid the sin of Sodom which "departed from the order of nature" (3:4).[28] *Testament of Levi* lists the sexual sins of Israel in a downward spiral and concludes with "your sexual relations will become like Sodom and Gomorrah" (14:6), suggesting the degradation of homosexuality. In Ezekiel the "abomination" *(toevah)* is surely a reference to sexual deviation (Ezek 16:50), and he does not specify the sin committed since the story was well known. Similarly, the author of *Jubilees* argues that Sodom and Gomorrah were judged for their fornication and impurity (*Jub.* 16:5; 20:5–6). Sexual promiscuity like that of Sodom is predicted by Benjamin (*T. Ben.* 9:1). Jude also focused on the sexual sin of Sodom and Gomorrah: they "gave themselves up to sexual immorality and perversion." The NIV uses the word "perversion," but the Greek literally says that they "went after other flesh" *(apelthousai opisō sarkos heteras).*

What comparison is drawn to v. 6 here? Was Jude saying that Sodom was like the angels in Gen 6:1–4 in the sense that they also wanted sexual relations with angels?[29] If so, the sin criticized was not necessarily homosexuality but the violation of the separation established between human beings and angels. It is unlikely, however, that Jude made this specific point. The sin of Sodom was not precisely like the sin the angels committed. The most important evidence against the proposed interpretation is that

[26] The words used clearly point to sexual immorality. So T. Fornberg, *An Early Church in a Pluralistic Society: A Study of 2 Peter,* ConBNT 9 (Lund: Gleerup, 1977), 47; W. J. Dalton, "The Interpretation of 1 Peter 3,19 and 4,6: Light from 2 Peter," *Bib* 60 (1979): 551, n. 11. Contra Paulsen, *Petrusbrief und Judasbrief,* 64. Surprisingly, Reicke identifies the sins with idolatry and self-exaltation (*James, Peter, and Jude,* 199).

[27] E.g., Vögtle, *Judasbrief, 2 Petrusbrief,* 43–45, though he sees a reference to sexual sin.

[28] Note the words ἐνήλλαξε τάξιν φύσεως αὐτῆς ("she changed the order of her nature").

[29] For this view see Kelly, *Peter and Jude,* 258–59; Bauckham, *Jude, 2 Peter,* 54.

the men in Sodom who had a sexual desire for the angels *did not know they were angels.*[30] Their sin consisted in their homosexual intentions and their brutal disregard for the rights of visitors to the city.[31] Furthermore, it would be strange to designate a desire for angels as a desire for "other flesh" *(sarkos heteras).* The term more naturally refers to a desire for those of the same sex; they desired flesh other than that of women. For various reasons some are attempting today to question the view that homosexuality receives an unqualified negative verdict in the Scriptures. Such attempts have been singularly unsuccessful. The biblical writers and the Jewish tradition unanimously condemned homosexuality as evil.[32]

The reason Jude introduced the example of Sodom and Gomorrah is that their punishment functions as an "example" *(deigma)* of what God will do to the opponents in the future. *Third Maccabees* drives home the same point: the consumption of the cities with fire and sulphur made them an "example" *(paradeigma)* for those to come (*3 Macc* 2:5). Jude characterized the punishment endured as "eternal fire" *(pyros aiōniou).* This fire functions as an example because it is a type or anticipation of what is to come for all those who reject God. The destruction of Sodom and Gomorrah is not merely a historical curiosity; it functions typologically as a prophecy of what is in store for the rebellious. The narrative stresses the devastation of the Lord raining fire and brimstone upon the cities (Gen 19:24–28). The brimstone, salt, and wasted nature of the land function as a warning for Israel and the church elsewhere in the Scriptures (Deut 29:23; Jer 49:17–18; cf. Isa 34:9–10; Ezek 38:22; Rev 14:10–11; 19:3; 20:10). Jewish tradition particularly emphasized that one could still see the horrible consequences of what had occurred in the area south of the Dead Sea. "Evidence of their wickedness still remains: a continually smoking wasteland, plants bearing fruit that does not ripen" (*Wis* 10:7, RSV). Josephus said: "In fact, vestiges of the divine fire and faint traces of five cities are still visible. Still, too, may one see ashes reproduced in the fruits, which from their outward appearance would be thought edible, but on being plucked with the hand dissolve into smoke and ashes. So far are the legends about the land of Sodom borne out by ocular evidence" (*J.W.* 4.484–85).[33] Philo made similar remarks (*T. Ab.* 141). He said: "Even to this day there are seen in Syria

[30] Rightly Moo, *2 Peter, Jude,* 242.

[31] Contra D. G. Horrell, *The Epistles of Peter and Jude,* EC (Peterborough: Epworth, 1998), 121.

[32] For further discussion of this point see T. R. Schreiner, *Romans,* BECNT (Grand Rapids: Baker, 1998), 93–97. See also Oecumenius in *James, 1–2 Peter, 1–3 John, Jude,* ACCS (Downers Grove: InterVarsity, 2000), 251. For a full treatment of the issue of homosexuality, see now R. A. J. Gagnon, *The Bible and Homosexual Practice: Texts and Hermeneutics* (Nashville: Abingdon, 2001).

[33] Josephus claims to have seen the pillar of salt that was Lot's wife (*Ant.* 1.203).

monuments of the unprecedented destruction that fell upon them, in the ruins, and ashes, and sulphur, and smoke, and the dusky flame which still is sent up from the ground as of a fire smouldering beneath" (*Moses* 2.56).[34]

We must also beware of overinterpreting the examples Jude presented of judgment in the past. Surely Jude was not implying that the opponents had had sexual intercourse with angelic beings (v. 6). Nor was he necessarily implying that they engaged in homosexual activity. His purpose was to emphasize that those who sin are judged, not to say that the opponents had committed the same sins as their predecessors. It is likely, however, that the intruders were guilty of sexual sin, as we will see in subsequent verses.

(2) Application to Adversaries: Three Sins Warranting Judgment (8–10)

[8]In the very same way, these dreamers pollute their own bodies, reject authority and slander celestial beings. [9]But even the archangel Michael, when he was disputing with the devil about the body of Moses, did not dare to bring a slanderous accusation against him, but said, "The Lord rebuke you!" [10]Yet these men speak abusively against whatever they do not understand; and what things they do understand by instinct, like unreasoning animals—these are the very things that destroy them.

After presenting three examples of God's judgment in history, we might expect Jude to say that the opponents would be judged as well. Instead of proclaiming their judgment, however, he announced their sins, providing a basis for their future judgment. The paragraph is connected with the preceding, as the words "in the very same way" (v. 8) demonstrate. Rendering the word "likewise" *(homoiōs)* "in the very same way," however, is slightly misleading, in that it may suggest that the intruders committed the exact sins of those judged in vv. 5–7. I have already argued that Jude did not intend in vv. 5–7 to say that the opponents were homosexuals or that they had sexual relations with angels. The connection between the two paragraphs is looser. A general analogy exists between the sins of those judged in vv. 5–7 and Jude's opponents. Jude's delight for triplets emerges again since the three sins for which the opponents will be judged in v. 8 are sexual sin, rejection of God's (or Christ's) lordship, and reviling of angels.[35] The connection between the sins itemized in v. 8 and the preceding para-

[34] Philo, *The Works of Philo* (Peabody: Hendrickson, 1993), 495–96.

[35] Bauckham (*Jude, 2 Peter,* 45 and *Relatives of Jesus,* 201–6) and Ellis ("Prophecy and Hermeneutic in Jude," 225) detect in the repetition of the word οὗτοι an interpretive formula, such as we see at Qumran or in apocalyptic literature. If this is the case, we have something similar to *pesher* exegesis. Bauckham admits, however, that the parallel is inexact, and it is unclear that Jude interprets Scripture in every case (*Jude, 2 Peter,* 45). J. Neyrey argues that the repetition of οὗτοι is rhetorical (*2 Peter, Jude,* AB [Garden City: Doubleday, 1993], 72). For a similar rhetorical pattern with οὗτος, see Acts 7:35–38.

graph is interesting to trace.[36] Sodom (v. 7) certainly committed all three sins since its inhabitants violated sexual norms, mistreated angels (though they did not know they were angels), and repudiated God's lordship. The angels in v. 6 also rejected God's sovereignty over themselves and transgressed sexual standards, but there is no evidence that they reviled other angels. Israel in the wilderness (v. 5) obviously rebelled against God's rule over them by refusing to obey his command to enter into the land of promise (Numbers 14), and they committed sexual sin with the Midianites (Num 25:1–9). Evidence that they blasphemed angels, however, is lacking unless one sees a repudiation of angels in their transgression of the law, but the connection in this case is scarcely clear. We can conclude, then, that the connection between vv. 5–7 and vv. 8–10 is general rather than exact.

Having traced the connection of vv. 8–10 to vv. 5–7, we should summarize the argument of vv. 8–10. The three sins for which the opponents deserved judgment are listed in v. 8. Michael's debate with the devil regarding the body of Moses introduces a contrast in v. 9. The intruders criticized demonic powers, but Michael, by contrast, did not even revile the devil and left the judgment of the devil to God. The breathtaking presumption of the adversaries is therefore featured. Jude resumed (v. 10) with two of the three sins mentioned in v. 8. The opponents mocked confidently even though they lacked any understanding of what they criticized. The one thing they did understand apparently was the power of physical appetites and sexual sin; they plunged right in by giving in to such desires, and they will be destroyed in the judgment on account of them.

8 We have already noted that three sins are featured in v. 8: sexual sin, denial of God's lordship, and blasphemy of glorious angels. The NIV translates the participle *enypniazomenoi* as "dreamers." This is fitting as long as the participle is understood to modify all three verbs, and the dreams are understood as the basis for the moral baseness of the opponents.[37] They appealed to their dreams as a source of revelation, as a justification for their lifestyle. Others understand Jude as criticizing the interlopers as ignorant, hypnotized, or dreamers,[38] but it is more likely that the opponents justified their moral laxity by appealing to dreams which they believed functioned as divine approval for their behavior.[39] The Scriptures, of course, do not rule

[36] See Bauckham, *Relatives of Jesus,* 188.

[37] Kelly understands the participle similarly; the sins are "a result of their dreamings" (*Peter and Jude,* 260–61).

[38] Osburn thinks Jude was merely saying that the false teachers were deluded ("Discourse Analysis and Jewish Apocalyptic in the Epistle of Jude," 298).

[39] So Horrell, *The Epistles of Peter and Jude,* 121–22. Hillyer says that they "claim to have visionary revelations" (*1 and 2 Peter, Jude,* 247). He cites *1 Enoch* 99:8, which speaks of those who "will sink into impiety because of the folly of their hearts, and their hearts will be blinded through the fear of their hearts and through the visions of their dreams."

out all dreams (cf. Joel 2:28; Matt 1:20; Acts 2:17). And yet false prophets also appealed to dreams and were criticized roundly for their delusion in the Old Testament (Deut 13:1,3,5; Isa 56:9–12; Jer 23:25–32).[40] The mere claim to have a dream from the Lord does not validate whatever one might say.

First, apparently the intruders appealed to dreams to justify their sexual licentiousness. The NIV translates the phrase "pollute their own bodies," and this is an accurate way of rendering the Greek "defile the flesh" (*sarka . . . miainousin*). The word "defile" *(mianiō)* often designates sexual sin in the Old Testament (e.g., Gen 34:4,13,27; Lev 18:24,27–28; Job 31:11; Jer 3:2; Hos 5:3; 6:10; cf. *Pss. Sol.* 2:13; *1 Enoch* 9:8; 10:11; 12:4; 15:3–4). It also fits with what Jude said about the angels and Sodom and Gomorrah in vv. 6–7.[41] The phrase "defile the flesh" to describe sexual sin is also found (*Sib. Or.* 2:279; Herm. *Mand.* 29:9; *Sim.* 60:2). Naturally the opponents did not think they were defiling the flesh. Presumably, they appealed to their dreams to say that their sexual freedom was from God himself, that they transcended moral norms.[42]

Second, the opponents also "reject authority." One could see a reference here to the rejection of human authorities, whether to church or governmental leaders. But the term *kyriotēs* never has this meaning in the Septuagint or the New Testament, and we would expect a plural if human authorities were intended. Alternatively, the reference could be to angelic powers (Eph 1:21; Col 1:16; cf. *2 Enoch* 20:1).[43] But once again a plural would be more likely, and since the next phrase likely refers to angels, Jude probably had in mind the lordship of God and/or Christ here (cf. Herm. *Sim.* 56:1; 59:1; *Did.* 4:1). Indeed, the translation "lordship" or "sovereignty" is preferable to "authority" (per NIV) since it more clearly points to God's sovereignty. The sin here is comparable to v. 4, where the opponents denied Jesus Christ as their Master and Lord. Again a specific doctrinal deviation probably is not intended. They denied the lordship of God or Christ by the way they lived.[44]

Third, the intruders "slander celestial beings." The NIV interprets the Greek for us here since the text literally says "slander glories" *(doxas)*. It is possible that the reference could be to human beings, with the result that

---

[40] For the connection to false prophets, see R. Heiligenthal, *Zwischen Henoch und Paulus: Studien zum theologiegeschichtlichen Ort des Judasbriefes,* Texte und Arbeiten zum neutestamenlichen Zeitalter 6 (Tübingen: Francke, 1992), 50; K. H. Schelke, *Der Petrusbrief—Der Judasbrief,* HTKNT (Freiburg: Herder, 1980), 156.

[41] Cf. Fornberg, *An Early Church in a Pluralistic Society,* 47; Fuchs and Reymond, *2 Pierre, Jude,* 166–67.

[42] That their sin was sexual is defended by Bauckham, *Relatives of Jesus,* 187, n. 13. Verses 5–7 do not necessarily indicate the sin in view was homosexuality (rightly Osburn, "Discourse Analysis and Jewish Apocalyptic in the Epistle of Jude," 299; Vögtle, *Judasbrief, 2 Petrusbrief,* 48).

[43] Paulsen, *Petrusbrief und Judasbrief,* 65.

[44] Fuchs and Reymond see a rejection of God's lordship (*2 Pierre, Jude,* 167). Hillyer sees a reference to v. 4 and thus thinks a denial of Christ's lordship is in view (*1 and 2 Peter, Jude,* 248).

honorable people are intended (cf. Pss 149:8; 23:8; Nah 3:10; 1QpHab 4:2; 4QpNah 2:9; 3:9; 4:4; 1QM 14:11).[45] And yet the plural Hebrew term *nikbadîm* is never rendered by the term *doxai* in the Old Testament. The notion that angels are glorious beings is quite plausible (Exod 15:11, LXX; *T. Jud.* 25:2; *T. Levi* 18:5; 1QH 10:8).[46] This interpretation fits best with v. 9, where Michael's struggle with the devil is recounted, and Michael desisted from reviling the devil. Some commentators see a reference here to good angels, arguing that Jude would not be worried about scorn heaped on evil angels.[47] But the parallel with v. 9, where Michael refused to pronounce his own judgment on the devil, suggests that Jude referred to *evil angels* in v. 8.[48] Jude's argument runs as follows: The intruders insult demons, but the archangel, Michael, did not even presume to blaspheme the devil himself but left his judgment to God. If Michael as an angel with high authority did not even presume to judge Satan, how can the opponents be so filled with pride that they insult demons, who have a certain glory, even though they have subsequently sinned?

Why were the angels receiving scorn from the opponents? We must admit our lack of knowledge here. Those who see the angels as good have proposed various answers. Some have suggested that the opponents were Gnostics who criticized the angels for their part in the creation of the material world. But this interpretation stands only if Jude is an anti-Gnostic polemic, and the evidence for such a theory is lacking. Others think the angels were criticized as mediators of the law of Moses (Gal 3:19; Acts 7:38,53; Heb 2:2; cf. *Jub.* 1:27–29; Josephus, *Ant.* 15.136).[49] This would fit with the antinomian character of the opponents, but it fails if the angels here are demons since there is no warrant (not even in Gal 3:19) to think that God's law was transmitted by demons.[50] Alternatively, others argue that the opponents held to a form of overrealized eschatology, and they disparaged angels because they knew believers would judge them (1 Cor 6:3). Another possibility is that angels were reviled because they would play a major role on the day of judgment.[51] But if the "glories" were demons,

---

[45] Some understand it to refer to civil authorities. E.g., M. Luther, *Commentary on Peter & Jude* (Grand Rapids: Kregel, 1990), 293; J. Calvin, *Commentaries on the Catholic Epistles* (Grand Rapids: Eerdmans, 1948), 438.

[46] Cf. Mayor, *Jude and Second Peter,* 35. A reference to angels is strengthened when we observe Jude's interest in angels (so I. H. Eybers, "Aspects of the Background of the Letter of Jude," *Neot* 9 [1975]: 116).

[47] E.g., Bauckham, *Jude, 2 Peter,* 57.

[48] Green, *2 Peter and Jude,* 168–69; Moo, *2 Peter, Jude,* 245–46. But we cannot read into this Gnostic dualism (against Fuchs and Reymond, *2 Pierre, Jude,* 167).

[49] So Bauckham, *Relatives of Jesus,* 272.

[50] Vögtle questions the antinomian thesis, noting that words like "commandment" or "law" are lacking (*Judasbrief, 2 Petrusbrief,* 55–56).

[51] Neyrey, *2 Peter, Jude,* 69.

another answer might be correct. It is difficult, of course, to discern from v. 8 alone whether the "glories" were good or evil angels, but v. 9 tips the scales in favor of demons. Michael did not take upon himself to pass judgment on the devil but entreated the Lord to judge him. Yet the intruders in Jude's community felt no compunction about reviling demons. The adversaries may have reviled these glories because they claimed that demons could not hurt those belonging to God. If this is the case, they underestimated the power of evil; for these angels, though evil, still retained glory, even though that glory had now been deformed by evil.

9 Verse 9 is a difficult verse, and so at the outset we should state its main point. The opponents insulted glorious angels who were demons, but Michael was so humble that he did not presume to condemn the devil but asked the Lord to rebuke him. The term "archangel" designates Michael's authority and prominence. In Dan 10:13,21 he is designated as a "prince" *(archōn)*—as "the great prince" (*ho archōn ho megas,* Theodotion) in Dan 12:1.[52] In Revelation he leads the battle against the dragon and the evil angels (Rev 12:7). His prominence continues in other Jewish literature (1QM 9:16; *1 Enoch* 9:1; 10:11; 20:5; 24:6).

Even though the Old Testament says the Lord buried Moses (Deut 34:6), speculation arose over his burial since no human being observed the burial place. The puzzling element in Jude is the reference to the argument over the body of Moses between Michael and the devil. The terms used suggest a legal dispute over Moses' body. By establishing Moses' guilt, the devil would deprive him of the right of an honorable burial and presumably claim ownership over his body. Michael had every right, it would seem, to criticize the devil since the devil was wicked and his motives were evil, but Michael did not presume to criticize the devil and utter a "reviling judgment" *(krisin blasphēmias)* against him.[53]

The words Michael pronounced, "The Lord rebuke you!" allude to Zech 3:2. The Old Testament context in Zechariah is significant, for the account in Zechariah represents another incident in which Satan attempted to establish the guilt of one of Yahweh's servants. Joshua, the high priest, was in the Lord's presence, but Satan accused him before the Lord (Zech 3:1). We might think that Satan rightly accused Joshua since his "filthy clothes" represented his sin (Zech 3:3–4). But Yahweh pronounced a judgment against Satan in saying "The LORD rebuke you" (Zech 3:2). God's word brings forgiveness, illustrated by the clean garments with which Joshua was clothed. As Kee has shown, the Lord was not

---

[52] "The great angel" ὁ ἄγγελος ὁ μέγας in B.

[53] The genitive βλασφημίας is an adjectival genitive, reflecting a Semitic idiom. So Mayor, *Jude and Second Peter,* 36; Fuchs and Reymond, *2 Pierre, Jude,* 168; Hillyer, *1 and 2 Peter, Jude,* 249; C. F. D. Moule, *An Idiom Book of New Testament Greek,* 2d ed. (Cambridge: University Press, 1959), 175.

merely reprimanding Satan so that the story merely concludes with a verbal rebuke.[54] Rather, the Lord's verdict was effective, sealing Satan's defeat in the courtroom and declaring Joshua's vindication. Those whom the Lord has chosen are vindicated in his sight (Zech 3:2,4–5).

Michael's words in Jude, similarly, do not merely indicate a desire for the Lord to reprimand Satan verbally for bringing an accusation against Moses, as if Satan would receive only a verbal "dressing down." The Lord's rebuke would function as an effective response to Satan's accusation so that Moses would be vindicated, and his vindication would secure his proper burial. The devil probably claimed authority over Moses' body because of Moses' sin in killing the Egyptian. Michael did not deny that Moses sinned or defend his behavior. He appealed to the Lord's rebuke with the confidence that Moses would receive forgiveness by God's word, with the result that God would remove his defilement (cf. Zech 3:3–5).

Where did Jude derive this story? Unfortunately, the account is not extant in any writing that has been preserved. Traditions of the account have come down to us, and these traditions are carefully sifted by Bauckham in an excursus.[55] The story is reputed to come from a book titled *Assumption of Moses*. The relationship between *Assumption of Moses* and *Testament of Moses* is keenly debated. In his thorough study Bauckham thinks there are two separate traditions in these two different works.[56] The issue need not be resolved by this commentary since we no longer possess the original version of the story. What we do learn from the traditions compiled by Bauckham is that the devil contested Moses' "right to an honorable burial," charging him with the murder of the Egyptian.[57] Michael asked the Lord to rebuke the devil, and the devil fled so that Michael could complete the burial.[58]

My interpretation differs in one significant respect from Bauckham's. Bauckham rejects the common view that Michael refused to slander the devil.[59] In his careful and fascinating study of the traditions of the account, he maintains that the story Jude drew on taught that *the devil slandered Moses* because Moses murdered the Egyptian. The key to grasping what Jude meant, suggests Bauckham, comes from a knowledge of the tradition

[54] H. C. Kee, "The Terminology of Mark's Exorcism Stories," *NTS* 14 (1968): 238–39.

[55] Bauckham, *Jude, 2 Peter,* 65–76; see also his careful study as reflected in the next note.

[56] Id., *Relatives of Jesus,* 238–70.

[57] See Bauckham's summary, *Jude, 2 Peter,* 72–73.

[58] Since the date of *Testament of Moses* is debated, it is possible that the story recounted by Jude derives from oral rather than written tradition (cf. J. D. Charles, "Jude's Use of Pseudepigraphical Source-Material as Part of a Literary Strategy," *NTS* 37 [1991]: 137, n. 31); cf. also Eybers, "Background of the Letter of Jude," 121, n. 15).

[59] Bauckham, *Jude, 2 Peter,* 60–62; id., *Relatives of Jesus,* 271–75.

he appropriated. Hence, the point of the story, according to Bauckham, is not that Michael refused to slander the devil.[60] Michael, according to Bauckham, did not presume to respond to the devil's accusation against Moses, appealing to the Lord's judgment, not his own authority as the leader of angels, to counter Satan. Bauckham's suggestion is intriguing, but I do not believe it is the most natural way to understand the verse.[61] In saying that Michael did not presume to bring "a reviling judgment," it seems most likely that this is a judgment *against the devil,* in the sense that Michael did not presume, though he seemed to have every right to do so, to speak against the devil. Although Bauckham's interpretation is ingenious, the words "did not dare to bring a slanderous accusation" are most naturally understood to say that Michael refused to utter a word of judgment against the devil. The verse, then, has a simple contrast. Michael did not dare to pronounce a condemning judgment upon the devil. He left the judgment of Satan in God's hands, asking God to finally judge him. Such a reading of the verse fits as well with our understanding of 2 Pet 2:10–11.[62]

Jude's reference to a noncanonical book is puzzling for many Christians today. Did he believe the account was historically accurate, or did he cite it to make a point?[63] It is difficult to be certain, but it seems likely that Jude believed the story was rooted in history. He gave no indication elsewhere that the traditions cited were unhistorical. But does that lead to the conclusion that the canon of Scripture should be expanded, or did Jude think *Assumption of Moses* was inspired? These are vexing questions, but we should not draw the conclusion that the citation from a book means that the entire book is inspired. Paul cited Greek poets and sayings without suggesting that the entire work was authoritative Scripture (Acts 17:28; 1 Cor 15:33; Titus 1:12). Jude did not intend to put a canonical stamp on *Assumption of Moses* simply because he cited it. He viewed this story as true or helpful, or he believed it was an illustration of the truth he desired to teach.

10 Michael fully understood the devil's wickedness and yet he did not presume to utter judgment against him, asking the Lord to judge him. Yet these men spoke abusively against "whatever they do not understand." The word *blasphēmousin* (v. 10, translated "speak abusively against" by the NIV but by "slander" and "slanderous accusation" in vv. 8–9) links the three verses together: note *blasphēmousin* in v. 8 and *blasphēmias* in v. 9. When Jude said that these people slandered what they did not comprehend,

---

[60] Bauckham, *Relatives of Jesus,* 273. He also argues that in 2 Pet 2:11 the purpose is not to say that the good angels treat demons with respect.

[61] See also here Vögtle, *Judasbrief, 2 Petrusbrief,* 61.

[62] See commentary for discussion of these verses.

[63] See also the discussion in Moo, *2 Peter, Jude,* 249–50.

he again had in mind the glorious angels of v. 8.[64] The intruders believed they understood heavenly things, but they were far out of their depth. The one thing they did understand, however, was the power of physical appetites. Their physical desires urged them on daily, and like irrational animals they were driven by sexual instinct rather than reason. Jude's language is highly ironic here, for presumably the intruders claimed a knowledge of heavenly matters, but their comprehension of truth did not exceed that of animals. Indeed by following their instincts they will be destroyed *(phtheirontai).* The destruction envisioned is not temporal (cf. 1 Cor 3:13; 2 Pet 2:12). Jude thought of their eternal judgment, when they will pay the consequences for being enslaved to their sinful desires, the only thing these people understood well.

2. Woe Oracle (11–13)

The text begins with a woe oracle where judgment is pronounced on those who have imitated the ways of Cain, Balaam, and Korah. The woe oracle, however, does not only point forward. It also reaches back to vv. 8–10 and functions as the conclusion of those verses. Hence, we see that the main proposition in vv. 8–13 is the pronouncement of woe upon the false teachers. The remainder of vv. 8–10 and 11–13 documents the reasons for the pronouncement of woe.

In vv. 12–13 Jude again used a triad, seeing these three men as types of the opponents infiltrating the church. Jude applied the woe oracle to the adversaries using the word "these" *(houtoi).* Thereby he brought the three dangers of the adversaries to the attention of the readers. They were hidden reefs in the love feasts; that is, the danger they posed was not immediately apparent, and hence they were as perilous as rocks that cause shipwreck when a ship is seeking harbor. They ate together with other church members shamelessly, fearing no judgment. Finally, they were leaders who did not shepherd the flock but only themselves, showing that they were bogus shepherds. Jude closed this section with four illustrations drawn from nature that depict the character of the opponents. Four different spheres of the natural world illustrate Jude's point: the clouds of the sky, the agricultural produce of the earth, the stormy sea, and the planets of the stellar regions. In the first two realms Jude criticized the teachers for not producing what they promised. They were long on words and short on substance.

---

[64] It exceeds the evidence to say, however, that they despised angels because of their "disdain for the malevolent OT Creator-god as well as his creation" (contra Charles, "Jude's Use of Pseudepigraphical Source-Material," 139).

The last two illustrations demonstrate that the opponents were shamefully evil, revealing that they were deserving of judgment.

(1) Three Types (11)

[11]Woe to them! They have taken the way of Cain; they have rushed for profit into Balaam's error; they have been destroyed in Korah's rebellion.

11 Woe oracles are common in the Old Testament prophets, and they are also prominent in the teaching of Jesus, especially Matthew 23 (vv. 13,15,16,23,25,27,29 par.).[65] Jude, following the example of others, gives the reason for the oracle (lit., "For they have taken; cf. Matt 23:13,15,23,25,27,29 par.). The NIV omits the "for" for some reason. Woe is pronounced on the opponents because they fit the type of evil persons in the Old Testament, and the three named are Cain, Balaam, and Korah. All three verbs are in the aorist tense, and yet the verbs do not denote past time in this context. Perhaps the aorists denote timeless action, signifying that each example functions as a type. In the last instance the aorist "have been destroyed" *(apōlonto)* seems to function as a prophetic aorist, communicating the certainty of the future destruction of the opponents. Jude naturally began with Cain since his sin is found in the earliest part of the Scriptures (Genesis 4), saying that the intruders "have taken the way of Cain."[66] Cain's sin, of course, was murder (Gen 4:8; 1 John 3:12). Jude was scarcely suggesting that the opponents were actually murdering others. Nor is it any more convincing to conclude that the adversaries were like Cain in the sense that they murdered the souls of others.[67] Even more speculative is Reicke's suggestion that the antinomian behavior of the opponents precipitated persecution that resulted in the martyrdom of believers.[68] Instead, Cain was naturally chosen in that he is an example of a person who chose wickedness over goodness. When God confronted him about his evil sacrifice (Gen 4:6–8), Cain grew angry and killed his brother instead of repenting. Cain became, therefore, an example of sin and envy in subsequent literature (1 John 3:12; *1 Clem.* 4:7; *T. Benj.* 7:5). Philo portrayed him as a man enslaved to self-love (*That the Worse Attacks the Better* 32, 78). In the Targums *Pseudo-Jonathan* and *Neofiti,* Cain said, "There is no Judgment, there is no Judge, there is no other world, there is no gift of good reward for the just and no punishment for the wicked."[69] Bauckham infers from this tradition that Cain is repre-

[65] See D. E. Garland, *The Intention of Matthew 23* (Leiden: Brill, 1979).

[66] Vögtle says that the verb ἐπορεύθησαν signifies the way of death (*Judasbrief, 2 Petrusbrief,* 66). The dative here may designate a locative of sphere. Cf. Moule, *Idiom Book,* 47.

[67] So Bigg, *Peter and Jude,* 332.

[68] Reicke, *James, Peter, and Jude,* 205–6.

[69] Translated by G. Vermes, "The Targumic Versions of Genesis 4:3–16" in *Post-Biblical Jewish Studies*, SJLA 8 (Leiden: Brill, 1975), 97–99.

sented by Jude as a heretic and a false teacher.[70] Such a conclusion overreads the evidence. It is unclear that Jude portrayed Cain as a false teacher, nor can it be established with certainty that Jude drew on this targumic tradition. The words about Cain should be construed more generally. The opponents had followed in Cain's way, the path of evil.[71]

The second of the three bad examples is Balaam.[72] The NIV understands Balaam's motive to be greed: "They have rushed for profit into Balaam's error." Interpreting the Old Testament account about Balaam is not easy. Some even believe that he is portrayed as a good character in Numbers 22–24 and then is criticized elsewhere in the Old Testament. Such a reading should be rejected because there are clues that point to Balaam's greed in Numbers 22–24. Furthermore, such an interpretation fails to read Numbers and the rest of the Old Testament as a canonical unity. The careful reader must explain why Balaam's donkey protected Balaam from death and rebuked him (Num 22:21–35). The narrator suggests that Balaam's intentions in going were impure, that he desired financial reward (Num 21:15–20). The point of the story is that the Lord sovereignly spoke through Balaam to bless Israel, even though the prophet desired to curse God's people (cf. Deut 23:4–5; Josh 24:9–10; Neh 13:2; cf. Josephus, *Ant.* 4.118–22; Philo, *On the Life of Moses* 1.277, 281, 283, 286; *On the Migration of Abraham* 114). The account in Numbers testifies to Balaam's true character since he was slain fighting against Israel (Num 31:8), and the sexual sin at Baal Peor in which the Midianites snared Israel is attributed to Balaam's advice (Num 31:16; cf. Rev 2:14; Josephus, *Ant.* 4.129–30; Philo, *On the Life of Moses* 1.295–300). This advice of Balaam's is portrayed as follows in *Pseudo-Philo,* "Pick out the beautiful women who are among us and in Midian, and station them naked and adorned with gold and precious stones before them. And when they see them and lie with them, they will sin against their Lord and fall into your hands" (*Bib. Ant.* 18.13).[73]

Jude saw a parallel between Balaam and the opponents, for like Balaam "they poured themselves out" ("have rushed," NIV) for the sake of money. The parallel with Balaam suggests that the opponents were false teachers, probably wandering prophets who spoke to make money.[74] The error of

[70] Bauckham, *Jude, 2 Peter,* 79–80; cf. Charles, "The Use of the Old Testament in Jude," 116.

[71] G. H. Boobyer understands all three aorists verbs to refer to death, so that Jude was saying that the opponents had gone to death in the way of Cain ("The Verbs in Jude 11," *NTS* 5 [1958–59]: 45–47). The interpretation is unconvincing, for the expression more naturally refers to the intruders copying Cain's sin (rightly Kelly, *Peter and Jude,* 269; Bauckham, *Jude, 2 Peter,* 80–81).

[72] For a survey of Jewish tradition on Balaam, see G. Vermes, *Scripture and Tradition in Judaism: Haggadic Studies,* SPB 4 (Leiden: Brill, 1961), 127–77.

[73] *OTP,* 2:326.

[74] On Balaam as a false prophet, see Heiligenthal, *Zwischen Henoch und Paulus,* 51, 61.

Balaam relates to his teaching. The active sense is nicely captured by Louw and Nida, "They gave themselves completely to the kind of deception that Balaam practiced for the sake of money."[75] In their teaching the opponents propagated error in order to make money, and yet at the same time they were deceived enough to believe their own error. Some have said that the error the teachers "rushed" into was sexual sin, but it does not make sense to say that they committed sexual sin for the sake of money.[76] It probably is the case, however, that their teaching included the idea of sexual license.

The last type hearkens back to Korah and his rebellion in the Old Testament (Numbers 16; cf. Ps 106:16–18; *Sir* 45:18–19; cf. *1 Clem.* 51:1–4). Once again we have a hint that the opponents were leaders since Korah had a priestly position but resented the authority of Moses and Aaron over him. Bauckham thinks the intruders were antinomians and spoke against the Mosaic law.[77] And yet no controversy over the Mosaic law is hinted at in the letter, and the word "rebellion" *(antilogia)* suggests instead opposition to leaders in the church.[78] The rebelliousness of the teachers against authority is mentioned elsewhere in the letter (vv. 4,8,12). Korah is listed last instead of in canonical order,[79] probably to emphasize the judgment in store for the opponents. Just as Korah and his followers were swallowed up suddenly by the earth, so too the false teachers will perish in a severe judgment. This fits with the observation that the three verbs in the verse progress in gravity ("go," "abandon," and "perish," NRSV) and climax with the verb "perish" *(apollymi)*.[80] We should note the connection to v. 5, where Israel in the wilderness was also "destroyed" *(apollymi)* because of failure to believe.

(2) Application to Adversaries (12–13)

[12]These men are blemishes at your love feasts, eating with you without the slightest qualm—shepherds who feed only themselves. They are clouds without rain, blown along by the wind; autumn trees, without fruit and uprooted—twice

[75] Louw and Nida, *Greek-English Lexicon of the New Testament,* 41.13. The genitive μισθοῦ is a genitive of price (N. Turner, *A Grammar of New Testament Greek, Volume 3: Syntax* [Edinburgh: T & T Clark, 1964], 238; Moule, *Idiom Book,* 47). Hillyer thinks it is a genitive of quality (*1 and 2 Peter, Jude,* 253).

[76] Against Bigg, *Peter and Jude,* 332.

[77] Bauckham, *Jude, 2 Peter,* 83–84.

[78] So Bigg, *Peter and Jude,* 332–33; Kelly, *Peter and Jude,* 268; Green, *2 Peter and Jude,* 173; Reicke, *James, Peter, and Jude,* 206. Though, contrary to Reicke, no evidence of rebellion against legal authorities is mentioned. Moo thinks we should not be overly specific, seeing a reference to the "rebellious, antinomian attitude" of the teachers (*2 Peter, Jude,* 258).

[79] Perhaps the dative is causal here. Cf. Moule, *Idiom Book,* 47.

[80] Rightly Charles, "The Use of the Old Testament in Jude," 110; against Boobyer, "The Verbs in Jude 11," 45–47. See n. 71 for the problem with Boobyer's interpretation.

dead. [13]They are wild waves of the sea, foaming up their shame; wandering stars, for whom blackest darkness has been reserved forever.

12 Jude proceeds to apply the woe oracle to the adversaries with the typical "these" *(houtoi),* warning his readers about three dangers in the lives of the opponents.[81] First, these people were "hidden reefs" (NASB) at love feasts. The NIV translates the word as "blemishes" instead of "hidden reefs." "Blemishes" is a possible translation. In that case the word *spilades* is related to the word *spilos,* which means "stain" or "spot," and some commentators think this view is correct.[82] The parallel text in 2 Pet 2:13 clearly refers to the opponents as stains or blemishes. Nevertheless, a different term is used here in Jude, *spilas* instead of *spilos,* and this word is commonly used in Greek literature for rocks; only in later literature does it mean "stains."[83] Since the word means "rocks" here, the idea is that the false teachers were like hidden reefs concealed from ships trying to make safe harbor.[84] Jude said they were "hidden reefs" in your "love feasts" *(agapais).*[85] During love feasts the early Christians shared a meal together that probably was consummated by the celebration of the Lord's Supper (1 Cor 11:17–34; Acts 2:42,46; cf. Ign. *Smyrn.* 8:2). Such feasts were a powerful symbol of the love that flowed among believers. Jude warned his readers that all was not what it seemed. Some of those in the love feasts were dangerous hypocrites, pretending to be full of love but hiding their dangerous teaching and lifestyle that threatened the church.

Second, in such feasts they were "eating with you without the slightest qualm." An alternate translation of *aphobōs* is "shamelessly."[86] They felt no

---

[81] Osburn maintains that Jude's metaphors in vv. 12–13 find their framework in *1 Enoch* 80:2–8 and 67:5–7 ("Jude 12–13," 296–303). Contrary to Osburn, however, it is unclear that the metaphors derive from *1 Enoch.* The alleged parallels do not share the exact wording, nor are they even remarkably similar in wording.

[82] Bigg, *Peter and Jude,* 333–34; Neyrey, *2 Peter, Jude,* 74–75; Paulsen, *Petrusbrief und Judasbrief,* 71.

[83] Cf. Mayor, *Jude and Second Peter,* 40–41; Kelly, *Peter and Jude,* 270; Bauckham, *Jude, 2 Peter,* 85–86.

[84] The word σπιλάδες is feminine and is in apposition to the participle οἱ συνευωχούμενοι (so Bauckham, *Jude, 2 Peter,* 77, 86). A. D. Knox argues that the term here means a dirty or foul wind, but this makes little sense in context ("Σπιλάδες," *JTS* 14 [1913]: 547–49).

[85] An interesting textual variant is ἀπάταις, but the variant represents assimilation from 2 Pet 2:13 and is clearly inferior. W. Whallon suggests the emendation οὗτοι εἰσιν αἱ ἐν τοῖς ἀχάταις ὑμῶν σπιλάδες, translated "these are the spots in your agates" ("Should We Keep, Omit or Alter the οἱ in Jude 12?" *NTS* 34 [1988]: 156–69). There is really no reason to accept the emendation since, contra Whallon, the text makes sense as it stands. Cf. the discussion in Landon, *A Text-Critical Study of the Epistle of Jude,* 103–7.

[86] Bigg and Kelly link ἀφόβως with ποιμαίνοντες instead of συνευωχούμενοι (Bigg, *Peter and Jude,* 335; Kelly, *Peter and Jude,* 271). The word ἀφόβως is closer to συνευωχούμενοι than to ποιμαίνοντες. A decision is difficult, but I incline to the reading in the NIV; so also Bauckham, *Jude, 2 Peter,* 86.

pang of conscience in participating in such meals, even though their lives were not characterized by love. Bigg thinks they excluded others from their part of the table or even had separate love feasts.[87] This is not the most natural way to read the Greek since *syneuōchoumenoi* means "eating together with," not eating in a separate venue.

Third, the opponents were "shepherds who feed only themselves." The words here reflect Ezek 34:2: "Woe to the shepherds of Israel who only take care of themselves! Should not shepherds take care of the flock?" Or, as Ezek 34:8 says, "My shepherds did not search for my flock but cared for themselves rather than for my flock." The reference to shepherds indicates that the opponents were leaders, claiming that they had the ability to guide and lead God's people.[88] But they had no concern for anyone but themselves. They did not exert effort and care for the flock but instead used their positions of leadership to establish a comfortable life for themselves.

The section concludes with four illustrations from the natural world.[89] The illustrations draw from every area in the natural world: clouds in the sky, trees on land, waves in the water, and stars in the upper atmosphere.[90] Jude began with an illustration from the atmosphere. The intruders were "clouds without rain, blown along by the wind." Palestine is a dry climate, tremendously dependent upon rains at crucial times to sustain life. When rain is desperately needed and thick clouds appear, the anticipation of and hope for rain climaxes. If no rain falls, bitter disappointment ensues. The opponents were like such clouds. They promised much but delivered little. Jude may have been alluding to the proverb, "Like clouds and wind without rain is a man who boasts of gifts he does not give" (Prov 25:14).[91] We probably should not read any significance into the idea that the adversaries were driven by the wind, as if the wind symbolizes the devil or others who influence the opponents. The idea is that the opponents were like clouds that hover overhead with the prospect of rain and then are blown away without providing water. So too the false teachers promised to slake the thirst of those who heard them but left them parched.

---

[87] Bigg, *Peter and Jude,* 334.

[88] So Bauckham, *Relatives of Jesus,* 190.

[89] The order of the universe in terms of the heavens, the earth, and the waters is also reflected in *1 Enoch* 2:1–5:4 and 80:2–7 (cf. Bauckham, *Relatives of Jesus,* 196–97).

[90] Ibid., 191.

[91] Jude's allusion must depend on a tradition rooted in the MT of Prov 25:14, for the LXX does not follow the MT here. Bauckham points out that Jude is also closer to the MT than the LXX in his allusions to both Ezek 34:2 (Jude 12) and to Isa 57:20 (Jude 13). Furthermore, Bauckham argues that Jude nowhere reflects the language of the LXX, suggesting, perhaps, that he was more familiar with the MT than the LXX (see *Relatives of Jesus,* 136–37). It must be admitted that the LXX is quite close to the MT in Ezek 34:2, and hence a conclusion cannot be clearly drawn in this instance.

The second illustration hails from the realm of agriculture. The intruders were also "autumn trees" that did not bear fruit. The word "autumn" *(phthinopōrina)* does not suggest that the tree previously had fruit that had already been picked since it was late autumn. Rather, it was late autumn and the tree still had not borne any fruit.[92] Some trees may bear their fruit late, but the time for waiting had passed, and now the hope for any fruit was extinguished. In saying that they were "twice dead" Jude may have meant that they were dead before their so-called conversion and had died again by virtue of their apostasy.[93] Or he may have been referring to their second death, in which they will die eternally.[94] I would suggest, however, that the expression is emphatic, a way of saying they were "totally dead." In the original "uprooted" follows "twice dead." Jude may have been saying, then, that they were dead in that they bore no fruit, and they were also dead because they had been pulled up from the ground. No one, of course, expects fruit from uprooted trees. Jude mixed different metaphors to convey the spiritual poverty of the intruders.

13 In the previous example Jude argued that the opponents lacked any good fruits. Here he used an illustration from the sea to depict the opponents. When he said the opponents were "wild waves . . . foaming up their shame," he focused on their evil works. Not only did they lack good works, but they specialized in evil ones. What they did is likened to the grimy foam that coats a beach, leaving a sticky residue of shame behind. Once again the Old Testament probably was in Jude's mind, "The wicked are like the tossing sea, which cannot rest, whose waves cast up mire and mud" (Isa 57:20).[95]

The last illustration comes from the realm of space, where the planets reside. The NIV translates "wandering stars," which is certainly possible, but it is even more likely that wandering planets are intended. To those living in New Testament times the planets strayed off course, not following an ordered course in the heavens. Hence, they were unreliable to guide people.[96] The opponents were likened to such in that they had wandered

---

[92] See Kelly's discussion (*Peter and Jude,* 272).

[93] Bigg, *Peter and Jude,* 335; Reicke, *James, Peter, and Jude,* 208. Hillyer thinks they were twice dead because the farmer destroyed them for not bearing fruit (*1 and 2 Peter, Jude,* 255).

[94] So Kelly, *Peter and Jude,* 273; Bauckham, *Jude, 2 Peter,* 88; Moo, *2 Peter, Jude,* 260. Vögtle says that the first death is moral and spiritual and that it leads to the second death (*Judasbrief, 2 Petrusbrief,* 68).

[95] Completely improbable is the suggestion of J. P. Oleson that we have an allusion to the birth of Aphrodite, who emerged from the foam of the sea ("An Echo of Hesiod's *Theogony* vv. 190–92 in Jude 13," *NTS* 25 [1979]: 492–503). The only connection with Jude is the use of the word "foam" (ἀφρός), which hardly inspires confidence in the proposed theory. Furthermore, Jude was inclined to use Jewish apocalyptic sources, not pagan myths (so Osburn, "Jude 12–13," 298–99, 301).

[96] So Bauckham, *Relatives of Jesus,* 191.

(planētai) from the straight way to the way of evil. A verbal connection to the "error" *(planē)* of Balaam is suggested here. Jude concluded vv. 12–13 with a promise of judgment. God has reserved the gloomy darkness for those who live in an evil manner (cf. 2 Pet 2:17). They will not experience the light of day but the darkness of God's wrath. We should note the parallel to v. 6, where the gloomy darkness is also the fate of evil angels *(zophon tetērēken* in v. 6 and *zophos . . . tetērētai* in v. 13).[97] Often the future judgment focuses on the fire reserved for the disobedient, though the theme of darkness is also common (Matt 8:12; 22:13; 25:30; cf. Tob. 14:10; *1 Enoch* 46:6; 63:6; *Pss. Sol.* 14:9; 15:10). Both themes together indicate that fire and darkness are metaphors of the future judgment since fire and darkness can hardly coexist. The future punishment of the wicked is not described literally, but the images indicate that it will be horrible.

3. Enoch's Prophecy (14–16)

Jude returned to a theme introduced in v. 4, namely, that the judgment of the false teachers was prescripted by God. The prophecy of Enoch demonstrates that the opponents were destined for judgment from the beginning. They had no hope of ultimately triumphing. The content of the prophecy comprises vv. 14–15. Enoch predicted long ago that the Lord would come and judge all those who lived ungodly lives. Their ungodliness reveals itself in both their works and their words. Jude used his characteristic "these" *(houtoi)* in v. 16, explaining that the opponents of his day were the object of Enoch's prophecy. The sins named in v. 16 reveal that they were the ungodly persons anticipated by Enoch.

(1) The Prophecy: Judgment on the Ungodly (14–15)

[14]Enoch, the seventh from Adam, prophesied about these men: "See, the Lord is coming with thousands upon thousands of his holy ones [15]to judge everyone, and to convict all the ungodly of all the ungodly acts they have done in the ungodly way, and of all the harsh words ungodly sinners have spoken against him."

14 The surprising element to most readers is not the content of the prophecy but its source. *First Enoch* is not considered to be canonical Scripture by any religious group, whether we think of Judaism, Roman Catholicism, the Greek or Russian Orthodox, or Protestantism.[98] It seems puzzling that Jude would cite

---

[97] So also ibid., 208.

[98] The venerable Bede rejects *1 Enoch* as canonical because it is a pseudepigraph and contains teachings that are contrary to apostolic doctrine (in *James, 1–2 Peter, 1–3 John, Jude,* ACCS [Downers Grove: InterVarsity, 2000], 255).

1 Enoch, for the quotation suggests to some that Jude believed *1 Enoch* was part of inspired Scripture and an inspired book.[99] Some church fathers concluded from this that *1 Enoch* itself was inspired (Clement of Alexandria, *Eccl. Proph.* 3; Tertullian, *De cultu fem.* 1:3), though this judgment never became persuasive to the church at large.[100] Others in the history of the church drew the same conclusion but then reasoned that Jude itself could not be part of the canon (cf. Jerome, *De vir ill.* 4). It was thought that any writing that considered *1 Enoch* to be canonical Scripture could not itself be canonical. Some have defended Jude's citation by saying that Jude cited an oral tradition from the original Enoch and that this tradition found its way into the pseudepigraphical book.[101]

The issue is not an easy one, but the following observations may be useful. Taking the last view first, it is difficult to see how Jude could have been citing an actual oral tradition from the historical Enoch since the book of Enoch was in circulation in Jude's day and was well known in Jewish circles. Jude almost certainly derived the citation from the book of *1 Enoch,* and the latter is clearly pseudepigraphical. We would be faced with having to say that Jude knew that *this specific quotation* from *1 Enoch* derived from the historical Enoch.[102] It is better to conclude that Jude quoted the pseudepigraphical *1 Enoch* and that he also believed that the portion he quoted represented God's truth. Jude's wording does not demand that he thought we have an authentic oracle from the historical Enoch.

We do not need to conclude, however, that the entire book is part of the canon of Scripture (rightly Augustine, *City of God* 15.23). Jude probably cited a part of *1 Enoch* that he considered to be a genuine prophecy.[103] Perhaps he referred to Enoch because the adversaries treasured the work, and thereby he used their own ammunition against them.[104] Vögtle suggests that the opponents rejected Christian tradition about Christ's coming and

---

[99] So Reicke, *James, Peter, and Jude,* 209; Müller, "Der Judasbrief," 280. Kelly says the revelations given to Enoch were thought to be inspired by Jude (*Peter and Jude,* 278).

[100] Some argue that the author of *Epistle of Barnabas* cites *1 Enoch* as Scripture (cf. *Barn.* 16:5 and *1 Enoch* 89:56–66). It is unclear, however, that *1 Enoch* is genuinely being cited here.

[101] E.g., G. Archer, *Encyclopedia of Bible Difficulties* (Grand Rapids: Zondervan, 1982), 430. This view is clearly mistaken (rightly Vögtle, *Judasbrief, 2 Petrusbrief,* 85; Schelke, *Der Petrusbriefe—Der Judasbrief,* 164). But contra Schelke, I think it is doubtful that Jude believed the prophecy was from the historical Enoch.

[102] Rightly Guthrie, *New Testament Introduction,* 915.

[103] For a view in harmony with mine see Moo, *2 Peter, Jude,* 271–74; Guthrie, *New Testament Introduction,* 914–16. W. M. Dunnett says, "Jude clearly accepted it [*1 Enoch* 1:9] as an inspired, apparently historical, and true utterance, without necessarily placing approval on the entire content of the Book of Enoch" ("The Hermeneutics of Jude and 2 Peter: The Use of Ancient Jewish Traditions," *JETS* 31 [1988]: 289). See also the next note.

[104] Charles, "The Use of the Old Testament in Jude," 112. See also his insightful comments on pp. 119–20, n. 4. Charles remarks that Jude may also have cited *1 Enoch* because it was valuable to his readers.

hence Jude cited the prophecy from Enoch.[105] Indeed, the content of the prophecy is not remarkable, assuring the readers that the Lord will truly judge the ungodly. Citing a quotation from another source does not indicate that the entire work is inspired, even if the saying drawn upon is true. For instance, Paul quoted Aratus (*Phaenomena* 5) in Acts 17:28, and he surely did not intend to teach that the entire work was inspired Scripture. Similarly, he quoted Epimenides in Titus 1:12, without any notion that he accepted the truth of the whole work. Some might think the citation here is different because Jude said Enoch "prophesied" *(proephēteusen)*. The verb "prophesy" *(propheteuō)* sometimes is used to designate canonical Scripture (Matt 15:7; 1 Pet 1:10). But the verb also is used to say that a certain utterance or saying is from God. For example, Caiaphas prophesied regarding the fate of Jesus even though he was an unbeliever (John 11:51). Zechariah prophesied when the Spirit filled him at the Baptist's birth (Luke 1:67). Women prophesied when the believing church gathered as well (1 Cor 11:4–5; cf. Acts 19:6; Rev 11:3). A prophecy may derive from God and still not be a part of canonical Scripture. We cannot necessarily draw the conclusion from the words "Enoch prophesied" that the work was considered to be Scripture. It would have been more telling if Jude had used the phrase "it is written" with reference to *1 Enoch*. Jude simply drew from a part of the work that he considered true. Bauckham rightly says, "It need not imply that he regarded the book as canonical Scripture. At Qumran, for example, the Enoch literature and other apocryphal works were evidently valued without being included in the canon of Scripture."[106]

The word *kai*, "also" (omitted by the NIV), could connect to either "prophesied" or "these men." If the latter, Jude said that Enoch prophesied to his own generation and also to those of Jude's day. More likely, however, the conjunction attaches to the verb, and in that case the NIV's omission is insignificant exegetically. The term *toutois* could be rendered "to these," but the dative probably is a dative of reference, so that it means "with reference to these," or as the NIV renders it "about these men."[107]

When Jude said that Enoch was "the seventh from Adam," he counted inclusively and began with Adam: Adam, Seth, Enosh, Kenan, Mahalalel, Jared, Enoch. Perhaps the number "seven" also is symbolic, designating completion and perfection. Does this indicate that Jude believed the quota-

---

[105] Vögtle, *Judasbrief, 2 Petrusbrief,* 84.

[106] Bauckham, *Jude, 2 Peter,* 96. See his more detailed and nuanced discussion in *Relatives of Jesus,* 225–33.

[107] For the former interpretation see Mayor, *Jude and Second Peter,* 44; Bigg, *Peter and Jude,* 336. For the latter, Turner, *Syntax,* 238; Moule, *Idiom Book,* 47; Reicke, *James, Peter, and Jude,* 208; Kelly, *Peter and Jude,* 275; Bauckham, *Jude, 2 Peter,* 93; Neyrey, *2 Peter, Jude,* 77.

tion came from the historical Enoch?[108] Such a conclusion is possible but seems unlikely. That Enoch was the seventh from Adam is stated explicitly only in the book of *1 Enoch* (60:8; 93:3; cf. *Jub.* 7:39).[109] It had to be widely known that the book itself was not written by the historical Enoch. Perhaps Jude designated the book he cited by calling Enoch the seventh from Adam. The historical Enoch was very interesting to Jews during the second temple period, since he did not die but was translated into God's presence (Gen 5:23–24). Hebrews confirms that this text was interpreted as saying that Enoch did not die (Heb 11:5; cf. *Sir* 44:16; 49:14). Jewish writers concluded from this that heavenly secrets were conveyed to Enoch, and it is not surprising that he is an agent of revelation in Jewish literature.

Scholars have attempted to discern the text Jude used in his citation of *1 Enoch*, and it is clear that he quoted from *1 Enoch* 1:9. For this verse we have the original Aramaic and a Greek, Ethiopic, and Latin version. Bauckham carefully compares Jude's citation with the texts we have.[110] Some believe that Jude cited the Greek version from memory.[111] Dehandschutter suggests that Jude used "a third form of the Greek text of Enoch."[112] Others think Jude was aware of the Greek version but supplied his own translation from the Aramaic.[113] Certainty on this matter eludes us. English readers can compare and contrast the differences by noting Isaac's translation of *1 Enoch* 1:9: "Behold, he will arrive with ten million of the holy ones in order to execute judgment upon all. He will destroy the wicked ones and censure all flesh on account of everything that they have done, that which the sinners and wicked ones committed against him."[114] The most interesting divergence in Jude's quotation is the insertion of *kyrios* ("Lord"). The term "Lord" is not in any of the other versions, representing Jude's Christo-

---

[108] Bauckham answers in the affirmative, arguing that Jude drew a link between Enoch's prophecy in the seventh generation at the beginning of history and the apostles' prophecies near the end of history (*Relatives of Jesus,* 225).

[109] Cf. Charles, "Jude's Use of Pseudepigraphical Source-Material," 143; C. D. Osburn, "The Christological Use of I Enoch i.9 in Jude 14, 15," *NTS* 23 (1976–77): 335; Guthrie, *New Testament Introduction,* 915.

[110] Bauckham, *Jude, 2 Peter,* 96–97.

[111] Kelly, *Peter and Jude,* 275.

[112] B. Dehandschutter, "Pseudo-Cyprian, Jude and Enoch: Some Notes on 1 Enoch 1:9," in *Tradition and Re-interpretation in Jewish and Early Christian Literature: Essays in Honour of Jürgen H. Lebram,* SPB 36 (Leiden: Brill, 1986), 114–20. See the discussion in Vögtle, *Judasbrief, 2 Petrusbrief,* 72–76.

[113] Osburn, "Christological Use of Enoch in Jude," 334–41; R. J. Bauckham, "A Note on a Problem in the Greek Version of I Enoch i.9," *JTS* 32 (1981): 136–38; id., *Jude, 2 Peter,* 97. Contra Dehandschutter, "Pseudo-Cyprian, Jude and Enoch," 117–19.

[114] *OTP* 1.13–14

logical interpretation of the judgment.[115] In applying a text that referred to God's judgment to Christ, Jude followed the precedent of other New Testament writers (cf. 1 Thess 3:13; 2 Thess 1:7; Rev 19:13,15; 22:12). The verb *ēlthen* is aorist but is rightly translated by the NIV as a future ("is coming") and is equivalent to a "prophetic perfect."[116] Jude spoke here of the second coming of Christ.[117] The "holy ones" with whom he will come are his angels.[118] The coming of Christ is patterned after God's theophany on Sinai, where he "came with myriads of holy ones" (Deut 33:2).[119] Zechariah looked forward to the day when "the LORD my God will come, and all the holy ones with him" (Zech 14:5). That angels will accompany Jesus at his coming is clearly taught in the New Testament as well (Matt 16:27; 25:31; Mark 8:38; Luke 9:26; 1 Thess 3:13; 2 Thess 1:7). The attendance of the angels at his coming indicates the event will be stunning and majestic.

15 The purpose of the Lord's coming is explained in this verse. He is coming to judge those who have opposed him and to reprove them ("convict," NIV) publicly. The "everyone" *(pantōn)* who will be judged refers only to unbelievers here.[120] Jude emphasized thereby that no unbelieving person would escape the judgment. He will "convict all the ungodly" *(pasan psychēn)*. Another connection to v. 4 exists in that the judgment is due to the "ungodliness" of the opponents. Indeed, Jude used three different terms from the "ungodly" word group in this verse. The false teachers are best described as ungodly. They lived their lives in disregard of God, as if he were not the sovereign and mighty God who deserves praise and honor and thanksgiving.

The judgment is specifically attributed to two matters—the evil works and words of the false teachers. We should note that the judgment includes "all the ungodly acts they have done." No evil action is exempted; nothing

[115] Osburn, "Christological Use of Enoch in Jude," 337; M. Black, "The Maranatha Invocation and Jude 14, 15 (I Enoch 1:9)," in *Christ and Spirit in the New Testament: Studies in Honour of Charles Francis Digby Moule* (Cambridge: University Press, 1973), 194.

[116] S. E. Porter, *Idioms of the Greek New Testament,* 2d ed. (Sheffield: JSOT Press, 1994), 37; Bauckham, *Jude, 2 Peter,* 93–94; Black, "Maranatha," 194; Osburn, "Christological Use of Enoch in Jude," 336. J. T. Reed and R. A. Reese argue that the aorist is not akin to a prophetic perfect. The aorist "is part of the background material. It provides an example or illustration rather than a direct statement about the subject" ("Verbal Aspect, Discourse Prominence, and the Letter of Jude," *FNT* 9 [1996]: 195).

[117] The reference is not to God here (contra Fuchs and Reymond, who say it may possibly refer to God or Christ; *2 Pierre, Jude,* 176).

[118] The word ἐν here means "with" (ibid., 176; Mayor, *Jude and Second Peter,* xxxviii).

[119] So Charles, "The Use of the Old Testament in Jude," 111–12; cf. Bauckham, *Relatives of Jesus*, 288. For the OT antecedents to Enoch's prophesy, see J. Vander Kam, "The Theophany of Enoch 1:3b–7, 9," *VT* 33 (1973): 129–50; Bauckham notes that the day of the Lord texts that predicted a theophany of Yahweh are now related to the coming of Christ and that applying such to Jesus Christ is rooted in early Palestinian Christianity (*Relatives of Jesus,* 288–302).

[120] Rightly Vögtle, *Judasbrief, 2 Petrusbrief,* 78.

wicked is erased from God's database. It is the ungodliness of the actions that is featured. Those who have rejected God demonstrate such by the way they live. Second, the judgment also is executed because of the "harsh words" of the ungodly. Once again the text emphasizes that every harsh word will be judged. And their harsh words stem from rebellion against God because they are "spoken against him." Some parallels to *1 Enoch* are instructive. Enoch said to the wicked, "You have not done the commandments of the Lord, but you have transgressed and spoken slanderously grave and harsh words with your impure mouths against his greatness" (*1 Enoch* 5:4).[121] The parallel to Jude is quite close in the Greek of *1 Enoch* 5:4, where the expression *sklērous logous* ("harsh words") is used. A similar idea appears in *1 Enoch* 101:3, "You utter bold and hard words *[megala kai sklēra]* against his righteousness."[122] Similarly, judgment is pronounced against "those who speak with their mouth unbecoming words against the Lord and utter hard words concerning his glory" (*1 Enoch* 27:2).[123]

(2) Application to Adversaries (16)

[16]These men are grumblers and faultfinders; they follow their own evil desires; they boast about themselves and flatter others for their own advantage.

16 The "these" *(houtoi)* opening v. 16 indicates that Jude's opponents were those about whom Enoch prophesied. Jude now explained why their judgment was deserved. Verse 15 grounds their judgment on both their ungodly actions and words, while v. 16 emphasizes their ungodly speech. The opponents were like Israel in the wilderness in that they were "grumblers" *(gongystai)* who complained against the Lord (cf. Exod 16:7–9,12; 17:3; Num 11:1; 14:23; 16:41; 17:5,11; Ps 105:25; *Sir* 46:7).[124] The succeeding word "faultfinders" communicates the same truth.[125] The false teachers were not joyous and loving but critical and quick to detect the weaknesses of others. Commentators debate about the object of grumbling. Some perceive complaints against the restrictions of the law.[126] Others think the intruders were Gnostic,[127] detecting grumbling against being imprisoned in a physical body. Kelly, however, is likely correct in saying that their grumblings were finally against God himself.[128] We have no evi-

---

[121] *OTP,* 1.15.

[122] Ibid., 82.

[123] Ibid., 27.

[124] Rightly Fuchs and Reymond, *2 Pierre, Jude,* 177.

[125] The term μεμψίμοιροι is not an adjective modifying γογγυσταὶ but a second noun (so ibid.).

[126] Bauckham, *Jude, 2 Peter,* 98.

[127] Cf. Fuchs and Reymond, *2 Pierre, Jude,* 177.

[128] Rightly Kelly, *Peter and Jude,* 278.

dence for reading the text in a more specific way.

They pursued pleasure by seeking to fulfill their own desires rather than thinking about how they could strengthen others. It is unclear that the "desires" here are sexual. Jude probably used the term in a general sense to describe their sinful passions, including perhaps the ideas of sexual sin and greed.[129] The NIV may be correct in rendering the next phrase "they boast about themselves," though the NRSV "they are bombastic in speech" is preferable. Both translations reveal that the false teachers were arrogant, but their arrogance was not so much in their boasting about themselves as in their rebellion against God himself (cf. vv. 9–10). The Greek expression used here (*lalei hyperonka,* "he speaks arrogant things") is also found in Theodotion's translation of the Septuagint (Dan 11:36), reflecting Antiochus Epiphanes' blasphemy against God (*lalēsei hyperonka,* "he will speak arrogant things"; cf. Dan 7:8,20).[130] Finally, they indulged in flattery for the sake of "advantage." The advantage is almost surely financial (cf. v. 11). They spoke smooth things so that people would reward them with the comforts of this life so that they could pursue their own desires.[131] The word "follow" *(poreuomai)* forms a link to v. 11 and anticipates v. 18.[132] The Greek expression "marveling to the face" *(thamazontes prosōpa)* stems from a Hebrew idiom "lifting up the face" that occurs in the Old Testament (Gen 19:21; Lev 19:15; Deut 10:17; 28:50; 2 Chr 19:7; Job 13:10; Prov 18:5; 24:23; cf. in Greek, Jas 2:1). The expression denotes showing partiality, which is consistently forbidden in the Old Testament. We cannot be sure that the opponents received bribes from those they were teaching (cf. *T. Mos.* 5:5) since the text is not clearly parallel to *Testament of Moses*.[133] We do not know what they said specifically to curry favor with their hearers, although we can imagine they taught what hearers thought was pleasant.

---

[129] So Kelly, *Peter and Jude,* 278; Moo, *2 Peter, Jude,* 271.

[130] Hence, there is no reference to glossolalia, against the suggestion of Sellin, "Die Häretiker des Judasbriefes," 222–23.

[131] Reicke speculates unduly when he says they may have negotiated with rich republican Romans to gain advantage (*James, Peter, and Jude,* 211).

[132] So Bauckham, *Relatives of Jesus,* 208.

[133] So id., *Jude, 2 Peter,* 100.

SECTION OUTLINE

IV. EXHORTATIONS TO BELIEVERS (17–25)
1. Remember the Apostolic Predictions (17–19)
   (1) The Apostolic Word (17–18)
   (2) Application to Adversaries (19)
2. Keep Yourselves in God's Love (20–21)
3. Show Mercy to Those Affected by Opponents (22–23)
4. Doxology (24–25)

IV. EXHORTATIONS TO BELIEVERS (17–25)

A new section commences with v. 17, and it is marked in the text with the term *agapētoi* ("beloved"), rendered "dear friends" by the NIV. The same term "beloved" commences the body opening of the letter in v. 3. Bauckham argues that a new section does not begin here since Jude continued to warn his readers about the false teachers.[1] Discerning where new sections begin can be difficult, and Bauckham rightly sees that Jude continued to admonish the church about the opponents. Nevertheless, we probably are justified in seeing a new section here.[2] The emphasis shifts from "these" *(houtoi)* to "you" (*hymeis,* v. 17).[3] The NIV, for the sake of English style, eliminates the "you" in v. 17, but the pronoun is emphatic, suggesting that Jude now turned toward exhortations for his readers. I have already noted that the use of "dear friends" signals the same intention. We should also note that Jude turned from the certain judgment of the opponents—the theme of vv. 5–16—to a reminder to his readers that their intrusion was predicted. Watson identifies this portion of the letter as a *peroratio,* where Jude summarized the main argument of the letter and drove home his conclusion. Jude turned from criticizing the opponents to encouraging and exhorting his readers.

Verses 17–23 should be divided into three subsections, which is not surprising given Jude's penchant for triads. First, Jude summoned the readers to remember the predictions of the apostles (vv. 17–19). The apostles pre-

[1] R. Bauckham, *Jude, 2 Peter* (Waco: Word, 1983), 102–3.

[2] Rightly J. N. D. Kelly, *A Commentary on the Epistles of Peter and Jude,* Thornapple Commentaries (Grand Rapids: Baker, 1981), 281; J. Neyrey, *2 Peter, Jude,* AB (Garden City: Doubleday, 1993), 84–85; D. J. Moo, *2 Peter, Jude,* NIVAC (Grand Rapids: Zondervan, 1997), 280.

[3] The term οὗτοι in v. 19 demonstrates, however, that Jude's exhortation still relates to the opponents.

dicted that scoffers would arrive and that they would be consumed with their own selfish desires. The church therefore should not be surprised at their intrusion into the congregation but should be prepared to fend off the insidious presence of the interlopers. Second, believers should remain in God's love (vv. 20–21). It is insufficient for believers to attack the false teachers. They must take positive steps to continue in the love of God, or their own love for God will slowly wither away. Love for God cannot thrive when believers devote all their attention to the deficiencies of others. They must continue to grow spiritually themselves. Three participles explain how the believers were to remain in God's love. They were to build themselves up in the faith, pray in the Holy Spirit, and wait eagerly for the mercy of the Lord Jesus Christ. Jude did not leave his congregation in suspense about how to keep themselves in God's love. He provided concrete instruction so that they would know how to do so. Third, Jude turned to how believers should treat those who were influenced by the false teachers (vv. 22–23). I see three admonitions in this section. Believers were to extend mercy to those who were wavering under the influence of the opponents and be patient with those struggling with doubts. Those who could be delivered from the intruders were to be snatched out of the fire, rescued from the impending peril. Those who were healthy, however, should keep a close watch on themselves and show mercy with fear. Those who get close to a fire may get burned, and so Jude admonished his readers to balance mercy with fear and caution lest they get caught in a whirlpool that sucks them into the evil perpetrated by the intruders. The three main segments of this section, then, focus on three different audiences. First, the readers should pay attention to the prophecies the apostles made about *the false teachers* (vv. 17–19). Second, the readers must not neglect *their own* spiritual growth but concentrate on how to preserve their own love for God (vv. 20–21). Third, the readers must show mercy *to those affected* by the false teachers, helping as many as possible to escape from imminent danger.

1. Remember the Apostolic Predictions (17–19)

(1) The Apostolic Word (17–18)

17But, dear friends, remember what the apostles of our Lord Jesus Christ foretold. 18They said to you, "In the last times there will be scoffers who will follow their own ungodly desires."

As stated above, a new section commences with the words "dear friends" *(agapētoi)* and the emphatic "you" *(hymeis)* of v. 17. Jude called on his readers to remember the predictions of the apostles, for they anticipated that scoffers would arrive in the last days and that these mockers would pursue their desires for ungodly actions. Jude's preference for the term "these" *(houtoi)* appears in v. 19, and Jude showed, as he did in v. 16 with the prophecy of Enoch, that the prophecy of the apostles was directed against the present opponents. In other words, the end-time prophecy was fulfilled currently, in the very lives of Jude's congregation. Hence, we should not understand the apostolic prophecies to relate to an era far in the future, distant from Jude's own concerns.

17 The term "beloved" signals that believers are specially objects of God's love. The NIV's "dear friends" does not convey adequately the reference to God's love in the term. What the readers must do is "remember" the words that the apostles previously spoke to them. Remembering in the Scriptures does not involve mere mental recollection, as when we remember a person's name that we had temporarily forgotten. Remembering means that one takes to heart the words spoken, so that they are imprinted upon one's life (cf. v. 5). The prophecies Jude referred to are those of the apostles. By apostles he did not refer to missionaries or messengers, though the term can bear that meaning (Rom 16:7; 2 Cor 8:23; Phil 2:25). Rather, Jude had in mind those who served as the foundation of the church (Eph 2:20), the authoritative interpreters and witnesses of the gospel (cf. 1 Cor 15:1–11). In this group belong the twelve, the apostle Paul, and perhaps Barnabas (Acts 14:4) and James, the brother of Jesus (Acts 12:17; 15:13; 21:18; Gal 1:19; 2:9; 1 Cor 15:7). Here Jude's words are closely matched by 2 Pet 3:2. Peter directed attention to those who denied the second coming of Jesus Christ, but Jude's warning is more general. The apostles anticipated mockers who would live to carry out their own desires.

Some scholars maintain that Jude could not have been written by Jude the brother of Jesus since he referred to the apostles, apparently conceiving of them as a collected group that had subsequently passed off the scene.[4] What Jude said about the apostles, however, does not require that the prophecies of all the apostles were collected, nor does it suggest that the apostles had died.[5] Jude merely said that the apostles uttered predictions about false teachers who would arise. These apostolic warnings probably were oral, so a written record of them is unnecessary.[6] And yet we have several texts that indicate

---

[4] E.g., J. B. Mayor, *The Epistle of St. Jude and the Second Epistle of St. Peter* (1907; reprint, Grand Rapids: Baker, 1965), cxlv; Kelly, *Peter and Jude*, 281–82; H. Paulsen, *Der Zweite Petrusbrief und der Judasbrief,* KEK (Göttingen: Vandenhoeck & Ruprecht, 1992), 79.

[5] I. H. Eybers rightly observes, "The reference to the predictions of the disciples of Jesus . . . need not be regarded as an indication that the letter of Jude is of late origin, because in the eyes of the author the *fact* of the prediction . . . was much more important than the lapse of time since the warning was uttered" ("Aspects of the Background of the Letter of Jude," *Neot* 9 [1975]: 115). See also Bauckham, *Jude, 2 Peter,* 103–4.

[6] Rightly Eybers, "Background of the Letter of Jude," 115.

that such warnings were part of the common stock of early Christian preaching. In Acts 20:29–30 Paul said: "I know that after I leave, savage wolves will come in among you and will not spare the flock. Even from your own number men will arise and distort the truth in order to draw away disciples after them." We see from Matthew that the apostles transmitted Jesus' warning about false prophets (Matt 7:15–20). Paul delivered similar cautions in both 1 Tim 4:1–5 and 2 Tim 3:1–5. For Jude to relay such words, then, does not require the death of the apostles, for what he said was part of the common stock of apostolic tradition, probably from the beginning of their ministry.

Nor does the verb "said" (an imperfect *elegon* in Greek, "they were saying") demonstrate that the instructions were from long ago. Bauckham rightly observes that we need to be careful about pressing too far the distinction between the imperfect and the aorist.[7] Moreover, Paul used imperfect verbs to describe his previous instruction of the Thessalonians, even though he had evangelized them in the recent past (cf. 1 Thess 3:4; 2 Thess 2:5; 3:10). This hardly is decisive evidence, then, for a late date for Jude. Indeed, Jude had already described himself as "brother of James" (v. 1), suggesting he was contemporary to the apostles rather than subsequent to them. Nor does this verse clearly separate Jude from the apostles, though he did not claim to be one (v. 1). Peter could use a similar expression to denote the predictions of the apostles (2 Pet 3:2) even though he was an apostle. The exhortation to remember the predictions of the apostles does not, therefore, necessarily exclude Jude from the apostolic office. Still, there is no other evidence that Jude claimed to be an apostle.

18 Indeed, Jude conceived of the apostles' words as directed to his hearers, and not as intended for some far off generation, for he said their admonitions were "said *to you*" (*hymin,* italics mine). The reference to "the last times" does not contradict the fact that the prophecies were directed to Jude's readers. New Testament Christians believed that the last days had dawned with the coming of our Lord Jesus Christ and with his death and resurrection. The author of Hebrews could say, therefore, that "in these last days" God "has spoken to us by his Son" (Heb 1:2; cf. Acts 2:17; 1 Pet 1:20), indicating that the last days had arrived. Similarly, in both 1 Tim 4:1 and 2 Tim 3:1 the entrance of false teachers is located "in later times" and "in the last days" respectively. In both cases Paul understood these predictions to be fulfilled in the false teaching troubling the Ephesian church. A connection is likely drawn here to v. 4, where Jude implied that the arrival and judgment of the intruders was prescripted. We have seen that the Old Testament prophesied such false teachers, and now Jude said that the apostles anticipated their coming as well.

---

[7] Bauckham, *Jude, 2 Peter,* 103.

The content of the prophecy, according to Jude, was rather vague. The apostles predicted that scoffers would arrive and that they would follow their own desires. Jude clearly had the intruders in mind since their mocking was clear in their rejection of God's lordship and their reviling of angelic powers (v. 8). To say that they pursued their own desires repeats almost exactly the indictment of the intruders in v. 16, but Jude added a nuance here. Their desire was to do what was ungodly. The NIV translates *tōn asebeiōn* as a descriptive genitive "ungodly desires." This is certainly a possibility. More likely, however, the term should be construed as an objective genitive, "desires for ungodly actions."[8] Again the word "ungodly" appears, one of Jude's favorite terms for the opponents (vv. 4,15,16).

(2) Application to Adversaries (19)

[19]These are the men who divide you, who follow mere natural instincts and do not have the Spirit.

19 Jude now connected the prophecy of the apostles to his own readers with the term "these" *(houtoi)*. The opponents in the readers' church were predicted by the apostles. Jude was not suggesting that the apostles were only thinking of one particular church. The apostles prophesied that the church in general would experience the entrance of false teachers. Once again we see another triad in Jude's description of the opponents. First, the opponents were those "who divide you." The term *hoi apodiorizontes* could mean that the intruders made distinctions between people. Some they classified as spiritual and some as unspiritual. Kelly sees support for this notion in the very next phrase, where Jude called the intruders "natural" *(psychikoi)*.[9] He thinks Jude turned back on the adversaries the language they themselves used. Such an interpretation fits with a Gnostic view of the opposition since Gnostics were famous for classifying some as spiritual and some as "soulish." Although such an interpretation is possible, it is more likely that Jude indicted the false teachers for causing divisions. The NRSV reflects this interpretation, "It is these worldly people, devoid of the Spirit, who are causing divisions."[10] The divisions are reflected in vv. 22–23.

---

[8] Rightly C. Bigg, *The Epistles of St. Peter and St. Jude,* ICC (Edinburgh: T & T Clark, 1901), 337; B. Reicke, *The Epistles of James, Peter, and Jude,* AB (Garden City; Doubleday, 1964), 218–19. E. Fuchs and P. Reymond point out that the genitive could also be construed as a subjective genitive, but they rightly opt for the objective genitive (*La Deuxième Épître de Saint Pierre, L'Épître de Saint Jude,* CNT [Neuchâtel–Paris: Delachaux & Niestlé, 1980], 181). Mayor supports a subjective genitive (*Jude and Second Peter,* 47).

[9] Kelly, *Peter and Jude,* 284–85; so also Fuchs and Reymond, *2 Pierre, Jude,* 181–82.

[10] So also Bauckham, *Jude, 2 Peter,* 105; C. D. Osburn, "Discourse Analysis and Jewish Apocalyptic in the Epistle of Jude," in *Linguistics and New Testament Interpretation: Essays on Discourse Analysis* (Nashville: Broadman, 1992), 308–9. See also the discussion of A. Vögtle, *Der Judasbrief, der 2 Petrusbrief,* EKKNT (Neukirchen-Vluyn: Neukirchener Verlag, 1994), 90–92.

Some of the congregation was under the influence of the teachers, and Jude had to write the letter (v. 3) under pressure because of their influence. They had wormed themselves into the love feasts (v. 12) and were causing all kinds of problems in the community, just as Balaam acted against Israel and Korah against Moses and Aaron (v. 11).

Second, the opponents "follow mere natural instincts." The NRSV translates the term *psychikoi* as "worldly people." The NIV's "who follow mere natural instincts" is unfortunate here since the emphasis is on who the opponents *were*, not what these people *did*. Hence, the NRSV is more in accord with the Greek in the translation "worldly people." The word *psychikoi* can also be translated "natural ones." Third, what Jude meant by this is best explained by the next phrase; they "do not have the Spirit."[11] To be "natural" means that one does not have the Holy Spirit. We know from Rom 8:9 that the presence of the Spirit is the mark of a Christian. Those who lack the Holy Spirit do not belong to God. Therefore, Jude excluded the opponents from the Christian community. They were "worldly people," not spiritual people, and they were not genuine Christians since they did not have the Holy Spirit. Believers, on the other hand, "pray in the Holy Spirit" (v. 20). Jude's words here remind us of Paul, who said that the "natural person" *(psychikos)* does not welcome the things of the Spirit, precisely because he lacks the Holy Spirit (1 Cor 2:14). Similarly, James said the wisdom of the world is "earthly, unspiritual *[psychikē]*, of the devil" (Jas 3:15). The opponents in Jude fall into the same category. They caused divisions because they did not belong to God at all, because they lacked the Holy Spirit.

The readers should not have been surprised by the intrusion of the opponents. The apostles foresaw that it would happen. Foreseeing their arrival should strengthen the faith of the church since it confirms the truth of the faith that was once and for all given to them (v. 3). No false teaching, no threat from the outside can be considered a genuine threat to the truth since it has all been foreseen and predicted. God never promised that the church would progress in the world without enemies from within. People are apt to think that blessing from God would mean that the people of God exist in a blissful state with no conflict. On the contrary, the apostles foretold that opponents would come, and now they had arrived. They were evident by their words and their works. It should be clear to all, therefore, that they were not part of the people of God. The church should recognize them, reject their teaching, and reach out to those wavering under their influence.

---

[11] Rightly Bauckham, *Jude, 2 Peter,* 106; Neyrey, *2 Peter, Jude,* 89.

2. Keep Yourselves in God's Love (20–21)

[20]But you, dear friends, build yourselves up in your most holy faith and pray in the Holy Spirit. [21]Keep yourselves in God's love as you wait for the mercy of our Lord Jesus Christ to bring you to eternal life.

The exhortation to believers continues in these verses, and a slight change of emphasis is indicated by the same phrase as opened v. 17, "But you, dear friends." Inexplicably the NIV omitted the emphatic "you" *(hymeis)* in v. 17 and retains it here. In both cases the Greek is exactly the same. In this instance Jude did not introduce a major new section but turned from emphasizing the intrusion of the opponents (vv. 17–19) to positive exhortations to believers. Jude recognized that his readers would not continue to be devoted to the faith if they concentrated only on resisting the opponents, as important as that was. The readers must also grow in the Christian faith themselves and keep themselves in the sphere of God's love. Most commentators see four independent commands in these verses. This is reflected in the verbs of the NRSV: "build yourself up," "pray," keep," and "look forward to." The NIV sees the first three imperatives as independent: "build yourselves up," "pray," and "keep." It relates the last verb, however, to the verb "keep" in translating "keep yourselves in God's love *as you wait*" (italics mine). I would argue that we should pay more attention to the specific grammar of the Greek text. Jude used only one imperative, the word "keep" *(tērēsate)* in v. 21. The other three verbs are all participles: building yourselves up *(epoikodomountes),* praying *(proseuchomenoi),* and waiting *(prosdechomenoi).* Each of these participles should be understood as instrumental participles, describing *how* we keep ourselves in God's love.[12] The participles in this case still virtually function as imperatives, but they modify the command to keep yourselves in God's love, setting forth the means by which the readers can do so. If this view is correct, then we have another example of a triad in Jude. He provided three means by which the readers could keep themselves in God's love, (1) by building themselves up in their faith, (2) by praying in the Spirit, and (3) by waiting eagerly for the return of Jesus Christ. Two other features of these verses should be noted. When we think of triads, the implicit Trinitarianism of the text should be observed. Jude referred to praying in *the Holy Spirit,* the love of *God,* presumably the Father, and the mercy of *our Lord, Jesus Christ.* Second, still another triplet emerges, at least conceptually, since Jude referred

[12] So R. Martin, "Jude," in *The Theology of the Letters of James, Peter, and Jude* (Cambridge: Cambridge University Press, 1994), 79–80; Osburn, "Discourse Analysis and Jewish Apocalyptic in the Epistle of Jude," 292; A. J. Bandstra, "Onward Christian Soldiers—Praying in Love, with Mercy: Preaching on the Epistle of Jude," *CTJ* 32 (1997): 138.

to faith, love, and the concept of hope in the return of the Lord.

20 As indicated above, I understand the two participles in this verse "building yourselves up upon" and "praying" (translated as imperatives by the NIV) to modify the imperative "keep" *(tērēsate)* in v. 21. Hence, Jude gave the first two means by which believers could preserve themselves in God's love. The instrumental participles also constituted commands, showing what must be done to remain in God's love. First, believers continue in God's love by building themselves up "in your most holy faith." The words "in your most holy faith" could be construed to say build yourselves up "by means of your most holy faith."[13] Or, conversely, the idea may be build yourselves up "on your most holy faith" (KJV, NASB, RSV, NRSV).[14] The latter interpretation is more likely. Jude used the metaphor of building something on a foundation. The foundation in this instance is "your most holy faith." Believers are to build on the faith's foundation in order to preserve themselves in God's love.

The metaphor of building on the foundation is used elsewhere in the New Testament. Paul said that the only foundation for the church is Jesus Christ, and people must build on that foundation rightly to receive a reward (1 Cor 3:10–15). The foundation upon which the church is built in Eph 2:20 is the apostles and prophets, with Christ Jesus being the cornerstone. Peter described believers as living stones that are being built up into a spiritual house (1 Pet 2:5). What Jude said here does not contradict Paul but represents a fresh use of the metaphor. The "most holy faith" upon which the church is built is the gospel of Jesus Christ, and this faith has Jesus Christ as its center.[15] When Jude spoke of "faith" here, he referred to the body of teachings, the doctrine of the church of Jesus Christ.[16] This fits with v. 3, where believers are exhorted "to contend for the faith that was once for all entrusted to the saints." So the first way believers remain in God's love is by continuing to grow in their understanding of the gospel, the teachings that were handed down to them at their conversion. This faith is "most holy" because it comes from the holy God, and Christian growth occurs through the mind, as believers grow in their understanding of God's word and of Christian truth. Jude did not think that growth occurred mystically or mysteriously. Instead, believers experience God's love as their understand-

---

[13] Apparently Bigg, *Peter and Jude,* 340.

[14] Kelly, *Peter and Jude,* 286; Moo, *2 Peter, Jude,* 284.

[15] Neyrey's suggestion that πίστει should be translated "faithfulness" does not fit the context as well (*2 Peter, Jude,* 90). Rightly Kelly, *Peter and Jude*, 285.

[16] So Paulsen, *Petrusbrief und Judasbrief,* 83; Fuchs and Reymond, *2 Pierre, Jude,* 183. Faith and the Spirit belong together in Jude; see R. Heiligenthal, *Zwischen Henoch und Paulus: Studien zum theologiegeschichtlichen Ort des Judasbriefes,* Texte und Arbeiten zum neutestamenlichen Zeitalter 6 (Tübingen: Francke, 1992), 69.

ing of the faith increases.[17] Affection for God increases not through bypassing the mind but by means of it.

The second means by which believers can remain in God's love is by praying "in the Holy Spirit." Some commentators think this describes speaking in tongues, but this is doubtful.[18] More likely the prayer in the Spirit is the ordinary prayer that should be part of the warp and the woof of the Christian life.[19] A striking parallel is found in Eph 6:18, "And pray in the Spirit on all occasions with all kinds of prayers and requests." The context in Ephesians clarifies that speaking in tongues is not primarily in view. Requests for the furtherance of God's will and resistance to the devil's attack are the focus. Similarly, in Jude the injunction to pray should be understood broadly. Believers cannot keep themselves in God's love without depending on him by petitioning him in prayer. Love for God cannot be sustained without a relationship with him, and such a relationship is nurtured by prayer.

21 The central command of the two verses now appears: "Keep yourselves in God's love" (v. 21). Was Jude exhorting believers to maintain their love *for* God, an objective genitive? Or was he saying that they should keep themselves in the place where they experience God's love for them, a subjective genitive? A decision is difficult. Probably we are faced with a false alternative. Our love for God depends upon his love for us. Hence, the two cannot and should not be rigidly separated.[20] It is interesting to note that in v. 1 believers are said to be "loved and kept by God." There God's love for believers receives the emphasis, the love by which he called us to be his people. What is remarkable is that Jude exhorted believers here to keep themselves in God's love. They must keep themselves in God's love to avoid apostasy, so as not to be corrupted by the opponents. We have already seen that being preserved in God's love will only be a reality if believers continue to grow in their understanding of the Christian faith and if they regularly pray. Ultimately, believers, as I argued in v. 1, are kept by Jesus Christ *(Iēsou Christou tetērēmenois)*. Or, as v. 24 says, God is the one "able to keep *(phylaxai)* you from falling." Those who trust in Christ remain in the faith because of the preserving work of God the Father. Nevertheless,

---

[17] The genitive θεοῦ includes a subjective idea, which fits with mercy coming from Christ in v. 21 (so Fuchs and Reymond, *2 Pierre, Jude,* 184).

[18] Supporting charismatic praying are Bauckham, *Jude, 2 Peter,* 113; J. D. G. Dunn, *Jesus and the Spirit: A Study of the Religious and Charismatic Experience of Jesus and the First Christians as Reflected in the NT* (1975; reprint, Grand Rapids: Eerdmans, 1997), 239–42. Against it is Vögtle, *Judasbrief, 2 Petrusbrief,* 100. Of course, speaking in tongues may be included in the wider idea of praying in the Spirit (so N. Hillyer, *1 and 2 Peter, Jude,* NIBC [Peabody: Hendrickson, 1992], 264).

[19] Cf. Moo, *2 Peter, Jude,* 285.

[20] Kelly suggests both ideas are intended and calls it a "comprehensive genitive" (*Peter and Jude,* 286–87). Vögtle rightly emphasizes that God's love has priority (*Judasbrief, 2 Petrusbrief,* 100).

the promise that God will keep his own does not nullify the responsibility of believers to persevere in the faith. God keeps his own, and yet believers must keep themselves in God's love. Jude represented well the biblical tension between divine sovereignty and human responsibility. On the one hand, believers only avoid apostasy because of the grace of God. On the other hand, the grace of God does not cancel out the need for believers to exert all their energy to remain in God's love.

The third means of remaining in God's love is explicated with the last participle, waiting (*prosdechomenoi*) "for the mercy of our Lord Jesus Christ." The word "waiting" is eschatological, focusing on the coming of the Lord. Joseph of Arimathea awaited God's kingdom (Mark 15:43). Simeon and Anna were waiting for God's redeeming purposes to be fulfilled (Luke 2:25,38). In Titus 2:13 believers are to await the hope of the Lord's return. Since believers are to wait for Christ's mercy, they will receive it at the coming of the Lord. We are reminded that Jude prayed for mercy to be multiplied for his readers in v. 2. The preposition *eis* should be construed as one of result, so "resulting in eternal life" is more precise than the NIV's "to bring you to eternal life," though the difference is not great.[21] Some commentators understand the phrase "resulting in eternal life" to modify "keep yourselves in the love of God."[22] The prepositional phrase, however, is closer to the participle, suggesting that the NIV reading is correct. Jude conceived of eternal life here, then, as something that will be received on the last day, as something that believers will possess at the coming of the Lord.

Referring to Christ's mercy is unusual in the New Testament. Why did Jude speak here of mercy? Probably because he thought of believers as needing mercy (not justice) on the last day when they meet Jesus Christ (cf. Matt 5:7; 2 Tim 1:18).[23] We have an indication here that grace is the basis upon which believers receive eternal life. Jude clearly taught that believers must remain in God's love until the end and avoid apostasy. He did not believe, however, that believers will ever be perfect in this world, and therefore they will need Christ's mercy on the last day. Jude emphasized that believers remain in God's love by waiting for Christ's return. Apparently Christians cannot remain in God's love if they immerse themselves in this world and cease to long for their future perfection before God (vv. 24–25). One of the means by which we continue in our love for God is if we continue to long for the day when Jesus Christ will show us his mercy, when he will grant us the gift of eternal life, and we will be perfected forever. Those who take their eyes off their future hope will find that their love for God is slowly evaporating, and it will be evident that their real love is for the present evil age.

---

[21] Reicke understands the εἰς to denote purpose, which is again close to the notion of result (*James, Peter, and Jude,* 214). Supporting result is Kelly, *Peter and Jude,* 287.

[22] E.g., Bigg, *Peter and Jude,* 340.

[23] Fuchs and Reymond, *2 Pierre, Jude,* 185.

3. Show Mercy to Those Affected by the Opponents (22–23)

[22]Be merciful to those who doubt; [23]snatch others from the fire and save them; to others show mercy, mixed with fear—hating even the clothing stained by corrupted flesh.

Before vv. 22–23 can be interpreted, we must establish the text, and, unfortunately, determining the original text is difficult since the textual tradition has a number of diverse readings. The most striking feature of the textual tradition is that some witnesses divide the text into two clauses, while other witnesses divide it into three.[24] The earliest text, 𝔓^{72}, divides the text into two clauses and can be translated as follows, "Snatch some from the fire, and show mercy to those disputing (or 'doubting') with fear."[25] Vaticanus (B) also splits the text into two groups: "And those to whom you show mercy when they doubt; save them by snatching them from the fire. For others you must have mercy with fear" (cf. NEB). The uncial C inserts the verb "reprove" or "convict" *(elenchete)* instead of "have mercy" *(eleate)* and reads as follows, "Reprove those who are disputing, and save others by snatching them from the fire." The Majority text (see K, L, P, S) also divides the text into two.[26] It is rendered by the NKJV, "And on some have compassion, making a distinction; but others save with fear, pulling them out of the fire" (cf. KJV).

The other noticeable feature here is that the term *diakrinō* ("doubt," "dispute," or "distinguish") is in the Majority text a nominative plural *(diakrinomenoi)* instead of an accusative plural as in all the other witnesses *(diakrinomenous)*. Since it is nominative in the majority text tradition, it must signify the action of those who are showing mercy, and it probably means that one must make distinctions between those who need mercy and those in a more perilous state who must be snatched from the fire. The three-clause text is supported especially by A and ℵ. Codex Alexandrinus (A) can be translated, "Reprove those who are disputing; save others by snatching them from the fire; on others have mercy with fear." The only major difference from Sinaiticus (ℵ) is that the first verb is "reprove" *(elenchete)* rather than "have mercy" *(eleate)*. The text of Sinaiticus is represented by the NIV, "Be merciful to those who

---

[24] Supporting the two classes are Bigg, *Peter and Jude,* 340–42; Kelly, *Peter and Jude,* 288.

[25] This reading is also attested with slight variations by syr^{ph} and Clement^{lat}. Scholars defending this view are J. N. Birdsall, "The Text of Jude in 𝔓^{72}," *JTS* 14 (1963): 394–99; C. D. Osburn, "The Text of Jude 22–23," *ZNW* 63 (1972): 139–44; Bauckham, *Jude, 2 Peter,* 109–10; Neyrey, *2 Peter, Jude,* 85–86; S. C. Winter, "Notes and Observations Jude 22–23: A Note on the Text and Translation," *HTR* 87 (1994): 215–22; D. G. Horrell, *The Epistles of Peter and Jude,* EC (Peterborough: Epworth, 1998), 130–31; C. Landon, *A Text-Critical Study of the Epistle of Jude,* JSNTSup 135 (Sheffield: Academic Press, 1996), 131–34. It should be noted that Osburn now thinks that the three-clause text is authentic ("Discourse Analysis and Jewish Apocalyptic in the Epistle of Jude," 292).

[26] Reicke thinks the Majority text preserves the correct reading (*James, Peter, and Jude,* 215).

doubt; snatch others from the fire and save them; to others show mercy, mixed with fear." The NRSV translates the text even more precisely, "And have mercy on some who are wavering; save others by snatching them out of the fire; and have mercy on still others with fear."

If we begin with smaller matters first, the imperative "have mercy" (*eleate* or *eleeite* in the texts) should be preferred to "reprove" *(elenchete)*. The former is supported by the wider textual tradition, and the latter was likely introduced by scribes to facilitate a progression from severity (reproving) to mercy. The Majority text, as noted, has the nominative "making a distinction" *(diakrinomenoi)* instead of the accusative *diakrinomenous* ("doubting" or "disputing"). But the latter is almost surely original, and the nominative probably was inserted to agree with the other two nominative participles in the text—"snatching" *(harpazontes)* and "hating" *(misountes)*.

Certainty on whether the text should be divided into two or three clauses cannot be attained. I believe, however, that the text as it is translated in the NRSV (and NIV) probably is original.[27] The two-phrase form of the text is more easily accounted for if there was originally a triad rather than vice-versa. Ross argues that the third reading does not fit as "an expansion of any of the shorter ones, and there would have been no motive for complicating an already obscure passage by adding a third clause."[28] Stylistically, however, such a decision fits with Jude's fondness for triads.[29] Some of the errors were likely introduced because it was difficult for scribes to determine the meaning of *diakrinō*. Should it be rendered "doubt" or "dispute," or even as "making a distinction" per the NKJV? Since the verb *diakrinō* occurs in v. 9 and clearly means "dispute," some scribes, in my judgment, thought the meaning of the verb must be the same in both verses. This would also explain the insertion of "reprove" *(elenchete)* since "reproving disputers" makes good sense. I would suggest, however, that in this context *diakrinomenous* means "doubters," and so Jude began by encouraging mercy for those who were doubting and wavering. The tripartite arrangement of the text is also supported by external evidence, especially the Alexandrian family. Metzger probably is correct in

[27] See especially S. Kubo, "Jude 22–23: Two-Division Form or Three?" in *New Testament Textual Criticism: Its Significance for Exegesis: Essays in Honour of Bruce M. Metzger* (Oxford: Clarendon, 1981), 239–53; cf. Vögtle, *Judasbrief, 2 Petrusbrief,* 102–5. Supporting a three-category form of the text is also J. M. Ross, "Church Discipline in Jude 22–23," *ExpTim* 8 (1989): 297–98, but he differs from Kubo in seeing the imperative ἐλέγχετε as original in the third clause rather than ἐλεᾶτε or ἐλεεῖτε. This view can be dismissed, for the textual evidence overwhelmingly supports "have mercy," and the text comes to a suitable climax in such a triad, since Jude concluded with the need for mercy coupled with fear. W. Bieder proposes the emendation ἐᾶτε here ("Judas 22f.: Oὓς δέ ἐᾶτε έν φόβῳ," *TZ* 6 [1950]: 75–77). Such conjectures should only be accepted as a last resort.

[28] Ross, "Jude 22–23," 297.

[29] Ross argues against 𝔓[72], noting that, "If Jude introduced the first category by *hous men,* he would have introduced the second by *hous de,* not by *diakrinomenous de*" ("Jude 22–23," 297).

concluding that Vaticanus (B), although an error was accidentally introduced, actually supports Sinaiticus (א).[30]

Before we examine the two verses more carefully, we should summarize the verses as a whole and their place in the argument. In vv. 17–19 Jude reminded his readers that the apostles predicted the opponents would arrive. Their presence did not constitute a surprise nor, ultimately, a threat to the faith once for all handed down to the saints. Then in vv. 20–21 he gave positive exhortations to believers. They must not think the faith will be preserved simply by attacking the false teachers and revealing their errors. The readers must be attentive to their own relationship with God. They must remain in God's love by growing in their understanding of the faith, by praying fervently in the Holy Spirit, and by waiting eagerly for Jesus to return and to grant them his mercy. We come to the third stage of the argument in vv. 22–23. Verses 17–19 focus on the opponents; and vv. 20–21, on the readers. Now Jude explained to the readers how they should respond to those who had been affected by the false teachers and perhaps even how they should treat the false teachers themselves. The exhortation is threefold. First, those who were wavering under the influence of the false teachers should not be rejected or ignored. By showing mercy to them, as they struggle with doubts, such people could be reclaimed. Second, others were close to being captured by the teaching and behavior of the opponents. Believers must not give up on them. Their lives could still be salvaged, and they could be snatched from the fire that threatened to destroy them. Third, others had already been defiled by the false teachers. Perhaps Jude even spoke here about the false teachers themselves, although this seems less likely. Probably Jude spoke of those who had fallen into the libertinism of the false teachers.[31] Even in this case mercy should still be extended. But the readers should be extremely careful, avoiding the danger of being stained by the sin of these opponents.[32]

22 Jude's preference for threes manifests again as he gave three exhortations to his readers. He began by saying "have mercy on some who are wavering" (NRSV). He likely referred to those in the church whom the false teachers were affecting. The word translated "wavering" (*diakrinomenous,* NRSV) could be rendered "disputing" or "arguing" (cf. Acts 11:2).[33] The parallel in v. 9 suggests to some that "disputing" was in Jude's

---

[30] *TCGNT,* 660–61.

[31] So Osburn, "Discourse Analysis and Jewish Apocalyptic in the Epistle of Jude," 292.

[32] J. S. Allen argues that all three clauses refer to the same group of people and not to three distinct groups ("A New Possibility for the Three-Clause Format of Jude 22–3," *NTS* 44 [1998]: 133–43). Allen's interpretation is unlikely. None of the parallels he lists match the threefold pattern found in Jude 22–23. He admits that the usage for which he argues is rare, and the parallel in Jude 10 is not close enough to warrant the interpretation he proposes for Jude 22–23. Therefore the view that three different groups are addressed should be retained.

[33] Bauckham, *Jude, 2 Peter,* 115.

mind here.[34] Birdsall argues that it means that mercy should be extended to "those who are under judgment."[35] In the middle voice, however, the word most commonly means "doubting" or "wavering" in the New Testament (Matt 21:21; Mark 11:23; Acts 10:20; Rom 4:20; 14:23; Jas 1:6).[36] This interpretation also fits with the progression of the text. Jude began with those who were least affected by the intruders. They were affected to the extent that they were beginning to doubt whether the opponents were correct or whether the faith they received at the inception of their Christian life was normative (v. 3). It is tempting to dismiss those struggling with doubts, to lose patience with them and move on to something else. Jude encouraged those who were strong to show mercy and kindness to those wavering with doubts, to reclaim them with gentleness (cf. 2 Tim 2:25).

23 Others in the church were in even greater danger. They had fallen under the spell of the intruders to a significant extent. Perhaps they had begun to embrace some of the latter's theology and were beginning to live in an antinomian manner. The "fire" here refers to future judgment in hell (cf. v. 7; cf. Matt 3:10,12; 5:22; 2 Thess 1:7; Heb 10:27; Rev 20:14–15). Jude did not say, then, that the opponents were already in the fire. They were to be snatched from the fire that would consume them unless they repented. Jude, as in v. 9, alluded to Zech 3:2 here. Joshua, the high priest, is described as "a burning stick snatched from the fire" (Zech 3:2; cf. Amos 4:11). The context of Zechariah 3 clarifies that he was destined for the fire because of his sin that was illustrated by his filthy garments (Zech 3:3–5).[37] The removal of his filthy clothes and his being endowed with clean ones symbolize the forgiveness of his sins (Zech 3:3–5). God's grace snatched him from the impending fire by cleansing him of his sin. Jude exhorted the readers to play a similar role in the lives of those influenced by the opponents. The NRSV catches the emphasis of the Greek better than the NIV. The readers are to "save others *by snatching* them out of the fire" (italics mine). The main verb is "save," and the participle "snatching" depicts how they are to save those entranced by the opponents. The image suggests that some have nearly been seduced by the false teachers. And yet there is still hope that they can be reclaimed, rescued from the judgment to come and restored to a right relationship with God.

Still another group of people are even more influenced by the false teachers, or perhaps Jude included some of the opponents in this category. Believers should "show mercy" even to those deeply ensnared in sin. They were

---

[34] So Bigg, *Peter and Jude,* 341.

[35] Birdsall, "The Text of Jude," 398.

[36] Rightly Kelly, *Peter and Jude,* 288; Moo, *2 Peter, Jude,* 287; Ross, "Jude 22–23," 297.

[37] The OT background demonstrates that the garment in Jude has nothing to do with the opponents being wandering charismatics (against G. Sellin, "Die Häretiker des Judasbriefes," *ZNW* 77 [1986]: 223–24).

not to despise them or abhor those so defiled by sin. And yet their mercy should be mingled with fear and hatred, knowing that sin had stained and defiled these people in a remarkable way. Some commentators think the fear here refers to the fear of God instead of the fear of contamination.[38] But contamination seems to be more fitting since Jude proceeded to speak of detesting even the garment defiled by the flesh.[39] If one gets too close, even the clothing will defile those attempting to show mercy.[40] Jude used the image of "clothing stained by corrupted flesh," drawing upon Zech 3:3–4, which speaks of the "filthy garments" on Joshua.[41] Joshua's soiled garments portrayed his sin (cf. Zech 3:5),[42]and similarly the tunic defiled by the flesh illustrates the sin of those in Jude's community.[43] The flesh here seems to be close to the Pauline view where it represents the principle of sin.[44] The Hebrew word for "filthy" is the word for excrement (Deut 23:14; 2 Kgs 18:27; Prov 30:12; Isa 36:12; Ezek 4:12), and it may be that Jude drew a connection between such excrement and the stained tunic *(chitōn),* which was the inner garment. Such a picture shocks the readers with how polluting and corrupting sin is. Believers are to beware lest their mercy is transposed into acceptance, and they themselves become defiled by the sin of those they are trying to help. Jude may have been thinking of Jewish purity laws where one would become unclean by coming into contact with something that was unclean. In contrast, believers will be presented before God "without blemish" (NRSV) in the last day, with every stain removed. Perhaps mercy is demonstrated especially through prayer in cases like these. The text constructs a nice balance between showing love and mercy and maintaining standards of purity and righteousness. Showing love for the sinner does not exclude an intense hatred for the corruption brought about by sin. Furthermore, believers need to beware of getting too entangled with some who sin, lest the sinner influence them rather than vice versa.

---

[38] Kelly, *Peter and Jude,* 289; Bauckham, *Jude, 2 Peter,* 116.

[39] So M. Green (*The Second Epistle General of Peter and the General Epistle of Jude,* 2d ed., TNTC (Grand Rapids: Eerdmans, 1987), 188; Moo, *2 Peter, Jude,* 289.

[40] Jude was not thinking literally here of garments being defiled (contra Fuchs and Reymond, *2 Pierre, Jude,* 186).

[41] Contra Winter, the letter of Jude indicts sexual license and does not advocate sexual asceticism. Hence, Jude was not suggesting that the body itself is a defiled garment that should be hated ("Jude 22–23," 219–22). The preposition ἀπό with the passive participle ἐσπιλωμένον designates agency rather than indicating that the defiled garment *is* the flesh.

[42] It should be noted that Zech 3:4 does not speak of the flesh (so Vögtle, *Judasbrief, 2 Petrusbrief,* 106), and so the parallel with Jude does not stand at every point.

[43] Reicke says the "flesh" stands for the sinful environment of the world (*James, Peter, and Jude,* 216). Vögtle rightly remarks that there is no anti-Gnostic polemic here (*Judasbrief, 2 Petrusbrief,* 106).

[44] Kelly, *Peter and Jude,* 289.

4. Doxology (24–25)

[24]To him who is able to keep you from falling and to present you before his glorious presence without fault and with great joy— [25]to the only God our Savior be glory, majesty, power and authority, through Jesus Christ our Lord, before all ages, now and forevermore! Amen.

Many letters close with a benediction (e.g., 1 Cor 16:23–24; 2 Cor 13:14; Gal 6:18; Heb 13:25; 1 Pet 5:14), but Jude concludes with a doxology, which is fitting for a sermon or in a liturgical setting. The doxology reminds the readers of the heart and soul of the Christian life. All glory and majesty and power belong to God. He will be praised forever and ever by believers in Jesus Christ. In particular, Jude reminded his readers that God is able and willing to keep them from succumbing to apostasy. The false teachers threatened, but those who truly belong to the Lord will not capitulate. They will continue to be faithful until the end. Their faithfulness until the end, however, is not due to their own nobility or inner strength. It is God himself who keeps his own from falling away. He grants the ability to stand before God blameless and joyful on the last day.

24 The doxology in Jude follows a form that is common in other New Testament doxologies. (1) God, the person who deserves the praise, is addressed in the dative case (Rom 16:25; Eph 3:20; 2 Pet 3:18); (2) glory and honor are ascribed to God (Rom 16:27; Eph 3:21; 2 Pet 3:18); (3) the endless duration of God's praise is featured (Rom 16:27; Eph 3:21; 2 Pet 3:18); and (4) a concluding "amen" is incorporated (Rom 16:27; Eph 3:21; 2 Pet 3:18). Jude shared all four of these elements, indicating that we have a common liturgical form here. Doxologies with a different form exist elsewhere in the New Testament (Rom 11:36; Gal 1:5; Phil 4:20; 1 Tim 1:17; 6:16; 2 Tim 4:18). Jude follows the fourfold format set forth above. (1) Like Rom 16:25 and Eph 3:20, the doxology begins by referring to God as "Now to him who is able" *(tō de dynamenō)*. (2) The glory ascribed to God is expanded by Jude in v. 25, where "glory, majesty, power, and authority" are ascribed to him. (3) God's honor, majesty and power are eternal, for they are "before all ages, both now and forevermore." We should note here the triad of past, present, and future.[45] (4) Finally, Jude concludes with the customary "amen."

When Jude spoke of God's ability to keep believers from falling, he did not merely mean that believers *might* be kept from falling. The idea is that God *will* keep them from falling by his grace.[46] The word for "keep" *(phylaxai)* is not the same term that has been used earlier in the letter (cf. *tēreō*, vv. 1,6,13,21), but the concept is the same. The promise that God will pre-

---

[45] The triad here was pointed out to me by Jim Hamilton.

[46] So Augustine in *James, 1–2 Peter, 1–3 John, Jude,* ACCS (Downers Grove: InterVarsity, 2000), 259.

serve believers from apostasy does not cancel out the exhortation of v. 21, "keep yourselves in God's love." Ultimately, however, believers obey this admonition because God will strengthen them to do so. He gives us the grace so that we desire to keep ourselves in God's love.

The preservation from "stumbling" *(aptaistous)* does not refer to sinlessness in this context. The verb "stumble" *(ptaiō)* does have that sense in James (2:10; 3:1). In Rom 11:11, however, the verb "stumble" refers to whether the Jews have stumbled irrevocably, so that they will be lost forever. Paul answered that question with an emphatic no! Peter used the verbal form of this word in reference to apostasy in 2 Pet 1:10. And that is how Jude used the adjective here. God does not promise that true believers will never sin. He promises that he will preserve us from committing apostasy, from abandoning the faith once and for all.[47] That this is what Jude meant is confirmed by the next clause, "to present you before his glorious presence without fault." Literally the term is "make you stand" *(stēsai,* NRSV) instead of "to present." Elsewhere in the New Testament the term "stand" refers to eschatological vindication at God's throne on the last day (Rom 14:4; 1 Cor 10:12; cf. Eph 6:11,13,14). What Jude said is that God is the one who will keep believers from committing apostasy so that they will be able to stand before God "with great joy" on the day of the Lord. Believers experience joy, and their joy brings honor to God as their patron and protector on the last day.[48]

On the day of the Lord believers will be "without fault" *(amōmous),* which is translated by the NRSV as "without blemish." The term "without blemish" is used of Old Testament sacrifices (Exod 29:1,38; Lev 1:3,10; 3:1,6; 4:3; Num 6:14; Ezek 43:22–23,25), of Jesus as a perfect sacrifice (Heb 9:14; 1 Pet 1:19), and of believers on the day of judgment (Eph 1:4; 5:27; Col 1:22). Jude used the term in the latter sense and with the same meaning. He was not suggesting that believers will in any sense be perfect in this life. The Lord will make his own, who have not abandoned him, blameless on the last day. God will complete his saving work on that day.

25 The one who is able to keep believers from falling is identified as "the only God our Savior" here. Some manuscripts add the term "wise," but the evidence for its inclusion is not strong, and scribes probably added it under the influence of Rom 16:27. In saying that God is the "only God," Jude did not counteract any form of Gnosticism.[49] He shared the common Jewish worldview that there is only one God, over against the polytheism of the Gentile world. In the New Testament, Jesus Christ usually is designated

---

[47] So also Kelly, *Peter and Jude,* 291; Bauckham, *Jude, 2 Peter,* 122; Moo, *2 Peter, Jude,* 300; Fuchs and Reymond, *2 Pierre, Jude,* 189.

[48] So Neyrey, *2 Peter, Jude,* 100.

[49] Against Kelly, *Peter and Jude,* 292.

as the Savior.[50] In some texts, however, God is said to be the Savior (Luke 1:47; 1 Tim 1:1; 2:3; 4:10; Titus 1:3; 2:10; 3:4), which represents the Old Testament as well (e.g., Deut 32:15; Pss 24:5; 25:5; 27:9; 65:5). The idea of God being the Savior fits well in a context in which false teachers threaten the church and believers need rescue from their clutches. The verse could be construed to say "God our Savior through Jesus Christ."[51] Green argues that the glory could not be through Jesus Christ "before all ages," and therefore Jude must have been ascribing glory to God "through" Jesus Christ. Comparable texts, however, suggest that Jude taught that glory, majesty, power, and authority are "through Jesus Christ" (Rom 7:25; 16:27; 2 Cor 1:20; Col 3:17; 1 Pet 4:11). An optative verb represented by "be" in the NIV might seem to be fitting, expressing a prayer wish. A prayer wish, however, does not fit with "before all ages." Believers cannot pray that God would be glorified and honored before time began since that period of history has ended, and no human being even existed during much of the past. An indicative verb like "are" is more fitting. Glory, majesty, power, and authority always belong to God for all of history. "Glory" signifies the honor, resplendence, and beauty that is ascribed to God for his saving work. Neyrey says that glory "refers to the public reputation or fame of someone."[52] And he emphasizes that such glory must be "publicly expressed and acclaimed." Since God does the protecting, saving, and preserving, he receives all the glory, acclamation, and praise. "Majesty" denotes his greatness and how worthy he is of honor given his exalted position. Kelly nicely captures its meaning with the phrase "His awful transcendence."[53] The idea that God is majestic hails from the Old Testament (Deut 32:3; 1 Chr 29:11; Pss 144:3,6; 150:2; Dan 2:20; cf. *Tob* 13:4). "Power" and "authority" are terms that are rather close in meaning. They indicate that God is sovereign and in control.[54] The direction of all things is in his hand (1 Tim 6:16; Rev 4:11; 5:13; 19:1). Glory, majesty, power, and authority have always belonged to God, before the world began and will be his forever and ever. This is not a prayer, which would be rendered by the term "may be," but a fact, and so the fitting verb is "are." Because of who God is and what he has done, the praise and power are his forever. Readers rest secure in this truth, and Jude did as well, signifying it by saying "Amen."

---

[50] Luke 2:11; John 4:42; Acts 5:31; 13:32; Eph 5:23; Phil 3:20; 2 Tim 1:10; Titus 1:4; 2:13; 3:6; 2 Pet 1:1,11; 2:20; 3:2,18; 1 John 4:14.

[51] Green, *2 Peter and Jude,* 207.

[52] Neyrey, *2 Peter, Jude,* 97.

[53] Kelly, *Peter and Jude,* 293.

[54] But there is no polemic against Gnosticism here (contra Fuchs and Reymond, *2 Pierre, Jude,* 190).

Selected Bibliography

1 Peter

Achtemeier, P. J. *1 Peter: A Commentary on First Peter.* Her. Minneapolis: Fortress, 1996.

Balch, D. L. *Let Wives Be Submissive: The Domestic Code in I Peter.* SBLMS 26. Chico: Scholars Press, 1981.

Bauckham, R. J. "James, 1 Peter and 2 Peter, Jude." In *It Is Written: Scripture Citing Scripture: Essays in Honour of Barnabas Lindars.* Edited by D. A. Carson and H. G. M. Williamson. Cambridge: University Press, 1988, 303–17.

Beare, F. W. *The First Epistle of Peter: The Greek Text with Introduction and Notes.* Oxford: Blackwell, 1947.

Bechtler, S. R. *Following in His Steps: Suffering, Community, and Christology in 1 Peter.* SBLDS 162. Atlanta: Scholars Press, 1998.

Best, E. *1 Peter.* NCB. Grand Rapids: Eerdmans, 1971.

———. "1 Peter and the Gospel Tradition." *NTS* 16 (1970): 95–113.

———. "I Peter II.4–10—A Reconsideration." *NovT* 11 (1969): 270–93.

Bigg, C. *The Epistles of St. Peter and St. Jude.* ICC. Edinburgh: T & T Clark, 1901.

Boismard, M.-E. *Quatre hymnes baptismales dans la premiére Épître de Pierre.* LD 30. Paris: Les Éditions du Cerf, 1961.

Brox, N. *Der erste Petrusbrief.* EKKNT. 2d ed. Zürich: Benziger/Neukirchen-Vluyn: Neukirchener Verlag, 1986.

Calvin, J. *Commentaries on the Catholic Epistles.* Grand Rapids: Eerdmans, 1948.

Campbell, B. L. *Honor, Shame, and the Rhetoric of 1 Peter.* SBLDS 160. Atlanta: Scholars Press, 1998.

Campbell, R. A. *The Elders: Seniority with Earliest Christianity.* Edinburgh: T & T Clark, 1998.

Chester, A., and R. P. Martin. *The Theology of the Letters of James, Peter, and Jude.* Cambridge: University Press, 1994.

Chin, M. "A Heavenly Home for the Homeless: Aliens and Strangers in 1 Peter." *TynBul* 42 (1991): 96–112.

Cranfield, C. E. B. *I & II Peter and Jude: Introduction and Commentary.* TBC. London: SCM, 1960.

Dalton, W. J. *Christ's Proclamation to the Spirits: A Study of 1 Peter 3:18–4:6.* AnBib 23. Rome: Pontifical Biblical Institute, 1965.

Daube, D. "Participle and Imperative in I Peter." In E. G. Selwyn, *The First Epistle of St. Peter.* 2d ed. Grand Rapids: Baker, 1981, 467–88.

Davids, P. H. *The First Epistle of Peter.* NICNT. Grand Rapids: Eerdmans, 1990.

Dubis, M. *Messianic Woes in 1 Peter: Suffering and Eschatology in 1 Peter 4:12–19.* SBL 33. New York: Peter Lang, 2002.

Elliott, J. H. *1 Peter: A New Translation with Introduction and Commentary.* AB. Garden City: Doubleday, 2000.

———. *A Home for the Homeless: A Sociological Exegesis of 1 Peter, Its Situation and Strategy.* Philadelphia: Fortress, 1981.

———. *The Elect and the Holy: An Exegetical Examination of I Peter 2:4–10 and the Phrase βασίλειον Ἱεράτευμα.*" NovTSup 12. Leiden: Brill, 1966.

———. "The Rehabilitation of an Exegetical Step-Child: 1 Peter in Recent Research." *JBL* 95 (1976): 243–54.

Erbes, K. "Was *bedeutet* ἀλλοτριοεπίσκοπος 1 Pt 4,15?" *ZNW* 19 (1919–20): 39–44.

Feinberg, J. S. "1 Peter 3:18–20, Ancient Mythology, and the Intermediate State." *WTJ* 48 (1986): 303–36.

Feldmeier, R. *Die Christen als Fremde: Die Metapher der Fremde in der antiken Welt, im Urchristentum und im 1. Petrusbrief.* WUNT 64. Tübingen: Mohr, 1992.

Francis, J. "'Like Newborn Babes'—The Image of the Child in 1 Peter 2:2–3." In

Papers on Paul and Other New Testament Authors, 111–17. StudBib 3. SNTSup 3. Sheffield: JSOT Press, 1980, 111–17.
France, R. T. "Exegesis in Practice: Two Examples." In *New Testament Interpretation: Essays on Principles and Methods.* Grand Rapids: Eerdmans, 1977, 252–81.
Goppelt, L. *A Commentary on I Peter.* Grand Rapids: Eerdmans, 1993.
Gross, D. "Are the Wives of 1 Peter 3.7 Christians?" *JSNT* 35 (1989): 89–96.
Grudem, W. *The First Epistle of Peter.* TNTC. Grand Rapids: Eerdmans, 1988.
Gundry, R. H. "'*Verba Christi*' in I Peter: Their Implications concerning the Authorship of I Peter and the Authenticity of the Gospel Tradition." *NTS* 13 (1967): 336–50.
———. "Further *Verba* on *Verba Christi* in First Peter." *Bib* 55 (1974): 211–32.
Hemer, C. "The Address of 1 Peter." *ExpTim* 89 (1978): 239–43.
Hill, D. "On Suffering and Baptism in I Peter." *NovT* 18 (1976): 181–89.
———. "'To Offer Spiritual Sacrifices …' (1 Peter 2:5) Liturgical Formulations and Christian Paraenesis in 1 Peter." *JSNT* 16 (1982): 45–63.
Hillyer, N. *1 and 2 Peter, Jude.* NIBC. Peabody: Hendrickson, 1992.
———. "First Peter and the Feast of Tabernacles." *TynBul* 21 (1970): 39–70.
Horrell, D. G. *The Epistles of Peter and Jude.* EC. Peterborough: Epworth, 1998.
Kelly, J. N. D. *A Commentary on the Epistles of Peter and Jude.* Thornapple Commentaries. Grand Rapids: Baker, 1981.
Luther, M. *Commentary on Peter & Jude.* Grand Rapids: Kregel, 1990.
Maier, G. "Jesustradition im 1. Petrusbrief." In *Gospel Perspectives: The Jesus Tradition outside the Gospels.* Vol. 5. Sheffield: JSOT Press, 1984, 85–128.
Martin, T. W. *Metaphor and Composition in 1 Peter.* SBLDS 131. Atlanta: Scholars Press, 1992.
McCartney, D. G. "The Use of the Old Testament in the First Epistle of Peter." Ph.D. diss., Westminster Theological Seminary, 1989.
McKnight, S. *1 Peter.* NIVAC. Grand Rapids: Zondervan, 1996.
Michaels, J. R. *1 Peter.* WBC. Waco: Word, 1998.
———. "Eschatology in I Peter iii.17." *NTS* 13 (1967): 394–401.
Merkle, B. "The Elder and Overseer: One Office in the Early Church." Ph.D. diss., The Southern Baptist Theological Seminary, 2000.
Moule, C. F. D. "The Nature and Purpose of I Peter." *NTS* 3 (1956–57): 1–11.
Oss, D. A. "The Interpretation of the 'Stone' Passages by Peter and Paul: A Comparative Study." *JETS* 32 (1989): 181–200.
Piper, J. "Hope as the Motivation of Love: I Peter 3:9–12." *NTS* 26 (1980): 212–31.
Reicke, B. *The Disobedient Spirits and Christian Baptism: A Study of 1 Pet. III.19 and Its Context.* ASNU 13. Copenhagen: Munksgaard, 1946.
———. *The Epistles of James, Peter, and Jude.* AB. Garden City: Doubleday, 1964.
Richard, E. J. *Reading 1 Peter, Jude, and 2 Peter: A Literary and Theological Commentary.* RNT. Macon: Smith & Helwys, 2000.
Richards, E. R. "Silvanus Was Not Peter's Secretary: Theological Bias in Interpreting διά Σιλουανοῦ . . . ἔγραψα." *JETS* 43 (2000): 417–32.
Schelke, K. H. *Der Petrusbriefe—Der Judasbrief.* HTKNT. Freiburg: Herder, 1980.
Schutter, W. L. *Hermeneutic and Composition in I Peter.* WUNT 2/30. Tübingen: Mohr, 1989.
Selwyn, E. G. *The First Epistle of St. Peter.* 2d ed. Grand Rapids: Baker, 1981.
Sevenster, J. N. *Do You Know Greek? How Much Greek Could the First Jewish Christians Have Known?* NovTSup 19. Leiden: Brill, 1968.
Snyder, S. "1 Peter 2:17: A Reconsideration." *FNT* 4 (1991): 211–15.
———. "Participles and Imperatives in 1 Peter: A Re-examination in the Light of Recent Scholarly Trends." *FNT* 8 (1995): 187–98.
Spicq, C. *Les Épîtres de Saint Pierre.* SB. Paris: Gabalda, 1966.
Talbert, C. H., ed. *Perspectives on 1 Peter.* Macon: Mercer University Press, 1986.
Thurén, L. *The Rhetorical Strategy of 1 Peter with Special Regard to Ambiguous Expressions.* Åbo: Academy Press, 1990.
———. *Argument and Theology in 1 Peter: The Origins of Christian Paraenesis.* JSNTSup 114. Sheffield: Academic Press, 1995.
Tite, P. L. *Compositional Transitions in 1 Peter: An Analysis of the Letter-Opening.*

San Francisco: International Scholars Publications, 1997.
van Unnik, W. C. *Sparsa Collecta: The Collected Essays of W. C. van Unnik. Part Two: I Peter, Canon, Corpus Hellenisticum, Generalia.* NovTSup 30. Leiden: Brill, 1980.
———. "The Critique of Paganism in I Peter 1:18." In *Neotestamentica et Semitica: Studies in Honour of Matthew Black.* Edinburgh: T & T Clark, 1969, 129–42.
Wand, J. W. C. *The General Epistles of St. Peter and St. Jude.* WC. London: Methuen, 1934.

2 Peter and Jude

Alexander, T. D. "Lot's Hospitality: A Clue to His Righteousness." *JBL* 104 (1995): 289–91.
Allen, J. S. "A New Possibility for the Three-Clause Format of Jude 22–3." *NTS* 44 (1998): 133–43.
Bauckham, R. J. "A Note on a Problem in the Greek Version of I Enoch i.9." *JTS* 32 (1981): 136–38.
———. *Jude and the Relatives of Jesus in the Early Church.* Edinburgh: T & T Clark, 1990.
———. *Jude, 2 Peter.* WBC. Waco: Word, 1983.
Bandstra, A. J. "Onward Christian Soldiers—Praying in Love, with Mercy: Preaching on the Epistle of Jude." *CTJ* 32 (1997): 136–39.
Black, M. "The Maranatha Invocation and Jude 14, 15 (I Enoch 1:9)." In *Christ and Spirit in the New Testament: Studies in Honour of Charles Francis Digby Moule.* Cambridge: University Press, 1973, 189–96.
Birdsall, J. N. "The Text of Jude in $\mathfrak{P}^{72}$." *JTS* 14 (1963): 394–99.
Boobyer, G. H. "The Indebtedness of 2 Peter to 1 Peter." In *New Testament Essays: Studies in Memory of Thomas Walter Manson,* 34–53. Manchester: University Press, 1959.
Callan, T. "The Christology of the Second Letter of Peter." *Bib* 82 (2001): 253–63.
Caulley, T. S. "The False Teachers in Second Peter." *SBT* 12 (1982): 27–42.
Cavallin, H. C. C. "The False Teachers of 2 Pt as Pseudo-Prophets." *NovT* 21 (1979): 263–70.
Chang, A. D. "Second Peter 2:1 and the Extent of the Atonement." *BSac* 142 (1985): 52–63.
Charles, J. D. "Jude's Use of Pseudepigraphical Source-Material as Part of a Literary Strategy." *NTS* 37 (1991): 130–45.
———. "Literary Artifice in the Epistle of Jude." *ZNW* 82 (1991): 106–24.
———. *Literary Strategy in the Epistle of Jude.* London and Toronto: Associated University Presses, 1993.
———. "The Language and Logic of Virtue in 2 Peter 1:5–7." *BBR* 8 (1998): 55–73.
———. "'Those' and 'These': The Use of the Old Testament in the Epistle of Jude." *JSNT* 38 (1990): 109–24.
———. *Virtue amidst Vice: The Catalog of Virtues in 2 Peter 1.* JSNTSup 150. Sheffield: Academic Press, 1997.
Danker, F. W. "2 Peter 1: A Solemn Decree." *CBQ* 40 (1978): 64–82.
———. "II Peter 3:10 and Psalm of Solomon 17:10." *ZNW* 53 (1962): 82–86.
Dehandschutter, B. "Pseudo-Cyprian, Jude and Enoch: Some Notes on 1 Enoch 1:9." In *Tradition and Re-interpretation in Jewish and Early Christian Literature: Essays in Honour of Jürgen H. Lebram.* SPB 36. Leiden: Brill, 1986, 114–20.
Desjardins, M. "The Portrayal of the Dissidents in 2 Peter and Jude: Does It Tell Us More about the 'Godly' than the 'Ungodly'?" *JSNT* 30 (1987): 89–102.
Donfried, K. P. *The Setting of Second Clement in Early Christianity.* Leiden: Brill, 1974.
Dunham, D. A. "An Exegetical Study of 2 Peter 2:18–22." *BSac* 140 (1983): 40–54.
Dunnett, W. M. "The Hermeneutics of Jude and 2 Peter: The Use of Ancient Jewish Traditions." *JETS* 31 (1988): 287–92.
Ellis, E. E. "Prophecy and Hermeneutic in Jude." In *Prophecy and Hermeneutic in Early*

Christianity: New Testament Essays. Grand Rapids: Eerdmans, 1978, 221–36.
———. "Pseudonymity and Canonicity of New Testament Documents." In *Worship, Theology and Ministry in the Early Church: Essays in Honor of Ralph P. Martin*. JSNTSup 87. Sheffield: JSOT Press, 1992, 212–24.
Fornberg, T. *An Early Church in a Pluralistic Society: A Study of 2 Peter*. ConBNT 9. Lund: Gleerup, 1977.
Fossum, J. "Kyrios Jesus as the Angel of the Lord in Jude 5–7." *NTS* 33 (1987): 226–43.
Fuchs, E., and P. Reymond. *La Deuxième de Saint Pierre. LÉpître de Saint Jude*. CNT. Neuchâtel—Paris: Delachaux & Niestlé, 1980.
Gilmour, M. J. "Reflections on the Authorship of 2 Peter." *EvQ* 73 (2001): 291–309.
Green, G. L. "'As for Prophecies, They Will Come to an End': 2 Peter, Paul and Plutarch on 'the Obsolescence of Oracles.'" *JSNT* 82 (2001): 107–22.
Green, M. T*he Second Epistle General of Peter and the General Epistle of Jude,* 2d ed. TNTC. Grand Rapids: Eerdmans, 1987.
Heide, G. Z. "What Is New about the New Heaven and the New Earth? A Theology of Creation from Revelation 21 and 2 Peter 3." *JETS* 40 (1997): 37–56.
Heiligenthal, R. "Der Judasbrief: Aspekte der Forschung in den letzen Jahrzehten." *TRu* 51 (1986): 117–29.
———. *Zwischen Henoch und Paulus. Studien zum theologiegeschichtlichen Ort des Judasbriefes*. Texte und Arbeiten zum neutestamenlichen Zeitalter 6. Tübingen: Francke, 1992.
Joubert, S. J. "Persuasion in the Letter of Jude." *JSNT* 58 (1995): 75–87.
Käsemann, E. "An Apologia for Primitive Christian Eschatology." In *Essays on New Testament Themes,* 169–95. Philadelphia: Fortress, 1964.
Kennard, D. W. "Petrine Redemption: Its Meaning and Extent." *JETS* 39 (1987): 399–405.
Kraus, T. J. "Παρὰ κυρίου, παρὰ κυρίῳ oder omit in 2Petr 2,11: Textkritik und Interpretation vor dem Hintergrund juristischer Diktion und der Verwendung von parav." *ZNW* 91 (2000): 265–73.
Kruger, M. J. "The Authenticity of 2 Peter." *JETS* 42 (1999): 645–71.
Kubo, S. "Jude 22–23: Two-Division Form or Three?" In *New Testament Textual Criticism: Its Significance for Exegesis: Essays in Honour of Bruce M. Metzger*. Oxford: Clarendon, 1981, 239–53.
Landon, C. *A Text-Critical Study of the Epistle of Jude*. JSNTSup 135. Sheffield: Academic Press, 1996.
Lövestam, E. "Eschatologie und Tradition im 2. Petrusbrief." In *The New Testament Age: Essays in Honor of Bo Reicke*. Edited by W. C. Weinrich. Vol. 2. Macon: Mercer University Press, 1984, 287–300.
Makujina, J. "The 'Trouble' with Lot in 2 Peter: Locating Peter's Source for Lot's Torment." *WTJ* 60 (1998): 255–69.
Mayor, J. B. *The Epistle of St. Jude and the Second Epistle of St. Peter*. London: Macmillan, 1907. Reprint, Grand Rapids: Baker, 1965.
Meier, J. P. "The Brothers and Sisters of Jesus in Ecumenical Perspective." *CBQ* 54 (1992): 1–28.
Miller, R. J. "Is There Independent Attestation for the Transfiguration in 2 Peter?" *NTS* 42 (1996): 620–25.
Moo, D. J. *2 Peter, Jude*. NIVAC. Grand Rapids: Zondervan, 1996.
Müller, P. "Der Judasbrief." *TRu* 63 (1998): 267–289.
———. "Der 2. Petrusbrief." *TRu* 66 (2001): 310–37.
Neyrey, J. *2 Peter, Jude*. AB. Garden City: Doubleday, 1993.
———. "The Apologetic Use of the Transfiguration in 2 Peter 1:16–21." *CBQ* 42 (1980): 504–19.
———. "The Form and Background of the Polemic in 2 Peter." *JBL* 99 (1980): 407–31.
Osburn, C. D. "Discourse Analysis and Jewish Apocalyptic in the Epistle of Jude." In *Linguistics and New Testament Interpretation: Essays on Discourse Analysis*. Nashville: Broadman, 1992, 287–319.
———. "The Christological Use of I Enoch i.9 in Jude 14, 15." *NTS* 23 (1976–77): 334–41.

———. "The Text of Jude 5." *Bib* 62 (1981): 107–15.
———. "The Text of Jude 22–23." *ZNW* 63 (1972): 139–44.
Paulsen, H. *Der Zweite Petrusbrief und der Judasbrief.* KEK. Göttingen: Vandenhoeck & Ruprecht, 1992.
Picirilli, R. E. "Allusions to 2 Peter in the Apostolic Fathers." *JSNT* 33 (1988): 57–83.
———. "The Meaning of 'Epignosis.'" *EvQ* 47 (1975): 85–93.
Riesner, R. "Der Zweite-Petrus Brief und die Eschatologie." In *Zukunftserwartung in biblischer Sicht: Beiträge zur Eschatologie.* Giessen: Brunnen, 1984, 124–43.
Roberts, J. W. "A Note on the Meaning of II Peter 3:10d." *ResQ* 6 (1962): 32–33.
Ross, J. M. "Church Discipline in Jude 22–23." *ExpTim* 8 (1989): 297–98.
Rowston, D. J. "The Most Neglected Book in the New Testament." *NTS* 21 (1974–75): 554–63.
Schrage, W. "'Ein Tag ist beim Herrn wie tausend Jahre, und tausend Jahre sind wie ein Tag.'" In *Glaube und Eschatologie: Festschrift für Werner Georg Kümmel zum* 80. Geburtstag. Tübingen: Mohr, 1985, 267–75.
Schreiner, T. R., and A. B. Caneday. *The Race Set Before Us: A Biblical Theology of Perseverance and Assurance.* Downers Grove: InterVarsity, 2001.
Sellin, G. "Die Häretiker des Judasbriefes." *ZNW* 77 (1986): 206–25.
Sidebottom, E. M. *James, Jude and 2 Peter.* NCB. London: Thomas Nelson, 1967.
Smith,T. V. *Petrine Controversies in Early Christianity: Attitudes toward Peter in Christian Writings of the First Two Centuries.* WUNT 2/15. Tübingen: Mohr, 1985.
Starr, J. M. *Sharers in Divine Nature: 2 Peter 1:4 in Its Hellenistic Context.* ConBNT 33. Stockholm: Almqvist &: Wiksell, 2000.
Talbert, C. H. "2 Peter and the Delay of the Parousia." *VC* 20 (1966): 137–45.
Thiede, P. "A Pagan Reader of 2 Peter: Cosmic Conflagration in 2 Peter 3 and the Octavius of Minucius Felix." *JSNT* 26 (1986): 79–96.
Thurén, L. "Hey Jude! Asking for the Original Situation and Message of a Catholic Epistle." *NTS* 43 (1997): 451–65.
Vander Kam, J. "The Theophany of Enoch 1:3b–7, 9." *VT* 33 (1973): 129–50.
Vögtle, A. *Der Judasbrief, der 2 Petrusbrief.* EKKNT. Neukirchen–Vluyn: Neukirchener Verlag, 1994.
Voorwinde, S. "Old Testament Quotations in Peter's Epistles." *VR* 49 (1987): 3–16.
Wall, R. W. "The Canonical Function of 2 Peter." *Biblical Interpretation* 9 (2001): 64–81.
Watson, D. F. *Invention, Arrangement, and Style: Rhetorical Criticism of Jude and 2 Peter.* SBLDS 104. Atlanta: Scholars Press, 1988.
Webb, R. L. "The Eschatology of the Epistle of Jude and Its Rhetorical and Social Functions." *BBR* 6 (1996): 139–51.
Wendland, E. R. "A Comparative Study of 'Rhetorical Criticism,' Ancient and Modern—with Special Reference to the Larger Structure and Function of the Epistle of Jude." *Neot* 28 (1994): 193–228.
Wenham, D. "Being 'Found' on the Last Day: New Light on 2 Peter 3:10 and 2 Corinthians 5:3." *NTS* 33 (1987): 477–79.
Wikgren, A. "Some Problems in Jude 5." In *Studies in the History and Text of the New Testament in Honor of Kenneth Willis Clark.* Salt Lake City: University of Utah Press, 1967, 147–52.
Wilder, T. L. "Psuedonymity and the New Testament." In *Interpreting the New Testament: Essays on Methods and Issues.* Nashville: Broadman & Holman, 2001, 296–334.
Wilson, W. E. "Εὑρεθήσεται in 2 Pet. iii.10." *ExpTim* 32 (1920–21): 44–45.
Wolters, A. "'Partners of the Deity': A Covenantal Reading of 2 Peter 1:4." *CTJ* 25 (1990): 28–44.
———. "Postscript to 'Partners of the Deity.'" *CTJ* 26 (1991): 418–20.
———. "Worldview and Textual Criticism in 2 Peter 3:10." *WTJ* 49 (1987): 405–13.
Wolthuis, T. R. "Jude and the Rhetorician: A Dialogue on the Rhetorical Nature of the Epistle of Jude." *CTJ* 24 (1989): 126–34.

Selected Subject Index

Person Index

Selected Scripture Index